Public Speaking
Strategies for Success

Second Edition

David Zarefsky

Northwestern University

Allyn and Bacon

Boston • London • Toronto • Sydney • Tokyo • Singapore

TO MY STUDENTS

Editor: Karon Bowers
Vice President, Editor in Chief: Paul Smith
Editorial-Production Administrator: Joe Sweeney
Editorial-Production Service: WordCrafters Editorial Services, Inc.
Composition Buyer: Linda Cox
Manufacturing Buyer: Megan Cochran
Cover Administrator: Linda Knowles
Text Designer: The Davis Group, Inc.
Photo Researcher: Sarah K. Evertson
Text Composition: Omegatype Typography, Inc.

Between the time website information is gathered and then published, it is not unusual for some sites to have closed. Also, the transcription of URLs can result in typographical errors.

Printed in the United States of America
10 9 8 7 6 5 4 3 2 1   VHP   01 00 99 98

Credits begin on page 453, which constitutes a continuation of the copyright page.

Contents

To the Instructor

While writing the first edition of *Public Speaking: Strategies for Success*, I asked myself why the market needed another public speaking textbook. My answer was that no book then available focused on the premise that successful public speaking is *strategic*. By that I mean that it involves understanding the circumstances in which one speaks, making deliberate choices about how to deal with these circumstances, and planning for achieving one's goals. The key elements in a strategic approach to public speaking are *critical thinking* and *strategic planning*, and these skills are emphasized throughout this book.

The response to the first edition was gratifying, suggesting that the book's basic approach made sense and was useful. Like all beginnings, however, in places it was rough-edged. This new edition aims to refine the approach and to incorporate new material, while maintaining the clear perspective for which the book became known.

NEW TO THIS EDITION

- **Carefully Revised Chapters**   Every chapter has been revised to streamline difficult material and make the text more accessible to students. An attempt has been made to achieve this important goal *without* compromising the integrity or complexity of the subject matter. Chapters 1 and 2 from the first edition have been blended into a single chapter to provide a more cohesive introduction to the course and an opportunity for students to begin making speeches earlier. Discussion of the public forum, formerly contained in Chapter 1, now appears in Appendix A.

Throughout the book, examples have been revised and updated as appropriate. Chapters on organization and on informing and persuading have been revised to flesh out details, streamline the structure, and incorporate additional practical guidelines. For example, in response to requests from reviewers and instructors who used the first edition, Chapter 7 (Organizing the Speech: The Body) now contains a more manageable number of organizational patterns to simplify students' options when deciding how best to organize their speeches, while still providing a wide range of choice. Chapter 14 (Persuading) now includes Monroe's Motivated Sequence for those who require it as a class assignment.

- **Enriched Emphasis on Learning from Others**   In every chapter there is a new boxed feature called *Applying Strategies* that features four real-life students from the University of Northern Colorado and describes their development throughout their public speaking course. Included are excerpts from their assignments, speeches, and journals, as well as comments and critiques from their instructor, Dr. Sherilyn Marrow. These boxes encourage students to learn from and be encouraged by others who are their peers.

- **Expanded Discussion of Technology**   Far greater emphasis has been placed on the use of information technology in the public speaking course. This is most obvious in Chapter 5, in which electronic research sources are given detailed attention, and in Chapter 12, which contains an expanded section on computer-generated visual aids. Every chapter includes a set of *Using the Internet* activities so that technology can be incorporated throughout the course. Special attention has been paid to the critical notion of evaluating material available on the Internet. While its use can be beneficial, students need to understand that the information must be evaluated carefully. Those of you teaching the course without access to advanced computer technology, however, will not be left behind, because the book still focuses on the art of rhetoric, with its traditions dating back to antiquity, long before the advent of the computer.

RETAINED FROM THE FIRST EDITION

While the changes described above have been made, the principal elements that distinguished the first edition have been maintained. These include a focus on strategies; integration of theory and practice; challenging examples and applications; stress on the skills of analysis, research, and reasoning; a holistic approach to the study of language and delivery; comprehensive treatment of visual aids and of occasions for public speaking; and a rich presentation of audience analysis and the public forum.

Focus on Strategies

The primary focus of the book—strategic thinking and planning—clearly has been retained in the second edition. Far too often students leave a public speaking class with nothing more than a recipe for how to prepare and deliver a seven-minute speech in class. Certainly, being able to prepare and deliver that classroom speech well is a start. The goal of this book, however, is to help students learn how to apply the skills required for the seven-minute classroom speech to the range of public speaking situations they will encounter throughout their lives. Students should recognize how often they will find themselves participating in speaking situations, whether as a public speaker or as an audience member. They need to think through and about the public speaking process and to develop strategies to achieve their goals.

This second edition includes *Choose a Strategy* boxes, which appear six times throughout the book and present students with a case study situation requiring that they decide how the skills and concepts discussed in the chapter (and in previous chapters) could be adapted to a concrete rhetorical situation. These case studies are geared toward students' level of experience and they focus on public speaking situations that students typically might encounter. After applying what they've learned to the initial scenario, students are asked to decide what impact a change in topic, audience, purpose, or other variable might have on the choice of strategies. These scenarios offer students a chance to explore the variables and tradeoffs that inevitably apply to any strategic decision. There are usually no "correct" solutions for these open-ended *Choose a Strategy* situations. Rather, they are exercises in what we have described as applied rhetoric: sizing up a situation, understanding its opportunities and constraints, assessing ideas, and reasoning with an audience in mind. These situations are realistic and encourage students to develop and refine their strategic thinking about the public speaking process.

Integration of Theory and Practice

An approach that views public speaking as a set of techniques or rules to be followed is of limited value. Few actual speaking situations will match exactly those for which the "rules" were written; students need instead to be able to adapt to the particular situations in which they find themselves. In order to do that, they must understand the theory behind the rules. Recognizing this fact, some books try to "import" theory, including all the latest specialized terms and jargon. This book instead integrates theory into the underlying discussions of practice, not by highlighting obscure writers or technical terms, but by explaining clearly what students should do and why. Theory and practice are treated as a seamless fabric.

A Variety of Challenging Examples and Applications

Because public speaking is situation-specific, this book includes a large number of cases and examples. The examples in this book have the following characteristics. First, they encompass a wide range of topics and issues, with some examples from actual speaking situations and some hypothetical examples to illustrate points in the text. Second, some examples compare speeches in the classroom with speeches in the field. Third, there are both brief examples and some extended examples that can be followed throughout an entire chapter. The examples throughout incorporate a diversity of cultural perspectives, partly to emphasize a need to analyze and respond to audiences as an integral part of the strategic thinking process.

Stress on the Skills of Analysis, Research, and Reasoning

This book, more than others, emphasizes practical applications of critical thinking skills that are so crucial to public speaking. These skills include active listening skills for mapping ideas and critical evaluation, and topic analysis to determine underlying issues. The investigation and research process is treated in considerable detail, with specific advice and guidance for analyzing a thesis to discover new subtopics and approaches. And there is a full chapter on reasoning in the context of the entire speaking situation (not limited to persuasive speeches), a subject often ignored or slighted in other public speaking texts. These practical skills and processes are summarized regularly for students in *Checklist* sections provided in almost every chapter.

A Holistic Approach to the Study of Language and Delivery

Public Speaking recognizes a fundamental irony about language and delivery. They are the features of a speech that are most immediately noticeable, and the aspects on which many beginning speakers wish to concentrate. Yet to focus intensively on the details of language and delivery may be the worst way to improve them; speakers may become so self-conscious that language and delivery are distracting mannerisms. This book, while quite specific in its treatment, focuses on language as a means to achieve a personal style and on delivery as a means to improve understanding of the message.

Comprehensive Treatment of Visual Aids and of Occasions for Public Speaking

The topics of visual aids and occasions for public speaking are common to public speaking books, but the treatment here is particularly comprehensive. A wide variety of visual aids are considered, including those that make use of contemporary computer technology. Although both deliberative and ceremonial occasions for public speaking are discussed, a much wider range of speaking occasions is presented—from everyday interchange to public forums to small groups.

A careful approach to the distinction between informing and persuading is noticeable in the later chapters. One of the most venerable traditions in public speaking instruction is to distinguish between speeches that inform and speeches that persuade. There is some value to that distinction, and yet we know that matters are not so simple. Most speeches are a blend of information and persuasion, sometimes so fine a blend that the elements cannot be separated. *Public Speaking* regards informing and persuading as headings for types of strategies speakers can use, and provides more specific coverage of speech purposes that may mix information and persuasion. Nevertheless, because of the time limitations of the classroom, instructors using this text can easily assign an informative speech and a persuasive speech without confusing students if they wish to do so. The realistic discussion of the blending and overlapping of informative and persuasive strategies is developed in Chapter 13 (Informing) and Chapter 14 (Persuading) in order to introduce students to the notion gradually.

A Rich Presentation of Audience Analysis and the Public Forum

Analysis of the audience is basic to any speaking situation, yet many books offer an unrealistic presentation of what audience analysis involves. They focus primarily on quantitative demographic information that the speaker often is unable to obtain. *Public Speaking* treats three separate levels of audience analysis and draws on awareness of audience psychology and culture—including responsiveness to cultural diversity—as well as demographics.

Public Speaking grounds public speaking in a concept of the *public forum*. All too often, the *public* dimension is missing from books on public speaking. Speakers will not always speak about personal issues to an audience made up only of their friends. Rather than treating the classroom situation as representative, this book argues that it is a simulation of the public forum. Audiences are called upon to make judgments about matters on which they cannot possibly have all the relevant information. The task of the speaker is to help in guiding listeners to make sound judgments. From this premise follow ideas about the importance of the speaker's *ethos,* about the responsibilities one incurs when speaking and the ethical standards one should meet, and about the collaborative nature of the speaker–audience relationship. These topics are all explored in this book. In addition, Appendix A focuses particularly on the public forum. It is intended to bridge the gap between the artificial speaking environment of the classroom and that of the "real world."

ORGANIZATION AND PEDAGOGY

Although unique perspectives and approaches are presented in almost every chapter, the structure of *Public Speaking* is relatively conventional, so that it might be adapted easily to public speaking classes at institutions of various types. An opening unit on the foundational skills of speaking and listening is followed by units that take up rhetorical invention, arrangement, style and delivery, and the contexts and occasions for speaking. Each chapter includes the following features:

- Learning objectives listed at chapter openings help readers anticipate key ideas they will need to keep in mind as the chapter develops.
- *Checklists* throughout every chapter provide students with a quick review and reinforcement of key guidelines as they read the chapter.
- Marginal glossaries remind students of key terms and concepts.
- End-of-chapter summaries encapsulate the highlights for easy review.
- *Using the Internet* activities at the end of each chapter offer students suggestions for exploring information on the Internet and learning about its use in the public speaking process. Through these activities, students can see the range of resources available while also understanding the limitations of that material.
- End-of-chapter questions, projects, and case studies, as well as footnote references, show background materials that interested students can pursue.

Appendix B contains ten full-length speeches for classes interested in analyzing the effectiveness of speakers in more depth. In addition to the seven contemporary pieces—three by students—there are three historical speeches that illustrate the power of applied rhetoric at key decision points in our national development. Headnotes call attention to features of the rhetorical situation for each of the ten speeches. An introduction, providing context and key information, precedes each speech.

SUPPLEMENTS

A full array of supplements has been developed to help instructors and students get the maximum benefit from working with this text.

FOR INSTRUCTORS

- *Annotated Instructor's Manual*
- *Test Bank*
- *Computerized Test Bank*
- *A&B Public Speaking Video*
- Student Speeches Video: Instructors may choose from one of a variety of student speeches videos offered by Allyn & Bacon.
- Instructional Video (featuring David Zarefsky)
- *A Guide for New Public Speaking Teachers*
- Public Speaking Transparencies
- Public Speaking PowerPoint Package (available only on the Allyn & Bacon website <www.abacon.com/speechcomm>)
- Digital Media Archive CD-ROM
- Communication Video Library

FOR STUDENTS

- *Speech Preparation Workbook*
- *Public Speaking in a Multicultural Environment* Essay
- Public Speaking Audio SoundGuide
- *Interactive Speechwriter* Software (Mac and IBM)
- *Preparing Visual Aids for Presentations* Guide
- *Quick Guide to the Internet for Speech Communication*
- Public Speaking Website <www.abacon.com/pubspeak>
- Companion website for *Public Speaking: Strategies for Success,* second edition <www.abacon.com/zarefsky>

ACKNOWLEDGMENTS

Articulating this perspective on public speaking in a textbook that is accessible to students has been a stimulating challenge. All or part of the manuscript was read by:

Ellen Arden-Ogle, Consumnes River College
Susan Baack, Montana State University

Ernest Bartow, Bucks County Community College

John Bee, Ohio State University

Sandra Berkowitz, Wayne State University

Vincent Bloom, California State University–Fresno

Faye Clark, DeKalb College

Marion Couvillon, Mississippi State University

Marilyn Cristiano, Paradise Valley Community College

Jim Dittus, Highland Community College

Susan Redding Emel, Baker University

Patricia Faverty, Thomas More College

William Fusfeld, University of Pittsburgh

Kathleen Galvin, Northwestern University

John Giertz, Bakersfield State University

Joseph Giordana, University of Wisconsin–Eau Claire

William Goodbar, Old Dominion University

Rose Gruber, Gloucester County College

Richard Halley, Weber State University

Diane Hill, Providence College

Carol Jablonski, University of South Florida

Karla Kay Jensen, Texas Tech University

Richard Jensen, University of Nevada–Las Vegas

Jack Johnson, University of Wisconsin–Milwaukee

William Jordan, North Carolina State University

Elizabeth Lamoureux, Buena Vista University

Al Montanaro, SUNY Plattsburgh

Stephen Neilson, University of Nevada–Las Vegas

Patrick O'Sullivan, Illinois State University

Cate Palczewski, University of Northern Iowa

Jay Pence, University of North Carolina–Chapel Hill

Lee Polk, Baylor University

Kenna J. Reeves, Emporia State University

Kurt Ritter, Texas A&M University

Kellie Roberts, University of Florida

Paul Sabelka, Iowa Wesleyan College

Noreen Schaefer-Faix, Kutztown University

Deanna Sellnow, North Dakota State University

Calvin Smith, Eastern Illinois University

Jessica Stowell, Tulsa Junior College

Robert Terrill, Indiana University

Denise Vrchota, Iowa State University

Beth Waggenspack, Virginia Polytechnic Institute and State University

Rita Kirk Whillock, Southern Methodist University

Roy Wood, University of Denver

The comments and suggestions of the reviewers listed above were quite helpful and often pointed the way for substantial improvement in the manuscript. The responsibility for what I have written, of course, remains with me.

My debt to Leah Ceccarelli, now on the faculty at the University of Washington, continues from the first edition. She helped in the development and selection of examples and end-of-chapter features. Victoria Gallagher, a member of the faculty at North Carolina State University, Glen Williams, now at the University of Akron, and Melissa Beall of the University of Northern Iowa developed the supplements for the first edition, and I remain grateful for their work.

I also appreciate the work of those who prepared the supplements for the second edition: Robert Brookey, University of Minnesota, who wrote the annotations and instructional material found in the *Annotated Instructor's Manual;* Robert Bookwalter, Marshall University, who provided excellent *Test Bank* questions and compiled questions for the *Online Study Guide* <www.abacon.com/zarefsky>; and Calvin Troup, Duquesne University, who brought his experiences and expertise in training public speaking instructors to *A Guide for New Public Speaking Teachers*. Additionally, Terry Doyle at Northern Virginia Community College assisted with the end-of-chapter *Using the Internet* activities. Finally, my thanks to Sherilyn Marrow at the University of Northern Colorado and her four students—T.J. Brinkerhoff, Carrie Biesel, Laura Breland, Latif Faraq— for allowing us into their lives during their public speaking course and contributing so much to the *Applying Strategies* boxed features.

At Allyn and Bacon, Steve Hull and Joe Opiela first persuaded me to undertake the task, and Bill Barke placed his faith in my ability to complete the book in a reasonable period of time. For the second edition, my editor has been Karon Bowers, who managed the marketing of the first edition and became intimately familiar with the book. Having her considerable editorial skills available for this new edition is an immense benefit. I also appreciate the conscientious attention to this work from Bob Weber, Production Administrator Joe Sweeney, and all the production staff at Allyn and Bacon, often working against short deadlines.

The title of the book, *Public Speaking: Strategies for Success,* has a twofold meaning. The book offers a strategic perspective that should lead students to become more successful public speakers. Additionally, the art of public speaking provides many of the strategies for students to succeed in many different walks of life. My hope is that this book will help you to empower your students to achieve that goal.

David Zarefsky

To the Student

In the fall of 1961, as a sophomore in high school, I enrolled in my first course in public speaking. As the saying goes, it changed my life. I had taken the course to become more comfortable in speaking before a group and to learn how to use my voice effectively and how to control distracting mannerisms. I accomplished those goals and so much more. I learned how to think analytically, how to organize ideas, how to do research, how to assess an audience, how to inform and persuade. It was not long before I realized that these skills and habits were valuable not just in public speaking but in every other course and, indeed, in almost every aspect of life. If I were to identify one course that provided the tools I have used in my personal and professional life, without a doubt Public Speaking would be that course.

Thirty years later, my daughter had an almost identical experience. After taking a course in public speaking, she suddenly realized that it was easier for her to write essays and research papers and that the papers were better. She began to read more critically and to analyze what she read. She, too, had found patterns for working with ideas that have been useful well beyond the confines of the course.

I hope that this book, and the course of which it is a part, will help you to have a similar experience. For over 2500 years men and women have studied the art of public speaking, both because it is valuable in its own right and because, in the best sense of the term, it is a liberal art—one that frees and empowers people. It does so by providing the knowledge, cultivating the skills, and modeling the habits of effective thought and expression that can be applied to any area of life.

APPLYING STRATEGIES

You will find Applying Strategies boxes in each chapter of this book. These boxes allow you to get to know four students (pictured at right) who attend the University of Northern Colorado in Greeley, Colorado. Just as you are doing now, these students took a public speaking course and experienced the same questions, fears, and uncertainties that you might encounter throughout the term. These students offer you their insight from their own public speaking experiences. The Applying Strategies boxes feature comments from the students as well as excerpts and sample material from their speeches that will provide you with tips and guidance. You will see how the necessary elements of a speech are implemented and how other students have used strategies discussed in this book. You will also hear from their instructor, Professor Sherilyn Marrow as she offers feedback on their outlines and speeches. From the experience of these students who have "been there," you will see that speaking in public is a valuable art and skill that is not as intimidating as it might appear at first.

Sherilyn Marrow: Greetings and welcome to the second edition of *Public Speaking: Strategies for Success* by David Zarefsky. I think you'll find Professor Zarefsky's textbook useful and friendly, just as my students at the University of Northern Colorado have. You'll learn a lot about speech making through the experiences of four of my students: Carrie, T.J., Latif, and Laura. No doubt you'll relate to one or all of these students. You'll read about their frustrations as well as their triumphs. They will share their perspectives on the "how-to's" of public speaking and offer suggestions to make your life a little easier. Much of their work is featured in the Applying Strategies boxes, along with my feedback as their instructor. It's our hope that this personalized approach will help you reach your public speaking goals. Consider us part of your strategy for success!

The title of this book is *Public Speaking: Strategies for Success*. That title has a double meaning. First, this book is about strategies for success in public speaking. Second, the premise of the book is that public speaking will provide you with strategies for success in life. Certainly it does not promise fame or fortune, but it does offer a blend of reflective judgment and carefully chosen action that should enable you, whatever your experience, to enjoy a life well lived.

I have chosen the term *strategy* to emphasize that public speaking is about *choices*. It is an art and not a science. When you speak, you will be faced with situations that offer both opportunities and constraints. You will want to decide how to work within this situation to achieve your goals, and your plan for doing so is a strategy. And even as you make choices in response to a situation, the pattern of your choices actually helps to define what the situation is. It affects you, but you also affect it.

Thinking strategically about public speaking means abandoning the belief that there is an all-purpose magic formula that will always produce a good speech. Although, as you will see, there are some general norms and expectations, a speech is good not because it follows some formula, but because it

Carrie Biesel

Carrie is a 21-year-old junior at UNC majoring in Speech Communication and Journalism. Her specific career goals are a position in either community affairs or public relations. She was born in California but has spent most of her life residing in Cortez, Colorado. Carrie has plenty of school spirit and enjoys combining her enthusiasm for school sports with her academic pursuits.

Laura Breland

Laura is a native Coloradan, having lived her 21 years in the Denver area. Currently a UNC junior, she plans on applying her English major and Sociology minor toward a teaching career or possibly working with adoption agencies in the future. She has overcome many challenges in her life, including Turner's Syndrome. Laura's hobbies include collecting dolls and running.

Latif Faraq

Latif is a 37-year-old, non-traditional student at UNC. Originally from Sudan, he has lived in the United States for the past five years. He is an extensive world traveler and has lived in many countries all over the world. At UNC he is a junior, majoring in Business and planning to continue with a Master's Degree. Formerly, he was an aircraft mechanic. Married with two children, Latif manages to work, study, and devote as much time as possible to his growing family.

T.J. Brinkerhoff

T.J. is a 21-year-old freshman at UNC majoring in Journalism and Mass Communication with an emphasis in Advertising. He is currently a quarterback for UNC's 1996 and 1997 Division II National Championship football team. In addition to juggling sports involvement, an academic career, and a part-time job, he loves to play guitar and create media-related memorabilia. T.J. is from Lakewood, Colorado, a suburb of Denver.

Sherilyn Marrow

Dr. Sherilyn Marrow (Ph.D., University of Denver) teaches in the Department of Speech Communication at the University of Northern Colorado. In addition to public speaking instruction, she teaches courses in family communication, research methodology, and interpersonal communication. She has presented and authored numerous works on how communication impacts the quality of personal and professional relationships. In the public speaking classroom, she remains professionally stimulated by facilitating the student's journey from reticence to confidence in public speaking.

deals effectively with a specific situation. A speech that is good in one context may be weak in another. It always is necessary to get down to cases.

For that reason, you will find many examples and case studies in this book. Some come from student speakers and some from speakers in the "real world." Some are actual situations and some are hypothetical ones. Some describe what speakers actually did and some ask you what you might do. Just as lawyers learn the law, in part, through the case method, so you will cultivate and sharpen the skills of public speaking by trying them out on specific cases.

Case material will be provided not only by this book, but also by your class. You will have the opportunity not only to present speeches, but to listen to many as well. Listening to speeches is also important, not just a necessary evil to be endured while you wait your turn to speak. You develop habits of analysis and memory, you see a large array of choices other students make in specific situations, and you gain skill in assessing whether strategies succeed or fail and in deciding whether or not they are strategies that you might wish to use.

At the same time, *Public Speaking* does not study cases in a vacuum. It draws on underlying theory to explain these situations. *Theory* does not refer to that which is impractical; nor does it refer to a lot of fancy terms or ideas that seem isolated from reality. Although sometimes the theory and practice of public speaking are studied in isolation, the premise of *Public Speaking* is that they need to be integrated at every step. Theory informs our understanding of practice by enabling us to explain what is happening in particular situations. And practice applies and modifies our understanding of theory. What you learn about theories of arrangement, for instance, will help you to organize a speech, but your experience in organizing speeches will also contribute to your thinking about theories of arrangement.

It is a pleasure to welcome you to this class in public speaking. This book, your own experience, and the interaction with other students and your instructor are all vital parts of the course. I hope that, like my daughter and me, you will find that you not only achieve your original goals, but actually transcend them.

David Zarefsky

Public Speaking

chapter 1
Welcome to Public Speaking

In This Chapter We Will:

- Identify the principal things you will learn in this course and how they will benefit you outside the classroom.

- Understand public speaking as a communication process in which the speaker and listeners jointly create meaning and understanding.

- Examine the main goals and strategies for developing a speech and learn how to prepare your first speech for this course.

- Discover how nervousness can be used to your advantage in public speaking and learn strategies to overcome anxiety.

- Recognize what makes a speech of high quality.

- Consider the ethical responsibilities of both speakers and listeners.

Welcome to Public Speaking, one of the most important courses you will ever take. If that sounds like a strong claim, consider what the following students had to say after completing a public speaking course:

> Before this class, I was extremely apprehensive about speaking in front of an audience. If the class hadn't been a requirement, I might have dropped it. Now I'm very glad that I took it. It helped a lot and gave me more confidence to speak in front of other people.

> My speeches have better content now, and I am more able to speak loudly and slowly without looking at notes.

> The most important thing that I've learned is how to organize my ideas—whether for a speech or a paper. I'm still not a great speaker, but now I know how to better communicate my ideas.

> After taking this class, I look more closely at arguments for their validity, and I'm more critical of other people's logic. I also have a better understanding of the ethical component of public speaking. I can recognize statements that are "loaded" and can respond to them appropriately.

WHY STUDY PUBLIC SPEAKING?

You may have enrolled in this course because you expect to be making public presentations and you want to learn how to do that better and more easily. Maybe your goal is to speak more forcefully or to be less nervous. Perhaps you want to become better organized, to learn more about how to pre-

Ethos, *your character as perceived by the audience, is influenced by first impressions. A self-assured, confident stance is the best possible beginning toward establishing positive* ethos.

pare a speech, or to think more clearly and more critically. You may even have chosen the course because it meets at a convenient time, is a requirement for graduation, or has a good instructor.

Apply What You Learn

Whatever your reasons for studying public speaking, this is one of the few courses you will take that combine theory and practice—that help you apply classroom content in your daily life. As you study creative and critical thinking, sensitivity to audiences, and effective speech presentation, the skills you learn will

- Help you critically evaluate messages and appeals of all kinds
- Make you more sensitive to people and situations
- Increase your self-confidence and your willingness to engage in serious dialogue with others[1]

Outside the classroom, these attributes will enhance your value as an employee and as a citizen. Employers and career counselors often put "good communication skills" at the top of the list of qualities they seek in people.[2] The reason is simple: Each year our economy becomes more dependent on information and the ability to communicate it.

Your study of public speaking will also help make you a more competent, more active citizen. The skills listed above will make you better able to understand public issues and social controversies, to decide what you think about them, and to participate effectively in resolving them—whether on your campus, in your neighborhood, or in the larger public forum.

Develop Specific Communication Skills

Here are some of the specific skills you will learn or improve by studying public speaking:

- How to listen carefully and critically in order to understand and evaluate what others say
- How to decide what you want to speak about and to select what to say
- How to find the material for a speech by examining your own experience, consulting with others, and using a library
- How to think critically about what you read and observe so that you will reason soundly when addressing an audience
- How to organize a speech to make it clear, coherent, sensible, and effective
- How to use language skillfully to convey both meaning and mood
- How to use your voice and your body to present yourself and your message in an effective, compelling way
- How to adapt general principles to your particular speaking situation, with emphasis on the dimensions of informing, persuading, and entertaining
- How to understand and benefit from reactions to your speeches so that the audience's response helps you improve your skills

In this chapter we will discuss each of these skills only briefly, so that you are able to get started practicing them. Each topic introduced here will be covered more fully later in the book.

This set of skills has been studied and taught for about 2,500 years (in different ways over the years, of course), so you are taking part in a very old and valuable academic tradition.

Focus on Critical Thinking and Strategic Planning

Besides improving these specific skills as a communicator, you also will be applying and refining two invaluable general skills that are emphasized throughout this book: critical thinking and strategic planning.

CRITICAL THINKING   Public speaking is in large measure an exercise in **critical thinking,** the ability to form and defend your own judgments rather than blindly accepting or instantly rejecting what you hear or read. Critical thinkers can analyze and understand various points of view, and they can quickly recognize the difference between fact and opinion.

Facts, as we will see in detail later, are statements that—at least in theory—can be *verified* by someone else. If a speaker says that the world's population has doubled every 25 years, that statement can be tested by checking population statistics. In contrast, **opinions** are *subjective* judgments that presumably are based on experience or expertise. If a speaker asserts that the world's population is growing too fast, that opinion cannot be verified externally; it stands or falls depending on the insight and judgment of the person who offers it.

Critical thinking is the basis of those "good communication skills" that employers seek and democracies need. As a listener, critical thinking will help you to recognize a speaker's unstated assumptions. As a speaker, it will help you to form precise statements that embody your thoughts. Overall, critical thinking will place ideas into a broader context, showing how they relate to other things that you already know or believe.

The particular skills of critical thinking are the focus of Chapter 2, but they will inform all your work in this course.

STRATEGIC PLANNING   A speaker operates in a world of choices: whether to speak, when to speak, what to say, how to phrase a particular point, how to explain or defend it, how to organize the message, what tone to give it, and exactly how to relate it to the audience. Even all these options do not exhaust the possibilities! Some speakers make these choices unconsciously, without real thought (and relying on luck). But effective speakers make their choices *strategically;* through **strategic planning** they identify their goals and then determine how best to achieve them.

Chapter 4 will focus on strategies relating to a speaker's many choices, but throughout the book you will be reminded—and encouraged—to think strategically.

PUBLIC SPEAKING AND COMMUNICATION

When you give a speech, you and your listeners are involved in **communication,** meaning that you interact in order to build some sort of connection whereby you can understand each other and recognize common interests.

---

critical thinking
The ability to form and defend your own judgments rather than blindly accepting or instantly rejecting what you hear or read.

facts
Statements that are capable of being verified by someone other than the speaker.

opinions
Subjective judgments based on experience or expertise, not capable of being verified by someone else.

strategic planning
The process of identifying your goals and then determining how best to achieve them.

communication
Interaction that builds connections between people that help them to understand each other and to recognize common interests.

How does this happen? And how does public speaking differ from other forms of communication such as personal conversation and written essays?

Early theories of communication viewed public speaking as a series of one-way messages sent from speaker to audience. In fact, however, the audience participates with the speaker in creating shared meaning and understanding. The speaker's ideas and values are tested and refined through interaction with the audience, and listeners' knowledge and understanding are modified through interaction with the speaker. Thus, public speaking is a *continuous* communication process in which messages and signals circulate back and forth between speaker and listeners.

From the audience's point of view, each listener comes to the speech with a framework of prior knowledge, beliefs, and values, and each listener "decodes," or interprets, the speaker's message within this personal framework. To a particular listener some ideas will be more important, or *salient,* than other ideas. If the speech is about vegetarian diets, for example, some listeners will approach it with special interest in health and nutrition, others will be concerned about the welfare of animals, and still others will view vegetarianism as a fad for eccentrics. The speech may support, challenge, or modify any of these frameworks, but each listener's framework will shape how he or she interprets and understands the speech. Audience members work actively to assess what the speaker says against what they already know or believe, and they constantly make judgments about the message and convey them back to the speaker through facial responses and other nonverbal clues.

From the speaker's point of view, knowing about the audience is crucial in preparing and delivering a speech. A speech about campus social life, for example, would be different for an audience of prospective students than for an audience of alumni. Even if the basic points of the speech were the same, the nature of the audience would affect how they are developed and explained and what tone or attitude the speaker projects. In preparing the speech, the speaker would analyze the audience and try to match listeners' expectations appropriately. Moreover, as listeners respond during the speech (by frowning, nodding approval, looking puzzled, etc.), the speaker would constantly modify how key points are organized and phrased and would try to acknowledge or respond to the audience's concerns.

Figure 1.1 on page 8 depicts this interplay between speaker and audience. Suppose that you plan to speak about the benefits of a vegetarian diet. In preparing the speech you'll remember that some listeners think vegetarianism is healthful, others think it is a passing fad, and still others associate it with eccentrics who don't really understand nutrition. As you speak, you'll be watching for **feedback,** responses from the audience that signal how they are reacting to what you say. Most responses will be nonverbal, such as frowns or nods of approval. Feedback might prompt you to acknowledge that some people doubt the merits of vegetarian diets; you might even admit that you had doubts yourself but now are a committed vegetarian. Throughout the speech—beginning with its preparation and lasting through its presentation—you will be sensitive to how well your ideas match your audience, and you'll use feedback to improve the fit as you speak.

Remember that audience members will not be passive. Each will assess everything you say against what he or she already believes. You may convince some to change their beliefs; others may interpret your message in ways consistent with their beliefs; and if the discrepancy between their beliefs and your

feedback
Responses from the audience to the speaker, often in the form of nonverbal cues.

FIGURE 1.1

Public speaking as a communication process.

message is too great, some listeners will reject your message. In any case, the audience will be actively involved as you speak, interpreting and testing what you say against their own beliefs and values and letting you know their reactions.

THE RHETORICAL SITUATION

From the preceding we can see that one way in which public speaking differs from other forms of communication is that *the speaker and listeners simultaneously participate in creating the message.* Another unique characteristic of public speaking is that it occurs *in response to a specific situation.* Unlike great dramatic or literary works, which "speak to the ages," the principal test of a good speech is whether it responds most effectively to the needs of the situation in which it is presented.[3]

The **situation** is the specific context in which a speech is given. Compared with poems and stories, which are read long after they were written, most speeches have a short life span. For example, student Mohammed Ghouse's first speech to his classmates concerned an important and timely issue:

> We read about people getting killed every day in Sarajevo—infants who are shot in their mothers' arms, children who dodge sniper fire to attend school in the bombed-out shell of a schoolhouse, young men who have lost limbs to this horrifying ethnic war. We must do whatever we can to stop the bloodshed—as individuals and as a nation.

situation

The particular context in which a speech takes place.

Although Mohammed's speech probably could be appreciated long after the war in Bosnia ended, it was created in response to a particular event and was designed primarily to be heard by a particular audience.

The study of how messages affect people has long been called **rhetoric.** This ancient discipline is concerned with the role that messages play in

- Shaping, reaffirming, and modifying people's values
- Binding people closer together or moving them farther apart
- Celebrating significant events
- Creating a sense of identity among people
- Conveying information and helping people to learn
- Nurturing, strengthening, or changing people's beliefs
- Leading people to take (or not to take) action

A **rhetorical situation,** then, is a situation in which people's understanding can be changed through messages.[4]

The following example shows how student Adam Paul Vales responded to a rhetorical situation by urging classmates not to park their cars on streets surrounding the campus:

> When you park on the streets, you make life miserable for the people who live in the apartments there. Sometimes, residents of those streets have to carry groceries four blocks through the snow because they are unable to find parking near their homes! When you go home, do you have to drive that far to find parking, or do you park on your own street? Is it fair to take that convenience away from our neighbors?
>
> I know you park on these streets because you have no place to park on campus. But the only reason the university is not building more parking lots is that they know the easier solution is just to force you to park on the street. This solution may be easy for the university, but it is very hard on the community. By refusing to park on the street and by demanding new parking lots, you will force the university to live up to its responsibilities to its students and to the local community.

Adam's message addressed a particular audience and asked its members to consider a specific problem and solution. The speech was timely and the message affected how listeners understood the situation. A well-conceived, well-presented speech can help resolve a problem that causes a particular situation, or it can help listeners to see the situation in a new light. An ineffective speech will leave the situation unchanged or may even make matters worse.

Determinants of the Rhetorical Situation

Figure 1.2 on page 10 shows the four basic factors that determine the success of any rhetorical situation: the audience, the occasion, the speaker, and the speech itself.

THE AUDIENCE   Whereas a poem or a novel is addressed to all potential readers over time, a speech is usually presented to a specific **audience.** Most speakers, most of the time, want to present their ideas in a way that achieves **identification** with the audience; that is, they try to find common ground between what they know about the audience and what they want to say. Bear in mind, though, that a speaker sometimes might want to *avoid* common ground and even to antagonize listeners to get their attention or to motivate them to participate.

rhetoric
The study of how messages affect people.

rhetorical situation
A situation in which people's understanding can be changed through messages.

audience
The people who assemble to listen to a speech.

identification
Formation of common bonds between a speaker and the audience.

FIGURE 1.2

Determinants of the rhetorical situation.

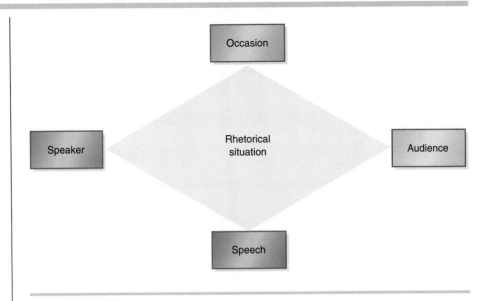

Listeners, as you know, are not passive receivers of the message. Instead, they form judgments about the speaker and message while the speech is in progress, and they communicate their judgments through feedback. Such reactions as eye contact, smiles, yawns, and frowns tell the speaker whether listeners understand the point being made, whether they are confused and need further explanation, whether they are paying close attention or seem distracted or bored, and whether the argument seems strong or needs additional support.

Ultimately, of course, the audience determines whether the speech was successful—whether a "speech to entertain" really was entertaining, whether a speech about a problem really did provide new information and insights, whether listeners actually will take the action that the speaker advocates. Because the audience is so important in determining the success of a rhetorical situation, Chapter 3 will explain in detail how to analyze the audience.

THE OCCASION (AND PURPOSE)   The **occasion** is the specific setting for the speech, the circumstances in which it occurs. The date, time, place, and purpose all influence the rhetorical situation. "A commencement speech about school reform, delivered at Western State University in June of 1998" is an example of an occasion; "growing unease about the quality of public education" is the rhetorical situation to which this speech was a response.

People speak on all kinds of occasions and for many reasons. Some speeches commemorate an important event or enact a ritual, such as presenting or accepting an award, delivering a eulogy, introducing or toasting someone, or entertaining an audience. Other speeches involve problem solving and decision making, such as giving an oral report or a sales presentation, advocating a policy, or refuting an argument. Still other occasions arise in which the speaker wants to lead the audience in deciding what is true, or in passing judgment on actions, or in applying some rule or social convention.

occasion

The specific setting for the speech; the context in which it takes place.

Whatever the occasion, the audience arrives with ideas about what is and what is not *appropriate behavior.* Such expectations have developed over time, and they limit what a speaker can do in responding to the rhetorical situation. For example, listeners expect a eulogy to offer a favorable view of the deceased, and they normally would think it inappropriate for a speaker to dwell on the person's failings. On the other hand, an after-dinner speech is usually expected to be lighthearted; a speaker who instead presents a highly technical lecture would not be responding appropriately to the occasion.

Simultaneous events further define the occasion. For example, the fact that a presidential campaign is underway helps to define the occasion for a speech about health reform. The retirement of a popular athlete helps to set the stage for a speech about retirement trends in industry. And if listeners only last week were urged to give up tobacco, that may affect their judgments about a speech that now asks them to give up red meat.

The *purpose* of the speech also defines the occasion, and we will look closely at three basic purposes (informing, persuading, and entertaining) at the end of this chapter. Most of the speeches that you will present will be **deliberative,** meaning that your purpose is to share information and to influence listeners' beliefs and actions. Much of this book therefore will focus on the skills needed to inform and to persuade. But we also will examine other reasons for speaking, such as celebrating and entertaining, and how they affect the rhetorical situation. Finally, Chapter 15 will explore the wide range of occasions for public speaking.

THE SPEAKER   The same speech delivered by different speakers will produce different reactions and effects in an audience. The concept of *ethos,* which we will examine in more detail later, refers to the speaker's character as the audience perceives it. Developing and maintaining positive ethos will contribute immeasurably to the success of a speech. If you appear interested in your topic, the audience will be more likely to be interested, too. If you appear to know what you are talking about, listeners will be more likely to trust your judgment and to follow your advice. Fortunately, you can learn the skills that enable a speaker to contribute positively to a rhetorical situation, and so we will focus on ways to develop and maintain positive ethos throughout the book.

THE SPEECH   Although we tend to think of the situation as something to which the speech *responds,* the message itself also works to *shape the situation.* Before Adam Paul Vales spoke about parking on campus, his audience thought of the side streets as a convenient parking lot; but during the speech they began to see those streets as symbols of campus politics and community responsibility. The message had redefined the situation.

In most cases, an audience's understanding of a situation can be improved by a speech that is organized effectively, that includes interesting examples and memorable phrases, and that is presented enthusiastically. Although many factors determine whether or not a speech responds successfully to a rhetorical situation, by understanding the basic factors involved you can better shape your message as a speaker and can participate more fully as a listener.

deliberative
Intended to give listeners new information and to influence their thought and action.

GOALS AND STRATEGIES FOR YOUR FIRST SPEECH

Most instructors assign a first speech early in the course, often asking students to introduce themselves or a classmate or to briefly develop a single main idea. Whatever your specific assignment is, two goals are important for any speech:

1. Your message should be clear.
2. You should establish positive ethos.

After examining what these goals entail, we will explore some strategies for achieving them.

A Clear Message

First, your speech should have a clear purpose and thesis. The **purpose** is your goal for the speech, the response you are seeking from listeners. The **thesis** is a statement of your main idea; it summarizes the basic point you want the audience to accept.

YOUR PURPOSE   Obviously, as a speaker you want listeners to pay attention to you and to think well of you. Beyond that, however, speeches can seek many different responses from the audience. Do you primarily want to impart information, to teach listeners something new? Or do you want to remind them of something they already believe so they will be more aware of it and how it affects them? Is it your goal to make listeners see the humorous side of something they regard as serious—or perhaps to see the serious side of what they may otherwise view as a joke? Do you want them to pay more attention to something that they may tend to ignore? Do you hope to change their beliefs or attitudes about something? Do you want listeners to take some specific action as a result of your speech?

Questions like these illustrate the many possible purposes that a speaker might have, but not all of them are suitable for a brief first speech. In your first

purpose
The goal of the speech, the response sought from listeners.

thesis
The main idea of the speech, usually stated in one or two sentences.

Checklist

1.1   *Goals for Your First Speech*

1. **Develop a clear message.**
   - *Choose a topic—the general subject area of the speech (unless your instructor has assigned the topic).*
   - *Determine the purpose of the speech.*
     Informing
     Persuading
     Entertaining
   - *State your thesis—the main idea of the speech.*

2. **Establish positive ethos.**
   - *Recognize that an audience's judgments about a speaker's character are:*
     Quite detailed
     Made quickly
     Durable

---

assignment you should aim to provide new information and ask listeners to think about it. For now, this is a more realistic goal than aiming to change your listeners' beliefs or attitudes. We will look more closely at the purposes of a speech later in the chapter. At this point, it is enough that you can state your purpose clearly in a sentence or two.

YOUR THESIS   After you have defined your purpose for speaking, you should clearly state the thesis, or main idea, that you want the speech to establish. After your speech is over, listeners should have little doubt about what you actually said or what you meant. If you find it difficult to state your main idea in a sentence or two, you may be trying to cover too much. Even complex technical claims should be reducible to simple, basic thesis statements.

If the effort to state your thesis results in a statement like "I'm going to talk about computers," you have not focused sharply enough on your subject; you have only identified a general area. A better, more specific statement of what the speech will seek to establish might be, "Using a computer has changed how I study." Similarly, if the purpose of your first speech is to introduce someone, simply saying "I am going to tell you about Jack Green" is too broad. Instead, a focused thesis statement like "Jack Green's life was greatly affected by his growing up in Europe" tells the audience exactly what your speech will claim. Stating your thesis in a single specific sentence will help ensure that you focus on the main idea rather than talking around it.

Establishing Positive Ethos

The second goal for your beginning speech is to establish positive ethos as a speaker. This Greek term was used by teachers of public speaking 2,500 years ago, and a rough translation is *character*.[5] But ethos does not refer to innate character traits, those at the core of a person's identity. Rather, **ethos** refers to the character that is *attributed to* a speaker by listeners on the basis of what the speaker says and does in the speech. Ethos is the character that you project when you are in a speaking situation. Some textbooks use the term *credibility* to describe this concept, but listeners make other judgments besides whether or not they should believe you. They also form impressions about what kind of person they think you are, based on what you say and project as a speaker.

Try the following experiment. Select a classmate whom you don't yet know well, and listen carefully to his or her first speech. Then, based only on the speech, jot down all the adjectives you can think of with which you would describe this person. Your list might look something like this:

nervous	funny
intelligent	slick
trustworthy	friendly
weak	unsure
deferential	happy
concerned	committed
respectful	tasteful

ethos
The speaker's character as perceived by the audience.

Even a list this long will not capture *all* the attributes you might perceive in a speaker upon hearing a short speech. What can we conclude from this simple exercise about ethos and its effects?

First, *an audience's judgments about a speaker's character can be quite detailed.* From this exercise you seem to know quite a bit about the speaker, based only on a very brief first speech. You have a sense of the person's intellect, emotions, judgment, relationships with others, power, confidence, and sense of self. Each of these is an important dimension of a person's character, and listeners make many such judgments about a speaker.

Second, *judgments about a speaker's character are made quickly.* Your classmate's speech probably lasted only a few minutes, and yet it gave you many insights into the person's apparent character. This exercise shows that assessments of ethos often reflect superficial first impressions. Whether the speaker walked confidently to the front of the room, looked at the audience, and then began speaking or whether the speaker seemed unsure, looked at the floor, and spoke before reaching the front of the room may give you clues about the person. As a listener you decide whether the speaker is nervous or comfortable, whether the speaker values the relationship with the audience, and how much confidence the speaker has in what she or he says. Your judgments may turn out to be wrong, of course, but you based them on the information you had. Listeners often only have first impressions to guide them in assessing a speaker, and they form judgments quickly.

Third, *assessments of ethos are durable.* Listeners' first impressions not only shape how they judge the speaker but also affect how they think about the speech and interpret what comes later. If the first impression you make is that you are very serious, it will seem out of character when you tell a joke later in the speech. The joke may cause listeners to revise their first impression ("Oh, that speaker's not so somber after all"), but it may also affect how they interpret the joke ("Such a serious person can't even tell a joke that's really funny").

The first speech is an icebreaker, an opportunity to learn about your classmates and to share things about yourself. Because an audience's assessments of a speaker are detailed, are formed quickly, and are durable, the goal of developing positive ethos in your first speech is just as important as having a clear statement of your purpose and thesis.

STRATEGIES FOR ORGANIZING YOUR SPEECH

Once you have in mind the twin goals of presenting a clear message and establishing positive ethos, the next step is to think strategically about ways to organize the speech in order to achieve these goals.

Basically, every speech has three parts: a beginning, a middle, and an end. We will call these the *introduction,* the *body,* and the *conclusion,* and we will examine them fully in Chapters 7 and 8. For now, it is enough to realize that each part of a speech includes certain elements and performs certain functions.

The Introduction

Your **introduction** should be designed to (1) get the audience's attention, (2) state your thesis, and (3) preview how you will develop your ideas.

introduction
The beginning of the speech, designed to get the audience's attention, to state the thesis, and to preview the development of the speech.

> ## 1.2 *Decisions about Organization*
>
> 1. **Develop an introduction.**
>   - *Get the audience's attention.*
>   - *State your thesis.*
>   - *Preview the development of the speech.*
> 2. **Assemble the body of the speech.**
>   - *Decide which kinds of supporting materials you need.*
>   *Experience*
>   *Narratives*
>   *Data*
>   *Opinions*
>   - *Decide how to organize the supporting materials.*
>   *Time order*
>   *Spatial order*
>   *Cause–effect order*
>   *Problem–solution order*
>   *Topical order*
> 3. **Prepare a conclusion.**
>   - *Draw together the ideas in the speech.*
>   - *Provide a strong note of finality.*

Often the third function can be omitted in a short speech that has only one main point.

To get listeners' attention and put them in the right frame of mind, you might startle the audience with a significant but little-known fact. If your speech is about recycling, for example, you could begin by asking, "Do you realize that the trees of an entire forest are harvested each year to make paper for textbooks?" Or if your speech is about the benefits of technology, you might begin with a story that illustrates what it was like to practice law before the advent of computerized databases. Your opening statement is the first impression of the speech that listeners will receive; you want to get their attention and focus it appropriately on your main idea.

The statement of your thesis further serves to put listeners in the right frame of mind by defining the context in which you want them to interpret what you are about to say. In speaking about recycling, for example, your thesis might be, "We need to get serious about conserving and replenishing our natural resources." If you identified your thesis clearly when preparing the speech, stating it in the introduction should be easy.

To preview how you will develop your thesis, the final thing the introduction should do is make a natural transition to the body of the speech by telling listeners what to expect. For example, you might follow your thesis statement with, "After examining how our forests have been reduced over the last fifty years, I will outline some simple measures that we can take to prevent further deforestation."

The Body

The **body** is the largest portion of the speech; it develops your thesis statement and offers whatever proof you need to support your claims.

SUPPORTING MATERIALS   **Supporting materials** are all forms of evidence that lend weight to the truth of your thesis, whether by explaining,

body
The largest portion of the speech; includes the development of supporting materials to prove the thesis and any subsidiary claims.

supporting materials
All forms of evidence that lend weight to the truth of a claim.

illustrating, or defending it. The many kinds of supporting materials can be grouped into a few broad categories:

- Experience
- Narratives (stories)
- Data
- Opinions

You can draw on your own *experience* with a topic or problem to make it clear that you are familiar with and have been affected by the subject of your speech. For example, if your thesis is "Health care takes too large a bite out of personal income," you could tell the audience what percentage of your own paycheck goes toward health costs. If your thesis is that travel broadens a person's mind, you could draw on your own travel experiences. To support the thesis that everyone needs to know about self-defense, student Teresa Madera described how she escaped from an assailant:

> It was late, and I was returning to the dorm after studying at the library. When I was passing an alley, a stranger jumped out at me. Luckily, I was carrying this key-chain. You'll notice that it has a small canister attached to it. This is mace, and it probably saved my life. I sprayed the guy who attacked me and then didn't wait around to see what happened.

Teresa went on to explain how her experience had convinced her that all students should be prepared to defend themselves.

You can use *narratives,* or stories, for supporting material; people often explain (and understand) situations in terms of a story. For example, in a speech about child abuse, student Stacey Gerbman illustrated the impact of the problem by telling the story of five-year-old Joey, who was abused by his father:

> Joey was afraid of his father. He hadn't meant to drop the milk jug, but it was so heavy. As he cringed in the corner of the kitchen, his father was screaming at him. Maybe he *was* a scrawny wimp, as his father said. Only a coward would whimper at the prospect of a beating. When the blows actually came, Joey couldn't stop crying. The next day, he had bruises on both body and soul.

Stacey ended the speech—and concluded the story—by telling how Joey later became a violent man himself:

> When Joey grew up and raised his own family, he too beat his children and showered them with verbal taunts. Sadly, he had learned that behavior all too well from his own father.

You can draw on *data* ("facts") for supporting material. If you claim that telephones outnumber people in the United States, you could simply use statistical tables to report the two total numbers. If the thesis is "Most American presidents have been lawyers," then naming all the lawyer-presidents would provide factual support.

You also can use *opinions* to support your thesis. As noted earlier, opinions are subjective judgments based on a person's experience; unlike facts, opinions cannot be verified. But if you use the opinions of experts to support your claims, those judgments are authoritative, because they are based on expertise in the subject. Opinions are especially useful in situations where you cannot observe things yourself or when you want to support promises or predictions. For instance, to support a prediction that inflation will not worsen over the next six months, you could cite the opinion of the chair of the Federal Reserve Board. In offering an opinion, of course, you want to be sure that the person really is an expert in the field and that he or she has no ax to grind and is not biased.

ORGANIZING THE EVIDENCE Whenever you offer more than one piece of supporting material, you must decide in what order to arrange your evidence. Suppose, for example, that you want to use facts, narratives, and opinions to support the claim that prisons are seriously overcrowded. Which type of material should you present first?

Sometimes the decision about organization is just a matter of preference—of what seems instinctively to have the most natural "flow." You might decide on this basis to begin with a narrative, then state the facts about prison overcrowding, and finally conclude with the opinions of some prisoners and corrections officers. In cases like this you should try several organizational arrangements to see which works best. You might ask some friends whether the thesis is clearer or more effective when you organize the supporting material one way rather than another.

At other times, the supporting material may suggest an organizational arrangement. If you are speaking about three times that your town was damaged by a flood, it makes sense to arrange the occasions chronologically—either from first to last or from last to first. Disrupting this natural pattern by describing the floods in random order would make the speech harder to follow.

Time order, as in this example, is one natural organizational pattern. Another is *spatial order*—arranging items according to their location. To discuss the varied geography of Texas, for example, you might proceed clockwise, beginning with the Panhandle in the far north, then describing the hill country of central Texas and the "piney woods" of the east, then dipping southward to cover the Gulf Coast and the Rio Grande Valley, and finally heading to western Texas and the Big Bend country.

Other common organizational patterns are *cause–effect* (beginning with conditions and then describing their causes, or vice versa); *problem–solution* (first explaining a problem and then pointing to the solution); and *topical structure* (mentioning all the economic facts, for example, before mentioning all the political facts). Strategies for using different organizational patterns will be explored in later chapters.

The Conclusion

The final part of the speech is the **conclusion,** which has two basic tasks. First, it should draw together the ideas in the speech so that they are memorable. This is sometimes done by a brief summary of the argument, sometimes by a restatement of the main points or ideas, sometimes by repetition of the thesis. Second, the conclusion should give a strong note of finality to the speech. It might restate the idea in the introduction to suggest a completed circle. It might challenge the audience with an interesting question. Or it might draw on the claims in the speech to appeal for a specific belief or action on the part of the listeners.

conclusion
The ending of the speech; draws together the main ideas and provides a note of finality.

BEGINNING ASSIGNMENTS

The One-Point Speech

A common first speaking assignment is the **one-point speech,** in which the speaker's task is to establish only one main idea (the thesis). This type of speech requires a thesis that is clear and simple, and it is developed as follows:

Introduction

1. Wake up!
2. This concerns you.
3. Generally speaking

Body

4. For example

Conclusion

5. So what?

As indicated, the first three steps enact the introduction to the speech. "Wake up!" is the device to get the audience's attention, such as an interesting story, a startling statistic, or an unexpected fact. "This concerns you" shows listeners how the topic relates to them; it gives them reason to pay attention and to take the speech seriously. "Generally speaking" states the thesis of the speech.

"Generally speaking" also forms a natural transition to the body of the speech, represented by the heading "For example." The body develops the thesis by presenting whatever supporting materials are needed to support the claims in the thesis—experiences, stories, facts, and opinions, arranged in whichever order is most effective.

Finally, "So what?" signals the twofold function of the conclusion: drawing together the important ideas of the speech and making a final lasting impression on the audience. Answering "So what?" points out what the supporting material leads to and gives listeners cues about what they should believe or do.

The following short example of a one-point speech has the thesis "Using a personal computer has changed how I study." The sections of the speech are indicated in brackets.

[WAKE UP!] When my parents went to college, they did their assignments with a mechanical typewriter and a slide rule. They aren't old, but this technology seems as ancient now as the slate tablets of the 1800s. [THIS CONCERNS YOU] When I told them I needed a computer for college, they were surprised. Some of you may also have had trouble explaining this to your parents. [GENERALLY SPEAKING] But using a personal computer has changed how I study. [FOR EXAMPLE] I take it to the library, and it's much easier to take notes about what I read. I can call up databases for my research class in political science. I actually revise papers

one-point speech

A speech in which only one main idea (the thesis) is offered and established.

after I've written them. I use electronic mail to ask the professor a question when there's something I don't understand. I download articles from the Internet. And I even write final exams on the computer whenever I can. [SO WHAT?] I can't imagine being a college student in the precomputer age. We should all stop to realize how much our lives have changed.

Being short and simple, the one-point speech is a good way to master the basic structure of a speech. For this first speech, you may have a day or more to prepare. But the five-step structure of the one-point speech is also useful whenever you have to speak impromptu—on the spur of the moment. When you raise your hand to speak at a meeting or in class, remembering the structure of the one-point speech will help you state your point briefly, clearly, and effectively.

The Speech of Introduction

Another common first assignment is a speech to introduce yourself, a classmate, or a famous person whom you imagine inviting to class. You can easily adapt the structure of the one-point speech to a speech of introduction if you avoid reciting all the details of the person's biography. Such a recitation would have no central theme; besides lacking a sense of unity, the speech would be dull. Instead, select a key aspect of the individual's experience, and devise your thesis from that. Then follow the structure of the one-point speech.

For example, you might open with a statement such as "Unlike most of us, John Patterson has never lived out of this town." The contrast between John and his classmates should capture the audience's attention and interest. This achieves the "Wake up!" function of the one-point speech.

Your next statement might be, "John's experience can give us insight into the sense of roots that many of our ancestors had but most of us lack today." This identifies how you will make John's experience relevant to the audience, fulfilling the "This concerns you" step in the one-point speech.

Then you might state the thesis: "This town is so much a part of John's identity that he cannot imagine himself apart from it." This step matches "Generally speaking" in the one-point speech. It both states the idea that you intend to establish and provides a natural transition to the body of the speech.

The next step is to support this thesis. You might do it by referring to key events in John's life that are closely identified with the town: growing up where everyone knew everyone else, participating in parades and celebrations, living as an adult in the same house that he occupied as a child, and watching things change around him as others moved into or out of town. These experiences are the supporting material, corresponding to "For example" in the one-point speech. Decide which order to present them in and how much detail to provide.

Finally, conclude by answering the implicit question "So what?" You might say something like, "So, the next time you read statistics about how often people move, or the next time you think about how many careers you might have during your life, remember that some people choose to nurture their roots where they stand. John Patterson is a thriving example."

THE SITUATION

You have three minutes to introduce yourself to your classmates and your instructor in your public speaking class. Three minutes is not enough time to describe everything there is to know about you, so choices must be made.

MAKING CHOICES

1. How should you decide what you want to share about yourself?

   Should you consider: the members of your audience? your classroom setting? your goals for the class? the course subject? how much or how little you want the audience to know about you?

   What else might you consider?

2. What is the most relevant information to relay to your instructor and fellow students?

   Should you describe: your primary likes and dislikes? where you are from? what your hobbies and personal interests are? why you are fearful of speaking in public?

   What other information about yourself might you include in your speech?

WHAT IF . . .

Let's assume you are given the same assignment but with a different audience and a different purpose. How would your decisions above be affected by the following conditions?

1. Your public speaking classmates are evaluating your speech for a grade.

2. Your speech of introduction assignment will not be graded.

3. Your audience is now the entire student body, and your purpose is to announce your candidacy for student president.

4. Your audience is the active members of a fraternity/sorority that you would like to join.

PRACTICING THE SPEECH

Now that you have analyzed how to put a speech together, you will soon be ready to speak. First, though, you should develop an outline of the speech and practice talking through its main ideas.

Outlining Your Speech

Sometimes speakers read a speech, word for word, from a fully written manuscript. On rare occasions they also commit the speech to memory.[6] These approaches may be helpful for highly formal speeches when every word matters and will be recorded for posterity. But for most of your speeches in this course, writing out and memorizing every word not only is a waste of time but may actually hinder your communication with the audience.

On the other hand, neither is it a good idea to speak impromptu—without preparation, trusting that a flash of inspiration will strike you as you speak. Most successful speakers aim for middle ground with an **extemporaneous** speech, meaning that they have a clear sense of the main ideas and how to organize them, but they have not planned the speech in advance word for word.

In speaking extemporaneously, an outline of the speech is a tremendous help. In fact, *two* outlines are even more helpful: a preparation outline and a presentation outline.

PREPARATION OUTLINE   Begin developing your speech with a **preparation outline,** which is more complete than the outline you will use when presenting the speech. The preparation outline helps you to identify your main ideas and to organize them sensibly, and it lists supporting materials and how you will use them. Write complete sentences in your preparation outline, as in this example for a section of the speech discussed earlier introducing John Patterson:

Main Idea: John has a clear sense of his roots.

Support

A. He still lives in the same house in which he grew up.

B. He marched in the Fourth of July parade every year.

C. He has never wanted to go anywhere else.

The rest of the speech would be outlined similarly.

PRESENTATION OUTLINE   Although the preparation outline is valuable in developing the speech, it is too complete to use while speaking. Your interaction with the audience will be limited if you are busy reading a fully elaborated, complete-sentence outline point by point. Instead, prepare a very brief outline of key words that will jog your memory and remind you of what comes next. You will use this **presentation outline** during the actual speech. Here is the previous example reduced to a presentation outline:

Main Idea: Sense of roots

Support

A. Same house

B. 4th of July

C. No desire to leave

Because you are familiar with the ideas of the speech, seeing the phrase "Same house" will remind you of the statement you want to make about how John still lives in the room he occupied as a child and how that experience has affected his perspective on life. You may never need to refer to the presentation outline while you are speaking, but if you do, a quick glance at the words "Same house" will remind you of the point you want to make.

You probably can reduce the presentation outline to fit on index cards, which are easier to handle than loose sheets of paper. For the first speech, you may need only one index card; three or four cards will usually be enough even for complex speeches.

extemporaneous
Descriptive of a presentation for which the main ideas and structure have been worked out in advance but specific wording has not been developed.

preparation outline
An outline used in developing a speech; main ideas and supporting material are usually set forth in complete sentences.

presentation outline
An outline used while presenting a speech; typically consists only of key words written on an index card.

Practicing Your Delivery

Because you are going to speak extemporaneously, practicing the speech is really a way to become familiar with the ideas by talking them through. You will not say exactly the same thing each time, but you will know the content of the speech well enough that the thoughts will come to you easily and you can express them naturally. To achieve this goal, use this sequence of activities:

1. *Develop and talk through the preparation outline.* In your complete-sentence outline, fill in the explanation of your thesis, and develop transitions between ideas. Don't worry about awkward pauses that occur while you figure out what to say next. These will smooth out as you practice.

   After you have talked through the preparation outline once or twice to yourself, make an audiotape recording and listen to it. Ask yourself whether your main point is clear and easy to identify. If not, change your explanation or your transitions to present the thesis more effectively. You might also ask a friend to listen to you. Check whether your friend can identify the thesis correctly, and ask for suggestions to improve the speech.

2. *Reduce the preparation outline to a presentation outline.* Write your outline with key words on an index card, and repeat step 1. Get familiar enough with the speech so that each key word triggers the same statement that you made when following the complete-sentence outline. If a key word doesn't prompt the same statement, change the key word.

3. *Develop exact wording for the introduction and the conclusion.* Unlike the body of the speech, which will be more effective if presented extemporaneously, you may want to memorize the introduction and conclusion because of their importance in shaping the audience's first and last impressions. Knowing exactly how you will start should give you a sense of security. Besides, if you write out your first and last *sentences* (no more) on the presentation outline, you'll be sure not to fumble for words when you begin to speak, and you won't have to rely on memory for strong finishing remarks.

4. *Simulate the conditions under which you will speak.* Find an empty room, and stand in front—where you will stand when you present the speech.

Imagine an audience present, and think about maintaining eye contact with them. (Don't present the entire speech looking either up at the ceiling or down at your notes.) Practice walking up to speak as well as returning to your seat. Both before and after speaking, pause a second or two to "size up" the audience and to signal a sense of self-control and confidence. If you will be speaking at a lectern, practice using it (avoid the tendency to grip it and hang on for dear life). Finally, when you are familiar with the content of your speech, practice how you will position yourself and move around and gesture. The more you can imagine yourself in the actual speaking environment, the less threatening the environment will seem.

STRATEGIES FOR OVERCOMING SPEECH ANXIETY

Even experienced speakers may be apprehensive when the time comes to speak.[7] In fact, researchers consistently report that most Americans fear public speaking more than anything. Being nervous is normal. You believe that what you have to say is important, and you value your listeners' judgment. Wanting to please your audience and to make a good impression, you may worry about making some innocent but colossal mistake.

In response to this emotional state, our bodies undergo numerous chemical changes. More blood sugar becomes available; insulin is secreted; blood pressure, respiration, and the conductivity of nerves all increase. In turn, these chemical changes induce feelings of anxiety or fear.[8] Although most people experience this to a modest degree, in some situations a person may become immobilized. Even the old term "stage fright" falls short of describing the deep-seated fear that some people have of speaking in public.[9]

Interestingly, though, the same chemical changes that cause extreme anxiety in some people bring others to a higher state of readiness and confidence. Many speakers get a boost of energy that, properly channeled, causes them to feel "psyched up" for the speech and hence in a position to do well. The

Checklist

1.4 *Overcoming Speech Anxiety*

1. **Acknowledge your fears, but recognize that you can overcome them.**

2. **Think about what you are going to say and the effect you want to have on your audience.**

3. **Act confident, even if you feel apprehensive.**

4. **Work carefully on the introduction so that you can start the speech on a strong note.**

5. **End the speech on a strong note, and pause for a second before returning to your seat.**

following five steps can help you tap into this extra energy and turn speech anxiety into an advantage.

1. *Acknowledge your fears, but recognize that you can overcome them.* Remind yourself that your listeners are not hostile; if anything, they will be supportive and sympathetic, especially for a beginning speaker. Also remind yourself that you have something valuable to say, that you know what you are talking about, and that it's important to share your ideas with the audience. This positive approach can convert nervous energy from a source of anxiety to a source of motivation.

2. *Think about what you are going to say and the effect you want to have on your audience.* The more you concentrate on your topic and on your relationship with the audience, the less anxiety you will feel—and the more likely you will do well. Becoming familiar with your outline through frequent practice will help boost your confidence.

3. *Act confident, even if you feel apprehensive.* Walk decisively to the front of the room, pause a moment to size up the audience, begin on a strong note, and maintain eye contact with your listeners. You may think of this as putting on a show, but remember that the audience has no idea how nervous you are. By acting confident, you will help listeners to feel positive about you, which, in turn, will help you *feel* more comfortable.

4. *Work carefully on the introduction so that you can start the speech on a strong note.* If you have written out the first few sentences of your speech and know exactly what you are going to say, this will propel you into the body of the speech. As you get into the speech and focus on what you are saying, your nervousness will probably subside.

5. *End the speech on a strong note, and pause for a second before returning to your seat.* Even if you *want* to rush back to your seat, present a well-prepared conclusion in a deliberate manner; then pause to let your closing thoughts sink into the listeners' minds before you return slowly to your seat.

Those seated behind the podium are listening to the speaker but also showing some signs of tension or anxiety as they wait their turn to speak. Pre-speech anxiety is perfectly natural; good speakers use it to help them focus on the occasion and on the speech.

How to Deal with Your Fear of Public Speaking

Latif Farag

Since English is not my first language, I was afraid of speaking in public because of making mistakes. When I talked to my teacher, he said that I speak English fluently and all I should do is: First, practice my speech many times; second, be confident of myself; and third, relax during the speech and say what I want to say.

Laura Breland

I got over my fears of public speaking by concentrating on my speech and thinking about what I was going to say. I usually tensed my whole body up and then relaxed it before every speech.

Carrie Biesel

I write out my speech outline and go over it in my head a lot, and then I feel prepared and don't stress about it. If you constantly think about it and about what could go wrong, you would make yourself crazy.

T. J. Brinkerhoff

In dealing with my fear of public speaking, I've tried to make a habit of familiarizing myself well with my text. To relax, I think it's also important to decide how and where you will stand while speaking, what you will do with your hands, and how to use your visual aids. I also find it helpful to take some deep breaths.

These simple steps will turn nervousness into an advantage for most speakers. In extreme cases of communication apprehension, however, nervousness becomes a pathological fear of relating to others in the public setting, and it may be necessary to treat the underlying anxiety through behavior modification—as is done with other phobias.[10] But such extremes are rare in a public speaking class. Even if you think that you are experiencing stage fright beyond the norm, remember this: You are in a relatively risk-free environment. Your classmates are likely to be friends and supporters because they are going through the same experience themselves. Your instructor's primary goal is to help you speak effectively, not to embarrass or intimidate you. Overall, there is probably no better setting in which to acknowledge your fears and then go ahead anyway. With practice, you are likely to find that speaking anxiety becomes manageable and actually helps you.

THE QUEST FOR QUALITY

With practice, you will overcome speech anxiety and will be able to get through your speech with confidence. Of course, you don't want to give just *any* speech; you want to give a *good* speech. So you need to know what makes a speech strong or weak. With practice you will develop an instinct about this. As a starting point, you can assess the quality of a speech by focusing on its purpose and on feedback from the audience.

Purpose and Quality

Speeches are presented to achieve a purpose, and so the overriding standard of quality is that a speech succeed in attaining its goal. As you learned earlier, the three most general purposes of speeches are to inform, to persuade, and to entertain:

- **Informing** provides listeners with new information or ideas.
- **Persuading** influences listeners' attitudes and behavior (either to strengthen existing beliefs or to support new ones).
- **Entertaining** stimulates a sense of community by celebrating the common bonds among speaker and listeners.

Although these general purposes may seem to be completely separate, they often coexist in a single speech—as when a speaker aims *both* to share new information and also to use that information in influencing attitudes and behavior (or to stimulate a sense of community). For this reason, in Chapter 4 we will classify purposes in a more detailed way. For now, though, focus on the general purposes and realize that you must have (1) something about which to inform the audience or (2) some position you want to persuade them to take or (3) some subject with which to entertain them. Therefore, any speech also has one or more *specific* purposes. Here are some examples:

General Purpose: Informing

Specific Purpose: Explaining the main steps in the construction of the college library

General Purpose: Persuading

Specific Purpose: Urging listeners to endorse the president's education proposal and to send telegrams of support

General Purpose: Entertaining

Specific Purpose: "Roasting" the boss on the eve of her retirement

In each case, the specific purpose is the standard to use in deciding whether the speech achieved its goal. Did listeners get a better understanding of the steps in constructing the college library? If so, then this specific example met the general goal of informing. Are audience members ready to send telegrams endorsing the president's education proposal? If so, then the speech succeeded at persuading. Can you and your coworkers empathize with the retiring boss and also share a laugh about the event? If so, then the entertaining speech achieved its goal.

Using purpose to assess the quality of a speech keeps things simple: Good speeches achieve the speaker's purpose; bad speeches do not. Yet few people are comfortable using only that standard. We do not want to regard as good a speech that misleads or manipulates the audience, even if it does achieve the speaker's purpose. And if the speaker's purpose itself is unworthy—such as reinforcing negative stereotypes, for example—we would evaluate the speech harshly even if it does achieve that purpose. Examples like these suggest that achieving one's purpose is not the only standard of quality in assessing a speech. It is a good place to begin, but the audience's reaction is another important factor.

informing
Providing listeners with new information or ideas.

persuading
Influencing listeners' attitudes and behavior.

entertaining
Stimulating a sense of community through the celebration of common bonds among speaker and listeners.

Feedback and Quality

Take a moment to look again at Figure 1.1. Recall that communication is mutual interplay between the speaker and the audience. As you speak, listeners provide *feedback,* nonverbal responses that help you sense whether you are achieving your purpose and how you might advance it better. One reason to maintain eye contact with the audience is to project that you are confident and trustworthy. But eye contact also gives you valuable feedback. If listeners frown or stare blankly when you make an important point, they may not understand you; you might want to explain that point further. If listeners appear lost, you might want to summarize your main points before moving on. If you've said something that you think is funny but no one laughs or smiles, you might either rephrase the comment or decide to let it pass. And when listeners nod supportively, you should feel confident and reassured.

After you speak, you are likely to receive more feedback in the form of comments from your instructor and classmates. They can tell you what was most effective about your speech and what could be improved. View such feedback as being constructive. Even if you think that someone missed your point completely, reconsider the organization of your speech and whether you might revise it to avoid "losing" some future listener. It's a good idea to take notes about listeners' comments; in the flush of energy right after you speak, you are unlikely to remember everything.

You probably also will receive unsolicited comments from classmates either after class or elsewhere on campus. If the comments are positive, express your appreciation. But realize that listeners are typically generous toward speakers; the fact that classmates liked your speech does not necessarily mean that you did everything exactly right! Sometimes, too, a classmate may express disagreement with your speech or may want to argue about your conclusions. Listen carefully to the person's point of view, and clarify your point if it was misunderstood. But don't feel that your success as a speaker depends on the approval of every single audience member. A listener whose mind is dead set against your point is not likely to change, no matter what more you might say. Be grateful that the person was honest, take whatever benefit you can from the criticism, but do not feel that you have failed if some audience members disagree with you.

In addition to your audience's reactions, you can get valuable feedback by reviewing a videotape of your speech. At first you may feel uncomfortable watching yourself on tape; you may be oversensitive to details that no one else would notice. But focus on the skills that you were practicing—a clear message and positive ethos—to glimpse yourself as the audience saw and heard you. The tape may reveal things about your delivery that you can change before giving your next speech.

ETHICS: RESPECT FOR AUDIENCE, TOPIC, AND OCCASION

Even though we sometimes say that "talk is cheap" or that "words can never hurt me," we know better. Speech has tremendous power, and the person who wields it bears great responsibility. Public speakers, in particular, set out to affect others, aiming to change what listeners believe or what they do. Furthermore, the act of addressing an audience may alter the speaker's own beliefs and values in response to listeners' reactions. Given this powerful interaction in public speaking, both speakers and listeners should seek high standards of ethical conduct.

As a listener you owe speakers your care and attention. Recognize and acknowledge the effort that went into preparing the speech, and appreciate that the speaker is disclosing something personal. Assume that the speaker is sincere, and listen intently to his or her message. Above all, listeners have the responsibility to think critically about the speech. Do not reject or refuse to consider the speaker's message simply because it differs from what you already believe. Nor, however, should you blindly accept the message. Assess the speech carefully to decide whether it merits your support. Whatever you decide, do so thoughtfully. Your agreement is especially valuable to a speaker when it reflects critical thought and you give it freely.

As a speaker you should demonstrate high ethical standards in four areas:

- Respect for your listeners
- Respect for your topic
- Responsibility for your statements
- Concern for the consequences of your speech

Respect for Your Listeners

Successful communication usually depends on evoking common bonds between the speaker and listeners. Audience members feel both that the speaker cares about them and that they are not just passive spectators. Rather, they feel that they are actively involved in the speech.

Because a speech is presented to a specific audience in a specific situation, a high-quality speech is sensitive to listeners' perspectives. A speaker who carefully analyzes the audience at hand will select materials and strategies that are appropriate and effective. In particular, the following principles demonstrate a speaker's respect for listeners.

MEET LISTENERS WHERE THEY ARE   One sign of respect is your willingness to acknowledge the audience's current position and to make it your point of departure—whether or not you agree with it. For example, in trying to convince opponents of capital punishment to rethink their position, student Mary O'Malley chose not to attack the audience's point of view but instead began by considering it:

> I understand that you have some reservations about the death penalty because you are worried that an innocent person might mistakenly be executed. This is certainly an important consideration. Death is final, and no one wants to be responsible for such a horrible mistake. Today I want to examine the possibility that a mistake might occur in the criminal justice system and to explore the consequences of such a mistake.

Rather than ignoring her listeners' views, Mary incorporated them into the speech, showing respect by meeting listeners on their own ground.

DON'T INSULT LISTENERS' INTELLIGENCE OR JUDGMENT   Besides starting her speech by acknowledging listeners' views, Mary also respected their judgment and intelligence by saying that she would examine their position in her speech. Likewise, when you prepare and present a speech, avoid patronizing or "talking down to" the audience. Don't devote the entire speech to what listeners already know or believe, making them wonder why they took the time to hear you. Also avoid suggesting that anyone who does not agree with you is somehow deficient in judgment. Steer clear of phrases that a listener might interpret as a put-down.

MAKE SURE YOUR MESSAGE MERITS THE AUDIENCE'S TIME   In general, although listeners could do other things with their time, they choose to attend your speech in the belief that you have something valuable and original to say. Recognize that you are receiving a gift of their time, and prepare a speech that deserves their gift.

RESPECT LISTENERS' ABILITY TO ASSESS YOUR MESSAGE   Because you respect listeners, you want them to understand your message thoroughly and to give their approval freely. Do not mislead listeners about your purpose or conceal what you want them to believe, feel, think, or do. If you are urging them to make a choice among alternatives, do not try to manipulate them by hiding options or by casting any particular option in unduly favorable or unfavorable light. If it is your goal to advocate one option over another, you will best defend your position by explaining how it is superior to the alternatives, not by distorting or ignoring the options that you dislike.

RESPECT THE CULTURAL DIVERSITY OF YOUR AUDIENCE   Not all listeners share your perspective. An audience often includes people with many diverse cultural backgrounds, and these affect their attitudes and experiences.

◀ Public speakers make claims on their listeners' attention and beliefs. Speakers therefore have a responsibility to say something worthwhile, to respect listeners' judgment, and to respect the diversity of viewpoint and cultural background that listeners represent.

As society becomes even more diverse, all public communicators must expect that some listeners will have different assumptions than their own. The tendency to imagine that one's own views are typical of everyone else is called *ethnocentrism*. It not only demeans listeners who have different cultural backgrounds but also reduces the likelihood of successful communication.[11]

Respect for Your Topic

Presumably, you will be speaking about a topic that matters to you, and you will have something important to say. When you speak, you are putting yourself on the record; your words will outlast the actual speaking situation. You are also asking listeners to accept you as a credible source of ideas about the topic. To justify their confidence in you, and to meet your own high standards, you need to know what you are talking about in enough detail that you can present it clearly and fairly. You must demonstrate that you care enough about the topic to study it thoroughly. Otherwise, why should the audience take your ideas about the topic seriously?

Responsibility for Your Statements

A public speaker makes claims on the audience, and so you must take responsibility for the accuracy and integrity of your statements. This is every bit as important in speaking as it is in writing, and similar guidelines apply.

Particularly in speaking (since listeners cannot see the printed word), you need to distinguish between fact and opinion, being careful not to misrepresent one as the other. Additionally, whether you are presenting fact or opinion, a statement is made in a particular context, and you must represent that correctly; if not, you will mislead or deceive the audience. The film critic who writes, "Nothing could be better than this film if you are looking for a cure for insomnia," does not want to be quoted as saying, "Nothing could be better than this film." Likewise, stating that the federal budget deficit has increased more than 300 percent over five years is not fair to the context if you fail to tell listeners that the source also said that, as a percentage of the economy, the deficit has actually shrunk.

As in writing, one of the most irresponsible things you can do as a speaker is to present another person's words or ideas as though they were your own. Such **plagiarism** is nothing less than theft. To avoid plagiarism:

1. Never present someone else's unique ideas or words without acknowledging it.
2. Specify who developed the ideas or said the words that you present ("As discovered by Professor Jones," "Socrates said," and so forth).
3. Paraphrase statements in your own words rather than quoting them directly, unless the exact wording of a statement is crucial to your speech.
4. Draw on several sources rather than relying on a single source.

Remember that it is also a form of plagiarism to present another student's speech as your own or to use the same speech in two different classes. Every speech you present should be your own original work.

plagiarism
Using another person's words as if they were your own.

Concern for the Consequences of Your Speech

Recognizing that your speech has consequences is another important ethical responsibility. You cannot be indifferent to how your speech may affect others, even though you may not know what all the effects will be. A listener might repeat an amusing anecdote you told, might feel more closely connected to someone whose life you celebrated, might get a psychological lift from your upbeat tone, or might change health insurance based on the reasoning in your speech. You cannot be held legally responsible for such effects, of course, but high ethical standards should lead you at least to think about how your speech might affect listeners.

Moreover, in any rhetorical situation, speakers and listeners together make up a community united by experience, interests, and values. Speech is the glue that holds a community together by making us aware of our common bonds and by giving us a vision to which we might aspire. Ethical public speakers take their membership in this community seriously, and they accept their responsibility to sustain the community by adhering to high ethical standards.[12]

Summary

By studying public speaking you will learn essential skills of thought and expression: reading, observing, and thinking critically; selecting what to say; using language effectively; presenting yourself skillfully; and responding to others' reactions to you. These skills, which you will study by blending theory and practice, will help you to be more articulate. They will apply to a variety of business and career situations, and they will enable you to participate more effectively as a citizen.

Public speaking is communication, the joint creation of meaning and understanding by speakers and listeners. A speech is given in a specific rhetorical situation, which is determined by the audience, occasion, speaker, and speech. Listeners interpret a message within their own framework of thought and knowledge, and they provide feedback as formal or informal responses to the speaker. The speaker takes listeners into account both in developing the speech and in responding to feedback.

You have two basic goals for your first speech: clarity of purpose and thesis and establishing positive ethos. The purpose is your goal for the speech, the response you seek from listeners. The thesis is the main point you want to make, which you should be able to state in one sentence.

Supporting materials—experience, narratives, data, and opinions—will lend weight to your thesis and help establish your claim. After choosing which supporting materials to use, you also must decide how to arrange them to advance your thesis. The basic structure of every speech includes an introduction, a body, and a conclusion—each of which serves distinct functions and raises strategic decisions. Common first speaking assignments are the one-point speech and the speech of introduction, both of which will give you practice in organizing a speech.

Outlining is an aid both in preparing and in presenting a speech. The preparation outline, usually written in complete sentences, details the structure and supporting materials of the speech. The presentation outline reduces this to key words and is used as a guide to cue you while you speak. Working with these two outlines, you can develop a sequence of practice exercises that range from informally talking through the speech to simulating the conditions under which you will deliver the speech.

Nervousness is a natural reaction to speaking in public, but you can turn it to your advantage by acknowledging your fears, reminding yourself of the strengths of your speech, concentrating on the topic and the audience, and carefully practicing your introduction and conclusion. Both during and after your speech you should seek feedback to improve subsequent presentations.

The overriding test of the quality of a speech is whether or not it achieves its purpose. Both formal and informal feedback will tell you whether your topic meets the requirements of the situation, whether your thesis is meaningful and important to the audience, whether your organization and presentation are effective, and whether the speech involves the audience and builds community. Beyond such practical matters, however, you also want to adhere to high ethical standards that reflect the mutual responsibilities of speaker and listeners and that recognize the significant power of public speaking as an act of communication.

In this chapter, we have introduced many concepts and skills. Each has been covered only briefly, so that you have the basic knowledge you need in order to begin giving speeches. Later chapters will cover each of these topics in more detail.

Welcome to what should be a unique, challenging, stimulating, and personally valuable class.

Discussion Questions

1. What is rhetoric? Why is it important to study rhetoric?

2. Develop two lists of adjectives, one describing what you consider to be positive judgments about a speaker's ethos and the other describing negative judgments. How might a beginning speech be strategically designed to develop positive judgments and avoid negative judgments? In answering this question, consider the following elements of strategy:
   Choice of topic
   Choice of purpose
   Presentation of supporting material
   Structure of the speech
   Delivery

3. The one-point speech is arranged in five steps:
   1. Wake up!
   2. This concerns you
   3. Generally speaking
   4. For example
   5. So what?
   Why is this a good model for developing a short speech? Discuss the strategic purpose of each step and how it contributes to the goals of imparting a clear message and building positive ethos.

4. Someone who is having trouble hearing a speaker usually leans forward to get closer to the sound. This is a cue to the speaker to increase the volume. What are some other common feedback cues that an audience might present? Discuss how a speaker might use each cue to modify either the message or the presentation.

5. View a speech with your classmates, and then, as a group, evaluate the quality of that speech. Take into account its purpose; the degree to which

the topic meets the requirements of the situation; sensitivity to cultural diversity; the meaningfulness and importance of the thesis; organization, support, and presentation; the way in which the speech builds community with the audience; and its ethical implications.

Which of these characteristics are most helpful and most important to you in distinguishing a good speech from a bad one? Is this the same for all speeches, or do different speeches call for different evaluative emphases?

6. What are the most important ethical considerations for a speaker and for a listener in your class? Using the guidelines in this chapter, work with your classmates to establish a code of ethics that individuals will abide by when they are speakers and when they are audience members.

Activities

1. For each of the following topics, devise a thesis statement that would be appropriate for a short speech.
   Affirmative action
   Date rape
   Job training
   Computers
   Summer vacation

2. Lay out three different types of supporting material for the thesis "Parking is a serious problem at most universities."

3. Following the recommendations in this chapter, develop both a preparation outline and a presentation outline for a speech of introduction, and practice the delivery of that speech.

4. Present the speech in activity 3 to a few friends or family members. Pay close attention to their feedback, both during the speech and when you discuss it with them later. Then strategically modify your speech to accommodate their concerns and suggestions. In one page, explain how the changes you made to your speech responded to the feedback you received.

5. Watch a speech, and then write a paper that evaluates its quality.

6. Examine your reasons for taking this public speaking course. What goals do you want to achieve? Based on your reading of this chapter, do you think this course will help you achieve your goals? Why or why not?

Using the Internet

1. **Using the Internet as a library.** The Internet does not replace the traditional library but should be used alongside it. You can find many valuable sources of information to use in your speeches, or you can find junk! One of the starting points for doing research on the Net is to use a site that has done some thoughtful screening of sources. An example of this is the **Librarian's Index to the Internet.** Point your browser to <http://sunsite.berkeley.edu/InternetIndex> and select one of the topic areas.
   • *Explore some of the sources that the creators of the list have included.*

(continued)

2. **Evaluating the information you find on the Internet.** You can judge for yourself what constitutes a quality source. The discussion of *ethos* in Chapter 1 is another starting point for evaluating the sources of information. Along with judging the character projected by a speaker, we can assess the accuracy and reliability of the information that the speaker chooses to present. To look at a way of making those judgments, do the exercise in the **Allyn & Bacon Public Speaking Website** entitled "Evaluating Sources of Information on the Web." We will be using some of the same basics for evaluating sources of information in Chapter 5. Point your browser to <http://www.abacon.com/pubspeak/exercise/evalsour.html> and do the exercise. Note that you have the option of having a copy of your results page sent to your instructor or to yourself. You may also print a hard copy of the exercise.

   - *The exercise references an editorial in JAMA (the online version of the* Journal of the American Medical Association) *entitled "Assessing, Controlling and Assuring the Quality of Medical Information on the Internet." To what degree do you think these criteria for judgment apply to your public speaking class?*

3. **The Internet and communication.** In this chapter, we've explored the concept of two-way communication, particularly in Figure 1.1, depicting the interplay between a speaker and audience. Explore how the concept of interplay works on the Internet. A good example of this is an online forum. One of the most widely respected forums is the Salon Magazine. Point your Web browser to <http://www.salonmag.com> to see the range of topics discussed in the magazine. Then, select "Table Talk" to join a forum. If this is your first time joining "Table Talk," you will need to sign on as indicated on the page.

   - *Click on one of the threads and observe how the interplay of users takes place.*

   - *You can also evaluate. Which participants, in your view, demonstrate ethos to speak on their topic?*

 Notes

1. These skills will help you succeed in college. See Rebecca B. Rubin and Elizabeth E. Graham, "Communication Correlates of College Success: An Exploratory Investigation," *Communication Education* 37 (January 1988): 14–27.
2. For example, business employers have named oral communication skills as the number 1 priority for college graduates seeking employment and the number 2 priority for successful performance once they have a job. Dan B. Curtis, Jerry L. Winsor, and Ronald D. Stephens, "National Preferences in Business and Communication Education," *Communication Education* 38 (January 1989): 6–14.
3. For a discussion of this difference between literature and oratory, see Herbert A. Wichelns, "The Literary Criticism of Oratory," first published in 1925, reprinted in *Methods of Rhetorical Criticism: A Twentieth Century Perspective,* ed. Robert L. Scott and Bernard L. Brock, New York: Harper & Row, 1972.
4. See Lloyd Bitzer, "The Rhetorical Situation," *Philosophy and Rhetoric* 1 (Winter 1968): 1–14.

5. Ethos is discussed extensively in Aristotle, *The Rhetoric,* translated by W. Rhys Roberts, New York: The Modern Library, 1954. See especially Book II.

6. A taste of how oratory was different in earlier U.S. history can be had by reading Garry Wills' description of Edward Everett's address at Gettysburg in *Lincoln at Gettysburg: The Words that Remade America,* New York: Simon & Schuster, 1992, pp. 21–22, 33–34.

7. For a summary of research done in this area, see Daniel Goleman, "Social Anxiety: New Focus Leads to Insights and Therapy," *New York Times* (Dec. 18, 1984): C1.

8. For a fuller description of the physical aspect of anxiety, see the table of physiological variables associated with anxiety in Raymond B. Cattell, "Anxiety and Motivation: Theory and Critical Experiments," *Anxiety and Behavior,* ed. Charles Spielberger, New York: Academic Press, 1966, p. 33.

9. For more about the study of speaker anxiety, see Joe Ayres, "Coping with Speech Anxiety: The Power of Positive Thinking," *Communication Education* 30 (October 1988): 289–296; and Michael Beatty, "Public Speaking Apprehension, Decision-Making Errors in the Selection of Speech Introduction Strategies and Adherence to Strategy," *Communication Education* 30 (October 1988): 297–311.

10. Some colleges have programs to treat severe communication apprehension. See Jan Hoffmann and Jo Sprague, "A Survey of Reticence and Communication Apprehension Treatment Programs at U.S. Colleges and Universities," *Communication Education* 31 (July 1982): 185–194.

11. One way to begin breaking down your ethnocentric views is to examine communication across cultures. See Robert Paine, ed., *Politically Speaking: Cross-Cultural Studies of Rhetoric,* Philadelphia: Institute for the Study of Human Issues, 1981.

12. For more on ethical considerations in the public speaking class, see Karl R. Wallace, "An Ethical Basis of Communication," *Communication Education* 4 (January 1955): 1–9. See also James A. Jaksa and Michael S. Pritchard, *Communication Ethics: Methods of Analysis,* Belmont, Calif.: Wadsworth, 1988; and Karen Joy Greenberg, ed., *Conversations on Communication Ethics,* Norwood, N.J.: Ablex, 1991.

chapter 2
Listening Critically

In This Chapter We Will:

- Distinguish between hearing and listening and learn why listening skills are important to speakers.

- Identify obstacles to effective listening.

- Learn how to listen carefully by mapping the central ideas of a speech and by taking notes.

- Explore how critical thinking is applied in the speaking situation.

- Consider how critical listening enables you to evaluate speeches.

I t's a standard scene in comic strips and television sitcoms: The husband sits at the breakfast table, face buried in the newspaper, seeming not to notice his wife seated across from him. The wife is trying to conduct a conversation about the day's events or about chores to be done around the house. Whenever she pauses, he mutters, "Mm-hmm"—never lowering the newspaper even to look at her. In desperation she finally grabs the paper and shouts, "You're not listening to me!" The husband calmly replies, "That's not true, dear. I heard every word you said."

ARE YOU REALLY LISTENING?

The husband and wife are both right, because hearing and listening are two different things. **Hearing** is a sensory process. Nerve endings in the ear receive sound waves and transmit them to the brain; the brain receives them, and we become conscious of sound. This is a physiological process.

In contrast, **listening** is a mental operation. It involves processing the sound waves, interpreting their meaning, and storing the interpretation in memory so that we can recall it, think about it, or act on it. The husband did *hear* every word, but he wasn't *listening*. His attention was focused entirely on the newspaper, and so he didn't interpret and store the information he heard. Now he can't repeat it, and he can't answer questions or make decisions about it.

Hearing comes naturally to most people and requires no special training. But listening is an acquired skill that takes practice. Even though people's ability to hear may be equally strong, some people are better listeners because they have trained themselves to:

- Focus attention
- Minimize distractions
- Process messages accurately
- Think critically[1]

In this chapter you will learn how to develop and improve these skills. First, though, we need to explore two questions: (1) Why should we concentrate on listening in our study of public speaking? (2) What makes listening so difficult that we need training to do it well?

Why Listening Is Important

CHECKING FOR ACCURACY   To begin with, we usually want to check the *accuracy* of what we heard, because the consequences of faulty listening can be far more serious than in the scene at the breakfast table. Students who don't listen to and correctly follow the professor's instructions could do the assignment but still get a failing grade. Employees who misunderstand the supervisor's instructions could jeopardize company profits—and their own jobs. Parents who don't really listen to a child's request for help could respond inappropriately, or not at all. And diplomats who don't listen carefully to each other could overlook an opportunity for a breakthrough in negotiations.

To avoid the consequences of faulty listening, we often check that we have heard and understood correctly. Students and employees ask questions

hearing
A sensory process in which sound waves are transmitted to the brain and someone becomes conscious of sound.

listening
A mental operation involving processing sound waves, interpreting their meaning, and storing their meaning in memory.

about instructions; parents try to find out what their child means; and diplomats "feel out" each other's statements before making a formal response.

GIVING (AND GETTING) FEEDBACK   Beyond checking the accuracy of communication, careful listening enables hearers to provide **feedback** to speakers. We saw in Chapter 1 that even in formal situations the speaker and the audience both send and receive messages. The audience members' reactions are usually nonverbal—applause, head nodding, bored or distracted looks, and indications that they are having trouble following the speaker's argument. Such feedback enables speakers to modify their message and improve the likelihood of achieving their purpose. During the speech, careful listening makes feedback possible; after the speech, it helps listeners to remember and think about the speaker's ideas.

You will spend far more time in this course listening to speeches than delivering them. By becoming a trained listener, you will provide appropriate feedback to other speakers. In addition, listening and responding to classmates' speeches will suggest ways to improve your own speaking. Your reactions to a speaker whose voice is too quiet, or who ends too abruptly, or who seems to lack confidence will make you more determined to avoid such problems. You'll also pick up tips from classmates who perform well. As you listen attentively, you will consider more and more factors that relate to your upcoming role as a speaker. You will develop ideas about what to do—or not to do—to make your own speeches successful. In short, your reactions to classroom speeches will provide feedback to yourself.

EVALUATING MESSAGES   Ensuring that you heard a message accurately and allowing you to provide feedback to the speaker and to yourself are two reasons why listening is so important. A third benefit is that you need to listen in order to *evaluate* what you hear. Unless you listen carefully, you seldom can know how to respond to or evaluate the message.

You have a vested interest in paying close attention to a classmate's message so that you can decide how it relates to you and to others in a broader audience. You need to be able to assess how the speaker's position and technique compare with yours and whether they are models to follow when it is your turn to speak. But you also should ask, "How will others whom I care about respond to this message?" Speeches often reach an audience beyond those who are present, and so you should consider how people who "tune in later" might react.

Finally—and unfortunately—not all speakers who seek our attention are scrupulous and ethical. Some urge listeners to do things that are unjustified or unacceptable. Be aware that their influence depends precisely on the fact that it is easy for people to hear without really listening. You need to know when a speaker is being unethical rather than just sloppy, insensitive, or misinformed. To protect yourself as a listener, you need to practice skills that will help you evaluate speakers and messages. Essentially, these are the skills of critical thinking, and you will learn to apply them to the speech situation later in this chapter.

Why Listening Is Difficult

So much, then, for the question of why speakers need to cultivate listening skills: Careful listening will help you both as an audience member and as a

feedback
Verbal and nonverbal audience response to a speech; usually taken seriously by a speaker and incorporated into the speech when possible.

speaker. But what makes listening so difficult that we need training in it? Why are so many people poor listeners? At least four factors deserve close attention:

- Listener distractions
- Limited attention span
- Jumping to conclusions
- Situational distractions

LISTENER DISTRACTIONS   We can think faster than we can listen. Since the processing of sound waves does not fully engage the brain, we can do something else at the same time we listen. Unfortunately, that "something else" may distract us from listening effectively.

Imagine a listener who is daydreaming during a speech, constructing a mental fantasy while listening. The fantasy may be more exciting and more personally relevant than the speaker's message. Gradually, without meaning to, this audience member will devote all energy to the daydream—still hearing, but not listening to, the speech. In fact, the distracting daydream may be stimulated by words in the speech. The word "video," for example, might trigger the thought "Oh, yes, I need to get my VCR cleaned," which, in turn, might lead to "I really enjoyed the movie I watched on video last night" and then to recollections about the movie. All these thoughts might lead to "I've got to remember to return the video tonight." Clearly, this is not careful listening.

Worse yet, the listener might be distracted several times during the speech before snapping to attention and thinking, "Oops! I'd better listen more closely to this speech." After tuning in again for a few minutes, the listener might then be distracted by some other word or phrase. The idea of "channel surfing"— of mindlessly switching among television programs without paying much attention to any of them—aptly describes how some listeners tune a speech in and out, seemingly at random. Although a speaker can't be held responsible for listeners' habits, a well-prepared, well-delivered speech is the best defense against listener distractions.

LIMITED ATTENTION SPAN   Another factor that makes listening difficult is that most people's **attention span**—the length of time they will attend to a message without distraction—is short. In the past, audiences were prepared for (and expected) lengthy speeches, sermons, lectures, and debates. During the eighteenth and early nineteenth centuries, political orations went on for hours, sometimes days. But today's public messages are much shorter. Until the creation of half-hour "infomercials" during the 1992 presidential campaign, the trend had been for shorter and shorter political messages. The same could be said of sermons, lectures, business presentations, and other forms of public speaking.[2]

Shorter messages are generally less complex and make fewer demands on listeners' powers of concentration. The speaker simply doesn't have time to try out many ideas, to develop them fully, and to suggest all their implications. Messages have to fit the short time available. This trend is especially clear in political advertisements, which shrank from about five minutes in the mid-1960s to only a few seconds in the late 1980s. Such short messages can present little except slogans or sound bites. And frequent exposure to short messages—whether advertising jingles or political slogans—weakens listeners' capacity to process and evaluate longer, more intricate messages.

The trend to make messages "short and simple" has been accelerated by television. Viewers are accustomed to changing channels frequently and may find it hard, even for entertainment, to pay attention for long. Also, the cost

- -

attention span
The length of time a person will attend to a message without feeling distracted.

of advertising time (or ad space, in print media) has led to shorter, simpler messages. And, of course, television is visually stimulating. As a result, many audience members today have only limited abilities to listen carefully to a speech—which may seem long, will not be primarily visual, and may not be entertaining.

JUMPING TO CONCLUSIONS People sometimes assume that they "know" what the speaker is going to say, but jumping to conclusions is no basis for effective listening. Early in the semester, student speaker Smita Shah gave an impromptu speech about why society should enforce capital punishment. Later in the semester, she again chose capital punishment as the topic for a different speech. But after doing her research, she changed her opinion and decided that capital punishment should be abolished. Nonetheless, when she rose to speak, some audience members were so sure that she would again favor capital punishment that they misinterpreted everything she said. Here are some of the questions they asked after she spoke:

"How can you support state-sanctioned murder?"

"What about innocent people who might be executed by mistake?"

"Doesn't it cost more to execute someone than to keep him in prison for life?"

"Isn't it true that a disproportionately large number of those executed are black?"

These audience members thought they were asking hostile questions, but they had jumped to conclusions and showed instead that they hadn't listened carefully.

Most untrained listeners sometimes make such assumptions and misinterpretations. People who attend a speech as committed supporters of the speaker's cause already "know" that they will agree with the message and hence do not listen to it carefully. They often find themselves endorsing a position that they don't really support. Other listeners who strongly oppose a speaker's cause almost instinctively reject every part of the message. In both cases, listeners jump to conclusions through **assimilation;** they blur the distinction between two similar messages and regard them as identical. If the speaker says something that in any way seems to confirm their position, they interpret that as the thesis of the speech. They also *disregard* any parts of the message that challenge their assumptions. They simply ignore those ideas. In both cases, hasty conclusions keep them from truly listening.[3]

SITUATIONAL DISTRACTIONS   Distractions in the specific speaking situation can also make listening difficult. Perhaps the wind blows the door shut while you are speaking, and listeners turn to look when they hear it slam. Or an audience member may arrive late, or some lights may go out, or loud laughter may erupt in the hallway. None of these events can be controlled, yet all can interfere with effective listening. The first thing a speaker can do in such cases is to try to offset the distraction by repeating or rephrasing the part of the speech that had to compete with it.

Each of these obstacles to effective listening can lead to a bad listening habit, which careful listeners can overcome through concentration. Figure 2.1 summarizes the obstacles, bad habits, and remedies for both listeners and speakers.

- Because *thinking is faster than listening,* your mind may wander and you may not pay attention. Some remedies are to concentrate harder on the speech and to take notes. As a speaker, you can offset this tendency by keeping the speech focused; rivet the audience's attention to each main idea by showing how it relates to your thesis.
- Because *your attention span is limited,* you may not be able to follow a long, complex speech. Besides concentrating and taking notes, you can stretch your attention span gradually by listening to longer speeches. As a speaker, work to combat this obstacle by dividing the speech into small segments that you can develop quickly and memorably; again, tie each segment to your thesis.
- Because *you jump to conclusions,* you may miss the speaker's precise point. You may think that statements you like are closer to your position than they actually are; and if you disagree with statements, you may magnify the differences between your views and the speaker's. The remedy is to set aside your prejudices and concentrate on the speaker's point of view. As a speaker, you can best overcome this obstacle through careful audience analysis, which is described in Chapter 3. Basically, if you analyze where listeners' preconceptions are likely to lead them, you can figure out exactly which points must be made especially clear.
- Because *elements in the situation distract you,* you don't listen carefully to what the speaker is saying. Again, try harder to concentrate; take notes, and exercise self-discipline. As a speaker, you can counteract distractions by remaining flexible, by adapting to the situation rather than being tied to your text. If you respond to a distraction quickly enough, you may even be able to turn it to your advantage.

assimilation
The tendency to regard two similar messages as basically identical, blurring the distinction between them.

Obstacles	Listener's bad habit	Remedy	
		Listener	**Speaker**
Thinking is faster than listening.	Listener's mind may wander.	Concentrate on the speech; take notes.	Keep the speech focused; tie each point to main thesis.
Listener's attention span is short.	Not hearing speeches that are long or complex.	Practice gradually to hear longer speeches.	Divide speeches into small, compact segments.
Listener jumps to conclusions.	Missing speaker's point; judging by listener viewpoint only.	Try to set prejudices aside.	Careful audience analysis; extra effort on clarity.
Situations contain distractions.	Following the distraction rather than the speech.	Concentrate on the speech and on self-discipline.	Stay flexible; adapt to situation.

FIGURE 2.1

Overcoming four obstacles to good listening.

As a speaker, the best defense against *all* obstacles to effective listening is precisely your awareness that listening is difficult. Knowing this, you can compensate for listeners' bad habits by finding clear and interesting supporting material, by repeating points appropriately, and by varying your delivery to fit the circumstances. Speakers must make a whole range of strategic choices about how to design and present a message, and we will examine those choices throughout this book.

As an audience member, understanding the difficulties of listening should strengthen your resolve to concentrate and to listen carefully and critically. Try to identify any bad habits in how you listen, and strive actively to correct them. In order to evaluate others' messages effectively and thus improve your own messages, become more sensitive to the obstacles of listening. By listening to others carefully and critically—discussed next—you'll gain information about audience beliefs and values that can help you make effective strategic choices as a speaker.

STRATEGIES FOR CAREFUL LISTENING

Some people try to overcome the difficulties of listening by going to the other extreme. They set the goal of focusing on *each and every word* the speaker utters. This approach rarely works, however, since the attempt to take in everything makes it less likely that you will think about, interpret, and assess what you are hearing. Similarly, students who try to take notes about every word in a professor's lecture often cannot explain what the lecture was about. They are so busy writing that they have little energy or time for thinking. It's a classic case of seeing the trees but missing the forest. Listening without thinking is just as flawed as hearing without listening.

Even careless listeners are quick to recognize the superficial strengths and weaknesses of a speech, such as whether the speaker tells an interesting story, mispronounces words, races through a quotation, or talks too loudly. Although these are important aspects of a speech, untrained listeners often fail to *think about* the ideas presented and whether or not those ideas support the thesis. They may be hearing the speech; they may even be listening to it; but they are not listening carefully.

Careful listeners, then, avoid both of these extremes. They do not try to remember every word, and they do not attend only to superficial aspects of a speech. They focus instead on the thesis and the main ideas that support it. Two techniques that can help you do this—and thus become a more careful listener—are *mapping* and *note taking*.

Mapping

Careful listening is encouraged by the technique of **mapping,** in which the listener draws a diagram showing the relationship between the thesis of the speech and the main ideas that support it. This involves four basic steps:

- Extracting the thesis
- Identifying the main ideas
- Assessing the main ideas
- Deciding whether the main ideas support the thesis

EXTRACT THE THESIS OF THE SPEECH Careful listeners should be able to identify not only the general topic of a speech but also its thesis, whether stated explicitly or not. You should be able to say, for instance, not only that the speech was about health care but also that the speaker claimed that the current system does not deliver care effectively. If the speaker states that thesis explicitly in the introduction, you can follow along and see how the claim is developed and supported in the body of the speech. But if the thesis is only implied by supporting material or is stated only in the conclusion of the speech, you have to listen carefully to extract the thesis and map its relationship to the main ideas.

Remember that your task in mapping a speech is not to reconstruct it word for word but to identify its main ideas and the appeals the speaker used. The thesis almost always can be expressed in one or two sentences; from this central point, the proofs and other supporting materials radiate.

IDENTIFY THE MAIN IDEAS THAT DEVELOP THE THESIS Suppose, for example, that the thesis of the speech about health care was "The current system does not deliver health care effectively." To support the thesis, the speaker offered three claims as main ideas:

A. Millions of people lack health insurance.

B. Health-care providers have few incentives to control costs.

C. The system emphasizes treatment and cure instead of prevention.

In this case, claims A, B, and C each represent a separate idea to support the thesis, and so a map of this speech would show each main idea as being connected to the thesis. Figure 2.2 shows two examples of how you might map this speech.

mapping
Diagraming the relationship between the thesis of a speech and its main ideas.

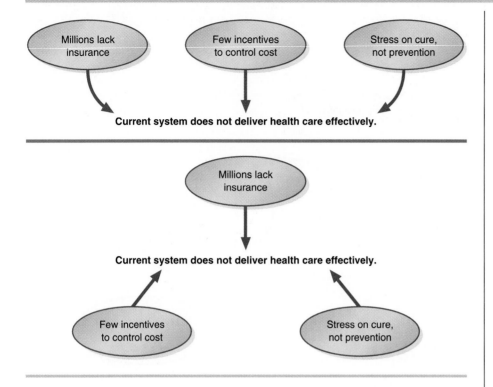

FIGURE 2.2

Mapping claims that separately support the thesis.

But suppose that the relationship among the main ideas was more complex, as in the following example:

A. Fear of high costs makes people postpone visits to the doctor.
B. Thus symptoms are discovered later than they might be.
C. Treating symptoms at a later stage is both more costly and more risky.
D. Hence fear of high costs leads to even higher costs.

In this example, each claim follows from the one before it; only together—and not individually—do the main ideas support the thesis. As shown in Figure 2.3 on page 46, a map of this speech would represent the relationship among the main ideas.

The structure of ideas in a speech map may or may not correspond to the actual structure of the speech. Again, the goal for careful listeners is not to recall exactly what was said but rather to be able to reconstruct the thesis and main ideas and to explain how they fit together.

ASSESS THE ADEQUACY OF THE MAIN IDEAS This is an evaluation step in which you judge whether the main ideas have been advanced solidly. For example, the thesis of a speech about techniques of self-defense might be "With knowledge of simple techniques, you can defend yourself if attacked." The main ideas that you diagram on your map are the following:

A. A victim can shout for help and run.
B. A victim can use mace to stop the attacker.
C. A victim can disable the attacker.
D. A person should walk only in safe neighborhoods.

FIGURE 2.3

Mapping claims that only together support the thesis.

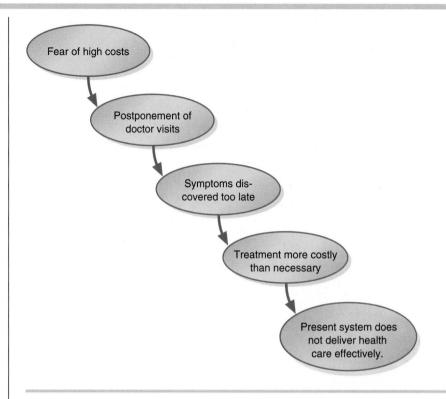

In evaluating the development of these points, you might decide that the claim about mace was not explored thoroughly. After all, you've heard that attackers sometimes grab the mace and use it against the victim. Or, in the speech referred to above about health care, you might conclude that the speaker failed to prove that medical providers have few incentives to control costs.

DECIDE WHETHER THE MAIN IDEAS TRULY SUPPORT THE THESIS

This second evaluation step moves beyond judging the main ideas in their own right to judge whether they really link to the thesis. Even if the ideas are true, they may not support the thesis. This was not a problem in the examples about mace and incentives to control costs; the ideas were in doubt, but their links were not. *If* mace were effective or *if* the health-care system lacked cost controls, then those ideas would provide support for their theses.

Now reconsider the speech about self-defense. The point about walking only in safe neighborhoods may be sensible, but it does not connect well to the thesis. It describes a preventive measure, not a technique for self-defense when you are attacked. So you would conclude that the link between this main idea and the thesis is weak. Or, in the health-care speech, suppose that the speaker convinced you that millions of people lack health insurance but did not prove that this makes the health-care system ineffective. After all, some people may not need insurance; others may be supported by relatives or friends; and others may not be eligible for insurance but do receive free or subsidized care. The main idea itself is not in question, but the link between that idea and the thesis is not established.

Mapping a speech enables you to listen carefully, because you have a clear purpose: to ferret out and evaluate the underlying structure of the speech in terms of its thesis and main supporting ideas. One handy shortcut in mapping a speech is to use plus and minus signs to record your appraisal both of the ideas and of their links. For example, a plus sign next to a claim indicates that you think the claim was established, whereas a minus sign next to a link indicates that you believe the link was not supported. Obviously, every speaker wants the audience to make positive evaluations of *both* the claims and the links.

Note Taking

You may not be able to complete the speech map while the speech is being delivered. Even if the main ideas were previewed in the introduction, you may not fully grasp them or see how they link to the thesis until the speaker has finished. And you probably will not be able to evaluate them until you have had some time to think about them. Sometimes your preliminary understanding of the thesis may turn out to be wrong, and mapping during the speech may lead you to jump to (wrong) conclusions. But if you wait until after the speech to make the map, can you confidently remember the thesis and main ideas? Most listeners cannot; they need notes to remind them.

Note taking is not a substitute for thinking about the speech during its presentation. Instead, disciplined note taking is an essential tool for careful listening. The goals are to record as much *significant* information as possible and to do so as *efficiently* as possible. The following suggestions will help you.

1. *Focus on the thesis and main ideas.* As the speech gets underway, try to identify these critical elements, and take notes that will help you recall their relationship. Avoid being sidetracked by examples and less important points.

2. *Use key words rather than sentences.* You need not record every word to remember the speech, and attempting that is inefficient and distracting. In particular, prepositions, articles (a, an, the), and even verbs often can be omitted without losing the sense of the idea being communicated.

3. *Organize the notes as a rough outline.* You don't need a formal outline of the speech; the crucial thing is to identify major headings and subheadings (claims and supporting ideas). If you leave plenty of space in the left-hand margin and between items in your notes, you can insert headings, subheadings, and related points wherever they belong—whenever the speaker presents them.

4. *Abbreviate and use symbols whenever possible.* By establishing some consistent, memorable abbreviations and symbols, you can take notes quickly without missing anything the speaker says. For example, some common abbreviations and symbols are w/ for "with," w/o for "without," = for "is," ≠ for "is not," < for "less than," > for "more than," and arrows pointing either up for "increasing" or down for "decreasing." Develop your own system of abbreviations and symbols for frequently used words and terms.

5. *Also make notes to help you evaluate the speech.* Since careful listening and evaluation are ongoing responsibilities, another level of note taking is to jot down comments that will help you prepare a critical assessment of the

speech. If you think that the thesis was supported well, write "good support"; if the structure of the speech confused you, jot down "disorganized." Put such evaluative comments in the margin, or write them in a different color, so that they don't interfere with your notes about what the speaker said. You can think of this as "making notes" to distinguish it from "taking notes."

The test of progress toward becoming a careful listener is whether, when a speech is over, you can reconstruct its basic form; not whether you have memorized the speech or can repeat it word for word, but whether you can identify the thesis and explain how it was developed.

LISTENING CRITICALLY

The title of this chapter is "Listening Critically," which moves far beyond listening carefully. **Critical listening** results not only in an accurate rendering of the speech but also in a personal interpretation and assessment of it. Thus the evaluation steps of mapping and note taking are developed more thoroughly. Basically, critical listening enables you to apply critical thinking to a speech.

Critical Thinking

You know from Chapter 1 that **critical thinking** is the ability to form and defend your own judgments rather than blindly accepting or instantly rejecting what you hear or read. *Critical* does not mean "negative," "hostile," or "adversarial"; but it does mean "judgmental." It is a conscious, systematic method of evaluating ideas wherever you encounter them—not only in speeches but also in conversation, in print, on television, in films and plays, and so on.

critical listening
Listening that enables you to offer both an accurate rendering of the speech and an interpretation and assessment of it.

critical thinking
The ability to form and defend your own judgments rather than blindly accepting or instantly rejecting what you hear or read.

Checklist

2.1 *Critical Thinking*

1. Characteristics of Critical Thinkers

- *Reluctant to accept assertions on faith*
- *Distinguish facts from opinions*
- *Seek to uncover assumptions*
- *Open to new ideas*
- *Apply reason and common sense to new ideas*
- *Relate new ideas to what they already know*

2. Critical Thinking Skills

- *Questioning and challenging*
- *Recognizing differences*
- *Forming opinions and supporting claims*
- *Putting ideas into a broader context*

THE CHARACTERISTICS OF CRITICAL THINKERS At least six characteristics are demonstrated by critical thinkers:

1. *Critical thinkers are reluctant to accept assertions on faith.* Unsupported assertions carry little weight with critical thinkers, who are skeptical and always imagine themselves asking, "What have you got to go on?"

2. *Critical thinkers distinguish facts from opinions.* **Facts,** at least in theory, can be independently verified by others. They are either true or false, and their truth is not subject to interpretation. The number of people who don't have health insurance is a fact, as is the historical claim that "Columbus sailed the ocean blue, in fourteen hundred ninety-two."

   Opinions are judgments that are *not* clearly true or false and so cannot be independently verified. For example, a person might hold the opinion that Paris is more beautiful than London or that the United States is the best country in which to live. Opinions may be highly individualistic, or they may be widely shared. Just because an opinion is widely shared, however, does not make it a fact—although it is not easily disregarded. Even so, remember that opinions *can* be changed. The importance of this to public speakers is that, often, the strength of an opinion depends on the ethos of the person who holds it (or who dismisses it).

   Facts are not necessarily better than opinions, and both are well suited for particular kinds of statements. But you should understand the difference between them. Critical thinkers listen carefully to be sure that a speaker does not mistake an opinion for a fact or a fact for an opinion.

3. *Critical thinkers seek to uncover assumptions.* **Assumptions** are unstated, taken-for-granted beliefs in a particular situation. For example, underlying the argument that we should mount extreme measures to cut the federal budget deficit is an assumption: that the budget deficit is a crisis. Often speakers and listeners assume that they share some crucial value—an assumption that is seldom noted until it is questioned. Critical thinkers not only uncover assumptions in what other people say but also identify and test their own assumptions as well.

4. *Critical thinkers are open to new ideas.* Although critical thinkers do not hold their opinions and beliefs lightly, they are willing to consider challenges to what they believe and are open to the possibility that they may have to change their minds.

5. *Critical thinkers apply reason and common sense to new ideas.* Critical thinkers ask whether a new idea makes sense, whether it seems internally consistent, and whether they can see and understand the links made by the speaker or writer in developing the idea. If reason and common sense tell them that everything is in order, they give the idea a good hearing—whether or not they expect to agree with it. But if reason and common sense tell them the idea is wrong, they are likely to reject it, even though it might support a conclusion with which they agree.

6. *Critical thinkers relate new ideas to what they already know.* They ask, *Is the new idea consistent with what I already think or know to be true?* If not, they ask how their existing attitudes and beliefs need to be modified and whether such modifications are justified. These steps enable them to put the idea into a broader context so that it does not exist in isolation but is incorporated into their constantly developing system of beliefs and attitudes.

facts
Statements that can be independently verified by others; they are either true or false.

opinions
Judgments that cannot be independently verified and that are not clearly true or false.

assumptions
Unstated, taken-for-granted beliefs in a particular situation.

What these six characteristics of critical thinking have in common is their emphasis on **reflective** judgment—neither blind acceptance nor automatic rejection of an idea, but a considered and thoughtful opinion about whether the idea and its support merit acceptance.

THE SKILLS OF CRITICAL THINKING   From these six characteristics of critical thinkers we can extract four basic skills that underlie critical thinking:

1. *Questioning and challenging,* both your own ideas and the ideas of others, so that you will neither accept nor dismiss an idea without thoughtful reflection.
2. *Recognizing differences*—between ideas, between facts and opinions, between explicit claims and unstated assumptions, and between easily explained events and anomalies or puzzles.
3. *Forming opinions and supporting claims* so that you can state and evaluate ideas.
4. *Putting ideas into a broader context* by seeing how they relate to what you already know and by understanding what they imply about other things you might assert or believe.[4]

Applying Critical Thinking to the Speech Situation

Earlier we noted that listeners form judgments about the strength of a speaker's ideas and about their links to the thesis. Now we will consider *how* listeners form such judgments.

Some judgments are made uncritically. A statement "sounds right," so you decide it must be true; or it is at odds with your beliefs, and you conclude immediately that it is false. If a speaker *seems* personable and sincere, you might accept the claims without investigation; but if the speaker's delivery is unappealing, you might reject the content out of hand. Each of these is an *uncritical* judgment, made without reason or reflection.

In contrast, if you apply critical thinking to the speech situation, you will make such judgments *critically*. **Critical judgments** are those that you can articulate and defend by providing the reasons for them. This does not mean that you are hostile or negative toward the speech. In fact, critical listening begins with the assumption that the speaker knows what he or she is talking about; but this assumption is balanced with skepticism, a reluctance to be pushed prematurely into conclusions.

Critical listening begins with mapping and is aided by note taking, but it adds the step of *reflection* before judgment. Reflective listeners think consciously about the speech and ask themselves questions about it. Here are some examples of questions that critical listeners might pose:

• Are the main ideas identifiable?
• Are the links among the ideas reasonable?
• Are the ideas supported where necessary?
• How does accepting or rejecting the thesis affect my other beliefs?

ARE THE MAIN IDEAS IDENTIFIABLE?   As emphasized earlier, it is important to know not just the general topic of the speech but also its specific thesis and the main ideas that support it. Critical listeners are especially concerned that the thesis be clear and precise.

reflective
Considered, thoughtful (as opposed to automatic).

critical judgments
Judgments that can be articulated and defended by providing the reasons for them.

2.2 *Critical Thinking about a Speech*

1. **Are the main ideas identifiable?**

2. **Are the links among the ideas reasonable?**

3. **Are the ideas supported where necessary?**

4. **How does accepting or rejecting the thesis affect my other beliefs?**

Suppose you were listening to a speech about multiculturalism in U.S. education. You might recognize quickly whether or not the speaker thinks multiculturalism is good. But as a critical listener you would ask yourself additional questions, such as:

- What does the speaker mean by "multiculturalism"?
- Does she mean the same thing each time she uses the term?
- Do others whom she quotes about multiculturalism mean the same thing that she does?
- Is she saying that multiculturalism is good in principle, as it is applied, or both?
- Is she saying that multiculturalism is good regardless of other values with which it may conflict? Or is she recognizing the conflicts and saying that multiculturalism is good on balance?

Notice that each of these questions is raised only to develop a precise understanding of the speaker's thesis, not to object to the thesis. Obviously, you cannot assess a speech critically until you know exactly what the speaker is trying to say.

ARE THE LINKS AMONG THE IDEAS REASONABLE? When we addressed this question earlier, we asked only whether the links seemed to square with common sense. But critical listeners want to know more than that; they will ask whether the speaker has proved the claims in a reasonable way.

Suppose that in a speech about the federal budget deficit the speaker claims that (1) excessive government spending is the primary cause of the deficit and that (2) the deficit is weakening the country's position in the world economy. As a critical listener you would ask such questions as:

- Does the speaker prove what he claims?
  This speaker is claiming that one thing *causes* another. But if he can show only that, as the deficit increases, international economic strength decreases, he has not proved a cause-effect relationship. A country's economic strength might result from some other factor or from a combination of factors.
- If the links *are* established, should you accept the speaker's claim?
  Even though the speaker might convince you that government spending adds to the deficit and that the deficit weakens the country's international position, you still might not find the conclusion acceptable. For example, you may have just read in the newspaper that delegates to the annual economic summit

conference clearly recognized the U.S. economy as being the strongest in the world. Something doesn't add up: If the deficit is so harmful, why is the U.S. economy so strong? In raising this kind of question, you are recognizing that the speaker has not examined the topic completely. You want to know more about other factors that apparently are offsetting the effects of the deficit, such as the highly trained labor force and the diversity of the U.S. economy.

ARE THE IDEAS SUPPORTED WHERE NECESSARY? As we have seen, some statements are accepted at face value by most listeners, whereas other statements need to be supported by facts, narratives, data, or opinions. As a critical listener, you require a speaker to support ideas that need it, and so you would ask such questions as:

- Does the idea need support?
  Even critical listeners accept some statements at face value. Maybe the idea is clear intuitively, or perhaps the speaker's explanation makes it seem so obvious that no further support is required. For example, if the speaker clearly defines the budget deficit as "the government's spending more than it takes in," you might see no need for additional support. But you probably will not be so quick to accept an opinion like "The budget deficit is mortgaging our economic future."
- Has the speaker offered enough supporting material?
  For most listeners, one or two examples of elderly people who cannot pay their medical bills will probably not be sufficient support for the thesis "The health-care system is hard on the elderly." The speaker doesn't offer enough examples to support a generalization about all elderly people. Insufficient support may lead listeners to conclude that there *is* no other support, and so they may not take the speaker's ideas seriously.

HOW DOES ACCEPTING OR REJECTING THE THESIS AFFECT MY OTHER BELIEFS? Critical listeners recognize that beliefs and values do not exist in isolation. Almost always, accepting or rejecting a speaker's thesis will have consequences for your beliefs about other matters. Believing, for example, that excessive government spending adds to the budget deficit may not square with another belief you hold—such as that government programs are generally effective and achieve beneficial goals.

These four sets of questions are intended to help you develop a clear understanding of what a speaker is asking you to think about, to believe, or to do. They will help you to form a careful and reflective judgment about whether or not to agree with the speaker. But listening critically does not mean that you have to subject a speaker to an inquisition before accepting anything he or she says. Rather, in the language of nuclear arms agreements, it is a way to "trust, but verify"—to accept the ethos of the speaker but not to depend entirely on that in deciding whether the speech makes sense.

APPLYING STRATEGIES

Thoughts about Listening

Laura Breland

I think listening is a very important skill that takes many trials and errors to become effective. I try hard to listen because I believe it is one of the most valuable skills to have. If someone is a good listener, then he or she will have a better chance to succeed in life.

T. J. Brinkerhoff

By listening to the other students, I have learned that an intense listening audience can be very helpful in developing quality speakers. By having an entire class focused on you, it helps build confidence in your speaking abilities. Receiving constructive criticism from a good listener can help you improve your skills even more. Listening, like speaking, is a skill that is developed and can be beneficial by helping you hear and understand more in depth a speaker's message. By developing good listening skills, you can learn to communicate better with others in everyday life by learning to overcome listening distractions.

Latif Farag

Before taking this class, I never thought about the difference between listening and hearing. I have always had the problem of hearing someone talking without really paying attention to what he or she is saying. Now I learned how to listen critically.

Carrie Biesel

I think that eye contact is the best way to show someone you are listening . . . Interrupting or looking off into space are totally obvious and can really hurt someone's feelings, making them think you don't really care about what they have to say.

EVALUATING SPEECHES CRITICALLY

So far we have considered one dimension of critical listening: judging whether or not a speaker's ideas are sound. We saw that the basic skills of critical thinking are used as well in thinking strategically about the thesis and supporting ideas of a speech. Now we will consider a second dimension of critical listening: assessing the strength of the speech *as a speech*. This evaluation centers on three questions:

- Did the speech demonstrate the principles and techniques of public speaking?
- What was strong and what was weak about the speech?
- How might the speaker improve the speech?

This dimension of critical listening is especially important in a public speaking class. Although your primary goal is to become more skilled at giving speeches, you will spend far more time listening to classmates speak than in speaking yourself. Your feedback as a critical listener will help others improve, and their assessments, in turn, will strengthen your abilities as a speaker. Outside the class, too, you will spend far more time as a listener than as a speaker.

Evaluation Standards

Like judgments about the content of a speech, assessments of its quality can be made uncritically—as when an audience member says, "Wow!" or

"That was a great speech!" without explaining why. But the goal is to make *critical* assessments, which depend on the four critical thinking skills described earlier: questioning and challenging, recognizing differences, forming opinions and supporting claims, and putting ideas into a broader context.

As you apply these skills to speechmaking, remember that a speech is a strategic communication. It is presented in a specific situation to achieve a specific purpose. By focusing on these two concepts—*the rhetorical situation* and *the speaker's purpose*—you will develop evaluation criteria that turn careful listening into critical listening.

RHETORICAL SITUATION   The discussion in Chapter 1 of the **rhetorical situation** made it clear that speeches are delivered not in a vacuum but in response to a specific context. Critical listeners thus realize that it is not fair to evaluate a speech without considering the situation in which the speaker prepared and delivered it.

Abraham Lincoln, to cite a historical example, has been criticized in recent years for not coming out more strongly against slavery in the period leading to the Civil War. Indeed, in his fourth debate with Stephen A. Douglas during the 1858 senatorial campaign in Illinois, Lincoln said:

> I will say then that I am not, nor ever have been in favor of bringing about in any way the social and political equality of the white and black races—that I am not nor ever have been in favor of making voters or jurors of negroes, nor of qualifying them to hold office, nor to intermarry with white people; and I will say in addition to this that there is a physical difference between the white and black races which I believe will for ever forbid the two races living together on terms of social and political equality.

rhetorical situation
The particular circumstances in which a speech is given, including especially an understanding of what must be done to achieve the desired effect on the audience.

This position seems far from the popular image of Lincoln as the "Great Emancipator," but some of the criticism ignores the specific situation in which he spoke—especially the fact that very few white Americans in the 1850s could imagine the races as equal. Nor did Lincoln have free rein about the content of speeches in these campaign appearances. Since his goal was to win the election, he could not antagonize listeners whose votes he was seeking. Any critique that altogether ignores the rhetorical situation in which Lincoln spoke would give a false impression of the realistic choices available to him.

The key questions, then, are:

- What was the specific rhetorical situation?
- What constraints and opportunities did it pose?
- How well did the speaker respond to the situation?

When evaluating a classmate's speech, consider *both* the constraints imposed by the immediate audience and the constraints imposed by the larger rhetorical situation. With respect to the immediate audience, ask whether or not the speaker adequately tailored the speech to the listeners' knowledge level. You also might consider whether the speaker's ideas and supporting material were interesting and effective for the specific audience. With respect to the larger rhetorical situation, ask whether or not the speaker understands current attitudes, beliefs, and practices regarding the issue at hand.

SPEAKER'S PURPOSE   Besides taking into account the speaker's rhetorical situation, also consider the speaker's purpose. It's easy to say that a speaker made the wrong choice in terms of purpose and should have aimed for something else. Generally, however, you should evaluate a speech *in light of* its stated or implied purpose. To condemn a speech for not accomplishing what the speaker never intended to accomplish is neither rational nor fair.[5]

If you understand the purpose of the speech, then the next key question is "How well did the speaker achieve the purpose?" This focuses on the means used by the speaker and whether they were the best choices available. If the purpose is to introduce a complicated subject, then a speech that assumes prior knowledge on the part of the audience and that fails to explain key concepts would not be well adapted to the purpose. The speaker may not recognize any problems, but critical listeners can point them out.

Evaluating a speech in terms of its purpose raises a third important question: "Should a speech be judged by its effects or by its artistry?" If the **effectiveness standard** is the only measure of a speech, then *whatever* is most likely to accomplish the purpose should be done. By this standard, to use an extreme example, Adolf Hitler would be regarded as a good speaker because he was effective in achieving his purpose.[6]

Most theorists, however, reject effectiveness as the sole basis for evaluating a speech. As noted in Chapter 1, the goal is not only to achieve a stated purpose but also to achieve it while following accepted principles and observing ethical norms. Public speaking is a practical art. The **artistic standard** asks whether the speaker followed the principles of the art and hence whether

effectiveness standard
Evaluation of a speech according to the effects it produced.

artistic standard
Evaluation of a speech according to its ethical execution of principles of public speaking without regard to its actual effects.

he or she did the best that could be done, consistent with ethical norms, in a specific rhetorical situation. If a classmate speaks in favor of some controversial topic—say abortion or gay rights—you should not fault the speech for failing to convince those listeners whose opposition is strongly entrenched. The artistic standard does not ignore the issue of effectiveness, however, because the application of public speaking principles and the observance of ethical norms generally make a speech effective.

Evaluating Classroom Speeches

To participate effectively in evaluating classroom speeches, you and your classmates must listen carefully and critically to each other. By exchanging valuable feedback, you will help each other become better speakers, and you will all sharpen your skills as critical listeners.

Typically, a classroom speaking assignment does not highlight all the dimensions of public speaking at once. One assignment may focus on how to organize a speech clearly; another may emphasize research skills and the selection of supporting materials. Therefore, when assessing a classmate's speech, be sensitive to the specific purpose of the assignment. If it is intended to focus on organization, for instance, that also should be the focus of your critique. To concentrate on some other factor, such as the speaker's gestures, would be unfair, since the whole point of this assignment is to deemphasize other aspects of speaking in order to put the spotlight on organization.

A constructive attitude is essential in evaluating classroom speeches, because that provides the best environment for learning from each other. If criticism is hostile or antagonistic, the speaker may become defensive and may ignore useful feedback. At the same time, listeners who are too eager to criticize a speech may not properly assess the speaker's situation and purpose. Do not overlook weaknesses in a speech, but remember that the purpose of the critique is to help your classmate improve the speech, not to undermine self-esteem. Emphasize what the speaker can improve and how to do that; and remember that the strengths of the speech need not be ignored in order to identify its weaknesses.

A classroom speech often develops only a limited number of points, and your critique, too, should focus on a few features of the speech that are most important. The value of feedback is greatly reduced when critics offer a blow-by-blow reaction to everything that was said. The speaker will not be able to benefit from the criticism, because the important points will be indistinguishable from superficial reactions. As a general rule, focus your critique on just a few features of the speech, and arrange them in order of importance. The critique itself is an attempt to influence others, and like a speech it should be composed in a way that best achieves its purpose.

Critiques of classroom speeches take a variety of forms. The most common is *informal discussion*. After a speech is presented, the class may spend some time talking about its strengths and about how it might be improved. Students are sometimes reluctant to participate in these discussions. Some may fear hurting their classmates' feelings, or they may believe that, if they critique others, their own speeches will be evaluated more harshly. These are shortsighted judgments. After all, a primary goal of this course is to become more skilled in speaking, and vigorous evaluation—as long as your attitude is constructive—is one of the best ways to achieve that goal.

Sometimes students fill out *rating forms* to evaluate classroom speeches. These emphasize the same features of public speaking that are stressed in the particular assignment. They are efficient—raters use check marks, circle key words, or assign numerical scores, for example—and they usually also include space to write more open-ended comments. If your class uses rating forms for evaluation, take the task seriously, and provide the most constructive feedback possible.

On some occasions, evaluation involves an *impromptu speech of criticism* in which the critic follows the speaker with a presentation that assesses the speech. This will sharpen your own critical skills and at the same time give you practice in speaking. Like any other speech, a speech of evaluation has a thesis and main ideas—in this case, whatever you think is most important to say in assessing a classmate's speech.

Evaluating Speeches in the Field

Most speeches are not delivered in a classroom for the purpose of practicing the art. Most are delivered in a variety of public settings such as banquets, commemorative celebrations, business meetings, churches and synagogues, political campaigns, and so on.

Many of the principles of classroom evaluation also apply to speeches in the field. In particular, critics need to have a clear understanding of the rhetorical situation and the speaker's purpose. Speeches are presented in specific situations to achieve specific goals, and the critique must take these into account. It is also helpful to become familiar with the speaker and his or her particular assets and liabilities in the speaking situation. As with classroom speeches, you need to decide which standards to use for evaluation, probably including such factors as the validity of the speaker's reasoning and assertions, any value judgments made consciously or unconsciously, and the ethical implications of the speech.

An advantage of assessing speeches outside the classroom is that they have more variety, since they don't all spring from the same assignment. No doubt you'll hear speakers who ignore some of the concepts and guidelines in this book or who give them a unique twist. By assessing speakers in the field, you will encounter a great range of speaking styles and can better develop your own distinctive approach to public speaking.

Rhetorical Criticism

Evaluating the speeches of others is an elementary form of **rhetorical criticism**—the analytical assessment of messages that are intended to affect other people. Careful, critical listening and evaluation of speeches will help you develop a mindset for rhetorical criticism. It will give you experience in thinking rhetorically about speeches: asking yourself what the speaker's purpose seems to be, what opportunities and problems are presented by the speaker's situation, how the speaker has chosen to go about the task, whether other choices were available, and whether the selected means and ends were the best possible in that situation.[7]

rhetorical criticism
The analytical assessment of messages that are intended to affect other people.

Engaging in rhetorical criticism has two major byproducts. First, it gives you insights into your own public speaking by providing a range of speakers to study and by drawing your attention to how they apply principles of public speaking. Second, it develops your sensitivity to public speaking and makes you more aware of how it works. Besides improving your own abilities as a speaker, this awareness should help you appreciate excellent public speaking and put you on guard against speakers who try to undermine listeners' critical abilities.

Summary

Although hearing is a natural physiological activity, listening is a cultivated skill that includes mental processing and assessment of what is heard. It is an important skill to develop to be sure you know what you heard, to provide feedback to the speaker, and to protect yourself from unethical or unscrupulous speakers.

Listening is difficult. People think more rapidly than they listen and therefore may be prone to daydream. They may engage in "channel surfing," tuning a speech in and out as they are stimulated by certain words to think about other things. For some people a limited attention span makes it difficult to take everything in; for others the commitment to listen to absolutely everything may get in the way of reflective judgment. People may jump to conclusions because they agree or disagree with the speaker, and they may regard what the speaker says as closer to or farther from their own beliefs than is really the case. Finally, factors in the situation such as noise or physical disruption may interfere with listening to the speech.

Overcoming these difficulties requires concerted effort to develop the skills of careful and critical listening. Careful listening includes decoding the message by identifying the thesis and mapping the links between it and the main supporting ideas. It also involves making at least some judgment about the content of the speech and the links within it. Careful listening can be aided by efficient note taking.

Critical listening begins with the skills of critical thinking and applies them to the speaking situation. Critical listeners are open to new ideas and arguments but assess them with skepticism and an insistence that they be explained and supported. The goals of critical listening are to be able to reconstruct the thesis and main ideas of a speech and to form a reflective rather than hasty judgment about them.

Critical listening makes it possible both to evaluate messages and to provide feedback to others about how they can improve their speaking performance. Clear standards of evaluation are needed, and the assessment should be guided especially by understanding of the rhetorical situation and the speaker's purpose. Although the effectiveness standard is an important criterion, by itself it usually is not the most appropriate basis for evaluating a speech. Instead, the artistic standard includes effectiveness but focuses on the question of how well the speaker applied public speaking principles and followed ethical norms in a specific situation. You will have the opportunity to practice rhetorical criticism both by critiquing classmates' speeches and by attending and evaluating speeches in the field.

Discussion Questions

1. We have all heard speeches that were interesting and speeches that were boring. What was it about the interesting speeches that grabbed your attention? What was it about the boring speeches that made them difficult to bear? Based on your answers, suggest some strategies for gaining and holding an audience's attention.

2. You are about to speak to a hostile audience. How do you get them to listen with an open mind rather than immediately discounting your position?

3. You are assigned the responsibility of grading a speech that you yourself haven't heard. You must consider the views of two critics who heard the speech and gave you their opinions about it. But their evaluations are contradictory: One says the speech was great, and the other thinks it was shoddy work. How would you reconcile these different evaluations and assign a grade to the speech?

4. You have just heard a speech that was particularly effective, but in your opinion it was ethically suspect. How would you evaluate the speech? Why?

Activities

1. Listen to a speech on television, in class, or at a lecture. Whenever your mind wanders, make a note about the last thing you heard and what you then began to think about. After the speech, write a short essay about your listening habits and how you would like to improve them.

2. Map a speech. Identify its thesis and main ideas, and evaluate its claims and links.

3. Write a three- to five-page essay to evaluate a speech. Analyze the rhetorical situation and the speaker's purpose; state and explain your evaluation standards; and apply rhetorical criticism to the speech.

Using the Internet

If you have access to a multimedia-equipped computer with sufficient processing power, you may be able to use your Internet access to listen to speeches. The exercises rely on using files in RealAudio or RealVideo format. Further details about using RealPlayer for listening are available at <http://www.real.com/products/player/index.html>. (However, if you are not set up for these formats, there are also text-based variations in the exercises below.)

1. **Listen to speeches in RealAudio or RealVideo format.** First explore some of the speeches in the Archive of speeches in the **Allyn & Bacon Public Speaking Website.** Go to <http://www.abacon.com/pubspeak/histsit.html>. *Note that for each speech on the page you can read text and/or listen to a RealAudio version.*

(continued)

If you do not have a sound card, consider having someone read the text aloud to you, or create your own recording with a tape recorder.

2. **Search for audio files and use mapping skills.** For this exercise, we will search for a speech presented by President Bill Clinton in one of his weekly radio addresses or a speech by the designated Republican spokesperson. Point your browser to the **White House Virtual Library** at <http://library.whitehouse.gov/?request=audio> and click on the choice "Radio Addresses of the President." From there type in a keyword for a topic area that you think President Clinton may have spoken about during his term that interests you. (If you come up empty the first time, try a different search term.)

Alternately, search **Weekly Republican Radio Address** by pointing your browser to <http://www.rnc.org/movie/response/index.html>. Notice that this is organized in reverse chronological order.

Note that the White House Virtual Library includes a text of the speech as well as the RealAudio file; the Weekly Republican Radio Address page provides only the RealAudio format.

Map the message you've found by

- *Extracting the thesis*
- *Identifying the main ideas*
- *Assessing the main ideas*
- *Deciding whether the main ideas support the thesis*

Notes

1. The complexity of an individual's cognitive processes is also responsible for differences in listening comprehension. See Michael J. Beatty and Steven K. Payne, "Listening Comprehension as a Function of Cognitive Complexity: A Research Note," *Communication Monographs* 51 (March 1984): 85–89.

2. Neil Postman provides an extensive social critique of how television is responsible for this trend in *Amusing Ourselves to Death: Public Discourse in the Age of Show Business,* New York: Penguin Books, 1985.

3. One example of this is seen in a study showing that when common citizens hear an argument about capital punishment, they judge the validity of evidence from the perspective they bring to the communication event, retaining their original beliefs regardless of the evidence presented. See Charles Lord, Ross Lee, and Mark Lepper, "Biased Assimilation and Attitude Polarization: The Effects of Prior Theories on Subsequently Considered Evidence," *Journal of Personality and Social Psychology* 37 (November 1979): 2098–2109.

4. For more about critical thinking, see Brook Noel Moore and Richard Parker, *Critical Thinking: Evaluating Claims and Arguments in Everyday Life,* 2nd ed., Mountain View, Calif.: Mayfield, 1989; and Leonard J. Rosen and Laurence Behrens, *The Allyn & Bacon Handbook,* 2nd ed., Boston: Allyn & Bacon, 1994, pp. 1–9. Although these textbooks focus on essay writing and evaluation, many of their directives apply as well to public speaking.

5. According to Mikhail Bahktin, we automatically tend to judge all utterances—from sentences to completed speeches—by what we imagine the speaker *wishes* to say. See "The Problem of Speech Genres," in *Speech Genres and Other Essays,* trans. Vern W. McGee, Austin: Univ. of Texas Press, 1986, p. 77.

6. Another example of why a speech should not be judged on effect alone is discussed in Edwin Black, *Rhetorical Criticism,* New York: Macmillan, 1965. For more about this debate in speech criticism, see Forbes I. Hill, "Conventional Wisdom—Traditional Form: The President's Message of November 3, 1969"; Karlyn Kohrs Campbell, "Conventional Wisdom—Traditional Form: A Rejoinder"; and Forbes I. Hill, "Reply to Professor Campbell," *Quarterly Journal of Speech* 58 (December 1972): 373–386, 451–460.

7. For more about rhetorical criticism, see James R. Andrews, *The Practice of Rhetorical Criticism,* New York: Longman, 1992.

chapter 3
Analyzing Your Audience

In This Chapter We Will:

- Discover how the success of a speech depends on the audience.

- Explore how the audience demographics, culture, and psychology affect listeners' receptiveness to a speech.

- Consider ways that speakers can adapt a message in particular circumstances to fit the audience.

- Identify both formal and informal methods of audience analysis.

- Examine how the speaker's ethos influences the audience and how speakers can improve their ethos.

Two students were presenting speeches to their classmates about the dangers of smoking. Both spent a great deal of time preparing, but they had strongly different attitudes about how to develop their speeches. The night before speaking, they met to compare their preparations. The first student said:

> I had no idea there was so much research information about this topic. I had to cut short my explanations in order to fit everything in. If I talk faster than usual, I just might make it within the time limit. I want everyone to know that I prepared thoroughly and that I take the topic very seriously.

His classmate took a different approach:

> Well, you may be right, but I don't think people want to hear about all the research. They need to know that the studies exist, but they really need to hear about how smoking has hurt someone they know. I want to tell a story that listeners can relate to, so that they'll be interested in my message.

The first student viewed the assignment only from his own perspective as speaker, worrying about how to include all the research and how to ensure a good grade. The second student considered the audience's perspective. She was determined to make the message interesting to classmates, and she carefully reviewed each bit of information from the viewpoint of someone hearing it in a short speech. Both speakers had the same general topic and goal, but to the audience the first speech was abstract, complicated, and dull, whereas the second was stimulating and full of common sense.

It may seem surprising that even your attitude toward preparing a speech can create such a difference in the audience's reaction, but it's natural for listeners to give appreciation, attention, and support to a speaker who considers their comfort, interests, and beliefs. Even though an audience can thus be a constraint on a speaker's freedom, you can work with that constraint by careful audience analysis on three different levels:

- By checking *audience demographics,* you will consider how your speech should respond to certain characteristics of the audience as a whole—such as its size, age range, and educational level.
- By respecting *audience culture,* you will become aware of how listeners approach your speech in terms of their interests, beliefs and values, prior understanding, and common knowledge.
- By understanding *audience psychology,* you will realize that listeners are selective about what they attend to and perceive.

The relationships among audience demographics, culture, and psychology are illustrated in Figure 3.1. After studying these three levels of audience analysis, we will examine strategies for learning about your specific audience and for assessing your own resources and ethos in relation to its members.

FIGURE 3.1

Levels of influence on audiences.

CHECKING AUDIENCE DEMOGRAPHICS

Size

How large will your audience be? The more listeners there are, the greater your sense of distance from them, and consequently the more formal your presentation is likely to be. Someone speaking to a dozen people in a small room clearly faces a different situation than someone addressing a large lecture hall or a mass-media audience.

Classroom speakers probably have an audience of about 20 to 25 listeners, an audience size that is typical of many speeches to service clubs, neighborhood groups, and work-related organizations. This size lets you address a public without losing sight of individuals, and the setting is a middle ground between highly formal and extremely informal.

Heterogeneity

Heterogeneity refers to the variety or diversity of audience members—the degree of dissimilarity among them. The smaller the audience, the more likely that its members will have similar assumptions, values, and ways of thinking. Of course, even a small audience may show marked differences in these criteria, but a large audience virtually ensures that members will have different values and assumptions as well as learning styles; the audience is said to be *heterogeneous*.

The two students speaking about the dangers of smoking assumed that their audience of American college students would be like them, would learn about the subject in the same way, and would respond favorably to their message. But a heterogeneous audience could include smokers and stockholders of tobacco companies who might oppose restrictions on smoking.

The more heterogeneous your audience, the more you need to find examples and appeals that will be meaningful to all kinds of listeners; or you might combine appeals that are relevant to different segments of the audience. Avoid materials that are significant only to some listeners but beside the point to others. The goal is to appeal meaningfully to a diverse audience without resorting to vague generalizations and **platitudes.**

An audience can be heterogeneous even if its members share the same cultural background, but a culturally diverse audience is particularly likely to be heterogeneous. The audience for the speeches against smoking might include a student or two from countries where smoking is unrestricted, and they may not share their classmates' concerns about the health risks of smoking.

Voluntary versus Captive Audience

Under what circumstances has the audience assembled? In general, people who have chosen to hear a speech are more likely to be interested and receptive than are people who have been coerced into attending. A captive audience may resent having to hear the speech, which may undercut the speaker's ethos and message.

Students who are required to attend an assembly, employees whose jobs depend on participation in a seminar, and churchgoers who find themselves listening to a political message when they expected a sermon are examples of captive audiences. Speakers cannot assume that captive listeners have any interest in them or their subject, and they must work particularly hard to interest and motivate them.

Some of your classmates may also be captive listeners, especially if the course is required or if individuals don't recognize the value of effective listening. With luck, you can turn them into voluntary listeners as they become interested in what you have to say and as they begin to see that they can improve their own speeches by listening carefully to yours.

If you assume that your audience is there voluntarily and you make no effort to motivate them, you could be setting yourself up for disaster. If you are wrong in your assessment and your listeners do see themselves as captive, their feelings of boredom or hostility are likely to overwhelm any message you present. For this reason, when you don't know the status of the audience, it is best to assume that listeners are captive and that you need to motivate them.

heterogeneity
Variety or diversity among audience members; dissimilarity.

platitudes
Buzz words or phrases that are devoid of specific content.

Composition

Sometimes, if it will help you make choices about your speech, you can analyze the audience in terms of such categories as age, gender, religion, ethnicity, educational level, or socioeconomic status. For example, it may be safe to assume that a young audience would be less interested in a speech about retirement planning than an older audience would be. Likewise, you might assume that listeners with a high level of formal education can think in figurative as well as literal terms and can deal with complex issues. And if an audience is made up mostly of members of a particular religious or ethnic group, you well may tailor your presentation to take advantage of their commonality.

Giving too much weight to demographic categories, however, may lead to false and unwarranted **stereotyping**—wrongly assuming that all members of a category are alike. For example, it is less true today than in the past that women and men differ in the likelihood of their being persuaded by a speaker. Nor do all people from rural areas think alike; and not everyone from a particular region has the same set of beliefs and values.[1] In short, demographic categories can provide important hints about an audience, but do not assume that the hints apply to everyone.

RESPECTING AUDIENCE CULTURE

Imagine that you are scheduled to speak about the joys of ham radio operation to a troop of Girl Scouts. Now imagine that your topic is the same but that your audience is a high school computer club or a convention of retired people. In what ways might you adapt your presentation to fit these different audiences?

No matter what your topic and purpose, to plan an effective message you must focus on the particular culture of your audience. **Audience culture** refers to subjective factors that characterize a particular audience and make its situation distinct: interests, beliefs and values, common knowledge and experience, roles and reference groups. Thinking critically about these factors will enable you to strategically plan a speech that fits your audience.

Self-Interest

Listeners have **self-interests;** they stand to gain or lose personally depending on what is done. For example, a proposal to raise students' tuition and fees would not be in the self-interest of those who are working their way through college, whereas a proposal to increase funds for financial aid *would* appeal to the self-interest of those same students. Self-interest goes beyond economic matters, however. A speech that advocates limits on listeners' freedom or power or that casts them in an unflattering role also will be at odds with the audience's self-interest.

Most listeners resist messages that clearly challenge their self-interest. If you feel that it is necessary to challenge the audience's self-interest, consider whether you can develop your message in a nonthreatening way while still

stereotyping
Assuming that all members of a demographic category are alike in all respects.

audience culture
Subjective factors that characterize a particular audience and make its situation distinct.

self-interest
Personal gain or loss resulting from an action or policy.

The Importance of Audience Analysis

Latif Farag

During all my speeches in this class, I have thought about my audience. This is because of the age difference. I'm 37 years old and the other students in the class are between 17 and 20 years. Also, I come from a different culture and I have to make sure that they understand the subject I'm talking about.

Dr. Marrow

Absolutely, Latif. Assessing the audience culture, including age and cultural background, is critical to speechmaking success. Take into consideration your audience's dominant ages and be careful not to stereotype, discredit, or undervalue them in any way. Also, when planning your speech, use examples or references that are universally recognized. Sometimes, culture-specific examples are obscure to the audience and can create a large psychological gap between the speaker and the audience.... Actually, the fact that you are older and from a different culture can enhance your credibility as a speaker. Just highlight some human experiences and beliefs shared by you and your audience, and your goal toward audience acceptance will be achieved!

being true to your beliefs. Perhaps you can plan the speech with a strong combination of appeals so that listeners will look beyond their self-interest to consider some broader concept of what is good.

For example, one common strategy for challenging listeners' self-interest is to suggest that their short-term sacrifices will bring long-term benefits (and so their self-interest will be satisfied in the long run). One student took this approach in arguing that course work should be more difficult. She began by admitting outright that her speech would challenge the audience's self-interest:

> Talk to any student at this college, and you'll hear about how busy they are, how much work they have to do, much time their classes take. I'm sure it's true, because many of us have never really been challenged to work hard before this. The last thing most students want is to hear someone say that classes should be made even harder. But if we can improve the academic reputation of this college, not only will it attract better students, but in the long run our own degrees will be more highly valued.

Personal Interests

Listeners also have **personal interests,** and so you need to assess how likely it is that your topic will interest others. Even though you may be an avid student of military history, you cannot assume that others will be captivated by a speech about battle planning. And although you may be thrilled by the details of auto mechanics, realize that many listeners only want to know how to turn the ignition key to start the car.

If you think that listeners will be strongly interested in your topic, a straightforward presentation may be fine. But if interest may be low, you should deliberately plan the speech in a way that captures the audience's

personal interests
What an individual regards as interesting or important.

attention and holds their interest. Usually, you should avoid technical language, jargon, and abstractions unless you know that the audience is familiar with and interested in the topic. On the other hand, startling statements, rhetorical questions, personal anecdotes, and narratives are especially good ways to involve listeners in your topic and enhance their interest in it.

Sometimes listeners do have a casual interest in your topic but do not regard it as particularly important or of high priority. Then your task is less one of arousing initial interest and more a matter of impressing the audience with the urgency of the situation and the significance of your message. In any case, by analyzing the audience's level of interest in your topic, you are better able to determine how to frame the speech.

Beliefs and Values

Beliefs are statements that listeners regard as true; **values** are positive or negative judgments that listeners make. For example, a listener might believe that homelessness is a serious problem (belief) and might also regard government aid for the homeless as a good thing (giving it a positive value). Another listener might agree that homelessness is a serious problem (belief) yet might object to government aid (giving it a negative value). Still another listener might not believe that homelessness is a serious problem and might think that its scope has been exaggerated. For the last listener, government aid is not an issue because no problem has been acknowledged.

As these examples show, an audience's beliefs and values are the starting point for crafting the strategy of your speech. You will want to uphold your own beliefs and values, of course, but you can do that and also advance your purpose if you emphasize the connections between listeners' beliefs and values and your own.

Assume that you wish to advocate increased government aid for the homeless. For the first listener your strategy might be designed to reinforce existing beliefs and values. For the second listener, you might briefly review the extent of the problem, but most of the speech would be designed to convince the listener that government aid works better than private solutions alone; your goal would be to change the listener's value about government aid from negative to positive. For the third listener, it is pointless to consider whether public or private solutions are better unless you can demonstrate that homelessness really is a problem. In this case much of your speech would be designed to illustrate the extent and severity of homelessness and the urgent need for action. Finally, if all three listeners are in your audience, your strategy should combine appeals in the hope that one thing or another would convince each listener.

This example has focused on topic-specific beliefs and values about homelessness. But listeners also hold many general beliefs and values about a host of topics—about human nature, about their responsibilities to others, about the status of their nation in the world, about the significance of science or religion, and so on. For example, if an audience believes that things generally are better (or worse) today than in the past, speakers in a political campaign might exploit that belief by claiming that their party (or the opposing party) is responsible for the situation. General beliefs and values, like topical ones, give you a good starting point from which to think strategically about how to reinforce some beliefs and attempt to change others.

beliefs
Statements that listeners regard as true.

values
Positive or negative judgments that listeners apply to a person, place, object, event, or idea.

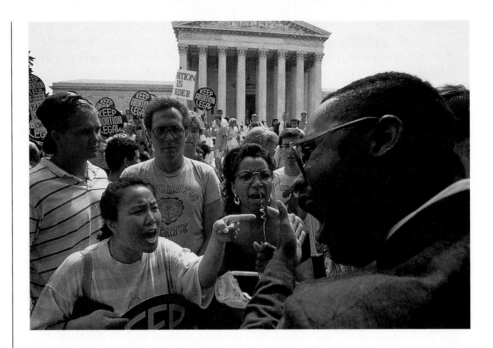

Sometimes listeners know a good deal about the topic and have strong feelings about it. To be successful, speakers must respond to what the audience already knows about the topic or situation.

Prior Understanding

How much do your listeners already know about your topic? Have they heard about any of your points before? Do they have enough background information to follow your reasoning? Answers to questions like these can help you design a powerful speech without boring or confusing your audience.

Speakers sometimes mistake intelligence for knowledge, thus overestimating what the audience knows. Fearful of **condescending** to listeners—of talking down to them and assuming that they can't think for themselves—some speakers cover complex material too quickly, omit important steps in an explanation, or relate events out of sequence. Another danger of poor audience analysis is telling listeners nothing that they do not already know. If the listeners believe a speaker is wasting their time and saying nothing new, they are less likely to pay attention. Worse, they may become angry or resent the speaker as a person. You can avoid all these dangers by analyzing what the audience already knows.

President Ronald Reagan was dubbed "The Great Communicator" in part because he could render complex subjects in simple, understandable terms. In a 1983 speech seeking support for his Strategic Defense Initiative, he used simple terms to describe sophisticated military and strategic concepts, and he also overcame complex arguments about defense spending:

> But first, let me say what the defense debate is not about. It is not about spending arithmetic. I know that in the last few weeks you've been bombarded with numbers and percentages. . . .The trouble with all these numbers is that they tell us little about the kind of defense program America needs or the benefits and security and freedom that our defense effort buys for us.

In simple language President Reagan then explained the importance of a defensive missile system: "I've become more and more convinced that the hu-

condescending

Talking down to an audience; assuming that listeners are not capable of thinking about a subject and reaching their own conclusions.

man spirit must be capable of rising above dealing with other nations and human beings by threatening their existence"; and "Wouldn't it be better to save lives than avenge them?" He admitted but downplayed the difficulties of developing this new system and called on the scientific community, "those who gave us nuclear weapons, to turn their great talents now to the cause of mankind and world peace, to give us the means of rendering these nuclear weapons impotent and obsolete." If President Reagan had focused only on technical and scientific issues in the belief that "everyone understood" the difference between offensive and defensive systems, his speech would have been far less effective.

Common Knowledge and Experience

What **cultural facts** in your listeners' general store of knowledge will be relevant to your speech? Surveys frequently report that embarrassing percentages of Americans cannot name their senator or representative, do not know when the Civil War was fought, or cannot locate a particular country on the globe. Such evidence does not argue that people are stupid or that a speaker must spell out everything for an audience. Rather, in recent years educators have been less concerned with teaching facts than with teaching students how to find information.[2] Thus, for a general audience, you may need to identify or explain cultural facts that are important to your argument. But if your audience is specialized—say a group of Civil War buffs—you can assume that listeners are familiar with basic information about your topic.

Speakers often make **allusions,** or brief references, to things that they assume listeners know about and understand. But if listeners don't "get" the allusion, they also will miss the point of the comparison. So you need to have a good sense of which allusions your audience will recognize. Well into the twentieth century, speakers could assume that most listeners were familiar with the Bible and with classic literature. Late in the century, however, popular culture—especially television—became the source of many allusions especially in the United States. For example, supporters of President John F. Kennedy fondly remembered his administration by referring to the popular musical *Camelot.* And during the 1984 presidential campaign, Democratic candidate Walter Mondale dismissed the argument of one of his primary opponents by asking, "Where's the beef?"—quoting a popular television commercial for a chain of hamburger franchises.

Similarly, in a classroom speech about nuclear power, Steve Cortez alluded to the animated television program "The Simpsons":

> What comes to your mind when you hear the words "nuclear power"? If you're like most Americans, you probably conjure up images of Three-Mile Island and Chernobyl. Or if you're a fan of "The Simpsons," you might think of the nuclear-waste-induced three-eyed fish found near the plant in a recent episode. Maybe you think of Homer Simpson eating doughnuts and sleeping while he's supposed to be monitoring the plant's safety equipment, or of Mr. Burns, the diabolical plant owner. Whatever your immediate impression of nuclear power, it's probably negative, and it shouldn't be.

By analyzing and understanding his audience's shared cultural experiences, Steve was able to allude to "The Simpsons" characters to build a strong introduction that captured interest and prepared listeners for his main point.

cultural facts
Facts that are commonly known among the members of a culture; common knowledge.

allusions
Brief references to something with which the audience is assumed to be familiar.

When a message is unfamiliar, listeners tend to perceive it in their own familiar context. This speaker should realize that his remarks about the new Americans with Disabilities Act may well be heard in the context of his listeners' personal experience in coping with disabilities.

Roles and Reference Groups

Each listener occupies a variety of **roles,** or socially assigned positions, and these are an important part of an audience's culture. An earlier example about ham radio operators referred to an audience made up of Girl Scouts. A listener who is a Girl Scout is also a young woman, a student, and a daughter; and she may be a member of a church, the Honor Society, and the dance club. Depending on which role is dominant for her at any given time, different topics and appeals are likely to be effective. If, while listening to a speech, she thinks of herself mainly as a Girl Scout, she may be more interested in physical adventure or social service than she would be if she thought of herself mainly as a dancer. In analyzing your audience, therefore, you need to decide which roles are most important to listeners while you speak.

Listeners also identify with many **reference groups,** whether or not they actually belong to them. Because reference groups serve as guides or models for behavior, they can influence listeners' beliefs, values, and actions. For example, a student may model his taste in clothes or hairstyle on the members of a popular band; he isn't a member of this band, but he likes people to think of him as sharing its characteristics. Another student may take cues about the importance of good study habits from older friends in her residence hall; they are a reference group for her because she likes to be thought of in reference to them. In other situations, however, each of these students will model different reference groups—family, friends, peers, public figures, and ethnic groups, for instance. By knowing which reference groups and values are important to your listeners, you can strategically plan effective appeals and supporting materials.

roles
Socially assigned positions, such as "parent," "student," "employee," and "citizen."

reference groups
Groups with which listeners identify, regardless of whether they belong to them. Reference groups serve as guides or models for behavior.

Cultural Diversity

We have been discussing culture as though audience members all share a common culture. In some respects they probably do, but a speaker who assumes that an audience has a single set of beliefs, values, or experiences is inviting disaster.

The United States has increasingly become a multicultural society, and today's audience members represent a diversity of cultures and backgrounds. This is true of public speaking classes particularly, because schools, colleges, and universities have sought to attract international students and students from various racial and ethnic groups. It is also true of society at large, as racial and ethnic minority groups make up a growing proportion of the population. Everyone, whether speaker or listener, must acknowledge and relate to people who reflect a wide variety of cultural backgrounds.

Chinese President Jiang Zemin learned this basic truth when he toured the United States in the fall of 1997. He championed the benefits of the Chinese system and dismissed calls for reform. But U.S. audiences were not impressed, and many protested his visit. Then, speaking at Harvard University, President Jiang acknowledged that China had made mistakes and said that his visit had taught him more about freedom. The protests did not stop, but these modest acknowledgments of cultural differences brought out expressions of respect—a key goal of Jiang's visit.

Speaking to a multicultural audience challenges you to become aware of your own cultural assumptions and predispositions. It is common for people to regard as universal the values of their specific culture. But reflection and careful self-analysis can help you avoid seeing your own values as universal and thus seeming insensitive to cultural differences.[3]

To use a simple example, U.S. culture traditionally has valued youth, whereas Japanese culture has valued age. In speaking to an audience of both American and Japanese listeners, it would not be a good idea either to discredit something by labeling it "old" or, on the other hand, to assume that our ancestors always understood things better than we do.

Another example is seen in cultural attitudes toward the role of women, which vary widely between more traditional and more modern cultures. Women's roles as professionals are not as widely recognized in some societies in the Middle East and Latin America as they are in the United States. So a speech about women in the business world might be planned and presented differently for an international audience composed mostly of men and for an audience of U.S. businesspeople.

Cultures differ even with respect to who is eligible to speak in public. During the early 1800s, women in the United States often were not allowed to appear on a public platform because that would violate their "feminine" role. As recently as 1976, U.S. Representative Barbara Jordan, one of the most prominent African-American politicians, began her keynote speech to the Democratic National Convention by observing:

> There is something different about tonight. There is something special about tonight. What is different? What is special? I, Barbara Jordan, am a keynote speaker.
>
> A lot of years passed since 1832, and during that time it would have been most unusual for any national political party to ask that a Barbara Jordan deliver a keynote address—but tonight here I am. And I feel that notwithstanding the past that my presence here is one additional bit of evidence that the American Dream need not forever be deferred.

Yet another example relates to people's attitudes about what is "correct" speech or language. The United States includes many regional, ethnic, and social dialects. In some circumstances these are perfectly acceptable ways of speaking; in others, listeners may regard them as substandard. If you plan to quote dialect in your speech, recognize that different language patterns are legitimate, and acknowledge the validity of "standard" patterns; yet do not disparage patterns different from your own.[4]

Regional differences in culture are also important. A student who grew up in the South and attends a university in the Northeast will not understand how classmates can survive winter. Likewise, they may be surprised by this student's unhurried pace and "laid back" lifestyle. But it is easy to misinterpret someone else based on the framework of your own background—unless you recognize and understand the validity of cultural differences.

Many beliefs about other cultures are based on negative, unflattering stereotypes, and it is particularly important to avoid these when addressing a multicultural audience. Consciously resist any such belief as that one culture is hard-working and another is lazy, or that one is educated and another is ignorant, or that one is compulsive and another is relaxed. The reality is far more complex, and such simple-minded attitudes will rightly both insult and antagonize an audience.

Speakers adapt to a culturally diverse audience in two basic ways. One approach is to derive examples from many cultures so that all listeners feel that they are being addressed within the framework of their own culture. Even if some cultures are not mentioned specifically, the speaker's acknowledgment of diversity may make everyone feel more included.[5] This approach, of course, requires the speaker to know which particular cultures are represented by audience members.

The other approach is to resist culture-specific references altogether and to search instead for appeals that transcend cultures. An appeal based on preserving the planet for the next generation, an appeal to the common interest in peace, or an appeal based on the beauty and wonder of nature may well transcend the limits of any particular culture.[6] In a speech in 1963, President Kennedy illustrated this approach. After speaking about the need to recognize diversity among nations and cultures, he noted that all people hold certain values in common:

> For in the final analysis, our most basic common link is that we all inhabit this small planet. We all breathe the same air. We all cherish our children's future. And we are all mortal.

UNDERSTANDING AUDIENCE PSYCHOLOGY

Selective Exposure and Selective Attention

Each day an infinite number of potential communication stimuli are available to us. We can converse with anyone we meet and can overhear the conversations of others; we can call or write to each other; we can read newspapers, magazines, and books; we can listen to the radio or watch television;

we can see films or videos; we can attend speeches, listen to lectures on tape, hear sermons, or join group discussions. And while we're busy doing all this, our computers can log on to the Internet to exchange mail and collect any information we specify.

Even if we did nothing else except engage in communication, there is clearly too much for any of us to do. How do we choose which speeches to hear, which magazines to read, which television programs to watch, and which Websites to visit? In short, how do we select the communications to which we will expose ourselves?

Selective exposure is the concept that our communication choices are not random; rather, we are inclined to expose ourselves to messages that are important to us personally and that are consistent with what we already believe. Few of us seek out messages that we do not think will be useful or pertinent to us; nor do we listen to speeches other than entertainment speeches merely for the pleasure of hearing them. And very few of us relish an attack on what we believe. Instead, we read magazines, listen to speakers, and make friends whose views are similar to our own.

Although selective exposure governs which messages we will seek out, sometimes audience members are not given a choice. Your classmates, for instance, are captive listeners who do not have the option of not hearing you, even if you disagree with them. But both captive and voluntary audiences can exercise a second level of control over potential communications. They are selective about whether or not to focus intently on a message, to follow it, absorb it, and take it seriously. These choices, sometimes made unconsciously, are called **selective attention.**

As we discussed in Chapter 2, it takes effort and energy to listen carefully and critically to a speech. Listeners' minds tend to wander—to events of the day, people they want to see, things they need to do, problems they hope to solve. Making the effort to listen requires motivation, and the speaker can help to supply that for the audience.

Student speaker Scott Poggi overlooked this opportunity when he decided to develop a speech based on his own special interests. On weekends Scott worked as a stagehand for a production company, and his speech demonstrated his expertise in the subject. He told his classmates all about the backstage area, introducing them to the light designer, the head light technician, and the light crew; mentioning the "FOH" (footlights and overheads), the electrics, and the cyclorama; telling them about the necessity of "testing and gelling the lights"; introducing them to the sound crew and their equipment; and finally describing the stage manager's many duties. By the time Scott finished, many in the audience were half asleep. Not only did he provide too much technical information without explaining it (classmates still had to ask, "What is an FOH, and how do you 'gel' a light?"); but he also never gave the audience any reason for wanting to know this information in the first place. Better audience analysis might have shown Scott that he would have to motivate listeners to help them pay attention.

The speaker can motivate the audience in at least three ways:

* Make the message personally important to listeners.
* Make the message stand out.
* Make the message easy to follow.

selective exposure
A tendency to expose oneself to messages that are important personally and that are consistent with what one already believes.

selective attention
Conscious or unconscious choice about whether or not to focus intently on a speech, absorb and process its contents, and take it seriously.

MAKE THE MESSAGE PERSONALLY IMPORTANT TO LISTENERS Listeners are better motivated to pay attention if the speech is personally meaningful and important to them, affects them, offers new information and insights they haven't considered, solves puzzles or paradoxes, or tells a story or makes a comparison with something they already know. When you plan the strategy for your speech, focus on making it clear how your message relates to audience members personally. In effect you are saying, "This concerns you. Sit up and take notice."

To apply these general principles, you might introduce your speech with an example that listeners will recognize or a story that describes an experience they might have had. Or you might translate statistics or abstract ideas into personal terms, as in the statement "Our national debt is now so large that each of you would have to work nonstop for 20 years just to pay off your share." You might even announce explicitly that listeners will benefit from your speech: "I'm going to tell you how you can get better grades in every course."

MAKE THE MESSAGE STAND OUT The message may stand out because of a contrast between what the speaker is expected to say and what he or she actually says. Listeners will sit up and take notice if a student suggests that professors do not assign enough work, if an athlete maintains that physical fitness is unimportant, or if a known advocate of gender equality speaks in favor of some gender-based distinctions. Alternatively, the contrast might be between the speaker and other elements in the situation. If you were to be the fifth speaker after four classmates had all discussed similar topics in the same way, you might deliberately modify your speech to do something different. Or the contrast might be within the speech itself, such as changes in pitch, volume, or rate of delivery.

A word of caution is necessary regarding the use of contrast. Any contrast effect you use should be closely related to the purpose of your speech; contrast for its own sake draws attention to itself and distracts from the message. Avoid attention-getting gimmicks, whether in the introduction or anywhere else in the speech. Even if you succeed in getting attention, the audience will remember the trick, not your message.

MAKE THE MESSAGE EASY TO FOLLOW Paying careful attention is work for listeners. The more you can do to minimize their task and to motivate them to make the effort, the more likely they will be attentive.[7]

Speakers can do several things to make their message easier to follow:

- Strategically plan the organization of the speech in a way that makes your thesis and overall argument clear to listeners.
- State your main ideas explicitly so that listeners can easily identify them.
- Speak at a rate that sustains listeners' interest but is not so rapid that they have to struggle to keep up with you.
- Repeat your main ideas and key points, signaling to the audience that these are important.
- Use pauses to mark the transitions in the speech.
- Summarize your thesis and main ideas memorably.

Perception

An audience is asked not only to listen carefully to a speech but also to *interpret* it as the speaker intends. **Perception** is the particular interpretation or understanding that a listener gets from a speech. When listeners decide what a speech "means," they are perceiving it in a particular way. Unfortunately, a speaker cannot ensure that the audience perceives the meaning of the speech in the same way that the speaker does. Even individual ideas may be interpreted differently by speaker and audience.

Any message is open to different interpretations and can result in different perceptions. Suppose, for example, that early in an election year the current president predicts economic growth over the next several months. Should you interpret that message as economic forecasting, or as a political appeal designed to win votes, or as wishful thinking by a candidate who does not really understand the economy? Or is it all of these? Clearly, speakers need to understand how most listeners perceive things.

Recall that perception, like attention, is selective; we interpret messages in ways that render them simple, stable, and consistent with our expectations. Complex or conflicting messages are simplified; qualifying statements and subtle distinctions may be lost. The following examples of how people perceive messages selectively are generalizations and obviously do not apply in every case. But they are based on research, and they can help you plan your speech. If applied *too* rigidly, however, they can result in stereotyping, which speakers should always avoid.

1. People tend to view their experiences as structured, stable, and meaningful rather than random, chaotic, or pointless. Seeking order, listeners are predisposed to accept any pattern that the speaker can offer to explain seemingly unconnected facts.

2. People tend to view events not as accidental but as having causes; they also tend to simplify the web of causal connections and sometimes even seek a single cause to explain complex effects. Given that the brevity of a speech also leads to simplification, speakers must be careful not to allow listeners to oversimplify the relationships among events.

3. People tend to view individuals as being responsible for their own actions and to assume that actions reflect a person's intentions.

4. People tend to view others as being basically like themselves. When a speaker discusses personal experiences, listeners often assume that the speaker thought and acted just as they would have in the same circumstances. And if the audience is heterogeneous, different kinds of listeners may perceive the speaker differently.

5. People tend to interpret things in the way that their reference groups do. The desire to fit in and to be accepted by important peers may cause some people to accept the group's perception as their own—without even being aware that they are doing it.

6. People tend to perceive messages within the framework of familiar categories, even at the risk of distorting the message. For example, if someone believes that Democrats generally favor government intervention in the economy and that Republicans do not, that person is likely to perceive any pro-Democratic message as calling for government involvement in the economy.

• • • • • • • • • • • • • • • • • • • •

perception
The interpretation or understanding given to a speech; the meaning it has for a listener.

CHOOSE A STRATEGY

Adapting to Your Audience

THE SITUATION

Over the last few months, your town has seen a rise in accidents related to underage drinking. Your local government is starting a campaign to crack down on underage drinking. You have decided that you want to support this cause and volunteer your time. Your first job is to speak to a group of students at the local college about this community problem.

MAKING CHOICES

1. How might you determine your audience's likely reaction to your message?

2. You suspect that some of your audience members will be somewhat hostile to your message. What strategies can you utilize to reduce the hostility of your audience and to gain their support and acceptance?

WHAT IF . . .

How would your choice of strategies vary if you were speaking to the following audiences who likely would be more supportive of your message from the start?

1. The local campus administration about the campaign to curb underage drinking

2. The general audience at the next town meeting

3. The families of students who have been involved in drinking-related accidents

Although the tendency of listeners to perceive selectively can distort the speaker's message, knowing about selective perception can help the speaker to plan the speech so that it will be interpreted as desired. Selective exposure, attention, and perception are characteristic of almost all listeners. Whenever you plan a speech, design strategies to overcome these tendencies.

STRATEGIES FOR ANALYZING THE AUDIENCE

Knowing that audience analysis is so important to your success as a speaker, how do you go about it? Various methods are available, ranging from the highly formal to the frankly speculative.

Formal Methods

Companies developing a new product typically engage in market research. They conduct surveys to learn the needs and desires of consumers (their "audience"); they ask the target group to select adjectives to describe a concept or product; they may convene small discussion groups (focus groups) to probe people's feelings about a product. In principle, methods like these are available to speakers, too, and such formal analysis often is used in large-scale efforts such as a political campaign. But for most speeches this approach is impractical. You will have neither the time nor the resources to conduct formal surveys or in-depth interviews of classmates in preparation for a speech.

FIGURE 3.2

Audience survey.

Audience Survey

Age _____ Gender _____ Year of Graduation _____

Home town _____

High school attended: Public   Private

Parents' occupation(s) _____

Taking course as: Requirement   Elective

Politically, I would describe myself as:

strongly	moderately	middle of	moderately	strongly
conservative	conservative	the road	liberal	liberal

In general, where do you fall along the following scale:

_____

Prefer the familiar   Prefer the new

What three adjectives most accurately describe you?

_____

What three adjectives would you most like to describe you?

_____

I regard college primarily as a time for

_____

What are the three most pressing problems confronting you in the next five years?

_____

What are the three most pressing problems confronting the country or the world in the next five years?

_____

[NOTE: The survey might well contain additional questions.]

Instead, a general audience survey like the one in Figure 3.2 can be invaluable. Your instructor might ask the class to complete such a survey and then might make the results available to everyone.

Informal Methods

Even if you can't conduct a formal audience survey, you still can learn quite a bit about your listeners. Here are some ideas:

1. Think back to what classmates said about themselves in their introductory speeches. They may have given you clues about their interests, their political leanings, their attitudes toward higher education, their family backgrounds, and other key aspects of audience culture.
2. In preparing to speak to an unfamiliar audience, ask the host or moderator some questions ahead of time. You may be able to find out which topics most interest audience members, who else was invited to speak to them recently, how attentive they are, and perhaps what their motives are for coming together to hear you.

3. If you know the demographic composition of your audience—its size, its average age, and the occupation of most members, for instance—interview people who represent this mix of variables. Although talking with just a few people is not a scientific sample, you may still get clues about the interests, beliefs, and values of the kind of people who will be in your audience.

4. If you know other speakers who have addressed an audience like the one you will face, talk with them ahead of time to learn what they encountered and what they think your audience will be like.

5. If you know which newspapers or magazines your listeners are likely to read, examine some recent copies before you speak. Besides getting a sense of what interests your listeners, you may locate allusions that will be especially meaningful to them.

6. Sometimes library research can help you analyze an audience. In Chapter 5 you will learn how to investigate your topic, and the same methods can help you investigate your audience. For example, you can find recent periodicals with surveys about the political attitudes of college students, or polls showing how older Americans feel about health care, or articles about how gender differences influence how people think or feel.

7. Don't overlook the most obvious method of audience analysis: direct observation. As your listeners assemble, size them up. About how many people are there? Are they all about the same age? What is the ratio of men to women? How are they dressed? Are they interacting or sitting apart? Do they seem enthusiastic? Such questions cannot give you perfect information about the audience, because they are superficial first impressions, but they often provide valuable insights that allow you to adapt your message appropriately and effectively.

Checklist

3.1 *How To Do Audience Analysis*

1. **Formal methods**
   - *Surveys*
   - *Focus groups*
2. **Informal methods**
   - *Prior knowledge of audience members*
   - *Interviewing*
       The host or moderator
       People similar to the audience members
       Others who have spoken to similar audiences
   - *Reading materials that the audience probably reads*
   - *Library research about the audience*
   - *Direct observation of audience members*
3. **Simplifying devices**
   - *Focus on the general public*
   - *Focus on specific audience roles or topic fields*
4. **Critical appraisal**
   - *What do you know? How reliable is the information?*
   - *What gaps remain? How important is it to fill them?*
   - *Are you relying on stereotypes or jumping to conclusions?*
   - *Would the speech satisfy a universal audience?*

Simplifying Devices

Although it seems desirable to get all the information you can about an audience, having *complete* knowledge is impossible. After all, audiences are often composed of people who are strangers both to each other and to the speaker. Their common interest in the speech may be all that brought them together, and the speaker often does not know who the specific audience members are.

In these respects, speaking in the classroom is atypical. You and your classmates get to know quite a bit about each other by giving and hearing multiple speeches. You may even have conducted formal audience analysis through a survey like the one in Figure 3.2. Given this depth of information, it is not very difficult to craft speeches that recognize the audience's position. Outside the classroom, however, detailed audience analysis is much more difficult, and many speakers employ simplifying devices to make the task easier.

FOCUS ON THE GENERAL PUBLIC For example, you might imagine your specific audience as the **general public**—listeners who share the characteristics of people in general, such as common sense, self-interest, sensitivity to others, and enthusiasm for a good story. The general public might be imagined as the readership of *Time* or some other mass-circulation magazine. In addition, this audience can be assumed to share whatever specific concerns or beliefs are reported in recent surveys of the population. Such surveys may show that people generally regard inflation to be a serious problem, or that they oppose U.S. military involvement in other lands, or that they object to tax increases to relieve the federal budget deficit. Not every member of any specific audience will share all these beliefs and values, of course; but the general public may be a reasonable substitute for the specific audience when you lack more precise information.

FOCUS ON AUDIENCE ROLES OR TOPIC FIELDS Another way to simplify audience analysis is to focus on the particular roles that you think your listeners play or on a particular field in which to place your topic. As we have seen, everyone occupies many different roles in society. A person may simultaneously be parent, child, sibling, student, classmate, employee, coworker, manager, and so on. Each such role may involve basic values and beliefs that are not as relevant to the other roles the person occupies. For instance, the standard of efficient communication that a woman uses at work is not the same standard that she uses as a wife or mother at home.

Similarly, we may think of speech topics as representing different **fields,** or subject-matter areas with different norms and assumptions. For example, most of us regard religion, politics, science, and art as distinct fields. We would not expect an audience to listen to a political speech with the same standards in mind that they would use in assessing a religious discourse. Nor would we expect science and art to evoke the same standards of quality.

In using roles or fields to simplify audience analysis, you should emphasize the particular role or field that seems most relevant to your speech. Addressing an audience at your church, for example, focus on members' moral and religious commitments. Speaking at a rally for student government candidates, focus on the common field of campus politics rather than on the many other topics about which listeners might disagree. And giving a speech to the

general public
Listeners who share the characteristics of people in general.

fields
Subject-matter areas with distinct norms or assumptions.

local Parents and Teachers Association, focus on listeners' common concerns for children rather than on their highly diverse concerns as public employees and taxpayers, men and women, and people of different ages.

In using simplifying devices to analyze an audience, keep in mind that generalizations often lead to stereotyping. Whether your assumptions about listeners' shared characteristics are true or not, you also want to show sensitivity to the many differences among audience members.

Critical Appraisal

Much of the information you have gained from these methods of audience analysis is inexact, even though you have done your best. For this reason you need to think critically about what you have learned. Ask yourself:

- How reliable, precise, and authoritative is your information about the audience? If the information seems questionable, can you devise strategies that compensate for error?
- Can you craft the speech so that it will be appropriate for listeners who are knowledgable about the topic and yet can be modified easily if listeners know less than you thought?
- Is your information about the audience really based on analysis, or might you be jumping to conclusions or relying on stereotypes?

One way to avoid jumping to conclusions is to view your listeners as representative of the **universal audience**—an imaginary audience made up of all reasonable people. No such audience exists, of course. The speaker constructs this image of an audience that accepts only those beliefs and values that no reasonable person would doubt.[8] Precisely because people are different, this is such a rigorous test that it could probably never be achieved. Yet it provides a norm or standard against which to assess your speech. It should prevent you from simply appealing to what you think are the audience's prejudices, or pandering to listeners' supposed beliefs and losing track of your own, or indulging in false stereotypes.

Thinking critically about your audience analysis will also promote your strategic planning. It will help you determine what you know that is useful to your speech and what questions remain unanswered. Although your knowledge of the audience will never be complete, critical thinking will help you decide whether you can afford to take chances and make guesses about the audience. And in planning strategies for presenting the speech, critical thinking will show you where you need to be especially sensitive to audience reactions.

Audience analysis is more an art than a science. As with every other aspect of public speaking, however, critical thinking and strategic planning will improve your information about the audience and will make your communication more effective.

ANALYZING YOUR OWN ETHOS

In Chapter 1 we introduced the concept of *ethos,* the character that an audience attributes to a speaker. In thinking about your audience, you also want to think about how its members are likely to characterize you.

universal audience
An imaginary audience made up of all reasonable people.

To begin with, you should determine similarities and differences between you and the audience with respect to demographics, culture, and psychology. Are you older or younger than most of your listeners? Is your ethnic, cultural, or economic background different? Are your personal interests similar to theirs? Do you have different general orientations toward change? If listeners judge you to be very different from themselves, they may be less likely to respond positively to your message. You will want to plan the speech so that you either minimize perceptions of difference when that is appropriate or acknowledge and compensate for differences when that is desirable.

Knowing what you do know about yourself and having thought about the similarities and differences between you and your listeners, consider how the audience members are likely to perceive you. Will they see you as knowledgable and competent or as arrogant and condescending? In the first case, you can expect listeners to welcome your efforts to share information and ideas; in the second case, expect them to resent your seeming to tell them what to do.

Critical self-assessment should point you to modifications that might improve your ethos. Sometimes minor changes will do the trick. Something as slight as different wording—"We all need to remind ourselves" rather than "I want to remind you," for instance—may help build a sense of community between you and your listeners rather than emphasizing your superiority and their dependence. Attention to this aspect of ethos is especially important when your audience is culturally diverse. What seems like a straightforward presentation to listeners from a single cultural background may be seen as patronizing to listeners whose backgrounds are different.

You also should think critically about your own beliefs and values. It is tempting to assume that they are self-evidently correct and hence should be accepted by everyone. But that assumption may misfire; if audience members question or reject your values, they may also question or reject your message. Although *you* may believe that everyone should appreciate the economic opportunities that our society provides, listeners who have recently lost their jobs, are struggling to make ends meet, or are victims of discrimination will probably see things very differently. If you take your personal values for granted in this situation, your speech will fail. The audience will judge you to be naive, if not misguided, and you will think them ungrateful or unmotivated.

Similarly, you may find that you and your audience have different role models, different common knowledge, and different life-shaping experiences. On each of these dimensions it is important to think critically about yourself and about how the audience is likely to perceive you. Then you can determine whether you want to make any adjustments in how you present yourself. As always, the goal is to remain true to yourself while also taking the audience's characteristics into consideration.

Adjustments in these areas are not so difficult to make, because the speaker controls much of the behavior by which an audience assesses ethos. After all, you can choose whether or not to establish eye contact, whether to smile or frown, whether to pause at the podium before returning to your seat, and so on. You decide which supporting materials to use, how to organize them, and such matters as word choice and gestures. All these aspects of presentation are under your control, and you can use them to influence how the audience judges you.

You want listeners' assessments of your ethos to be positive, and not only because you like to have others think well of you. Your concern goes back to the belief, first articulated by Aristotle, that a speaker's apparent character may well be the most important resource to use in persuasion. How listeners perceive your ethos will affect what they think about your speech.

Summary

In this chapter we examined ways to analyze an audience in order to develop a sense of how listeners are likely to approach your message. The most important dimensions of audience analysis are demographics, culture, and psychology.

Demographic variables that affect an audience include size, heterogeneity, whether listeners are captive or voluntary, and composition in terms of age, gender, occupation, religion, economic status, and similar criteria. The assumption is that differences in these dimensions may result in different patterns of thought and action.

Audience culture includes elements that are more subjective. One of these is interest, both the listeners' self-interest and the topics that they find personally interesting. Other cultural factors include listeners' beliefs and values, their prior level of understanding about the topic, their common knowledge and experiences, and their roles and reference groups. Cultural diversity characterizes many audiences today, and speakers need to be sensitive to how listeners from different cultures might react to a speech.

Audience psychology involves matters of exposure, attention, and perception—all of which listeners do selectively. Because the audience's presence and attention are not guaranteed, you must make every effort to motivate the audience to listen. You should try to make your message personally relevant and important to listeners, to make your message stand out, and to make your message easy to follow. Even if the presence and attention of an audience are achieved, you must design the speech in ways that discourage distortion of the message through selective perception.

As important as audience analysis is, procedures for doing it are usually inexact. Large-scale campaigns use surveys, focus groups, and other research techniques. But audience analysis is less precise in most situations. You can read newspapers or magazines that your audience is likely to read, interview people who represent the makeup of your audience, talk with other speakers about what to expect, do library research about your audience, and observe the audience as it assembles. You also can simplify your analysis by thinking of the audience as the general public or by focusing on listeners' roles and specialized fields. Because audience analysis is imprecise, you need to think critically about your information and to plan strategies that let you adjust your message effectively.

The final step in audience analysis is to analyze yourself to determine how listeners are likely to judge your ethos. Consider any significant similarities and differences between you and your listeners that may affect how they will perceive you. Then make any adjustments that might improve their perceptions of your character, but remain true to yourself. The fact that you control much of the behavior which influences judgments of ethos is a strong reason to undertake careful self-analysis.

1. In preparing a speech about the dangers of smoking, how might your strategies differ for an audience of fourth-graders, an audience of college students, and an audience from a retirement community? Would you make different appeals to an audience of men and an audience of women? What changes would you make in presenting this speech to an audience of Caucasians and to an audience of Mexican Americans? How might these modifications draw on stereotypes that could offend your listeners?

2. Has culture been enriched or impoverished by the fact that its basic store of allusions often comes from popular culture rather than, as in the nineteenth century, from classic literature and the Bible? Does this difference really matter? Why or why not?

3. In 1997 Republicans in Congress proposed to overhaul the Internal Revenue Service. President Clinton first opposed this plan but changed his mind when he realized it would pass. He said that alterations in the proposal now made it possible for him to support it. In what way did Clinton use his audience's beliefs and values to reach his goal? Do you believe that this was an honest presentation of his beliefs, a strategic appeal to the audience, or both?

4. Identify some universal values that you could use in a speech to a diverse audience. Challenge your most fundamental beliefs as you and your classmates try to determine whether or not the values truly are universal.

Activities

1. In one page, explain how you would use the strategies of relevance, contrast, and simplicity to motivate your audience to pay attention to the message in your next speech. In what ways are you planning to appeal to the self-interest and personal interest of your audience?

2. Complete the audience survey in Figure 3.2, make copies of your answers for your classmates, and exchange them so that each person in the class has a booklet of questionnaire responses. Use this booklet to make a list of the commonalities and differences among audience members that you are likely to encounter when presenting a speech in this class.

3. Compare your questionnaire answers to those of your classmates. In what ways are you similar to your audience members? In what ways are you different? How will this affect how your audience perceives you? After critically analyzing your own ethos, create a short speech designed to develop a positive ethos for you as a spokesperson for a particular topic.

4. Using more informal modes of audience analysis, answer the following questions:
   a. What beliefs and values do your classmates hold regarding the topic you have chosen for your next speech?
   b. What do your classmates know about your topic?
   c. What common experiences do you and classmates share with regard to this topic?

   After answering these questions, write a short essay explaining the specific ways that you plan to use this information in developing strategies to maximize attention and to help the audience perceive your message in a way that advances your goal.

Using the Internet

1. **Audience analysis of your class.** Use one of the three exercises included in the **Allyn & Bacon Public Speaking Website.** Go to <http://www.abacon.com/pubspeak/analyze/analyze.html>. Select "Draw a Demographic Profile of Your Audience," "Draw a Psychographic Profile of your Audience," or "Credibility Self Assessment." The exercises are about halfway down the page and are identified with an icon for a pencil. You can print out a copy of the results page after completing the exercise, send it to your own e-mail address, and/or send it to your instructor.

2. **Audience analysis based on scientific survey results.** Check out the subject categories of studies done by the **General Social Survey** at the University of Michigan. This database includes findings on surveys on a variety of topics. Go to <http://www.icpsr.umich.edu/gss/subject/s-index.htm> for an alphabetical list of subject areas.

   Another good source is the **Institute for Research in Social Science Public Opinion Poll Question Database,** which is maintained at the University of North Carolina at Chapel Hill. Go to <http://www.irss.unc.edu/data_archive/pollsearch.html>. From this database you can enter search terms to find questions and results from polls taken in the last 30 years. The database features results from polls conducted by Lou Harris & Associates and a number of polls done in the South.

3. **The audience as a constraint.** Listen to and/or read one of the following speeches for critical analysis:

   Queen Elizabeth II addressing a worldwide audience on the death of Diana, Princess of Wales. Go to <http://www.abcnews.aol.com/sections/world/queenspeech905/index.html/>, provided by ABC News.

   Kate Michelman, President of the National Abortion and Reproductive Rights Action League, speaking before the 1996 Democratic National Convention. Go to <http://www.naral.org/naral/spdnc.html>. This page is from the National Abortion Rights Action League.

   President Bill Clinton speaking about the problem of hate crimes at the White House Conference on Hate Crimes, November 10, 1997. Go to <http://www.whitehouse.gov/Initiatives/OneAmerica/whc.html>. You can also listen to the RealAudio version of the radio address given by the President on June 7, 1997, to announce the plan for this conference. Go to <http://www.whitehouse.gov/WH/html/1997-06-07.html>. This page also includes text documents of each piece of discourse.

(continued)

To evaluate how the makeup of the audience was a constraint that influenced what the speaker said, consider some of the following:

- *How did the speaker address the listeners as a particular audience?*
- *How did the speaker address the listeners as part of a universal audience?*
- *Form a judgment as to how well you think the speaker adapted to the audience.*

Notes

1. Joshua Meyrowitz makes the argument that traditional social differences between gender and age groups have been eroded in postmodern culture by the backstage information provided through television. See *No Sense of Place: The Impact of Electronic Media on Social Behavior,* Oxford, England: Oxford Univ. Press, 1985.
2. See E. D. Hirsch, Jr., *Cultural Literacy,* Boston: Houghton Mifflin, 1987.
3. Cultural differences may even influence expectations about the form and purpose of a speech. See Alessandro Duranti, "Oratory," *International Encyclopedia of Communications,* New York: Oxford Univ. Press, 1989, vol. 3, pp. 234–236.
4. To get an idea of the different words and phrases used in regional dialects, see Eric Partridge, *A Dictionary of Slang and Unconventional English: Colloquialisms and Catch-Phrases, Solecisms and Catachreses, Nicknames, and Vulgarisms,* New York: Macmillan, 1984.
5. To gather examples that include the concerns of different cultural groups, you might want to examine some speeches created by and directed toward those different cultural groups. One compilation of culturally diverse speeches is *American Public Discourse: A Multicultural Perspective,* ed. Ronald K. Burke, Lanham, Md.: University Press of America, 1992.
6. Michael Osborn has written about how language is often used to appeal to universal themes. See "The Evolution of the Archetypal Sea in Rhetoric and Poetic," *Quarterly Journal of Speech* 63 (December 1977): 347–363.
7. Another list of guidelines for overcoming selective attention can be found in Howard W. Runkel, "How to Select Material that Will Hold Attention," *Communication Quarterly* 8 (September 1960): 13–14.
8. The concept of a universal audience is discussed in more detail by Chaim Perelman in *The Realm of Rhetoric,* trans. William Kluback, Notre Dame, Ind.: Univ. of Notre Dame Press, 1982.

chapter 4
Choosing a Topic and Developing a Strategy

In This Chapter We Will:

- Consider when it is appropriate for you to choose the topic of your speech and when the choice is beyond your control.

- Learn how the audience, the occasion, the speaker, and the speech together determine the rhetorical situation.

- Identify the characteristics of a good topic and the steps involved in choosing a good topic.

- Examine how to determine the specific purpose of a speech and how to identify the constraints and the opportunities you face.

- Explore what is meant by strategic planning in preparing a speech and how your constraints and opportunities can be used to achieve your purpose.

- Discover how to formulate statements of the specific purpose and thesis of your speech and how these statements will influence other strategic decisions.

- Determine how to analyze your thesis to figure out which issues you need to discuss and which ideas need support.

From your audience analysis you know as much as you can about your listeners, and now you are ready to make the choices that will shape your speech. Since ancient times a speaker's choices and activities have been grouped under five major headings:

- **Invention** is the generation of materials for the speech. You produce (or "invent," to use the classical term) these materials through a combination of analysis, research, and judgment. You begin by identifying what *could* go into the speech, then you conduct research to determine what ideas are supportable, and then you select the most effective materials for your purpose and audience.
- **Arrangement** is the structuring of ideas and materials in the speech. This includes the organization of materials for each main idea, the ordering and connecting of main ideas within the body of the speech, and the overall structure of the introduction, the body, and the conclusion.
- **Style** is the distinctive character that may make a speech easily recognizable or memorable. Style is achieved primarily through language, and it reflects the speaker's awareness of how language can be used both to "show" and to "tell"—both to evoke emotions and to convey descriptive meaning.
- **Delivery** is the presentation of the speech. Whereas the preceding activities are performed by the speaker alone, delivery involves actually sharing the message with the audience. Skillful delivery involves the effective use of voice, gesture, facial expression, physical movement, and visual aids.
- **Memory** was an extremely important category of skills at a time when most speeches were memorized. Today, however, most speakers use either **extemporaneous presentation** (referring to an outline) or **manuscript presentation** (reading a written script). Even so, some dimensions of memory are still very important—for example, keeping track of your main ideas, phrasing ideas so that listeners will remember them, and precisely wording an effective introduction and conclusion. Memory skills also are critical in rehearsing your speech mentally and in practicing it aloud before presentation.

In this chapter and the next two we will address matters of invention. Then, in Parts 3 and 4, we will study the skills of arrangement, style, and delivery. Although no chapter focuses solely on memory skills, those concerns will surface throughout our study.

All your decisions as a speaker should be made *strategically,* that is, with a view to what will best achieve your purpose. But first you need to know what your purpose is; and to decide that, you need to know what your **topic** is.

For many students, deciding what to talk about is the hardest part of a speech assignment. Fortunately, elements in the situation will often make that decision for you. Suppose, for example, that you are committed to a specific public issue, such as protecting the ozone layer against further depletion. The issue itself defines your topic, and *personal commitment* determines why it is important for you to speak. Or your *experience and knowledge* may lead to an invitation to speak about a specific topic. If you are an expert on bicycle safety, for example, a group of amateur cyclists might invite you to speak

invention
The generation of materials for a speech.

arrangement
The structuring of materials within the main ideas, the organization of main ideas within the body of the speech, and the overall structure of introduction, body, and conclusion.

style
The distinctive character that may make a speech recognizable or memorable.

delivery
The presentation of the speech to an audience.

extemporaneous presentation
A mode of delivery in which the speech is planned and structured carefully but a specific text is not written in advance nor memorized.

manuscript presentation
A mode of delivery in which the speaker reads aloud the prepared text of the speech.

topic
The subject area of the speech.

about safety tips. If you instead discussed U.S. foreign policy, or the pleasures of sailing, or the need for reform in the university, you would not be meeting your responsibility to the audience.

Sometimes the *occasion* will determine your choice of topic. Many speeches are delivered on ceremonial occasions. If you are accepting an award, the award and what it represents will decide your topic. If you are delivering a eulogy, the achievements of the person who died become the subject of the speech. If you are roasting a coworker who is about to retire, your subject matter will be humorous traits or events involving that person.

Sometimes a classroom speaking *assignment* will specify the topic. More typically, the choice of topic will be left to you, with the understanding that you will address an audience of people your age, in your school. Selecting a topic is an important step in creating a speech, and you need practice in matching your topic to the situation. In addition, you probably will be more effective if you talk about something that interests you rather than an assigned topic.[1] In the classroom it is particularly important that you size up the situation and then stand up for what interests you, for what you believe and can share with others.

Outside of class, the primary occasion when you will have freedom in choosing your topic occurs when the audience is interested in hearing *you,* almost regardless of what you have to say. Such an open-ended invitation may arise out of respect for your achievements, interest in your experiences, curiosity about your personality or general approach, or the desire to learn whatever is on your mind.

UNDERSTANDING THE RHETORICAL SITUATION

Whether your topic is determined by the occasion, assigned by your host, or selected by you, you will not begin in a vacuum. Your speech will be influenced by the **rhetorical situation** to which it responds. No two speeches are exactly the same, because the rhetorical situations are not identical. Moreover, your speech not only responds to the situation but also modifies it. In doing that, you face opportunities as well as constraints. Your goal is to devise a **strategy**—a plan of action—that will respond to the constraints and take advantage of the opportunities.

An example will illustrate the double-sided nature of the rhetorical situation. When the Space Shuttle *Challenger* exploded in 1986, the nation watched the tragedy unfold on television. Many children were shocked to see the first school teacher in space killed before their eyes. Many adults wondered whether the space program was in trouble. Others concluded that developing the capability for space travel was not worth the cost. Still others believed that the vaunted American technology had failed. The nation suddenly needed reassurance, and that would be provided in a speech by President Ronald Reagan.

This context defined a rhetorical situation. The audience was the American people, who needed to be consoled. The occasion was one of collective grief, uncertainty, and doubt. The speaker was President Reagan, widely known as "The Great Communicator." And the speech consisted of both the text that was prepared and its oral presentation by the President.

rhetorical situation
A situation in which there are challenges or needs that can be met through effective messages.

strategy
A plan of action to achieve stated goals.

As it happened, on the night of the tragedy President Reagan had been scheduled to deliver the annual State of the Union address. He instead chose to deliver a eulogy prepared by White House speechwriter Peggy Noonan. Clearly the speech was written to respond to the situation by honoring the *Challenger* crew: "They, the *Challenger* Seven, were aware of the dangers—and overcame them, and did their jobs brilliantly. We mourn seven heroes." At the same time the speech was designed to turn the audience away from sorrow and toward a new commitment to the space program: "The *Challenger* crew was pulling us into the future—and we'll continue to follow them." By comparing the astronauts to Sir Francis Drake, an early explorer of the North American continent, the speech transformed the senseless tragedy into a heroic need to open a new frontier. The speech succeeded in redirecting the audience's emotions; it provided a transformation from mourning to renewed dedication. Careful evaluation of the situation allowed President Reagan and Ms. Noonan to plan an effective strategy.

Similarly, when you give a speech in class, your rhetorical situation is influenced by the audience and by the values its members hold. These are **constraints** within which you must work. At the same time, you have the opportunity to modify listeners' beliefs and values by what you say. You want to understand the constraints and the opportunities in a rhetorical situation so that you can use both to achieve your purpose.

As we noted in Chapter 1, the key elements that create the rhetorical situation for any speech are the audience, the occasion, the speaker, and the speech itself (see Figure 4.1). Each element warrants further brief discussion now.

constraints
Factors beyond your control that limit your freedom of choice.

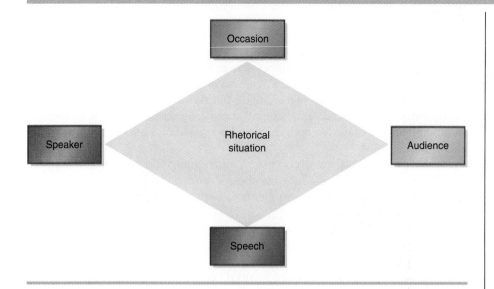

FIGURE 4.1
Determinants of the rhetorical situation.

The Audience

Unlike a poem or a novel, a speech is presented for a specific audience, and its success in achieving its goals depends on the reactions of those listeners. This is why audience analysis, discussed in Chapter 3, is so important. The audience helps create the rhetorical situation by affecting, among other things, your choice of what to emphasize in the speech, what level of knowledge to assume, how to organize the speech, and what your specific purpose will be.

Most speakers, most of the time, want to present their ideas in ways that achieve **identification** with the audience; that is, they try to find common ground between what they know about the audience and what they want to say.[2] Without distorting their own message, they try to emphasize the elements that are most likely to strike a responsive chord among audience members. Thus, an African-American speaker who is addressing a mostly white audience might emphasize their shared American dream.

Sometimes, though, a speaker may deliberately *avoid* identification with the audience and may even try to antagonize listeners. The same African American might point out that the American dream is *not* shared equally by all citizens. Such a tactic may suggest that the speaker is a person of high integrity who will not hold back punches simply to gain the audience's approval. Or, the strategy may be intended to influence some other audience that is overhearing the speech.[3] Whether the goal is to identify or to criticize, however, knowledge of the audience is critical in assessing the rhetorical situation.

The Occasion

Some speech occasions are **ceremonial,** such as presenting or accepting an award, introducing someone, delivering a eulogy, or commemorating an event. Others are primarily **deliberative,** such as making an oral report, delivering a sales presentation, advocating a policy, or refuting another person's argument. Ceremonial speaking focuses on the present and is usually concerned

identification
Formation of common bonds between the speaker and the audience.

ceremonial
Speaking that focuses on the present and is usually concerned with praise or blame.

deliberative
Speaking that focuses on the future and is usually concerned with what should be done.

with what is praiseworthy in the subject. Deliberative speaking focuses on the future and is usually concerned with what should be done.

Many occasions combine ceremonial and deliberative elements. For example, the manager of a firm that is losing money during a recession might speak to employees. The occasion is deliberative in that the manager informs workers about the company's financial circumstances, announces new policies, and seeks reactions to proposed changes; but the occasion is also ceremonial because the manager's presence demonstrates a personal interest in workers' well-being and because the speech provides reassurance and motivates workers to do their best.

A third category of speech occasion, traditionally known as **forensic,** is concerned with rendering judgments about events in the past. Although this is the dominant form of speaking in courts of law, it plays only a small role in public speaking generally.[4]

Each type of occasion raises certain expectations about what is appropriate behavior, and these expectations help to define the rhetorical situation. For example, if an engineer is presenting the features of a new product to the marketing group, everyone will be focused on the product's best features and how to make them more salable. The occasion will be deliberative. Unlike a ceremonial occasion, it will not emphasize good wishes or feelings about the product or the staff. And unlike a forensic occasion, it will not concentrate on the company's past sales performance with other products. Rather, the focus will be on how best to design the new product to achieve a strong sales record in the future.

The Speaker

The same speech delivered by different speakers can produce quite different reactions and effects. Your interest in the subject—as made evident through voice, delivery, and the vividness of your imagery—helps to determine how the audience will react to the speech. Your ethos affects whether or not listeners will pay attention and will regard you as believable. This is why we stressed the goal of developing a positive ethos in Chapter 1 and why audience analysis, detailed in Chapter 3, includes the important step of analyzing your own ethos.

Fortunately, many of the skills that enable speakers to contribute positively to a rhetorical situation can be learned. Previous public speaking experience will also affect your comfort level, and the ability to respond to audience feedback will make you more flexible in any rhetorical situation.

The Speech

Although we tend to think of the rhetorical situation as predating the speech, the message itself works to shape the situation. The length of the speech, the clarity of its structure, the variety of supporting materials used, the degree of formality, the extent to which the speech tells a story, and the degree to which it is adaptable in response to feedback—all will affect its power in the rhetorical situation. In general, a speech is more likely to contribute positively to the situation when its structural pattern is simple and clear, when it is engaging to the audience, when its approach is informal, and when it is adaptable during delivery.

forensic
Speaking that focuses on the past and is usually concerned with rendering judgment.

Checklist

4.1 *Characteristics of a Good Topic*

1. **Importance to the Speaker:** A good topic is one that matters to you.

2. **Interest:** A good topic will gain and hold the audience's interest.

3. **Worthy of Audience's Time:** A good topic is one that listeners feel is worth their time to hear about.

4. **Appropriateness of Scope:** A good topic is manageable within the time available.

5. **Appropriateness for Oral Delivery:** A good topic is one that can be understood from a speech, without having to go back over the ideas.

6. **Clarity:** A good topic is one that audience members can easily identify.

WHAT MAKES A GOOD TOPIC?

If the topic of your speech is dictated by the issue, occasion, or audience, it is easy to decide what will make a good topic: whatever is pertinent and appropriate to the situation. You talk about what you were asked to discuss or about what the issue or occasion seems to require.

But what should you talk about if you have complete freedom to select the topic? Figure 4.2 identifies some potential speech topics, and the following criteria will help you to decide whether the topic you have in mind is a good one. (As you read, you might want to apply these criteria to the topics listed in Figure 4.2.)

Public Issues	Personal Experience	Occasions
Campaign reform	Extreme skiing	Death of friend
Gun control	Computer networking	Commencement
TV violence	Poetry writing	Wedding
Northwest logging	Hunting	Anniversary of club
Euthanasia	Cardiopulmonary resuscitation	Annual company party
Bioengineering	Amateur radio operation	
Gay rights	Sign language	
Hate speech		
Affirmative action		
Core requirements		

FIGURE 4.2
Sample speech topics.

IMPORTANCE TO THE SPEAKER   A good topic is one that matters to you. If you do not care about the subject, it will be very hard to make it interesting or important to the audience. Consider how the following three students used their personal interests to develop good speech topics:

- Elvin Torres attended night school to earn his degree and advance his career with the Federal National Mortgage Association. A recent promotion at work would soon require him to make publicity speeches on local cable access television for activities such as the annual Home Buyer's Fair. Elvin used his public speaking class to prepare the sort of talk he would soon be giving to a larger public audience.
- Sindi Jonas was appalled at what she experienced when she went hunting with her boyfriend last month. To her the sport seemed unnecessarily violent and cruel. Sindi used her speech class as an opportunity to explore arguments to convince her boyfriend and others to put away their hunting rifles and find another hobby.
- Phillip Marcus was angry. During a closed-book exam in a sociology class, he saw another student copying answers from a sheet of paper. Phillip had heard that cheating on exams had become a serious problem, but until now he had not seen such a blatant example. At first he was stunned by what he regarded as outrageous conduct; then he became upset that his work and the work of other honest students was devalued by this incident. He decided to give a speech in his public speaking class to make others aware of what was happening, to evoke in them similar feelings of anger, and to channel their emotions toward doing something about cheating. How Phillip chose his topic and developed his strategy will be seen throughout this chapter.

In speaking about a topic of personal interest, you must be careful that your own interest does not harden into bias. You must be able to discuss the subject impartially and must recognize the value of other people's points of view.

INTEREST TO THE AUDIENCE   Even though the topic matters to you, you still must gain the interest of the audience. Audiences will be interested if your topic provides new information they can use, if it offers a solution to a puzzle or problem that affects them, if it connects what is unfamiliar to what they know, or if it reports stories or experiences similar to their own. Phillip Marcus decided that his story of the student who was cheating on the exam would interest others and also would arouse their anger.

Keep in mind as well that an audience's strong interest in the topic potentially may lead to *mis*communication. For example, when a manager addresses employees to describe the company's new policy about personal telephone calls, the audience has a strong interest in the message because it clearly will affect them. But there is also a risk that the audience will feel threatened or will believe that the company has become less friendly. Thus, even when listeners are strongly interested in the topic, they may resist the message related to it. Their personal interest may actually weaken their ability to listen critically.

WORTHY OF LISTENERS' TIME   A related criterion is that the topic should be something that listeners regard as worth hearing about. If the topic is frivolous or trivial, they may feel that they have wasted their time by listening to you, especially if they came voluntarily and could have been doing something else. Unless there is something unique about the approach, a topic such as "How to open a beer can" probably would not meet this test. This does not mean that your topic must be profound or deadly serious; light-hearted humor or new insights on familiar subjects can work very well in a speech. The question to keep in mind is whether the audience will feel that what you have had to say was worth their attention and time.

APPROPRIATENESS OF SCOPE   A speaker has to cover the topic to an appropriate degree within the time available. A topic that includes a very large number of points that can be covered only superficially—for example, a five-minute analysis of U.S. foreign policy—should probably be avoided. Similarly, a very narrow topic that can be covered completely in a short time—such as a description of how to stop when skating in-line—is probably not a good choice either.

Even in a five-minute speech you might discover that you are repeating yourself several times. Although the topic of cheating on exams might invite a long philosophical discussion of ethics and morality, it also could be focused enough to be covered in a short speech. It is a good topic because it offers rich possibilities for the development of ideas without excessive repetition.

APPROPRIATENESS FOR ORAL DELIVERY   Sometimes a topic can be developed better in an essay than in a speech. Because readers proceed at their own pace, they can reread any passage that is difficult to understand. But a speech is delivered in real time and at the same pace to all listeners, some of whom will not be able to recall it after delivery. Listeners who miss a particular link in a speaker's chain of ideas cannot rewind the live speech and replay it; if the link was critical, the rest of the speech might become meaningless.

Topics that depend on technical formulas or elaborate arguments are usually better presented in print than in oral delivery. Still, if a speaker's main ideas and examples are planned carefully and presented clearly, even technical and complex topics can be understood by a nonspecialist audience.

CLARITY   Finally, of course, the speaker should make it clear to all listeners what the topic is. Speakers often fail to refine their topics sufficiently, and the result is a confused jumble of poorly connected ideas. If you are confused about the ideas in your speech, you can be sure that your audience will be confused too. Even if you think you understand the topic, the fact that you know more about it than the audience does may lead you to present it in a way that is beyond comprehension. For this reason you should always strive to understand and be sensitive to the audience's level of knowledge.

HOW TO CHOOSE A GOOD TOPIC

The preceding discussion of the general characteristics of a good speech topic may still leave you wondering what is the right topic for you. This section offers some suggestions to help you identify a good topic.

Checklist

4.2 Steps in Choosing a Good Topic

1. **Conduct a personal inventory.**
   - *What public issues do I care about?*
   - *What experiences have I had that might be generalizable?*
   - *Which of my interests overlap with those of the audience?*

2. **Use finding aids.**
   - *Brainstorm.*
   - *Browse through printed materials.*

3. **Narrow the topic so that it can be covered adequately within the time available.**

Conduct a Personal Inventory

In Chapter 3 you learned how to ask questions to analyze your audience. Now it is time to ask some questions about yourself.

WHAT PUBLIC ISSUES DO I CARE ABOUT? Public issues are those that concern people generally. Because most audience members are likely to be affected by these issues, they often make good speech topics—but only if you yourself also care about them. It is important, then, to be aware of current events and to think about how you and others are affected by them.

Suppose you decide that animal rights, homelessness, child abuse, and shifting ethical standards really matter to you. These are topics about which you feel strongly. On the other hand, to be perfectly honest, you are not very interested in international trade, health-care financing, and school voucher systems. You probably could develop the first group of topics into effective speeches; the second group would probably not inspire you.

WHICH OF MY EXPERIENCES MIGHT BE GENERALIZABLE? Everyone has had unique experiences, but these do not always make good speech topics. If audience members do not believe that your experience could happen to them, they may react to your speech with the same boredom that many people feel when watching someone else's home videos. On the other hand, if something about your experience can be generalized so that others can imagine themselves in the same situation, you may be onto a good topic.

The fact that your car broke down on the highway on a dark rainy night might matter only to you. But if you can generalize the experience—for example, to the fear that many people share of being overwhelmed by technology—your experience might make a good topic. Audience members who don't care at all about your car might still become interested in a speech about a more general problem that they share. Likewise, Phillip Marcus's anger at seeing a classmate cheat could be generalized if he relates the experience so that listeners can imagine how they would feel if it had happened to them.

WHICH OF MY INTERESTS OVERLAP WITH THOSE OF THE AUDIENCE? Another question to ask in your personal inventory is whether you and your listeners share a common interest in any topic. If so, you'll have a good match.

You will have an incentive to speak about the topic, and they will be motivated to listen.

Sometimes the match may be exact. For example, you may find that both you and your audience are interested in the Beatles. At other times you will have to match a specific interest with a more general category. For example, you are interested in the Beatles, and your audience is interested in rock stars. In that case you'll want to relate the more specific to the more general, explaining how the Beatles exemplify the general subject of rock stardom. If you can do that, you have a good topic.

Use Finding Aids

If your personal inventory did not uncover a good topic for your speech, you can use certain procedures and sources to find a topic. One such finding aid is **brainstorming,** a mental exercise in which you identify the first things that come to mind when you are presented with a given term or category. Do not censor your thoughts; just record them without evaluation. For example, you might divide a sheet of paper into columns with such category headings as "Heroes," "Places to Visit," "Hobbies," and "Favorite Books." (These are just examples, of course; pick whichever categories you want to explore through brainstorming.) Under each heading, jot down the first five things that occur to you. For example, you might list five heroes or five characteristics of a hero, or you might name five places you have visited or five places you hope to visit. Do not stop to evaluate your ideas; write down whatever first comes to mind. Then study the list to see whether you can find any patterns. You may discover, for example, that your lists of heroes, places to visit, hobbies, and favorite books all include items related to the Civil War. Since you seem to have an interest in the Civil War, some aspect of that could become your speech topic.

Another kind of finding aid is printed source materials, such as newspapers, magazines, encyclopedias, dictionaries, and atlases. Browse through these materials, and jot down notes about topics that interest you. Even if you have not given much thought to these topics before, perhaps now you can see how they could lead to a good speech.

Narrow the Topic

The final step in selecting a good topic is to narrow it so that it fits the situation. If your speech is limited to only ten minutes, for example, you could not begin to explore a topic like "America's Shifting Ethical Standards." But suppose that you narrowed the topic down to the specific standard of honesty, then narrowed that to cheating as an example of dishonesty, and then narrowed that to cheating by college students and finally to "Cheating on This Campus." *Now* you could cover the topic within the allotted time, and your topic would relate to the broader subject that caught your interest in the first place.

Narrowing the topic is like pouring it through a funnel: What goes into the large end is too much to manage, but what comes out the small end can be focused effectively. Time constraints are one obvious reason to narrow the topic. But you also should narrow it to be sure that you can learn enough about the topic before your speech is due and to be sure that the topic fulfills your specific assignment.

brainstorming
A mental free-association exercise in which one identifies, without evaluation, the first thoughts that come to mind when one is presented with a given term or category.

APPLYING STRATEGIES

Choosing an Appropriate Topic

T. J. Brinkerhoff

By choosing an appropriate topic for a given speech, you can better

capture your audience and avoid losing their attention. A topic with universal application or understanding and new insightful material regarding that topic can make a speech more useful, entertaining, and/or informative.

The best speeches that I have heard were on common subjects that gave greater insight to the topic. I particularly liked a speech by one of my classmates, Ryan Gibson, on how the media uses gimmicks to sell products while avoiding the reality of the products they sell, for example, alcohol and cigarettes. He

also showed the different ways women are exploited in mass media. His speech opened my eyes to some obvious things that I had not seen before, and he made it interesting and entertaining.

Appropriateness of a topic is also determined by the audience that you address and how they will react to the material presented.

Dr. Marrow

Yes, T. J. Choosing a topic for your speech is like throwing the football as quarterback of

our UNC football team—they both require a strategy! In the speech-writing arena, it all starts with conducting a personal inventory of your interests and then identifying which of your interests overlap with those of the audience. Then, as you stated, once you find a common subject that appeals to the audience, you can develop it with more insight or from a different perspective. This strategy of choosing a topic and developing it is a sure-fire way to win over your audience!

Whatever else you do, resist any urge to postpone selecting a topic. If you wait until the last minute, you won't have time to inventory your interests, to use finding aids, and to narrow the topic appropriately.

DEVELOPING A STRATEGIC PLAN

So far, we have examined the elements that *create* a rhetorical situation (audience, occasion, speaker, and speech). And now that you understand how to select a topic, it is time to consider how your speech will *respond* to the rhetorical situation.

Because any speech will affect or change the situation in some way, giving a speech may be thought of as intervention in the rhetorical situation. This intervention should be strategic, not random; the speech is planned so that it becomes the means to a desired end. Consequently, a crucial early step in preparing to give a speech is to discern your purpose, any factors that might limit your strategies, and the options and opportunities available.

In preparing to respond to and intervene in the rhetorical situation, you need to develop a **strategic plan** that identifies the purpose of your speech, the constraints on it, and the opportunities it provides (see Figure 4.3, which expands on Figure 4.1). Then you select the best means to achieve your purpose. Ideally, the strategic plan also should indicate how you will know whether your purpose has been achieved.

strategic plan
An identification of the objectives to be sought in a speech and the means for achieving them.

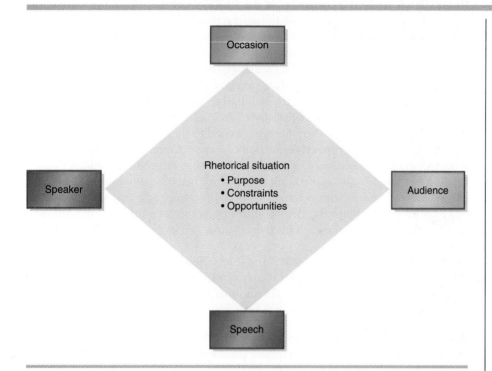

FIGURE 4.3
Intervening in the rhetorical situation.

Identifying the Purpose

The classroom assignment to "make a speech" may mislead you into thinking that fulfilling the assignment is an end in itself. That approach courts disaster, however, because strong public speeches have a clear sense of **purpose.** The speaker plans to achieve a particular goal and wants the audience to respond in a specific way. A speaker's purpose provides the criteria that determine whether the speech was successful or not.

We saw earlier that speeches traditionally are classified as ceremonial, deliberative, or forensic, depending on their purpose. Ceremonial speeches entertain but also celebrate shared values and strengthen commitments to them. Deliberative speeches explore what public policy ought to be. And forensic speaking seeks justice with respect to past events. In addition, recall that in Chapter 1 we described the purposes of a speech in terms of informing, persuading, and entertaining.

Both of these conceptions of purpose are of some use, and yet both are limited. For example, many speeches combine deliberative and ceremonial elements, and it is not uncommon for a single speech to both inform and persuade. For the rest of our study, then, we will use a more precise classification that identifies seven common speech purposes:

- Providing new information or perspective
- Agenda setting
- Creating positive or negative feeling
- Strengthening commitment
- Weakening commitment
- Conversion
- Inducing a specific action

purpose
The outcome the speaker wishes to achieve; the response desired from the audience.

PROVIDING NEW INFORMATION OR PERSPECTIVE   Sometimes the audience generally knows about a topic but is unfamiliar with its details. Your goal as speaker may be to fill in such gaps by providing new information. For example, listeners may be aware that U.S. political campaigns are expensive, but they may not know that costs are escalating, or the reasons for this trend and its implications, or whether there are practical alternatives. Thus, the purpose of a speech about campaign finance might be "to deepen and enrich the audience's understanding of campaign costs."

Alternatively, listeners may be accustomed to thinking about a topic only from a certain **perspective,** or point of view. Commuting to work, for instance, might be seen only as a source of tension, frustration, and lost time—all outcomes that make commuting seem negative. But commuting can be viewed much more positively—as "buffer time" to prepare for the workday or to "decompress" before returning home, as a time to catch up on news with the help of the car radio, or as time to handle paperwork while on the bus or train.

Changing listeners' perspective about a subject may alter beliefs and values relating to it. At the very least it may convince listeners that the subject is more complicated than they thought and that how they think about the topic is affected by the perspective from which they view it.

AGENDA SETTING   One purpose of a speech is **agenda setting,** causing people to think about a topic that they previously knew little about or ignored. The goal of the speech is to put the topic "on the agenda," to draw attention to it. Many environmental threats, for example, were not taken seriously until advocates put them on the agenda by speaking about them.

College freshman Mark Gordon sprained his wrist while in-line skating for the first time. In talking with the doctor who treated him, Mark discovered that skating accidents were the number-one cause of injuries on campus. He used this information to create a speech about skating injuries, alerting many of his listeners to a problem that had escaped their notice:

> Did you know that the current sports craze is also the most dangerous sports activity on campus? More people are hurt in skating accidents than are hurt in rugby, football, or diving. The most common injuries are wrist fractures, sustained when a skater tries to break a fall. By telling you about the danger of in-line skating, I hope to provide you with the information you need to make an informed choice about whether or not to try this sport.

CREATING POSITIVE OR NEGATIVE FEELING   Sometimes a speaker's goal is more general: to leave the audience with a positive or negative feeling about the occasion, the speaker, or the message. Political candidates, even as they discuss specific policy issues, are often really more interested in making listeners generally feel good or bad about themselves or the world.

Student speaker Craig Hinners prepared a speech of this type when he took a short, nostalgic look at the Chicago elevated train, called the "El" by locals:

> On the El, you are always entertained. If you gaze out the window, you are treated to an intimate look at the lives of people whose backyards and windows face the tracks. If you set your sights inside the train, you can see and hear the stories of people from all walks of life—office workers, mothers with children, old men. You glance at the bright color of gum casually placed on the back of the seat by a teenager who no longer tasted its flavor, and hear the sound of old vehicles and snow-damaged tracks.

perspective
The point of view from which one approaches a topic.

agenda setting
Causing listeners to be aware of and to think about a topic that previously had escaped their attention.

Craig's purpose was not to get listeners to do anything about the El, or even to change their beliefs about its rundown condition; he wanted to share a wistful, comfortable feeling with them.

Likewise, many ceremonial speeches aim to evoke or strengthen common bonds by reference to a shared event or experience. The speakers wish to have the audience feel as they do, most often in a positive way. The audience's general attitude, not a belief or action, is the measure of success.

STRENGTHENING COMMITMENT   Many speeches are like "preaching to the converted"; they are delivered to listeners who already agree with the speaker. In such cases the goal is to motivate audience members to become even more strongly committed. It is one thing to casually favor a candidate's election to office, but it is quite another thing to contribute money to the candidate's campaign, to display the candidate's poster on one's lawn, or to mobilize friends to vote for the candidate on election day. Increasing the intensity of listeners' commitment makes them more likely to act on their beliefs.

Marc Kishfy was in a public speaking class at a commuter college where students routinely arrived late for class because they could not find a parking space. Marc knew there was smoldering resentment about the parking situation, and he decided to mobilize students to spark change:

> So many students spend hours trying to find a parking space, and their chances of finding one are as good as their chances of finding a needle in a haystack. Rumor has it that the college will add 80 more parking spots next summer. But 80 spots is nothing when hundreds of students are driving around trying to park. My fellow students, now is the time to come together and take action to put an end to this nonsense. Now is the time to demand that our needs are met. Now is the time to demand more parking spaces on campus!

WEAKENING COMMITMENT   Speakers also sometimes want to reduce the intensity of listeners' commitment to a belief—not so much to get them to change their minds as to acknowledge some sense of *doubt*. Recognizing that an issue has more than one legitimate side may be the first step in *eventually* changing people's minds. Even if listeners remain committed to their position, a reasonable but contrary argument may weaken their support for it. Although you may believe, for example, that higher defense spending is necessary, you may at least think twice about it after hearing a speech that argues that much defense spending is wasted.

Dorte Hoerst knew that her listeners strongly believed taxes were too high. She also knew that a single ten-minute speech was unlikely to change their belief. But she might be able to chip away at their position if she could show that their tax dollars supported many of the public agencies that they took for granted:

> I know that you think taxes are too high already. But in the Netherlands, where I come from, we pay much more in taxes. We do this because we benefit from the public services provided by that money. The streets you drive, the schools you attend, the police who protect you, the public agencies that assist you when you need help—all of these are supported by the tax money you pay each year.

CONVERSION   Although it happens rarely on the basis of a single speech, sometimes listeners actually *are* persuaded to change their minds—to stop believing one thing and to start believing another. In short, listeners are converted. **Conversion** involves the replacement of one set of beliefs with

conversion
The replacement of one set of beliefs by another that is inconsistent with the first.

another set that is inconsistent with the first. For example, a listener who believes that homeless people are themselves to blame for their condition might be persuaded by a speaker that homelessness reflects faulty social policy, not faulty individuals.

Student speaker Rachel Samuels converted some of her audience by explaining the need for adult teachers to act as editors to censor high school newspapers. Her classmates initially bristled at the idea of curtailing students' freedom of speech. But when Rachel demonstrated that libel lawsuits could bankrupt the public school system, they began to understand her position:

> The editing of high school newspapers is not government censorship of political or religious speech. Rather, it is editing by an authority to avoid the danger of libel lawsuits. In the world outside high schools, editors often keep journalists from printing the whole story in order to protect citizens' privacy. High school newspapers should be no different.

INDUCING A SPECIFIC ACTION   The last purpose we will consider is the most specific and most pragmatic. Often speakers do not really care about the beliefs and attitudes of individual listeners, as long as they can persuade people to take a specific action—to make a contribution, to purchase a product, to vote for a specific candidate, and so on.

When the goal is action regardless of the reason, the speaker may use widely different appeals. One listener may be induced to vote by the argument that it is a civic duty; another may favor a particular candidate's economic proposals; a third may know one of the candidates personally. The speaker does not care whether listeners have the same reasons for voting; all that matters is that they be prompted to take the same action.

Linda Morales, a student in charge of a new recycling program at the university, gave a speech urging students to recycle paper, bottles, and cans. She started with an appeal to the audience's social consciousness:

> We must recycle if we want to preserve the world in which we live. It takes work to ensure a clean and unpolluted environment. But it is our responsibility to ourselves and our future.

Although this was a strong argument, it was unlikely to motivate all students. Knowing that others might be moved more by an appeal to school spirit, Linda described a recycling competition against their collegiate rivals:

> Students at other universities in town have already recycled thousands of pounds of newspapers and bottles this year. Our rivals to the south have pulled ahead of us with a vigorous recycling effort. Are we going to allow ourselves to be left in the dust?

Linda figured that still other listeners might recycle if they thought they could gain something immediately. To appeal to them, she also talked about a promotional contest among dormitories:

> And don't forget the prize money! The dorm that gathers the most junk gets $500 to spend on food, drink, and music at the end of the year.

Linda's only real concern was whether or not audience members would participate in this recycling program. She didn't care whether they were motivated by social consciousness, by school spirit, or by personal gain. She used multiple appeals to achieve her purpose with as many listeners as possible.

These seven categories of purpose certainly do not exhaust the possibilities, but they illustrate some common reasons why people give a speech.[5] Identifying your purpose is a critical step because that will help you to plan strategies which accomplish your goal.

Identifying the Constraints

After you identify the specific purpose of your speech, the next step in developing a strategic plan is to identify the constraints within which you must maneuver. As noted earlier, constraints are factors beyond your control that limit your options. Constraints may arise from:

- Audiences in general
- Your specific audience analysis
- Your ethos as a speaker
- The nature of your topic
- The rhetorical situation

FROM AUDIENCES IN GENERAL   As we learned in Chapter 2, the attention span of most listeners is limited, and it has shrunk over the years. Today most audiences begin to get restless when a speech exceeds 20 or 30 minutes. And even when listeners are generally attentive, the degree of attention varies. At one moment your speech may be the most important thing on their minds; at another moment, something you say may trigger an unrelated thought; and at yet another moment listeners may be distracted by something else altogether.

Knowing that attention spans are so limited, you will want to help the audience remember your main ideas by phrasing them simply, organizing them in a structure that is easy to follow, and repeating them during the speech. Another strategy is to use interesting examples and to choose language that captures attention. In the 1992 presidential campaign, for example, candidate Ross Perot drew audiences to his rather long television speeches by using simple visual aids and by spicing his speech with short, clever sayings (such as that deficit reduction could be achieved by "rolling up our sleeves and getting under the hood to fix the car").

Besides having limited attention spans, audiences tend to have a high opinion of themselves and naturally resist being talked down to. They may believe that they have exerted great effort or even done you a favor by coming to hear you speak. You should always show respect to the audience and recognize that they will be the ultimate judges of your speech.

FROM YOUR SPECIFIC AUDIENCE ANALYSIS   You also will be constrained by the analysis you performed of your specific audience, as described in Chapter 3. Your audience analysis may tell you that some appeals are out of bounds and that others are far more likely to succeed. For example, the manager who speaks to employees about the company's strained economic conditions has many choices; to succeed, however, she or he *must* deal with the fact that workers are worried about losing their jobs. This fear, identified through audience analysis, is an important constraint on what the manager can say.

FROM YOUR ETHOS AS A SPEAKER   The audience's perceptions of the speaker's character, or ethos, are another important constraint. If listeners see you as competent to discuss the subject, as trustworthy, as dynamic and energetic, and as having goodwill toward them, you enjoy a positive ethos. As we saw in Chapter 3, you want to evoke positive assessments of your ethos because an audience's perceptions of your character strongly affect whether that audience will be influenced by what you say.

Even a generally positive ethos can constrain you, however, because then you must craft a speech that sustains or builds on the audience's high expectations. When well-loved comedian Bill Cosby gives a speech, the audience expects lighthearted humor and would be confused if he presented a serious lecture. Even when he resumed speaking after the tragic death of his son, people expected him to be good-natured and funny. Although his ethos is positive, he must work within its constraints.

If, for whatever reason, your ethos is generally perceived as negative, then your challenge is either to change it or to overcome it. When former President Richard Nixon spoke publicly after he was forced to leave office, he often had to contend with the perception that he was not being honest. His negative ethos was a strong constraint on his effectiveness as a speaker.

FROM THE NATURE OF YOUR TOPIC   Some topics constrain a speaker more than others do. A highly technical subject that is difficult to make interesting strains the audience's attention span even more than usual. And a topic that seems far removed from listeners' concerns is unlikely to spark and hold their interest.

In such cases the challenge is to plan strategies that evoke and heighten interest. This is what student John Casey did in speaking about the research underway in the university's laboratories. Rather than droning on about details of antibodies and peptides, he made the topic interesting by describing the scientific community's quest for a "magic bullet" to cure cancer.

FROM THE RHETORICAL SITUATION   Every speech is a one-shot effort to influence the audience, but the occasions when a single message will change anyone's attitudes are few. For example, a classroom speech about abortion is unlikely to convince strong believers on either side to switch allegiance. Moreover, a speaker's range of stimuli is limited to only words and, sometimes, visual aids. Yet most cases of successful persuasion involve multiple messages and a variety of stimuli—verbal, visual, and experiential. Of course, a one-shot effort may be more likely to succeed when your goal is to reinforce the commitment that listeners already feel. Even so, a speaker should never overestimate the effect that a single speech can have on an audience.

We see, then, that a speaker cannot plan a speech with complete freedom. The constraints imposed by the audience, the audience analysis, the speaker's ethos, the topic, and the rhetorical situation must all become part of the strategic plan. Then the challenge is to be creative and find opportunities within these limits.

Identifying the Opportunities

Your opportunities as a speaker result from the special assets that you bring to the situation and from the choices that you *are* able to make. But to take advantage of the opportunities in developing a strategic plan, you first need to be aware of them.

Probably your most important asset is that you have an *information advantage* over listeners; you are likely to be better informed about the topic than they are. This may offset the constraints that the audience imposes. After all, you selected the topic because it matters to you, and you have researched it, as we will describe in Chapter 5. You have given the topic sustained attention, and so you should be able to awaken interest in it, to provide new information about it, and to explain difficult concepts.

A second opportunity arises from your *audience analysis* (see Chapter 3). It will tell you something about the composition and attitudes of your specific listeners. Furthermore, almost any topic can be presented in various ways; there is no single "correct" approach but many different paths to the same goal. Your audience analysis will enable you to select which path to pursue and to plan strategies that are most likely to succeed.

For example, the proposal that college graduates should be required to perform some sort of national service is controversial. Many students might be expected to oppose such limits on their personal freedom. If you favor such a proposal, you might argue that the sacrifice of individual freedom is justified by social needs. Or you might contend that those who have social advantages also have responsibilities to those who do not. Combining these justifications, you might say:

> For my generation, national service is an idea whose time has come. We are among the most privileged people in society. We've been given tremendous advantages, and we have a responsibility to give something back by providing needed service. Not only will we benefit those less fortunate than ourselves, but we will make our country better.

However, because these justifications depend on such values as patriotism and altruism, this argument would probably be more effective in reinforcing commitment among listeners who already favor national service than in converting those who oppose it. The strategy of stressing the personal benefits to those who serve might be especially effective for listeners who oppose national service because it would limit their freedom. For them you might add this section:

> And not only that, but national service will offer benefits to those who serve. They will expand their knowledge of themselves, learn valuable skills, make important contacts, and perhaps start on the way to a new career path. So this is not really a charity or a welfare program; it's a chance for those who serve to gain.

Speakers sometimes choose their means without much thought, but, as this example shows, attention to the specific audience can help you plan strategies that will advance your ideas effectively.

Selecting the Means

If you have been thinking strategically, by this point you have articulated the purpose of your speech and have identified your constraints and opportunities in proceeding toward that goal. The final step in strategic planning is to select the means that you will use to achieve your purpose.

In many respects this decision is the most important, because it touches on virtually every aspect of your speech. How will you lead your audience in reasoning through to the conclusions you want to establish? How will you structure the speech? What supporting materials will you use? What choices will you make about wording, emotional language, and repetition? How will you actually present the speech? All these matters will be explored in later chapters, but here you should recognize that each of them involves a choice which can be made either by accident or by design. The essence of strategic planning is to avoid accident and to design means that are most appropriate for achieving your purpose.

DEVELOPING THE PURPOSE STATEMENT AND THE THESIS STATEMENT

From this understanding of strategic elements—purpose, constraints, and opportunities—you can begin to construct the skeleton of your speech. You have already determined the topic. The next steps are to formulate a clear statement of purpose and a thesis for the speech.

The Purpose Statement

Our earlier discussion suggested seven general categories of purpose: agenda setting, providing new information, weakening commitment, and so on. Review those categories to determine which one best describes the overall purpose of your speech. Then you need to develop a **specific purpose statement.** This focuses on the outcome of your speech by specifying what you want to achieve, and for that reason it is audience centered. It follows from the seven general purposes described earlier; those general purposes are made more specific by relation to a particular topic.

For example, if you were going to discuss cheating at the university, you might proceed as follows:

TOPIC: Cheating at the university

GENERAL PURPOSE: To provide new information

SPECIFIC PURPOSE: To inform listeners of widespread cheating on this campus

The specific purpose is an instance of the general purpose, to provide new information.

Notice that the specific purpose statement has several important characteristics. First, it focuses on the audience rather than on the speaker. It identifies the outcome you seek, not how you will achieve that outcome. Second, it summarizes a single idea. Although some speeches are complex and have more than one purpose, you are likely to be more effective if you can state your purpose as a single succinct idea. Third, the specific purpose statement is precise and free of vague language. It tells exactly what you are trying to achieve, and so you can determine whether or not you succeed.

Next, think critically about your specific purpose statement. Remember that listeners are giving their time and energy to hear you speak, and ask yourself whether your specific purpose is worthy of their efforts. If you are telling them only things that they already know, if your purpose is too grand to be achieved in the time available, if the topic is too technical or seems trivial, listeners are unlikely to pay close attention. In that case, of course, you cannot achieve your purpose.

specific purpose statement
Statement of the particular outcome sought from the audience; a more specific version of a general purpose.

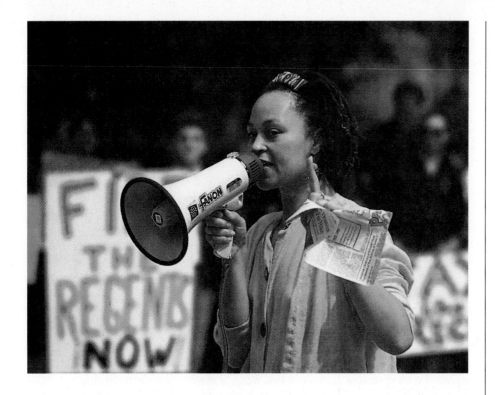

The thesis statement sums up what you most want listeners to remember. It should be possible to translate the thesis statement into a slogan for a poster.

The Thesis Statement

The final step in preparing the overall design of the speech is to identify the **thesis,** a succinct statement of the central idea or claim made by the speech. Whereas the specific purpose statement indicates what you want the audience to *take from* the speech, the thesis statement indicates what you want to *put into* it. The thesis sums up the speech in a single sentence that you most want listeners to remember. Here is how the thesis statement about campus cheating might evolve:

TOPIC: Cheating at the university

GENERAL PURPOSE: To provide new information

SPECIFIC PURPOSE: To inform listeners of widespread cheating on this campus

THESIS STATEMENT: Far more students engage in cheating than most of us think.

Notice how the topic (itself the result of a narrowing process) has been narrowed into a thesis statement that summarizes exactly what the speech will say.

Many of the tests of the specific purpose statement also apply to the thesis. Both should be stated in a single phrase or sentence. Both should be worded precisely. And both should fit the time available and other constraints in the situation.

Occasionally a speaker does not state the thesis explicitly, relying instead on all the supporting ideas to imply it. There are advantages and disadvantages to letting the audience determine the exact thesis. If listeners participate actively in figuring it out, they are likely to stay interested in the speech and

thesis
The central idea or claim made by the speech, usually stated in a single sentence.

perhaps may even be more likely to accept the thesis. On the other hand, if the thesis is not stated, the audience might not identify it accurately, or different listeners might identify different theses. Even though accomplished speakers sometimes trust the audience to identify the thesis, students of public speaking are well advised to state it explicitly.

ANALYZING THE THESIS STATEMENT

The thesis statement governs various choices about the content of a speech. By analyzing your thesis statement, you can determine just what your choices are.

Identifying the Issues

First you must identify the issues contained within the thesis statement. People often use the term "issue" quite loosely, as when they say, "Don't make an issue of it." But the term has a more precise meaning. An **issue** is a question raised by the thesis statement that must be addressed in order for the thesis itself to be addressed effectively.[6]

Issues are identified by posing questions about your thesis statement. Because the statement is so simple and brief, it always leaves much unsaid. By raising questions about the thesis statement, you'll discover what it seems to take for granted. Then your speech can flesh out these underlying assumptions and show that they are correct, giving listeners reason to accept the thesis statement itself.

Consider the thesis statement in the example above: "Far more students engage in cheating than most of us think." It seems straightforward. But notice what happens when we ask questions about the statement:

"Far more students"	→ How many? Is that number more than we think? Is it "far more"?
"Engage in cheating"	→ What is covered by the term "cheating"? And what must one do to "engage in" it?
"Than most of us think"	→ Who are "most of us"? What do "most of us" think? Why do we think this?

These questions identify the issues in the thesis statement. You may decide that some of the answers are obvious or that some can be covered together. You may decide not to take them up in the same order in the speech. But these essentially are the questions you'll need to answer if you want listeners to accept that "far more students engage in cheating than most of us think."

Now consider a thesis that is not yet well formed. Bill Goldman wanted to explore whether "voting in local elections is a worthwhile effort for me as a student." He had not yet framed an explicit thesis, but even this more broadly phrased statement can be questioned to discover the issues. Bill had to think about what "worthwhile" means for a student, whose stake in local elections is usually small; he also had to think about what "effort" is required to vote and why even that is an issue. He then began to question whether it was "harder" for him to vote than for others or harder than it "should" be. Gradually, he came to believe that low voter turnout can be explained by the fact that voting is inconvenient. This process of discovering issues helped Bill both to refine and to test his thesis statement.

Finally, consider the example of Angela Peters, who wanted to talk about the college admissions process. After doing some research, she might begin to develop her speech like this:

TOPIC: The college admissions process

GENERAL PURPOSE: Weakening commitment to a position

SPECIFIC PURPOSE: To cause listeners to doubt their belief that admissions decisions are made rationally

THESIS STATEMENT: Most colleges and students lack clear criteria for making admissions decisions.

ISSUES:

1. What are "most colleges"? Who are "most students"? How do we know?
2. What makes the criteria for admissions clear or unclear?
3. What are a college's or a student's criteria? Are they "clear" or not?
4. What are the admissions decisions about which we are concerned?

Now Angela can complete her research by looking for the answers to these specific questions. When she speaks about "the college admissions process," she will know what she wants to say, and she will have the supporting material she needs to weaken listeners' commitment to the belief that admissions decisions are made rationally.

Why Identify the Issues?

Analyzing the topic to identify the issues is important for several reasons. First, it enables you to determine what the speech must cover. Without knowing the issues, you risk giving a speech that listeners will dismiss as being beside the point.

Recall that Bill Goldman initially wanted to explore whether "voting in local elections is a worthwhile effort for me as a student." Through the process of discovering issues he eventually came to believe that low voter turnout reflected the fact that voting is inconvenient. At this point his topic became "Why Americans don't vote," and his thesis was "Because voting is inconvenient, many people don't vote." He was able to document that even in presidential elections voter turnout is low and that it is declining. He also was able to show that polling places may be inconvenient to get to, that people don't like waiting in line, and that the form of the ballot is often complex. He proposed as his solution that people be allowed to vote from home through the use of a touch-tone telephone. This solution seemed appropriate *as he described the problem,* but he did not really analyze the issues and causes fully. His thesis statement was too vague and did not consider alternative explanations.

After the speech an audience member challenged whether Bill had really thought through the problem. The listener pointed out that, since people will endure inconvenience if they believe that the rewards justify it, perhaps a more significant cause for failing to vote is the belief that one's vote will make no difference or that the voter will have nothing to show for the effort. Although the "costs" of standing in line at an inconvenient location and being confronted by a confusing ballot may explain why many citizens do not vote, a deeper reason may be that they see no real "benefit" from casting their votes. If so, then voting by telephone is unlikely to improve the turnout rate. Had Bill analyzed his thesis more carefully, he might have seen that the costs and benefits of voting were likely to be an issue, and he would have been prepared to address this.

A second reason to analyze the thesis statement is to direct your research, which otherwise could be endless. Combing your own experience and ideas, talking with others, and investigating library resources could go on indefinitely. A search of books and articles in just a single library will probably turn up hundreds of sources that have something to say about voting rates (and on the Internet, an unfocused search will yield truly unmanageable results).

One way to make your research task manageable is to focus your inquiry. By analyzing your thesis to determine the issues, you can better decide what and how to research. For example, in giving a speech about voting rates, you may decide that the key issue relates to voting at state and local levels. As a result, you would not pay much attention to the vast literature comparing turnout rates among countries or turnout rates in national elections. Your research would be directed to the questions that bear on the issues you have identified.

A third reason to identify the issues is that doing so may lead you to modify your thesis. If your initial thesis is "Americans are too busy to vote," analyzing the issues might convince you that your thesis should be "Americans are too lazy to vote" or "Americans are too confused to vote" or "Americans feel that they have no reason to vote." The differences among these statements are obvious. Which one (or more) claim you try to develop and defend in the speech will be influenced by your analysis of what the issues really are.

Finally, as you will see in Chapter 7, analyzing your thesis is also helpful when you turn to organizing your speech.

 Summary

In this chapter we investigated the initial steps in preparing a speech: understanding the rhetorical situation, choosing a topic, and developing a strategic plan—an action plan that reflects a clear sense of purpose and that identifies your constraints and opportunities.

Whether or not you choose your own topic, it is important to understand the factors that determine the rhetorical situation: the audience, the occasion, the speaker, and the speech. Sometimes speakers do not choose their own topics, which instead are determined by the issue, the occasion, or the audience. But in situations where you do choose the topic, your speech will be more effective if the topic matters to you, if you can make it interesting to the audience, if its scope fits the time available, if it is appropriate for oral delivery, and if it is clear.

When you are able to choose your own topic, you should follow certain steps. Conduct an inventory of your interests and those of the audience, use finding aids such as brainstorming and general reading, and narrow the topic so that it can be addressed adequately within the time available.

With a topic in mind, speakers formulate an overall strategy for responding to the rhetorical situation. Strategic planning is guided especially by the purpose of the speech: whether to provide new information or perspective, to raise issues, to create positive or negative feeling, to strengthen or weaken commitment to a position, to change listeners' minds, and/or to induce a specific action by audience members.

Achieving your purpose depends in part on the constraints and opportunities in the rhetorical situation. Constraints limit what you can do and may result from what you know about audiences in general, from your analysis of the specific audience, from your ethos as a speaker, from the nature of your topic, or from the fact that a speech is a one-shot appeal that is primarily verbal. Opportunities arise from the fact that you probably will know more about your topic than listeners do and from the fact that you may draw on and respond to the audience's attitudes and values. Your strategy should use constraints and opportunities to achieve your purpose.

The process of identifying your topic, your general and specific purposes, and your thesis statement allows you to focus on the strategic development of the speech. You know what you want to say and what effect you want to achieve. You might modify these ideas as you learn more about the subject or refine your audience analysis, but the purpose and thesis statements will influence the following strategic decisions:

- What you need to know about the topic in order to establish that the thesis is true
- Which main ideas you need to develop to establish the thesis
- Which inferences must be made to link the main ideas to the thesis
- How best to organize your development and support of the thesis
- Which elements in the design of the speech will make listeners most comfortable about accepting the thesis statement

We will focus on these important strategic choices in the next several chapters.

Discussion Questions

1. When a small liberal arts college decided to change its core curriculum, the issue of core requirements became important to students in a public speaking class, many of whom spoke about that topic. Discuss the issues in this rhetorical situation that seemed to call for speech.
2. How do the purpose of a speech and its subject matter relate to one another? Discuss the speech purposes described in this chapter, and identify some potential topics for each purpose.
3. Imagine that you are giving a six- to eight-minute speech to a group of fraternity members in which your purpose is to weaken their commitment to the idea that alcohol is desirable at parties. What constraints and opportunities do you face in this situation? How will you use those constraints and opportunities in your strategic plan for this speech?
4. Now imagine that you are giving a six- to eight-minute speech to a meeting of Students Against Drunk Driving in which your purpose is to strengthen their commitment to the idea that alcohol is dangerous at parties. How do the constraints and opportunities of this situation differ from those in item 3? In what ways would your strategic plan for this speech be different?

Activities

1. Choose a good topic for a speech in this class. In doing so, conduct a personal inventory and use finding aids such as brainstorming and source browsing. Make sure that you narrow the topic so that it is appropriate for the time available.
2. Produce a list of constraints and a list of opportunities for the topic you have chosen. Consider the audience, the occasion, the speaker, and

the speech. In a few paragraphs, describe your purpose and how you are going to achieve it within the bounds of these constraints and opportunities.

3. Provide the following information about your speech:

TOPIC:
GENERAL PURPOSE:
SPECIFIC PURPOSE:
THESIS STATEMENT:

Evaluate each of these decisions, explaining why you made the choices you did.

Using the Internet

1. **Classical perspectives on occasions for public speaking.** In this chapter we examined the three types of speaking occasions: ceremonial, deliberative, and forensic. Read an online version of Cicero's writings on speaking occasions by going to <http://www.towson.edu/~tinkler/reader/cicero.html>.

2. **Choosing your topic with online resources.** Is your intention to share information or to persuade? Use the "Assess Your Speechmaking Situation" page from the **Allyn & Bacon Public Speaking Website** to consider topic ideas and to clarify your purpose. Point your browser to <http://www.abacon.com/pubspeak/assess/topic.html>. From there you can sort out a range of topic choices and subject areas that might be fruitful starting points for planning your speech.

Do a personal inventory and analyze your audience:

• *Which topics on this list are meaningful and interesting to you?*

• *How do you assess your audience's interest level?*

• *Which of your interests overlap with those of your audience?*

• *How can you narrow your topic to fit the constraints of the situation?*

Some of the sources on this page are general search tools. You can learn more about using search tools by clicking on the link for "Notes on Using Search Tools." It is identified by the blue icon for "Notes from the Instructor." You may also go directly to that source by pointing your browser to <http://www.abacon.com/pubspeak/research/notetool.html>.

3. Use of Thomas or Project Vote Smart for legislative topics: **Thomas** is the Website of the Library of Congress that describes action in the U.S. Congress. **Project Vote Smart** provides a number of valuable links for finding out about debates in Congress.

1. See Craig R. Smith and Paul Prince, "Language Choice Expectation and the Roman Notion of Style," *Communication Education* 39 (January 1990): 63–74.
2. *Identification* is a rhetorical concept treated by Kenneth Burke in *A Rhetoric of Motives,* Berkeley: Univ. of California Press, 1969.
3. The strategy of speakers who do not seek identification is examined in Robert L. Scott and Donald K. Smith, "The Rhetoric of Confrontation," *Quarterly Journal of Speech* 55 (February 1969): 1–8.
4. These three categories are described in Aristotle, *The Rhetoric,* trans. W. Rhys Roberts, New York: The Modern Library, 1954, Book I, Chapter 3.
5. This classification system is original. Although the broad categories served our purposes in Chapter 1, we will use this more precise system of purposes for the remainder of our study.
6. For another list of purposes, see Sonja K. Foss and Karen A. Foss, *Inviting Transformation: Presentational Speaking for a Changing World,* Prospect Heights, Ill.: Waveland Press, 1994, pp. 10–16.
7. Classical rhetoric addresses the subject of issue identification as "stasis theory." For more on this theory, see Otto Alvin Loeb Dieter, "Stasis," *Communication Monographs* 17 (November 1950): 345–369; Ray Nadeau, "Classical Systems of Stases in Greek: Hermagoras to Hermogenes," *Greek, Roman, and Byzantine Studies* 2 (January 1959): 51–71; and Ray Nadeau, "Hermogenes on Stases: A Translation with an Introduction and Notes," *Communication Monographs* 31 (November 1964): 361–424. For a modern approach to classical stasis theory, see Lee S. Hultzen, "Status in Deliberative Analysis," *The Rhetorical Idiom: Essays in Rhetoric, Oratory, Language, and Drama,* ed. Donald C. Bryant, Ithaca, N. Y.: Cornell Univ. Press, 1958, pp. 97–123.

chapter 5
Researching the Topic

In This Chapter We Will:

- Identify the kinds of material that are available to support the ideas in your speech.

- Explore how to find supporting materials through your personal experience, interviews with others, library research, and electronic searches.

- Describe a strategy for conducting research efficiently and productively.

- Explain how to cite sources and how to take notes about your research.

n this chapter you will learn how to investigate your topic so that you can speak about it intelligently. Since you are making claims on listeners' time and attention, both you and they will want to be confident that you know what you're talking about.

The process of finding supporting material for your speech is called **research.** It is closely linked to the process of **analysis** that you studied at the end of Chapter 4. Indeed, the available materials guide you in identifying the issues related to your topic, and searching for material without knowing which issues you need to investigate would be pointless.

Sometimes analysis precedes research. This is the right sequence when you already know what your thesis statement is. You then determine which questions must be answered in order to make that statement, and you go to find the answers. Sometimes, though, you don't yet know your thesis statement; you know only the topic. Angela Peters wanted to talk about the college admissions process (topic), but she didn't know enough about it to be sure what she wanted to say (thesis). In this case, she should begin not with analysis but with research. She needs a general understanding of the topic before she can frame the thesis statement. Then she should analyze her thesis statement as described in Chapter 4 and, finally, return to research for answers to the specific questions she identified.

Whether your research precedes or follows your analysis, you will want it to accomplish three basic goals:

- To develop or strengthen your own expertise on the topic
- To find the evidence that will support your ideas
- To make your ideas clear, understandable, and pertinent to your audience

Keep in mind that these different goals may not all be achieved by the same kind of material. If you conceive of the research process too narrowly, you may find that you have obtained great background knowledge but have no specific material to include in your speech. Or you may find that your evidence is clear and meaningful in the context in which you found it, but it may mean little to your audience without that context.

TYPES OF SUPPORTING MATERIAL

To do research for your speech, you first have to decide which types of supporting material you need. The following seven types illustrate the array of possibilities:

- Personal experience
- Common knowledge
- Direct observation
- Examples
- Documents
- Statistics
- Testimony

research
The process of looking for and discovering supporting materials for the speech.

analysis
Exploration of a speech topic to determine which subordinate topics must be covered.

5.1 Types of Supporting Material

1. **Personal experience**
2. **Common knowledge**
3. **Direct observation**
4. **Examples**
   - *Brief example*
   - *Hypothetical example*
   - *Anecdote*
   - *Case study*
5. **Documents**
6. **Statistics**
   - *Surveys and polls*
   - *Rates of change*
   - *Experiments*
7. **Testimony**
   - *Factual testimony*
   - *Opinion testimony*

Personal Experience

Sometimes you can support your ideas on the basis of your own experience. Suppose your topic concerns the difficulties that first-year students have in adjusting to college life. You might well illustrate your main points by referring to your own first college days. If you were speaking about volunteerism, your experience in tutoring elementary school students or working in a soup kitchen would certainly be relevant. Student speaker Mitch Apley

5.2 Testing the Strength of Supporting Material

1. **Personal experience**
   - *Are you sure your memory is reliable?*
   - *Is your experience generalizable?*
   - *Will others interpret it the same way?*
2. **Common knowledge**
   - *Are you sure the audience shares it?*
   - *Are you sure it is correct?*
3. **Direct observation**
   - *Are you sure of what you saw?*
   - *Might you have any bias?*
4. **Examples**
   - *Are they representative?*
   - *Are there enough of them?*
5. **Documents**
   - *Can they be trusted?*
   - *Are they properly interpreted?*
   - *Is the context made clear?*
6. **Statistics**
   - *Are appropriate measures used?*
   - *Are they reliable and valid?*
   - *Have they been interpreted properly?*
7. **Testimony**
   - *Does the person have access to the data?*
   - *Is the person expert on the subject?*
   - *Is the person reasonably objective?*

used a personal story to introduce his speech about the need to teach children that getting drunk is not a social coup:

> Last quarter, I went out with some buddies of mine to have a good time. We were partying hard, and I got really wasted. I mean, I've never been so trashed in my life! A few weeks ago, I saw some pictures of myself that I don't even remember being in. It was great! That is—until I rolled my new sports car. The police tell me that I was lucky to walk out of there alive. I was even more lucky to avoid hurting someone else. Many drunk drivers aren't so lucky.

Mitch gained credibility—and the audience's attention—because he knew what he was talking about. He used his experience to illustrate his main points, and since his listeners could relate to him, they found his experience pertinent to them as well.

Common Knowledge

An often-overlooked type of supporting material is **common knowledge,** the understandings, beliefs, and values that members of a society or culture generally share. Such beliefs are sometimes called "common sense." Some writers use the term "social knowledge" to emphasize that we know these things to be true on the basis of broad social consensus.[1]

Common knowledge is often expressed in the form of *maxims,* such as "Work expands to fill the time available for its completion," "You can't trust the people who made the mess to clean it up," "Nature abhors a vacuum," or "If you want something done right, do it yourself." Sometimes common knowledge takes the form of *generally held beliefs.* For example, whether correctly or not, most Americans believe that the Great Society programs of the 1960s failed, that taxes are too high and definitely should not be increased, that the war in Vietnam was a mistake, and that God plays a role in their lives. Common knowledge also is expressed in *value judgments,* such as the importance of protecting the environment, the commitment to a right to privacy, and a preference for practical solutions over ideological disputes.

One student speaker used common knowledge as supporting material when he said:

> We all know why we're here in college: to have fun and to get a good job when we leave. With this in mind, let me tell you why the Greek system is a benefit to any student.

When asked later, audience members agreed that the speaker's claim about students' goals was commonly shared by students at that school.

Common knowledge is not always correct, of course; people certainly can believe things that "ain't so." But common knowledge has the status of **presumption**—that is, we consider it to be right until we are shown otherwise. Precisely because the knowledge is "common" and widely shared, it can often be useful as supporting material.

Direct Observation

Sometimes you can support your claim on the basis of simple, direct observation—the heart of the scientific method. If you are speaking about whether drivers obey basic traffic laws, you can stand near a traffic light or stop sign and count how many drivers ignore these signals. If you are speak-

common knowledge
The beliefs and values that members of a society or culture generally share.

presumption
The assumption that a statement or claim is true until shown otherwise.

ing about the widespread use of telephone answering machines, you can call various friends and organizations and observe how often the calls are answered by a machine. Student speaker Kari Potts used direct observation to support her claim that dormitory food was priced competitively:

> When I first came to school, I thought the dorm food was really overpriced. So I decided to check the local restaurants to see if I could do better. Imagine my surprise! When I went to Jimmy John's sandwich shop, I priced a moderate lunch— just a sandwich and a drink—at $4.66. A light lunch at Burger King, only a salad and a drink, costs $4.48. In comparison, lunch at the dorms costs $4.95, and you can eat as much as you want.

Examples

When you offer an example, you make a general statement more meaningful by illustrating a specific instance of it. You can provide this kind of support for a claim by using a brief example, a hypothetical example, an anecdote, or a case study.

BRIEF EXAMPLE If you wanted to support the claim that the structure of the United Nations does not adequately reflect the current balance of power in the world, you might cite as an example the fact that Germany and Japan— despite their economic strength—do not have permanent seats on the Security Council. You might cite as another example the dominance of the General Assembly by "third world" nations. And you also might cite the UN's inability to compel member nations to pay their assessments. You would not develop any of these examples in detail, however; they are important because *together* they support your claim that the structure of the United Nations is outmoded.

HYPOTHETICAL EXAMPLE In using a hypothetical example to support a claim, you ask listeners to *imagine* themselves in a particular situation. You might say, "Suppose that year after year you spent more money than you took in. What would you have to do about that?" Listeners might conjure up images of severe cuts in their budget, selling their home or car, or even bankruptcy. You then could use this example to help the audience understand the difficult choices Congress makes in fashioning the federal budget.

ANECDOTE An anecdote, or story, allows you to develop an example in great detail. If your topic is the frustration of dealing with a bureaucracy, you might tell a story about someone's failure to get a problem resolved within the system. You could describe the maze of telephone inquiries and form letter replies and your hero's trek to the seat of power, only to be directed to the wrong office. Finally reaching the appropriate official, the person is patronized by a clerk who says, "According to our records, you are dead." Such an extended, engaging story would illustrate your point and help the audience relate to the issues.

CASE STUDY You often can support a general claim by zeroing in on one particular true case and discussing it in detail. If your topic were about whether or not campus codes to regulate offensive speech can be effective, you might describe one or two campuses that have tried this approach and then argue that their experiences illustrate whether such codes are workable in general. If you believe that making Election Day a national holiday would increase voter turnout, you might support your claim by drawing on case studies of nations where Election Day is a holiday.

Notice that all these types of examples work by relating a part of something to the whole. By examining a particular instance of whatever is being discussed, you may be able to support claims about the topic as a whole.

Documents

Authoritative documents are another source of supporting material. The Declaration of Independence is often quoted to support the belief that there are natural rights. For many people the Bible is the document most often quoted. Crucial support took the form of White House tape recordings in the investigations of the 1972 break-in at the offices of the Democratic National Committee in the Watergate complex in Washington, D.C. One recording has been called the "smoking gun" of the Watergate scandal because it provided evidence that President Nixon knew about the break-in and had participated in covering up the crime until 1974.

The student who spoke about cheating on campus referred to a university document to show that academic dishonesty would not be tolerated:

> According to the student handbook we got as freshmen, cheating is "a serious breach of our commitment to ethical behavior as students" and will be punished with "a failing grade in the class and possible expulsion from the university."

Documents can be a solid form of evidence if your audience regards them as trustworthy—and if you quote them accurately. The exact words of a document provide a record that is not skewed by the opinions and interpretations of others.

Referring specifically to key documents can be a good way to show authoritative and specific support for your claims. ▶

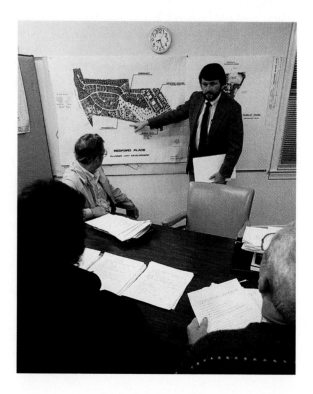

Statistics

Supporting material presented in quantitative form, as statistics, is especially useful when the scope of the topic is vast. But if you are speaking about your family or your college class, the scope of the topic is narrow enough that you probably don't need statistical support; you can just provide a set of examples or case studies. When your topic involves the state or the nation, however, one or two examples are unlikely to represent the diversity of the population.

Statistics are numbers recording the extent of something or the frequency with which something occurs; they take such forms as medians, averages, ratios, indices, and standardized scores. Such numbers become meaningful when they are compared with some base line or other pattern to permit an inference about the relationship between the two. For example, you might support a claim by comparing the median family income for different professions or different ethnic groups or different nations.

Although statistical statements take a great variety of forms, the following three types are especially valuable for supporting material in speeches.

SURVEYS AND POLLS   Suppose your topic was about how most Americans regard the public educational system. In theory, you or someone else could interview all Americans and then tabulate the results. But that approach is doomed to fail. Not even the Census Bureau has been able to find and count all Americans, and the time and expense involved would make the task impossible. Moreover, the data would be obsolete by the time you completed your survey.

Instead, you can *infer* the attitudes of the people as a whole from the attitudes reported by a sample of the population, as long as the sample is representative of the whole. In the case of public opinion about the U.S. educational system, a 1992 Gallup Poll reported that 68 percent of the sample interviewed believed that public schools fail to educate the nation's children. That statistic would be used to suggest that the general public—not just the people interviewed in this survey—give American public education a vote of no confidence.

Surveys and polls are widely used in the physical and social sciences and to gain information about public opinion on matters of policy.

RATES OF CHANGE   Often, what is noteworthy about a statistic is not its absolute size but its rate of change. For instance, it may be more important to know that the national debt doubled during the 1980s than to know the total dollar amount. Similarly, knowing that medical costs have increased at a much faster rate than personal income may be more useful than knowing either of the exact amounts. And knowing that the world's population is doubling faster and faster may have greater implications than knowing what the total population is. Speakers often can illustrate and emphasize such dramatic rate changes through visual aids.

Rates of change show what is happening and can help an audience compare the situation to some known benchmark. By themselves, however, statistics may not tell much and may easily mislead.[2] For example, one student speaker supported the claim that the university was not promoting affirmative action by citing what seemed like an important statistic:

> Did you know that fewer African Americans were admitted to this school this year than last year? There's no excuse for that! It proves that this school has no commitment to diversity.

statistics
Numbers recording the extent of something or the frequency with which it occurs.

The speaker had fallen into a statistical trap, however, by failing to note that the *total* number of students admitted was lower this year than last. The percentage of African-American students in the entering class was actually slightly higher and had increased for three years in a row.

EXPERIMENTS   Experiments are controlled tests of the effect of one thing on another. They are conducted by comparing situations that are essentially similar except for the factor being tested. A claim that secondhand smoke leads to lung cancer, for example, would be supported by comparing the cancer rates of two groups that were similar in all essential respects except that one had been exposed to secondhand smoke and the other had not. Similarly, the claim that African-American drivers are stopped by police officers in a particular neighborhood more often than are Caucasian drivers could be tested by sending the same model car through the same neighborhood at the same time of day at the same speed with drivers who differ only in the color of their skin.

Testimony

Testimony is information or an opinion that is expressed by someone other than the speaker, who uses the testimony to support some claim. When using testimony, you rely on someone else's judgment, and so you need to assess that person's competence and credibility. You may also need to convince the audience that your source is knowledgable and trustworthy.

FACTUAL TESTIMONY   *Facts* are pieces of information that can be proved true or false. Speakers often support ideas by reporting facts that were gathered by others, such as quoting the secretary of state about developments in the Middle East, or quoting a public health expert about the dangers of secondhand smoke, or quoting a campus security officer about the number of crimes reported last year. When you quote facts, you are implying that you cannot verify the information yourself but are willing to accept it because you think the source is credible.

OPINION TESTIMONY   *Opinions* are beliefs formed from experience and judgment. When you offer another person's opinion to support a claim, you are indicating that someone whose judgment is trusted, whose expertise is valued, or who is in a better position to know than most people are has reached a certain conclusion. You are asking the audience to accept that conclusion because of the person's expertise, judgment, or knowledge, not because you can verify the statement. Thus you might quote an expert in Middle Eastern politics to support a point about the peace process in that region, or you might quote campus security officers about whether the campus is a safe place to be after dark.

When using opinion testimony for support, consider whether the audience will know and trust the person you are quoting. You may have to establish why your source's opinion is more valuable than the average person's.

testimony
Information or an opinion expressed by someone other than the speaker, cited to support some claim.

CHOOSE A STRATEGY

Using Research to Support Your Speech

THE SITUATION

Since you started school a year ago, you've often heard students on campus complaining about the level of financial assistance available. Many of the students on your campus must work part time to pay for tuition and expenses. You and some friends have joined together to form a group to lobby for more financial aid—and a larger variety of types of aid. You have one week to prepare for a ten-minute presentation in front of the director of financial aid to convince her that more aid is needed for students on campus.

MAKING CHOICES

1. What types of information do you need to back up your arguments about the situation on your campus?
2. What types of information do you need to illustrate that your situation is worse than on other similar campuses across the country?
3. What other types of information will be relevant and effective?

WHAT IF . . .

Suppose that your research shows that: (a) your school falls within the national average for amounts of financial assistance awarded; (b) your school has a higher-than-average percentage of students who work; (c) there are fewer types of financial aid programs available at your school than at similar schools; and (d) tuition is higher at your school than the national average.

1. With one of your key arguments lacking in support, what additional information should you get to support your overall case?
2. What other arguments might you make based on the evidence and how might you support them?
3. What will you do with the information that does not support your case?

FINDING SUPPORTING MATERIAL FROM PEOPLE

The word "research" conjures up images of the scientist in the laboratory, the solitary scholar in a musty library, or the introvert peering for hours into a computer screen. Although laboratories, libraries, and computers are indeed places where evidence can be found, do not overlook your personal observations and interviews with others as potential sources of support.

Personal Experience

Your memory is an important source of evidence. Experiences you've had, events you've observed, and things other people have said to you all become part of your personal stock of supporting material.

Besides the things you remember, your own observations may be a source of evidence. If your topic is about the quality of campus housing, you might visit a variety of living units and observe what conditions are like. In your speech you then could state, "I visited six kinds of living units on campus, and here is what I found." Your reported observations would become evidence.

Interviews

Sometimes the best source of supporting material is other people. Interviews enable you to ask exactly the questions that you need to have answered, and the give-and-take of the interview routine permits follow-up discussion. Moreover, people sometimes will make statements in an oral interview that they would not be willing to make in print.

It is not only national and international experts who provide valuable interviews. The manager of the local department store has a perspective on how economic conditions affect consumer confidence. Faculty members have expertise on a variety of issues in every academic discipline. And fellow students can tell you about all aspects of campus life, including, say, how changes in funding for student loans may affect their educational plans. Clearly, potential interviewees are everywhere, and your strategic planning should consider all options.

If distance or time constraints prevent you from conducting face-to-face interviews, you can question sources by telephone, mail, or the Internet. However you actually contact your sources, the following guidelines will help make your interviews effective.

PREPARE FOR THE PERSON Learn as much as you can about the people you plan to interview. How long have they held their current position? What experiences have they had with the subject? Are they prominently identified with some issue or aspect of your topic? Are they well known, or will you need to establish their credentials? Thinking about such questions in advance of the interview process will allow you to derive the greatest benefit from your sources' expertise in the time available.

PREPARE FOR THE SUBJECT It is a waste of your sources' time if you ask them very general questions or seek information that you can get easily in other ways. Don't let the interview substitute for your own background reading and research. Be familiar with general aspects of the subject, including its history, its current state, and relevant issues. Make sure that you understand basic concepts that are likely to come up in the interview so that you can focus your questions on unique information that your source can provide.

Checklist

5.3 *Guidelines for Interviewing*

1. **Prepare for the person.**
2. **Prepare for the subject.**
3. **Prepare for the format.**
4. **Conduct the interview competently.**
5. **Take notes or record the interview.**
6. **Determine what can be used.**

PREPARE FOR THE FORMAT   An interview is a particular kind of communication event that proceeds through questions and answers. Before the interview, formulate your questions carefully so that they are not vague and not leading or hostile. Your questions should be simple and direct and should not anticipate answers or favor any particular viewpoint. Instead, you should give your sources the opportunity to make their own judgments, to explain why they think as they do, and to comment on different points of view that others may have expressed.

Also be aware that different types of questions elicit different types of information. A **closed question** limits the respondent to a fixed number of choices, such as "Would it be more efficient for campus security to invest in (1) an escort system or (2) a shuttle bus?" This type of question directs the respondent to pick one option from those you have offered, which is helpful when you want to commit the person to a definite position. A closed question also allows you to count and compare the answers of different respondents, since they all choose from the same optional answers. But closed questions do not reveal much about respondents' thinking and opinions.

In contrast, an **open-ended question** does not limit or direct the person's response, as in "What do you think should be done to enhance campus security?" Although an open-ended question does permit full expression of opinions, the answer may stray far from the information you most need for your speech, and you may have to refocus the interview repeatedly.

Time is another factor to consider in formulating questions. A closed question can be answered quickly and may allow you to interview more respondents; but you will need time to collect, tabulate, and analyze responses before you can use the information in developing your speech. Open-ended questions take more time to answer, which may limit how many respondents you can interview (and how many are willing to be interviewed). Also, respondents often introduce important matters that you did not consider in your original questions, and you should allow time to pursue them.

CONDUCT THE INTERVIEW COMPETENTLY   Being a competent interviewer includes such basic matters as arriving on time, reminding the person who you are and the purpose of your interview, and thanking him or her for taking the time to help you. But competence also includes the ability to adjust your questions in response to the flow of the interview itself. The person may say something that answers several of your questions or parts of them, or a comment may bring up a question that you had not planned on asking. Do not regard your questions as rigid and inflexible; adjust them as the interview evolves. On the other hand, if the interviewee seems to ignore a question, you may need to ask it again, perhaps phrasing it differently. Or you may need to ask a **follow-up question** that explores the implications of a previous response. Finally, you must take care to reach an agreement with the respondent about what information, if any, you can quote directly and what information is solely for your own use. If you do intend to quote directly, be sure that your understanding of the person's answers is accurate and exact.

TAKE NOTES OR RECORD THE INTERVIEW   Don't assume that you will remember everything important that is said during an interview. Arrive prepared, with notebook in hand, so you can keep track of important points. If you prefer to tape-record the interview, be sure to ask ahead of time whether that will be all right; no one should be recorded without permission. Think carefully

closed question
A question with a finite number of choices from among which the respondent must pick.

open-ended question
A question that does not restrict the range of possible responses.

follow-up question
A question that explores the implications of a previous response.

about using a tape recorder, however. Although it does free you from the burden of note taking and ensures an accurate record of the interview, it also may make the respondent more guarded and less candid, knowing that every word is being "recorded for posterity." Besides, later on you'll have to transcribe the entire recording in order to organize notes for your speech. It may be more practical and more effective to take notes during the interview itself, while you have the opportunity to follow up and clarify the person's remarks.

DETERMINE WHAT TO USE IN YOUR SPEECH   Not everything that you obtain in an interview will be useful in your speech; nor should the interview be your sole source of information. As you assemble materials for the speech, ask yourself which points can be supported most effectively by the interview and which points can be supported just as well by other sources. For example, you may decide to rely on printed sources for general or statistical information about your topic and then draw on the interview for opinion testimony and for real-world examples.

FINDING SUPPORTING MATERIAL IN PRINT

Although your personal knowledge and experience with others are valuable sources of evidence, you probably will need to rely heavily on printed material—especially when your topic is of public significance. In that case, you'll want material of broader scope than what you have experienced or what people have told you. The library is the best source of printed material, and often of audiovisual material as well. An added benefit of doing library research for your speeches is that you will learn much about how to use the library and will probably discover that it is an inviting rather than a forbidding place.

Books

When you think of printed materials, you probably think first of books. Both general and specific books about your topic—as well as anthologies of essays by different authors—can be valuable sources of supporting material. In most libraries the fastest way to locate relevant books is to consult the subject index in the card catalog. Subject cards may be a separate section of the catalog or may be filed together with title cards and author cards. Many libraries now rely on computerized catalogs, and some also have incorporated databases from other libraries or from the Library of Congress. Today's computerized catalogs are easy to use and make research remarkably efficient and productive. Don't hesitate to ask a librarian for help in using a computerized catalog.

Whether on cards or computer, the subject entry will give you important information about a book: its author, title, length, date and place of publication, other subjects under which the book is listed, and its call number (see Fig. 5.1). The entry also may guide you to other closely related subjects. For example, the subject heading "labor unions" may direct you to such categories as "trade associations," "labor-management disputes," and "collective bargaining." Don't hesitate to explore these headings as well.

FIGURE 5.1

Example of a catalog card.

The book's call number will tell you where to find the book on the library's shelves. If the stacks are "open," meaning that you have access to them, browse the books with call numbers near to the book that you want. You may discover related titles that you hadn't identified by other means.

Sometimes, particularly if your library is small, you may run across a citation to a book that cannot be found. Fortunately, most libraries can arrange an interlibrary loan, using specialized indexes to help you identify other libraries that have the book and arranging to borrow it for you. Be aware, however, that this takes time. If you anticipate needing books that your library doesn't have, request them far ahead of when you will need them for your speech. The librarian in charge of interlibrary loans can explain the procedure and time frame to you.

Reference Works

Although usually published in book form, reference works are a special category of printed sources. They are seldom intended to be read from cover to cover; they do not develop a sustained argument or claim; and they usually are not written in narrative form. Rather, they are convenient collections of facts and information. Typically, reference works are shelved in a special section of the library, where a reference librarian can help you find and use the following common types of materials.

Dictionaries not only tell you the definitions of a word but also trace its origin and usage. Besides general dictionaries, you can find specialized dictionaries that identify the terms and usage within particular fields.

Encyclopedias are also either general—the kind found in many homes— or specialized in particular subjects, such as *The Encyclopedia of Philosophy* and the *International Encyclopedia of Communications*. Encyclopedias contain brief essays that will give you an overview of a subject. If that subject is incidental to your speech, this level of understanding may be all you need. If you need a deeper understanding, the encyclopedia will give enough background information to steer you to more specialized sources.

Abstracts are short summaries of articles or books related to a particular discipline. Many academic and professional groups publish abstracts of the articles appearing in their current journals. By reading abstracts instead of entire journals, you can discover which articles include material that may be useful.

Fact books are compilations of statistical information that you can consult when you need specific data to support a point in your speech. Almanacs, for example, are published every year and supply up-to-date facts about an enormous range of subjects.

Biographical references identify particular individuals and outline their backgrounds and achievements. *Who's Who* is the best-known biographical reference, but a vast number of such sources can tell you about both contemporary and historical figures.

Compilations and yearbooks are edited collections of material of a given type. For example, *Editorials on File* is a digest of selected newspaper editorials arranged by topic; it is published regularly and then compiled into a yearbook each year. Other examples of such compilations are *Facts on File* and *Congressional Quarterly Almanac,* an especially useful guide to the status of issues currently before the U.S. Congress. *Congressional Quarterly* also publishes a pamphlet called *CQ Researcher,* which examines a different issue of public interest each week. This compilation of facts and opinions includes background information, editorials about each side of the issue, and a bibliography of important books and articles to help you start researching the issue.

Atlases provide geographical information, including the exact location and physical characteristics of specific sites, cities, and regions.

Collections of quotations are useful both for tracking down the origin of popular sayings and for finding maxims or brief quotations related to a particular topic.

Periodical indexes, found in the reference section of the library, are described in the next section.

Periodicals

Periodicals (sometimes called "serials") are published at regular intervals—usually weekly, monthly, or quarterly—and have the advantage of being more up to date than books.

GENERAL-INTEREST PERIODICALS   These are usually sold on newsstands and by subscription, and they thus circulate widely; examples include *Time, Newsweek, U.S. News & World Report,* and *People.* Periodicals like these may have useful information about current events, but their coverage of issues is fairly brief and not deep, with the exception of feature articles. Given their mass circulation, they may be useful in identifying topics of interest and prevalent attitudes among many readers.

Other general-interest periodicals are more focused journals of opinion that delve more deeply into issues and often espouse a particular point of view. Examples include *New Republic* and *Progressive* (liberal) and *Commentary* and *National Review* (conservative). Consult sources like these when you are interested in a particular political perspective on your topic. Other opinion journals, such as *Atlantic* and *Harper's,* tend to represent more diverse and eclectic viewpoints.

SPECIAL-INTEREST PERIODICALS   These are intended for readers who have particular interests, which may be as broadly defined as business *(Fortune* and *Business Week)* or rock music *(Rolling Stone* and *Spin)* or may be as narrowly focused as snowmobiles, digital imaging, or coin collecting. Whatever your topic is, you probably can find a periodical that is devoted to it. Some are aimed at specific demographic groups—based on age, gender, ethnicity, and so on—and even cities are the focus of magazines named after them.

TECHNICAL PERIODICALS   These are written primarily for specialists in a given field. Scholarly journals are the obvious example, with one or more publications dedicated to most academic disciplines: *American Political Science Review, Journal of the American Medical Association, Journal of American History, American Bar Association Journal, Quarterly Journal of Speech,* and so on. Colleges and universities also sometimes publish scholarly journals, such as *Critical Inquiry* and *Yale Review.* Law reviews also fit into this category. Although journals like these are intended mainly for subject-matter specialists, they sometimes include material that can be very helpful for a speech, such as the results of surveys, experiments, and historical and critical analyses conducted by experts in various fields.

INDEXES TO PERIODICALS   You can locate periodical articles by consulting published indexes, the most common of which is the *Reader's Guide to Periodical Literature.* This easy-to-use subject-matter index can be found in virtually every library, and you probably have used it in the past. With few exceptions, however, it indexes only popular, general-interest periodicals.

To locate articles in special-interest and technical periodicals, consult the large number of specialized indexes that are available. The *Bulletin of the Public Affairs Information Service* is useful for many topics dealing with public policy issues. The *Social Sciences Index* and the *Humanities Index* can point you to journals and periodicals relating to those many disciplines. The *Business Periodicals Index* can help you research topics about the economy and business conditions, and the *Index to Legal Periodicals* covers law reviews and journals. Finally, the *International Index to Periodicals* can guide you through journals published in other countries. If the subject of your speech falls outside these categories, ask the reference librarian to suggest appropriate periodical indexes.

Newspapers

Newspapers are the most important source of ongoing current information. Besides reporting the latest news, many newspapers analyze and interpret it and publish related feature articles. Your own daily newspaper will be a valuable source of information for speeches. If you do not already do so, develop the habit of reading the paper regularly and clipping material that you think may be useful in developing a speech.

Especially if you live outside a major metropolitan area, it's a good idea to consult newspapers that cover current events and opinions more comprehensively than your local paper does. Many of these have their own indexes, including *The New York Times* (probably the most comprehensive), the *Wall Street Journal* (especially good on business and economic issues), the *Christian Science Monitor,* the *Washington Post* (particularly on matters of national politics), the *Chicago Tribune,* and the *Los Angeles Times.*

Like most of us, libraries discard all but the most recent newspapers, but first they usually record them on microfilm. You can read the film on machines designed for this purpose, and you can take notes or make photocopies of material that you want to use in your speech.

Government Publications

An often-overlooked source of supporting material is the vast range of publications by state and national governments. Many college and university libraries are government depositories, which means that they regularly receive copies of most federal (and sometimes state) government publications. Some also include the publications of foreign governments and of the United Nations.

Covering virtually every public issue, government publications include bulletins, reports, pamphlets, research studies, congressional deliberations, judicial opinions, and agency publications. Often, however, these are not indexed in the card catalog or general periodical indexes. If your speech topic is of concern to government bodies, you are well advised to visit the government publications section of your library and to consult with the librarian in charge. Although government documents may seem intimidating at first, you can learn to use them effectively by following their few printed directions and seeking the help of the librarian if necessary.

The most comprehensive federal index is the *Monthly Catalog of U.S. Government Publications,* in which titles are arranged alphabetically under the government agency that published them. The subject index is probably the best place to start. When you look up the subject of your speech, you will find a series of entry numbers, one for each document in the alphabetical listing. When you find the entry number, return to the front of the index and locate the document with that entry number. You will then be able to identify the issuing agency, title of the document, call number, and Superintendent of Documents number. Although the *Monthly Catalog* is the most comprehensive index, it is not annotated. You will have to guess from the issuing agency and the title whether the document will be useful to you.

The *Congressional Information Service* is an especially valuable index to congressional publications because it includes abstracts, or brief summaries, of their contents. Again, the subject index lists entry numbers that you can use to look up the abstracts. This is particularly useful in approaching multivolume transcripts of congressional testimony. The *Congressional Information Service* includes all the publications of the legislative branch: hearings, committee reports, commissioned studies, and other documents. It does not index the executive or judicial branches, and it does not cover years before 1970. Nonetheless, for matters that are currently before Congress or that have been considered in the recent past, it is an invaluable reference source.

Other indexes to federal government publications include the *Congressional Record Index,* the *American Statistics Index,* and the *Index to U.S. Government Periodicals.* The librarian in charge of the government periodicals section can help you locate and use these. Similarly, because state and international documents are indexed in a variety of ways, ask the librarian for help.

FINDING SUPPORTING MATERIAL ELECTRONICALLY

The development of the World Wide Web (Internet) has made a wealth of supporting material available. Some of the material is very useful, such as online library card catalogs, information from organizations, and subject-specific information that you can't find anywhere else. Properly used, the Web can be a valuable supplement to library research. Keep in mind, though, that *anyone* can publish on the Web; with no assurance of quality control, you also will find information that is inaccurate, useless, tasteless, or even willfully misleading. For this reason, no matter how critically you assess information on the Web, you should not rely entirely on it for your research but should use electronic sources *in addition* to sources you find from people or in print.

The Web got its name because each site on it usually contains *links* to other related sites, thus forming a kind of web. Having found a site that contains useful information, you can follow its links to other sites that seem interesting. This is like using the bibliography of one book to find other books, only much faster.

Searching for Information on the Web

BROWSERS To navigate through the links on the Web, you need a *browser,* a computer program that keeps track of where you are on the Web and of the path you took to get there. The browser also displays a particular site's infor-

◀ While the Internet can provide quick access to a wide variety of information and research about your speech topic, you should evaluate information obtained on the Internet critically before relying on it as supporting material.

mation on your computer monitor. The two most widely used browsers are Netscape Navigator and Microsoft Internet Explorer.

A browser will enable you to:

- *Go to a specific site by entering its address into the computer.* Each site has a distinct address, called a *Uniform Resource Locator (URL).* This always begins with the letters <http://>. The colon and the two slash marks are required and are followed by the specific URL. For example, the Website for Allyn & Bacon, the publisher of this book, is <http://www.abacon.com>.

- *Move to a new site by selecting an on-screen link.* When you look at a page displayed by the browser on your monitor, you'll often see words and phrases that are highlighted, usually by being underlined and appearing in a different color from the main text. Highlighted phrases are the links to other pages on the Web. Click your mouse on a highlighted phrase, and the browser will jump you to the selected location. Some links lead to programs or data files that you can download to your computer.

- *Return to previous sites.* Clicking the mouse on the "Back" button retraces your path through the linked pages of the Web. Clicking on the "Forward" button returns you to the site you left when you began retracing your path.

- *Go to your home page.* When you start your browser, it always brings you to the same starting point, or *home page.* Clicking the mouse on the "Home" button returns you to that page.

- *Set bookmarks to locate specific sites.* A *bookmark* brings you directly to a Web page without having to go through the other links. This is useful when, after dozens of links, you finally find what you were searching for, or when you discover a site that you may want to explore later. Netscape Navigator files bookmarks under the "Bookmark" menu, and Microsoft Internet Explorer files them under "Favorites." In either case, when you reach a site that you want to bookmark, select the "Add" option under those menus; to return to a bookmarked site, pull down the menu and select the name of the bookmark. Figure 5.2 lists some subject-specific sites that you might want to bookmark.

- *Revisit any recent site.* The browser creates a *history file* that records the name of every site you visit as you "surf the Net." This lets you return to any recently visited site. In Netscape Navigator you'll find the history file in the options under the "Windows" menu, and in Microsoft Internet Explorer it is under the "Go" menu.

- *Print the currently displayed page.* When you find information that you want to keep, you can print it out by clicking the "Print" button.

SEARCH ENGINES   There is no overall organization for Websites that is similar to a library's card catalog. Thus, when you are researching a speech, it is difficult to know where to look for useful information. You have to roam the Web until you happen to find what you're looking for. With a browser, your search might be immediately productive, or it might take a good deal of time and still you might miss key sites altogether. With so many diverse sites on the Web, it's impossible to visit them all yourself in search of information.

To solve this problem, you need a kind of program called a *search engine,* which scans a gigantic index that is created by robot programs that roam

IdeaList	http://www.contact.org
DejaNews	http://dejanews.com
Thomas, Legislative Information on the Internet	http://thomas.loc.gov
Yahoo! Chat Events	http://events.yahoo.com
ForumOne	http://www.forumone.com
Timecast	http://timecast.com

FIGURE 5.2
Frequently used subject-specific sites.

the Web collecting and indexing its pages. The largest search site is Alta Vista (**<http://altavista.digital.com>**). It contains information from 31 million pages on 476,000 Websites, and its search engine looks through this massive index in a fraction of a second to find key words and phrases.

Another popular search engine is maintained by Yahoo! (**<http://www.yahoo.com>**). Whereas Alta Vista is based on key words, Yahoo! is based on categories, and it shows links to Websites that cover the topics you specify. The difference is dramatic. For example, Yahoo! recently returned a list of 133 categories and 12,284 sites that had the words "Supreme Court decisions" in

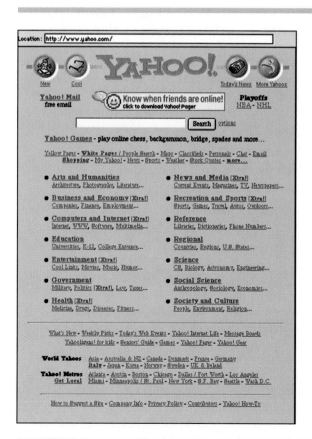

FIGURE 5.3
Search engines such as Alta Vista and Yahoo! are good places to start if you are having difficulty locating information for your speech. Remember, however, that the search engines do not evaluate the reliability of websites—they only identify their availability.

their title or category name. Alta Vista, in contrast, found more than 2 million pages of information using the same search words.

Avoiding Information Overload

Because search engines have massive indexes, they are likely to give far more information about sites than you can absorb, much less use. By making your search as specific as possible, you can trim down the number of sites returned. Suppose that your topic is about drunk driving. Using Alta Vista, type "drunk driving" in the search box and click the "Submit" button. Alta Vista will search its index for all Web pages that have the words "drunk" and "driving." Within seconds you will see that "drunk" was found about 8,000 times and "driving" was found over 43,000 times. There is no way you can consult all those sources, even if you had weeks to prepare your speech. And even if you could, you would find that most of the pages are not pertinent to your topic. How can you avoid this problem?

Try again, but this time type "drunk+driving" in the search box. The + sign ties the two search words together, so now Alta Vista will find only sites that contain them as a phrase. (You can accomplish the same goal by putting the words inside quotation marks.) The new search results in about 200 sites.

Now, if your topic is mainly about laws that govern drunk driving, you can modify the search further. Typing "drunk+driving laws" will make it more likely that you will find what you need within the first several sites.

Now conduct the same search using Yahoo! Type "drunk driving" in the search box, and click the "Search" option. You will find 7 categories that have these words and only about 211 sites with "drunk driving" in the title. Then type "drunk driving laws" and search. You'll find fewer than 10 sites with those words in the title.

Why the big difference between Yahoo! and Alta Vista? Because Yahoo! is looking for titles and categories, whereas Alta Vista is looking only for the words. Conduct searches in both sites, and see which you like better. Following are some other search engines that you may want to explore:

Excite	http://www.excite.com
Info Seek	http://www.infoseek.com
Lycos	http://www.lycos.com
Web Crawler	http://www.webcrawler.com

The + sign is one way that you can narrow the scope of the search. Here are some other possibilities:

- **AND** This command causes the search engine to find only Web pages that include *all* the key words you specify (but not necessarily together). For instance, if you entered "drunk AND driving," the search engine will find only Web pages that use both words.
- **NEAR** This command is used to find Web pages on which two words are close to each other. For example, "drunk NEAR driving" will lead you to pages that include such phrases as "driving while one is drunk." Various search engines have different tolerances for "closeness," but usually the search terms must be within six or eight words of each other.
- **NOT** The NOT command allows you to make a distinction between closely related terms, when you know which key words you

want to eliminate. For example, "DWI NOT DUI" will locate pages with the term "DWI" (driving while intoxicated) but not any related pages that use the term "DUI" (driving under the influence).

Finding Useful Information

Since anyone can construct a Website for any reason, the Web includes information that is biased, out of date, or simply inaccurate. But it also contains the most recent information about topics of current interest. You have to figure out where to look.

Pay special attention to the home pages of government agencies and think tanks. These organizations conduct extensive research and release policy papers on a range of issues. One of the most comprehensive is the Electronic Policy Net, <http://www.epn.org/>, which includes an easily navigated image map. Clicking a location on this map brings you to the home page for a particular subject, such as "Health Policy." When you arrive at the page for health-related issues, you will see a variety of specific subjects. Click on one of these, and you will enter a hypertext analysis of the issue.

Think tanks are often not neutral but are supported by organizations with a particular ideological perspective. The Electronic Policy Net, for instance, labels itself a progressive organization. You can find a wide range of think tanks at **Allyn & Bacon's Public Speaking Website** under the link for "Social Problems and Social Policy" (<http://www.abacon.com/pubspeak/topic.html>).

Evaluating Internet Evidence

In Chapter 6 we will consider how to decide whether your supporting materials are of good quality and really do support your claims. Here, however, because the presence of information on the Internet is almost completely unregulated, we need to note some special precautions about supporting materials from electronic sources. The following questions are especially pertinent.[3]

- *Who set up the Website?* If you cannot tell who sponsors the site, be suspicious of its contents. People or organizations with an ax to grind can disguise their motivations or identity, leading you to regard biased information as though it were neutral. One clue to a site's reliability is its *domain name*—the last portion of its URL. As a general rule, URLs that end in **<.gov>** (government agency) or **<.edu>** (educational institution) may be more reliable sites than those ending in **<.org>** (organization) or **<.com>** (commercial source).

- *When was the site last updated?* The value of the World Wide Web is that it can supply up-to-the-minute information about current topics. Often, however, sites are not updated regularly, and the information becomes obsolete. If you cannot tell when a site was last updated, that may be a reason to be wary of its content.

- *Can you confirm the information?* If something seems too good to be true, it probably is. And if you find information on the Web that seems to make your case airtight or to refute someone's ideas conclusively, be careful. A good general rule is to check electronic information against other sources. Even if you can't find the exact same facts or ideas, what you obtain from the Web should be compatible with what you learn from people or in print.

APPLYING STRATEGIES

The Hardest Thing about Doing Research

Laura Breland

When investigating a topic, I try to find the most outrageous things about it. The more unique, the better for me. Gather many sources and eliminate some of them that will hurt more than help the speech.

Latif Faraq

The hardest thing about doing research is the literature review. After going to the library and bringing all the books and journals you need, you have to sit down and read the materials and find out which ones are useful for your topic.

T. J. Brinkerhoff

The hardest thing about doing research is searching the material thoroughly, and concentrating on it long enough to extract the important information.

Carrie Biesel

I did my persuasive speech on automobile safety and I needed to have statistics to back up my personal experience. I went to the library, and all the books I found were very outdated or checked out. I ended up getting on the Internet and finding a lot of information there.

A STRATEGY FOR RESEARCH

Researching for a speech can seem overwhelming. At first the topic may seem so vast that you don't know where to begin. You may not be able to think of any people you should interview, or you may identify so many people that you don't have time to question them all. The resources of a major library can be daunting, and specialized indexes and finding aids may only compound the problem by revealing an even larger mass of material to consider.

Checklist

5.4 Research Strategy Checklist

1. Start early.
2. Determine where you need to go.
3. Bring necessary materials and supplies.
4. Learn the library's layout and the locations of various materials.
5. Develop a preliminary bibliography.
6. Set priorities within the bibliography.
7. Read progressively.
8. Read selectively.
9. Read efficiently.
10. Be open to new ideas.
11. Use multiple sources and evidence of various types.
12. Keep a speech material file.
13. Know when to stop.

A research strategy can make these burdens manageable. Just as you need to understand your speech goals and the means to achieve them, you need to approach research strategically. The following suggestions will help you devise a research strategy.

START EARLY   Your instructor no doubt has warned you not to wait until the last minute to begin preparing your speech. This is sound advice. Research does take time and involves a certain amount of trial and error. The sooner you begin thinking about and working on the speech, the better.

DETERMINE WHERE YOU NEED TO GO   Your topic may require you to do research in the field, in the library, on the Internet, or by a combination of methods. The analysis described in Chapter 4 of the issues related to your topic should help you determine which questions you need to answer and which kinds of research will help you answer them. Keep those questions in mind as you do your research.

BRING NECESSARY MATERIALS AND SUPPLIES   It's frustrating (and often embarrassing) to arrive at the research site and discover that you don't have the materials you need. For example, if you are conducting interviews, you may need a tape recorder, tapes, and batteries or an extension cord as well as a notebook and pen. In the library you may need notecards, pencils or pens, computer disks, and correct change for the photocopying machine. Think ahead, and be prepared.

LEARN THE LIBRARY'S LAYOUT   You do not want to waste valuable research time figuring out how the library is arranged and where things are. You should know your way around. Learn where to find the card catalog, the reference room, and the stacks. Find out where periodicals, newspapers, and government publications are kept. Learn whether copying and computer equipment is available and what the library's hours and procedures are. If your library offers an orientation tour, arrange to take it even before you begin intensive research for your speech.

DEVELOP A PRELIMINARY BIBLIOGRAPHY   Consult the various indexes and reference works described in this chapter to develop a list of potential sources. To save time later, this preliminary bibliography should include the call numbers or other identifying numbers you will need to locate the material.

SET PRIORITIES WITHIN THE BIBLIOGRAPHY   The order of items in your bibliography will probably not reflect the order in which you want to read the materials. Decide what is most important to locate right away. It may be a particular aspect of the topic or a certain kind of source.

READ PROGRESSIVELY   If you are not yet very familiar with your topic, begin by reading general works to gain a background understanding of key terms, major issues, and the origins and development of the subject. This background will prepare you for in-depth reading about the specific issues that you will highlight in your speech. Finally, there probably are particular claims or arguments for which you will need support: a specific example, a particular statistic, or a certain piece of testimony. As you proceed through your research, be clear about what level of understanding you seek. In general, if you find yourself reading about the same points repeatedly in different sources, it is time to move on to a more specialized level of research.

READ SELECTIVELY   Very likely you will discover far more information than you can read—or even skim—in the time you have to prepare your speech. The key is to be selective in what you read. For example, check the dates of available sources. For some topics, such as whether a recession is likely to occur in the next year, very recent material is crucial. For other topics, such as the origins of the Social Security system, older material may actually be more valuable. If the date seems inappropriate for your purpose, don't bother consulting that source.

READ EFFICIENTLY   Doing research is not like reading a novel; you want to read quickly and efficiently, not from cover to cover. The goal is to identify which elements of a document or source are most pertinent for your speech. Skim material, looking for key words and a general sense of the context. Use guides—such as a book's table of contents, index, and headings—to determine which sections to read carefully and which you may skim or skip. Stay alert, however; efficiency is not haste, and you do not want to make a wrong turn somewhere that causes you to misunderstand the context of key points.

BE OPEN TO NEW IDEAS   Even though you are reading with a particular goal in mind, keep open the possibility that your research may change your perspective or uncover something about your topic that you had not considered. You might discover issues that you did not originally anticipate, and you might even decide to change your thesis statement.

USE MULTIPLE SOURCES AND EVIDENCE OF VARIOUS TYPES   Your speech will be less credible if all the supporting material comes from a single source or is of one type. If you use a single source to support your claims, the audience may think that you are simply parroting the thoughts of someone else, which may leave you open to the charge of **plagiarism.** Although plagiarism usually involves the use of someone else's words as though they were your own, it also applies to the use of someone else's ideas. Even if you cite the source properly, you may invite trouble. For example, one student's speech about recycling presented the same information, in the same order, as did a pamphlet that had been distributed to every student on campus. Not only did this student bore the audience with information they already had, but she made them angry, since they thought she was trying to avoid the work of amassing evidence from different sources and arranging it creatively for their benefit.

Likewise, the speech will be less interesting if all your evidence is of the same type. A mix of examples, testimony, statistics, and other types of support not only will hold the audience's attention but also will add credibility to your claims by suggesting that the same conclusion was reached through several different methods.

KEEP A SPEECH MATERIAL FILE   Sometimes you will find materials that could be useful in a speech while you are doing something else—reading the newspaper, watching television, conversing with others, or studying for other courses. Don't lose track of this material or assume that you can find it when

plagiarism
Using someone else's words or ideas as though they were your own.

you need it. If you think that you may want to talk about a subject later in the term, begin now to save relevant material as you come across it.

Experienced speakers develop a **speech material file.** The file might be a notebook in which you jot down ideas, quotations, stories, poetry, or interesting examples. It might be a file of clippings from newspaper or magazine articles. The form of the file is not as important as the habit of keeping one. You will be pleasantly surprised by how much easier it is to prepare a speech when you do not have to start literally from scratch, when you already have materials about topics that interest you.

KNOW WHEN TO STOP   Research is an ongoing activity, and you can always learn more about any topic—especially if you enjoy the subject and like doing research. But there comes a point at which you must stop collecting evidence and assemble the speech, which, after all, has limits of time and scope. Besides, you want to leave enough time for the other steps of preparation; further research will only tell you more about what you already know—and more than you can possibly tell the audience. Considerations like these should help you to determine when it is time to move on to the other steps of speech preparation. As you develop the speech, you can return to research as needed to fill specific holes.

NOTE TAKING AND FILING

No matter how thorough or extensive your research is, it will do you little good if you forget what you learned or where you learned it. Sometimes, something will seem so vivid or so obvious that you cannot imagine forgetting it, but most people remember far less than they think they will. Experienced speakers have learned to keep track of their speech material by establishing some system of note taking. Be guided by whatever works best for you, but the following suggestions should help you to establish an effective note-taking system.

USE A FLEXIBLE SYSTEM   Recording each idea, statistic, example, quotation, and the like on an individual notecard or sheet of paper is better than taking continuous notes about different topics or taking notes in a spiral notebook or other bound book. A flexible system is one that makes it easy to sort and rearrange material in organizing the speech, to locate related materials, and to discard items that you decide not to use. Taking notes on a computer may be the most flexible system, as long as you can rearrange the notes easily in developing the speech.

When taking notes from electronic sources, you can follow the same methods described here—copying material from the monitor onto notecards or sheets of paper. But there are also programs that enable you to take notes electronically. One such program, distributed by Allyn & Bacon, is Q•Notes. It enables you to select electronic information for later reference and to capture the source information. The program creates notecards with the information, allows you to add comments to each card, and organizes and files the notecards for later use. It also allows you to keep track of sources and to build references and footnotes.

speech material file
A file of clippings, quotations, ideas, and other gleanings on a variety of subjects that may be used as supporting materials.

Author Card—Computer Display

Search request: **F PA MISHARA, BRIAN**
Search result: **5 records at all libraries**

Type **HELP** for other display options.

1.
Author: **Mishara, Brian L.**
Title: **Alcohol and old age / by Brian L. Mishara
               and Robert Kastenbaum.
                 New York : Grune & Stratton, c1980.**
Description: **ix, 220 p. ; 24 cm.**

Series: **Seminars in psychiatry.**

Notes: **Includes bibliographical references and
               index.**

Subjects: **Aged -- Alcohol use.
               Alcohol -- Physiological effect.
               Geriatric psychiatry.**

Other entries: **Kastenbaum, Robert, joint author.
               Seminars in psychiatry (New York, N.Y. :
               1975)
               (Record 1 continues on the next screen.)**

Press **RETURN** to see the next screen.
- > f su aged alcohol use

INCLUDE FULL BIBLIOGRAPHIC CITATIONS   A "full" citation contains all the material needed to find the source from which you took notes. This step may seem time consuming, but you can make it more efficient through careful use of abbreviations. In any case, it should not be omitted. First, you often will need to go back to the original source to verify your notes, to check their context, or to compare them with other sources. Second, the bibliographic information will often be helpful in evaluating the strength of evidence or in choosing among different sources of evidence. It takes far more time and effort to find the source a second time than to note its full bibliographic citation while doing research.

Because standard guides for citing sources often neglect electronic material, the following suggestions should be helpful:[4]

- If the Internet material has a print equivalent, begin with the citation for the hard-copy version, and then proceed through the following steps.
- If the Internet posting has no apparent print equivalent, identify the name of the article in quotation marks, then identify and italicize the name of any larger complete work or any institutional association that sponsors the information.
- Give any other identifying file number or version number that is available.
- Give any available date for the origin or the posting of the document, without parentheses.

- Give an exact citation of the Internet address or the URL locator for the Website. Preserve slashes, mechanics, and spaces within the address. Do not add a final period.
- Follow this immediately with the date of your access to the posting, enclosed within parentheses, followed by a period.

DECIDE WHETHER TO QUOTE OR TO PARAPHRASE THE SOURCE
It takes less thought but more time simply to copy the exact words of the source. Unless an exact quotation is necessary, it is more efficient to paraphrase, to summarize the gist of the idea in your own words. Obviously, your note-taking system should signal to you at a glance whether a note is quoted or not. A good method is to enclose the words of others in quotation marks but to omit them from your own paraphrases or summaries.

CLEARLY IDENTIFY DELETIONS AND ADDITIONS IN QUOTED MATERIAL
Sometimes the quotation you want to use is interspersed with other material that is unrelated to your purposes or is longer than you want to quote. At other times the quotation may not be clear unless you add some words—for example, to identify the reference of a pronoun in the quotation.

When you use a quotation, you must make certain that all deletions and insertions are faithful to the context of the original source. Your notes should identify any variations from the exact text of the quotation. The most common practice is to identify deletions in your notes with an ellipsis (a series of three dots, like this . . .) and to identify insertions in notes with brackets (like this [ ]). It is important to use brackets rather than parentheses, because parentheses would indicate that the inserted words were in the original source. (In the speech itself, use changes in pitch or rate to identify insertions or deletions.)

TAKE NOTES ONLY ONCE
If you take notes in longhand, be sure that you write legibly so that you do not have to recopy or type the notes. Duplicate note taking is a waste of time. Increasingly, laptop computers are used for note taking, which overcomes the problem of unclear handwriting. A computer also lets you take notes in continuous fashion and later print them out on separate sheets of paper, as recommended earlier. Or you may keep your notes in electronic files that you can search and manipulate as needs arise.

Summary

Research locates the supporting materials to be used in the speech. These materials are of many types, including personal experience, common knowledge, direct observation, examples, documents, statistics, and testimony. They can be found from people, in print, and electronically. Supporting materials from people include personal experience and interviews. Among printed sources of supporting material are books, reference works, periodicals, newspapers, and government publications. There are special indexes and finding aids for many of these sources of supporting material.

Computer technology makes it possible to find supporting material on the World Wide Web by using a browser or a search engine. With appropriate search strategies you can avoid information overload and find useful material. Because few if any restrictions govern Internet publication, electronic evidence must be evaluated with special care.

Although the process of researching a speech can seem overwhelming, it can be managed by developing a research strategy. Such a strategy includes beginning early, being clear about what is needed and where it can be found, setting priorities and reading materials progressively and efficiently, taking useful notes, and developing the habit of maintaining a speech material file.

Discussion Questions

1. Which types of supporting material would you need to back up the thesis "Television programs have too much violence"? Evaluate each type of supporting material, and determine which part of the thesis each type would best support.

2. With a group, discuss the pros and cons of the following sources of supporting material, including the situations in which each type would be most appropriate:

   Personal experience
   Interviews
   Library research
   The Internet

Activities

1. In researching a thesis of your choice, find an example of each type of supporting material. Test the strength of each type to determine which material would best support your thesis.

2. Conduct an interview, following the guidelines offered in this chapter.

3. Follow the directions in this chapter for using the Internet to research your speech. Did the browsers and search engines work effectively? Did you find relevant information without being swamped by irrelevant material? How did you determine which material was relevant and trustworthy?

Using the Internet

1. **Using online library resources.** The Internet can be useful to assist in traditional library research. You can use the Internet to access the card catalogs of many libraries. This will help you determine what kind of resources are available on your topic.

   Check out the **Library of Congress** for starters. Point your browser to <http://lcweb.loc.gov/homepage/lchp.html> and click on the link for searching the catalogs. The online librarians will provide instructions for doing Web-based searching with key words and for browsing online. In addition, you will see an explanation of how to use Telnet, a different computer program than your Web browser, to do "Command Search."

   You may also be able to find the card catalog for your college library or a public library near you. A good clearinghouse for finding the online resources to use in your area is **Libweb,** located at the University of California, Berkeley campus. Go to <http://sunsite.berkeley.edu/Libweb/>. Notice that you can find links to libraries of various kinds—and from all over the world.

(continued)

Libraries differ in their protocols for doing online searches. Many use the types of searching that you learned how to do at the Library of Congress site: Web-based searches with key words, browsing through lists, or using Telnet commands.

2. **Finding information from U.S. government agencies.** Check especially at **FedWorld,** which links you to most of the agencies of the U.S. government. Point your browser to **<http://www.fedworld.gov/>**. A second valuable source for online government information is **FedStats.** This page reports on studies that have been done by various government agencies, and particularly empirical studies that gather statistical data. Go to **<http://www.fedstats.gov/>**. Of special note is the A–Z search function, which lists topics in alphabetical order. Or click on the link for "Agencies," which takes you to pages for different federal offices.

3. **Finding and citing online research sources.** Do an interactive exercise from the **Allyn & Bacon Public Speaking Website** that guides you through the process of doing a variety of types of online research. You will also learn how to cite an online source using the MLA (Modern Language Association) guidelines. Go to **<http://www.abacon.com/pubspeak/exercise/mlaexer.html/>**.

Note, once again, that you have the option of sending a copy of your results page to your professor or to yourself. You may also print a hard copy. Click on the various links to pages that will take you step by step through:

Using search engines such as Alta Vista and Yahoo!

Sources for finding and citing online periodicals and journals

An exercise for finding an online speech text and citing it

4. **Finding online newspapers.** There are thousands of newspapers worldwide online. Find most of them at **Editor & Publisher MediaINFO** links. Go to **<http://www.mediainfo.com/ephome/npaper/nphtm/online.htm/>**. From there you can browse by continent or enter a keyword search term to find a newspaper. Some newspapers will require that you register with them. This service is usually free, and may require that you provide an e-mail address.

Notes

1. Thomas B. Farrell, "Knowledge, Consensus, and Rhetorical Theory," *Quarterly Journal of Speech,* 62 (February 1976): 1–14.
2. For more on the misuse of statistics, see John Allen Paulos, *Innumeracy: Mathematical Illiteracy and Its Consequences,* New York: Hill and Wang, 1988.
3. Some of the problems with doing electronic research are explained in Steven B. Knowlton, "How Students Get Lost in Cyberspace," *The New York Times,* "Education Life" section (Nov. 2, 1997): 18, 21.
4. For more information about how to cite electronic sources, see Janice R. Walker and Todd Taylor, *Columbia Guide to Online Style,* New York: Columbia Univ. Press, 1998.

chapter 6
Reasoning

In This Chapter We Will:

- Examine the nature of rhetorical proof in public speaking and learn how it differs from proof in formal logic or mathematics.

- Identify the three components of rhetorical proof: claim, supporting material, and reasoning.

- Explore six basic patterns of reasoning, focusing on their types, appropriate tests of their soundness, and how to use them in a speech.

- Learn what a fallacy is and identify both general fallacies and fallacies that correspond to particular patterns of reasoning.

- Appreciate how an understanding of reasoning processes helps in preparing and delivering a speech and in being an active, critical listener.

By now, you have analyzed your situation, picked a good topic, and assembled some useful supporting materials. But how do you know whether these materials actually prove the point you want to make? In this chapter you will learn about proof in public speaking and how to strengthen the reasoning in your speech.

Consider the following claims:

- 2 + 2]= 4
- The sum of the angles of a triangle equals 180 degrees.
- Light travels at 1,086 miles per second.
- *The Mona Lisa* is Leonardo da Vinci's most beautiful painting.
- The semester academic calendar is best for our university.
- The government's economic policy is bad for the country.

The first three statements are mathematical or scientific claims; they are based on a system of rules by which they can be proved with absolute certainty—as long as you operate within that system. The last three claims are different; they involve beliefs, values, and judgments. Although for any of these three you could find evidence that convinces *you* of their truth, someone else might be unimpressed by your evidence or might find counterevidence to argue an opposing point. Therefore, the "proof" of these claims is not offered with the same level of certainty that supports the first three claims.

PROOF, SUPPORT, AND REASONING

The ideas in a speech almost never take the form of a fixed mathematical principle as in the first three claims above. Instead, the basic material of public speaking is like the last three claims, involving matters of belief or value, judgments about what ought to be, norms of conduct, or predictions about the future. Such statements require agreement between the speaker and listeners, not only about the truth of the claim but also about what should count as proof in the first place.[1]

Rhetorical Proof as Support

Rhetorical proof is established through interaction in which the speaker and listeners reason together. This type of proof does not *ensure* that a conclusion is correct, but it offers *support* for a conclusion. It gives listeners confidence that the conclusion is probably correct and that they can share it, make it part of their working knowledge, and act on it if they are able to do so.

Suppose you are speaking to first-time employees about how they should save and invest their money. Research and analysis have convinced you that buying stocks is the best investment, but you can't prove that conclusion because it involves value judgments, predictions, and speculations. To help listeners reach the same conclusion, your speech might draw on statistics, historical accounts of the growth of the stock market, and examples of successful investors. These are called "supporting materials" precisely because their function is to *support* your conclusion. They do not guarantee that your conclusion is correct, but they give listeners good reasons to accept what you say and to act on it.

rhetorical proof
Proof established through interaction between the speaker and the listeners; provides support for a conclusion but not assurance that it is true.

Even as you select proofs that are suited to the specific audience, one standard for a reasonable and ethical argument might be what you would consider suitable for a jury of your peers. With that standard in mind, what would be your strongest arguments in justifying a military action for this audience?

Unlike mathematical proofs, then, rhetorical proofs have degrees of support ranging from strong to weak. As a result, both speakers and listeners must evaluate rhetorical proofs critically, testing them rather than taking them for granted. Your goal as a speaker is to provide the strongest support possible for your conclusion. What factors make rhetorical proof strong?

Proof and the Audience

The overriding factor in supporting a claim is, of course, the audience. Listeners who pay attention to the reasoning in a speech are critical and active; they are willing to be convinced but are skeptical enough to ask whether the speaker's reasoning withstands scrutiny. Critical listeners will ask whether your causal links are valid, whether your comparisons are apt, and whether the people you quote are authorities in the subject—all tests that you will study in this chapter. Knowing that you will face a critical audience helps you as a speaker, because you will make sure that your reasoning is strong. In this way you and your listeners work together to achieve the highest possible standard of rhetorical proof.

Audiences differ, of course, and so you might need different proofs to convince, say, an audience of Democrats that the administration's economic policy is flawed than you would need for an audience of Republicans. But if you focus too narrowly on the immediate audience, you could run into a serious ethical problem: Yes, you may be *able* to convince the audience, but *should* you? Not all audiences are made up of critical listeners (as advertisers know only too well). Indeed, some listeners probably would accept just about any conclusion.

When Adolf Hitler's devoted followers accepted his claims about German racial superiority, did that prove his statements true? The answer to this difficult question turns out to be "yes and no." In a purely functional sense, yes: For those people in that situation, Hitler's claims could be considered proved; believers made the claims part of their working knowledge and acted on them. But in a larger sense, no: Regardless of what Hitler's supporters did or did not believe, they *should not have* accepted his claims, because his reasoning and evidence were flawed.

Speakers need to focus not only on proofs that listeners *actually do* regard as solid but also on proofs that they *ought to* regard as solid. Generally, a proof is **reasonable** if it would be taken seriously by a broad and diverse group of listeners exercising their best critical judgment.[2] Such an audience includes people who actually hear your speech as well as a larger, more culturally diverse audience who might "overhear" it through word of mouth or the media. Think of a well-selected jury of peers in a well-run courtroom as your audience; if such a group of critical listeners would accept your proof, the inference is reasonable.

Even if your actual audience does not resemble such a group, do not abandon your standards. In offering a rhetorical proof, you must satisfy the immediate audience and also must meet a broader standard of reasonableness that would satisfy a larger imagined audience of critical thinkers.

Components of Proof

Any idea in the speech—whether a main point or a subordinate point—can be regarded as a *unit of proof* that has three components: the claim, the supporting material, and the reasoning.

CLAIM   The **claim** is the statement that you want the audience to accept; it is what you are trying to prove. The claim could be your broad thesis ("Popular music has changed greatly since 1960"), or one main idea ("Music videos have added a new dimension to popular music"), or a specific subpoint ("Having a video aired on MTV is now as important as getting radio time").

SUPPORTING MATERIAL   This second component of a proof, examined in Chapter 5, provides *evidence* for your claim. To prove your claim, you must link supporting material to it.

REASONING   It is reasoning that links the supporting material to your claim so that you and your listeners together can decide whether the evidence really does support the claim.

Usually the claim and the supporting material are stated explicitly in the speech and are easy to identify. But the essential link, reasoning, is usually implied; it involves a mental leap from the supporting material to the claim. This leap is called an **inference.** The inference enables us to say that, even though we are going beyond what the supporting material literally says, we feel justified in doing so because similar inferences in the past have usually led to acceptable results.[3]

reasonable
Would be inferred by most people when exercising their critical judgment.

claim
A statement that a speaker asks listeners to accept and that the speaker tries to prove.

inference
A mental leap from the supporting material to the claim.

An Example of Rhetorical Proof

After introducing a speech about the effect of tax increases on a family's budget, student Catherine Archer claimed:

> Taxes have taken a bigger bite out of the average paycheck each year. Just look at the record. Our state sales taxes have gone up faster than our income. Local property taxes have gone through the roof. And now the federal government is proposing to raise gasoline taxes again. Where does it all stop?

After the speech, she invited questions from the floor. "What about Social Security?" one woman asked. Catherine replied:

> Thank you. That's still one more example of a tax that has gone up faster than income. In fact, many people today pay more in Social Security tax than in their income tax.

Then a man in the audience said, "Since you mentioned income taxes, I want to remind you about the tax cuts passed by Congress in 1997, especially the capital gains cut"; he seemed to imply that Catherine had not considered *all* the possible taxes and had jumped to a conclusion. She didn't disagree with the man but restated her claim: "You're right about capital gains, but other taxes have gone up so much that my main point is still true."

This example illustrates five important aspects of rhetorical proof:

1. Reasoning plays the crucial role in linking supporting material to the claim. Catherine's reasoning connected specific examples to her claim that taxes take a larger share of the paycheck each year.

2. Reasoning depends on an inference but cannot guarantee that the inference is "right." Nonetheless, we still can apply tests of soundness. In this case, for instance, do the examples really represent the overall tax picture, or has Catherine left out some important categories?

3. An inference often takes the form of an implicit statement that some general rule is being followed. Catherine's reasoning implied: "These examples of tax increases are significant and representative."

4. The speaker and listeners together decide whether the inference is sound. This audience participated by asking questions that helped to identify possible problems with Catherine's inference, and she had a chance to address their concerns. Together, speaker and audience probably became more confident about the inference.

5. Nothing can guarantee that the inference of a rhetorical proof is correct, but over time tests have evolved to distinguish between good and bad inferences. Asking whether Catherine's examples represent all categories of taxes is one such test.

Using Rhetorical Proof in Your Speech

Figure 6.1 on page 152 shows the relationships among claims, supporting material, and reasoning. It shows the "inner workings" of the speech, thus enhancing the view of the rhetorical situation depicted in Chapter 4 (see Fig. 4.3).

The best time to construct effective reasoning relationships is after you research the speech. Your outline (discussed briefly in Chapter 1 and fully in Chapter 9) will help you to see what is used as supporting material for each

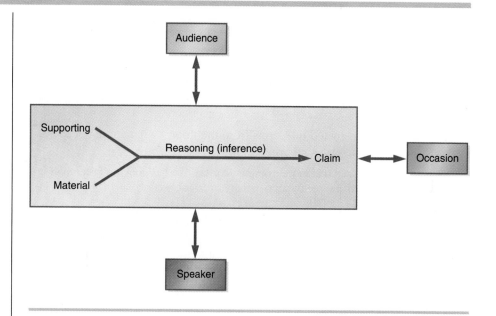

claim. As Figure 6.2 shows, each Roman numeral in the outline identifies a main idea that supports your thesis statement, and each capital letter represents supporting material for that main idea. At a smaller level, each capital letter marks a claim that is supported by all the Arabic numbers under it, which, in turn, are supported by the lowercase letters, and so on.

Beginning with the smallest claims in your outline, examine the supporting material for proofs; then identify what kind of link (inference) will best connect the supporting material to each claim. In this chapter are practical methods to help you discover appropriate links and to test whether they will make the connection that you want to make with your audience.

To help you develop convincing rhetorical proofs, next we will discuss six broad categories of reasoning: example, analogy, sign, cause, testimony, and narrative. For each category the discussion first will focus on the variety of types, then on some tests to discover errors in reasoning, and finally on suggestions for using each reasoning pattern in a speech.

FIGURE 6.2

An outline reveals links in reasoning.

II. Lack of variety is not a valid complaint against Campus Food Service.
  A. You get more choices than you would at home.
    1. Each day there are 3 main entrees and a vegetarian meal.
    2. There also are other options.
      a. A salad bar
      b. Cereals
      c. Breads
      d. Soups
  B. A special dinner is offered once each month.

APPLYING STRATEGIES

The Use of Reasoning in Speeches

Laura Breland

I think [the way to decide on] a strategy for reasoning is to find the one that best suits the speaker when he or she is preparing a speech. If the speaker adapts to inductive reasoning, then he or she should use that strategy more in his or her speech. If the speaker adapts to deductive reasoning, he or she should use that strategy more in his or her speech.

Carrie Biesel

I guess my best example of that would be in my persuasive [speech], too. I didn't just spout a bunch of meaningless facts and statistics. I talked about a car accident I was in personally and the effects it had on me, physically and emotionally, and on my family, the families of others that were involved in the accident, etc. That made it hit home more and seem more like "that could happen to me."

Latif Faraq

I noticed in the speeches given by the students in my class that if there is no reasoning in a speech, the audience will be doing something else rather than listening to it. But, if there is reasoning in the speech, all the class will pay attention and support the speech.

T. J Brinkerhoff

Using reasoning in speeches is important in supporting your topic, especially in a persuasive or argumentative speech. Speeches that are filled with facts and statistics, but are absent of supporting logic, do not help listeners develop an opinion of the subject. Using a line of reasoning one way or the other helps an audience form an opinion either for or against your stance. Hopefully, using effective, sound, and documented reasoning will help your speech have more strength and credibility.

STRATEGIES FOR REASONING THROUGH EXAMPLE

Probably the most common reasoning pattern in public speaking is inference from example. **Examples** are specific instances that are used to illustrate a more general claim; the inference is that the specific is typical of the general. For *example:*

- A tourist notices that three downtown streets are deserted at midday and infers that businesses in that town are not doing well.
- On four occasions a student succeeds in visiting faculty members during their office hours and infers that instructors are conscientious and accessible.

examples
Specific instances used to illustrate a more general claim.

- A researcher discovers that 15 percent of the people in one community lack health insurance and infers that about 15 percent of the country's population has no health insurance.

- Believing that most politicians cannot be trusted, a citizen infers that neither of the candidates for mayor can be trusted.

In each example someone has brought together a statement about a particular situation and a statement about a general claim and has attempted to relate the two. Whether proceeding from specific to general (the first three examples) or from general to specific (the last example), the inference is that particular cases are **representative** of the general category. To say that they are representative is to say that they are typical cases, that there is nothing unusual about them.[4]

A moment's thought shows why representativeness is important. Suppose that, although three downtown streets were deserted, traffic jams occurred near all the city's shopping malls; then the tourist would not be justified in drawing a general conclusion from the specific case observed. Or imagine that the student's four successful visits were all on days when faculty members were careful to hold office hours because they were advising majors for next semester's registration; then it would not be valid to infer that instructors are accessible at other times.

In short, if the particular cases are *not* typical (not representative), then we cannot confidently infer that what is true of them is true in general. Again, inferences cannot be guaranteed as mathematical proofs can be. But even if we can't be absolutely certain that examples are representative, we can still try to select them in a way that removes all known causes of distortion or bias.

Types of Inference from Example

Speakers use many different types of examples, depending on their purposes. The following three considerations are especially pertinent in selecting examples.

INDIVIDUAL VERSUS AGGREGATE EXAMPLES Sometimes a speaker describes individual occurrences of an example. John, Martha, and Claude, for instance, are all friends of the speaker who had to interrupt their education for financial reasons; by talking about each of them, the speaker supports the inference that the cost of a college education is a serious concern.

At other times, individual cases will be less convincing than an aggregate statistical example. Because 50 percent of students in a national survey report that they have seen someone cheat on an examination, the speaker infers that probably half the students on campus have witnessed such behavior.

FACTUAL VERSUS HYPOTHETICAL EXAMPLES Factual examples are actual occurrences; whether individual or aggregate, they are "real." In

representative
Typical of the larger category from which a case is selected.

When your argument is based on quite specific examples, you must try to show that these examples are typical. This speaker believes, as her poster claims, that "many people" deal with the problem of HIV by denial.

This is the way many people deal with HIV.

contrast, a speaker may construct hypothetical examples, creating a vivid (but imaginary) illustration of something abstract. To describe the problems of homelessness, for example, a speaker might invent a hypothetical character whose daily experiences are typical of homeless people generally.

A speaker may have good reasons to offer a hypothetical example rather than a factual one, but the invention should be acknowledged and should never be treated as fact. One journalist received a Pulitzer Prize for a series of stories describing the plight of a child who was addicted to drugs; when it came to light that this child was hypothetical rather than a real person (as the stories had intimated), the prize was withdrawn.

BRIEF VERSUS EXTENDED EXAMPLES   Sometimes a quick list of examples is effective, because the speaker's emphasis is on the existence and number of cases rather than on their details. Thus, to establish that many students are worried about the cost of education, a brief mention of John, Martha, and Claude should support the claim.

But suppose the speaker wants listeners to understand what students go through when financial problems make them leave school. Then it would be more effective to offer a more complete description of just one case. Better than to simply report that John had to leave school for financial reasons would be to describe the events that led to his decision—the conversations between him and his parents, how he broke the news to his friends, and what his life has been like since leaving.

Checklist

6.1   *Tests for Inference from Example*

----

1. **Are there enough examples?**
2. **Do all the examples represent the category?**
3. **Are the examples ambiguous?**
4. **Are the examples fallacious? Do any examples assume that**

- *what is true of the part must be true of the whole (fallacy of composition)?*
- *what is true of the whole must be true of the part (fallacy of division)?*

Tests for Inference from Example

Inference from example will be accepted as reasonable if listeners have no reason to doubt it. Ask yourself these questions when using inference from example to support your claim:

1. *Are there enough examples?* If the number of examples is very small, particularly in making a statistical generalization, the sample may not include significant features of the population as a whole. If you claim that more students are graduating from high school than ever before, because *your* high school graduated a record number of students, the audience may doubt your inference; your high school is only one of thousands.

2. *Do the examples represent the whole category?* If all the cases you cite are alike in some way that distorts your inference—say you use only fraternity members as examples to support some point about *all* college students— your claim will be weakened.

3. *Are the examples ambiguous?* Sometimes a single example can support different inferences, making it a poor example. If 70 percent of employees are dissatisfied with the company's new computer system, one speaker may claim that the new system is flawed; but another speaker may claim that employees need more training to understand the new system. Which claim is the audience to believe?

4. *Are the examples fallacious?* Although the point of an inference by example is to relate the part and the whole, be aware that the parts do not always add up to the whole. The **fallacy of composition** results from assuming that what is true of the part is automatically true of the whole. ("The instructor enjoys this class very much, and so the students must enjoy this class, too.") Conversely, the **fallacy of division** results from assuming that what is true of the whole is automatically true of the part. ("The students are excited about the homecoming game, and so the instructor must be excited, too.")

Guidelines for Reasoning through Example

1. *Limit the number of examples.* You want enough examples to indicate a pattern that supports your inference, but you don't want to risk boring the

fallacy of composition
Assuming that what is true of the part is automatically true of the whole.

fallacy of division
Assuming that what is true of the whole is automatically true of the part.

audience with unnecessary examples. Consider your purpose and audience carefully; a single example may be enough.

2. *Make sure each example is believable.* Even one unbelievable example can undermine your inference—and your entire point.

3. *Avoid obvious, overused examples.* If you tell listeners what they already know, your inferences may seem trivial or trite. Seek novel examples that might surprise the audience. Arguing against censorship, for example, student Sarah McAdams skipped the standard example of book burning in Nazi Germany; instead, she surprised listeners by citing examples of U.S. censorship:

> In 1925, anyone caught teaching Darwin's *Origin of Species* in a Tennessee public school was fined. In 1933 a young actor was arrested for smuggling an illegal item into the United States. That item was James Joyce's *Ulysses*—a book that is now considered a literary masterpiece. In 1980, some high school students were forced to read an edited version of Shakespeare's *Romeo and Juliet* because parents and teachers thought the original play was too racy.

4. *Match the details of examples to your purpose.* If your main point is the very existence of the example, few details are needed. But if you want to show the audience exactly how the example illustrates your inference, supply more detail.

5. *Make the examples memorable.* After selecting enough believable, fresh examples, bring your inference to life for the audience by carefully selecting details and describing the examples vividly. We will pursue this goal in Chapter 10, "Achieving Style through Language."

STRATEGIES FOR REASONING THROUGH ANALOGY

An **analogy** is a comparison of people, places, things, events, or more abstract relationships. Whereas the key feature of inference from example is the link between the parts and the whole, the key feature of inference from analogy is a comparison between the known and the unknown.

Suppose your college is considering a major investment in the athletic program, hoping to increase alumni contributions through successful athletic competition. You don't know whether that will happen, but you do know that a similar school increased alumni contributions after overhauling its athletic program, and so you infer that your school will benefit similarly.

An inference from analogy asks the audience to accept the idea that items that are basically alike in most respects will also be alike in the particular respect being discussed.

Analogical inferences are prominent in public speaking because they are psychologically appealing to an audience. They enable us to accept something that is unknown because it is similar to something that we do know.[5]

Types of Inference from Analogy

Depending on whether the comparison between things is direct or concerns their relationships, an analogy is either literal or figurative.[6]

analogy
A comparison of people, places, things, events, or more abstract relationships.

LITERAL ANALOGIES A **literal analogy** is a *direct* comparison of objects, people, or events. A speaker who says, "Illinois will not be able to escape the recession, which has already hit Michigan—another Midwestern industrial state" is directly comparing Illinois to Michigan. The inference is that, because Illinois is basically like Michigan, it too will probably face recession.

Speakers often use literal analogies to suggest that one action or event is a *precedent* for another—that actual experience with one enables us to predict what will happen with the other. Student Cecilia Villa took this approach in arguing that the proposed budget for the space station was too optimistic:

> The experts tell us that the space station will cost only $37 billion. But this figure will surely increase. Look at the Hubble space telescope. This piece of NASA engineering went $60 billion over budget, and it still didn't work when it was launched!

FIGURATIVE ANALOGIES A **figurative analogy** compares the *relationships* between objects, people, or events in order to make complex or abstract statements more vivid and more concrete. Again, the comparison begins with something the audience already knows.

Suppose you wanted to claim that the Social Security System will face financial problems around the year 2020 as "baby boomers" reach retirement age. You could support your claim with statistics, of course, but that could be tedious and would work far better in print than in a speech. But if you said, "Depending on Social Security for your retirement income is like playing Russian roulette with your future," your comparison would make the statistics— and your point—clear: Social Security is a gamble.

Similarly, the speaker predicting a recession in Illinois might add, "Trusting the politicians to find a way to avoid it is like putting the fox in charge of the chicken coop." This speaker is not directly comparing politicians to foxes or the recession to a chicken coop. Rather, the comparison is figurative; it points to *relationships*. The politicians stand in the same relationship to the recession that the fox does to the chicken coop. In both cases those who supposedly are protecting something are really a grave threat to it.

literal analogy
A direct comparison of objects, people, or events.

figurative analogy
A comparison of the relationships between objects, people, or events.

Tests for Inference through Analogy

As we saw concerning inferences from example, things may be *similar*, but they are never completely *identical*. Thus, as with examples, we can never be sure that an analogy is completely valid. No matter how similar things are, they are also different in some respects.

Checklist

6.2 *Tests for Inference from Analogy*

1. **Are there basic differences as well as similarities?**

2. **Do the differences outweigh the similarities?**

For an analogy to be strong and compelling, listeners have to believe that the basic similarities between two items outweigh their basic differences. An analogy raises two closely related questions:

1. *Are there basic differences as well as similarities?* Suppose a speaker claims that Detroit and Chicago have similar economic concerns because they are alike in so many ways: Both are northern metropolitan areas, both have large populations, both are surrounded by suburbs that erode the tax base, and so on. Besides these similarities, however, there is an obvious and important difference between the two cities: Detroit's economy has depended on one industry, automobiles, whereas the economy of Chicago is more diversified.

2. *Do the differences outweigh the similarities?* The discovery of differences between items being compared is not, in itself, reason to question the analogy. One has to demonstrate that the differences really do matter. For instance, if a diversified economy protects a city better against recession because workers who lose jobs in one industry can find new jobs in another, then this difference outweighs the similarities between Detroit and Chicago, and the analogy is questionable. But if a weak national economy hurts cities in general—whether or not they have a diversified economy— then this difference between Detroit and Chicago would not matter much, and the analogy would stand.

Guidelines for Reasoning through Analogy

1. *Avoid analogies that are trite or farfetched.* An overused analogy will lose the audience's attention and make the entire speech seem stale, while an analogy with no basis in common sense may call so much attention to itself that it distracts from the point it is supposed to prove. The televised public service announcement that compares the brain to an egg and drugs to hot butter that "fries" the brain has become both farfetched and trite. Its target audience of young people know that their friends who use drugs do not immediately and irreversibly "burn out" their brains. The comparison is exaggerated, and so the target audience dismisses it. In addition, over-exposure to this analogy has led to the sarcastic response, "Does bacon come with that?"

   Financial manager Manuel Gonzalez was more effective in using an analogy to convince operations managers that the company was overextended and risked being bogged down by a product competition it could not win. He compared the company's situation to that of the United States trying unsuccessfully during the 1960s to win the war in Vietnam. He fleshed out the analogy by showing how a lack of understanding of local conditions in each market, plus an unmeasured outpouring of resources in pursuit of vague objectives, was putting the company in the kind of no-win situation that the United States faced in Vietnam. Because the comparison of a company's sales and a nation's military strategy was fresh and because Mr. Gonzalez developed it in detail, the audience paid attention and did not find it farfetched.

2. *Analyze what you are comparing.* Make sure that you understand the essential similarities and differences of the items in your analogy so that you

can argue convincingly that their similarities outweigh their differences and will not be surprised if a listener suggests otherwise. The speaker who compared Detroit's and Chicago's economic outlooks must be ready to respond to a listener's observation that the cities differ in the important factor of economic diversification. If that difference wasn't important to the speaker's main point, the analogy could be defended.

3. *Use analogies sparingly.* Although analogies are a form of inference, they also are like ornaments (to use an analogy of our own). Too many ornaments may hide what they are intended to decorate, and too many analogies in a speech may obscure the main point. Political speaker Ross Perot, for example, uses so many attention-grabbing figurative analogies that they sometimes overwhelm the audience.[7]

STRATEGIES FOR REASONING THROUGH SIGNS

A **sign** is something that stands for something else—which is usually an abstraction or something that we cannot observe directly. The presence of the sign causes us to infer the existence of what it stands for.

If the number of students absent from class increases suddenly, that may be a sign of a flu epidemic. If today's average grades are higher than ten years ago, that may be a sign that grading standards have changed. If homeless people are living on the streets, that may be a sign that public policies are not meeting the needs of the disadvantaged. If wages differ for male and female workers doing similar jobs, that may be a sign of gender discrimination. In each case, we infer that something exists based on something else that presumably is a sign of it.

Types of Inference from Signs

In theory, anything can stand for anything else. In practice, however, inferences from signs fall into several types:

- Physical observation
- Statistical indexes
- Institutional regularity

PHYSICAL OBSERVATION   If the alarm goes off and you don't check the time but you look out the window and see a bright sun, you probably infer that the sun means it's morning. Similarly, through **physical observation** of a bulldozer on an empty campus lot a student inferred that the university was about to construct a new building. The sun and the bulldozer were observable signs of other things that could not be observed.

STATISTICAL INDEX   Many statistical measures are taken as signs. High scores on exams, for instance, are widely accepted as a sign of intelligence. Similarly, the ups and downs of the Dow-Jones Industrial Average are seen to indicate the health of the economy, and a rising Consumer Price Index is regarded as a sign of inflation. Intelligence, economic health, inflation—these are all abstract concepts that cannot be observed directly. But in each case some **statistical index** that we *can* see is regarded as a sign of something that we cannot observe.

sign
Something that stands for something else.

physical observation (as a sign)
Regarding something that can be observed as a sign of something that cannot.

statistical index (as a sign)
A statistical measure that is taken as a sign of an abstraction.

INSTITUTIONAL REGULARITY   **Institutional regularity** is an observable pattern that results from some norm or social convention. For example, since athletic competitions usually begin with the singing of the national anthem, if you turned on your TV and heard people singing it, you might infer that a game was about to begin. In the same way, since diplomatic disagreements often are described by such polite phrases as "They had a frank exchange of views," that phrase in a news story about international negotiations might be a sign that discussions had reached an impasse.

Tests for Inference from Signs

If a sign *always* stood for the same thing, then whenever we observed the sign, we could infer that the abstract concept was present as well. Thus, *whenever* someone scored high on a test, we could infer that the person was intelligent; and *whenever* we heard the national anthem, we could expect a sports event to follow. So certain a sign would be said to be *infallible,* meaning that it predicts with certainty the existence of the thing it signifies.

Reality offers few (if any) infallible signs. To say that something is a sign, then, means that it *usually* signifies something else, although in a given circumstance it might not. The high rate of absenteeism from class may well signify an epidemic, but are students suffering from the flu or spring fever? Because most signs are *fallible* and can be interpreted variously, critical listeners and speakers will subject them to the following tests of reasonableness.

1. *Is an alternative explanation more credible?* Is it more reasonable to suppose that today's higher grades signify harder-working students, or changes in grading standards, or changes in admissions policies? The question can be resolved by gathering other information. If the credentials of entering students have been similar for the past ten years, then it is more reasonable to infer that the higher grades signify changes in grading standards. Examine alternative explanations for a sign before accepting inferences based on it.

2. *Can the alleged sign be found* without *the thing for which it stands?* Although the national anthem is often sung before an athletic contest, it also is sung on many other occasions—at the opening of a patriotic rally, for example, or at the end of a television station's broadcast day. A sign that can be found in a variety of circumstances is not a solid basis for an inference.

3. *Is the sign part of a pattern, or a single unusual case?* If only one instance of gender-based wage differences can be found, that is not a strong sign of discrimination. But if a *pattern* of wage differences can be identified, it is more reasonable to see that as a sign of gender discrimination.

● ● ● ● ● ● ● ● ● ● ● ● ● ● ● ● ● ● ●

institutional regularity (as a sign)
A sign relationship that results from norm or social convention.

Checklist

6.3   *Tests for Inference from Signs*

1. **Is an alternative explanation more credible?**

2. **Can the alleged sign be found *without* the thing for which it stands?**

3. **Is the sign part of a pattern, or a single unusual case?**

Guidelines for Reasoning through Signs

1. *Use sign inferences to link the abstract with the concrete.* Keep in mind that the primary purpose of a sign inference is to predict the existence of something that cannot be observed on the basis of something that can be. Use sign inferences to convince listeners that something they cannot see does, in fact, exist.

2. *Explain the sign relationship clearly.* Make sure your listeners understand exactly *what* you are alleging to be a sign of something else and *why* you think it predicts what you claim. The student speaker who said, "All we have to do is turn on the television set to see signs of the glory of modern civilization," left the audience wondering. Was she referring to the technological achievements of broadcasting? Did she believe that the content of television programs showed the triumph of the human spirit? Or was she actually being sarcastic and preparing to criticize typical television fare?

3. *Point to multiple signs of what you want to infer.* Student Roger Berkson used several signs in a speech. Alone, each sign could be fallible, but together they all pointed in the same direction and gave his inference credibility:

   When I saw that many more students were absent from class lately, I wasn't sure that it meant that they were sick. After all, it was close to midterm exams, and everyone could use more time to study. But then I found out that visits to the infirmary went up, sales at the pharmacy were on the rise, and more beds were in use at the city hospital. Those signs suggest to me that we have a flu epidemic on campus.

4. *Do not claim more for a sign inference than it can establish.* A sign inference claims a predictable relationship between the sign and the thing for which it stands, but it does *not* establish that either one affects the other. Although a rise in the Consumer Price Index may predict inflation, it certainly does not influence, cause, or lead to inflation. This last point highlights an important distinction between sign inferences and our next form of reasoning: inference from cause.

STRATEGIES FOR REASONING THROUGH CAUSE

Unlike a sign inference, a **causal inference** explains the relationship between things by pointing to the influence of one thing on the other.

Suppose the state legislature significantly raises the gasoline tax, which service stations pass along to consumers by raising the price of gasoline, and sales then decline. Is this chain of events a coincidence? We can never know for sure. But it may be reasonable to infer that the price increase affected consumption patterns—that as the cost of gasoline rose, more consumers decided to limit their driving and to conserve gasoline as well as their money.

A causal inference relates things by identifying one as the cause (higher price) and the other as the effect (lower sales). The cause, of course, must both precede and lead to the effect. The scientific method offers procedures for deciding whether to infer such a cause–effect relationship, or *causality*.

cause

A pattern of inference that suggests that one factor brings about another.

Researchers devise controlled testing situations that are alike in every respect and are held constant; then the researchers vary the one factor that they think is the cause. If they get different results, they infer that the difference was caused by the one factor that they changed.

This method of inferring causality is not available to public speakers, who deal with subjects on which a "laboratory" cannot be controlled. The speaker must examine the subject as it is and cannot possibly hold constant its many complex variables. The method for inferring causality, then, is to demonstrate reasons why the cause—effect relationship makes sense and to ask whether any alternative explanation is more plausible.

Types of Inference from Cause

PREDICTION   Some causal inferences explain changes by predicting what leads to what. In a speech about the loss of the ozone layer over the South Pole, a speaker might say, "When we release fluorocarbons from aerosol cans and air-conditioners, we cause the thinning of the ozone layer"; the inference is that fluorocarbons in the atmosphere destroy the layer of ozone that shields us from the sun's ultraviolet rays.

ASSIGNMENT OF RESPONSIBILITY   Another common use of causal inferences is to assign responsibility for something, to explain why it occurred. Suppose you were asked to speak about the question "Why would someone run for president if there were no chance of being elected?" In thinking about the question, you may see other reasons to run for office: to get publicity, to establish political relationships, to add certain issues to the agenda for public discussion, to position oneself to run for vice-president, to have a good time, and to be ready in case leading candidates falter. Through a causal inference, you could present these as reasons or motivations—as causes—for the decision to run.

EXPLANATION   A causal inference also can be used to explain something that otherwise doesn't make sense. Consider this paradox: Why, in the richest nation on earth, are there shortages of funds for virtually every social program? Answering such a question involves finding some element—often unexpected or obscure—that explains the situation. If your inference explains that Americans strongly prefer private over public investment, you would have identified a possible cause of the paradox.

STEPS TO A GOAL   A causal inference also can relate the means to the ends, as when we know our goals and want to determine the best way to attain them. This form of reasoning is used often in problem–solution speeches. If you advocated the development of solar power in order to avoid risking an energy shortage, you would be employing this type of causal inference.[8]

Tests for Inference from Cause

As with the other patterns of reasoning, the rhetorical proof in a causal inference is not ironclad. We may think we understand how one aspect of a situation influences another and yet may be mistaken—as examples throughout

6.4 Tests for Inference from Cause

1. **Has a sign relationship been confused with a causal relationship?**
2. **Does some common cause of both factors make them seem like they have a cause–effect relationship?**
3. **Does the fact that one event occurred after another falsely signify a cause–effect relationship?**
4. **Have important multiple causes or multiple effects been overlooked?**

this chapter have shown. Any of the following analytical errors will make a causal inference less reasonable.

1. *Has a sign relationship been confused with a causal relationship?* Because we know that two things are somehow related, we mistakenly assume that one causes the other. Student Michael Leu, for example, let enthusiasm for his subject overpower his ability to test inferences when he made the following argument:

   The cities of our nation have a desperate problem with gangs. Teenagers shoot each other in the streets in broad daylight with semiautomatic weapons. Now consider the fact that England doesn't have this same level of gang violence in its inner cities. That's because, in England, guns are illegal. Comparing the United States to England, we can see that easy access to guns has caused gang activity in our cities.

   Had Michael tested the inference in his last sentence, he might have recognized a serious flaw in his reasoning. Although an increase in guns may be a *sign* that gangs are active, that sign (guns) is not the *cause* of gangs.

2. *Does some common cause of both factors make it seem like they have a cause–effect relationship?* This reasoning error alleges that one factor is the cause of another, although in fact *both* manifest some third cause. If you fall prey to the **common cause fallacy,** you may mistakenly remove what you think is the cause of a problem, only to discover that nothing changes.

   For example, the fact that students in wealthy school districts generally score higher on standardized tests than do students in poorer districts may seem at first glance to prove that higher spending for education results in higher test scores. But some have argued that the real reason why wealthy districts score better is that the families who live in them can afford to give their children reading and travel experiences and even personal computers—and that this enrichment at home leads *both* to higher test scores and to pressure on school districts to spend more for education.

3. *Is there a* post hoc *fallacy?* In Latin *post hoc* means "after this"; thus a **post hoc fallacy** occurs if you assume that, because one event occurred *after* another, it was *caused by* the earlier event. This reasoning error comes up often in political speeches. Republicans observe that the Cold War ended after President Reagan took office and assume that he should get credit for

common cause fallacy
Assuming that one thing causes another when in fact a third factor really is the cause of both.

post hoc fallacy
Assuming that, because one event occurred before another, the first is necessarily the cause of the second.

it; Democrats point to a recession while President Bush was in office and blame him for it. Can we reasonably infer that the end of the Cold War and the onset of recession were caused by these two presidents?

4. *Have important multiple causes or multiple effects been overlooked?* If a problem has multiple causes, acting to remove a single cause is unlikely to solve the problem. Consider the high cost of health care. One important cause is the inefficient distribution of doctors—most practice in large cities rather than in smaller communities and rural areas. But forcing doctors to move will not solve the problem, because other factors also cause health costs to rise: the small total number of doctors, their inability to control fees, the costs of advances in medical technology, and changes in the insurance industry.

Likewise, a particular action may have multiple effects, some of which may be undesirable. Student speaker Demetris Papademetriou overlooked this when he used a causal inference to argue for the legalization of marijuana:

No one wants to lose the forests of America. But in our modern society, we need paper, and wood is an essential ingredient in paper. Even with recycling, we are forced to cut trees at an alarming rate. But we shouldn't lose all hope. There is a type of plant that could save our trees. By legalizing marijuana, we could use the hemp to make paper, just as our forefathers did when they produced the paper on which the Constitution is written.

Talking with classmates after his speech, Demetris found that he had not convinced them because he had neglected another possible effect of legalizing marijuana. Besides producing more paper, his "solution" could lead to increased use of other drugs—an effect the audience wasn't willing to risk.

Guidelines for Reasoning through Cause

1. *Analyze what the alleged cause is and how it exerts its influence on the effect.* A student speaker who ignored this advice argued that the position of the stars on a person's birthday causes that person to show certain personality traits. When listeners asked questions, though, the speaker was unable to explain the astrological cause or how it worked its influence.

2. *Realize that causal relationships are often complex and subtle.* A cause can have multiple effects, and an effect can have multiple causes. Be sure that your analysis of the cause–effect relationship is plausible and that your inference will be accepted as reasonable.

STRATEGIES FOR REASONING THROUGH TESTIMONY

When you rely on other people for the accuracy of supporting materials, their *testimony* stands in for your own direct encounter with the materials. You have confidence in their judgment and are willing to argue that the claim is true because they say so.

When a claim involves, for example, various economic indicators, or the long-term significance of a Supreme Court decision, or adequate safeguards for removing toxic waste, few speakers know enough to support the claim based on their own knowledge. In such cases both speaker and listeners are usually willing to defer to the judgment of someone whose training, experience, or esteem might all be reasons to trust that person's judgment.

Types of Inference from Testimony

In Chapter 5 you learned that testimony can be either fact or opinion. Each of these forms of testimony can be classified further according to (1) the type of person who offers it and (2) whether it is quoted or paraphrased.

EXPERT VERSUS LAY TESTIMONY   In most cases we seek **expert testimony**—the support of someone who is recognized as an authority on a particular subject, who has studied the subject in detail, and whose knowledge and interest in the subject far exceed the average person's. It is not unusual, however, for an expert in one field to make judgments about another field, as when a sports figure endorses a breakfast cereal or an economist comments on fashion trends. When experts testify about matters outside their field of expertise, we should examine their claims closely.

Although expert testimony usually provides stronger support for a claim, sometimes a speaker deliberately uses **lay testimony,** citing the opinions of "ordinary people" to show what nonexperts think about the subject. President Reagan's speeches often cited ordinary citizens as heroes to make the point that patriotism is not abstract or complex and can be expressed by anyone in daily life.

QUOTED VERSUS PARAPHRASED TESTIMONY   Quoted testimony repeats the exact words of the source, whereas paraphrased testimony gives only a general idea of what the source said. The statement "Police Chief Walters said,

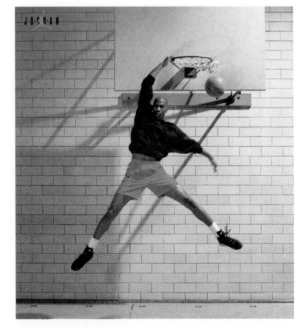

If your argument is based on testimony, your audience has a right to ask if the person quoted is really an expert or authority on the subject.

expert testimony
Testimony from a person who is generally recognized as an authority on a particular subject.

lay testimony
Testimony from a person who is not an expert.

'The rate of burglaries in our town is an embarrassment to civilized society' " is quoted; to paraphrase this you might say, "Police Chief Walters said that the burglary rate was unacceptably high."

Although quoted testimony usually provides stronger support, at times a quotation is too long, too confusing, or too technical for listeners to follow. In that case a paraphrase may allow you to cite what the source said without losing the audience's attention. The paraphrase, of course, must render the quotation accurately, or else you will *misquote* the source.

Tests for Inference from Testimony

Enticed by fame or fortune, some people will say just about anything. Therefore, even the quoted testimony of an expert is not always strong support for a claim. Like other forms of reasoning, inferences from testimony must meet certain tests.

1. *Does the statement accurately reflect the source's views?* In arguing that creationism should be taught in public schools, imagine that a student paraphrased a well-known paleontologist as saying that Darwin's theory of evolution is wrong. Listeners could find this hard to believe, and their doubts would turn out to be well-founded if the paleontologist actually said:

   Darwin was wrong. Natural selection is not the most important way in which evolution occurs. Other mechanisms that Darwin did not consider play a role just as crucial to the evolution of species.

   This exact quotation shows that the scientist would not have questioned Darwin's theory but only the importance of one proposed means of evolutionary change. The speaker's paraphrase of the statement as an attack on the theory of evolution was not accurate, and the audience rejected the claim.

2. *Is the source an expert on the topic?* As noted earlier, an expert in one field sometimes offers opinions about other fields. But a physicist is not necessarily an expert on international relations, nor is an actor the most credible source for a claim about nuclear energy. It is not enough that a source be regarded as *generally* well qualified; the source needs to be an expert in the *particular* subject about which you are making a claim. (This test was discussed in Chapter 5. Although it always applies to expert testimony, adapt it to assess lay testimony by asking, "Does this ordinary person have experience relating to the claim?")

   Student speaker Trisha Butcher gave a speech about the benefits of using ethanol as a fuel source. She based many of her arguments on what she had heard from her father, a corn farmer:

   According to my dad, ethanol causes less pollution than petroleum, and we all know how important it is in today's environment that a fuel burn clean. My father also told me that the production of ethanol-burning automobiles would be an economically sound investment for the country. It might cost a lot of money at first, but the long-term financial benefits outweigh the short-term costs.

   Listeners were unconvinced—as they should have been, since this testimony failed several tests. As a farmer, Trisha's father was hardly in a position to analyze fuel emissions; nor was he qualified to make national economic predictions. And since he sold the corn from which ethanol is produced, his opinion as a source was biased. But Trisha recovered when she revised this speech for her final class project. She found a chemical engineer to comment about fuel emissions and an economist to assess how ethanol fit into the national economic picture. Then she used her father's testimony to illustrate the personal struggles of a corn farmer trying to sell his bumper crop in a saturated market—a point on which he *was* well qualified to speak.

3. *Is there a basis for the source's statements?* A speaker who offers judgments without providing any basis for them is said to **pontificate.** Unfortunately, experts as well as lay people can do this. But if the source is offering judgments, listeners need to be confident that he or she is familiar with all aspects of the topic and has reasons for making the claim.

4. *Is the source reasonably unbiased?* No one is completely free of bias, of course, but if a source has a vested interest in a claim, the pressure will be strong to offer testimony consistent with that interest. An environmental engineer who owns land at a particular site, for example, may be more likely to downplay hazards on the site than would an engineer who has no economic interest in the matter. Similarly, claims by industry experts— whether automakers, cigarette manufacturers, or health-care providers— should be scrutinized. On the other hand, just because an expert stands to gain from the consequences of his or her testimony does not mean that the testimony itself is wrong. When expertise and self-interest are mixed, however, you need to be a skeptical, critical listener.

5. *Is the testimony up to date?* Some issues are truly timeless, and so it will not matter when a person's testimony was offered. Moral and philosophical principles may be timeless matters, although even here advances in knowledge and technology may affect what once seemed settled matters. On most matters, though—and particularly when data and statistics are involved—recent testimony may be more valuable than older support.

Even when testimony meets all these tests, you still may have to choose among the conflicting claims of qualified experts who disagree. Do not simply pick what supports your thesis and ignore other testimony. Instead, (1) ask what each expert's record of previous statements may imply about the quality of judgment in this case; (2) ask which expert's testimony is closest to consensus in the field; and (3) ask which expert's statement is most consistent with other things you already know or believe.

pontificate
To offer judgments without providing any basis for them.

Checklist

6.5   *Tests for Inference from Testimony*

1. **Does the statement accurately reflect the source's views?** 2. **Is the source an expert on the topic?** 3. **Is there a basis for the source's statements?** 4. **Is the source reasonably unbiased?** 5. **Is the testimony up to date?**	**When qualified experts disagree, ask:** 1. **What does each expert's record of previous statements imply about the quality of judgment in this case?** 2. **Which expert's testimony is closest to consensus in the field?** 3. **Which expert's statement is most consistent with other things you already know or believe?**

Guidelines for Using Inferences from Testimony

1. *Be sure you quote or paraphrase accurately.* Obviously, a direct quotation must be exactly what the source said. But it is equally important that a paraphrase be faithful to the context and meaning of the original statement and that it fairly reproduce its subtleties. Thus, if the context suggests that the source favors an action but has reservations about it, you would not paraphrase accurately if you suggested that the source wholeheartedly supports the action.

2. *Usually, draw on multiple sources of testimony.* If all your testimonial evidence comes from a single source, listeners may infer that no one else agrees or that your research is shallow; this could undermine even an authoritative source's credibility.

3. *State the credentials of your source.* Because an inference from testimony depends on listeners accepting the source as an authority, you should specify whom you are quoting or paraphrasing. Don't include every credential of the source, but list qualifications that support the claim in the quotation. Similarly, in selecting sources to quote, focus on people whose credentials are pertinent to your subject. The endorsements of celebrities who lack subject-matter expertise carry little weight.

4. *Your own ethos affects the credibility of testimony you cite.* If listeners regard *you* as highly credible, they will be more likely to accept what you say; they will make inferences about the truth of your claims based on your own credibility. When basketball star Magic Johnson, after being diagnosed HIV-positive, urged others to avoid contracting the virus, he was a highly credible source because he was directly affected. Beyond that, if listeners love basketball and admire Magic Johnson, your use of his testimony will be more credible than it would be if they had no apparent interest in him or the sport.

STRATEGIES FOR REASONING THROUGH NARRATIVE

This final category of inference, called narrative, comes into play when a speaker tells a story. A story is often more powerful than other ways of developing an idea. First of all, it is *personalized;* it presents a broad, general, or abstract idea as a specific situation involving particular people. Listeners become involved in the action and wonder what will happen; the story thus adds an element of suspense. A narrative works just like an extended example, and so *representativeness* serves to test the inference, just as it does for inference from example.

The dramatic structure of a narrative inference makes it powerful, which is apparent to anyone who reads novels or watches television and movies. The narrative structure consists of *characters,* a sequence of episodes or moves (often called a *plot*), the resolution of some sort of *conflict* (broadly defined), and an *ending* to which the resolution points. But the ending—the "moral of the story"—often is not stated explicitly. Audience members infer it for themselves.[9]

Checklist

6.6 Tests for Inference from Narrative

1. **Is the narrative coherent?**
2. **Is the narrative plausible?**
3. **Are characterizations consistent?**
4. **Does the narrative have resonance?**

Narratives take many forms in speeches and have many uses. They may be personal—a story in which the speaker is the main character—or they may be about other people. They may describe real events or a hypothetical situation; fictional narratives are also common in speeches, as in the retelling of children's stories, fables, biographical accounts, and historical scenarios.[10]

Tests for Inference from Narrative

To test whether a narrative inference is sound, examine various elements of its structure. Some important questions follow.

1. *Is the narrative coherent?* Does the story hang together and make sense? Is everything tied together at the end? Or do unexplained factors and loose ends make the story seem "unfinished" and its point seem unclear?

2. *Is the narrative plausible?* Is the story realistic, or is it farfetched? Since the narrative is offered to explain or support some claim, an implausible narrative will call that claim into question as well.

3. *Are characterizations consistent?* Do individuals in the story act as the audience has been led to expect? Just as you must be credible as a speaker and just as the experts you quote must be credible as authorities, so the characters in a narrative must be credible. If they are not, the audience will question the story—and the claim.

4. *Does the narrative have resonance?* **Resonance** is a feature that makes a narrative strike a responsive chord with listeners, allowing them to identify with the story and to relate it to their own experience. If your narrative has resonance, listeners will realize that you are telling the story not for its entertainment value but to speak directly to them and to make them understand your point.

AVOIDING ERRORS IN REASONING

We have examined a variety of inferences and some tests for each of them. The best way to ensure that your reasoning is sound is to apply those tests to specific inference patterns. But there are also some general errors in reasoning, called *fallacies*. A **fallacy** is an inference that appears to be sound

resonance
The quality of striking a responsive chord with listeners, causing them to identify with what one is saying.

fallacy
An inference that appears to be sound but that, on inspection, contains a significant flaw.

> ## 6.7   *General Tests for Inferences*
>
> 1. **Does the claim follow from the supporting material?**
> 2. **Does the claim advance our understanding beyond the supporting material?**
> 3. **Is the claim relevant to the issue?**
> 4. **Is the language clear and unequivocal?**
> 5. **Has probability been clearly distinguished from certainty?**
> 6. **Is the speaker's emotional response appropriate to the situation?**

but that, on inspection, contains a major flaw. Although fallacies often seem persuasive, critical listeners quickly realize that the reasoning goes astray.

Sometimes the term "fallacy" refers very broadly to any claim that people disagree with or any statement that they do not like. At other times the term refers very narrowly to defects in formal logic only. In public speaking, however, fallacies are inferences that would generally be regarded as unreasonable by a broad and diverse audience of listeners exercising their best critical judgment.[11]

Six General Tests of Inferences

1. *Does the claim follow from the supporting material?* This is the most basic question. If a speaker stated, "Because our school is 100 years old, it needs higher academic standards," we would be hard pressed to find any relationship between the supporting material (the age of the school) and the claim (that higher academic standards are needed). The claim might be correct, but it probably could not be inferred from *this* supporting evidence. The technical term for an inference in which the claim does not follow from the supporting material is **non sequitur** (Latin for "It does not follow").

2. *Does the claim advance our understanding beyond the supporting material?* Since we reason from what we already know (the supporting material) to what we wish to establish (the claim), an inference moves beyond the supporting material. But sometimes an inference has no real movement; the claim simply restates the supporting material in slightly different words. Such an inference is said to be **begging the question**, as in this statement: "Freedom of speech is for the common good [claim] because the expression of opinions is ultimately in the best interest of all [supporting material]."

3. *Is the claim relevant to the issue?* Sometimes a speaker makes a claim that is not pertinent to the topic at hand. Consider the following argument from a student who was claiming that the Scholastic Assessment Test (SAT) does not predict academic success:

> The test numbers do nothing to measure a student's potential for success in college. I am so tired of the way the modern world reduces us all to numbers. The college admissions process has become a clear example of this. When students want most of all to be seen as unique persons, they are instead reduced to an SAT quotient.

non sequitur
A claim that, on its face, is unrelated to the supporting material.

begging the question
Only restating the claim in slightly different words, rather than supporting the claim.

By noting the dehumanizing effect of using test scores to assess college applicants, the speaker *was* making a point about the SAT, but the point did nothing to support the claim that the exam is a poor measure of students' potential. An inference that diverts attention from the issue is said to be **ignoring the question.** (More commonly it is called a *red herring,* from the practice of dragging a smoked fish along a trail to confuse hunting dogs.)

4. *Is the language clear and unequivocal?* In Chapter 10 we will study the specific roles of language in a speech. The important point here is that the clarity of language may affect the quality of an inference. When the language of a speech can have multiple meanings, it is said to be **equivocal;** and any inferences based on that language will also be open to interpretation.

   Suppose that a politician promises "no tax increases." This sounds straightforward but can be interpreted in many ways. Is the politician promising that there will be no new taxes? Or that the current tax rate will not increase? Or that the percentage of a family's income paid in taxes will not change? Or that the family will spend no more on taxes this year than last year? Furthermore, what is a "tax"? Is it limited to such obvious categories as income, sales, and property taxes, or does it also include fees for driving on toll roads or camping in national parks?

5. *Has probability been clearly distinguished from certainty?* Speakers sometimes forget that inferences cannot be guaranteed, and they regard as *certain* what is really only *probable.* A speaker might argue, for example, that viewing violent television programs unquestionably inspires people to act violently. But this claim is hardly a sure thing; some research suggests that television violence may have little or no effect on behavior, and some even argue that television violence reduces aggression by providing a relatively harmless outlet for it. When a speaker suggests that all the evidence is clear-cut in one direction, listeners will do well to be wary that he or she is overstating the case.

6. *Is the speaker's emotional response appropriate to the situation?* During the 1988 presidential debates, Democratic candidate Michael Dukakis, who opposed capital punishment, was asked whether he would favor it were his wife raped and murdered. Dukakis virtually ignored the hypothetical situation posed by the questioner and proceeded in analytical fashion to restate his position on capital punishment:

   I think you know I've opposed the death penalty during all my life. I don't see any evidence that it's a deterrent, and I think there are better and more effective ways to deal with violent crime. We've done so in my own state. And that's one of the reasons we have had the biggest drop in crime of any industrial state in America.

   Many viewers reacted negatively to this response because Dukakis seemed to show no emotion; nothing in his answer suggested the rage people might expect from a husband in this situation. As a result, many listeners both discounted Dukakis's views on capital punishment and decided that he was not credible. Both conclusions were reached by inference from the mismatch between Dukakis's emotional reaction and what would be expected.

   The key issue is the *appropriateness* of the speaker's emotional response. Some situations, such as the presentation of scientific research, call for straightforwardness and calm; others, such as the one Dukakis

ignoring the question
Making an inference that diverts attention from the issue at hand.

equivocal
Having multiple meanings.

faced, call for a passionate response. But since the meaning of situations is not given and since inferences from emotions—like other inferences—cannot be guaranteed, how do we know what a particular situation calls for? The real point is that most people in a given audience or even a given culture will regard a situation in a certain way, and a speaker should analyze the norms of appropriate emotional response as part of the audience analysis.

Second, should speakers *always* respond in the "appropriate" way? Like other principles of public speaking, this one is not universal. At times a speaker deliberately violates listeners' expectations by making an "inappropriate" response, perhaps becoming emotionally aroused about a subject that the audience regards as "no big deal" or finding humor in a subject that the audience takes seriously. Usually, when a speaker violates norms of appropriateness, the purpose is to shock listeners, to make them sit up and take notice, and to convince them to reexamine their ideas about the situation. But such a strategy is risky, because the discomfort produced by an inappropriate response may turn the audience against the speaker instead of stimulating analysis.

Finally, be aware that emotional responses are sometimes misused, as when a speaker labels ideas as being "anti-American" or "sexist" or "racist." Unsupported appeals to fear, to prejudice, or to pride are actually devices to *prevent* inference, an attempt to substitute emotional reactions for substantial proof.

REASONING IN PUBLIC SPEAKING

It is time to apply our exploration of the reasoning process to preparing, delivering, and listening to speeches.

When preparing a speech, ask yourself why listeners should regard the supporting material as grounds for your claim. Then apply the tests for the particular kinds of inferences (Checklists 6.1 to 6.6) and the general tests for inferences (Checklist 6.7) to determine whether your reasoning seems sound. Then imagine a relatively skeptical listener—not someone hostile to the topic but someone who really does need to be convinced. Would that person regard your reasoning as sound?[12]

Proceed to higher levels of claims and repeat this process. Finally, ask whether all the Roman numerals in your outline taken together provide a basis for inferring your central claim. If so, then you have done a good job in working with your speech materials. But if you find any questionable inferences, your listeners are likely to find them, too.

When presenting a speech, remember that the audience is a critical factor in establishing rhetorical proof; the speaker and listeners reason together. You will not always make every step in your reasoning explicit; sometimes the supporting material or, more likely, the inference will seem to be assumed. This means that you are drawing on the audience's knowledge and expectations to establish the inference.

For example, audience analysis might suggest that your listeners believe that imports of foreign automobiles threaten American jobs. You might never mention that inference explicitly in your speech, instead saying, "This week's newspapers report a huge increase in the number of imported cars. We know what that means for the auto plant in our town." Occasionally, of course, the audience analysis will be mistaken. Suppose that the last statement were met by blank stares—or, worse, by frowns. Such feedback signals that the audience is not ready to participate in this inference. Even while giving the speech, you may modify your strategic plan, deciding in this case to make the inference explicit—not only stating that imported cars threaten American jobs but also giving evidence to support your claim.

You can help listeners follow your reasoning process by signposting its steps and inferences. Saying "Let me provide three examples" or "An analogy is in order here" will prompt listeners to anticipate the inference and its appropriate tests. Asking (and later answering) such a question as "How do we know that the statistical sample was representative?" will suggest that you know the relevant tests of reasoning and are confident that your speech satisfies them. Even the use of reasoning terms ("consequently," "therefore," "the premise is," "the implied conclusion is," and so on) will help listeners understand where you are in reasoning through the speech.

Summary

In this chapter we have seen that rhetorical proof in public speaking is different from proof in mathematics or science. Rhetorical proof depends on an interaction between the speaker and the audience; although their joint conclusions cannot be guaranteed absolutely, they can be supported and shown to be probable.

A rhetorical proof includes three components. The claim is the statement that listeners are asked to accept. Supporting material provides the foundation for the claim. And reasoning links the supporting material to the claim; it involves making an inference—a mental leap—that the supporting material really does support the claim. Although inferences cannot be guaranteed, certain patterns of inference can be shown to be generally reliable. An inference is reasonable if it would be made by most people when exercising their critical judgment.

We distinguished among inferences from example, analogy, sign, cause, testimony, and narrative. Each of these reasoning patterns has several different types, and for each certain tests are appropriate. In addition, we studied six general tests of reasoning to help you avoid such fallacies as the non sequitur, begging the question, ignoring the question, equivocal language, confusing probability with certainty, and inappropriate emotional response. These are fallacies because their inferences seem to be sound but actually are seriously flawed.

The chapter concluded with suggestions for using your understanding of the reasoning process in preparing, delivering, and listening to speeches.

Discussion Questions

1. In class, watch a videotape of a recent political speech, and discuss its reasoning process. What patterns of inference were used? Why do you think the speaker chose to use those patterns? Did they work? Did you recognize any fallacies?

2. If you knew that your audience would be uncritical, why would you take time to test your inferences before speaking? With a group of peers, discuss the ethics of proper reasoning.

3. In what ways might emotion help someone or prevent someone from making a proper inference? Discuss situations in which particular emotions (love, fear, hate, anger, boredom) might advance or detract from the reasoning process.

Activities

1. In Chapter 2, you studied how to listen critically to a speech and to develop a map of what was said, evaluating each link between support and claim with a plus or minus sign. Now expand your evaluation of each link on that map. Identify each type of inference, and conduct appropriate tests to understand why each link is positive or negative.

2. Identify examples of each type of inference that you plan to use in your next speech. Which reasoning patterns are most appropriate for your topic? Which do you think will be most effective with your audience? Which types of inference are you most comfortable using?

3. For the next few days, think critically about the everyday communication events around you. Using Checklist 6.7 as a guide, identify a recent claim that fails one of the general tests, and explain its fallacy. Pay close attention to television commercials, news editorials, and "heat of passion" arguments.

Using the Internet

Effective reasoning must be based on evidence that is carefully gathered and analyzed critically. In addition, we can engage in further critical thinking about a piece of evidence or the claims we infer from it by taking part in discussions. Both exercises presented use critical thinking on four levels:

- *Gathering evidence*
- *Selecting evidence*
- *Forming inferences*
- *Testing evidence and inferences through discussion*

1. **Using effective rhetorical reasoning.** The effective use of reasoning depends on solid critical thinking as one makes inferences through the use of examples, analogy, signs, causality, testimony, and narratives. Examine how some of these types of inferences were made through a historic case study of the Salem witch trials. How did reasoning go awry?

   Go to the site created by *National Geographic* entitled **"Salem, Witchcraft Hysteria"** by pointing your browser to <http://www.nationalgeographic.com/features/97/salem/>. After taking part in the hypertext, go to the forum created by *National Geographic* at <http://www.nationalgeographic.com/features/97/salem/newdiscussframe.html/>. There you can see how other people have responded to the situation.

(continued)

2. **Responding as a critical listener.** We note in this chapter that listeners must evaluate rhetorical proofs by testing them rather than taking them for granted. Be a listener/reader who responds to issues critically using some of the topics in the **Allyn & Bacon Public Speaking Forum.** Each forum is organized as a discussion group on the Simon and Schuster News Server.

To locate the discussions, go to <http://www.abacon.com/pubspeak/assess/netforum.html#ab/>. There you will see a variety of topics for public discussion. Scroll down the list, noting that there are links to online documents and online statements made by public speakers and writers. After reading or listening to these statements, form a judgment about whether you think one of the advocates has made a reasonable claim. Then join one of the groups to express your view. To join, click on the link that begins with the expression <news://ssnews.prenhall.com> located just below each of the topics in the forum, such as:

Should the Internet be privatized?

Is Social Security going broke?

Should the state regulate physician-assisted suicide?

Chemistry, cancer and our diet

Notes

1. Although scientists and mathematicians may argue about what counts as proof, their institutional standards for agreement are usually clearly defined. See Philip J. Davis and Reuben Hersh, "Rhetoric and Mathematics," *The Rhetoric of the Human Sciences: Language and Argument in Scholarship and Public Affairs,* ed. John S. Nelson, Allan Megill, and Donald N. McCloskey, Madison: Univ. of Wisconsin Press, 1987, pp. 53–68; Gyorgy Markus, "Why Is There No Hermeneutics of Natural Sciences? Some Preliminary Theses," *Science in Context* 1 (Spring 1987): 5–51.

2. See the discussion of "universal audience" in Chapter 3. See also Chaim Perelman and Lucie Olbrechts-Tyteca, *The New Rhetoric: A Treatise on Argumentation,* trans. John Wilkinson and Purcell Weaver, Notre Dame, Ind.: Univ. of Notre Dame Press, 1969, pp. 31–35.

3. For a more detailed map of the reasoning process, see Stephen Toulmin, Richard Rieke, and Allan Janik, *An Introduction to Reasoning,* 2nd ed., New York: Macmillan, 1984. See also J. Ramage and J. Bean, *Writing Arguments,* 3rd ed., Boston: Allyn & Bacon, 1995.

4. Also consult a theoretical discussion of inferences from example in speeches, such as Scott Consigny, "The Rhetorical Example," *Southern Journal of Speech Communication* 41 (Winter 1976): 121–134.

5. Researchers have shown that both figurative and literal analogies are persuasive for audiences. See James C. McCroskey and Walter H. Combs, "The Effects of the Use of Analogy on Attitude Change and Source Credibility," *Journal of Communication* 19 (December 1969): 333–339.

6. Our modern understanding of literal and figurative analogies developed from the classical tradition. For more on the genesis of analogical reasoning, see James S. Measell, "Classical Bases of the Concept of Analogy," *Argumentation and Advocacy* 10 (Summer 1973): 1–10.

7. For more on the use of analogies in speeches, see James R. Wilcox and Henry L. Ewbank, "Analogy for Rhetors," *Philosophy and Rhetoric* 12 (Winter 1979): 1–20.

8. For a more detailed theoretical discussion of inferences from cause, see David Zarefsky, "The Role of Causal Argument in Policy Controversies," *Argumentation and Advocacy* 13 (Spring 1977): 179–191.

9. According to some, storytelling is the most important aspect of speechmaking. See Walter R. Fisher, "Narration as a Human Communication Paradigm: The Case of Public Moral Argument," *Communication Monographs* 51 (March 1984): 1–22.

10. For a good practical discussion of the power of narrative in speeches, see A. Cheree Carlson, "Narrative as the Philosopher's Stone: How Russell H. Conwell Changed Lead into Diamonds," *Western Journal of Speech Communication* 53 (Fall 1989): 342–355.

11. Several books explore fallacies in detail. See Alex C. Michalos, *Improving Your Reasoning,* 2nd ed., Englewood Cliffs, N.J.: Prentice-Hall, 1986; T. Edward Damer, *Attacking Faulty Reasoning,* 2nd ed., Belmont, Calif.: Wadsworth, 1987; Howard Kahane, *Logic and Contemporary Rhetoric,* Belmont, Calif.: Wadsworth, 1980.

12. It has been said that "arguments are found in people," meaning that listeners are responsible for making the inferential leaps between supporting material and claim. See Wayne Brockriede, "Where Is Argument?" *Argumentation and Advocacy* 11 (Spring 1975): 179–182.

chapter 7
Organizing the Speech: The Body

In This Chapter We Will:

- Explain why the organization of a speech is important for both the speaker and the audience.

- Identify criteria for selecting the main ideas to include in your speech and the characteristics that a main idea should have.

- Learn how to arrange the main ideas into recognizable patterns and which patterns of arrangement you might use.

- Examine ways to decide how much and which kinds of supporting material you need and how to arrange the support for each idea.

f you have used all the strategies suggested in Chapters 4 and 5 for investigating your topic, you now should have a better understanding of the issues that are implicit in your thesis. You also should have located a variety of supporting materials for your ideas—examples, statistics, testimony, and so forth. You have probably investigated many more ideas than you can discuss in the time available, and you very likely have located far more supporting materials than you can use, even after applying the tests of reasoning that we examined in Chapter 6. For all this effort, your ideas and materials may show no evident pattern and may not seem to fit together well. What, then, do you do with all the ideas you have explored and all the evidence you have gathered?

Identifying and locating material for the speech is not enough; you also need to organize it in strategic ways that advance your purpose. **Organization** is the selection of ideas and materials and their arrangement into a discernible and effective pattern. This process is so crucial that we will discuss it in three chapters. Here we will focus exclusively on the body of the speech. Then, in Chapter 8, we will consider introductions, conclusions, and transitions. Finally, in Chapter 9, we will learn how to apply the principles of organization in outlining your speech.

WHY IS ORGANIZATION IMPORTANT?

To help orient new students to the college, the Counseling Office offers a program in which seniors give speeches about how to develop good study habits. The first speaker, Burt Wilson, maintained that "good habits depend on several important factors. For one thing, you have to avoid procrastination. Good reading skills are also helpful to college students. Oh yes, and by the way, you also need to be self-motivated." The incoming students looked puzzled and unconvinced; they stopped taking notes, and no one asked questions. The very next speaker, Laura Simmons, covered the same ground, but she said: "Good study habits depend on a balance of skills plus motivation. On the one hand, you have to develop good reading skills; on the other hand, you need to overcome procrastination. You can do both if you focus on the priorities that motivate you to study." The audience responded very differently to Laura's speech; they took notes and asked a number of questions when she finished.

This example illustrates that audiences will understand, remember, and be influenced by an organized message more than by a disorganized one. The reason is obvious. Careful listening is difficult under any circumstances, and it is even more difficult when listeners cannot tell where the speaker is going or how the parts of the speech relate to one another. An idea or example that is not connected to anything else is easy to forget.[1] The mental energy that listeners use in reconstructing a confused or disorganized speech is not available for absorbing and reflecting on its main points.[2] Moreover, listeners may resent this additional work and may express their resentment by resisting the message.[3]

Beyond such basic considerations about the audience, a speaker should recognize that organizational pattern, or form, itself is persuasive. If listeners can identify a clear pattern in the speech, they can anticipate what idea is coming next. If a speaker describes the development of intercollegiate athletics by talking first about the past and then about the present, listeners reasonably can expect to focus next on the future. As the speaker develops the main ideas aloud, listeners follow along and develop the ideas in their minds.

organization
The selection of ideas and materials and their arrangement into a discernible and effective pattern.

The ability to follow a speaker's organizational pattern is important for several reasons:

- An audience can better remember the main ideas of a speech when the speaker presents them in a recognizable pattern. For example, the past/present/future pattern is one category of arrangement that prompts the recall of specific ideas. Listeners are more likely to remember the first idea if they can connect it mentally to the heading "past."
- Effective organization encourages active rather than passive listening. It engages listeners' attention and helps them to ignore or override distractions.
- Being able to anticipate what's coming next makes listeners feel that they are "in the know." They may believe, for example, that the next natural step in the speaker's organizational pattern is to discuss the present influence of television revenues on college sports. If that is indeed the next main idea, listeners are likely to feel personal satisfaction at having "called it right."[4]

In short, form is persuasive because listeners are more likely to be disposed positively toward ideas that they have helped to shape, that they can remember well, and about which they feel personally satisfied.

Organization is important for the speaker as well. In Chapter 4 you were introduced to the idea of *strategic planning* for a speech. In any rhetorical situation the goal is to respond to your constraints and to take advantage of your opportunities to achieve your purpose. Organization is a major strategic resource that greatly affects the outcome of a speech. You need to bring critical thinking and reflection to such organizational decisions as the number and order of ideas, how you group them, what you call them, and how you relate them to the audience. In devising your strategic plan, you should question what your options are, how each option relates to your purpose, and how different choices are likely to be perceived by listeners.

Moreover, in planning your speech, organization can be a guide to check that you haven't accidentally left anything out. For example, noticing that your speech covers both the past and the present of your topic, you recognize that the audience will be likely to think, "But what about the future?" This prompts you to find the materials needed to discuss the future as well. During your presentation, too, keeping the organization in mind can prevent the embarrassment of suddenly forgetting what the next point should be.[5]

Organization has two basic components: *selection* and *arrangement*. We will discuss each component with respect both to the main ideas of the speech and to the supporting materials.

SELECTING THE MAIN IDEAS

Identifying Your Main Ideas

As you remember from Chapter 4, the thesis statement is the principal claim of your speech, the statement you want listeners to accept. When you ask questions about your thesis statement, you identify the issues that you must address in order to establish the thesis. **Main ideas** are the claims that

main ideas
Claims that address the issues in the thesis statement; the primary divisions of the speech.

address the issues in your thesis statement, and they are the major divisions of the speech. In Chapter 9 you'll see that main ideas are signaled in the speech outline by Roman numerals.

You can identify the main ideas in your speech from (1) your thesis or specific purpose or from (2) patterns in your research.

FROM YOUR THESIS OR SPECIFIC PURPOSE   Stuart Kim used this approach to identify his main ideas in a speech seeking to persuade the audience to contribute to the United Way. Like many college students, Stuart was a community service volunteer; he tutored reading and math at an after-school center for children from low-income families who had no parent at home during the day. Stuart enjoyed the work and felt that he was really helping the children, but toward the end of the year he was startled to learn that the center would have to close. It was funded by the United Way, and contributions were down. Appalled that "his" children would have nowhere to go, Stuart decided to speak to community groups and urge them to support the United Way. He used his public speaking classmates as a test audience to practice the speech.

Because Stuart's purpose was to persuade the audience to contribute to the United Way, he thought immediately of several ideas that he needed to address. He would have to tell listeners what the United Way is, that the agencies it supports (such as Stuart's after-school center) were important and valuable, and that the United Way needed and merited *their* support. If the speech failed to address any of these elements, the audience was unlikely to be persuaded to donate money. Stuart regarded these as the main ideas, and he divided the speech into corresponding sections:

I. The United Way is a federation of health, recreational, and social service agencies.
II. The activities of these agencies are important and valuable to our community.
III. These activities cannot be continued unless we support the United Way.

In this example, Stuart was able immediately to see the main ideas that derived from his thesis and purpose. But sometimes the connection is not so obvious. If Stuart had not identified his main ideas at once, he might have worked them out by quizzing his thesis statement, using the method you learned in Chapter 4:

TOPIC: The United Way

GENERAL PURPOSE: Inducing a specific action

SPECIFIC PURPOSE: Convincing listeners to give money to the United Way.

THESIS: Everyone should contribute to the United Way.

ISSUES:

1. Everyone   → Why me?
2. Should contribute → Why? What does it do?
3. The United Way   → What is it?

MAIN IDEAS:

1. The United Way needs and merits *your* support.
2. The United Way supports important and valuable programs.
3. The United Way is an umbrella organization to raise money for social service programs.

> ### 7.1 Questions to Help Identify Main Ideas
>
> | | |
> |---|---|
> | 1. What does it mean? | 11. How will it happen? |
> | 2. How to describe it? | 12. Who is involved? |
> | 3. What are the facts? | 13. What are some examples? |
> | 4. What are the reasons? | 14. Why is it strange? |
> | 5. How often does it occur? | 15. What are the objections? |
> | 6. What is my view? | 16. Compared with what? |
> | 7. What are the parts? | 17. What is the effect of this? |
> | 8. What is the reasoning? | 18. Any stories to tell? |
> | 9. What is the cause? | 19. How often? |
> | 10. Which ones? | 20. What is preventing it? |

Looking over this list, Stuart would probably decide to put main idea 3 first in the speech and to end with main idea 1. Why? Because listeners need to know what the United Way is before they can decide whether to support it and because the direct appeal in main idea 1 provides a strong conclusion. Applying these analytical steps, Stuart would derive the same main ideas that he was able to recognize instinctively.

Checklist 7.1 contains some of the standard questions to ask about a thesis statement in order to identify your main ideas.

FROM PATTERNS IN YOUR RESEARCH   Another approach to identifying main ideas is to observe patterns in the research that you have completed. If the people you interview and the literature you read repeatedly mention certain subjects, those may well be the main ideas about your topic.

For example, suppose that almost everything Stuart Kim read about the United Way mentioned its low administrative costs and suggested that its reliance on volunteers meant that most of the money raised can be spent directly on providing services. This idea may not have emerged from Stuart's initial conception of a strategy to meet his purpose, and yet it may be very important to include the idea in the speech. It suggests that it is better for people to contribute to the United Way than to support a host of individual charities that do not use their funds as efficiently.

Choosing among Main Ideas

The thesis and purpose of a speech as well as the process of research are sources of main ideas. Often, however, you'll have more ideas than you have time or energy to pursue—and more than your audience will be willing and able to consider.

Suppose, for example, that Stuart's research suggested all the following points:

The administrative costs of the United Way are low.

Organizations in the United Way must be nondiscriminatory.

The United Way had its origins in charitable organizations of the late nineteenth century.

Some groups within the public object to the programs of certain United Way organizations.

The United Way is staffed largely by volunteers.

It is not clear whether someone who lives in one community but works in another should support the United Way at home or at work.

The United Way substitutes a single annual campaign for what otherwise would be continuous solicitation for each of the member agencies.

The alternative to supporting the United Way is to expand the government's social welfare programs.

Each of these topics could be discussed at length, and each might be supported by a variety of materials. Yet no speech of reasonable length could address them all. Therefore, like most speakers, Stuart will need to select from among the possible main ideas which ones to use in the speech.

Criteria for Selecting the Main Ideas

Most speeches cover between two and five main ideas. Although there is no magic to these numbers, they do generally represent what an audience expects and can likely follow and remember.

If you have derived more than five main ideas from your thesis and purpose and from your research, you can reduce their number and select which ideas to include by asking two questions:

- Is this idea really essential to the speech?
- Can a more general statement combine several ideas?

IS THIS IDEA ESSENTIAL? In researching a speech, you may discover many interesting things about your subject that are, frankly, sidelights. Although they may be fascinating to you, they distract from your specific purpose. For example, knowing that the United Way developed from nineteenth-century charitable organizations may reveal quite a bit about American attitudes toward charity or about how organizations evolve. But remember that Stuart Kim's purpose is to persuade audience members to donate money. Most people don't need to know about the United Way's origins and history in order to decide whether to contribute. Likewise, if Stuart's goal is only to persuade people to give, it may not matter whether they do so at work or at home.

This first criterion is often difficult to apply. Speakers are reluctant to omit ideas that interest them, and valuable research time seems wasted if the results do not find their way into the speech. But including nonessential material may distract the audience and prevent you from achieving your ultimate purpose. It is necessary, then, to be hard-nosed and to subject all potential main ideas to this rigorous test: If an idea—no matter how interesting—is not essential to your specific purpose, it does not qualify as a main idea and should be excluded.

CAN SEVERAL IDEAS BE COMBINED? When you find yourself considering a large number of main ideas, consider whether some of them are not main ideas at all but illustrations of, or support for, more general statements. You may be able to combine what you thought were distinct main ideas into one general statement, thereby reducing the number. Your thesis should suggest these more general statements into which you could combine elements.

In the United Way example, the low administrative costs, the nondiscriminatory policies, and the convenience of a single annual campaign might turn out not to be separate main ideas but examples to support a general statement like "The United Way is the best way to contribute to charity." The three statements all answer the question "Once I've decided that it's important to make a charitable contribution, why should I do so through the United Way?" That question is a longer form of "Why me?" which was derived from the thesis statement. All these examples thus could support the main idea, "The United Way merits *your* support." By referring to the issues suggested by the thesis statement, or just by asking whether a more general statement could be made, we reduced three statements of main ideas to one.

Characteristics of the Main Ideas

Unfortunately, just cutting the number of main ideas—as difficult as that is—may still result in a speech that does not seem complete, coherent, or persuasive. It is also important that the selected main ideas have the following characteristics.

SIMPLICITY   Because the main ideas serve as memory aids for both speaker and audience, they should be stated simply and succinctly so that they can be remembered. "The United Way is efficient" is a better statement of a main idea than is "The United Way has low administrative costs, economies of scale from combining campaigns, and simple distribution mechanisms." As a general rule, a main idea should be stated in a single short sentence.

DISCRETENESS   Each main idea should be separate from the others. When main ideas overlap, the structure of the speech becomes confusing, and it is difficult to remember what was said under each main heading. For example, if one main idea is "The United Way supports agencies that meet social needs" and another main idea is "The United Way supports health and recreational agencies," the two ideas overlap; they are not discrete. After all, health and recreation are also among our social needs. Such a structure will not be clear to listeners, and the speaker will not know where to put supporting material.

PARALLEL STRUCTURE   When possible, main ideas should be stated in similar fashion. Sentences should have the same grammatical structure and

Checklist

7.2 *Characteristics of Main Ideas*

Taken together, the main ideas of the speech should be characterized by:

1. **Simplicity**
2. **Discreteness**
3. **Parallel structure**
4. **Balance**
5. **Coherence**
6. **Completeness**

should be of approximately the same length. This principle, known as **parallel structure,** makes the pattern easy to follow and to remember. For example, Stuart Kim might use this pattern:

> The United Way is effective.
>
> The United Way is efficient.
>
> The United Way is humane.

In this example, "effective," "efficient," and "humane" are the key terms that listeners are asked to remember. Each of these value judgments can be supported with different types of evidence, but the basic structure of the speech is parallel.

BALANCE   Taken together, the main ideas should not be loaded toward one particular aspect of the subject. Rather, they should add up to a balanced perspective. In the preceding list, each of the three key terms refers to a different aspect of the United Way: what it accomplishes, what it costs, and what values it represents. These are three different factors that would affect the decision to contribute, and together they offer a balanced perspective. If, on the other hand, three or four main ideas related to the United Way's finances and only one dealt with its underlying values, the organization of the speech would appear unbalanced. Finances would be covered in detail, but other important aspects of the topic would be treated superficially or ignored.

COHERENCE   **Coherence** means that the separate main ideas have a clear relationship and hang together; listeners can see why they appear in the same speech. If Stuart Kim wished to persuade listeners to contribute to the United Way but offered one main idea about the origins of charitable organizations, another about efforts to extend the United Way to Eastern Europe, another about controversial agencies that the United Way supports, and another about accounting procedures, it is hard to imagine how the speech could be coherent. These topics are not clearly related to each other (except that they all involve the United Way), and they do not come together to support any conclusion—certainly not the ultimate claim that "you should contribute to the United Way."

COMPLETENESS   Finally, the main ideas taken together should present a complete view of the subject, omitting nothing of major importance. If Stuart wants to convince the audience to contribute to the United Way but fails to explain what the organization does with the money it receives, the pattern of main ideas would not be complete. Most people who make charitable gifts want to know how their contributions are used.

ARRANGING THE MAIN IDEAS

Having selected the main ideas for your speech, the next step is to decide upon their order—which ideas to put first, last, or in the middle. We'll look at the factors you should consider in arranging your main ideas and then at a variety of organizational patterns that you can use.

parallel structure
Structure in which phrases are of similar syntax and length.

coherence
Clear relationships among ideas and topics so that the speech appears to hang together as a natural whole.

APPLYING STRATEGIES

Organizing Your Speech

Carrie Biesel

I guess when I start thinking about a speech in my head, I automatically think in terms of the main body. I hate extensive introductions that have to be re-stated in the conclusion. I like an attention-getter and then the story and that's it. The main body IS the speech; it is the point you are trying to make. It's not the little things.

Dr. Marrow

You're right, Carrie, to a point. The main body IS the speech, but the *little things* do count. If the speaker's total message seems disorganized and hard to follow, the audience is likely to tune out quickly. The audience does not want to waste time and energy searching for the speaker's main points. Besides, David Zarefsky

reminds us that audiences will remember, understand, and be influenced more by an organized than a disorganized message. Therefore, a good, solid organizational structure consisting of a clear introduction, body, and conclusion is essential. Pay close attention to the little things AND the main body in your speech, and you can't lose!

Factors Affecting Arrangement

ARE THE MAIN IDEAS DEPENDENT?   Ideas can be arranged in a pattern that makes them either *dependent* or *independent*.

Logically dependent ideas are like links in a chain, because the strength of each depends on all the others. If one link is broken, the chain is destroyed. Here is such a chain of logically dependent main ideas:

> If we develop regulations for campus speech, they will necessarily be vague.
>
> If regulations are vague, people will not know whether or not the regulations apply to them.
>
> If people are unsure whether regulations apply to them, they will hesitate to speak out about controversial issues.
>
> If people do not speak out about controversial issues, intellectual debate is undermined.

This speaker, obviously, would argue that codes to regulate speech would undermine the vital intellectual exchange of campus life. The links in this argument need to be arranged precisely as shown if the audience is to follow the speaker's reasoning.

Logical dependence is common in telling a story. With obvious exceptions (such as flashbacks), you should relate events in the order in which they occurred so that listeners can follow the plot. Likewise, if you arrange ideas in a spatial pattern—talking, for example, about colleges in different regions of the country—then you need to maintain that pattern of geographical movement. You might move from east to west or from west to east, but you would not want to zigzag from New England to the Southwest and then to the mid-Atlantic states.

• • • • • • • • • • • • • • • • • • •

logically dependent idea
Cannot stand on its own but requires that some other claim or statement be true.

In contrast, **logically independent ideas** stand alone, and the truth of each in no way rests on the others. Again using the example of a proposed code to regulate campus speech, here is a logically independent pattern of reasoning:

Campus speech codes are unacceptably vague.

Campus speech codes discourage the airing of controversial issues.

Campus speech codes bring bad publicity to the college.

This speaker also wishes to oppose campus speech codes, but notice the difference in the structure of main ideas. In this case, each idea bears *independently* on the conclusion. Any one of these claims by itself could give the audience good reason to oppose speech codes, regardless of the other claims. Speech codes are undesirable if they are too vague, *or* if they chill the discussion of controversial issues, *or* if they bring unfavorable publicity.

A dependent pattern of reasoning can be risky, because the defeat of any one link will cause the chain to break. For this reason, some writers advise the use of an independent pattern whenever possible. But a dependent pattern also offers advantages. It is highly coherent and easy to follow. And if each link is established successfully, the force of the overall pattern may cause the whole chain to seem even stronger than the sum of its links.

The choice of a dependent or an independent pattern is influenced most strongly by your thesis statement. Use whichever pattern is more effective in establishing your claim. But one thing is certain: If your main ideas are dependent on each other, their arrangement is virtually decided. You can begin at either end of the chain, but you must connect the ideas in order, link by link. With an independent pattern, however, you do not have to present the main ideas in any particular order. In that case, additional questions will arise.

ARE SOME MAIN IDEAS RELATIVELY UNFAMILIAR?

Because most people comprehend unfamiliar ideas by linking them to familiar ideas, you may wish to begin your speech with a main idea that is already familiar to listeners. This will attract their interest and get them thinking about your topic. Then you can move to the less familiar ideas, knowing that the audience is working with you.

Your audience analysis may suggest that most people realize that campus speech codes attract adverse publicity but that they may not be familiar with the vagueness of such codes and may not have thought about their effect on the airing of controversial issues. You therefore might begin with the familiar idea that campus speech codes attract negative publicity, making the point that this is just the tip of the iceberg. Speech codes also have two less obvious problems: They are too vague to be administered fairly, and—even worse—they stifle discussion of controversial issues. If your audience analysis is correct, you have succeeded in arranging the ideas from most familiar to least familiar.

There is another reason to begin with the familiar. If your first main idea were completely unfamiliar to the audience, it would be much more difficult for listeners to grasp. You might distract them by making them stop to think about what you mean by "the inherent vagueness of speech codes,"

logically independent idea
Does not require the truth of any other claim or statement as a condition for its own truth.

When you have a strong idea that you plan to present emphatically, as this speaker does, should it be placed first or last in your speech?

and they might miss your next point. On the other hand, discussion of a familiar main idea can be used to explain a less familiar idea. For example, knowing that listeners might quickly recognize that campus speech codes cause adverse publicity, you might ask why the publicity is so adverse. This question would provide a natural transition into your second, less familiar idea.

SHOULD THE STRONGEST IDEA COME FIRST OR LAST?   This question comes into play under two conditions: when the main ideas are independent and when they are not equally strong. (A "strong" idea is one that will seem compelling to an audience of critical listeners. An idea is not considered to be strong if it does not make much difference to listeners—even if it is true and well supported.)

Should you present your strongest main idea first in order to make a strong first impression on the audience? Or should you present it last, to end with a bang and leave the audience on a positive note? Many researchers have studied the relative merits of a **primacy effect** (strongest idea first) versus a **recency effect** (strongest idea last), but the results are inconclusive.[6] Too many other factors also influence the impact of arrangement. However, if one idea seems weaker than the others, you should present it in a middle position rather than either toward the beginning or toward the end.

Often, the strength of an idea depends not on any inherent feature of the idea itself, but on how well the idea sits with the audience. This involves such factors as whether the idea relates to listeners' experience, whether it strikes most people as being consistent with common sense, and whether—if it is true—it makes a major or only a minor contribution toward the overall goal of the speech. Because the strength of an idea depends on listeners' perceptions, your audience analysis is not finished when you first select a topic, purpose, thesis, and strategy; the audience affects all major decisions about speech preparation and delivery.

primacy effect
A tendency for what is presented first to be best remembered.

recency effect
A tendency for what is presented last to be best remembered.

Patterns for Arranging Main Ideas

In theory, you can arrange main ideas in an infinite number of patterns. But several common patterns are easy for an audience to follow, and they work well for a variety of topics. You first should focus on these general patterns, which are described next. Then, if your topic, purpose, or audience seems to call for a different pattern, you can develop your own.

CHRONOLOGICAL   The passage of time is the organizing principle in the chronological approach. The units of time (most often the past, the present, and the future) become the main ideas. For example, in discussing the topic "What personal computers can do," you might organize the speech as follows:

I. Personal computers could do only a few things in the early 1980s.

II. Personal computers are far more powerful today.

III. Personal computers will be even more versatile in the future.

This example proceeds in normal chronological order, beginning with the past and ending with the future. But you can start at any point in the chronology. For example, you might reason that a speech about recycling would be clearest if you begin with the state of recycling programs today, then move backward in time to examine the origins of today's programs, and finally conclude with a discussion of recycling in the future.

SPATIAL   Whereas chronological order organizes main ideas according to time, spatial order arranges them according to place or position. A speech might begin with the aspects of the topic that are nearest and then proceed to the aspects that are farther away. This pattern might work well for a speech about the effects of inflation, in which the main ideas are:

I. Inflation affects an individual's spending power.

II. Inflation affects state and local funded projects.

III. Inflation affects the federal budget.

Another common spatial arrangement would be to present ideas literally in geographic order:

I. Inflation hurts trade on the Eastern seaboard.

II. Inflation hurts farmers in the Midwest.

III. Inflation hurts the oil industry in the West.

Checklist

7.3 *Basic Organizational Patterns*

1. **Chronological**	5. **Problem–solution**
2. **Spatial**	6. **Comparison and contrast**
3. **Categorical (topical)**	7. **Residues**
4. **Cause–effect**	

CATEGORICAL (TOPICAL)   In the categorical pattern, each main idea that you identified in analyzing your topic becomes a major division of the speech. For example, in researching the advantages of studying abroad, you may have decided that such study enables students to experience another culture, to visit places of historical or cultural interest, and to meet interesting people with different experiences and lifestyles. Each of these topics becomes a major heading in your speech. Especially because a topical pattern has no required order (for example, from past to present or from left to right), it is important that main ideas be stated in parallel fashion and that they be easy to recognize and remember. The major headings for this speech might be:

I. You can experience another culture.

II. You can visit interesting places.

III. You can meet people with different experiences.

Sometimes the topical pattern is even easier to remember if the categories have an obvious or standard structure. "People, places, events" is an example of such a simple, memorable structure.

CAUSE–EFFECT   In Chapter 6 you learned how to infer causes and effects. Cause–effect is also an organizational pattern, and it can proceed in either direction. You can focus on causes and then identify their effects, or you can first identify effects and then try to determine their causes. For example, a speech about the depletion of the ozone layer might proceed like this:

I. Society has increased the use of aerosol spray cans.

II. These release fluorocarbons into the atmosphere.

III. Fluorocarbons erode the ozone layer surrounding the earth.

IV. Depletion of the ozone layer exposes people to additional ultraviolet radiation.

Or, rather than moving from cause to effect, you might proceed from effect to cause:

I. We are becoming more vulnerable to ultraviolet radiation.

II. This effect results from the release of fluorocarbons into the atmosphere.

III. Widespread use of aerosol cans is one source of the problem.

The choice between these two arrangements would be governed by which topics you wanted to present first and last, not by anything intrinsic to the cause–effect organizational pattern.

PROBLEM–SOLUTION   A variation of the cause–effect pattern is one that focuses on problems and their solutions. A speech using this pattern first lays out the dimensions of the problem and shows why it is serious; then it considers one or more potential solutions and explains why a particular solution is best. For example, a speech about the difficulties of the college registration system might be structured something like this:

I. The current registration system is both inefficient and unfair.

II. Registration by touch-tone telephone, processed by computer, would solve these problems.

You can use a variation on ▶
cause-effect organization
when your speech describes
a problem for which you
offer a solution. South African
President Nelson Mandela
often used this approach
throughout his efforts to
end apartheid in South Africa.

The development of the first major heading might claim that the current registration system does not match students with their preferred courses as well as possible and that it gives an unfair advantage to students who happen to be first in line. Perhaps after considering some other solutions, the speaker would then claim that these problems can be overcome by using computer and telephone technology.

Often, problems are not self-evident to an audience. A speaker has to motivate listeners to feel that some important need is not being met before they will regard a situation as a problem. A variation on the problem–solution pattern, then, is to emphasize *psychological order*. The speaker first motivates listeners to perceive a problem and then provides the means to satisfy that feeling by identifying a solution. If Stuart Kim had chosen this approach in speaking about the United Way, his speech might have been organized as follows:

I. We all have a responsibility to others.

II. This responsibility includes financial support for the social service organizations that help others.

III. Giving to the United Way helps us to meet our responsibilities.

In this example, the first step is to arouse an attitude, motive, or desire among the audience members. Subsequent steps then refine that motivation and show how it can be satisfied by a particular action. In Chapter 14 we will examine an elaborated version of this organizational pattern, called the "motivated sequence."

COMPARISON AND CONTRAST   Sometimes it is easiest to examine a topic by demonstrating its similarities to, and differences from, other topics with which the audience is likely to be familiar. From your studies of American history, for example, you know that women and racial and ethnic minorities have sometimes been subjected to prejudice and discrimination in the workplace. Your speech might be organized to compare the experiences among these groups:

I. Women often are not promoted to senior positions because executives do not think they will remain on the job while raising children.

II. Mexican Americans, in many parts of the country, are hired only for the most menial jobs.

III. Earlier, German Americans and Japanese Americans were fired from their jobs because employers thought them to be unpatriotic.

IV. Today, immigrants from the former Soviet Union are at risk because they are seen as competing for existing jobs.

V. African Americans have been limited in work opportunities because many whites believe that they do not want to work.

Now the question is whether you want to highlight the differences or the similarities among these groups. You might select either of the following as your last main idea:

VI. Although some groups have managed to overcome the effects of discrimination and have succeeded in the workplace, others have not been so lucky.

or

VI. Although the experiences of these groups are very different, they have one factor in common: Society's prejudice places an artificial ceiling on their economic opportunities.

In either case, the earlier main ideas are brought together in the last one, which shows either how differences outweigh similarities or the reverse.

RESIDUES   A final organizational pattern is to arrange the speech by process of elimination. This pattern works well when there are a finite number of possibilities, none particularly desirable, and you want to argue that one of them represents "the least among the evils." For example, in a political campaign in which you find no candidate particularly appealing, you could use this pattern to rule out all but one candidate, whom you then support as being the least objectionable.

Student speaker Jennifer Aiello used organization by residues to convince her classmates that tuition increases, although certainly unpopular, were necessary. She arranged her main ideas to rule out the other options available to the school:

No one wants to pay more money. But let's look at the other options. Does anyone want larger classes? . . . How about fewer discussion sections? . . . Can we afford to make cuts in campus security? . . . What about student health care?

By talking about each of these other options, Jennifer was able to convince most of her audience that a moderate tuition increase was warranted and would be better than any alternative.

THE SITUATION

Last week, you had twenty dollars stolen out of your wallet. This was one incident in a wave of many recent campus thefts. Your advisor has asked you to speak to the other students about your experience as well as what you've learned about campus safety and how to protect yourself in the future.

MAKING CHOICES

1. How should you decide what main points you want to relay to your audience?

2. What organizational pattern will be most effective in conveying that information to your audience?

3. What information is most important to relay and where should that be placed in your speech?

WHAT IF . . .

How would your organizational decisions change if the following were true:

1. Your speech was to precede a speech by the chief of campus security.

2. The campus crime problem wasn't a recent phenomenon.

Choosing the Organizational Pattern

The organizational patterns described here do not exhaust all the possibilities, but they illustrate that you have many options from which to choose.[7] How should you decide which organizational pattern to use in your speech? Does it matter, for example, whether you use a cause–effect pattern or a comparison and contrast pattern? How do you know whether, say, the costs and benefits of voting are more important than the convenience of voting? The answers to questions like these are complex and must take into account your subject, your purpose, your audience, and your culture.

BASED ON YOUR SUBJECT Certain subjects lend themselves to particular organizational patterns. For example, because the collapse of communism in Eastern Europe is a historical event, it has a dramatic structure that would be emphasized by telling a story in chronological order. On the other hand, a speech about the components of air pollution would more likely suggest a topical pattern.

BASED ON YOUR PURPOSE Your purpose or strategy also influences the selection of an organizational pattern. For instance, if you want to urge the audience to lobby for the regulation of cable television, then an analytical pattern that emphasizes problems and solutions will be especially appropriate, because it will focus attention on the specific proposal for which you want listeners to lobby.

BASED ON YOUR AUDIENCE   Your audience is another influence on the arrangement of your speech. For example, listeners who have paid little attention to developments in Eastern Europe would probably be more interested in an overview of the collapse of communism since 1989 than in a country-by-country analysis. But an audience composed mostly of people with Eastern European origins might be strongly interested in hearing about events in their "old countries." And listeners who are involved in foreign policy issues would probably be most interested in the implications of changes in Eastern Europe. These differences can help you decide which points to put first and last.

BASED ON THE CULTURE   Finally, the culture will affect your organizational pattern. For example, mainstream American culture is strongly oriented toward pragmatism, and so a pattern that focuses on problems and solutions would resonate well for many listeners. But other cultures and subcultures have a much greater concern for ideology, for myth and ritual, for narrative, or for authority; the preference for these values would affect the pattern of analysis.

Joanna Watkins was about to address an audience with a high proportion of Asian students. She had studied some Roper Poll surveys about dominant values among various cultural groups in the United States and had learned that many Asians value family and group loyalty and mutual support more than such mainstream American values as competitiveness and individual achievement. Since Joanna's topic was about how to get ahead in college, she needed to arrange her speech carefully. In this case, a highly pragmatic cause–effect pattern—which might be just right in other situations—would probably be inappropriate.

Clearly, no organizational pattern is automatically "right" for any given speech. You need to think critically about the implications and effects of any pattern and choose an arrangement that suits your strategy. Moreover, although we have considered these basic patterns as though they were mutually exclusive, you obviously can combine them. For instance, you could use a chronological pattern but at each step in the chronology you might examine developments topically or by reference to causes and effects. Or you could organize your speech using both a topical pattern and comparison and contrast. In theory, the potential combinations of patterns are limitless. Particularly when audience members have different cultural backgrounds, value systems, and priorities, a creative combination may be most effective.

SELECTING AND ARRANGING SUPPORTING MATERIALS

Many of the same considerations we have discussed about selecting and arranging main ideas also apply to the materials you will use to support your main ideas. In Chapter 5 you studied research techniques to help you *locate* supporting materials; now you should consider which materials to select and how to arrange them.

Selection of Supporting Materials

HOW MUCH AND WHAT KIND?   Probably the most important question, and the hardest to answer, is "How much support is enough?" You need to offer enough evidence to establish your claims but not so much that the

Checklist

7.4 *Selecting Supporting Materials*

1. **Does the supporting material meet tests of strength for its type? (These are given in Chapter 5.)**
2. **Will the supporting material be easily understood?**
3. **Is the supporting material vivid and interesting?**
4. **Is the supporting material consistent with other things you know?**
5. **Will the supporting material be efficient to present?**

speech becomes repetitive and boring. But where is the middle ground between these extremes?

The only all-purpose answer to this question is, "It depends."[8] It depends, most of all, on your audience analysis. In examining listeners' prior understanding of your topic, you may find that your main idea is one with which they are likely to agree. If so, a relatively modest amount of support will be enough. But if the audience is likely to find your main idea controversial, you will need more support to convince doubters.

For example, a speaker who tells a college audience that the legal drinking age should be lowered to eighteen is probably "preaching to the choir." These listeners have likely already accepted the claim, and so the speaker needs only a few pieces of reliable supporting material. But a speaker who tells the same audience that the legal drinking age should be kept at twenty-one will probably need to supply much more evidence to convince listeners that the benefits of such a change would outweigh the disadvantages. In contrast, if the audience were composed of older people, the reverse would likely be true: The speaker who wants to raise the drinking age might need less supporting material than the speaker who wants to lower it.

Besides listeners' beliefs about the specific topic, their common knowledge and experience will affect how much supporting material you need. Also, if they are skeptical by nature, you will want to add more support. If they are impatient or are not good listeners, you will want to keep the speech short and the supporting materials simple. If they are accustomed to asking questions after a speech, you will want to anticipate their major questions and to incorporate supporting material that prepares you to answer them.

The following general procedure can help you decide how much supporting material you need:

1. As shown in Figure 7.1, imagine scales, each ranging from low to high, labeled "Knowledge," "Beliefs and Values," and "Willingness to Act."
2. Based on your audience analysis, place an **X** on each scale at the position which you think characterizes your audience.
3. Based on your strategic planning, place an **O** on each scale at the position which the audience needs to occupy if you are to achieve your specific purpose.
4. Examine the distance between the **X**s and the **O**s. In general, the greater the distance, the more supporting material you need.

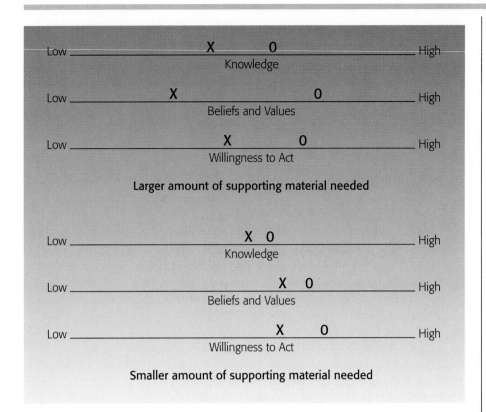

FIGURE 7.1
How much supporting material?

In any case, supporting material should not be redundant; each piece of evidence should add something new to the speech as a whole. The testimony of three different people who say exactly the same thing is not likely to be higher in value than one person's testimony. Nor will you strengthen the speech by citing the same example from multiple sources.

Regarding the types of supporting materials to use, the general goal is to aim for *variety*. The speech should not depend entirely on statistics, on testimony, on examples, or on primary documents. The reasons are simple. First, you are more likely to hold the audience's interest by varying the types of evidence you offer. Although it is important that the audience be able to anticipate your general pattern, too much repetition induces boredom. Second, different listeners will be persuaded by different kinds of evidence. If your audience is heterogeneous, then using a variety of support helps you to strike a responsive chord among many different listeners.

WHAT CRITERIA?　Having decided how much and what types of support you need, you still face other choices. For example, you may have decided that testimony is the form of support you need and that one quotation from an expert will be enough. But your research may have accumulated the testimony of four or five experts. How do you decide which one to use? Similarly, you may have found multiple examples, various statistical measures, or more primary documents than you might need.

What criteria can you use to assess these supporting materials? Obviously, your choices should not be random. The following guidelines will help you to select supporting materials that will contribute the most to your speech:

1. Apply the criteria for strength of supporting material that were given in Chapter 5. For instance, with regard to testimony you should ask which authority has the greatest expertise on the subject, which statement is most recent (if timeliness is a factor), and so on. With respect to examples, you want to use a case that is representative. And if you are choosing among pieces of statistical evidence, consider the reliability and validity of each.

2. Select the supporting material that is easiest to understand. Remember that you want to direct the audience's thinking toward your main ideas. If listeners have to work hard to understand and remember your supporting material, they will be distracted from the focus of your speech.

3. Select vivid or interesting supporting material when you can. Not every piece of evidence will be graphic and easy to remember, of course. But when you have a choice, select supporting material that will interest listeners and will hold their attention. Less interesting material requires the audience to give it greater concentration, which again will distract from your main ideas.

4. Select supporting material that is consistent with other things you know. It is always possible, of course, that your prior beliefs and the audience's common sense will turn out to be mistaken. But a useful test of supporting material is whether it is consistent with what you already know to be true. If you use material that challenges commonly held beliefs, you should be prepared to defend it and explain why the audience should not reject it out of hand.

5. When you have a choice, select supporting material that will be efficient to present. In general, a short anecdote is better than a long narrative, if they make the same point. And a statistical measure with categories that are clear is more useful than one that needs lengthy explanations.

Arrangement of Supporting Materials

Just as the main ideas of a speech can be arranged according to a variety of patterns, so too can the supporting materials that establish each main idea. The same considerations—your purpose and your strategy—govern the arrangement of main ideas and of supporting materials.

Suppose, for example, that for a main idea you want to demonstrate that the percentage of eighteen-year-olds who attend college has been increasing steadily. Because your objective is to demonstrate a rate and direction of change, a chronological pattern might serve best. It would enable you to "take a snapshot" of how many eighteen-year-olds were in college at different points in time. You could show your audience that in 1960 about 24 percent of high school graduates attended college; in 1970 the number had increased to 33 percent; in 1980 it remained about the same; but in 1990 it jumped to almost 40 percent (see Fig. 7.2). By arranging these "snapshots" in chronological order, you can convey the message of ongoing progress.

For another example, suppose you want to establish that alienation from politics is a nationwide occurrence. You might use a spatial pattern,

Year	Percent
1960	23.8
1970	33.3
1980	32.3
1985	34.3
1988	37.6
1989	38.5
1990	39.6
1991	41.4

FIGURE 7.2

Percentage of high school graduates attending college.
Source: *Statistical Abstract of the United Staes,* 1992.

drawing on examples from the East, the Midwest, the South, and the West. In yet another speech you might want to emphasize trends in the training and preparation of popular music singers. You could use a topical pattern to focus on each singer you want to discuss, or a comparison and contrast pattern that would let you demonstrate important similarities and differences among the singers.

You also can combine the patterns of arrangement in a single speech. In discussing the apathy of American voters, you might use both a chronological and a spatial pattern, as follows:

I. Voter apathy has become a growing concern.

   A. During the years before World War I, voter turnout was high.

   B. In the modern age, the height of voter participation came in 1960.

   C. Since 1960 there has been a slow but steady decline in political participation.

II. Voter apathy is widespread.

   A. It can be found in the East.

   B. It can be found in the Midwest.

   C. It can be found in the South.

   D. It can be found in the West.

Such a combination, aside from clarifying each main idea in the most appropriate way, also brings variety to the speech—a desirable objective in itself.

Summary

Organizing the body of the speech involves two sets of choices: what to include and what pattern of arrangement to use. Both decisions relate to the main ideas of the speech as well as to materials that support those ideas.

Organization helps both the audience and the speaker. A well-organized speech is more persuasive and more easily remembered—partly because form itself is persuasive, partly because a recognizable form makes content easier to remember, and partly because listeners can anticipate what is coming next. For the speaker, organizational structure is an aid in preparing the speech, in evaluating its main ideas, and, when presenting, helping you remember what comes next.

Main ideas are chosen by reference to the speaker's strategy and purpose and also by reference to the themes that are most frequently identified through research. Main ideas should be relatively few in number, simple in phrasing, parallel in structure, coherent, and complete in their treatment of the topic.

Arranging the main ideas raises such considerations as their dependence on one another, the value of beginning with the familiar, the importance of first and last impressions, and especially the nature of the audience. Speakers should be familiar with seven general patterns of arrangement: chronological, spatial, categorical (topical), cause–effect, problem–solution, comparison and contrast, and residues.

Selection criteria are also invoked with respect to supporting materials for the speech. These criteria begin with audience analysis, which helps to determine how much and, perhaps, which types of supporting material are needed. Supporting material should be easy to understand, interesting, varied in type, representative of the available evidence, easy to present, credible, and consistent with what already is known. The same factors that affect the arrangement of main ideas also affect the arrangement of supporting material. Materials that support different main ideas may be arranged in different patterns.

From this discussion of how to organize the body of the speech we move next to focus on the introduction, the conclusion, and transitions. Then we will examine the organization of a complete speech.

Discussion Questions

1. In this chapter we examined Stuart Kim's strategic plan to select and organize main ideas for a speech to convince listeners to donate to the United Way. But what would Stuart's speech be like if he faced a different rhetorical situation? Imagine that he is planning to speak to fellow volunteers at a yearend gathering to celebrate the United Way. Using the list of ideas that Stuart developed in his research, and drawing on your own imagination, discuss the selection and arrangement of appropriate main ideas for such a speech.

2. Which organizational pattern would you recommend for each of the following rhetorical situations? Why?

   To inform an audience of high-school students about their college options

   To explain the historical development of baseball to a group of British tourists

   To teach a group of coworkers how to use a new computer program

   To strengthen the commitment of fellow party members to a candidate's campaign

   To persuade a hostile audience that cigarettes should be regulated more strictly

   To introduce an award-winning journalist who is about to give a lecture at a school assembly

3. What is the best organizational strategy for your next speech in this class? Gather in groups of four or five, and discuss your strategic plan with your classmates. Answer the following questions about each group member's strategy:

   a. Do the main ideas satisfy the criteria of simplicity, discreteness, parallel structure, balance, coherence, and completeness?
   b. Which other organizational patterns might be more suitable for the purpose and audience of this speech?
   c. Which type of supporting material is needed to develop each main idea in the speech?

1. Select the main ideas for your next speech.

   a. Use Checklist 7.1 to generate a list of potential main ideas.
   b. Subject each idea in the list to the tests described in this chapter: Is the idea essential? Can a more general statement combine several main ideas?

2. Arrange the main ideas for your next speech.

   a. Identify the pattern of arrangement that you have chosen.
   b. Write a paragraph or two to justify the pattern that you have selected. In doing so, ask yourself the following questions:

      Are the ideas dependent on or independent of one another?
      Are you beginning with the familiar or with the unfamiliar?
      Are the first and the last ideas strongest?
      Why is this pattern most appropriate for your audience and purpose?

3. Select the supporting material for your next speech.

   a. Draw scales like those in Figure 7.1 to determine how much supporting material you need.
   b. Choose the supporting material that you will use to develop each main idea in the speech.
   c. Using the criteria in Checklist 7.4, write a sentence or two to explain why you have chosen each piece of supporting material.

1. **Using journalistic questions to develop a thesis and main ideas.** Journalists are advised that a coherent newspaper story answers the questions: who, did what, when, where, and why? You can also use this principle to think about selecting information to organize your speech. Do an interactive exercise at the **Allyn & Bacon Public Speaking Website.** The exercise will start with one of the journalistic questions as a way of exploring topic ideas. From there you will focus on the goal for an informative speech. Based on that goal, you can develop your thesis and identify main ideas to use in a speech. Lastly, you can choose a pattern of arrangement to use.

(continued)

Point your browser to <http://www.abacon.com/pubspeak/exercise/5wtopic.html> and complete the exercise. Note that you have the option of having a copy of your results page sent to your instructor, or to yourself. You may also print a hard copy of the exercise.

2. **Finding patterns of arrangement.** Observe the pattern of arrangement used in speeches by listening to RealAudio files or by reading texts of speeches. Go to the **Allyn & Bacon Public Speaking Website** link "Develop an Organizational Pattern" by pointing your browser to <http://www.abacon.com/pubspeak/organize/patterns.html>. After listening to the speech, assess the organization critically:

   - *Do the main ideas satisfy the criteria of simplicity, discreteness, parallel structure, balance, coherence, and completeness?*

   - *Is the organizational pattern chosen appropriate for the purpose of the speech and the audience?*

   - *Does the speaker use supporting material to develop each main idea?*

3. **Assessing principles of organization on Web pages.** What principles of organization work best for a Web page? Use the questions outlined below to assess the organizational strategy used in each of the following Web addresses:

   The World Wide Web Virtual Library: <http://vlib.stanford.edu/Overview.html>

   State and Local Government on the Net: <http://www.piperinfo.com/state/states.html>

   Yahoo! News: <http://www.yahoo.com/headlines/news/>

   The Federal Court Locator: <http://www.law.vill.edu/Fed-Ct/fedcourt.html>

   HotWired Magazine: <http://www.hotwired.com>

   The Washington Post: <http://www.washingtonpost.com>

   - *To enable a user to navigate from one main idea to another, does the Web page designer use the criteria of simplicity, discreteness, parallel structure, balance, coherence, and completeness?*

   - *Is the Web page effectively organized by using one of the patterns of arrangement used in speechmaking: chronological, spatial, categorical, cause–effect, problem–solution, comparison and contrast, and residues?*

   - *Does the organizational strategy for the page seem to work for the type of content on it and for the audience for whom the page is written?*

1. Experiments show that an audience retains more of a message that is organized than one that it is not. See Ernest C. Thompson, "An Experimental Investigation of the Relative Effectiveness of Organizational Structure in Oral Communication," *Southern Speech Communication Journal* 26 (Fall 1960): 59–69.

2. Research confirms that organized speeches are comprehended more fully than unorganized speeches. See Arlee Johnson, "A Preliminary Investigation of the Relationship between Message Organization and Listener Comprehension," *Communication Studies* 21 (Summer 1970): 104–107.

3. One study suggests that an unorganized persuasive message may actually produce an effect that is opposite to what the speaker intended. See Raymond G. Smith, "An Experimental Study of the Effects of Speech Organization upon Attitudes of College Students," *Communication Monographs* 18 (November 1951): 292–301. Another study simply concludes that an extremely unorganized speech is not very persuasive. See James C. McCroskey and R. Samuel Mehrley, "The Effects of Disorganization and Nonfluency on Attitude Change and Source Credibility," *Communication Monographs* 36 (March 1969): 13–21.

4. Rhetorical theorist Kenneth Burke envisions form as "the creation of an appetite in the mind of the auditor, and the adequate satisfying of that appetite." See "Psychology and Form," *Counter-Statement,* Berkeley: Univ. of California Press, 1931.

5. One study demonstrated that speakers who have a plan and practice that plan have fewer pauses in their speeches. See John O. Greene, "Speech Preparation and Verbal Fluency," *Human Communication Research* 11 (Fall 1984): 61–84.

6. See Howard Gilkinson, Stanley F. Paulson, and Donald E. Sikkink, "Effects of Order and Authority in an Argumentative Speech," *Quarterly Journal of Speech* 40 (April 1954): 183–192; and Halbert E. Gulley and David K. Berlo, "Effect of Intercellular and Intracellular Speech Structure on Attitude Change and Learning," *Communication Monographs* 23 (November 1956): 288–297.

7. For a few more ideas, see James A. Benson, "Extemporaneous Speaking: Organization which Inheres," *Argumentation and Advocacy* 14 (Winter 1978): 150–155.

8. Some researchers who have tried to determine experimentally the place of evidence in a speech have concluded that there are just too many variables (such as the prior beliefs of the audience members, the credibility of the speaker, and the different types of evidence) to draw deterministic conclusions. See Kathy Kellermann, "The Concept of Evidence: A Critical Review," *Argumentation and Advocacy* 16 (Winter 1980): 159–172; and Richard B. Gregg, "The Rhetoric of Evidence," *Western Journal of Speech Communication* 31 (Summer 1967): 180–189.

OCCIDENTAL

COLLEGE

chapter 8

Organizing the Speech:Introductions, Conclusions, and Transitions

In This Chapter We Will:

- Discover why an introduction and a conclusion are needed to complete a speech and give it a satisfying sense of form.

- Examine the main purposes and some common types of introductions and conclusions.

- Offer strategies for preparing an introduction and a conclusion.

- Explore how speakers use transitions to connect the elements of a speech and give its structure a dynamic quality.

- Determine the elements of a transition, which may be either explicit or implicit.

The body of the speech (Chapter 7) is certainly its most important part; it takes up the most time, and it expresses and supports the main ideas. But if a speaker launches directly into the first main idea and ends abruptly after the last, you probably would think something was strange, perhaps even insulting, about the speech. It would be like joining a conversation that was already well along, having missed the beginning completely. The ending would seem abrupt, too—like reading a book that was missing its last few pages or walking out of a movie in its last minutes. You would be surprised that the speaker had stopped, because the speech would not seem "finished."

An audience reacts this way because a speech that is composed only of its body is not really complete. It does not satisfy listeners' expectations about form. Listeners expect a beginning, a middle, and an end. They expect to be guided into a topic, not dropped in its midst, and they expect the discussion to conclude naturally. Audiences notice when a speaker departs from this customary sense of form; if they are not disturbed by it, they at least are likely to be distracted.

In this chapter we will explore the two elements of a speech that surround its body: the introduction and the conclusion. We will focus on the purposes of these elements, some common types, and strategies for preparing them. Finally, we will look at how speakers use transitions to connect the introduction, body, and conclusion and thus give the speech a dynamic quality.

INTRODUCTIONS: BEGINNING THE SPEECH

Both daily life and studies in the psychology of persuasion tell us that first impressions are extremely important. When you meet someone new, you quickly form impressions about that person, often based on little more than superficial characteristics like the person's clothing and hairstyle, or car, or way of speaking. Moreover, many first impressions are likely to prove durable; they will influence how you interpret what this person says and does.[1]

The Purposes of an Introduction

The **introduction** to a speech powerfully affects the audience's first impressions of the speaker. It gives the audience clues about the speaker's personality, intentions, style, and overall perspective. These first impressions shape how the audience will perceive the entire speech.

The introduction also prepares the audience for the speech by giving clues about what will follow. It establishes the context for the speaker's ideas, thus putting listeners in the right frame of mind to attend to those ideas.

The overall purpose of using your introduction to prepare the audience can be broken down into four specific goals:

- To gain the attention and interest of your audience
- To dispose the audience favorably toward you and your topic
- To clarify the purpose or thesis of your speech
- To preview the development of your topic

introduction
The beginning of the speech, which affects listeners' first impressions of the speaker and prepares them for the speech.

GAINING THE ATTENTION AND INTEREST OF YOUR AUDIENCE   The introduction should make the audience want to hear what will follow. Accomplishing this goal is critical because, like someone switching television channels, listeners can choose whether or not to pay attention. Even when the audience cannot escape a speaker physically, individuals can decide whether or not to be active listeners. They can pay careful attention and follow the speaker's thought process, or they can fidget and daydream until the speech ends—unheard.

The primary way to make listeners pay attention is to convince them that what follows will be interesting. An effective introduction suggests to listeners that they will be stimulated by the speech. The suggestion may be explicit, as when a speaker says, in so many words, "This concerns you." But often it is the form of the introduction as much as its content that captures the audience's interest. A lively narrative, startling or unexpected information, or a personal experience that listeners can identify with obviously has content; perhaps more important, however, is that such introductory techniques suggest that the speech will be interesting and thus warrants attention.

DISPOSING THE AUDIENCE FAVORABLY TOWARD YOU AND YOUR TOPIC   It is not enough merely to get the audience's attention. Indeed, a speaker can easily gain attention by turning the audience hostile, but such an introduction would be counterproductive. No one likes to be assailed by a speaker, and few listeners will respond positively to someone they distrust or someone who seems to know little about the topic. How much energy would you invest in following a speaker who is overbearing, pompous, or dogmatic?

Beyond sparking attention, then, the introduction aims to make the audience favorably disposed toward you and your topic so that listeners will be sympathetic and attentive. This is not to suggest that they will listen uncritically and accept whatever you say but rather that they will be charitable in interpreting and responding to your speech. You can create a favorable first impression not only by being well prepared and confident but also by offering examples and narratives that fit your listeners' interests and perspectives. As you learned in Chapter 3, the audience analysis will indicate the basic predispositions of your listeners. By identifying with these predispositions in your introduction, you make it more likely that the audience will be favorably disposed toward you and your topic.

Like most generalizations, this one needs to be qualified a bit. Sometimes a speaker will choose deliberately not to gain the audience's favor. For example, a dissenter who feels the need to speak out against the majority opinion may intentionally make an audience hostile by, say, accusing them of denying rights to those who are less powerful. Even though the immediate audience is unlikely to be persuaded by such a direct attack, the dissenter may, in fact, be addressing those listeners primarily to gain the attention and favor of some other audience. The real intended audience is composed of people who will hear about the speech and conclude that the dissenter is a person of courage and principle for venturing into hostile territory. This audience, of course, will then be favorably disposed toward the speaker and the topic; the dissenter will have gained both their attention and their goodwill.

CLARIFYING THE PURPOSE OR THESIS OF YOUR SPEECH   Listeners are more likely to follow your speech and be influenced by it if you clearly identify what you want them to believe or to do. Most introductions include an explicit statement of the speaker's thesis or purpose, such as: "I will argue that the United States cannot compete economically without strengthening public education" or "After you consider the facts, I hope you will call the Red Cross and volunteer to donate blood."

Speakers often state their purpose after making introductory remarks that gain the audience's interest and make listeners favorably disposed. But sometimes speakers can assume that the audience is interested and favorably disposed. In this case the entire introduction might focus on an explicit statement of purpose.

PREVIEWING THE DEVELOPMENT OF YOUR TOPIC   Besides capturing the audience and clarifying your purpose, the introduction also previews how you will develop your topic in the body of the speech. Classical theorists of public speaking refer to this step as the **partition;** the speaker divides the body of the speech into selected categories for discussion.[2] For example, a speaker might say, "First I will explain how higher education got into financial trouble, then I will describe the consequences of this for students and faculty, and finally I will tell you what we can do about it." Basically, the speaker has revealed the pattern for the body of the speech (in this case, a problem–solution pattern) and what the major headings will be. As we saw in Chapter 7, such a "road map" helps listeners to follow the speaker's thinking and to anticipate what will come next. If listeners recognize the form of the speech early along and participate in following it, they will be more likely to find the speech effective and to be influenced by it.

An Example of an Introduction

Only your own imagination and creativity limit you in devising an introduction that achieves the four primary goals. Even so, several types of introductions show up frequently in successful speeches, and you should be aware of them to decide whether they will be effective for your speech and audience. Before examining them individually, let's look at how one student used her introduction to prepare the audience.

Michelle Ekanemesang was the third speaker to give an informative speech in her public speaking class. To gain her listeners' attention (after all, they had already heard two speeches), she walked to the podium, paused, looked at the audience, and then suddenly dropped a large book on the floor. The resounding thud brought all eyes to Michelle as she began to speak: "Just as easily as that book fell to the floor, the innocence of a child can crash." Then, walking around to the front of the podium to retrieve the book, Michelle continued:

> However, unlike this book, a child's innocence cannot be picked up and placed back on the pedestal where it was. Children today encounter many experiences that lower the level of their innocence. Along with gangs, guns, and drugs, they also face another monster that is not so well publicized. This monster is sexual abuse. Approximately one child out of four is sexually abused by the age of 18. This means that perhaps four people in this classroom have been abused. Today I want to give you some insight into the causes and effects of childhood sexual abuse as well as some tips about preventing it and what to do if you or a child you know has been a victim of sexual abuse.

Michelle's book-dropping trick could have turned into a resounding flop if she had not explained how it connected to her speech. She quickly and effec-

partition
Division of the body of the speech among selected categories for discussion.

tively gained her listeners' attention and then maintained it by saying that some of them might be victims themselves, thereby emphasizing the personal relevance of her topic. From the outset it was clear that Michelle was going to talk about the horrors of child abuse. She took a serious tone of outrage and disposed the audience favorably toward her treatment of the subject. Her final statement in the introduction then clearly previewed which main topics the audience could expect her to cover: the causes, effects, prevention, and treatment of childhood sexual abuse.

Types of Introductions

In deciding which of the following types of introductions to use, always try to relate the introduction directly to your speech, as Michelle did. If you quote someone famous or tell a joke without showing how that connects to the speech itself, you risk raising the audience's expectations, which your speech may not fulfill. The speech, after all, should be a unified whole. The introduction and the conclusion should work together with the body of the speech to create the response or action that you desire.

IDENTIFYING WITH YOUR AUDIENCE One obvious way to build goodwill and capture the audience's interest is to draw on something that you share—a common experience, common acquaintances, common values, or common goals. If listeners perceive you as being basically like themselves, they automatically form a good first impression of you. And their interest should be high because, in effect, you may be telling them something about themselves or speaking on their behalf.

Student speakers often find it easy and effective to identify with their audience because, typically, they do share many common experiences with their listeners. One student began a speech about the evils of bureaucracy by referring to a common campus experience:

> You've probably noticed, as I have, how slow the lines get during class registration. It seems as though the peak traffic periods always come just when all the staff are on break. A process that ought to make things efficient for students is devoted instead to making things comfortable for the staff. Actually, that's what most bureaucracies are like.

Having gained the interest and goodwill of the audience by identifying with them, and having stated the thesis, the speaker was then well positioned to

Checklist

8.1 *Types of Introductions*

1. **Identifying with the audience**
2. **Referring to the speech situation**
3. **Stating the purpose**
4. **Stating the importance of the topic**
5. **Citing statistics or making claims**
6. **Telling a story (anecdote)**
7. **Using an analogy**
8. **Asking a rhetorical question**
9. **Quoting someone**
10. **Using humor**

---

complete the introduction by previewing how the discussion of bureaucracy and its evils would be developed in the speech.

REFERRING TO THE SPEECH SITUATION   Another way to establish common bonds with an audience and to strike an appropriate opening note is to refer directly to the situation. Many speeches are delivered on ceremonial occasions (for example, commencement addresses, wedding toasts, speeches of welcome or farewell), and these often are introduced effectively by an explicit reference to the occasion. At other times the content of the speech, rather than its ceremonial character, may dictate a reference to the occasion. The student who is speaking about campus bureaucracies, for example, might now preview the development of the topic by tying it to the situation: "Since today is the beginning of registration for next semester, it's high time to do something about the inefficient, ineffective bureaucracy that controls our academic destinies."

Other situational factors also can be the touchstone for an effective introduction. For example, the location of the speech might be important, as it was when Martin Luther King, Jr., began his famous address "I Have a Dream." Dr. King's introduction noted that he stood symbolically in the shadow of Abraham Lincoln; indeed, he was delivering his address from the Lincoln Memorial.

Referring to a previous speaker might be a natural introduction to your own speech. If your reference endorses or builds on something a previous speaker said, it creates a bridge between the two speeches and a seemingly logical flow to the discussion. And if the previous speaker was competent and credible, you even may inherit the audience's favorable disposition toward that speaker.

On the other hand, your reference does not have to support the previous speaker. In fact, that speech might provide the ammunition needed for you to disagree with something the speaker said. In this case your introduction is both a bridge that maintains continuity and a stop sign that signals the differences between the two of you. For example, imagine that a student in a public speaking class just spoke about the underappreciated beauty of snow. By coincidence the next speaker has planned to extol the joys of summertime. Adapting the introduction to fit this situation, the second speaker could say, "Snow is nice if you're looking at it from afar. But speaking as a Midwesterner who is tired of sloshing through an icy mess on my way to school, I celebrate something far more beautiful: summertime."

STATING YOUR PURPOSE   Sometimes an introduction that explicitly states your purpose can be very helpful, especially if the audience is captive or is known already to be favorably disposed to your ideas. This approach is also effective when your thesis is startling or unexpected: "In the next hour, many children in this town will suffer from abuse and neglect. We will see why this happens. Then I want you to volunteer one day a week to help stop this." Your direct challenge will probably make the audience take notice. You've alerted them that you expect something of them, and so they are likely to pay attention in order to decide whether or not to grant your request.

STATING THE IMPORTANCE OF YOUR TOPIC   Another effective opening device is to alert the audience to the significance of your topic before actually stating what the topic is. For example, a speech about preventing AIDS might begin with the statement "I have information that literally can save your lives." Similarly, a speech about purchasing a home might begin with "Today I want to discuss the most important financial decision most of us will ever make."

This type of introduction demands the audience's attention. Just by saying that your topic is important, you ask people to take notice. This strategy also has an element of mystery, which leads the audience to wonder just what it is that is so critical. Be aware, however, that this approach has been overused, and audiences sometimes react to such claims by being skeptical. A speaker who opens with "This speech could change the course of your life" may actually prompt listeners to think, "Oh, sure; I've heard that before." Consider your topic and your audience carefully to ensure that this type of introduction will help you and will not backfire. Remember: One goal of your introduction is to dispose the audience favorably toward your point of view. If listeners react skeptically at the outset, you may never regain their interest.

If your speech has a formal title, be sure that its specific wording is accurate and complete. Then your introduction can "unpack" the title to forecast what will follow and to highlight your main points. In 1984 Governor Mario Cuomo of New York illustrated this introductory strategy in a speech at the University of Notre Dame:

> I would like to begin by drawing your attention to the title of this lecture: "Religious Belief and Public Morality: A Catholic Governor's Perspective." I was not invited to speak on "Church and State" generally. Certainly not "Mondale versus Reagan." The subject assigned is difficult enough. I will try not to do more than I've been asked.

Governor Cuomo then proceeded to state his perspective and to indicate how he planned to develop his ideas.

CITING STATISTICS, MAKING CLAIMS Listeners sit up in interest when a speaker cites startling statistics or makes a surprising claim. Their astonishment on hearing the information causes them to pay attention. For example, to introduce the topic of academic dishonesty, a student might begin:

> A highly reliable national survey recently found that over 70 percent of college students admitted that they at some time had cheated in a class. If we are typical college students, that means that fourteen out of the twenty of us are cheaters. I couldn't believe this until I began to examine what academic dishonesty is. Let me share with you what actions it includes.

This type of introduction works best when the statistics are accurate but not well known—when there is a gap between what listeners think they know and what is actually the case. Statistics can show that our common assumptions are not accurate, that a problem is greater than we know, that a condition we viewed as worsening is actually improving, and so on. But the risk with this approach is that listeners may become defensive about their predispositions. Rather than considering the possibility that academic dishonesty really is more serious than they thought, for example, they may react by doubting the statistics or by denying the claim. You certainly want to encourage listeners to think critically; but if their very first response to your introduction is to doubt what you say, it will be difficult to build goodwill and regain their interest. Keep your primary purposes in mind when developing your introduction.

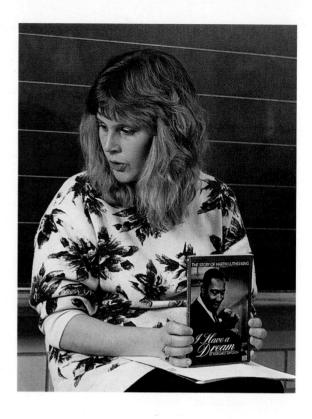

TELLING A STORY   Speakers often begin with an anecdote—an extended illustration or example that is cast in narrative form. In other words, an anecdote tells a story, which may be true or fictional. A speaker introduces the topic by relating a personal experience or something that happened to others. For example, when student Michael Green gave a speech about the harmful effects of spanking children, he began by relating an experience he had as resident advisor in his dormitory:

> Last Friday night, a guy from the fourth floor was making a lot of noise and disturbing the other residents on the floor. This guy is a troublemaker, and that night he was really drunk. When I told him to chill out, he mocked me and said, "What are you going to do about it?" I was really mad, because here was this punk, who weighs about half as much as I do, challenging my authority. It would have been so easy to use physical force to teach him a lesson. But I restrained myself. I knew that hitting this student would only teach him that violence is the proper way to respond to problems. Similarly, when parents spank their children, they are letting their anger speak for them, and they are sending the wrong message.

The power of an anecdotal introduction lies in its narrative form. The story is engaging, and the chronological sequence is easy to follow. A narrative is concrete—it involves specific characters in a particular situation—and therefore listeners can attend to it with less effort than is needed to follow something more abstract. A narrative encourages the audience to sympathize and even identify with its characters. In contrast, opening with statistics or a quotation removed from its context seems less natural to listeners, and they may wonder what your point is.

One potential drawback in using an introductory anecdote is that it may overshadow the preview of your topic or even the body of the speech. It may be so interesting that it distracts attention from your main points. To avoid this, use an anecdote that leads directly into your thesis statement and partition. Try to create unity between the anecdote and the main points so that each reminds the audience of the other. If you can achieve unity, the anecdote alone will remind listeners later of what you said.

USING AN ANALOGY   Closely related to the anecdote is an analogy, which, as you learned in Chapter 6, is a comparison. An analogy draws attention to the similarities or the differences between two objects, events, or situations. A speaker can use an analogy to clarify an unfamiliar subject by comparing the subject with something else that the audience already understands.

Like anecdotes, analogies help to make abstract concepts concrete. They are especially useful in introducing technical material to listeners who are not specialists in the speaker's field. For example, to inform his audience that the presence of human immunodeficiency virus (HIV) in a person's blood does not necessarily mean that he or she has AIDS, student Dan Kinsella began with the following analogy:

> At the university, many students carry backpacks. So if you entered a building filled with people wearing backpacks, you probably would assume that it was a college building. However, the building could just as well be a restaurant where students hang out. Just as finding backpacks in a building does not always mean that you are on campus, the sighting of HIV in a person's blood does not always mean that the person has AIDS. I am going to explore with you some of the causes and consequences of mistakenly assuming otherwise.

This analogy translated what could be a difficult point—that the presence of HIV does not necessarily indicate an active disease state—into a concept that the audience could grasp easily.

During World War II President Franklin D. Roosevelt was gifted at using analogies to explain the complexities of foreign policy to average voters. Discussing why, in 1940, the United States should lend (rather than sell) war materials to Great Britain and its allies, he offered the analogy of a man whose neighbor's house was on fire. When the neighbor ran up to ask for a garden hose, the man did not first demand payment; instead, he gave the hose to the neighbor on the promise that it would be returned when the threat was past. In just this way, Roosevelt reasoned, the United States should approach lending supplies to cash-strapped allies. This simple analogy both explained and dramatized the president's perspective, and it helped make his case with the public.

Analogies are persuasive (and thus advance the purposes of an introduction) because most listeners find it easy to focus on similarities and differences. To be effective, though, an analogy should be fairly simple and direct, like Roosevelt's. A complex comparison will force your listeners to puzzle out just what it is that you think is similar about the two things, and they will be distracted from the body of your speech. And if your analogy is too farfetched (as some students thought Dan Kinsella's was), listeners' first impressions of you may be negative, and they may not take your main ideas seriously. In both cases the analogy would undercut the purposes of the introduction. An analogy should be fashioned with care. If it doesn't advance your purposes, look for some other way to begin your speech.

ASKING A RHETORICAL QUESTION   Do you think you need to know what a rhetorical question is? Like the sentence you just read, a **rhetorical question** is one for which no answer is really expected. Instead, simply asking the question will cause an audience (or a reader) to think about the answer.

When a speaker poses a rhetorical question, the real goal is not to come up with an answer but, rather, to make the audience think. This device may prompt listeners to imagine themselves in some other time, place, or situation. For example, in urging white Americans to be sensitive to the role of race in the lives of African Americans, a student speaker might begin by asking, "How would you feel if, at the time you were born, your earning capacity and life expectancy were automatically reduced for no reason but the color of your skin?" Then, to preview the development of the speech, the student might ask, "Why is it that, forty years after Brown v. Board of Education, educational opportunities still are not equal?" The first question gets the audience thinking, and the second question previews the development of the speech. Since the goal is to make the audience think, the speaker in this case would probably not state the thesis explicitly just yet.

The pitfall in asking rhetorical questions is that speakers have overused or misused this device. Some may ask an introductory question merely to ask it, rather than to induce listeners to imagine a situation or to preview the speech. An even greater risk is that listeners will answer the question in their minds—with an answer that is different from what the speaker wants to discuss. In the worst case of all, someone in the audience may offer a response that undermines the entire introduction. One student began a speech about popular films of the 1960s by asking, "What do you think of when you hear the name 'James Bond'?" From the rear of the classroom another student called out, "A third-rate movie." As beginning lawyers learn (sometimes the hard way), you should never ask a question unless you already know the answer.

QUOTING SOMEONE   The introductory device of beginning a speech with a quotation is especially common and useful in sermons; the scriptural quotation then serves as the text on which the sermon is based. In secular settings, too, speakers often open with a quotation that captures the essential idea they intend to develop. Besides gaining the audience's attention, the quotation leads naturally into the development of the speaker's main ideas.

Quoting an opposing viewpoint is a variation of this type of introduction. Abraham Lincoln did this superbly in a famous speech he made at Cooper Union in 1860. He began by quoting what his political rival, Stephen A. Douglas, had said about the intentions of the country's founders; then Lincoln used the Douglas quotation to highlight and advance his own thesis and main points.

Beginning a speech with a quotation is such a common introductory device that whole books of short quotations are published for this purpose. The warning about introductory quotations, however, is exactly the same as for anecdotes and analogies: Your introduction must relate directly to what you plan to say in your speech. If the audience cannot see the connection clearly, the introduction will seem superfluous and, therefore, will be counterproductive. A good test is to ask yourself whether the quotation will lead naturally to your thesis statement and partition, and then to the body of the speech.

rhetorical question
A question for which no answer is expected but which encourages listeners to think.

USING HUMOR   Perhaps the most common introductory device is to begin the speech with a humorous reference or a joke. Humor relaxes the audience, disposes listeners favorably toward the speaker, and disarms skeptics. It also tells both the speaker and the audience to keep their perspective about the topic and not take themselves too seriously.

Despite all these advantages of humor, the worst advice for preparing the introduction to a speech is that "every speech should start with a joke." Humor is not always appropriate to the subject (or the occasion or the audience), and the joke does not always relate directly to the speech. Again, unless the connection is clear to the audience, at best a joke delays the "real" speech, and at worst it detracts from the speech.[3]

In 1964 President Lyndon Johnson used the occasion of commencement at the University of Michigan to proclaim the values of the Great Society. Unfortunately, his opening was more of a warm-up than an introduction:

> It is a great pleasure to be here today. This university has been coeducational since 1870, but I do not believe it was on the basis of your accomplishments that a Detroit high-school girl said, "In choosing a college, you first have to decide whether you want a coeducational school or an educational school."

The president's good humor continued:

> I came out here today very anxious to meet the Michigan student whose father told a friend of mine that his son's education has been a real value. It stopped his mother from bragging about him.

These jokes clearly had nothing to do with the Great Society, as was apparent when the president's tone changed abruptly: "I have come today from the turmoil of your Capital to the tranquility of your campus to speak about the future of your country." That was the real beginning of the speech; the humorous references were not developed further. President Johnson's joke got listeners' attention and may have disposed listeners positively toward him, but it did not achieve the other purposes of an introduction.

This survey of the types of introductions is extensive, but it is not meant to be complete.[4] Anything can be used to begin a speech if it will achieve the four purposes of an introduction: gaining your audience's interest, disposing listeners to think well of you and your topic, clarifying your purpose or central theme, and previewing how you will develop the topic. The great variety and range of introductory devices, however, does not mean that you should select one hastily or without care. The introduction is clearly critical in making an effective speech, and you should prepare it as carefully as you do the body and the conclusion.

Strategies for Preparing an Introduction

The multiple purposes of an introduction and the great variety of ways to achieve them may seem daunting, but the following strategies and suggestions should help you plan a successful introduction for your speech.

PREPARE THE BODY OF THE SPEECH FIRST   Just as this book explains how to organize the body of the speech (Chapter 7) before focusing in this chapter on introductions and conclusions, you should follow that same sequence in preparing your speech. After all, it helps to know what you are introducing. Having already prepared the body, you now know what your main ideas are and how you will develop them. That information will help you craft an appropriate introduction that prepares the audience effectively. Another good reason to follow this strategy is that you will be less likely to delay preparing the entire speech just because you haven't yet thought of the "perfect" introduction.

RELATE THE INTRODUCTION TO THE BODY   Keep in mind that the introduction has to prepare your listeners and then lead them naturally into the body of your speech. The connection between the introduction and the body should be clear and direct. A particular anecdote, joke, or quotation might well arouse your audience's interest, but if it seems unrelated to your main points, it may not lead listeners in the direction you intend. Indeed, some introductions—no matter how engaging—may undercut your purposes, weakening the entire speech. Although this book examines each element of a speech individually, your goal is to convey a satisfying sense of form to the audience. The introduction is the obvious place to start doing this.

KEEP THE INTRODUCTION BRIEF   Remember that the focus of the speech is on the main ideas that you will develop in the body; the introduction should lead listeners to these ideas, not obscure them. A too long, too strong introduction could turn into the tail that wags the dog, running away with the speech and ultimately confusing your audience.

Some speechwriters advocate that an introduction should take 10 to 20 percent of the total time for the speech. Although we resist such precise measurement, the key point remains: Limit the length of your introduction so that it does not become a speech in itself.[5]

MAKE THE INTRODUCTION COMPLETE   As you experiment with potential introductions, assess how each one advances (or hinders) the purposes that an introduction serves. Although exceptions exist, most introductions include the following elements: a device to gain your listeners' interest and to dispose them favorably toward you as a speaker, a statement of your thesis or purpose, and a preview of how you will develop the topic.

KEEP A FILE OF POTENTIAL INTRODUCTIONS   In developing an introduction, you doubtless will run across ideas, quotations, examples, and other materials that are not immediately useful but that you can imagine shaping into an introduction for a future speech. Keep track of such materials. Do not rely on memory to recall them or find them at just the moment you need them. You might make notes on index cards or sheets of paper, just as you did when researching a speech (Chapter 5), and establish a file of introductory material arranged by topic. Then, when you start preparing your next speech, you already have resources and will not have to depend entirely on either memory or inspiration.

BE GUIDED BY THE EXAMPLES IN THIS BOOK   In this chapter you have studied the most frequently used types of introductions; Appendix B and other speeches in the book also illustrate a variety of introductions. Consider these examples not as models to be followed blindly but as guidelines to help you think creatively about the best way to introduce your particular speech. Developing an introduction is a creative process; use the examples to spark your own thinking and imagination.

PLAN THE INTRODUCTION WORD FOR WORD   Especially in the opening lines of the speech, you want to be sure that you say exactly what you intend. An extemporaneous opening is risky even for very confident, very experienced speakers, because no one can entirely control the speech setting and circumstances. Nor is it wise to carry a written script to the podium, planning to read the introduction aloud. A good first impression is unlikely when your face is buried in notes. Instead, prepare and practice your opening words carefully so that you can begin speaking with confidence and good effect even if your listeners haven't quite settled down. Remember that one of your goals is to capture their attention, and you must be ready to do it with your first words.

Preparing and practicing the introduction word for word will enable you to create the clearest, most compelling first impression on the audience. Moreover, knowing exactly what you are going to say at the beginning of your speech will give you greater confidence and a sense of security. So armed, you can overcome the anxiety that even experienced speakers feel when they stand to address an audience.

CONCLUSIONS: ENDING THE SPEECH

Just as you want to begin your speech on the right note, so do you want to develop an appropriate, effective ending. A speech should neither end abruptly nor trail off into oblivion. As we did with introductions, we will approach conclusions by focusing on their purposes and their types and then looking at some strategies for preparing them.

The Purposes of a Conclusion

Like your introduction, your **conclusion** needs to accomplish several specific goals:

- Complete the sense of form by anticipating the end
- Summarize the main ideas
- Make a final appeal to the audience

COMPLETING THE SENSE OF FORM BY ANTICIPATING THE END   Perhaps the most basic function of the conclusion is to signal to listeners that the speech is ending. No doubt you have heard a speaker who seemed to be finishing several times before the speech actually ended. Such a speech has "false conclusions"—misleading signals that the end is near. Summary statements, the use of the word "finally," and similar cues alert the audience that the speech is wrapping up. But if you send such signals prematurely, you will

conclusion
The closing of the speech, which draws together what the speaker has said and indicates what the audience should believe or do in response to the speech.

confuse listeners and may even arouse their impatience when the speech does not end as expected.

On the other hand, you probably also have heard a speaker who ended so abruptly that you were surprised. Suddenly, although you thought the speaker was still developing a major idea, he or she came to the end of a sentence, said "Thank you," and sat down. Somehow, that approach did not seem right either.

In both cases the speakers failed to provide a satisfying sense of form. Listeners notice when a speaker departs from customary form, and they are bothered by it. If you confuse them with false endings or surprise them by stopping abruptly, your conclusion has not completed the sense of form. Listeners do need to be signaled that it is time to draw together their perceptions about the speech; but you should send this signal only at the appropriate time.

SUMMARIZING THE MAIN IDEAS   A second important purpose of the conclusion is to draw together the main ideas in your speech in a way that helps listeners to remember them. Even trained and experienced listeners rapidly forget what they have heard. If you want the audience to remember what you have said, you need to issue reminders at appropriate points throughout the speech. And no place is more appropriate for a **summary** than the conclusion is.

To end a speech about the messages embodied in popular music, for example, you might summarize by saying, "As we have seen, popular music tells us about our own values, about our relationships with others, and about our obligations to nature, society, and the next generation." As this example shows, a summary does not entirely repeat the main ideas, and it certainly does not reprise their development. Rather, it reminds the audience of key points, often by highlighting particular words or phrases in a way that listeners can remember—as in the parallel structure of the three "about" phrases in this example.

An effective summary, then, is an aid to memory. By including a summary in your conclusion, you will increase the chances that listeners will recall your main ideas correctly.

MAKING A FINAL APPEAL TO THE AUDIENCE   The conclusion is also an opportunity to say exactly what response you want from the audience. It is your last chance to remind listeners about whatever you want them to think or do as a result of your speech.

Sometimes a speaker wants listeners to take a very specific action, such as signing a petition, donating money, writing to their legislators, or purchasing a particular product. At other times the desired response is a belief rather than an action. For example, suppose you want the audience to agree that the current president and administration have set a correct course in foreign policy matters. You are not asking listeners to take any specific action, but you do want them to be favorably disposed toward the president's international policies. Your conclusion might say, "I hope I've convinced you that the president's foreign policy is on the right track." Although you are not asking for anything directly, you do want to intensify or to change your listeners' beliefs. Either response may lead to actions later, but that is not your purpose in making this concluding appeal.

summary
A condensed restatement of the principal ideas just discussed.

Sometimes the response you seek may be even more general, as in these concluding remarks:

> The next time you go to a fast-food restaurant, think twice about whether you'll get a nutritious meal.
>
> Whether or not you agree with my beliefs about abortion, I hope you will think about what I have said.
>
> The next time you wake up and see the sunrise, stop to think about the miracles and wonders of nature.

None of these concluding statements calls for action, and yet each of them asks listeners to "do" something: to become more aware of something they had not recognized or to think critically about something they had accepted. Virtually any speech—whether or not it is billed as a "persuasive" speech—asks for some response from the audience. In developing the conclusion of a speech, your goal is to make the audience understand exactly what response you seek.

An Example of a Conclusion

Here's how Michelle Ekanemesang ended her classroom speech about the sexual abuse of children:

> Remember that children are our future generation and should be safe from plagues like sexual abuse. Committed by psychologically damaged men and women of all ages, sexual abuse is a crime that leaves a lasting scar on its childhood victims. Through education and knowledge we can help these children and prevent them from having to encounter experiences which will affect them forever after. I hope that the information I've shared with you today will be passed on to a younger audience and will help to stop sexual abuse in the future. Remember, prevention is always better than cure!

Michelle's first concluding sentence hinted to the audience that her speech was coming to an end. The next two sentences summarized the points she had made in the body of her speech. Finally, she asked the audience to take action and help stop sexual abuse by passing on the information that children need in order to prevent abuse from occurring.

Types of Conclusions

You already know that the types of introductions are bent toward a purpose and can be developed in various ways to achieve that purpose. The same is true for conclusions. Indeed, some of the following types of conclusions mirror the types of introductions you have studied; others introduce new elements into the speech.

Checklist

8.2 *Types of Conclusions*

1. **Summarizing**
2. **Quoting someone**
3. **Making a personal reference**
4. **Challenging the audience**
5. **Offering a utopian vision**

(In addition, many of the types of introductions in Checklist 8.1 can also be used as concluding devices.)

SUMMARIZING   We observed earlier that one purpose of the conclusion is to summarize the main points of the speech. Sometimes summary is the dominant purpose. In that case the concluding summary would be more extended than in the preceding examples. It would remind the audience not only about major topics addressed but also about the details of your argument, even repeating some memorable thematic phrases. Such an extensive concluding summary may need a "miniconclusion" of its own, to avoid ending abruptly or trailing off into insignificance.

In contrast, sometimes a succinct, bare-bones restatement of key phrases may make the most rousing finish. Consider the following conclusion from a 1937 speech by President Franklin D. Roosevelt warning about the dangers of isolationism:

> America hates war. America hopes for peace. Therefore, America actively engages in the search for peace.

These three simple statements (note their parallel structure) are a brief but highly memorable recapitulation of the main ideas. They suggest finality, they summarize main ideas, and they indicate the action that will be taken.

QUOTING SOMEONE   Just as many speeches begin with a quotation, so many end with one. In both cases, remember to tie the quotation clearly to your speech. A concluding quotation, however, may also go beyond your central ideas and give the audience something to think about; the risk of confusing listeners is much lower at the conclusion, because they have already heard your main points.

Student speaker Kim Davis found a quotation that succinctly summed up her ideas in a speech about gays in the military. Quoting a gay soldier who had been discharged for his sexual preference, she read: "'They gave me a medal for killing two men, and a discharge for loving one.'" Closing quotations should be like this one and like President Roosevelt's: a few neatly balanced, memorable words that sum up your central idea or advance your main purpose.

MAKING A PERSONAL REFERENCE   Particularly if your speech is about impersonal or abstract issues, it may be appropriate in the conclusion to personalize the issues by making reference to yourself. Such a concluding device (1) illustrates your own identification with the subject—you embody the ideas and values in the speech—and (2) encourages the audience to identify with you. In this way listeners might imagine that they feel the same you do about the topic.

Student Romila Mushtag used this type of conclusion effectively after arguing that hate speech should not be outlawed on campus. She ended the speech by showing the audience a handwritten racist note that had been taped to her locker door. By revealing that she had been victimized by hate speech and yet would defend someone's right to use such speech, she demonstrated a level of integrity that the audience couldn't help endorsing and trying to emulate. Her personal reference made listeners identify with her—and with the ideas in her speech.

CHALLENGING THE AUDIENCE   Particularly when your speech asks the audience to do something, concluding with a direct challenge may be effective. This type of conclusion not only creates a common bond between

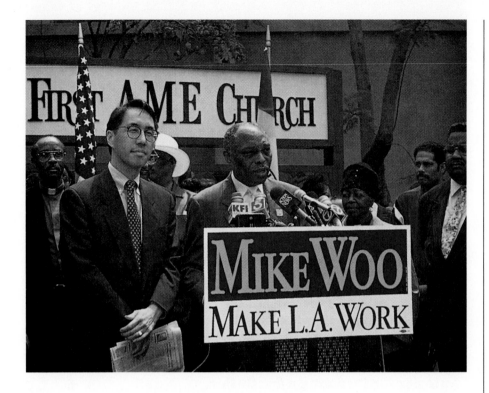

◀ A challenge to the audience is often a good way to end a speech that asks listeners to do something. In this case, the challenge is to "make L.A. work" by voting for Mike Woo.

speaker and audience but also transfers to the audience some of the responsibility for achieving the speaker's goals. For example, student speaker Cathy Cummins, after summarizing her main ideas, ended a speech about the breaking of gender stereotypes with this challenge:

> Together, we must evaluate the definitions set up for gender in our society and realize that we are limiting ourselves and future generations by continuing to reproduce gender roles. It's time we stopped limiting ourselves and our children. I for one am going to raise my children with the knowledge that boys can play with dolls and that girls can have chemistry sets. I hope you will do the same.

OFFERING A UTOPIAN VISION   Closely related to challenging the audience is this type of conclusion, which offers an idealized, positive vision of what can be achieved if only the audience will work together with the speaker. Rather than focusing on the challenge itself, however, this approach emphasizes the results of meeting the challenge successfully. The vision is called "utopian" not to dismiss it but to emphasize that it usually transcends the immediate, practical world.

One of the most famous examples of a conclusion containing a utopian vision is Martin Luther King, Jr.'s "I Have a Dream" address, delivered in 1963 at the March on Washington:

> . . . When we allow freedom to ring—when we let it ring from every village and every hamlet, from every state and every city—we will be able to speed up that day when all of God's children, black men and white men, Jews and Gentiles, Protestants and Catholics, will be able to join hands and sing in the words of the old Negro spiritual, "Free at last! Free at last! Thank God Almighty, we are free at last!"

Even speeches about less momentous topics may conclude by envisioning how things will be once a problem is solved or a goal is achieved. Offering a utopian vision is particularly effective when the speaker is calling on the audience to make sacrifices or to take risks to achieve a distant goal. By predicting ultimate success, the utopian vision assures listeners that what the speaker is calling for will be worth the efforts they make.

Abraham Lincoln used this type of conclusion often. After warning of the perilous situation facing the Union in 1861, at the time of his first inaugural address, Lincoln confidently predicted in his conclusion that "the mystic chords of memory, stretching from every battlefield and patriot grave to every living heart and hearthstone all over this broad land, will yet swell the chorus of the Union, when again touched, as surely they will be, by the better angels of our nature." Yes, clouds may darken the sky at the moment, Lincoln was saying, but he promised his listeners that together they could achieve positive results in the fullness of time.

Besides these specific types of conclusions, notice that many of the introductory approaches discussed earlier also can be used for the conclusion, including narratives, anecdotes, and rhetorical questions.[6] In the same way, some types of conclusions can be adapted effectively for use in an introduction. A quotation or a personal reference, for instance, can be as powerful at the beginning of the speech as at the end.

Strategies for Preparing a Conclusion

Several of the earlier suggestions for preparing an introduction apply as well to preparing a conclusion:

- Work on the conclusion after developing the body of your speech; again, it helps to know what you are concluding.
- Connect the conclusion clearly to the body of the speech so that listeners will grasp how it relates to your main ideas.
- Keep the conclusion relatively brief so that it does not detract from the speech itself.
- Aim for a complete conclusion, including both a wrap-up of your major ideas and a clear indication of how you want listeners to respond. (1) Summarize your argument memorably; (2) tell the audience what belief or action you seek.

The following guidelines and suggestions will help you develop an effective conclusion.

BE SURE THAT IT TRULY IS THE CONCLUSION   This first principle is simple to state but no less important for that. As you begin to develop the conclusion, take care to put it at the end of the body, and lead the audience naturally into your summary and final appeal.

Recall once more that listeners get distracted or confused when a speech departs from customary form. On the one hand, avoid any wording that might signal a false (premature) conclusion. On the other hand, indicate clearly when you are ready to move from the body of your speech to its conclusion.

RETURN TO YOUR INTRODUCTORY DEVICE WHEN POSSIBLE   One way to enhance the sense of form and unity in a speech is to conclude by referring again to the device you used in the introduction. If you began with a quotation, you may be able to repeat that same quotation in your conclusion, teasing a different meaning from it now that the audience has heard how you developed your topic. If your introductory device was an anecdote or a rhetorical question, your conclusion might return to that same device and embellish it based on the ideas you developed in your speech.

Of course, this suggestion cannot always be followed. The ideas in the speech may have moved far beyond where they were in the introduction, and returning to the introductory device would seem jarring ("Isn't this where we came in?"). But when you can return to the introduction, listeners will feel that the speech hangs together well, that it has a satisfying sense of form.

PRACTICE THE CONCLUSION   The inspiration of the moment is no more dependable at the end of a speech than at the beginning. Just as you developed your introduction word for word, so should you prepare a conclusion by writing out key phrases and sentences that summarize your ideas and make a strong appeal. In addition, practice the conclusion orally. Your speaking rate is likely to slow down by the end of the speech; you probably will pause briefly between the body and the conclusion; and specific words and phrases will need careful emphasis. Practicing the conclusion out loud a few times before you present the entire speech will help you craft both its content and its ultimate effect.

TRANSITIONS: CONNECTING THE ELEMENTS OF A SPEECH

Introduction, body, conclusion—these structural elements seem so static that, in planning one of them, you can easily forget how dynamic a speech actually is. From beginning to end the speech represents movement. You begin with a set of ideas and a strategic objective; by moving through the ideas, you also move toward achieving the objective. Similarly, listeners begin with a certain level of understanding about the subject and a certain disposition toward you as speaker; careful listening and thinking move them through the speech as well.

This dynamic movement of both speaker and listeners is achieved by—and depends on—connections that the speaker provides to bridge any gaps between elements. **Transitions** connect the introduction to the body, connect each main idea within the body, and connect the body to the conclusion. Ultimately, transitions create the sense of form that makes a speech successful.

The Purposes of Transitions

The most important purpose of transitions is to create this sense of movement and form; transitions make the speech dynamic and satisfying. Along the way, they also help listeners follow the speaker's movement throughout the development of the speech, and they help listeners remember what the speaker said. Equally important, transitions keep the speaker from lapsing into

transition
A connection, or bridge, between the main elements of the speech and between the main ideas within the body of the speech.

APPLYING STRATEGIES

Introductions, Conclusions, and Transitions

Excerpts from Latif's Informative Speech on Problem-Solving

Introduction:
The most critical activity a business organization undertakes is problem-solving. To solve a problem you need to make a good decision. And this is not an easy task. You have to go through steps to do that. There are five stages for problem-solving and these stages are: the intelligence stage, the design stage, the choice stage, and implementation and monitoring. The first three stages are the decision-making phase. This model, the decision-making phase, was developed by Herbert Simon. And then later that model was incorporated by George Huber into an expanded model of the entire problem-solving process which included implementation and monitoring.

Transition from Introduction to Body of Speech: And let's talk about each stage.

Transition between Main Points: Let's talk about the other two stages.

Dr. Marrow's Comments

Latif, why don't you narrow your focus and discuss either problem-solving or decision-making, but not both . . . too much for a four-minute speech. Therefore, let's focus on problem-solving.

Your attention-getter is weak. Why not start with telling a story that emphasizes the importance of good problem-solving skills? I recall the other day you were telling me how sick your little boy was and how you decided to take him to the emergency room at the hospital. At the end of this story, you could emphasize your credibility in problem-solving and why it is important for the audience to have a plan when problem-solving. Perhaps that story would pull your audience in better than "Problem-solving is the most critical activity a business organization undertakes."

You have given attention to the transitions after your introduction and between main points. There also needs to be a transition between your main points and your conclusion, such as "Now you know the five steps involved in effective problem-solving" or "Now that you understand the alternatives involved in the process as well as how problem-solving includes and goes beyond decision-making . . ." In addition, consider tying your transitions more into the main point of each area of your speech's body rather than into the specific stages of the process. Overall, it will have a more unifying effect.

Conclusion:

These are the most effective steps for decision-making and problem-solving. At the end, I really encourage you to use these stages to solve a problem. Because everyone in his or her life has a problem and needs to solve it.

You have attempted to summarize your speech and call the audience to some kind of action, which is entirely appropriate. However, you need to summarize the five steps that you mentioned in your introduction. I also like to use the word "conclusion" here so the audience knows you are wrapping up your message. Example: "In conclusion, we have discussed the five steps involved in effective problem-solving—intelligence, design, choice, implementation, and monitoring." Then, for maximum effectiveness, refer to your story in your introduction. Remind them that effective problem-solving can sometimes be a matter of life or death, as in the case of your son. That strategy works well in conclusions. Let's rewrite the main points in this speech as well ... we'll problem-solve your speech on problem-solving!

nervous mannerisms that would accentuate the gaps between ideas, eroding the connections that give a speech movement and form.[7]

Even accomplished speakers sometimes neglect to think about transitions. They may organize the body of the speech carefully, labor to devise an effective introduction, and craft a compelling conclusion; yet they assume that transitions will spring up spontaneously. Facing the audience, however, their spontaneous connections may be as pedestrian as "My next point is . . ." or "Next, let me discuss . . ." The movement is halting; the sense of form is unclear.

Even worse is a speaker who bridges gaps and moves forward on the basis of sheer nervous energy and repetition. You probably have heard a speaker who punctuated every pause with "Ahh . . ." or who completed every thought with "Okay" or "Right?" or who moved to each new point with "Now, then . . ." Such mannerisms can become so obvious and distracting that the audience starts counting them rather than listening to the speech.

From your experience as a listener, then, you know that an effective speaker understands the nature of transitions and includes them consciously to create movement and form. The rest of the chapter focuses on how to provide such connections in your speeches.

Elements of Effective Transitions

We cannot list and describe "types" of transitions, as we could with introductions and conclusions. Although the following three elements—internal previews, internal summaries, and links—may seem to be separate types of transitions and can sometimes be found in isolation, they are really three elements that together make up a complete transition.

INTERNAL PREVIEWS   A preview is a compressed version of what the speaker is about to develop; it prompts the audience to anticipate what is coming, in terms of both content and form. As you saw earlier, the introduction will probably preview your main points. Beyond the introduction, however, consider whether an **internal preview** will help prepare your audience

internal preview
A preview within the body of the speech, leading into one of the main ideas.

to follow along every time you move from one main idea to another. Here are some examples of how to do that:

1. If the preview in your introduction suggested that there are three main reasons to abandon the quarter system at your college, an internal preview might point out, "One of the most important reasons is that in a semester system students will have a longer time to learn what is offered in each course."

2. In a speech arguing that both students and faculty would benefit if the school offered more sections of closed courses, an internal preview between the first and second main points might tell the audience, "The second reason to have more sections is that the faculty will be able to give each student more attention."

3. In a speech about the size of the federal budget deficit, the body of the speech might start with an internal preview of the first major argument: "Some argue that the budget deficit is not a serious problem. I don't agree, and let me tell you why."

4. In a speech about multiculturalism, an internal preview might signal that you are going to tell a story about how cultural diversity became a concern on campus.

Whether obviously or subtly, each of these internal previews tells the audience what to expect—each is a kind of early alert system for the audience. An internal preview signals that listeners should get ready to move on to some new aspect of the speech, and it provides clues about the nature of the movement or about the new aspect itself.

INTERNAL SUMMARIES   Just as previews are not confined to the introduction, summaries can appear both in the conclusion and at certain points within the body of the speech. Like a concluding summary, an **internal summary** draws together the central points that were just discussed, serving both to aid memory and to signal closure to those points. An internal summary does not wrap up the entire speech; it reviews only a portion of it. The following simple examples are internal summaries for the internal previews you just looked at:

> So, as we've seen, abandoning the quarter system would permit students to take classes that last longer, allowing them to learn more about a particular subject and reducing the pressures they face.

> I hope I've made it clear that one benefit of additional sections of closed courses is more individualized attention. The faculty will be able to answer more questions in class and students will get prompt feedback.

> So the federal budget deficit really is a serious problem, because it depletes the capital needed for private investment and because it makes us economically dependent on other nations.

> As I see it, then, our commitment to cultural diversity came about through this and other key incidents that embarrassed us by showing the limitations of our perspective.

Each of these internal summaries wraps up one main idea of the speech. It gives the audience a brief reminder of the idea and also signals the point of completion.

Whether previewing or summarizing the entire speech or just a part, you can use repetition and restatement to alert the audience that you are beginning

internal summary
A summary within the body of the speech, drawing together one of the main ideas.

or ending one of your key points. For example, the first internal preview described above might be elaborated as follows:

> One of the reasons that we should abandon the quarter system is that students will have longer to learn what is offered in each course: more time to learn means less rush. Let me explain why this is so.

Similarly, the second internal summary above might be drawn out in this way:

> I hope I've made it clear that one benefit of additional sections of closed courses is more individualized attention. The faculty will be able to answer more questions in class and students will get prompt feedback. Opening up more sections of closed courses will truly help our teachers to interact more with us and that, in turn, will benefit us.

LINKS All these examples illustrate that transitions contain links from one idea to the next. Some links are subtle and are established through careful word choice; others are explicit.

The construction "not only . . . but also" is an example of a subtle link. It moves from the point that was just discussed to the one that is coming up next, as in "Not only are closed classes bad for the students, but they're also bad for the faculty." The speaker thus links two ideas that previously were separate in the speech.

Conjunctions such as "in addition," "furthermore," and "moreover" have the same effect. They suggest the cumulation of ideas, linking the ideas by hinting that the one to come will build on the one just considered. In contrast, conjunctions like "however," "nonetheless," and "on the other hand" signal that the speaker is going to move from one point of view to an opposing viewpoint or in some way will qualify or limit the force of what was just said.

Sometimes links are more explicit. The speaker who finishes one idea with an internal summary and then says, "But here's the proverbial fly in the ointment," is announcing that the point just made is about to be rendered troublesome or problematic or that something calls it into question. And the speaker who says, "It's not enough to focus on the cost of higher education; we also have to be concerned with quality," is telling the audience that they need to consider one more important factor.

How subtle or explicit should a particular link be? That depends on several factors. If the connection seems obvious and listeners can be expected to see it without help, an explicit link may be insulting. But if the connection between points is complex or seems to contradict common sense, an explicit link may be appreciated. Audiences can follow narrative and chronological links more easily than they can follow analytical links. Similarly, links based on "common knowledge" and general understanding do not have to be as explicit as links that require specialized knowledge or training.

COMPLETE TRANSITIONS As we have suggested, not every element of every transition need be made apparent. But a complete transition would include an internal summary of the point being concluded, a link to connect it to the next point, and an internal preview leading into the new point. For example, a complete transition in the speech about abandoning the quarter system might go like this:

> So there's no doubt that students will benefit from the change. Abandoning the quarter system will give them more time to write papers and study for final exams

and will reduce their level of pressure and stress. [Internal summary] But students aren't the only ones who will gain from this change. [Link] The faculty will gain two benefits as well. Let me tell you about them. [Internal preview]

Strategies for Preparing Transitions

Besides deciding how explicit to make each transition and whether to use repetition to emphasize the transition, consider the following brief suggestions.

IDENTIFY MAIN IDEAS SUCCINCTLY In internal previews and internal summaries, quickly and clearly identify the main idea being referred to; that will make it easier to remember. Rather than restating an idea completely, use a memorable word or phrase to highlight it in the transition.

USE PARALLEL STRUCTURE IF POSSIBLE When related ideas are identified in a similar or parallel fashion, that repeated pattern may make the link more memorable. Whenever possible, internal previews and internal summaries should use one of the organizational patterns described in Chapter 7.

USE SIGNPOSTING **Signposting** alerts the audience to where you are in the speech. If you say that you will discuss three advantages of something, in previewing each advantage it will be helpful to identify it as "first," "second," or "third." Listeners will have no doubt that you have completed the discussion of one advantage and are about to talk about the next; and they also will clearly perceive the structure that you intended. Similarly, you can use pauses, repetition, and changes in speaking rate, pitch, or volume as signposting to guide the audience.

· ·

signposting
Using verbal cues to indicate to an audience where you are in the structure of the speech.

Checklist

8.3 *Transitions: Critical Thinking and Strategic Planning*

1. **Questions to ask yourself: At this point in my speech**

   - *Do my listeners need a reminder or an alert about how far I've come?*
   - *Do my listeners need a reminder of how my last point relates to my next?*
   - *Do I need some verbal markers to help me and my listeners follow my outline?*
   - *Will my listeners follow my ideas better if I give them a brief preview?*

2. **If the answer is "Yes," here are some things worth doing:**

   - *Construct brief phrases that identify main ideas in the speech, and use them as markers and reminders at key intervals.*
   - *Set up your points in parallel structure whenever possible. Check your outline to help you do this.*
   - *Include verbal signposts that briefly show where you are and what comes next.*

This chapter has offered a catalog of the purposes, types, and guidelines for preparing introductions, conclusions, and transitions. The introduction shapes the audience's first impressions. Its purposes are to gain attention and interest, to dispose the audience favorably toward the speaker and topic, to state the thesis or purpose of the speech, and to preview how the topic will be developed. The types of introductions we examined are identifying with the audience, referring to the speech situation, stating the purpose of the speech, stating the importance of the topic, citing statistics and making claims, telling a story (anecdote), using an analogy, asking a rhetorical question, quoting someone, and using humor. The introduction should be prepared after the body of the speech is well in hand; it should be related to the body, should be brief but complete, and should be worded (and practiced) carefully.

The conclusion completes the speech and gives it a sense of form by signaling to the audience that the end is near. It summarizes the main ideas and may make a final appeal to listeners, asking them for a particular belief or action. Among the types of conclusions are summarizing, quoting someone, making a personal reference, challenging the audience, and offering a utopian vision. Guidelines for preparing the conclusion are similar to those for the introduction. When possible, the conclusion should return in some way to the introductory device; this enhances the unity of the speech.

Transitions give a sense of movement or progression to the speech by guiding listeners clearly from one point to another as the speaker develops the topic. Transitions help the audience remember the main points and the structure of the speech; they also reduce a speaker's distracting nervous mannerisms in trying to move from one idea to the next. A complete transition has three elements—internal preview, internal summary, and link—but not all elements are presented explicitly in every transition. Transitions should be succinct, should use parallel structure if possible, and should provide signposting to guide the audience.

1. a. Which type of introduction would be most effective in each of the following speech situations?

   A speech introducing the recipient of a lifetime achievement award

   An informative speech to classmates about how to improve study skills

   A speech to warn boaters about the dangers of "mixing water and alcohol"

   A speech to strengthen volunteers' commitment to helping the homeless

   A speech to reverse opposition to the death penalty

   b. In those same speech situations, which type of introduction would be least appropriate? Why?

2. What does an introduction need in order to prepare the audience effectively for the speech? Meet in small groups to answer this question. Each group member will present the introduction to a speech, and the other group members then will guess the speaker's purpose, the rhetorical situation, and the content of the speech. After everyone has made a guess, the speaker will reveal the actual purpose, situation, and content so that the group can compare intent and effect and then discuss ways to improve that introduction.

3. Which factors should a speaker consider when deciding how complete to make a particular transition? Discuss how the following constraints and opportunities might or might not influence your decision:

Your main points are organized in a dependent pattern.

Your main points are organized in an independent pattern.

You are moving between main ideas in the speech.

You are moving between subpoints within a main idea.

You are giving a speech that teaches a difficult concept to a group of students.

You are giving a speech to a group of protesters that enumerates well-known reasons to reinforce their commitment to the movement.

Activities

1. Attend a speech in your community or read a speech manuscript that you have retrieved from the library or the Internet.

   a. Identify the strategies used in the introduction and in the conclusion.

   b. Closely examine at least one complete transition in this speech, identifying the internal summary, link, and internal preview.

   c. Evaluate the introduction, conclusion, and transitions of this speech. Are they effective? If so, what makes them effective? If not, how could they be improved?

2. Create three potential introductions and conclusions for your next speech. Choose the best one of each, and explain why you think it is best.

3. Follow the instructions in Checklist 8.3 to strategically plan transitions for your next speech.

Using the Internet

1. **Exploring resources online for your introduction and conclusion.** Go to the **Allyn & Bacon Public Speaking Website** page entitled "Writing Your Beginning and Ending" at <http://www. abacon.com/pubspeak/organize/begend.html/> where you will find ideas and examples for being more creative as you write your introduction and conclusion. There are also links to other resources for finding useful material for an introduction or conclusion.

2. **Analyzing overall organizational structure.** After finding one of the two sites below, analyze whether the speech creates a sense of dynamic movement from start to finish. Particularly, consider how the speaker began with a set of ideas and a strategic objective. Did the speaker/writer successfully make the types of connections that move the audience from the introduction to the body and on to the conclusion?

   Martin Luther King, Jr., "Letter from Birmingham Jail," first published in *Atlantic Monthly* in August 1963, now online at **Atlantic Unbound,** the digital version of the magazine, at <http://www. theatlantic.com/unbound/flashbks/black/mlk.htm/>.

(continued)

Abraham Lincoln, "First Inaugural Address," presented in 1861, online at <http://www.columbia.edu/acis/bartleby/inaugural/pres31.html/>. Inaugural addresses by other American presidents can also be found at <http://www.columbia.edu/acis/bartleby/inaugural/>. This site from Columbia University is the Bartleby collection of inaugurals.

3. **Assessing principles of organization on web pages.** Do the principles we've looked at for creating effective introductions, conclusions, and transitions enhance the quality of a Web page? Find several Web pages that have been reviewed by **Lycos.com** and included in its rankings for the top 5 percent. Lycos' reviewers visit a site that has been recommended and assess its content, design, and overall effectiveness. Point your browser to <http://point.lycos.com/categories/> and then evaluate the sites you've chosen, considering the following:

   • *Does the page create a favorable first impression? How, or why not?*
   • *Does the page achieve the goals of an introduction?*
     Gaining attention and interest
     Disposing the viewer favorably to the site and its source
     Clarifying the purpose of the site
     Previewing the content of the site as a whole

Notes

1. See Norman H. Anderson and Alfred A. Barrios, "Primacy Effects in Personality Impression Formation," *Journal of Abnormal and Social Psychology* 63 (September 1961): 346–350.
2. Classical theorists often used words like this, from the language of architecture, to describe the organization of speeches. See Leland M. Griffin, "The Edifice Metaphor in Rhetorical Theory," *Communication Monographs* 27 (November 1960): 279–292.
3. For more on the effects of humor in speeches, see C. R. Gruner, "Advice to the Beginning Speaker on Using Humor—What the Research Tells Us," *Communication Education* 34 (April 1985): 142–147.
4. For another list of introduction types, see Richard Whately, *Elements of Rhetoric*, Carbondale: Southern Illinois Univ. Press, 1963, originally published 1828, pp. 170–172.
5. One early study found that, on average, introductions made up 9 percent of the total speech and conclusions made up 4 percent. See Edd Miller, "Speech Introductions and Conclusions," *Quarterly Journal of Speech* 32 (April 1946): 181–183.
6. For a discussion on the use of metaphor in conclusions, see John Waite Bowers and Michael M. Osborn, "Attitudinal Effects of Selected Types of Concluding Metaphors in Persuasive Speeches," *Communication Monographs* 33 (June 1966): 148–155.
7. Research shows that transitions make it easier for listeners to comprehend a speech. See Ernest Thompson, "Some Effects of Message Structure on Listeners' Comprehension," *Communication Monographs* 34 (March 1967): 51–57.

chapter 9
Outlining the Speech

In This Chapter We Will:

- Explore why outlining is a valuable part of speech preparation and presentation.

- Learn how to create a preparation outline that uses proper principles of subordination and coordination.

- Determine how to adapt the preparation outline into a presentation outline that you can use in delivering your speech.

A speech **outline** is simply a display of the organizational pattern of the speech. It serves several purposes:

- The outline helps you clarify and choose the best organizational strategy for your speech.
- The outline helps you check your organizational pattern to see that it is sensible and consistent. It lets you determine easily whether the main ideas support your thesis statement, whether your reasoning is strong, whether the supporting materials are linked to your claims, and whether the overall design of the speech advances your purpose.
- The outline is a written memory aid that helps you become familiar with the claims you want to make and the order in which you plan to make them.

Speakers depend on outlines at two stages: when they put the speech together and when they deliver it. Each stage requires a different kind of outline. The **preparation outline** is used in composing the speech and is developed in enough detail to show how each idea and piece of evidence fits into the overall structure. The **presentation outline,** or speaking outline, is simpler and briefer and is used as a memory aid while you deliver the speech. Although the character and use of these outlines are different, the preparation outline should lead naturally into the presentation outline.

THE PREPARATION OUTLINE

In making your preparation outline, you pull together many of the subjects you studied in previous chapters. You decide on your purpose and thesis statement; you identify the issues and supporting material; and you organize the introduction, body, and conclusion. As you develop your ideas, you plan a strategy for your speech, thinking about what to put where and why. You map out this plan by testing your thesis against the material that supports it. You think critically, inspecting the outline to ask which sections of the speech are complete and which need further development. Outlining a speech is like exercising; it is a "rhetorical workout" that helps you get in shape.

The preparation outline is relatively formal. If your instructor has asked for an outline of your speech, it is the preparation outline that you should submit. Usually you should write it in complete sentences so that anyone reading the outline can make reasonable guesses about what your speech includes. Student speakers sometimes think of the preparation outline as drudgery. "After all," they might say, "I took this course to learn how to speak, not how to write outlines." And it is true that some very accomplished speakers can do without a fully developed outline. But for beginning speakers the preparation outline is extremely important, and you should approach it with care. It enables you to clarify your own thinking, to be sure that the structure of your speech is clear, and to rehearse on paper the main ideas you will develop and the relationships among them.

What Does a Good Outline Look Like?

An outline indicates the hierarchy of importance of ideas within a speech. Typically, the main ideas are signaled by Roman numerals, and each succes-

outline
A display of the organizational pattern of the speech.

preparation outline
A detailed outline, usually written in complete sentences, used to develop a clear organizational structure during preparation of the speech.

presentation (speaking) outline
A brief outline, usually containing only key words, used as a memory aid during delivery.

sive level of less important ideas is designated first by capital letters, then by Arabic numerals, and finally by lowercase letters.[1] In short, you proceed from the most important ideas to the least important, indenting each level appropriately. The overall structure of your outline would look something like this:

I. Main idea

   A. Support

   B. Support

      1. Subpoint

      2. Subpoint

   C. Support

      1. Subpoint

         a. Sub-subpoint

         b. Sub-subpoint

      2. Subpoint

   D. Support

II. Main idea

An outline may extend to additional detail, of course, with deeper indentations for each level of "sub-sub-subpoints." But if the structure of a speech is that complex, the audience probably will not be able to follow it carefully. If your preparation outline needs more than four levels of importance, your thesis is probably too broad and unfocused.

A variation of this common outline pattern is the *decimal outline,* in which numbers and decimal points signal the levels of importance. The main ideas are designated with whole numbers; the next level of importance uses numbers with one decimal place (such as 1.1 and 1.2), then numbers with two decimal places (1.1.1, 1.1.2, 1.2.1), and so on. Again, the levels of the outline are indented to show the relationships among the ideas, like this:

1. Main idea

   1.1 Support

   1.2 Support

      1.2.1 Subpoint

      1.2.2 Subpoint

   1.3 Support

Constructing the Preparation Outline

Whether you use Roman numerals or decimals, the following principles will help you construct your preparation outline.

STATEMENT OF TOPIC, GENERAL PURPOSE, SPECIFIC PURPOSE, AND THESIS   These elements, discussed in Chapter 4, should be displayed above the outline. By keeping them in view as you develop the outline, you can check the emerging plan against the goals it is designed to achieve.

APPLYING STRATEGIES

Outlining Your Speech

T. J.'s Outline

TOPIC: The process of calling a football play in an offensive huddle.

SPECIFIC GOAL: To let my audience know more about the process of calling a football play in the huddle and how it translates to the field.

THESIS: There are three main parts to an offensive play, including the formation, play, and snap count.

Introduction

   I. "3 Double Wing U right 61 Double Cross X comeback Fullback corner." Those terms probably have little meaning and value to you.

  II. Unlike other team sports, football requires precise coordination between players. (Other sports do too but in a different way.)

     A. Football is the only game that requires a team regrouping after every play.

     B. With between 100 and 150 plays in an offensive scheme per week, the huddle is an important tool in team success and unity.

     C. Football is a coded game to keep secrets from the defense (much like war).

 III. Playing football for fifteen years, I've had the opportunity to learn a lot about the game.

     A. Even with all my experience there is still plenty I don't know.

 IV. Offensive football contains three important parts, including formation, play, and snap count.

Transition: The first part of play calling is the formation.

Body

   I. According to <u>Winning Football with the Forward Pass</u>, "The quarterback must...be in total control of the huddle."[1]

     A. When beginning a play call, the quarterback must be confident in his offense.

     B. He begins by calling a specific formation in the huddle.

     C. A formation is usually designated in the huddle by a number, color, or name (at UNC, a number).

       1. An even number tells the tight end to line up on the right side of the formation.

Dr. Marrow's Comments

First of all, T. J., kudos on your outline... however, you can make this effort a little easier on yourself. This outline is very comprehensive—more than you need for this assignment. The complete sentences are required, but you do not need to write out most of the sentences that you will say in your speech.

Don't forget that for every "A" you need a "B", and that for every "1" you need a "2". For example, if you cannot come up with a second subpoint for III in your introduction, you should leave "A" out of your outline.

Overall, this speech outline reads well. The sentences are short enough for good listening power, and the language is descriptive and vivid. Your use of transitions throughout your speech is most helpful.

2. The specific number called (say 6) tells the running backs which linemen to set up behind.

3. The wide receivers line up based on the tight end's position.

<u>Transition</u>: The next part of play calling is the actual play.

II. The quarterback must "know the proper selection of plays for specific situations," as stated in <u>The Coach's Guide to Developing a Passing Attack</u>.[2]

    A. There are two main types of plays.

        1. Running plays.

        2. Passing plays.

    B. Running plays are usually designated by another number and a blocking call.

    C. Passing plays have numbers and tags assigned to them.

III. To let the team know when to start the play the quarterback must give a snap count.

    A. The snap count is a series of words arranged to give instructions to the offense and to confuse the defense.

    B. The snap count is an important tool in coordinating an offense.

        1. It unifies their attack.

        2. It allows time to look over a defense and prepare for their assignments.

<u>Transition</u>: Now let's look back at the specifics of play calling.

Conclusion

I. When a quarterback calls a play in an offensive huddle he must call a formation, play, and snap count to precisely coordinate an offensive unit.

    A. Along with that responsibility, the quarterback "must always exude confidence when calling the play in the huddle," as stated in <u>The Coach's Guide to Developing a Passing Attack</u>.[2]

II. So the next time you watch a football game, remember what I've told you today and know that those players out there in the huddle are listening to a quarterback say something like "one weak zoom Z right fake 37 call quarterback keep pass right on one." And make sure to see if they do everything right.

Bibliography

1. LaVell Edwards and Norman Chow, <u>Winning Football with the Forward Pass</u>, Boston: Allyn & Bacon, 1985, p. 46.

2. Jerry Howell, <u>The Coach's Guide to Developing a Passing Attack</u>, New York: Leisure Press, 1982, p. 23.

Make sure your sentences are parallel in structure throughout your outline. You do a good job of this in some places, but it's important to be consistent!

The only major thing that I would want you to change is item IA in your conclusion, "Along with that responsibility, the quarterback 'must always exude confidence when calling the play in the huddle,' stated in <u>The Coach's Guide to Developing a Passing Attack</u>." This information should be stated earlier in your speech. Your audience expects a review in a conclusion, not any new information to process.

For the speech about Campus Food Service, discussed in Chapter 7, you might precede the outline with the following:

TOPIC: Campus Food Service

GENERAL PURPOSE: Conversion

SPECIFIC PURPOSE: To convince listeners that the often-criticized Campus Food Service is really quite good.

THESIS: Campus Food Service is vastly underrated.

COMPLETE SENTENCES   One function of the preparation outline is to test the clarity and precision of your claims. Sometimes you may have a general idea of what you want to say but are unsure of the exact idea you want to express. By writing the outline in complete sentences, rather than just highlighting general topics, you will force yourself to specify exactly what claims you want to make. This will make you less likely to "talk around the subject" when you deliver the speech.

For example, if your outline simply says "Voting bad," you would have little idea what you really want to say—other than that there is something negative about voting patterns. In contrast, the complete sentence "Voting in presidential elections has declined over time" is much more precise and focuses your attention on your essential message.

SUBORDINATION   A primary purpose of the preparation outline is to map out the relationships between claims and supporting materials. The outline should clearly show **subordination;** supporting materials for a given idea should be outlined as indented under that idea. If you designate the main idea with Roman numerals, for example, then you should identify its supporting materials with capital letters. It is easy to mistake subpoints for main ideas or for supporting points when your outline does not show their subordinate structure.

Look again at this fragment of an outline from Chapter 7:

I. Voter apathy has become a growing concern.

   A. During the years before World War I, voter turnout was high.

   B. In the modern age, the height of voter participation came in 1960.

   C. Since 1960 there has been a slow but steady decline in political participation.

II. Voter apathy is widespread.

   A. It can be found in the East.

   B. It can be found in the Midwest.

   C. It can be found in the South.

   D. It can be found in the West.

Details about the voting in different eras would be subordinate to a claim that voter apathy has increased over time. Likewise, information about voting rates in different regions of the country would be subordinate to a main idea about the geographic spread of the problem. Each subordinate point supports the idea under which it is indented. The distinction between main ideas and supporting points helps to make the subordinate structure clear and easy for an audience to follow.

subordination

Designating the supporting materials for a main idea with the subordinate symbol and indentation system in an outline—for example, supporting materials, indicated by capital letters, indented under their main idea, indicated by Roman numerals.

COORDINATION   Closely related to the principle of subordination is that of **coordination:** Ideas with the same level of importance should be designated with the same symbol series—all with Roman numerals, or all with capital letters, and so on. Items so designated are not subordinate statements; they are parallel, or coordinate, statements.

The preceding outline appropriately identifies the two statements "Voter apathy has become a growing concern" and "Voter apathy is widespread" as main headings. These are equally important ideas, and they are both parts of an overall topical organization that coordinates two aspects of the topic: chronology and geography. It would be a mistake to label as main headings "Voter apathy has become a growing concern" and "It can be found in the South." These statements are not united by a topical plan and might even be said to conflict, since the first statement implies a national problem and the second focuses on a single region. In the same way it would be a mistake to label "Voter apathy has become a growing concern" as a main idea and "Voter apathy is widespread" as a supporting point, because the second point is on equal footing with the first, not subordinate to it.

It is easy to see in the abstract that these patterns are in error. But it is also easy to make these types of errors when you are not consciously thinking about outlining and organizational schemes—especially if, say, you happen to find compelling supporting material about voting rates in the South. As you compose your preparation outline, ask whether the ideas that you have designated with the same symbol series are really *coordinate*—whether they are of the same importance and (often) parallel in structure.[2]

Checklist 9.1 provides an opportunity to practice the principles of coordination and subordination.

Outlining Introductions and Conclusions

Including the introduction and conclusion of your speech in the preparation outline is fairly straightforward. They are developed as separate sections of the outline, and the primary numerical divisions identify the elements of the introduction and conclusion. For the introduction these elements typically are:

I. Attention-getting device
II. Statement of thesis or purpose
III. Preview of the speech

coordination
Designating all ideas that are on the same level of importance with the same symbol series and level of indentation in an outline.

Checklist

9.1   *Subordination and Coordination*

Arrange the following statements into an outline that illustrates subordinate and coordinate relationships:

- *Food service responds to students' complaints.*

- *Variety is not a valid complaint.*

- *Taste is not a valid complaint.*

- *Food service offers three main entrees and a vegetarian meal.*

- *Being ignored is not a valid complaint.*

- *A special dinner is offered once each month.*

- *All food on the line is taste-tested.*

And for the conclusion the key elements usually are:

I. Summary of main ideas

II. Action desired from audience

III. Closure device

Here is how you might outline the introduction and conclusion of the speech about Campus Food Service:

Introduction

I. **Attention-getting device:** [*Take on persona of student going through food service line.*] "Oh great! Another meal at Campus Food Service. Let's see . . . what do I want? What is that? Uh . . . no mystery meat tonight, thanks. What? Chicken again. There's some pasta. Ugh, it looks like three noodles and a gallon of water. That's it. I'm ordering in tonight."

II. **Thesis:** Campus Food Service, however, is vastly underrated.

III. **Preview:** By showing how Campus Food Service keeps costs to a minimum, keeps offering a good variety, keeps a democratic system sensitive to the needs of the consumer, and keeps maintaining high quality standards, I am going to prove that Campus Food Service is the best meal program for students.

Conclusion

I. **Summary:** The Campus Food Service plan is a fair way for students at the university to eat. It keeps charging students a low price for meals, keeps offering a wide variety of food selections, keeps trying its best to meet the student's needs, and keeps maintaining freshness and taste standards.

II. **Action step:** The next time you hear people making ill-founded complaints about Campus Food Service, don't hesitate to set them straight.

III. **Closure:** We are just left with one problem, though. Now that we know all the benefits of eating at Campus Food Service, what are we going to complain about at dinner?

Outlining Transitions

The preparation outline will also help you check the flow of your reasoning and the structural "joints" of your message. Look over the outline to check that the sections naturally link to one another. Is it clear, for example, that B is the next logical step after A? Can you envision how you will wrap up the discussion of idea I and then move to idea II?

If you need to make the transitions of your reasoning explicit, incorporate them into your preparation outline. The easiest way to do this is to make parenthetical notes between the items in the outline that the transition will link. In the example about voter apathy you might include an explicit transition between items I and II in the body of the speech. The relevant part of the preparation outline might look like this:

D.

(Transition)

II.

Citing Supporting Materials in the Outline

You also can use the preparation outline to fit supporting materials into the speech. You can do so physically, by sorting your note cards according to the designations on your outline. For instance, you could put in one pile all the notes that bear on item I. A in the outline; separate piles would contain notes that relate to items I. B, II. A, and so on. This process has two obvious benefits:

- You can easily evaluate the supporting materials for a given idea in the speech and can select which evidence to include.
- You will discover which ideas still lack supporting materials, indicating that further research may be needed.

After you have selected supporting materials, incorporate them into the outline. The following three alternative ways to do this all have both benefits and drawbacks:

1. In the outline, reproduce the supporting material immediately below the idea to which it relates. This approach most closely resembles what you will do in the speech and is probably easiest for a reader of the outline to follow; but it will make your outline longer and may disrupt the clarity of its structure.

2. Use footnotes in the outline, and then reproduce the supporting materials at the end. This method preserves the clarity of your structure, but you'll have to flip back and forth between the outline and the supporting materials.

3. Attach a bibliography to the outline indicating the sources of supporting materials. This approach will keep your structure clear and will let a reader of the outline know, in general, where supporting materials came from; but it will not match up specific evidence with specific ideas.

THE PRESENTATION OUTLINE

As important as the preparation outline is, you probably will not want to use it during your speech. It is cumbersome and wordy; and it may encourage you to read the outline as though it were a manuscript, rather than speaking extemporaneously and adapting to the situation. Therefore, when you are satisfied with the preparation outline, you should develop a presentation, or speaking, outline. This will be the main source of notes you'll use during the speech itself.

Guidelines for the Presentation Outline

Some basic principles will help you develop a useful speaking outline.

MATCH STRUCTURE OF PREPARATION OUTLINE   This first principle is the most obvious. The whole point of carefully developing the preparation outline is to devise a clear and meaningful structure for the speech. The outline from which you speak, therefore, should follow the same pattern.

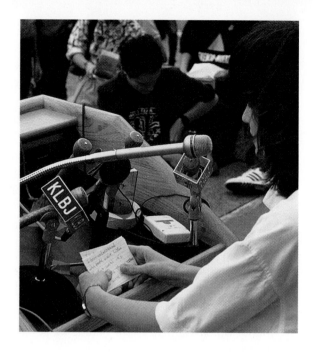

Using small note cards is a practical way to keep simple cues in front of you as you speak. This speaker could have placed the cards on the lectern or held them in one hand and kept the other free to gesture.

USE KEY WORDS   The complete sentences that you used in the preparation outline will distract you in the speaking outline; there will be too much to stop and read while you are speaking. Instead, the speaking outline should use key words that remind you of your ideas. For example, the preparation outline for the speech about voter apathy might be translated into this presentation outline:

   I. Growing
      A. Before WWI
      B. 1960
      C. After 1960
  II. Widespread
      A. East
      B. Midwest
      C. South
      D. West

Each key word should recall to your mind the complete statement that appears in the preparation outline. If a key word does not reliably prompt your memory, change the key word.

INCLUDE INTRODUCTION, CONCLUSION, AND TRANSITIONS   Just as your preparation outline includes entries for the introduction, the conclusion, and transitions, your speaking outline can have separate sections for the introduction and the conclusion and can show transitions as parenthetical notes. In keeping with the key-word nature of the speaking outline, however, state these as briefly as possible, with only enough detail to ensure that you will remember them.

    There are two exceptions to this general statement. Because the exact wording of your introduction and conclusion may be important to create the desired initial and final impressions, the attention-getting step in the introduction and the closure-developing step in the conclusion may be written out word for word or even committed to memory.[3]

Your speaking outline may refer to transitions in the form of parenthetical notes, such as "(Cause–effect link here)," "(On the other hand)," and the like. These will remind you of how you intend to signal transitions, thereby making the movement through your outline apparent to listeners.

Use of Note Cards

Most speakers find it better to use note cards than large sheets of paper for the speaking outline. Note cards are more compact, sturdier, easier to rearrange, and less distracting. You can set them on the lectern (if you are using one) or hold them in one hand without limiting your freedom of movement or gesture. You can outline each Roman numeral on a separate note card, or you can put your entire speaking outline on a single card. Some classroom assignments may limit you to a single note card so that you will make your keyword outline as simple as possible.

Reference to Supporting Materials

The speaking outline should cue you about which supporting materials to use. If the actual materials are not simple enough to remember, put them on separate note cards. If you are speaking at a lectern, you can stack the cards in the order you'll use them. If not, you may want to hold them with your speaking outline cards.

Here is a simple illustration of how you might identify supporting materials in your speaking outline:

III. Voting not thought important
    A. Makes no difference—[quot. from Dionne book]
    B. No real choice—[on-campus interviews]

Point A would remind you to read the quotation that supports idea III (you can write the quotation on a separate note card if you don't want to handle a large book). Point B will similarly remind you to recount your informal talks with people on campus who said that there is no real difference between the major political parties and hence no reason to vote.

Use of Stage Directions

Your speaking outline also can include reminders to yourself, as long as they are brief and don't interfere with the structure. Reminders like the following will alert you to things you plan to do during the speech:

  I. Growing [REPEAT]
    A. Before WWI [SLOW DOWN]
    B. 1960
    C. After 1960
    [SUMMARIZE / PAUSE]
 II. Widespread [REPEAT]
    A. East
    B. Midwest
    C. South
    D. West
    [RESTATE POINT]

Broadcasters may use Tele-
PrompTers to cue themselves.
Often the TelePrompTer will
present the text in outline
form similar to note cards.

In this way your speaking outline not only will remind you of the structural pattern of the speech but also will help you coordinate your actions during its delivery.

Using an Outline in Rehearsal

In Chapter 11 you will learn how to practice presenting your speech. The speaking outline plays an important role in rehearsal. Be sure that its key words remind you of all the solid thinking you've done and the supporting material you've found. If a key word doesn't immediately prompt you to recall the details, change the key word to one that will. As you rehearse, it will become easier to see and remember the relationship between key words and the overall structure you have devised. Also keep your preparation outline handy; you'll want to check during rehearsal that you are not leaving any gaps and that all your careful work is included in the speaking outline.

SAMPLE OUTLINES

The "Applying Strategies" box in this chapter shows a sample student outline with the instructor's comments. Here are two more examples, one of a preparation outline and one of a presentation outline. They are based on a speech by Maude Bauschard, a student at the University of Denver. Also included are comments, questions, and suggestions. As you examine them, consider how the outlines might be strengthened.

PREPARATION OUTLINE

Slave Labor   by Maude Bauschard

TOPIC: Slave labor

GENERAL PURPOSE: To inform the audience about slave labor as a human issue.

SPECIFIC PURPOSE: To make the audience aware that slave labor affects everyone and can be controlled, possibly stopped, if certain actions are taken by the general public.

THESIS: Slave labor is an issue that is widespread today and is due to companies allowing slave labor to be used as a means of producing goods, countries allowing slave labor to occur, the lack of education about the reality of slave labor within the industrialized world, and the lack of education in underdeveloped countries.

Introduction

I. **Attention-getting device:** In my first speech I told you about Iqbal Masih, the four-year-old boy who was sold into slave labor, forced to work twelve-hour days, and kept chained to the wall. I want you to keep in mind the image of this boy throughout my speech, because this is the image that you will hopefully fight against after I have stated my argument. [RELATE DIRECTLY TO LISTENERS]

Notice how the first few sentences are written out. The specific example makes the introduction interesting, and mention of details brings Maude's first speech back to mind.

II. **Thesis:** Slave labor is an issue that is widespread today and is due to companies allowing slave labor to be used as a means of producing goods, countries allowing slave labor to occur, the lack of education about the reality of slave labor within the industrialized world, and the lack of education in underdeveloped countries. [GESTURE TO COUNT CAUSAL FACTORS]

This is probably an overly complex statement of the thesis. Is it necessary to include all the specific causal factors in the thesis statement? Compare this statement with the more succinct version in the presentation outline.

III. **Preview:** I will redefine slave labor, explain human rights violations American companies are involved in, explain how education of the industrialized world can help prevent the continuation of slave labor, and explain how the education of underdeveloped countries directly affects the economy of a nation. [PAUSE]

Body

I. Slave labor is when any human being is forced physically or economically to work in unhealthy conditions and, if the individual is paid, he or she is paid below a living wage. [REPEAT DEFINITION]

Since the definition of "slave labor" used here is unusual, Maude makes a good choice to make it explicit and to repeat it for emphasis.

II. Several American companies use slave labor in their plants in other nations. [ACKNOWLEDGE THIS IS UNPLEASANT NEWS]

A. In November of this year, workers at a factory in Nicaragua that produces goods for a major retailer wrote to the Chief Executive Officer and asked him to visit the factory site.

Are these statements coordinate? A and B seem to relate to one manufacturer, C and D to another. Would it be more sensible to group them? Also, consider whether there are enough examples and whether the evidence given supports the claim in main idea II.

B. Such conditions the workers are forced to work in were forced overtime and being fired for trying to organize unions. [VOICE TO EMPHASIZE INJUSTICE]

C. Another retailer has factories in 32 foreign countries employing 450,000 to 500,000 people; only 11,000 are employed in the United States. [CITE SOURCE]

D. The Director of Labor Practices of that retailer wants to adhere to three standards of conduct:

1. Does the company meet the basic standards of labor conduct in the country?

2. How does the company compare in labor practices to other companies in the same industry?

3. How has the company improved since the last year?

[TRANSITION to contrast these standards with those coming next]

III. The National Labor Committee wants to create three standards of conduct in American-owned companies in foreign countries.

Notice that this main heading is not included in the preview. Should it be? Or should it come after the discussion of China, in Roman IV?

A. All American companies in foreign countries should create a "living wage."

B. American companies should agree to independent monitoring of labor laws by human rights and religious groups.

C. American-owned companies should allow all workers the right to free association and the ability to unionize.

[REPEAT EACH FOR EMPHASIS]

[TRANSITION to move from U.S. companies to other nations]

IV. China is a major violator of human rights that should not hold any business ties with America; unfortunately too many products come out of China, just look on the bottom of any toy. [SMILE]

Maude focuses here on only one example and treats it as if it were the main idea. Is this a wise choice in light of the thesis? Should other countries be discussed too? Also, note that this main idea is not mentioned in the preview.

A. Henry Wu is living proof of the slave labor forced upon political prisoners in China. [CITE BIO SOURCE]

A powerful example that Maude might wish to develop in greater detail.

B. We the citizens of the world have to tell our governments to stop trading with countries such as China that allow slave labor to occur.

This is an example of a misplaced point in the outline. It is not related to main idea IV and actually fits better under main idea V, which introduces solutions.

V. The industrialized world's ignorance of slave labor can no longer be excused; it is up to each of us to teach others about this issue and to learn more about it ourselves.

A. It is not only the industrialized world that must become educated on the subject matter at hand, it is those who are subject to the cruelties of slave labor.

B. First we must understand why underdeveloped countries can benefit from education.

Notice how the substructure of this main heading refers to "underdeveloped countries" rather than to the "industrialized world," as the heading says. A benefit of outlining your speech is that you can discover places like this where your development actually veers away from your stated main idea.

1. Traditional economic resources have been defined as land, labor, and capital.

2. However, today's economists have added a new category: human capital.

3. Human capital cannot have a number value placed on it; it is defined as the technical knowledge a person possesses.

4. This technical knowledge increases the person's ability to produce greater economic resources. [CITE ECONOMIC STUDY]

[TRANSITION to suggest self-interest]

    C. The industrialized world cannot change thousands of years of a culture, but if these countries wish to compete in the global economy, or at least pull themselves out of national poverty, then more individuals will have to be educated in how to compete in the new global economy.

An important point which the outline might want to develop in fuller detail. This probably deserves at least as much attention as the NLC standards that are mentioned above.

Conclusion

I. **Action step:** We are part of the solution.

    A. We must write the CEOs of companies and tell them that we will not use their products.

    B. We must write to legislators and tell them to stop trade with countries that allow slave labor to occur within their borders.

    C. We must teach others of the reality of slavery in the twentieth century.

Notice that Maude has omitted a summary step in the Conclusion. Why might she have done so? Is this a wise choice for this speech?

These are good examples of how solutions can be brought to the level of what the individual can do.

II. **Closure**: Ultimately it is up to the people of the countries that allow slave labor to determine whether or not it will continue.

    A. America cannot force its values on other cultures.

    B. The people of the individual countries must enforce education of the main populace.

Is this the strongest possible closing for the speech? There is a potential to return to the image of the introduction, especially since Maude said she wanted listeners to remember that image at the end of the speech.

Bibliography

Peterson, Wallace C., and Paul S. Estenson. Income, Employment, and Economic Growth. New York: Norton, 1996.

Livingston, Nancy. "Ex-Prisoner Wu Asks Americans Not to Buy Chinese Goods Made by Slave Labor." Knight-Ridder/Tribune News Service, October 31, 1995.

Senser, Robert A. "The Crime of Child Slavery: Child Labor in South Asia." Current, March–April 1994, p. 29.

Western Canada's Media Information Magazine "Iqbal," http://www.media-wave.com/Bookmarks/Slavery/Slavery.2.html.

SPEAKING OUTLINE

<u>Slave Labor</u>   by Maude Bauschard

Introduction

I. Attention getter: In my first speech I told you about Iqbal Masih, the four-year-old boy who was sold into slave labor, forced to work twelve-hour days, and kept chained to the wall. I want you to keep in mind the image of this boy throughout my speech, because this is the image that you will hopefully fight against after I have stated my argument. [RELATE EXAMPLE TO AUDIENCE]

Even in the speaking outline, the first part of the introduction is written out so that Maude will start off on a sure footing.

II. Thesis: Slave labor is widespread and has various causes.

III. Preview [GO SLOWLY]

This simply reminds Maude to be sure to include a preview. She trusts that she will remember what it should say.

Body

I. Definition [REPEAT]

II. US companies use

A. Nicaragua letter [QUOTE TEXT]

B. Have minimal standards

Here the main ideas are identified only by a key word, which can be done easily when there is parallel structure.

Maude's note reminds her to quote from the statement by the factory workers.

[TRANSITION: Contrast]

III. NLC objectives

IV. China [HARRY WU EXAMPLE]

V. Education re: economics of human capital [USE CHART & TESTIMONY / REMOVE VISUAL AID WHEN DONE]

Here there *is* a specific transition. Maude wants to heighten the difference between the standards she has just described and those that she will support.

Maude's stage directions remind her both to use specific types of supporting material and to put her visual aid away when she has finished with it.

Conclusion

I. Action step: Write to companies and politicians [SUGGEST NAMES].

II. Closure: Ultimately it is up to the people of the countries that allow slave labor to determine whether it shall continue or not.

Notice how, even in the speaking outline, Maude has written out the last sentence or two so that she will know exactly how she wants to finish the speech.

Summary

We have completed our three-chapter discussion of organization by considering speech outlines, which display the formal structure of the speech in terms of numbers and letters. An outline is important both in preparing and in presenting the speech.

The preparation outline allows you to visualize the form of the speech, providing an opportunity to check your reasoning and organizational pattern. Rules of coordination and subordination should be followed in constructing an outline. Ideas that are equally important should be coordinated at the same level on the outline. Supporting materials should be outlined as subordinate to the main points they demonstrate. The preparation outline is usually written in complete sentences and includes primary sections for the introduction and the conclusion. Transitions are inserted as parenthetical comments, and citations are included within the outline or at the end in footnotes, a reference list, or a bibliography.

Because the preparation outline can be rather long and cumbersome, a presentation outline, or speaking outline, should be used during delivery. The speaking outline follows the form of the preparation outline but is written in key words rather than complete sentences. It can be reproduced on note cards, with separate note cards for supporting materials. Because only the speaker sees this version of the outline, it may include short notes about stage directions.

The sample preparation outline and speaking outline provided at the end of this chapter show some of the issues to be addressed in order for the parts of a speech to come together into a well-planned, purposeful presentation.

Discussion Questions

1. Many beginning speakers write speeches without first developing an outline. How does the construction of an outline help a speaker to prepare a better speech? What are the disadvantages of creating an outline?

2. When developing an outline, how do you determine which ideas are subordinate to others? How do you determine which ideas are coordinate? As a class, construct an outline of this chapter, and discuss how it demonstrates the principles of subordination and coordination.

3. In small groups, share the preparation outline for your next speech with your classmates. Discuss the following questions:
   Do the main ideas support the thesis?
   Are the main ideas parallel and on the same level of importance?
   Do the subpoints support the claims made in the main ideas?
   Are the subpoints parallel and on the same level of importance?
   Are there places where transitions are especially needed?

Activities

1. Attend a speech or read a speech manuscript that you have retrieved from the library. Create an outline of this speech, and use the outline to critique its structure.

2. Construct a preparation outline for your next speech. Then annotate your outline, explaining why you made the decisions that you made. Model the page layout of your outline after the sample preparation outline at the end of this chapter, using marginal notes to describe your strategic choices.

3. Create a speaking outline for your next speech, and use it to rehearse. Practice and modify the speaking outline until your delivery becomes smooth.

1. **What does a good preparation outline look like?** Use guidelines for creating a preparation outline by doing an outline of a historic speech from **The Douglass Archive of American Public Address.** Point your browser to **<http://douglass.speech.nwu.edu/>** and select one of the speeches from the archive.

   Use the format for a preparation outline that includes:

   • *Statements of the Topic, General Purpose, Specific Purpose, and Thesis*

   • *An outline of the key elements of the introduction*

   • *An outline of the organizational pattern of the body of the speech, in complete sentences. Be sure to identify subpoints in a way that subordinates them to the main ideas.*

   • *An outline of the conclusion*

2. **How do you cite sources that you found on the Internet?** You can look up guidelines for the APA (American Psychological Association) or the MLA (Modern Language Association). For APA guidelines, point your browser to **<http://www.lib.usm.edu/userguides/apa.html/>**. For MLA guidelines, use **<http://www.cas.usf.edu/english/walker/mla.html/>**.

   You can also do an interactive exercise at the **Allyn & Bacon Public Speaking** Website for finding and citing some of the most common types of online sources, using MLA guidelines. Point your browser to **<http://www.abacon.com/pubspeak/exercise/mlaexer.html/>**. There you will find an exercise developed from the *Allyn & Bacon Handbook 3/e.*

Notes

1. For another way of creating preparation outlines, see Collin Rae, "Before the Outline—The Writing Wheel," *Social Studies* 81 (July–August 1990): 178.
2. If you are having trouble with the mechanics of outlining, see James Gibson, *Speech Organization: A Programmed Approach,* San Francisco: Rinehart Press, 1971. Also see the instructions about outlining in the computer program by Martin R. Cox, *Interactive Speechwriter,* Boston: Allyn & Bacon, 1995.
3. It has been shown that apprehensive speakers are less likely to follow the strategy that they had planned for the introduction of a speech. See Michael J. Beatty, "Public Speaking Apprehension, Decision-Making Errors in the Selection of Speech Introduction Strategies and Adherence to Strategy," *Communication Education* 37 (October 1988): 297–311. By including a detailed introduction in your speaking outline, you may be more likely to follow your plan, despite apprehension at the beginning of a speech.

chapter 10
Achieving Style through Language

In This Chapter We Will:

- Develop an understanding of style as the personal choices that distinguish or characterize speakers.

- Examine the role of language in contributing to the style of a speech.

- Learn the key differences between oral style and written style.

- Explore how definitions affect the stylistic significance of individual words and phrases.

- Identify means to achieve clarity, rhythm, and vividness.

- Distinguish among levels of style and determine how variety, balance, and conciseness affect judgments of the overall style of a speech.

- Suggest things you can do to enhance the stylistic quality of your speeches.

I f you told your friends that a popular singer has an intimate style or that a politician displays a presidential style, they probably would know what you meant. Something about that person stands out and makes him or her easy to describe. There is a pattern in the person's behavior—conscious or not—that you can recognize and that may let you characterize the person as being, say, a folk-rock singer or a "New Age" politician. Or the pattern may be unique, allowing you to distinguish that individual from all other singers or politicians.

WHAT IS STYLE?

These examples offer a working definition of **style** as the pattern of choices attributed to a person by others to characterize or to distinguish him or her. We can elaborate on several aspects of this definition.

First, style is a pattern of *choices* that are not predetermined.[1] That is, the politician does not *have* to appear presidential. Nor does choice necessarily imply strategic awareness. The politician may or may not be conscious of all aspects of behavior that lead voters to regard one as seeming presidential. Even so, if you set out to cultivate a positive style, you *are* engaged in strategic planning, as we will see in this chapter.

Second, although we commonly say that a singer "has" a certain style, as though that style was possessed by him or her, in fact it is the fans who observe a pattern of choices, who label it as a certain style, and who then attribute the style to the singer. Style is perceived by others whose inferences and judgments attribute it to the person. Style is always audience dependent.

Third, style can be used either to set someone apart from others or to identify someone with a particular group. Some singers, actors, or politicians have a highly individualistic style; their patterns of choices make them unique among all other singers, actors, or politicians. In such a case we say that the person's choices create a distinct **signature.** Just as your handwriting is slightly different from anyone else's and your actual signature is unique, so too can your speaking performance have a unique signature.

On the other hand, when a person's style is identified with a particular group, we say that the style is of a certain **type.** There are at least three ways in which a style may be of a given type:

- *Generic types* are styles that fit into a category, such as mysteries, jazz, or tragedy.[2]
- *Culture types* identify the basic styles of a culture, such as the pioneering spirit or the work ethic.[3]
- *Archetypes* are patterns of basic human experiences that recur across time and across cultures, such as the rhythm of birth and death or of struggle, defeat, and triumph.[4]

Style in a Speech

Even if we understand style in general, two common problems arise when we talk about a speaker's style. First, style is not always a positive attribute. If a politician has a bullying manner or a preacher is known for mumbling, style

style
The pattern of choices attributed to a person by others to characterize or to distinguish him or her.

signature
An individual pattern of stylistic choices that characterize a particular person.

type
A pattern of stylistic choices that characterizes a group with which a person identifies.

will hurt rather than help their effectiveness. Recognize that the distinctive style of a speech can sometimes be negative, as when a speaker keeps saying "uh," or peppers the speech with "like," or repeats "you know" so often that listeners start counting the repetitions. These are stylistic patterns, to be sure, but they are also nervous mannerisms; they detract from the message rather than helping it. For some speakers the goal is to *remove* negative characteristics from a speech. In removing them, however, the speaker is not removing style but is *changing* it from a nervous, unsure style to a smooth, confident one.

The other problem is that we often think of style in a speech as ornamentation that is added to the content rather than as part and parcel of the content. In this view, it is enough just to speak plainly and clearly without concern for style. Abraham Lincoln's Gettysburg Address is often cited as an example of a plain speech that is remembered far better than the highly stylistic two-hour address delivered on the same day by Edward Everett. The mistake is to think that Lincoln's speech was pure, distilled content while Everett's had a great deal of added style. In fact, it simply is not possible for a speech to be "without style." Every speaker makes choices. In Lincoln's case, obvious stylistic features include plainness of structure, simplicity of wording, abstraction, and even brevity.[5]

More recently, style and content were merged inseparably in President John F. Kennedy's inaugural address. Although few can identify the main points in Kennedy's outline or his thesis and supporting materials, the speech is recalled for its well-crafted phrases: "Let us never negotiate out of fear. But let us never fear to negotiate," and "Ask not what your country can do for you—ask what you can do for your country." For most people today, these statements embody what the speech *said*. They are stylistic elements, to be sure, but they also represent the content of the speech.

If we avoid viewing style either as distracting mannerisms or as unnecessary ornamentation, we will see that the concept of style in public speaking is the same as in art, music, literature, and politics. With speeches too, style is a pattern of choices—as recognized and interpreted by the audience—that may categorize or distinguish the speaker. Speeches may have distinctive signatures; may reveal generic types, culture types, or archetypes; or may be a mixture of signatures and types.

Style and Language

Like other aspects of public speaking, style is best approached through strategic planning: identifying your resources and using them to achieve your purpose. The most significant resource for creating an effective speaking style is language. But speakers often take language for granted, paying little attention to the words they choose to express their ideas. This is bad strategy because it surrenders control over a resource that can transform a dull speech into a memorable one. Language exerts such effects by influencing the audience's perceptions of both the speech and the speaker.

PERCEPTION OF THE SPEECH A speaker's word choices direct listeners to view the message in one way rather than another. Suppose, for example, that one speaker describes the federal government as "the engine of our economic strength" and that another refers to the federal government as "a cancer destroying our independence." Although both phrases create a concrete image for the abstraction "the federal government," notice the difference in perspective. The first phrase is a *favorable* evaluation; it gives the federal government credit for driving the economy and urges us to view economic regulation positively. The second phrase invites exactly the opposite reaction: The government is evaluated *unfavorably* and is viewed as a threat. The simple matter of word choice signals how each speaker feels about the subject and encourages us to evaluate it in the same way. Notice also that the word choices are inseparable from content; both phrases make arguments and inferences implicitly as well as explicitly.

This brief example illustrates what happens repeatedly throughout a speech. Ideas have meaning for listeners only as those ideas are expressed in language, and the language chosen shapes the meaning of the ideas that are expressed.[6]

PERCEPTION OF THE SPEAKER   Additionally, language influences how the audience perceives the speaker as a person. And since the appeal of ideas cannot be separated completely from the appeal of the person who expresses them, word choices influence a speaker's ethos.

Again, consider some simple examples. The speaker who begins every other sentence with the word "now" will drive the audience to distraction. The speaker who needlessly uses obscure or "highfalutin'" words may impress some listeners but also may seem distant, arrogant, or condescending. The speaker who uses words inaccurately or imprecisely may seem ignorant. And the speaker whose language offends listeners—as with racist, sexist, or ethnic slurs—usually loses credibility.

In contrast to these negative examples, if you effectively repeat a key word or phrase, you will actively involve listeners in your speech by helping them to anticipate what comes next. Colorful, appropriate language can lead listeners to see things from a new perspective, perhaps convincing them that your topic deserves more attention than they thought. By creating a memorable "sound bite," you can cause listeners to think of you more positively. And if your wording avoids jargon, technical terms, and excess verbiage, you probably will be judged pleasing to hear.

Oral Style versus Written Style

A situation comedy on television requires different stylistic elements than an opera does, and the same characteristics that make a novel stylistically strong may be unacceptable in a newspaper column. In short, a style that is powerful in one medium may be ineffective in another. Stylistic decisions respond to the constraints of the situation and the medium.

In the same way, the stylistic goals that you might aim to achieve in an essay are different from the goals you would pursue in a speech. Try delivering as a speech what you have written recently as a term paper in another course. Your audience will easily recognize that this "speech" is inauthentic, difficult to follow, and perhaps even boring. Your term paper will not succeed as a speech because you have been trained to write for the eye, not for the ear.

Some differences between written and oral presentations are fairly obvious. You can read written material at your own pace, skimming some sections and reading other parts more closely. If something is unclear, you can go back and reread it. If there's an unfamiliar concept, you can stop and look it up. If you lose track of the author's main argument or organizational structure, you can go back and review it. And if you get tired, you can put the writing aside and return to it later.

A speech offers none of these characteristics. Although you could tape a speech and replay it later, this is rarely done. In most cases a speech is ephemeral—it is delivered, and then it is gone. Listeners cannot control the pace of delivery; each of them must attend to the same idea at the same time. There's no "pause" button that makes the speaker wait while you consult a source to check something that you don't understand. If you forget the speaker's main points or structure, you can't review them. For all these reasons, listeners are much more dependent on the speaker than readers are on the writer. And because concentration is always important and always difficult, the speaker must make the speech as easy as possible for listeners to follow and remember.[7]

Given these differences between writing and speaking, you will want to consider the following factors when developing an oral style.

SIMPLICITY   Oral style is simpler than written style. Speakers use shorter and more common words. Descriptions are briefer. Sentences are shorter and less complex. Jargon and technical language are avoided. The organization of the speech is clearly identified through previews, transitions, and summaries. All these features of oral style reflect the fact that, unlike the writer, the speaker must seek instant understanding. If listeners have to puzzle out the speaker's meaning or intention, they have less mental energy for concentrating on what comes next. Because the speech can't be stopped in midstream, the speaker's goal is to avoid distracting the audience from following along.

REPETITION   Oral style is more repetitive than written style. A speaker might repeat key ideas for emphasis or to ensure that listeners did not ignore them. A catchy phrase or refrain might recur throughout the speech. Even the structure of the speech might follow a repetitive pattern. (This element of oral style is found in print as well. Notice that each heading in this section is followed by the words "Oral style is . . . ")

If not overdone, repetition serves several purposes. It can highlight your main ideas and provide emphasis, much like italic or boldface type in print. Similarly, repetition of a particular sentence structure can help listeners "see" the pattern of your speech, allowing them to follow and anticipate its organization. Repetition is also a memory aid for both speaker and listeners.

INFORMALITY   Oral style is more informal than written style. Few of us always speak in complete sentences. Nor do we observe all the grammar rules of standard English. In fact, were you to transcribe and read one of your speeches, you probably would find a number of grammatical errors and incomplete sentences; yet when you deliver the speech aloud, these aren't noticed. Speeches often do not read well, just as essays often do not sound well.

REFLEXIVITY   Oral style is more **reflexive** than written style, meaning that speakers often refer to themselves and to the audience and situation. In contrast, your English composition teachers probably have told you to limit the use of "I" in your essays and to avoid statements that—although perfectly clear to you and your classmates—might be unclear to outsiders. Recall that written material is usually composed without a specific audience in mind; indeed,

. . . .

reflexive
Making self-reference to the speaker or situation.

writers often intend to transcend particular audiences. Speakers, on the other hand, usually intend to have an impact on a specific audience, which they analyze as described in Chapter 3.

Speakers are also more likely to make their organizational structure explicit, saying things like "Here's how I'm going to develop my idea," "Let me review my three main points," and "Now we're ready for the conclusion." Because listeners cannot stop your speech to check its organization, or put it aside when their concentration wavers, you must help them follow your train of thought. You do this by referring explicitly to your outline and by such devices as signposting, internal previews, and internal summaries (see Chapter 8).

POTENTIAL FOR CLUTTER   Oral style is more likely to include clutter, because speakers are thinking on their feet and cannot revise their remarks as writers can. Sometimes the thinking and the speech get "out of sync," and—often unknowingly—a speaker may fill the gap with unrelated and unplanned words until the thinking and the speech are brought back into line. The result is clutter: vocalized pauses ("um," "er," "ah"), digressions, pointless repetition, and distracting words like "right," "you know," and "okay."

Because clutter usually occurs when you need some time to think about what you will say next, the remedy lies in your preparation. Before speaking, make sure that you have a strong sense of your outline, your main ideas, and how you will develop your thesis. Preparation helps you to avoid clutter and makes the speech flow smoothly.

Basic Requirements for Effective Style

Before we examine some specific stylistic resources that are available to speakers, it is important to recognize two basic requirements for effective style in all speaking situations:

- The accuracy of what you say
- The appropriateness of what you say

ACCURACY   Some philosophers think that there is no such thing as an "accurate" or "inaccurate" use of words, since the connection between a word and the thing for which it stands is just a matter of social convention, which changes. In everyday usage, however, it is meaningful to talk about using words accurately. Speakers who have no understanding of a word's dictionary definition or who use a word in a way that is significantly different from common usage will appear not to know what they are talking about. Sometimes this can be funny, as when a student speaking about medical research said, "I know that there is a cadaver shortage, but we can train new ones in two weeks." The student obviously didn't understand what "cadaver" meant. And although his slip delighted listeners, they were not just laughing along with a jovial speaker. At the least, they were distracted. And the impression that the speaker was inept weakened his credibility.

Mrs. Malaprop, a character in an eighteenth-century play, repeatedly misused words and has given her name to another kind of inaccurate usage. A **malapropism** is the seemingly unintentional but possibly meaningful confusion of words or usages. For example, in defending the behavior of Chicago's police during the 1968 Democratic national convention, Mayor Richard J. Daley told the press, "The police aren't there to *create* disorder; the police are there to *preserve* disorder." The Mayor obviously meant something different from

malapropism
Unintentional but possibly meaningful confusion of words or usages.

Verbally as well as visually, an appropriate style is one that shows your own personal, social, and cultural identity while also showing respect for those in the audience whose identity is different from your own.

what he said. But his malapropism caused many listeners not to take him seriously and even to suppose that he had made a "Freudian slip" which revealed his "deeper" thoughts.

The character B. O. Plenty in the "Dick Tracy" comic strip is a constant source of malapropisms; so is Archie Bunker on the 1970s sitcom "All in the Family." Although audiences are delighted by gross usage errors in humorous situations, a malapropism can be devastating to a speaker's credibility.

APPROPRIATENESS TO THE AUDIENCE AND SITUATION   The second basic requirement for effective style is that your words be appropriate to the audience and situation. You want to show listeners that you are sympathetic and respectful. If your words make them feel patronized, insulted, or taunted, your style will undercut your message.

Be especially careful of wording when your listeners have different cultural backgrounds. If you are insensitive to how various cultures use language, you may easily offend someone. Also make sure that your overall tone matches what is expected in the situation. Vulgar language, for instance, would be jarring in a formal lecture. And although you may think you have an engaging dry wit, you might be surprised to discover that listeners perceive sarcasm that went beyond the bounds of acceptable irony.

Because every situation is different, it is hard to say just what word choices will make your style seem appropriate. But the following general guidelines can help support your message:

1. *Avoid sounding self-important or pretentious.* Do not use language that will make listeners think you are arrogant. The physics major who made fleeting references to "dark matter" and "superstring theory" without

explaining what he meant was probably showing off rather than genuinely trying to communicate. Similarly, when a student speaker argued that the university should require more core courses, her language implied that her classmates were culturally illiterate:

A broad liberal arts background is essential for our generation to cope with the postmodern condition in which we find ourselves thrown. The fact that most of you cannot name the last ten presidents and that many of you have no concept of even the most basic political, social, or literary theory signals an epistemological breakdown in our culture.

Remember that you are seeking a favorable response from your audience. Usually the most effective routes toward that goal are to establish common bonds and to stress significant points of similarity between you and the audience. No one enjoys being talked down to or called to account by a speaker. Listeners will resist your message if your language or attitude seems superior.

2. *Avoid signs of disrespect.* Racial slurs, sexist references, and ethnic jokes clearly fall into this category. Because such comments debase and degrade other people, most listeners regard them as inappropriate even if not directed at them personally. The best rule is the simplest: Don't use such language, not even to poke fun at yourself.

3. *Avoid inappropriate emotion.* Just as you obviously would not choose the occasion of a funeral eulogy to speak badly of the deceased, neither would you prepare an after-dinner speech that is somber or gloomy. Cultures vary in what emotions are considered appropriate for a given occasion. Situational expectations also are not absolute, and speakers sometimes deliberately violate them in certain circumstances. But that should happen only for a clear purpose. As a general rule, analyze the nature of the speaking situation, and aim to keep your style and tone within the boundaries of what the audience expects.

Once you are certain that your speech meets these minimal conditions for effective style, you can consider various stylistic resources and make language choices that enhance your appeal. You can choose and arrange words to capitalize on their descriptive or persuasive power; to achieve clarity, rhythm, and vividness; and to create interest and balance in your speech.

As we examine the major resources available, understand that we will not even come close to the limits. Centuries ago, handbooks listed two hundred or more variations in word usage that could be adapted by eager speakers.[8] Clearly, in this chapter we are just beginning to scratch the surface.

DEFINING TERMS APPROPRIATELY

definition
The process of giving meaning to a word.

One of the most important stylistic resources is **definition,** the process by which you establish the meaning of a word for your audience. In defining a word, your choices range from neutral to persuasive, and your decisions should take into account all aspects of the rhetorical situation.

Neutral Definitions

Sometimes a speaker defines words in a fairly neutral way, with no goal other than being precise and clear. Although no definition is entirely neutral, in this case the speaker does not really want to change listeners' views about the thing described. The following definitional strategies are relatively neutral.

REPLACING A COMMON MEANING WITH A MORE TECHNICAL MEANING
A teacher of rhetoric might begin an introductory lecture this way:

> Many people, when they think about "rhetoric," conjure up images of endless political speeches full of bombast and posturing which really don't end up saying anything. But to the Romans of antiquity, rhetoric was one of the seven liberal arts, a set of skills which was not inherently good or inherently bad, but capable of use for good or evil alike.

In this case the teacher's goal is to make students equate the term "rhetoric" with classical antiquity rather than with contemporary usage. The common meaning is inadequate for the teacher's purposes.

DEFINING BY SIMILARITIES AND DIFFERENCES You can convey to listeners a more precise meaning of a term if you can both distinguish the term and compare it with something the audience already knows. A guidance counselor might say, "Cocurricular activities are a fundamental part of a child's education. They are like the curriculum in the demands they make of students but unlike it in their informality and the degree of control invested in student leaders." Thus the term "cocurricular activities" is defined both by comparing it with the academic curriculum and also by showing how it is different.

OPERATIONAL DEFINITIONS An abstraction can often be defined by an **operational definition,** which explains the meaning of the term by identifying specific operations to be performed. A speaker might ask, "How will we know when we have dealt effectively with worldwide famine?" The answer to the question—"When we have doubled the amount of food aid and when the rate of death by starvation is cut in half"—makes the abstract concept of "effective famine reduction" concrete by defining it in terms of what must be done to achieve it.

In each of these neutral examples of definitions, any shift in the audience's perceptions and attitudes about the topic is incidental to the speaker's goal of clarifying meaning and usage. Often, however, as shown in the next two sections, speakers use definition *precisely* to change listeners' perceptions and judgments.

Denotation and Connotation in Definitions

Words have meaning on at least two levels. A word's **denotation** is what it refers to, or "denotes"; its denotation is similar to its dictionary definition. For example, the denotation for "chair" is "a seat with four legs and a back intended for one person." At the same time, a word also evokes feelings. This second dimension of meaning is **connotation.** The connotation of "chair" is relatively neutral. But if a speaker referred to this object as a "throne," listeners might respond with feelings of respect or dignity (unless, of course, the speaker was being ironic or sarcastic).

---

operational definition
Explaining what a term means by identifying specific operations to be performed.

denotation
The referent for a given word.

connotation
The feelings or emotional responses associated with a given word.

Moving from physical objects to abstractions, the influence of connotation is even stronger. "Liberal" denotes a person who adheres to a particular political philosophy, but its connotation has changed considerably over the years. During the 1930s, and again during the 1960s, "liberal" typically had positive connotations, suggesting farsightedness, vision, and idealism. During the 1980s and 1990s, however, the same word with the same denotation took on quite different connotations, suggesting poor judgment, impracticality, and waste. Because of these shifts in connotation, someone who might have been proud to be called a liberal in the mid-1960s would probably have preferred a designation like "moderate" or "progressive" in the late 1990s.

As a speaker, you naturally will want to use words whose connotations are consistent with your goals—positive connotations if you want to praise or advocate, negative connotations if you want to condemn or dissuade. But you also should be careful to select connotations that reflect listeners' views, based on audience analysis. If you choose negative connotations for an idea that most listeners regard as neutral or positive, you may be accused of "stacking the deck," "loading the issue," or "begging the question." All these phrases suggest that you are *assuming* by definition what you really need to *demonstrate* by reasoning and argument.

Consider, for example, the connotations in student Zana Kuljanian's speech about why the death penalty should be abolished. She never used the words "capital punishment," instead saying:

> There is no reason why we should sanction state-sponsored murder. State-sponsored murder is immoral, unconstitutional, and dangerous. Nevertheless, we allow these organized public assassinations to proceed at an alarming pace.

Because Zana used words like "murder" and "assassinations," she was not very successful at persuading listeners who didn't already agree with her. Similarly, the white student who called capital punishment "justice for barbaric criminals" was not well received by black listeners, who saw racism rather than justice behind the fact that black prisoners are executed in disproportionately large numbers.

Persuasive Definitions

The shifting connotation of "liberal" illustrates the persuasive power of definitions. Its connotation changed not by accident but by the deliberate choice of "conservative" politicians to make "liberal" a word of criticism rather than of praise. To do this, they associated the previously positive word with phrases that have negative connotations, such as "big government," "special interests," and "tax and spend." These new associations allowed them to shift the commonly accepted connotation of "liberal" while preserving its denotation.

Persuasive definition can take two forms. In this example, the denotative meaning of "liberal" remained the same while its connotative meaning changed. The word identified the same people as liberals, but its connotation changed from positive to negative. Alternatively, connotative meaning can stay the same while denotative meaning changes. Consider the phrase "special interests." Its connotations are negative because "special interests" are seen in contrast to the general or public interest. Throughout much of the twentieth century "special interests" was associated with big business and with people of great wealth. During the 1980s, however, it came to be associated with advocates for women's rights, for multiculturalism, for labor, or for abortion.

persuasive definition
A shift in connotation applied to the same denotation or a shift in denotation applied to the same connotation.

Although the phrase retained its negative connotations, the people to whom it referred were considerably different.

You may be wondering how one goes about persuasive definition. Connotations, after all, are not easily abandoned. How does one break the connection between a word and what it "means"? The recent history of the phrase "equal opportunity" illustrates this process. Traditionally—at least until the 1960s—people were thought to have equal opportunity to achieve a goal if no discriminatory barriers were placed in their way, such as state or local laws that prevented blacks from voting, from using public accommodations, or from having equal access to education. "Equal opportunity," therefore, meant the elimination of officially sanctioned discrimination; indeed, this was the goal of the civil rights movement during the late 1950s and early 1960s.

Then some people began to argue that the removal of legal barriers was not truly providing equal opportunity, since African Americans were still hurt by a legacy of racial discrimination, inferior education, and poverty. In this view, equal opportunity meant the chance to compete with an equal probability of success. In a famous speech in 1965, President Lyndon Johnson used the analogy of a footrace, saying that even if two runners were brought to the same starting line to begin the race at the same time, the race would not truly be fair if one runner had previously been hobbled by chains and was therefore unable to train effectively. President Johnson identified the seemingly clear concept of equal opportunity, suggested that it was not so simple, equated the traditional view with only the appearance of equality, and then offered a new definition: Real equality of opportunity would result only when everyone had both an equal chance to compete in the race and also an equal chance to succeed.

During the 1990s the connotations of "equal opportunity" shifted again. The affirmative action programs that were designed to help make opportunities equal were criticized by some as calling instead for "racial preferences." To these critics, equal opportunity can be achieved only by dismantling the programs that an earlier generation had created in pursuit of the same goal.

Persuasive definition, as in these examples, occurs not only in public life but also in the public speaking classroom. Student Jon Peterson wanted to convince listeners that licensed deer hunting was not a bad thing. Unfortunately, most of his audience had the image of Bambi's mother in mind whenever he uttered the word "deer." To alter this connotation, Jon created a different vision of what deer are like:

> The Disney cartoon version of a deer is touching. But the innocent creature portrayed in *Bambi* is just as inaccurate as Disney's version of a mouse called Mickey that stands on two feet and wears gloves. To farmers trying to protect their crops, suburbanites trying to grow shrubbery, even nuns trying to tend their garden, overpopulated deer have become large rats with hooves. They eat everything in sight and leave a wake of destruction in their path.

Every speaker has important resources of definition. If your topic is an unpopular proposal to increase students' tuition and fees, you will induce very different reactions in listeners by characterizing the proposal as "extortion" rather than as "fair pricing." Likewise, even though you cannot affect how society views an issue like health care, you *can* affect how your audience will view it—by deciding, for instance, whether to define national health insurance as "cost containment" or as "socialized medicine." Your ability to use language in defining a situation will affect how your audience perceives and reacts to it.

Clarity	Rhythm	Vividness
• Concrete words • Maxims • Limiting jargon and defining technical terms • Word economy • Active voice • Careful use of irony • Purposeful ambiguity	• Repetition • Parallel wording • Antithesis • Inversions of word order	• Description • Stories • Comparisons: simile and metaphor • Vivid sounds: alliteration and onomatopoeia • Personification • Reference to hypothetical people: dialogue and rhetorical questions

FIGURE 10.1

Achieving clarity, rhythm, and vividness.

ACHIEVING CLARITY, RHYTHM, AND VIVIDNESS

Just as you can affect the style of a speech by making persuasive definitions, so you can affect its style through language that creates clarity, rhythm, and vividness. Figure 10.1 lists the strategies that we will consider to achieve these three goals.

Clarity

Because listeners usually cannot replay your speech, you should make the speech as easy to comprehend as possible. The following stylistic resources can increase the clarity of your message.

CONCRETE WORDS   If listeners have to puzzle out the meaning of your words, they will be distracted from your train of thought. And if they don't decipher your meaning correctly, your message will not get through to them. Because most people process images more easily than abstract concepts, your message will be clearer if you use concrete words and images. The speaker who tries to help listeners grasp the magnitude of "a trillion dollars" by calculating the length of a line of dollar bills laid end to end may be offering a trite example, but the effort is sensible. Concrete, clear images help an audience grasp and remember a message; as a result, they are more likely to be swayed by it.

MAXIMS   **Maxims,** or aphorisms, are short, pithy statements—often in the form of proverbs—that are familiar to most people and can be used to describe a situation or idea. The speaker who explains scandals in government by saying, "We've put the fox out to guard the chicken coop," succinctly expresses an idea that most listeners will grasp instinctively: Those with a motive to cause trouble should not be put in a situation that permits them to do so. Maxims contribute to clarity by offering listeners a memorable phrase that encompasses a larger argument or theme.

LIMITING JARGON, DEFINING TECHNICAL TERMS   Virtually every field of knowledge has **jargon**—specialized or technical terms that outsiders find difficult to understand. Lawyers, for example, speak of "torts," "probable

maxim

A concise statement of a principle, often in the form of a proverb; also called an *aphorism.*

jargon

Specialized or technical terms within a given field of knowledge.

cause," and "incompetent testimony," but few who are not trained in law will know exactly what these terms mean. Similarly, when student Tracy Hocutt gave a speech about artificial turf, she tossed around such terms as "turf burns" and "staph infections." Although this is common language for athletes, Tracy was talking over the heads of most of her audience.

Science, athletics, religion, medicine, music, accounting, and even public speaking have specialized languages that make it easier for people within the field to discuss issues and to understand each other. But because specialized terms and jargon may confuse outsiders, you should avoid using them in a speech. The reason is simple: Unless all your listeners are familiar with the specialized meanings, such terms will make your speech difficult to comprehend. And unless *you yourself* are very familiar with the field and its specialized language, you run the risk of using the terms inaccurately or inappropriately.

Even places can generate a specialized language. Every college campus, for example, has its own terms to designate campus landmarks, types of courses, procedures and rules, and the like. If you're speaking on campus or addressing an alumni audience, you can use these terms freely, especially to help establish common bonds with your audience. Jargon is not a problem when everyone knows what it means. But if you're speaking to a general audience, you should avoid specialized terms for the same reason that you avoid professional jargon—to make your meaning clear.

It's not always possible to rid your speech of every last **technical term.** There may be no easily understood equivalent for the term, or it may be important to distinguish the technical term from a more general, popularized concept. In such cases, use technical terms as needed, but be sure to define them clearly and carefully. Some good strategies are to repeat the definition, to restate it differently, or to offer examples that illustrate it.

WORD ECONOMY You can increase the clarity of your message through **word economy**—using words efficiently and avoiding unnecessary words. Listeners find it difficult and tiresome to follow a speech that beats around the bush, that is cluttered with digressions, extraneous ideas, inexact wording, and nervous asides such as "like," "okay," "now," or "right" in nearly every sentence. If you tape and listen to one of your speeches, you may be surprised to discover the amount of such clutter and to hear how it obscures the clarity of your message. Try to identify the things you do that create clutter; then make a conscious effort to reduce it. Especially avoid overly complex sentences, excessive use of adjectives and adverbs, and needless hedging terms or qualifiers.

ACTIVE VOICE In writing and speaking, we can distinguish between the **active voice,** which focuses on *who did what;* and the **passive voice,** which focuses on *what was done.* The sentence "John hit the ball" is in the active voice and emphasizes the person performing the action. In contrast, "The ball was hit by John" is in the passive voice and emphasizes the consequences of the action. Notice that the passive voice is much less personal than the active voice.

For clarity, you generally should use the active voice. It makes clear who does what, and it usually requires fewer and simpler words to express an idea. Use the passive voice only when the person really does not matter to your point or when the person might distract attention from the act or consequences you want to emphasize.

technical term
A term that is not widely used in ordinary conversation but that has a specific meaning within a particular field of knowledge.

word economy
Efficiency in the use of words; avoidance of unnecessary words.

active voice
A word pattern that focuses on who did what and prominently features the agent.

passive voice
A word pattern that focuses on what was done and largely ignores the agent.

CAREFUL USE OF IRONY   Speakers use **irony** when they say the opposite of what they mean, often with a shift in vocal tone or some other nonverbal clue that they do not intend to be taken literally. If you recite a long list of complaints about the quality of the campus food service and then conclude by saying, "No one, it seems, can find fault with the food on our campus"—while really meaning the opposite—you have made an ironic statement. Listeners may chuckle as they realize the great gulf between what you're saying and the reality that you have just described. Carefully used, irony also can be a way for speakers to signal to the audience that they take their ideas seriously but don't take themselves too seriously.

Be aware, however, that irony can make a speech less clear if listeners cannot recognize it as irony. Student Mark Nielson tried to mock animal rights activists in a speech ironically "praising" them:

> We have come here to praise those brave souls, standing out in the rain with their dogs shivering in the cold as they stand up against the inhumane treatment of animals.

Mark thought that his use of irony was clear; to his dismay, however, he learned that most listeners thought he was sincere in commending the activists. If you decide to use irony, be certain to provide enough clues so that listeners will clearly understand what you really mean.[9]

PURPOSEFUL AMBIGUITY   Until now, we have assumed that clarity is a desirable goal in a speech and that you should avoid **ambiguity**—words or phrases that can be interpreted in various ways. That assumption is generally sound, but in some cases a speaker deliberately and purposefully uses ambiguity to provide a rallying point for listeners who have different interests and agendas. In this case the ambiguous reference is called a **condensation symbol,** because it condenses harmoniously in one word or phrase a variety of attitudes that might diverge if the reference were more specific.[10]

The phrase "family values" is a good example of a condensation symbol. Virtually everyone can be expected to value families, but "family values" may conjure up an array of very different themes. For example, both pro-life and pro-choice supporters believe that their position on the abortion issue better promotes "family values." Most people—whether loggers protesting the loss of jobs because of laws that protect forests or environmental activists concerned about the future of "the human family"—may view their own position as the one that most values families. In this case, without ambiguity it would be impossible to enlist the power of family imagery to draw support from listeners with so many different opinions and interests.

Condensation symbols are especially useful when addressing an audience that is culturally diverse. They are **multivocal,** meaning that they communicate on many different levels at once. Diverse audience members hear a condensation symbol as having different denotations but a common connotation, whether positive or negative. When a politician advocates "putting children first," one listener will see the need for new government programs to benefit children. Another, thinking the budget is tight, will want to cut other programs to redirect resources to children's programs. A third, who supports children's legal rights, will want to give priority to their well-being even if it means removing them from abusive adults. The term means something different to each listener, but all three agree that protecting children is a high priority.

irony
Saying or writing the opposite of what is meant.

ambiguity
Lack of clarity in the meaning of a word or phrase because it can be interpreted with more than one meaning.

condensation symbol
A word, phrase, or thing that harmoniously accommodates (condenses) diverse ideas or references within a single positive or negative connotation.

multivocal
Speaking simultaneously with different "voices" or on different levels of denotative meaning but with similar connotations.

The multivocal term enabled the speaker to embrace different levels of meaning. The goal, then, is not to avoid ambiguity altogether but to limit it to the appropriate level for your specific audience and situation.

Rhythm

Because a speech is heard, not read, the sound of the message contributes greatly to its stylistic effect. Language choices that affect the **rhythm,** or pace, of the speech can help to convey a mood—of loftiness, of momentum, or of equilibrium, for example. Moreover, listeners who grasp the pattern of the rhythm can anticipate what is coming next. This feeling of being in the know makes them more active participants in the speech situation.

The following stylistic resources are especially useful in affecting the rhythm of a speech.

REPETITION   Repeating a key idea, argument, or theme is a way to emphasize its significance. The speaker who says, "Interest on the national debt is now the largest item in the federal budget—larger than defense, larger than Social Security, larger than any other domestic program—the largest item in the federal budget," has left little doubt that the central point is the magnitude of the federal deficit. Properly used, repetition acts like bold or italic type in printed material. It tells the audience: "Here really is the central idea." Use repetition selectively, however, or its power will diminish.

Another kind of repetition is a refrain that the speaker begins and the audience joins in or completes. Knowing that the speaker will be pausing for the refrain holds listeners' attention, and shouting out the refrain involves them actively in the speech. Political speakers often use such a repetitive refrain to rally support, and it is also common in protest rallies. Preachers, too—particularly in some mostly African-American communities—are fond of using this pattern of **call and response** with their congregations.[11] This form of repetition helps the speaker and listeners bond as they jointly create the rhythmic pattern.

PARALLEL WORDING   A speaker who uses one of the familiar organizational patterns described in Chapter 7 will find that listeners are following along and can guess what will come next. Assume that your topic is unemployment. If you begin by saying, "Here's how unemployment developed in the past," and then you ask, "What's the nature of unemployment in the present?" a careful listener will guess that your next major organizational unit will have something to do with the future. You can further emphasize this pattern, and heighten its effect, by using parallel wording:

Unemployment has been a tragedy in the past.
Unemployment is a tragedy in the present.
Unemployment will continue to be a tragedy in the future.

Parallel wording is stylistically useful even at levels lower than the statement of main ideas. The challenging candidate who insists that the incumbent is "out of luck, out of touch, and come November will be out of office" has created a parallel pattern that listeners can follow easily and in which many can participate. By the time the speaker says "come November," most listeners can probably figure out that the last item will be "out of office." The rhythm of the three-part pattern is catchy and easy to remember, and being involved in creating it will make listeners more likely to accept it.

rhythm
The sense of movement or pacing within a speech.

call and response
A pattern in which the audience responds to a speaker's questions or prompts, often with a repetitive refrain.

ANTITHESIS   Another rhythmic resource is **antithesis,** the pairing of opposites within the speech. Besides suggesting to listeners that the speaker is clever, antithesis also creates a kind of equilibrium, or balance, in which competing views are weighed and taken seriously. As was mentioned earlier, President John F. Kennedy was noted for his stylistic effectiveness as a speaker, and most particularly for his use of antithesis. In his inaugural address, for example, he said, "Let us never negotiate out of fear. But let us never fear to negotiate." Later, in promoting individual responsibility and voluntarism, he said, "Ask not what your country can do for you—ask what you can do for your country." The first parts of these statements acknowledge that there are limitations and concerns; the second parts transcend them. The use of antithesis suggests that the speaker is aware of the concerns but is prepared to deal with them.

INVERSIONS OF WORD ORDER   Variations from normal word order, even if they are not antitheses, may cause listeners to sit up and take notice because an unusual phrase is memorable. In spoken English the normal word order is subject–verb–object. A variation on this, if not overdone, will attract notice simply because the sound of the speech is different from what is expected. In Kennedy's speech the phrase "Ask not" differs from the more normal word order, "Do not ask." This inversion attracts extra attention to the sentence.

Vividness

Beyond clarity and rhythm, a third stylistic resource is the ability to make sentences or paragraphs **vivid**—to present in words what are really compelling visual images, pictures that listeners can see in their mind's eye. Not only does vividness add color and interest, but it also makes the speech easier to understand. Again, a variety of stylistic resources are available to make your speech vivid.

DESCRIPTION   Probably the most common way to paint mental pictures is by **description,** by giving specific details. Nearly every day we describe someone in terms of gender and age, height and weight, color of eyes and hair, occupation and interests, style of dress, characteristic attitudes, relationships with others, and so on. The composite of all these details creates the mental picture or image of that person.

Similarly, a speaker can use an accumulation of details to describe an event, a place, or a situation. Student speaker Jennifer Frantz used that strategy to set the tone for an antidrug speech; she began by describing a Swiss park called the Platzspitz:

> It was once a tranquil park, where families could picnic and children could play. Now it is covered with syringes, infested with rats, and inhabited by addicts who no longer have hope. When you see a mother, a father, and a small child lying on the ground and suddenly the mother wakes up, reaches out, and violently shoves a needle into her leg, you begin to wonder what the world is coming to.

STORIES   A story has power not only because of its familiar narrative form but also because it permits listeners to "see" what is going on and to identify with it. An issue like homelessness, for example, is much more compelling to

---

antithesis

The pairing of opposites within a speech, often to suggest a choice between them.

vivid

Graphic, easy to picture. A speech is vivid if its language enables listeners to develop mental pictures of what is being said.

description

A cumulation of details that suggest a mental picture of a person, event, or situation.

---

listeners when the speaker tells a story rather than discussing it in the abstract. The speaker might describe a typical day in the life of a particular homeless person: the contempt in the eyes of passersby, the daily search for food, the difficulty of bathing and grooming, and the cold and dangerous night on the street. The sequence of events will make vivid for the audience what it is like to be homeless even for one day. Listeners will be drawn into the story and will be better able to empathize with the homeless and to understand their problems.

COMPARISONS: SIMILE AND METAPHOR   In Chapter 6 we saw that analogy is a powerful form of reasoning; a comparison can help people to accommodate a new idea or new information by deciding that it is similar to what they already know or believe. Comparisons can be made vivid by using similes and metaphors.

A **simile** is an explicit statement that one thing is *like* another. Responding to a proposal that the drinking age be reduced to sixteen, a speaker might say, "That's *like* giving a stick of dynamite to a baby." The simile clearly invites the audience to see the new or the unknown in familiar terms. Knowing the obvious absurdity of giving a stick of dynamite to a baby, listeners can see that the proposed lower drinking age is a bad idea.

A **metaphor** discusses one thing *in terms of* another. Rather than stating that one thing is *like* another, it assumes as much and names the thing as though it actually were the other. A speaker who refers to a new dormitory as "the Taj Mahal" is not explicitly saying that the dorm is like the Taj Mahal but is assuming so and is inviting listeners to see it in terms of the Taj Mahal. The metaphor thus makes more vivid the disparity between the new dorm and older, less luxurious housing.[12]

VIVID SOUNDS: ALLITERATION AND ONOMATOPOEIA   You also can create vividness in a speech through patterns of sound.

Alliteration is a repetitive consonant sound, as in "Tiny Tim" and "Big Bang." Former Vice-President Spiro Agnew reveled in such phrases as "the nattering nabobs of negativism." Another politician called for reform "in our communities, our countryside, and our classrooms," repeating the hard *c*. The value of alliteration is that it makes it easier to remember the items arranged in a parallel pattern.

Onomatopoeia is the use of sounds that resemble what they describe. In the phrase "the hissing of the snake," the *s* sounds simulate the very hissing that the speaker wants listeners to imagine. Similarly, people often describe the slow passage of time simply by saying, "tick-tock, tick-tock."

When used sparingly and purposefully, both alliteration and onomatopoeia add sound to mental images, making them more vivid.

PERSONIFICATION   A powerful means of achieving vividness is through **personification,** the discussion of abstract or complex ideas in human terms. To return to the example of homelessness, talking about "a day in the life of Sam Walters" is likely to be far more vivid than talking about homelessness as a set of abstract social problems. Personification makes issues concrete and enables listeners to identify with another specific person.

President Ronald Reagan often used personification in his speeches. In his 1987 State of the Union address, he talked about "the kids on Christmas Day

simile
An explicit statement that one thing is *like* another.

metaphor
Naming one thing *in terms of* another; discussing one thing as though it were another.

alliteration
Repetitive consonant sounds.

onomatopoeia
Use of sounds that resemble what they describe.

personification
Discussion of abstract or complex ideas in human terms.

looking out from a frozen sentry post on the 38th Parallel in Korea or aboard an aircraft carrier in the Mediterranean—a million miles from home but doing their duty" and "farmers in tough times, who never stop feeding a hungry world," and "the volunteers at the hospital choking back their tears for the hundredth time, caring for a baby struggling for life because of a mother who used drugs." By using these personifications the President made the point that Americans are heroes far more vividly than he would have by simply stating it as an abstract proposition.

REFERENCE TO HYPOTHETICAL PEOPLE   The charge is often made that speeches are one-way communications in which listeners are passive and don't participate in the give-and-take of ideas. A speaker can combat the sense that a speech is unexciting by incorporating hypothetical people into it, either through dialogue or by asking rhetorical questions.

Dialogue draws the audience in by reproducing a conversation within the speech, including what both dialogue partners said. Here's how student Beverly Watson used dialogue in a speech about student government:

> I was discussing campus elections yesterday with my roommate. She said, "People don't vote because the elections are a mockery." But I insisted, "The problem is just that there isn't enough publicity." She said, "You're very naive." I said, "And you're far too cynical." Then she began to defend her position.

Although the listeners are still spectators, to be sure, dialogue lets them witness a lively interaction between people. The "overheard" conversation gets them more involved in the speech.

Sometimes a speaker uses dialogue to refer to opponents' objections—usually anonymously—and then to answer them. Comments like "There are those who say . . . " or "And then you might ask . . . " or "I hear it said . . . " allow the speaker to state and refute a variety of arguments. Richard Nixon's famous "Checkers" speech of 1952 (when he was a senator running for the vice-presidency) took this approach to respond to charges that he had benefited personally from a secret fund established by his political supporters. Nixon admitted there was a fund but insisted that "Not one cent of the . . . money of that type ever went to me for my personal use." To more fully satisfy his critics, he then engaged in hypothetical dialogue: "But then some of you will say, and rightly, 'Well, what did you use the fund for, Senator? Why did you have to have it?' " Nixon speaks as though "some of you" were actually present, talking with him. He states "your" concerns and then proceeds to answer them, and "you" as a listener hear both sides of the dialogue. If the speaker has analyzed the audience well and identifies the real concerns on listeners' minds, this can be an effective way to respond to them.

The use of **rhetorical questions** is another way to involve others hypothetically. As you learned in Chapter 8, a rhetorical question is one for which you do not really expect an answer. You ask the question solely to make the audience think about an issue and to quickly reach the obvious answer, which you already know. The "Checkers" speech illustrates this approach to vividness as well. To talk about why the secret fund was necessary, Nixon first asked listeners some questions:

> Do you think that when I or any other senator makes a political speech, has it printed, [we] should charge the printing of that speech and the mailing of that speech to the taxpayers?

dialogue
Reproducing a conversation within a speech.

rhetorical question
A question for which no answer is expected; it is asked to get listeners thinking so that they quickly recognize the obvious answer.

Do you think, for example, when I or any other senator makes a trip to his home state to make a purely political speech that the cost of that trip should be charged to the taxpayers?

Do you think when a Senator makes political broadcasts . . . that the expense of those broadcasts should be charged to the taxpayers?

Nixon raised these questions because he assumed that listeners would agree that the answer is "No." That set the stage to say that a special fund was needed because these expenditures should not be "charged to the taxpayers."

APPLYING STRATEGIES

Using Language Effectively

Excerpts from Laura's Speech on Adoption

Imagine that you're alone, no one to care for you, no one to love you. You're scared, you're uncertain. Now replace those feelings with excitement as you're running around playing outside with your new family just having a really good time. I'm talking about adoption. There are many options when a couple wants to have a child.

Another benefit concerning adoption is that there are closed and open adoptions. An open adoption means that a person chooses to have contact with the biological family. A closed adoption is that they do not choose to have contact with the biological family.

Another advantage of adoption is that there was a law passed in 1980, Public Law 9762, that helps with adoption. This law helps with the planning of permanency of each separating child.

Dr. Marrow's Comments

You're off to a good start here, Laura. I love your use of description, rhythm, and reference to a hypothetical situation. Now let's work on clarity by mincing some unnecessary words and adding some to avoid ambiguity. Try this: Imagine you're a child alone, no one to care for you, no one to love. You're scared, you're uncertain. Now replace those feelings with joy as you're playing outside with your new family, having a really good time. These feelings happen and can happen every day with a process called adoption—one of many options to consider when wanting a child."

Your parallel wording is effective ("An open adoption means that a person chooses to have contact with the biological family. A closed adoption is when they do not choose to have contact with the biological family.") Remember to keep your pronouns consistently singular or plural ("a person," "they"). Also, Laura, you may want to add a clarifying phrase to your first sentence, as I'm not sure that closed and open adoptions, as written, equal a benefit. Try this approach: "Another benefit of adoption is that the adoptee can legally select the amount of contact he or she desires to have with the biological family."

Use "benefit" instead of "advantage" for consistency. Again, for clarity purposes, I'm not sure that the law is a benefit, but rather you're telling what the law does. You can omit details like the number of the public law. You may want to add a simile here for comparative power as well. Try this: "Another benefit of adoption is that there is a law that helps plan the permanency of each separating child. It's like an insurance policy or a binding contract."

(continued)

Excerpts from Laura's Speech on Adoption	Dr. Marrow's Comments
In an article written by Patricia Kane called "Bringing Kids All the Way Home," even troubled families who have adopted from overseas said they would do it all over again. Some couples prefer private adoption agencies but in some states they are illegal, such as Delaware, Michigan, and North Dakota. This according to Eleanor Rosenberg.	Laura, please tell us a story about a specific troubled family in Kane's article . . . the story can be short, but it would add tremendous credibility to your powerful statement that families adopting from overseas would do it all over again. Also, you need a transition statement to talk about private adoption agencies. Try this: "Even though there are many public agencies that handle adoption here and overseas, many people prefer private adoption agencies. According to Eleanor Rosenberg, there are . . ."
In a story about an adopted person, she chooses to find a biological family and she states, "My return to the agency has given me belief in my birth and early childhood as real events."	I like the theme you're emphasizing here—searching for one's roots as a means of reaffirming identity and early childhood. How about some more testimony or quotations from other adopted persons to reinforce your theme? Also, you may want to add a rhetorical question, like, "Can YOU imagine what it would be like to discover new information about your birth and early childhood?" This language device gets your audience to visualize themselves in this situation. This could be especially strategic with your thought-provoking topic of adoption.

STYLE AND THE ENTIRE SPEECH

Having examined a variety of stylistic resources relating to word choice and arrangement, it is time to step back, change our perspective, and consider the style of the speech as a whole.

Choosing the Right Level of Style

Classical writers on public speaking distinguished among three levels of style: The *grand style* is majestic, lofty, and formal; the *plain style* is simple and colloquial; and the *middle style* falls somewhere between those two poles.[13]

Our society has largely abandoned the grand style, but not entirely. African-American speakers such as Jesse Jackson often bring the grand style of the church sermon into the political arena. Similarly, speakers from some Latin cultures may use indirection or flowery language that characterize the grand style, and some speakers from Eastern cultures may use a style that relies more on embroidered narrative than on logical demonstration.

Still, most people in mainstream U.S. society overwhelmingly favor the plain style, viewing the grand style as a relic of nineteenth-century orations that often lasted several hours. Most of us prefer understatement to overstatement. We use figures of speech and other stylistic resources not so much for ornamentation as for how they contribute to the clarity of an argument. It is a serious mistake, however, to confuse plainness with artlessness. The "plain" style is not as plain as it sometimes seems. Nor is it natural. Rather, it is carefully crafted of simple sentences, familiar words, the active voice, and a clear progression from one idea to the next.

Finding the Right Pace and Proportion

VARIETY   Using all the stylistic resources we examined in connection with words, sentences, and paragraphs—or using the same few over and over—will call attention to your style rather than to your ideas. This detracts from the audience's perception of the speech as a unified whole. The alternative is variety—in the resources you use, in how often you use them, and so on. Stylistic variety will keep any particular technique from calling attention to itself and will contribute to a pleasing overall impression of the speech.

BALANCE   A speech that is uniform in style may not sustain the audience's attention and interest. If the entire speech is concrete and anecdotal, listeners may miss the larger point that the examples are trying to make; but if the speech is completely abstract and theoretical, they may not see how it relates to their own experience. If the speech is entirely intense and gripping, listeners may experience "emotional overload"; but if it is completely dispassionate and low-key, they may decide that the speaker does not really care about the subject.

A speech loaded with alliteration and antithesis may call attention to these devices rather than to the purposes for which they are used, but a speech that has no interesting turns of phrase may strike listeners as dull. In these cases and in all matters of style, an effective balance among available resources will enhance the overall style of the speech.

CONCISENESS   Many writers say that it is easier to write a long book than a short one, because editing one's own thoughts is so difficult. In the same way, it often is easier to speak for thirty minutes than for ten. (Although that may surprise you, it's true. As you research your topic, you'll find more and more material that you want to include, and deciding to omit any of it will be difficult.) Particularly in modern American culture, however, speeches that go on for too long or that lack a clear, compact thesis and structure usually will not be judged as exhibiting good style. Today's audiences tend to value messages that are brief, stripped of adornment, to the point, and concise.

Memorable Phrases

Many classic speeches are remembered because of a particular line or phrase. Examples include William Jennings Bryan's "Cross of Gold" speech; Martin Luther King, Jr.'s, "I Have a Dream" speech; and Sojourner Truth's "Ain't I a Woman?" speech. A pithy phrase or quotable quote that somehow captures the essence of the speech is today called a **sound bite,** because it is often the only part of the speech that receives media coverage. President George Bush's 1988 acceptance speech is remembered for the sound bite "Read my lips. No new taxes!" Similarly, the popular-culture phrase, "Show me the money," is a sound bite that conveys a sense of skepticism or distrust. But whether you are addressing twenty-five classmates or a national television audience, a memorable phrase prevents listeners from forgetting your speech and also enhances their judgment of its style.

sound bite
A memorable phrase that is recalled from a speech and used to identify the speech.

Congruence of Language and Delivery

Finally, the language of the speech should match your style of delivery (which we will examine in Chapter 11). If your topic and language are serious and formal, your delivery should not be casual and informal, and vice versa. Generally, classroom speeches are informal in both style and delivery. But you may sometimes speak in a more formal situation, and it is important that your choice of language and style of delivery match.

ACHIEVING GOOD STYLE

We have been talking about stylistic choices that involve careful planning and forethought. But if you deliver a speech extemporaneously and cannot labor over each word, how can you possibly pay so much attention to language? And isn't it better, anyway, to focus on the content of your message and just talk naturally? Is it realistic to expect any speaker these days, especially a beginning student speaker, really to focus on style?

These are good questions, and you probably have thought about them. Obviously, no one expects to attain the stylistic talent of Winston Churchill or Ronald Reagan, at least not right away. But you have to start someplace. And lurking behind those questions are two erroneous assumptions about speeches. If you can correct those errors, you will be on the way to understanding how to develop a good style.

Erroneous Assumptions about Speeches

One mistaken assumption about speeches might be called the "plain-style myth"—the belief that people naturally speak in the plain style and have to exert effort only to achieve the grand style. Far from being impromptu, how-

---

Checklist

10.1 *Strategic Language Choices*

1. **Questions to ask yourself: After outlining my speech . . .**

   - *Am I sure this will sound like a speech, not an essay?*
   - *Will my key terms have the connotations I want?*
   - *Does the language suggest momentum for the speech?*
   - *Is the language vivid and interesting?*

2. **If the answer is "No," here are some things you might want to consider:**

   - *Review your key-word choices, and put them in the speaking outline so you won't lose sight of them.*
   - *Tape-record as you practice the speech; review the tape, and modify word choices to make the speech clearer and more oral.*
   - *Identify alternative ways to express your main ideas, and test whether they improve clarity or rhythm.*
   - *Insert appropriate figures of speech into the outline to make the speech more vivid.*

Practicing the speech and then viewing yourself on videotape, trying to anticipate how you look and sound to an audience, can be an important step in achieving an effective speaking style.

ever, the plain style may require several outlines and hours of preparation. Few of us speak extemporaneously as clearly or as precisely as we would like. (To test this claim, tape-record an impromptu speech and play it back; you may be surprised at how unclear or awkward your language usage is.) Most of us have to force ourselves to simplify, to consolidate, to focus, and to delete language in order to make the speech artfully plain. *Any* style requires preparation.

Equally mistaken is a second belief: that a focus on style is somehow at odds with attending to the content of the speech. As we've seen in this chapter, "content" and "language" are not completely separate categories. Content becomes meaningful as it is expressed in language, and speakers' choices about style and language affect listeners' perceptions of what the content actually is. When we talk about what a speaker "said," then, we are talking about both content and language. So yes, it pays for speakers—even beginning speakers—to focus on achieving style through language.

Suggestions for Developing and Improving Style

1. Review your preparation outline and your presentation outline from the standpoint of style and word choice. Incorporate key phrases and stylistic choices into the preparation outline so that you won't lose track of them when you speak.

2. Practice composing speeches in writing. Although you will seldom speak from manuscript, actually writing out a speech can help you focus on style; it creates a specific text that you can examine and revise to improve your style. This exercise also will help you make stylistic choices when you speak extemporaneously.

3. Be your own worst critic when revising your outline or manuscript for style. Are key ideas and arguments worded as effectively as possible?

Does your language make the message easy or difficult for the audience to remember? Does the speech seem interesting or tedious? Use the stylistic resources discussed in this chapter to modify your speech and enhance your style.

4. Practice your speech, not only to become more familiar with its contents and to gain self-confidence but also to listen to its overall rhythm. Does the speech "move" in the way you would like? Does the climax occur at the place in the speech where you intend it to be? If the answers to these questions are negative, you can revise the speech to make appropriate adjustments.

5. Consider how your speech might incorporate the stylistic resources discussed in this chapter. For example, identify any similes or rhetorical questions that you might use. Then practice the speech, and ask yourself whether the stylistic devices really enhanced the overall quality. If not, be ruthless in omitting them. But if a device seems to work, don't be afraid to keep it in. You can apply this process to each of the stylistic devices in this chapter: Invent alterations, try them out, and assess their contributions to the speech.

6. Raise your awareness of other speakers' styles. Read some classic speeches, and try to identify how each speaker achieved the style for which the speech is known. Watch videotapes of contemporary well-known speakers, and analyze their stylistic choices. Listen carefully to classmates' speeches, and try to characterize each person's style. Listening critically to speeches of the past and present will make you more sensitive to the whole idea of stylistic choices—and also occasionally may give you ideas about how similar choices might enhance your own speeches.

7. Don't work on too many things at once. One advantage of giving several speeches in a course on public speaking is that you can focus on different skills in different speeches. It's unrealistic to expect solid research, flawless reasoning, perfect organization, and effective style all in the same beginning speech. But it's also true that all these elements work together to produce an effective speech. By focusing on and practicing a few skills at a time, you will make gradual progress toward integrating all of them.

 Summary

Style is attributed to speakers by listeners, based on the distinctive pattern of choices made by speakers to express themselves. The language of a speech affects listeners' perceptions of both the message and the speaker. Oral style differs significantly from written style in its simplicity, repetition, informality, and reflexivity. The basic requirements for effective style are accuracy and appropriateness to the audience and situation.

The speaker's powers of definition—particularly the connotative aspect and the concept of persuasive definition—are especially important. Other important considerations are clarity (achieved through the use of familiar and concrete terms, limiting the use of jargon, removing clutter, and employing the active voice); rhythm (including such matters as repetition, parallel wording, antithesis, and inversion of normal word order); and vividness. For the speech as a whole, the important criteria are the stylistic level (grand, middle, or plain), variety, balance, conciseness, memorable phrases, and congruence of language and delivery.

Conscious efforts to improve style may seem at odds with a natural or conversational tone, but the plain style is itself a work of art, not an off-the-cuff presentation as it sometimes may seem. Becoming more sensitive to other people's speeches and practicing composing your own are the recommended routes for enhancing your own speaking style.

Discussion Questions

1. What does it mean to say that content and style are interconnected? Try rewording the following statements. Do they have the same impact when you rephrase them? Discuss the ways in which word choice helped to convey the meaning in these passages.
   a. "I have a dream that my four little children will one day live in a nation where they will not be judged by the color of their skin but by the content of their character."—Martin Luther King, Jr., "I Have a Dream" Speech
   b. "The mystic chords of memory, stretching from every battle-field and patriot grave to every living heart and hearthstone all over this broad land, will yet swell the chorus of the Union when again touched, as surely they will be, by the better angels of our nature."—Abraham Lincoln, First Inaugural
   c. "I remember: It happened yesterday or eternities ago. A young Jewish boy discovering the kingdom of night. I remember his bewilderment, I remember his anguish. It all happened so fast. The ghetto. The deportation. The sealed cattle car. The fiery altar upon which the history of our people and the future of mankind were meant to be sacrificed."—Elie Wiesel, Nobel Peace Prize Acceptance Speech
2. What connotations do people give for the following words? If you wanted to draw on the positive connotations for these words, what terms would you use?
   Technology
   Rhetoric
   School
   Marriage
   Rap music
3. As a class, watch the videotape of a great orator. Discuss that orator's style. In what ways does he or she use language to achieve clarity, rhythm, and vividness? How do the language choices of that orator help achieve the purpose of the speech?

Activities

1. Adapt a written form to an oral form, and vice versa. (*Note:* To complete this activity, you will need a video or audio recorder.)
   a. Read an essay that you wrote for another class. Then put the essay aside, and with a video or tape recorder capturing the event, describe the information in that essay as though you were making an oral presentation before a class. Do not look at the written essay when you make the presentation. When you are done, play the tape, and compare the written essay to your oral presentation. In what ways are they different?
   b. Record yourself giving an extemporaneous speech. Listen to the tape and transcribe that speech, word for word. Then transform that transcription into a form that is appropriate for a written essay. What did you have to change, and why?

2. Read the manuscript of a speech, and seek to discover which language devices are used to develop the style of the speech. Identify the use of at least five stylistic resources (such as persuasive definition, maxim, irony, purposeful ambiguity, repetition, parallel wording, antithesis, metaphor, alliteration, rhetorical question, and dialogue; see Figure 10.1 for a complete list). What effects do these resources have on the audience? How do they create those effects? Why does the speaker use these resources in the way he or she does?

3. Write out your next speech in manuscript form, whether or not you plan to deliver it in that form. As you write this speech, think carefully about the language you are using. In the margins or in footnotes, annotate your manuscript, identifying the language resources that you chose and explaining why you used them in the way you did.

Using the Internet

1. **Assessing style in a famous speech.** Analyze President Kennedy's inaugural address for style choices. Point your browser to <http://oyez.at.nwu.edu/history-out-loud/jfk/>. Then, after reading or listening to the inaugural address, determine if Kennedy used the principles of oral style and made effective stylistic choices. Evaluate his language choices in light of the way his words

   - *expressed simplicity*
   - *created repetition*
   - *achieved an appropriate level of formality or informality*
   - *demonstrated reflexivity*
   - *achieved accuracy*
   - *were appropriate to the audience and situation*
   - *expressed clarity*
   - *created rhythm*
   - *created vividness*

2. **Using online dictionaries.** In a library you will find many different types of dictionaries. You can also do this online. From the **Allyn & Bacon Public Speaking** Website, you can access a variety of types of dictionaries at <http://www.abacon.com/pubspeak/organize/dict.html/>. Dictionaries are especially useful for finding denotative meanings of words.

3. **Assessing a famous speech for use of persuasive definitions.** Persuasive definitions are developed as speakers attempt to shift the meaning of a word or phrase, especially its connotation. Read or listen to a speech by President Franklin D. Roosevelt, which he delivered to the American people as a radio address. The speech is entitled "Fireside Chat on the Reorganization of the Judiciary, March 9, 1937." Point your browser to <http://oyez.at.nwu.edu/history-out-loud/fdr/> to find the speech. After listening to it or

(continued)

reading the text, describe how Roosevelt attempts to define the following terms:

- *reorganization*
- *policy-making body*
- *independent judiciary*
- *justice under the Constitution*
- *packing the Court*

Notes

1. For more about style as choice, see Geoffrey N. Leech, *Style in Fiction: A Linguistic Introduction to English Fictional Prose,* New York: Longman, 1981; especially Chapter 1, "Style and Choice."
2. For more about generic types, see Kathleen Hall Jamieson, "Generic Constraints and the Rhetorical Situation," *Philosophy and Rhetoric* 6 (Summer 1973): 162–170.
3. For more about culture types, see Michael Calvin McGee, "The 'Ideograph': A Link between Rhetoric and Ideology," *Quarterly Journal of Speech* 66 (February 1980): 1–16.
4. For more about archetypes, see Michael Osborn, "Archetypal Metaphor in Rhetoric: The Light–Dark Family," *Quarterly Journal of Speech* 53 (April 1967): 115–126.
5. The style of Lincoln's Gettysburg Address is discussed in detail in Garry Wills, *Lincoln at Gettysburg: The Words that Remade America,* New York: Simon & Schuster, 1992.
6. Since classical times, rhetorical theorists have commented on the connection between ideas and language. See Marcus Tullius Cicero, *De Oratore,* trans. H. Rackham, Cambridge, Mass.: Harvard Univ. Press, 1982, pp. 23–24.
7. For a more thorough examination of the differences between written and oral forms, see Marcia Irene Macaulay, *Processing Varieties in English: An Examination of Oral and Written Speech across Genres,* Vancouver: Univ. of British Columbia Press, 1990.
8. A modern handbook of such stylistic tools also exists. See Arthur Quinn, *Figures of Speech: Sixty Ways to Turn a Phrase,* Salt Lake City: Gibbs M. Smith, 1982.
9. For more about irony, see Wayne Booth, *Rhetoric of Irony,* Chicago: Univ. of Chicago Press, 1974.
10. However, it should be noted that ambiguity can have positive immediate effects that are followed by negative long-term effects. See David Zarefsky, *President Johnson's War on Poverty: Rhetoric and History,* Tuscaloosa: Univ. of Alabama Press, 1986.
11. See Jack L. Daniel and Geneva Smitherman, "How I Got Over: Communication Dynamics in the Black Community," *Quarterly Journal of Speech* 62 (February 1976): 26–39.
12. Much has been written about the way in which metaphors work. For a start on this subject, see I. A. Richards, *The Philosophy of Rhetoric,* New York: Oxford Univ. Press, 1965, Chapters 5 and 6; Max Black, "Metaphor," *Proceedings of the Aristotelian Society* 55 (1954–1955): 273–294; and George Lakoff and Mark Johnson, *Metaphors We Live By,* Univ. of Chicago Press, 1980.
13. For example, see Marcus Tullius Cicero, *Orator,* trans. H. M. Hubbell, Cambridge, Mass.: Harvard Univ. Press, 1939, pp. 69–111.

chapter 11
Presenting the Speech

In This Chapter We Will:

- Identify the desirable characteristics of speech presentation, especially naturalness, support of the speaker's purpose, and empathy with the audience.

- Explore how the aspects of a speaker's voice (volume, pitch, rate, pauses, articulation, enunciation, and pronunciation) can support the presentation, and consider how variety in each aspect enhances the speech.

- Examine how the speaker's body (physical appearance, movement, gesture, and facial expression) can help make the presentation effective.

- Distinguish among four basic modes of speech presentation and explore the advantages and limitations of each.

- Suggest a general procedure for practicing the speech before presenting it formally.

People who fear speaking in public are usually anxious about some aspect of oral presentation. "What will I do with my hands?" "What if I forget my speech?" "How will I know if I'm talking too fast?" "Suppose I start shaking and can't control it?" Concerns like these often lead people to avoid public speaking altogether.

CHARACTERISTICS OF EFFECTIVE PRESENTATION

Given this common anxiety about speaking in public, it might seem strange that we haven't focused on presenting the speech until now. We've explored how to analyze the audience, select and research a topic, test reasoning, organize the speech, and use language effectively. Why put off the very subject that so many speakers worry about most?

Well, strange as it seems, one of the *least* effective ways to improve your presentation is to concentrate on it directly. If you are self-conscious about what to do with your hands, for example, thinking about them will make you feel even more awkward—they'll suddenly seem like fifty-pound weights. Worrying about using your hands naturally will distract you (and your audience) from the subject of your speech. In fact, the best way to improve your presentation is to keep your attention on the speech and on the audience.

Why, then, should you study presentation at all if it might make you even more self-conscious? Because by learning about the aspects of presentation and by practicing certain strategies you can train yourself to speak "naturally" even if you *are* nervous about facing an audience.

Presentation is also called **delivery;** the two terms are used interchangeably to refer to how the voice and body help create the effect a speaker wants. The same ideas, even the same words, can elicit different reactions from an audience, depending on how you present them. Delivery, then, is much more than simply a way to "embellish" a speech. *How* a speaker says something affects *what* is really said, and so it also affects what listeners actually hear and understand.

Delivery that contributes positively to the overall effect of the speech has three general characteristics. First, as already noted, it does not call attention to itself or divert attention from the ideas in the speech. Rather, effective delivery will seem natural and uncontrived.

Second, effective delivery helps the audience to listen, understand, remember, and act on the speech. Listening carefully and critically to a speech is difficult; the presentation, if well done, will make it less so. Perhaps by lowering your voice you can make the audience listen more carefully when you state your main idea. Or, well-timed pauses may signal the transitions in your argument, making it easier to follow. Or, a gesture that points to the audience may help you personalize your call for action in the conclusion of the speech. Such examples of effective presentation can help you overcome the hurdles that listeners unconsciously put up to protect themselves from being influenced.

Third, effective delivery builds a sense of community between speaker and audience. It bridges potential gaps in communication, connecting people even if the setting is formal and highly ritualized. In most situations the speaker wants to identify with listeners, wants to symbolize that they are

delivery
The presentation of the speech, using the voice and body to create the desired effect.

all members of the same speaking/listening community. In other words, the speaker wants to show **empathy** with listeners, to give them a sense that he or she knows what they think and can feel what they feel. Empathy is achieved through an intimate, informal presentation that is based on careful audience analysis and strategic planning.

Now we will look closely at how both your voice and your body can enhance the presentation of a speech and help you build the desired relationship with listeners.

THE VOICE IN PRESENTATION

Unlike a singer, a speaker doesn't cultivate the voice as an end in itself, just to be expressive. Rather, a speaker uses the voice to advance the overall purpose of the speech. Particularly important to realize is that vocal cues are among the audience's earliest evidence in judging a speaker's ethos.

Six dimensions of the voice can be drawn on to enhance your effectiveness as a speaker: volume, pitch, rate, pauses, articulation and enunciation, and pronunciation (see Figure 11.1). Any vocal pattern—no matter how pleasant it first sounds—can easily become monotonous and hence distracting. Therefore, to keep a speech interesting and to keep the audience listening, you want to create *variety* in the six dimensions of your voice.

Volume

Volume refers to loudness; the higher the volume, the louder the voice. But how loud should you speak? That will depend on the size and the shape of the setting and on whether or not you use a microphone. To check and adjust your volume in any setting, watch listeners' reactions carefully when you begin to speak.

Besides regulating the overall loudness of your voice, remember to vary the volume at key points in the speech. You can emphasize an idea either by speaking louder or by lowering your voice. In both cases, listeners renew their attention because the vocal variety signals that they should listen carefully. By changing your volume, you can either understate an idea or overclaim it, depending on your purpose and the situation.

FEEDBACK Most audiences will let you know quickly if they cannot hear you, and their feedback will help you decide how loudly to speak.

empathy
Feeling what listeners feel and knowing what they think.

volume
Loudness of voice.

Volume	Loudness
Pitch	Placement on the musical scale
Rate	Speed; number of words per minute
Pauses	Silences for emphasis or transition
Articulation and enunciation	Clarity and distinctness of individual sounds or words
Pronunciation	The accepted way to sound a given word

FIGURE 11.1
Dimensions of vocal quality.

Also pay attention to the volume of other speakers and to how the audience reacts to them.

Students Brad Cummings, Alicia Lee, and Rosa Dominguez all gave classroom speeches on the same day. Brad was first, and he began in a very soft voice. Listeners had so much trouble hearing him that they moved forward in their seats and even cupped their ears with their hands. Unfortunately, for the first two minutes of his speech Brad looked only at his notes, and he missed the signal from the audience that he should speak more loudly. Alicia noticed the problem and was determined to avoid it when she spoke. But she overcompensated, speaking in a booming voice that made some listeners so uncomfortable that they actually pushed their chairs farther away. When Rosa's turn came, she knew that her volume should be somewhere between Brad's and Alicia's.

AMPLIFICATION   Before microphones and electronic amplification, speakers seldom had the option of using a low volume, because they could not be heard by the listeners farthest away. Speakers had to talk loudly and to project the voice from deep in the diaphragm so that it had greater carrying power. Today, if the audience is large, you can choose to use a microphone to amplify your voice; this gives you the option of speaking at lower volumes.

It takes some practice to use a microphone effectively, however. You need to speak more slowly and to articulate words more distinctly so that they will not become slurred through amplification. Position your mouth a few inches from the microphone, and speak directly into it. If you hear static or noises or your voice feeds back to you, move farther from the microphone and speak more softly. Don't wait until the time of your speech to test the microphone, and make sure that it is turned on if you plan to use it. You'll undercut the power of your introduction if you have to stop to ask, "Can everyone hear me?"

Since most classroom speeches are not amplified, you need to learn to project your voice adequately by controlling volume and the other dimensions of vocal quality. But because so many auditoriums, large meeting rooms, and outdoor rallies require the use of amplification, you also should look for opportunities to practice speaking with a microphone.

Pitch

When we say that someone's voice is "high" or "low," we are referring to its **pitch**—the placement of the voice on the musical scale. A soprano has a higher pitch than a bass. The pitch of a voice is determined by the speed with which sound waves vibrate. The faster the vibration, the higher the pitch—and voice.

As shown in Figure 11.2, the normal pitch for any speaker is fairly narrow. But extending higher and lower than normal pitch is a larger range within which both speaker and listeners will be comfortable. You can raise or lower your pitch within this range for emphasis, and listeners will still find it pleasant to hear you. The widest range that the speaker is physically able to produce includes extreme pitches that are difficult for an audience to listen to. Extremely high pitches grate on the ears, like fingernails scratching a chalkboard; and extremely low pitches are distorted and too resonant, which most listeners also find displeasing.

Probably the most distracting pitch range for listeners is a **monotone**—a very narrow, unchanging range that is used for the entire speech. Such a delivery is monotonous and uninteresting. Audiences quickly tire of it, and they

pitch
Placement of the voice on the musical scale, ranging from high to low.

monotone
A very narrow, unchanging pitch range.

FIGURE 11.2
Ranges of pitch.

Low	Medium low	Medium	Medium high	High
Possible but uncomfortable	Comfortable for variation	Normal	Comfortable for variation	Possible but uncomfortable

tune it out; some people even fall asleep, lulled by the droning voice of the speaker. Since most people have a wider range of comfortable pitches than they customarily use, there's no reason to speak in a monotone. By varying your pitch, you can sustain the audience's interest, signal transitions in the speech, and emphasize important ideas.

If you tape-record yourself delivering a speech, you may well discover that your pitch is higher on tape than it sounds to you when you are speaking. Two factors account for this. First, your ability to hear your own voice is always distorted. Second, pitch rises under stress, and giving a speech is stressful for many people. The key to a pleasant pitch is to relax as much as possible. Control your breathing so that you have enough air to complete each sentence; relax your shoulder muscles; and project your voice from deep in your body rather than forcing it from your throat.

Rate

Stereotype has it that Southerners talk slower than Midwesterners do and that Easterners talk faster. Whether true or not, these ideas refer to **rate,** the speed at which a person speaks. The average rate is between 120 and 150 words per minute, but successful speakers vary considerably. John F. Kennedy typically spoke at a faster rate than did Ronald Reagan, and yet both presidents were immensely persuasive speakers.

Two factors that we considered in connection with pitch—stress and variety—also apply to rate.

STRESS   Like pitch, rate goes up when a person is under stress. Students who practice their speech and time it to fill the ten minutes required by the assignment may be surprised that the speech takes only six minutes when they deliver it in class. This happens not because they timed it inaccurately or forgot a large portion of the speech but because they sped up their rate under the stress of presentation.

Racing through your speech makes it difficult for the audience to follow and comprehend your ideas; listeners simply don't have time to process and react to what they hear. The remedy, as with pitch, is to control your breathing and relax. Pause frequently for breath, taking in enough air to complete each statement. And remember to watch for feedback from the audience, since you also want to avoid speaking too slowly. A speech delivered at a very slow rate will tire listeners and will give them time to think about things other than your ideas.

VARIETY   Just as a monotonous pitch can seem boring, so a monotonous, unchanging rate can displease listeners. A speaker who utters every word and sentence at the same rate—no matter how significant or suspenseful the ideas

rate
The speed at which a person speaks, measured in words per minute.

are—gives no clues about what's really important. All ideas receive about the same treatment, and listeners tend to tune out.

Beginning speakers sometimes think that the only way to vary rate is to speed up at critical places in the speech. In fact, *both* speeding up and slowing down can convey movement or suspense and can compel attention and interest. Indeed, the choice of rate may itself communicate a message. Slowing down suggests that the speaker is serious and that every word matters; the audience had better pay attention. It may also create a mood like calmness or sadness or may suggest that the speaker thinks the ideas are difficult to grasp. Speeding up may propel a narrative forward or may evoke feelings of suspense, excitement, or outrage.

Most speakers vary their rate less than they think they do, and most could benefit by cultivating greater variety. Exercises in which you read a sentence or a list of words at differing rates will help you see how variety in rate can enhance interest in the message. Tape-record yourself reading part of a famous speech at different rates. The playback may surprise you by showing that changes in rate may change meaning as well. This exercise should also give you a sense of which "normal" rate is most comfortable for you personally.

Pauses

Pauses are the brief silences within a speech. Although it may seem strange to include silence among the dimensions of voice, silence as well as speech can be highly communicative. The message in a pause is one of completeness and finality.

Properly used, pauses enhance a speech in two ways. First, they emphasize what the speaker said, providing a kind of verbal underlining. While the speaker is silent, listeners can think about what they have just heard, storing the thought in memory. A speaker who never pauses will move on to a new idea before listeners can make sense of the last one—and can unintentionally convey that all ideas are equally important or that none is really important. Without pauses, the audience will remember less and will be influenced less.

Second, pauses mark transitions in a speech. Since speaking doesn't have "punctuation marks," pauses—and variety in pitch and rate—can serve that function, telling the audience that the speaker has ended a section and is about to move on to a new topic or idea. This gives the audience time to absorb what was just said before switching again to active listening. It also gives speakers time to collect their thoughts before moving to the next idea.

Simple as the concept of pauses might seem, like the other dimensions of voice, pausing requires practice to be used effectively. You will want to avoid the following common problems.

PAUSING TOO OFTEN A pause can signal the end of a paragraph in a speech, but that signal will be undercut if you also pause for every comma or semicolon. Too many pauses make a speech jerky and make the speaker seem nervous. Use pauses sparingly for effect.

PAUSING AT THE WRONG PLACES Since pauses are like punctuation marks, use them at the same places in the text as you would write the marks for which they stand. Pausing in the middle of sentences or ideas can confuse

pauses
Periods of brief silence within a speech.

Using pauses to emphasize a parallel speech structure is a good way to let the audience know what to expect next. Rev. Jesse Jackson made especially good use of such pauses in his "Common Ground" speech to the 1988 Democratic National Convention.

listeners and make comprehension difficult. President Jimmy Carter had problems with this aspect of delivery.

On the other hand, powerful effects can result from unusual pausing. One of the most memorable speeches of recent times was delivered by Dr. Martin Luther King, Jr., on August 28, 1963. Standing in front of the Lincoln Memorial in Washington, D.C., he summoned his audience to work peacefully to attain civil rights for African Americans. He inspired listeners with his vision of the American Dream, closing with lines adapted from the song "America":

> So let freedom ring from the prodigious hilltops of New Hampshire. Let freedom ring from the mighty mountains of New York. Let freedom ring from the heightening Alleghenies of Pennsylvania! Let freedom ring from the snowcapped Rockies of Colorado! Let freedom ring from the curvaceous peaks of California!

Instead of pausing after each sentence, Dr. King stopped briefly after each refrain of "Let freedom ring," building intensity and creating the musical effect of a crescendo. His midsentence pauses emphasized the repeating pattern in his examples and let the audience know what to expect next. The Reverend Jesse Jackson used the same strategy in a speech at the 1988 Democratic National Convention, pausing each time he repeated the phrase "common ground." In both cases, unusual choices of when to pause created the desired effect by providing emphasis.

NOT PAUSING LONG ENOUGH   Uncomfortable with silence, speakers are notoriously poor judges of how long their pauses are; most imagine them to be much longer. Again the tape recorder is a valuable aid. Time your recorded pauses, and compare them with how long you *thought* you paused when you spoke. All pauses should be relatively brief, of course, but the effects of a one-second pause and a five-second pause are considerably different.

USING VOCALIZED PAUSES   Sounds such as "uh" and "umm" are **vocalized pauses,** meaningless sounds that a speaker produces during moments of silence. These almost always arise from nervousness and can be highly distracting to listeners. (Have you ever been in an audience that began to count the speaker's "uhs" and "umms"?) Sometimes vocalized pauses are words or phrases such as "like," "you know," "now then," and "okay?" Such repetition is a nervous response; the speaker is uncomfortable stopping for even a few seconds.

Whether syllables or words, vocalized pauses call so much attention to themselves that they interfere with the message. The remedy is easy to state but difficult to carry out: When you pause, *be silent*. Again, the tape recorder is useful, because most speakers are not aware of their vocalized pauses. Listen to yourself, and discover how often you vocalize during a pause. If you do it frequently, make a mental note to *remain silent*.

Articulation and Enunciation

The related concepts of articulation and enunciation have to do with precise, distinct speech. **Articulation** refers to the clarity of individual sounds; **enunciation** refers to the distinctness with which words are sounded.

ARTICULATION   Common articulation problems include difficulty in forming the *th* sound (saying "dese" instead of "these") and dropping the final *g* from a word ("workin' " and "makin' "). Articulation can be improved through specific vocal exercises for particular sounds. The easiest way to diagnose articulation problems is to have someone else listen with you to a tape of your speech and to identify any sounds that call attention to themselves.

Not everyone articulates in the same way, of course. Speakers whose native language is not English, for example, often have difficulty with standard English articulation. Their goal should be not to articulate like native English speakers but to articulate clearly enough that they can be heard and understood. By the same token, listeners should make reasonable efforts to understand speakers whose articulation patterns are unfamiliar. In our increasingly diverse society we all meet people who "speak differently." We should not allow cultural differences in articulation to block successful communication.

ENUNCIATION   The distinctness with which words are sounded is another aspect of clarity that speakers need to consider. One specific problem is the tendency to slur words together. This is fairly common in informal settings, where "Whaddaya know?" and "Whatcha doin'?" may replace "What do you know?" and "What are you doing?" In a speech, however, such lack of enunciation will seem inappropriate; unless it is being used for effect, it is likely to influence the audience's perception of the speaker.

The other extreme to avoid is being too precise in enunciation, saying each word so distinctly that you seem pompous and condescending to the audience. Speaking too distinctly not only distracts attention from the message but also may arouse negative feelings in listeners, who believe the speaker is "putting on airs."

Pronunciation

Even when a word is familiar to the eye, we sometimes wonder how it should be sounded. Correct **pronunciation** refers to the accepted way to

---

vocalized pauses
Pauses filled with sound, such as "uh" or "umm."

articulation
Precision and clarity in the production of individual vocal sounds.

enunciation
Precision and distinctness in sounding words.

pronunciation
Sounding of a word in the accepted way.

sound any given word. This includes such matters as which syllable to accent, whether to sound a vowel as short or long, and which optional consonant sound to use (for example, whether to give a *c* a hard sound, like a *k,* or a soft sound, like an *s*).

THE IMPORTANCE OF PROPER PRONUNCIATION   First, the meaning of a spoken word may depend on its pronunciation, and mispronouncing it may prevent listeners from sensing which meaning you intend. The word "desert," for example, means something different when you accent the first syllable (noun = "hot, dry place with lots of sand") than when you accent the second syllable (verb = "to abandon"). Second, like some of the other dimensions of vocal quality, mispronunciation calls attention to itself and may overshadow your ideas and message. Third, faulty pronunciation reflects negatively on a speaker's credibility; listeners may (mistakenly) get the impression that the speaker is ignorant or incompetent and hence is not to be trusted.

The phrase "proper pronunciation" may conjure up images of Eliza Doolittle, the British street vendor in *My Fair Lady* who could not speak "the king's English" and was stigmatized because of her lower-class **dialect,** or pronunciation pattern. Today in the United States, however, people are more likely to recognize and to accept that pronunciations vary according to geography (and according to economic and other cultural factors). Different regions have developed different dialects. Many New Englanders, for example, add an *r* sound to words ending in *a,* as John F. Kennedy did when referring to "Cuber" or to an "idear." Similarly we can point to the "Southern drawl," the broad *a* that is said to be a "Chicago accent," and the Midwestern "nasal twang."

For a long time such pronunciation patterns also gave rise to negative regional stereotypes ("Southerners are lazy," "New Yorkers are rude," and so forth). But with greater mobility and the impact of the mass media, we have become more aware of the many cultural traditions in U.S. society. Today we are more likely to hear speakers with a variety of dialects, and so we are less likely to view such differences as highly unusual.

On the other hand, just as slang is sometimes inappropriate, it remains important to speak standard American English in some situations. If the audience is highly diverse, many listeners may be distracted by an unfamiliar dialect. And in highly formal situations *any* sort of dialect may be seen as a distraction.

PRONUNCIATION AND AUDIENCE ANALYSIS   In thinking about pronunciation and dialect, analyze your audience in relation to yourself, asking the questions listed in Checklist 11.1 on page 290. Depending on your answers, design a strategy for your speech as suggested in the checklist.

As you learned in Chapter 3, cultural diversity is a feature of many audiences. Even though dialects have become more familiar and less distinct, the acceptance of cultural diversity (and its variations in the use of language) is still somewhat at odds with the striving for national unity (and its goal of a common mode of speaking). Knowing that, you should plan your presentation in a way that increases the chances of achieving your goals.

INFLECTION   Articulation, enunciation, and pronunciation relate to the sound of individual syllables and words. **Inflection** is a similar concept

dialect
A pronunciation pattern that characterizes a particular geographic area (or economic or cultural factors).

inflection
Pronunciation pattern for a sentence as a whole.

Checklist

11.1 Pronunciation and Audience Analysis

Questions to Ask:

- *Am I culturally different from most of my immediate listeners?*
- *If so, how might this affect their impressions of me and my speech?*
- *How do cultural differences affect my ability to achieve the goals of my speech?*
- *Does my pronunciation make me vulnerable to stereotyping by the audience? Conversely, is there a danger that I may stereotype the audience?*

Strategic Decisions to Consider:

- *Should I confront stereotyping, either directly or indirectly?*
- *How should I try to manage the impression that my pronunciation might give the audience?*
- *Should I modify my volume or rate, the amount of explanation I provide, or any of my supporting material?*

except that it applies to the sentence as a whole. Appropriate inflection is important for the same reasons we have already discussed: Without it, you risk distracting listeners' attention, distorting your message, and damaging your credibility.

For example, one normal inflection pattern is to raise the pitch toward the end of a question and to lower the pitch toward the end of a statement. Speakers who reverse this pattern sound strange, and the audience may have trouble figuring out what they mean. Some speakers are so unsure of themselves that they raise their pitch after nearly every statement, hoping to discover whether the audience understands and agrees with their point. But this inflection pattern only makes ideas more difficult to follow, since they sound like questions rather than statements.

A given sentence may have more than one appropriate inflection pattern, and yet its meaning will change greatly when the wrong pattern is used. Student Jeremy Rivers, for example, was extolling the merits of a particular brand of luggage and confidently told the audience, "Nothing could be better than this brand." He thought this statement was strongly positive, and so did most listeners. But Jeremy was surprised to discover that a few audience members understood this remark differently, concluding that they really would be better off with *nothing* than with this brand. Careful attention to inflection would have given the audience a better clue about which meaning Jeremy intended.

In general, think about the audience when you work on improving your speaking voice. Watch for feedback to ensure that your volume, pitch, rate, and degree of pauses are comfortable for listeners and to see that your enunciation, articulation, and pronunciation make your ideas clear. To avoid distracting from your message, aim for a presentation voice that has variety, that seems natural, and that captures and holds listeners' attention.

APPLYING STRATEGIES

How to Improve Your Delivery

Carrie Biesel

Stay calm. It's only a speech. Getting worked up over it will just cause you to mess up. Stand straight and breathe. Don't hold your breath or fidget as you speak. Walk side to side in front of the audience. Don't move forward and backward, as this will make some information seem more important than other information. Smile and be genuine. It's obvious when a speech is recited with no feeling, and that loses the audience's attention right away.

Latif Farag

I think the two most important elements in delivery are the bodily action and the eye contact. Speakers should be very careful and shouldn't put their hands in their pockets or rock or swing them. They should be careful with their movements and not wander. They shouldn't just look at their note cards all the time and forget about the audience.

Laura Breland

I think that presentation of a speech is very important. I try to focus on the idea that it is important and on how I want to present and what I want to present.

T. J. Brinkerhoff

The most important thing to do when presenting a speech is to be yourself rather than trying to be a speaker. When somebody is comfortable in front of a group, it is easy to see. The best speakers that I have seen are the ones who treat public speaking like they are speaking to you just as they would talk to their friends. People who try to deliver a speech in a persona other than their own are easily recognizable and irritating. Presenting a speech really comes down to how well you know your material so that you can deliver it effortlessly. I personally think that memorized speeches are the most effective because they are easy to listen to and more personal for the audience.

THE BODY IN PRESENTATION

Just as the voice gives the speaker important *auditory* and *verbal* resources, the body provides equally valuable *visual* resources. Not surprisingly, the same general principles relating to the voice in presentation also apply to the body. The speaker's body is used to enhance the message, not to call attention to itself. The body and its movements influence listeners' first impressions of the speaker and, hence, their willingness to take the speaker seriously. And changes in body placement and movement can mark transitions in the speech and add enough variety to keep the audience interested in and focused on the message.

Physical Appearance

Even before you begin to speak, audience members are forming impressions of the sort of person you are. This happens quickly and on the basis of superficial judgments, but those judgments are durable. (See the discussion of ethos in Chapter 1.) Consequently, you want to avoid doing anything that will make you seem unprepared, incompetent, or unreliable.

BEFORE YOU SPEAK   Consider the physical arrangement of the speaking space before deciding such things as how to approach the podium and what to wear. Is the setting large and impersonal or small and intimate? How formal or informal is the setting (and occasion)? Will you be able to establish eye contact with listeners, or will you be far away from them and speaking with a microphone?

Your appearance to an audience at an outdoor rally will be far different from how you appear to the same audience in a cathedral. Similarly, the settings for a retirement banquet, a business meeting, a commencement address, and a medical lecture are all different and can influence how the audience perceives you. Whenever possible, then, you should examine the speaking space and practice in it before presenting your speech.

APPROACHING THE PODIUM   Your physical appearance begins to create impressions as you walk to the podium. If you start speaking while you walk, before facing the audience, you may seem in a hurry to finish and so unsure of yourself that you won't look the audience in the eye. Likewise, if you shuffle uncertainly toward the podium, the audience may think you lack confidence and don't know what you are talking about. Such assumptions may be wrong, of course, but they affect your ethos and can create a "credibility deficit" that you'll have to overcome.

No matter how you feel about speaking, create the best first impression that you can. Walk firmly and purposefully to the podium, pause to collect your thoughts, look directly at the audience, and then begin with confidence. In Chapter 12 you will learn that your body acts as a visual aid for the speech—the audience will be *looking at you*. Try to make your body's message match and reinforce the message of your words.

CLOTHES AND GROOMING   What you wear and your personal appearance—everything from hairstyle to footwear—are the stuff of first impressions and will affect your ethos. A badly dressed, unkempt speaker easily becomes the focus of attention and distracts the audience from the message. If you constantly push hair out of your face, wear a baseball cap that makes eye contact impossible, or fiddle with keys or jewelry, you practically beg the audience to focus on the distractions rather than the speech.

Typically, speakers dress a bit more formally than audience members do.[1] The general public may attend a speech in sports attire, but the speaker is a major figure and is expected to look the part. In recent years this unwritten "dress code" has relaxed considerably. President Jimmy Carter made a point of appearing in shirtsleeves without a tie, and President Bill Clinton's jeans and running clothes became part of his image. Yet both men were well advised to wear suits and ties when addressing the public—when they wanted to project a serious image.

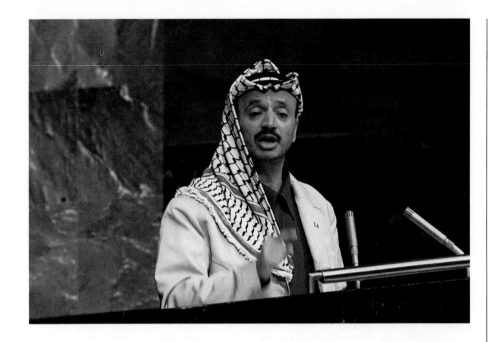

◀ Some speakers, such as Yasser Arafat, wish to make an important cultural statement through distinctive clothing. In such a situation, you need to be sure that physical features such as hair, jewelry, and head gear do not detract from the positive ethos you hope to establish through your speech.

Sometimes a speaker will want to make a cultural statement through clothing and hairstyle and will resent any advice about adapting to the audience's expectations. But here, as elsewhere, audience analysis is critical; plan your personal appearance to advance your strategic goals.

Movement

How and where you position your body while speaking can also enhance or distract from the message. When student speaker Rachel Samuels stood behind the large, heavy podium in her classroom, only her head was visible. Recognizing the problem, Rachel stepped away from the podium to present her speech.

Even if the height of the podium does not affect your appearance this way, it's a good idea to step away from it occasionally. Many beginning speakers grip the podium as though tensely steering a car that is out of control. This may give a sense of security, but it also puts a barrier between you and the audience. Instead, if you loosen your grip and step away from the podium at points in the speech, your body language will provide visual cues. For example, you can signal transitions in the speech by moving a step or two forward or to the side. And by moving toward the audience, you can show your trust and break down any imaginary walls between you and listeners.

The 1992 presidential debates among Bill Clinton, George Bush, and Ross Perot included one format that resembled a town meeting in which citizens in the audience asked questions. At one point, when Bill Clinton was asked how the federal budget deficit had affected him personally, he did not respond right away. First he took a few steps toward the questioner and established eye contact. Although he was actually speaking to a television audience of millions, Mr. Clinton seemed to be responding to this citizen one on one. The unstated message was that they had a common bond. And because Mr. Clinton had to face the cameras to answer his questioner, television viewers also felt that he was responding directly to them—and had a bond with them.

Although purposeful, planned movement will benefit your presentation, constant or aimless movement will be a great distraction. A speaker who moves all around the room for no apparent reason puts a burden on listeners; it's up to them to follow the movements and maintain eye contact. Many will simply stop trying—and stop listening as well. Speakers also should avoid shifting their weight from side to side. Like vocalized pauses, this nervous response calls negative attention to itself.

Just as you should not begin speaking until you have reached the podium and sized up the audience, so should you not gather up notes and start returning to your seat while you are still speaking. The audience will not have a chance to absorb your final thoughts, and your conclusion will be weakened. You also will give the impression that speaking to them was painful and that you want to finish as soon as possible. Take your time, and take control over the situation. When you do return to your seat, walk confidently without calling attention to yourself.

Gesture

The term **gesture** refers to the movement of hands and arms during the speech as a means of emphasis. Many speakers are especially self-conscious about their hands and what to do with them while they speak. Some put their hands into their pockets—not to create an informal, conversational tone but just to get them out of the way. These speakers usually seem tense, as though they are tightly clenching something buried deep in their pocket. Other untrained speakers fidget, moving their hands and arms aimlessly as a nervous reaction. Since such movements are not coordinated with the speech, they call attention to themselves and detract from the message.

In contrast, a well-timed, purposeful gesture heightens the power of both your text and your voice. But what is such a gesture like? Centuries ago, theorists of public speaking believed that certain gestures went naturally with particular words or ideas. They wrote manuals illustrating hundreds of gestures and their matching words so that speakers could learn the gestures by rote and perform them automatically when reciting the matching text.[2] Today this approach is considered nonsense; such a presentation is so artificial and contrived that it seems funny.

Even so, not all speakers are naturally expressive with their hands. Whether you use many or few gestures does not matter; what matters is that your gestures support your message, not draw attention away from it. If you videotaped yourself in informal conversation, you probably would discover gestures that you are unaware of—they simply come out naturally when you talk. A few possible uses of gestures are to emphasize the importance of a point, to suggest balance or opposition ("on the one hand," "on the other hand"), and to position ideas in space and time.[3]

Above all, gestures used in presentation should appear natural. Achieving this is less a matter of memorizing gestures than of becoming familiar with the general rhythm of gesture. It begins with an **anticipation step,** which simply means that you bring your hands to a position from which a gesture can easily be made. If you are gripping the podium or handling several pages of notes, gesturing will be difficult and awkward. First you need to be in a position that lets you execute a gesture naturally.

gesture
Movement of hands and arms during the speech as a means of emphasis.

anticipation step
The first step of a gesture; involves bringing the hands into a position from which the gesture can be made.

Being ready to gesture, you next move to the **implementation step**—the few seconds in which you execute the movement as you intended. Typically, a speaker's gestures occur somewhere between the waist and shoulders, an area that eases natural movement and is also visible to audience members. Perhaps most important in implementing the gesture is to *follow it through*. Untrained speakers often make a half-gesture, raising a hand partway without completing the movement. Such a gesture has little purpose or effect, suggesting instead that the speaker is nervous.

Having implemented the gesture, during the **relaxation step** you return your hands to their normal position, whether at your side, in front of you, or resting on the podium. Without this step you risk being trapped in continuous gesture. Since your hands are in the visual space where gestures take place, and you haven't returned them to rest, you may find yourself gesturing repeatedly and in the same way for every word or idea. That, of course, dilutes the power of the gesture when you really do want to emphasize something.

Finally, don't worry too much about gestures. Although "what to do with my hands" is a concern for many speakers, the issue is relatively unimportant. Gestures tend to take care of themselves as long as you avoid distracting mannerisms, practice the three steps of gesture, and concentrate on your message.

Facial Expression

The speaker's facial expressions are another powerful element of nonverbal communication that can heighten or detract from the speech. Obviously, a smiling speaker communicates something much different from a frowning one. But someone who smiles and grins throughout the presentation will seem out of place and hence not believable, as will a speaker who delivers a lighthearted message but shows no facial expression at all. Again, it is valuable either to videotape your speech or to have someone observe you practicing it. Discover whether your facial expressions are consistent with and support the message in your text.

EYE CONTACT   One aspect of facial expression, **eye contact,** deserves special attention. Speakers who do not look the audience in the eye may lose credibility. In mainstream American culture, not looking at someone is widely thought to mean that the person is lying or has something to hide. In fact, speakers from cultures with different norms about eye contact may be misunderstood and misjudged by an American audience.

Another important point is that eye contact lets you see how the audience is responding to the speech; it provides feedback. Listeners' facial expressions often indicate whether the message is clear or needs explanation, whether claims seem persuasive or not, and so on. Such feedback helps you adjust your presentation to fit the audience while you speak. But if you stare at your notes or gaze at the back wall, you cannot make eye contact and take advantage of feedback.

SPEAKING TO A LARGE AUDIENCE   Maintaining eye contact with a large audience presents problems. You can't look at everyone, but if you focus on nearby listeners, those farther away will feel left out. And if you keep turning your head to look briefly at many groups in the audience, the constant movements will be a distraction, and you won't really make eye contact with anyone. The remedy is not to fix on particular audience members but to focus on

implementation step
The execution of a gesture, raising the hand and moving it in the intended manner.

relaxation step
Returning the hands to a normal relaxed position at the conclusion of a gesture.

eye contact
Looking directly at members of the audience.

For most American audiences, ▶
eye contact is important if
the speaker wishes to appear
credible. Hillary Rodham Clinton maintains direct eye contact with her audiences both
to enhance her credibility
and to see how listeners are
responding to her speeches.

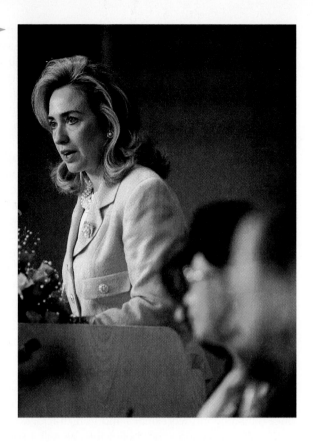

general areas of the audience. Mentally divide listeners into three or four
groups, and shift your focus among them to correspond to transitions in the
speech. This lets all listeners feel—to some degree—that you are talking directly to them, and you can monitor the groups for feedback. At the same
time, your shifting focus helps to signal transitions in the speech.

SPEAKING FOR THE CAMERA   Different problems arise when speaking for
the camera. Even though you *are* addressing a very large audience, you are
speaking only to a camera—a single "listener" who provides no direct feedback through eye contact. On camera, if you move your head from side to side
as you would with a large audience, you create an impression of shiftiness.
And since the camera is close in, it exaggerates your shifts in eye contact. You
will seem to be rolling your head around, which can only detract greatly from
the speech. When speaking on camera, then, it is wiser to imagine only a single listener and to look directly into the camera to address that person. And
because you cannot modify your presentation on the spot through feedback,
careful audience analysis and strategic planning are extremely important.

MODES OF PRESENTATION

Most theorists identify four general modes of presentation: impromptu,
memorized, manuscript, and extemporaneous. No matter which mode
you choose, you can use voice and body to enhance the presentation. But

the modes themselves also involve choices that can strengthen or weaken the speech.

Impromptu Presentation

When you have little or no time to prepare specifically for a speech, you make an **impromptu presentation.** Perhaps someone at a meeting says something that inspires you to respond, and so you raise your hand to offer your views. You thereby give a speech seemingly without any preparation at all. In fact, you may have "spent a lifetime" preparing for that speech. The issues are important to you, and you've thought about them a great deal. But you never imagined that you would be speaking about them on this particular occasion.

Structure an impromptu presentation as simply and clearly as possible. Because you do not have a chance to plan the speech in detail, you may become entangled in the web of your argument. The key is to focus on a very small number of main ideas, previewing and summarizing them so that listeners have no doubts about your thesis or how the ideas develop it. Impromptu speaking also often takes cues from previous speakers, referring to their specific points and suggesting how their message relates to yours.

Memorized Presentation

A **memorized presentation** is the opposite of impromptu; you pay such close attention to your text that you commit it to memory. This mode of speaking was highly valued in the past. School children studied famous orations and recited them by rote. Great orators often wrote out their entire speeches and then committed them to memory. Such speeches were long; it was common during the early 1800s for a U.S. senator to speak for hours, delivering a memorized presentation.

Today few theorists advise anyone to memorize a speech. Besides the unnecessary investment in energy, speaking from memory has other problems. First, because the text is memorized, the speaker might not take feedback into account and adapt to the audience's needs. More likely, the speaker will ignore the audience and deliver a soliloquy. Second, if you write and then memorize a speech for oral delivery, the recital may be stiff and stilted. It will sound memorized, which quickly causes an audience to lose interest. Finally, a memorized text raises concern about what might happen if you forget a line. Some speakers can ad lib and patch things up quickly, but many become flustered; having forgotten the memorized words, they don't know what to say.

Although memorized presentation has these problems and is generally discouraged, it can be helpful to memorize the first few sentences of your introduction and the last few sentences of your conclusion. Then you will begin the speech confidently and end it solidly, without trailing off. And if you want to use a particular phrase or line in the speech, you might commit that to memory and plan where it would fit best. But the practice of memorizing an entire speech has fallen into disuse—deservedly.

Manuscript Presentation

Like a memorized speech, **manuscript presentation** also involves a text that is prepared word for word, but the speech is read rather than delivered from memory. This speaking mode is useful in highly formal situations, when

impromptu presentation
A mode of presentation in which the speaker has done little or no specific preparation for the speech.

memorized presentation
The opposite of speaking impromptu; the speaker pays close attention to a prepared text and commits it to memory.

manuscript presentation
A mode of presentation in which the speaker reads aloud the prepared text of the speech.

specific wording is critical. The president of the United States uses manuscript presentation for the State of the Union address and for most speeches about major policies. The risk of saying the wrong thing is too great to rely on other presentation modes.

Manuscript presentation also is useful when precise timing is important, as when speaking on radio or television. This was clearly illustrated in 1952, when vice-presidential candidate Richard Nixon appeared on television to defend himself against charges of financial irregularities (the speech is discussed in Chapter 10). He ended by urging listeners to express support for him by writing to the Republican National Committee. But Mr. Nixon was not speaking from manuscript, and he ran out of time as he was telling the audience where to write. Millions of listeners were able to respond anyway, but if you watch that speech on tape, you will see how awkward the ending is.

Although manuscript presentation may be appropriate in these specific circumstances, as a general rule it is not the best mode. First, reading a paper aloud is not the same as speaking directly to an audience. Audiences recognize the difference and are less attentive; the manuscript interferes with direct communication between the speaker and listeners.

Second, very few people are well trained in the art of reading aloud. Even a text that is rich in imagery, that identifies with the audience, and that offers solid argument may be negated if it is read indifferently or with vocal patterns that do not match the intent of the message.[4]

Third, presenting a speech from manuscript makes it difficult to maintain eye contact and profit from feedback. Accomplished speakers sometimes can do it—taking in a sentence or two of their text and then gracefully looking up and speaking to the audience. But many speakers do this awkwardly, which is distracting at best, and they often lose their place in the text.

Extemporaneous Presentation

A speech that is prepared and rehearsed but is neither written out nor memorized is called **extemporaneous presentation.** This mode is recommended for most speakers and speeches, because it encourages a conversational quality and is flexible enough to permit adaptation to feedback. Extemporaneous speaking is not impromptu; the speaker has outlined and planned the speech carefully, has a specific structure in mind, and probably uses prepared notes during presentation. But no word-for-word text exists in advance of delivery, and the speech is not memorized or read aloud.

The advice in earlier chapters that you develop a preparation outline and a presentation outline assumed an extemporaneous mode of presentation. The preparation outline helps you identify your main ideas, their relation to each other and to your thesis, and the order in which to present them. The presentation outline includes enough key words to help you keep the ideas straight and to present them as intended. As you practice the speech, you will try out different ways of verbalizing the ideas, getting a sense of how the speech sounds and what you mean. But you will not memorize or write down the specific wording (other than introductory and concluding sentences). Speaking extemporaneously lets you discuss ideas informally and conversationally. Your focus will be on ideas rather than on specific words, making it easier to maintain eye contact and modify your message in response to feedback.

extemporaneous presentation
A mode of presentation in which the speech is planned and structured carefully but a specific text is not written in advance nor memorized.

PRACTICING FOR SPEECH PRESENTATION

The idea of practicing to appear natural may not seem quite so strange, now that we have explored how the speaker's voice and body can be used in a planned way to bring about that result. Yet the easiest way to fail at the goal is to focus too much on your voice or body rather than on what you are going to say and on what you are trying to achieve.

Thinking consciously about your strategic objectives—what you wish to share with the audience, how you want to affect listeners, or what you want audience members to believe or do after hearing your speech—should focus your attention on the purpose of the speech. If you keep content and purpose clearly in mind, then you can practice using your voice and body to *contribute* to those goals rather than being ends in themselves.[5]

The most important advice about practice is to begin early. Skills of presentation take time to perfect, and you will learn them best when you are relaxed, not tense. Unless the assignment really calls for an impromptu speech, waiting until the last minute is never a good idea. Things will not seem to fall into place. The speech may seem disorganized or not artfully crafted; or the content and presentation may be out of sync; or the gestures, movement, and vocal variations may be distracting. Admittedly, the advice to start early on a task is easier to give than to follow, but it will pay great dividends in the case of speech presentation.

Each person takes a unique approach to practicing a speech, and you should find methods that work well for you. In general, however, a four-step process is likely to be effective:

1. Develop the presentation outline.
2. Mentally rehearse the speech.
3. Practice the speech orally.
4. Simulate the speech setting.

The Presentation Outline

Develop your presentation outline as discussed in Chapter 9, and talk it through several times. By referring only to the outline, you should be able to articulate your main ideas and the links in your thought. Each key word should

---

Checklist

11.2 *Practicing the Speech*

1. **Develop the presentation outline.**
   - *Talk through the outline several times.*
   - *Write out or memorize any portion for which exact language is essential.*
2. **Mentally rehearse the speech.**

3. **Practice the speech orally.**
   - *With no one else present.*
   - *With a small group of friends.*
   - *On videotape if possible.*
4. **Simulate the speech setting.**

trigger a more complete thought. If this does not happen, revise the presentation outline to include more key words, different words, or a different structure.

This is also the time to write out or memorize any portion of the speech for which exact language is essential, such as a few introductory sentences or your conclusion. You might include your thesis statement, if you want to have its precise wording in front of you. Although excessive memorization is discouraged, some parts of even an extemporaneous speech depend on exact wording, and this is the time to develop the words you plan to use.

Mental Rehearsal

Picture an imaginary audience, and run through the speech in your mind while holding this image. Try to see yourself in the speaking situation, and think through what you would say. As you rehearse mentally, you may hit upon a particular transitional phrase or may discover the most effective way to express an idea clearly. Speakers who skip the step of mental rehearsal often fail to consider the big picture of how the speech will look and sound when everything comes together. As a result, the speech may seem fragmented or unnatural to an audience.

Oral Practice

Practice the speech orally, several times, under a variety of conditions. **Distributed practice** (brief periods of practice spread over time) is likely to be more effective than **massed practice** (a few lengthy sessions shortly before you speak).

The first few times, deliver the speech with no one else present. Although this will not give you feedback, you will become sensitive to the sound of the speech, to its length and timing, and to opportunities to enhance your use of voice and body. Because you are both speaker and listener, you'll want to satisfy yourself that everything fits together correctly.

Then practice with a small group of friends. Even two or three people are enough, if you trust them to give candid reactions that might improve the speech. This stage of practice will let you actually share your thoughts with others and see how the speech is affected by having an audience present. Use such "early reviews" to check whether the design of the speech will achieve your purpose. Ask especially whether listeners got a clear sense of your thesis, whether the speech moved clearly from one point to another, whether you spent too much or too little time on anything, and whether the speech seemed too slow or too fast. Raise any other specific concerns you have about the speech. The more feedback you get from these first listeners, the stronger your final presentation will be.

Videotape your presentation, if possible, and study the tape to see how the speech looks and sounds to others. This step makes many people uncomfortable, because they think they look and sound different from what the tape reveals. But try to set aside such feelings, focusing instead on what listeners will see and hear. For example, if the tape shows that you are looking only at your notes and are not making eye contact, you can correct this by the time you deliver the speech. The tape also might reassure you about some aspect of performance, such as gestures—perhaps they appear more natural than you thought. Look for positive feedback as well as negative; the tape can build your confidence even as it reveals areas that need improvement.

distributed practice
Brief periods of practice spread over time.

massed practice
A few lengthy practice sessions shortly before delivering the speech.

Simulation

Either practice the speech in the room where you'll speak, or simulate that setting as closely as possible. For instance, if you will be speaking in a large auditorium, practicing there or in a similar space will show you how much you should exaggerate gestures and movement so that they can be seen at a distance. If the setting will be smaller and more intimate, you may need to practice modulating your voice so that you don't seem to be shouting. And if you will be using a microphone, practicing with it will help you control and adapt your voice in ways that avoid distortion and slurring. Finally, this step will make you more comfortable with the setting so that, when the time comes, you can focus on your audience and your message.

Summary

The principles and guidelines that we explored in this chapter should be qualified by the important statement that presentation of a speech should appear natural. A speaker's technique should not call attention to itself or in any way distract from the message. But seeming natural is not simple; you must understand the resources of your voice and body and must practice using them.

Besides being a resource for the speaker, voice gives the audience insights into the speaker's personality. Variety in voice keeps listeners interested and adds emphasis to the speech. Six vocal dimensions that a speaker can use to enhance a speech are volume, pitch, rate, pauses, enunciation and articulation of individual sounds, and pronunciation.

Similar general principles apply to the speaker's use of the body. Movement and gestures should appear natural and should contribute to the overall goals for the speech. Resources of the body include physical appearance (posture, grooming, attire, and the like), movement of the body, gesture, and facial expression.

We examined four presentation modes: impromptu, memorized, manuscript, and extemporaneous. Each mode has its strengths and limitations, and each is appropriate for specific speaking situations. For most purposes an extemporaneous presentation is preferred, although parts of the speech—the introduction, the conclusion, and perhaps the thesis statement—may be committed to memory.

Like most skills, speech presentation is improved by practice, including practicing how to appear natural. Each speaker develops a unique practice routine, but a four-step process is recommended: develop the presentation outline, mentally rehearse, practice orally with feedback, and simulate the speech setting as closely as possible.

Discussion Questions

1. How does delivery vary according to purpose? In what ways might delivery be different for a eulogy, an instructional speech, and a speech of dissent?

2. In what ways does delivery style contribute to or detract from a speaker's strategy? Discuss and compare the strategies and styles of some famous speakers—for example, Ronald Reagan, George Bush, Bill Clinton, Ross Perot, Newt Gingrich, and Jesse Jackson. Discuss both their manuscript delivery in formal televised speeches and their extemporaneous delivery in debates and press conferences.

3. In what ways might you improve your delivery? Each student should present a short introduction to a speech, and classmates should then discuss the strengths and weaknesses of presentation. Focus especially on aspects of delivery that the speaker is unlikely to recognize by examining a tape, such as articulation, enunciation, and pronunciation.

 Activities

1. Select a passage from a speech that you can obtain in manuscript form. Tape-record yourself presenting this passage first at a very slow rate, then at a moderate rate, and finally at a quick rate. Then vary the rate *within* the passage, slowing down or speeding up as needed to best convey the message. Repeat this process varying the volume of your delivery. Listen to the tape of these variations, and identify how changes in rate and volume affected the presentation.

2. Write out the introduction and conclusion of your next speech. Before you practice the delivery of these sections, decide where you want to include pauses and which words you want to emphasize by changes in volume and pitch.

3. Watch a videotape of yourself presenting a speech. Pay close attention to your delivery style—your volume, rate, and pitch variations; whether you use vocalized pauses; your eye contact, posture, and gestures; and so on. List the things about your delivery style that currently detract from your message and that you would like to improve. How might you go about improving them?

Using the Internet

1. **How important is the voice in a presentation?** Make that judgment after listening to at least two speeches from the **History Channel Archive of Great Speeches.** Point your browser to <http://www.historychannel.com/historychannel/gspeech/> where you can find the speech featured for the day. Then, click on the link for "Archive" to browse the whole list of offerings. After listening to the two speeches, draw conclusions about which speaker made the best use of vocal qualities: volume, pitch, rate, pauses, articulation, enunciation, pronunciation, and inflection.

2. **How important is physical delivery?** Read the article from the *Time Magazine* issue of October 10, 1960, entitled "The Campaign: Candid Camera," which contrasts the response of television viewers to that of radio listeners in their judgments of who won the first Kennedy–Nixon Debate. Point your browser to <http://allpolitics. com/1996/analysis/back.time/9610/03>.

3. **Assess your own delivery choices.** Do an interactive exercise at the **Allyn & Bacon Public Speaking** Website entitled " Yeas and Nays of Delivery" to explore common attitudes that speakers have toward delivering a presentation. To do this, point your browser to <http://www.abacon.com/pubspeak/exercise/delex.html>

1. Studies have shown that a speaker's attractiveness has an influence on the persuasiveness of the message. Attractiveness can be achieved at least partly through clothing and grooming. See Shelly Chaiken, "Physical Appearance and Social Influence," *Physical Appearance, Stigma, and Social Behavior: The Ontario Symposium,* Vol. 3, ed. C. Peter Herman, Mark P. Zanna, and E. Tory Higgins (Hillsdale, N.J.: Lawrence Erlbaum, 1986), pp. 143–177.

2. For examples of this, see John Bulwer, *Chirologia: Or the Natural Language of the Hand;* and *Chironomia: Or the Art of Manual Rhetoric,* first published 1644, ed. James W. Cleary (Carbondale: Southern Illinois Univ. Press, 1974); and Gilbert Austin, *Chironomia: Or, A Treatise on Rhetorical Delivery,* first published 1806, ed. Mary Margaret Robb and Lester Thonssen (Carbondale: Southern Illinois Univ. Press, 1966).

3. For more discussion of gestures in informal conversation and in speeches, see Peter E. Bull, *Posture and Gesture* (New York: Pergamon Press, 1987), especially Chapter 10: "The Use of Hand Gesture in Political Speeches: Some Case Studies."

4. Researchers Herbert W. Hildebrandt and Walter W. Stevens discovered this rather accidentally when trying to determine whether extemporaneous or manuscript delivery was more effective. See their "Manuscript and Extemporaneous Delivery in Communicating Information," *Communication Monographs* 30 (November 1963): 369–372.

5. It is important to remember that delivery should match the speaker's material, intent, and personality. See Harry W. Bowen, "A Reassessment of Speech Delivery," *Communication Quarterly* 14 (November 1966): 21–24.

chapter 12
Using Visual Aids

In This Chapter We Will:

- Identify the main benefits of using visual aids in a speech as well as the potential drawbacks of using them.

- Examine major categories of visual aids and how each might contribute to the effectiveness of the speech.

- Describe materials for making visual aids and address some considerations governing the choice of materials.

- Explain the principles of preparing visual aids and of using them during the speech.

- Consider how computer technology expands the options for preparing and presenting effective visual aids.

n a classroom speech about the benefits and harms of computers, Tom Baltrushaytis used an overhead projector to show cartoons that related to each point he made. Similarly, in a speech about diabetes, Dimitra Apostolopoulos showed her listeners a blood-sugar tester and a syringe, explaining how each is used by a diabetic. And in a speech arguing that the legal drinking age should be lower, Justin Whitney presented a graph to show the relationship between age and drunk-driving accidents. All three speakers enabled their listeners to *see as well as hear* by using one or more **visual aids** (any materials shown to the audience during the speech). Such materials are "aids" because they help the speaker by adding a visual dimension to the verbal message.

Each of these speakers carefully selected visual aids by keeping the audience and specific purpose in mind. Tom knew that his audience regarded computers as powerful machines, and so he thought that humorous cartoons would serve his purpose of making technology seem less imposing. Dimitra decided that her speech would be clearer if listeners could see the instruments she described. And Justin believed that the information in his speech would be more memorable if the audience saw it in chart form.

BENEFITS OF USING VISUAL AIDS

Not every speech calls for visual aids. Sometimes the message and its structure are so simple that visual aids aren't needed. Sometimes a speaker prefers to achieve an effect through voice and personality alone. And sometimes visual aids may even distract the audience from the message. Nonetheless, visual aids often can be used to good effect. And in some situations, such as a sales presentation, they are virtually required; audiences expect to see visual aids and will regard the speaker as unprepared without them.

There are three main benefits of using visual aids:

- Visual aids make the speech more interesting.
- Visual aids enhance the speaker's credibility.
- Visual aids improve comprehension and retention.[1]

Interest

Throughout our study we have seen that a speech is strengthened by variety—in the speaker's voice, gesture, and movement, for example. Similarly, visual aids can enhance listeners' interest by adding variety to your message. When you stop to point to a chart or graph, or to show a slide, you alter your delivery pattern. Moreover, adding visual to aural stimuli is itself a means of making the speech interesting. Because listeners must "switch gears" to look at a poster or a map, they are less likely to fall into the trap of passive listening and more likely to attend to the message.

Credibility

A speaker who prepares and uses visual aids well often makes a better impression on the audience.[2] Carefully prepared and appropriate visual aids suggest to the audience that you know the subject and think highly enough of them to do extra work. Again, careful audience analysis is the key to knowing how visual aids might enhance your credibility. When Tom Baltrushaytis

visual aids
Materials that the speaker shows to the audience during the speech.

12.1 Strategic Planning for Visual Aids

1. In making decisions about visual aids, ask yourself these questions:

- *Does the audience expect me to use visual aids, making their absence distracting?*
- *Would my speech be clearer if I illustrated important points?*
- *Can I retain the audience's interest through visual aids?*
- *Can visual aids make it easier for listeners to remember and understand my important points?*
- *Can I prevent visual aids from distracting from my message?*

2. If any answer is "Yes," then proceed to:

- *Decide which type of visual aid would best serve your purposes.*
- *Determine the appropriate size and material for the visual aid, based on the audience and the circumstances.*
- *Design the visual aid.*
- *Practice the speech including the use of the visual aid.*

used cartoons to illustrate his speech about computers, he knew that these aids were appropriate for an audience that expected to be entertained. But had his audience been computer experts who anticipated a technical presentation, the cartoons might have backfired and caused listeners to downgrade Tom as a speaker.

In some cases the absence of visual aids can undermine a speaker's ethos. For example, if you were making a presentation to a board of directors and the norm was for such presentations to include slides and transparencies, your failure to use visual aids might suggest that you hadn't done the necessary preparation, didn't have your speech ready ahead of time, or weren't taking the audience seriously.[3]

Comprehension and Retention

A critical benefit of visual aids is that they often make it easier for listeners to understand and remember the speech.[4] Words by their nature are abstract; listeners have to translate them into mental images. But visual aids are concrete. They make it easy for listeners to see what you are talking about and to remember what you said. Listeners may remember a map, a graph, or a picture and associate it with a particular idea in your speech.

For instance, you can effectively supplement a listing of the components of the federal budget by showing a pie chart in which each component is a proportionate slice of the overall pie. You can strengthen a statement like "Interest on the national debt has grown from 8 percent to 30 percent of the budget" by using two side-by-side pie charts that show listeners exactly how the proportion of debt has grown over time. Similarly, listeners may not immediately grasp a verbal description of highway directions from Chicago to Detroit; but showing them a simple map is an effective way to strengthen the message.

Even in printed messages—when readers have the luxury of proceeding at their own pace and can go back over the text—complex material is often accompanied by visual aids. In public speaking, when the message cannot be slowed down or replayed, the variety achieved through visual aids is even more important.

To these three benefits of using visual aids we must add one major drawback. Visual aids can be a powerful distraction, drawing attention to themselves rather than to the heart of your speech. If listeners begin to notice how frequently you change slides or that you have misspelled a word on a chart, then they are not paying attention to the main idea of the speech, and they will be far less likely to remember what you said.

Usually, however, when visual aids distract, it is because the speaker did not use them properly. If posters and charts are not large enough for audience members to see or read easily, they may frustrate or bore the audience. But that is not a reason to avoid all use of posters and charts. If slides are out of focus or are changed so quickly that audience members fail to grasp their purpose, they will distract from the message of the speech. But that is not a reason never to use slides. These problems can be avoided. The fault lies not in the decision to use visual aids but in how they are used.

From this discussion it should be clear that the preparation and use of visual aids are not casual matters; in fact, they are an integral part of your strategic planning for the speech. The remainder of this chapter will describe different types of visual aids, the materials from which they can be made, and some guidelines for their preparation and use.

TYPES OF VISUAL AIDS

The varieties of visual aids can be grouped conveniently under five headings: charts, graphs, representations, objects or models, and people.

Charts

A **chart** simplifies complex material by arranging it visually according to some obvious principle. The listener is helped not only by being able to see as well as hear the information but also by the way in which the chart organizes the material.

One common type of chart is the *statistical chart* (see Fig. 12.1). Because statistics are so abstract, they are often hard to comprehend or remember when heard; displaying them on a chart makes them easier to grasp. But remember that the purpose of a statistical chart is to *simplify* complex information. All too often, statistical charts used in speeches contain too much information, making them hard to read and hard to grasp. The energy that the audience spends trying to decode them is a distraction from the main point of the speech. Generally speaking, a statistical chart should illustrate only one point or support only one conclusion. A series of simple charts is easier to understand than is a single complex table that includes all the information.

Another common chart is one that shows the *sequence of steps* in a process. Many speeches give instructions about how to do something, or they describe the evolution of a process. For example, a speech about how to apply for college might cover the steps of (1) determining which criteria are

chart
A visual arrangement of words or numbers according to some obvious principle.

Entitlements and Projections			
The Biggest Entitlements in 1993 (In Billions)		Projections for 1999 (In Billions)	
1. Social Security	$302	1. Social Security	$408
2. Medicare	$143	2. Medicare	$264
3. Medicaid	$76	3. Medicaid	$151
4. Federal civilian retirement	$39	4. Federal civilian retirement	$51
5. Unemployment compensation	$35	5. Supplemental Security Income	$35
6. Military retirement	$26	6. Military retirement	$35
7. Food stamps	$25	7. Food stamps	$30
8. Supplemental Security Income	$21	8. Unemployment compensation	$26

FIGURE 12.1

A statistical chart should show important relationships clearly. Here the figures are contrasted in parallel columns and arranged in order of size.

Source: Congressional Budget Office and *The Atlanta Journal Constitution,* Feb. 7, 1994.

most important—such as size, cost, distance from home, or the presence of special curricular programs; (2) assessing your aptitudes and interests; (3) determining a range of schools that satisfy your criteria and match your interests; (4) obtaining literature about those schools and eliminating some as options; (5) arranging to take whatever standardized tests are necessary; (6) obtaining application materials; and (7) filling out the application forms and mailing them, along with any supplementary material. These seven steps might form the subheadings of the speech. A chart listing the seven steps in order would help listeners to remember the steps and to keep track of where you are in the speech. The chart would make clear not only what the steps are but also the appropriate sequence to follow in completing them.

Although the entire sequence of steps in a process might be listed on a single chart, consider whether you could heighten interest in the speech by developing the chart gradually. You could use a *series* of charts, with each one revealing additional new information. For example, in a speech about how the territory of the United States expanded beyond the original thirteen colonies, you might start with a chart listing only the Northwest and Southwest Territories. After discussing those acquisitions, you might then flip to another chart that lists those territories and also adds the Louisiana Purchase as a second stage in the sequence. By using a series of charts, you can control the information so that it evolves as your speech progresses, and listeners will not be distracted by items that you have not yet discussed.

Another common type of chart that emphasizes a sequence of steps is a **decision tree.** In this case the focus is on the points at which *choices* are made—and the likely consequences of various choices. Suppose that your speech about selecting a college focused on the question "Should I go to a selective private university?" You could present this question as one that requires the answers to a series of other questions. The first question might be "Can I meet the academic standards?" If so, proceed to consider the main question; if

decision tree
A chart showing points in a sequence at which decisions must be made, and the likely consequences of various choices.

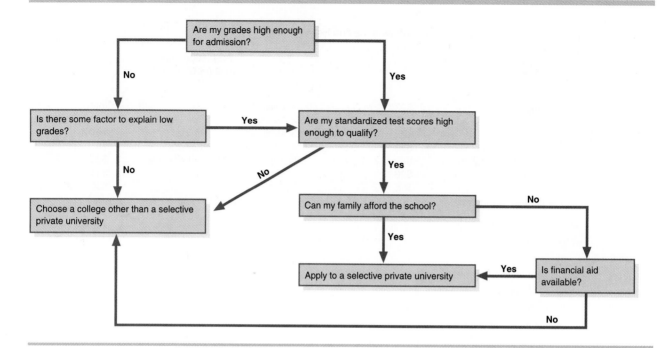

FIGURE 12.2

A sample flowchart

flowchart

A chart showing the "flow" or progress through several steps, with alternative paths showing the outcome of different decisions.

not, that issue is moot. But if the answer were "Yes, I can meet the standards," the next question might be "Can I afford a private school?" If so, then write for information about the school. If not, there might be another question, such as "Am I eligible for financial aid?" The decision tree identifies the points at which each choice must be made, and lines on the chart connect each decision with its consequences.

Another way to present a decision tree is as a **flowchart,** which—rather than arranging the sequence as a tree with branches—suggests how each decision "flows." The chart consists of labeled boxes connected by arrows; at key points, one decision flows in one direction, and a different decision leads in a different direction. Figure 12.2 shows a flowchart on the topic of "How to choose whether to apply to a selective private university."

Even when you are not presenting a series of statistics or describing a sequence of events, a chart can be a helpful visual aid. For instance, as you present a verbal list in your speech, you might support it with a *visual list*. Lists fly past an audience rather quickly, and without visual support your point might be lost. A visual list also helps listeners to recognize and follow the structure of your message. For example, in a speech describing different types of home remedies, student speaker Amy Ahlfeld displayed a chart that named each remedy, identified its most probable active ingredients, and listed the ailments it was supposed to cure. The chart helped listeners to organize and remember all this information.

A slight variation of the visual list is a *columnar chart* that conceptually maps the main ideas or key terms by relating them to others. The items in one column of the chart are keyed to corresponding items in another column. An example is shown in Figure 12.3, which was prepared by student Maria Rosado at a campus in the southwestern United States, where she was speak-

FIGURE 12.3
A columnar chart for discussing drug names.

Drug name	English street name	Spanish street name
Heroine	Horse, Smack	_____
Cocaine	Coke, Flake, Snow	_____
LSD	Acid	_____
Mescaline	Mesc	_____
Peyote	Buttons, Cactus	_____
Phenocyclidine	PCP, Angel dust, Hog	_____

ing about the prevalence of drugs in the region and their potential harm to teenage users. Because some listeners were Anglo and others were Latino, Maria thought that some would recognize drug names in English and some in Spanish. Knowing little Spanish herself, she prepared a three-column chart that listed the drugs in one column and their English street names in the adjacent column. The third column she left blank. Then she asked the audience to help her fill the blanks by providing the Spanish street names. This "unfinished" visual aid thus helped Maria to make the point that it was important to recognize these common names anywhere in the region.

Graphs

A **graph** is a visual display of relationships that shows how change in one thing affects another thing. The most common types are line graphs, bar graphs, and pie graphs (see Fig. 12.4 on page 312).

A **line graph** charts one variable as a function of another. The values for one variable are shown on the horizontal axis, and those of the other variable are shown on the vertical axis. Any pair of values can thus be represented by a point on the graph. A line connects the various points to show the relationship between the variables.

For example, suppose you wanted to demonstrate that the crime rate increases in hot weather. The two variables might be "temperature" (on the vertical axis) and "average reported crimes per hour per 1,000 population" (on the horizontal axis). At 60 degrees Fahrenheit you find that there are an

graph
A visual display of relationships, showing how change in one thing is related to change in another.

line graph
A graph in which a line connects points, each of which represents a combination of the two items being compared.

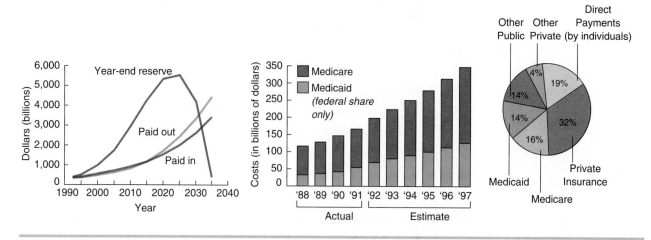

FIGURE 12.4

Graphs should be kept as simple as possible, with all elements labeled and a minimum number of variables displayed. Left to right: line graph, bar graph, pie graph.

Source: U.S. Congress, House Committee on Ways and Means, "1992 Report of The Board of Trustees of the Federal Old-Age and Survivors Insurance and Disability Insurance Trust Funds," 182.

average of 25 reported crimes per hour per 1,000 population, so you would find the point on the chart where a horizontal line from the "60 degrees" mark and a vertical line from the "25 crimes" mark intersect. Suppose that at 80 degrees Fahrenheit there are an average of 40 reported crimes and at 100 degrees Fahrenheit there are 65. These points could also be located on the graph. Then a line could be drawn to connect all three points. The line would show clearly that the crime rate goes up as the temperature increases. The relationship between the crime rate and the temperature will be clear and memorable.

Sometimes, however, things are more complicated. The trend will go one way up to a point, but then it will reverse. For example, grades have been shown to motivate improved student performance. Up to a point, a teacher who gives more As may prompt students to do better work. But if it becomes clear that large numbers of students will receive an A, there is *less* incentive to do better work because students know that grades will be high anyway. Line graphs can show complex relationships as well as simple ones.

A **bar graph** is used to show comparisons and contrasts among one or two variables. Unlike a line graph, a bar graph shows units of measurement on only one axis (usually the vertical); the other axis identifies the categories to be assessed. Then, for each category, a bar is drawn to the appropriate value. The relative lengths of the bars permit easy comparison.

For instance, you might wish to show how gender or race affects the likelihood of completing a college degree. In this graph the two genders and the various races are the primary variable. The vertical axis could show percentages from 0 to 100. On the horizontal axis are labeled the categories of the variable. One space would be labeled "Men," and another would be labeled "Women." Then bars would be drawn to the appropriate percentages for each

bar graph

A graph in which the length of bars indicates the amount or extent of items being compared.

gender, making it easy for listeners to compare them. Farther along the horizontal axis, additional spaces might be labeled "White," "Black," "Hispanic," "Asian," and so on, and again bars would show the appropriate values.

You can extend a bar graph to make comparisons using a second variable as well, such as time. For example, the first space could have three bars showing how many men completed college degrees in 1970, in 1980, and in 1990. The spaces for women, whites, blacks, and so on, would show the same information. Visual inspection of the sets of three bars will let the audience see how completion rates vary for each gender/race as well as whether the gap between men and women or between races has widened, narrowed, or stayed about the same over time.

Finally, a **pie graph** is used to show proportions, or percentages, of a whole. (It is called a pie graph because it is usually round and shows the different components as slices of the pie.) If you were speaking about how tax dollars are spent, for example, you might show a pie graph with slices of different sizes representing the proportions of tax money spent on defense, social security, education, welfare programs, interest on the national debt, and so on. Like bar graphs, pie graphs can be used to illustrate two variables. Two pies—one showing the distribution of the budget of the United States and the other showing its distribution in Canada—will make clear that a larger percentage of the federal budget has been required for defense in the United States.[5]

Representations

Representations are visual portrayals of reality. They include textual graphics, diagrams, maps, still photographs or slides, and film or videotape.

A **textual graphic** is a display of words. It is used so that the audience can simultaneously see and hear the words. At the most basic level, a teacher is using a textual graphic when he or she writes an unfamiliar word on the chalkboard. Seeing the word helps students to learn it. In speeches, textual graphics may be used to show a simple outline of the main ideas, to show the central thesis of the speech, or to show the action the speaker wants the audience to take. If you are asking listeners to write to their senator, for example, you could use a textual graphic that shows the senator's address.

A **diagram** is a simple drawing or sketch that represents a more complex object (see Fig. 12.5 on page 314). A diagram is more abstract than a photograph, and because it leaves out many details, you can emphasize the parts of the object that you think are most important. If you were describing how to raise a sail, you might display a diagram of a boat in order to refer to its parts as you proceed. The diagram will not look exactly like a boat, as a photograph would, but it will let listeners know what the principal parts are and how they are used in the process of raising the sail.

Maps can be particularly useful visual aids if the speech focuses on directions to, or relationships among, places. For example, a speech about the history of U.S. Route 66 would be aided by a map showing the major points on the famous highway that, in the years before interstates, stretched from Chicago to Los Angeles. But a map almost always needs to be simplified for a speech. Even an enlarged Rand McNally map would not be effective in this case, because it would include so much detail that the audience would not be able to see or focus on Route 66. A much simpler map, showing only the outline of the states and the approximate path of Route 66, would be much

pie graph
A graph in the shape of a circle in which the various components of the whole are shown as portions of the circle, like various-sized slices of a pie.

representations
Visual portrayals of reality.

textual graphic
A display of words so that the audience can both see and hear them.

diagram
A simplified drawing or sketch that represents a more complex object.

FIGURE 12.5

A diagram for instructional purposes should show only the key features needed for demonstration, as in basic sail instruction.

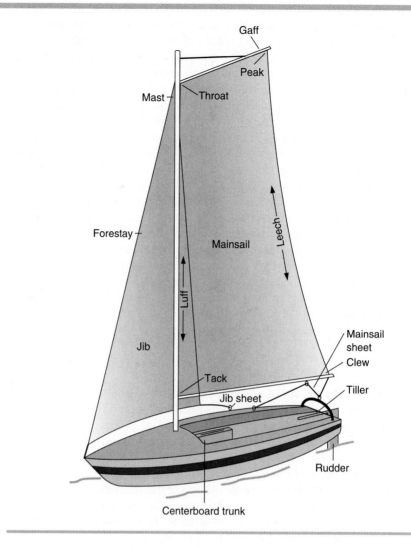

more useful (see Fig. 12.6). Nor should the map identify all the points of interest along this famous road; it should show only the points featured in the speech—perhaps three or four. Finally, the map need not be drawn to scale or provide an exact representation, since you are using it primarily to help listeners picture the relationships among the places on Route 66.

Photographs, too, should be used cautiously as visual aids. Because a photograph portrays reality in all its complexity, it may contain far more information than is important to the speech. What you wish to emphasize may not stand out from the background, and background elements may distract the audience from your intended focus. For example, if you show a slide of a traffic accident to support your speech about safe driving, your point will be obscured if the audience instead pays attention to the unusual billboards near the scene of the accident.

Some photographs, however, so clearly capture the essence of their subject that they are indeed "worth a thousand words." Examples include such famous photos as the soldiers raising the U.S. flag at Iwo Jima in World War II, President Truman holding up a newspaper headline that had mistakenly

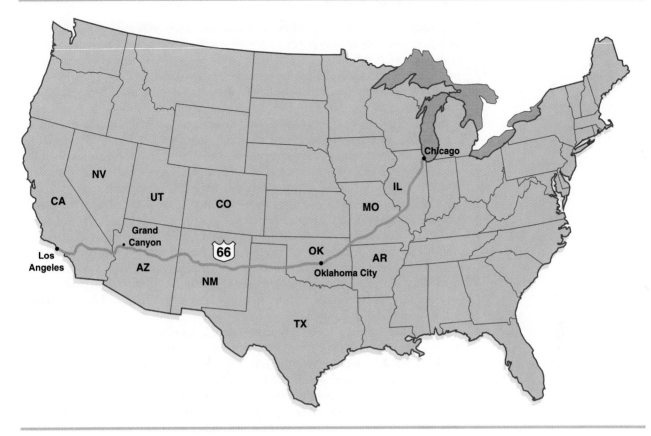

FIGURE 12.6

Maps should be simplified to display only the key features needed for the presentation—in this case the states and main stopovers on Route 66 from Chicago to Los Angeles.

announced his defeat in 1948, President Johnson taking the oath of office aboard *Air Force One* in 1963, and the explosion of the space shuttle *Challenger* soon after its launch in 1986. But such photos are rare. Before deciding to illustrate your speech with a photograph, ask yourself (1) whether what you want to show in the photo is clear enough and easy enough to see that it will engage listeners' attention and (2) whether any background elements in the photo will distract the audience from what you want to emphasize.

Film and videotape add the dimension of motion to still photography and raise the possibility of editing to remove distracting scenes (but not to remove distractions in any given shot). These visual aids require special equipment, of course, but videocassette recorders and monitors, in particular, are now easy to carry and set up. There is, however, a potential danger in showing moving images. Videos are like television, in front of which people have learned to become relatively passive. Once you turn on the video, your audience may expect to be entertained and may stop listening actively. To offset this danger, show only short segments of film or tape, and surround them with your oral presentation. Probably the biggest mistake would be to make a short introduction and then just turn the presentation over to videotape. Active listening will decrease markedly.

Objects and Models

Sometimes the best visual aid is the actual object you are talking about—as when a lawyer holds up key evidence for the jury to see. Chefs on television, for instance, usually explain recipes by using real ingredients, real pots and pans, and real ovens to demonstrate the process. Similarly, to speak about the different types of seashells found off the coast near your town, you could display examples of shells and point out their unique features. Be aware, though, that objects require you to use your hands more extensively than if you were just pointing to a diagram.[6] You will need to hold things, to manipulate them, and to move them around. All this may solve the problem of what to do with your hands, but you must be careful. Hold the objects firmly and steadily, avoid accidentally knocking them over with sweeping gestures, and be sure to put them away when you are finished with them so that they will not distract the audience.

If it is not feasible to use the actual object, either because it is too large or because it is not portable, you may be able to use a model of the object. For example, a developer who is making a presentation about how a pedestrian mall would improve the downtown area might find it useful to prepare a scale model of the development to refer to during the talk. Similarly, lawyers trying to fix responsibility for an accident might find it useful to refer to a scale model of the accident scene. The one general principle to follow in using a model is that it must be large enough for listeners to see easily. If they have to strain to see the model or you have to apologize because some feature of it is not visible to everyone, it will not be an effective visual aid.

Finally, animals should not be used as objects or models. Too many problems arise, for example, if you try to use your pet to demonstrate obedience training. The animal will be in a most unfamiliar situation, it may react with fear, and you may lose control. Animals may make noise, get loose, move about, perform bodily functions, or otherwise embarrass you. Even at best, they will distract from your speech by drawing the audience's attention immediately to whatever they are doing rather than to what you are saying.

People

Having just warned against using live models in a speech, it may seem odd that the final category of visual aids is people; it may seem odd, too, to think of yourself or others as visual aids. It almost sounds demeaning. But people presumably are better behaved than animals are, and there are obvious and simple ways in which they can add visual impact to the content of a speech.

Your own body can serve as a visual aid. For example, if your topic is "Power walking," you can demonstrate the high-intensity movements involved in this type of walking. The demonstration not only will show listeners how to do it but also will help make credible your claim that power walking is vigorous exercise.

Your appearance and grooming can also serve as a visual aid. It obviously makes a difference whether you arrive for a business presentation in a suit or in sweatshirt and jeans. Your clothing either reinforces or undercuts your message that you are seriously interested in obtaining the account. This is not to say that you always have to wear a suit to make a good impression as a speaker. The critical thing is to match your appearance to the situation. If your speech is about lifeguarding, a pair of shorts and a Red Cross T-shirt may be the most effective clothing.

For many people, dress is an important means of asserting cultural identity. Covering your head, wearing non-Western clothing, or dressing in dark colors may be ways to express your heritage and values. At the same time, however, less conventional styles of dress may lead listeners to stereotype you and perhaps to be distracted from your message by your unfamiliar (to them) appearance. Your audience analysis and strategic planning may need to focus on this aspect of the situation. Should you dress to accommodate the expectations of your audience? Or should you "be yourself" and deliberately assert your different cultural identity? The answers to these questions should reflect your analysis of the audience and your specific purpose.

Other people can also serve as visual aids. The obvious example is a speech in which someone helps you demonstrate something. If you plan to use the help of others, it is best to make arrangements with them ahead of time. You will avoid being embarrassed if no one responds when you ask for a volunteer, and you will also be able to coordinate the presentation so that the "volunteer" doesn't seem surprised and you don't seem poorly prepared. Talk candidly with the volunteer about why it is important to perform the task skillfully but quietly, without visible facial responses or other reactions that might upstage you and draw attention away from your speech.

Of all these different types of visual aids, which is the best to use? Charts? Graphs? Representations? Objects and models? People? By now you know, of course, that there is no "correct" answer to such questions.

CHOOSE A STRATEGY
Using Visual Aids

THE SITUATION

Your campus organization is underfunded, especially when compared to similar campus organizations. You're getting ready to present your case for more funding to the fifty members of the student government. You've put the final touches on the text of your speech, but now you need to consider using visual aids.

MAKING CHOICES

1. What type(s) of visual aids might you use? Why?
2. How should you determine what visual aids would be most appropriate and most useful for this speaking situation?

WHAT IF . . .

Your choice of visual aids likely will be affected not only by the type of information available to you but also by the audience to whom you are speaking and your purpose. Decide what type(s) of visual aids you might use and why you would use them for the following situations:

1. You are speaking to a group of ten student government officers instead of the entire student government.
2. You are speaking to the entire 10,000 students on campus.
3. You are speaking to ten members of the administration instead of the student government.

The decision depends on your topic, on where you are speaking, on the size of the audience, on what the audience is likely to expect, and on how comfortable you are with using visual aids. Any visual aid can be used well or badly. The important thing is to choose it knowingly and with a specific purpose in mind. Once again, critical thinking about your rhetorical situation and strategic planning to achieve your goal will help you make decisions about visual aids.

CHOOSING MATERIALS FOR VISUAL AIDS

Besides your decisions about the types of visual aids to use, you have many options about the materials from which they can be made. Some materials are simple and are available almost everywhere, while others depend on sophisticated equipment and technology. Here we will examine the chalkboard, flip charts, posterboard, handouts, transparencies, slides, and videotape.

Chalkboard

In many speaking situations, using the chalkboard is the easiest way to provide visual aids. Student speakers in classrooms can almost always count on the availability of a chalkboard, and most meeting rooms and presentation settings also include one. Or you might find a variation on the chalkboard—the white board on which you can draw with erasable markers.

Although chalkboards are easily accessible, using them for visual aids presents some problems. For one thing, a chalkboard drawing usually has an amateur quality that may affect the audience's impressions of your speech. Moreover, there is the problem of deciding *when* to draw the visual aid. If you try to draw and talk at the same time, you risk losing eye contact with the audience as well as your concentration. Your vocal qualities will be affected, because your voice will be directed toward the board rather than the audience. But if you stop speaking while you draw, there is an obvious break in the flow of your speech and in the audience's attention. Finally, if you draw the visual aid before beginning to speak, it will remain visible throughout the speech and may distract listeners. (You might avoid this last danger by covering the chalkboard until you are ready to present the visual aid. In some rooms this can be done conveniently by pulling down a screen that is already attached to the chalkboard; but if there is no screen, it may be difficult to cover the visual aid.)

If you do decide to use the chalkboard, make every effort to maintain eye contact with the audience; avoid turning your back on listeners to face the chalkboard. Also make sure that your body does not block anyone's view of the visual aid. Using a ruler or some other object to point to it and practicing where to stand and how to move around will help you to remember that the critical relationship is between you and your listeners, not between you and the visual aid.

Flip Charts

A **flip chart** is a writing tablet made of large sheets of paper, usually newsprint, that rests on an easel; you can "flip" each sheet over the binding at the top of the tablet after you have used it. You can create a flip chart by

flip chart
A writing tablet made of large sheets of paper, usually newsprint, the pages of which can be flipped over after they are used.

using markers that let you write large enough, wide enough, and dark enough for the audience to see without difficulty.

Flip charts are as easy to make as chalkboard drawings, but they offer two advantages. First, you can develop your visual aids in a sequence. This is especially effective when you want to show the audience a verbal list without including everything at once. For example, you can prepare a series of charts that gradually reveal and elaborate the outline of your speech. The first chart might show only your first main heading. After discussing that idea, you could flip the chart to reveal the next heading; or you could repeat the first heading in one color but also show the new main heading in a contrasting color. As you move through the outline, you can make the audience focus only on the idea that you are discussing at that particular time.

Second, you can easily hide a particular visual or dispose of the flip chart when it is not in use. Instead of erasing or covering up the chalkboard, all you have to do is flip the chart to a blank page. Because you are unlikely to need the chart at the beginning of the speech, you can leave the top sheet blank; simply flip it over when you are ready to discuss your first visual aid.

Posterboard

Anything you can draw on a flip chart can also be prepared on posterboard. Posterboard is as firm as stiff cardboard, making it easier to hold and to handle than a flip chart. If you do not need a lot of visual aids, posterboard may be easier to use.

Where do you put the posterboard? Like other visual aids, it should be concealed when you are not referring to it. You might lay it face down on a table or stand it in the tray of a chalkboard, with the poster facing away from the audience. Or you might attach a blank posterboard to the front of your poster until you are ready to show it. All these methods will prevent listeners from focusing on the poster until you want them to do so. Just be sure that your means of concealment does not make the posterboard hard to reach and uncover when you are ready to use it.

How to display the poster is another consideration. You could hold it, of course; but if it is large and bulky or you need to display it for a long time, holding it will limit your ability to make other appropriate gestures and movements. Another possibility is to place the poster on an easel, much as you would a flip chart. If you prepare several posters, you could stack them on the easel in the order you plan to use them. (Remember to make sure that the easel is available when you begin to speak.) Or you might mount the poster to the wall with thumbtacks or tape (being careful not to damage the wall, of course). This approach can make it harder to remove the poster during your speech, after you have used it, but the short distraction might be offset by the freedom of movement that you gain when you don't have to worry about holding the poster up.

Handouts

The logical extension of the chalkboard, flip chart, or poster is the **handout**—one or more sheets of paper that you or an assistant literally hand out to audience members to refer to during the speech.

Teachers of public speaking disagree about using handouts. On the positive side, handouts make it easier for a speaker to present complex informa-

handout
One or more sheets of paper given out to audience members before or during the speech; at some point the speaker refers to the handout.

tion, since listeners have their own copy of key terms and definitions or can follow the details of a diagram. Handouts reduce the need for audience members to take detailed notes, which *may* permit them to concentrate more fully on the substance of the speech. And in some situations—such as a sales presentation—leaving a handout with prospective customers is a highly desirable way to reinforce the message.

But handouts are also a potential source of distraction. The audience may pay more attention to the handout than to what you are saying. This is especially likely to happen if you distribute a handout at the very beginning of the speech but do not refer to it until several minutes have elapsed. Nor is it a good idea to distribute handouts in the middle of the speech; that breaks the flow of thought and disturbs listeners who want to concentrate on the speech.

The difficulties with handouts are magnified if you do not have enough copies for everyone. Although some people will share, others are likely to be left out. The worst situation is to pass photographs or a book around the audience while you are speaking. Listeners' attention will lapse in waves as the material reaches them and they focus on it rather than on your speech.

Transparencies

Transparencies are celluloid sheets that are projected onto a screen with the use of an overhead projector. The celluloid sheets are inexpensive, and the projector enlarges the transparency and makes it easily visible to the audience. Finally, since the room does not have to be as dark for an overhead projector as for slides or film, there is less disruption of the speech.

Transparencies are easy to prepare. Using special markers you can draw charts or diagrams, or you can write key words. (Prepare transparencies only with permanent-ink markers; all your efforts will be wasted if the ink lifts off.) You also can photocopy text, graphs, or charts onto transparencies. Like flip charts, you can develop and display transparencies in sequence. You can even add to a transparency by drawing on it while it is being shown. And you can stand at the projector and use a pencil or a pen to point to specific objects on the transparency.

Like any visual aid, however, you have to plan the use of transparencies. First, you will need to stand next to the overhead projector if you want to work with your transparencies as you are speaking. If the size of the print on the transparencies requires you to be a certain distance from the wall, or if the electrical outlet is located inconveniently, you might have to stand behind some members of the audience. You can limit this difficulty by checking the room carefully in advance to determine how large the print should be in order to place the projector where you want it.

Second, you will need to check the projection equipment carefully. To have greater flexibility in positioning it, you might bring a long extension cord with you (but find out whether the cord needs a three-pronged plug; a household extension cord may not be suitable). And it's always a good idea to carry a spare lightbulb for the projector. If the bulb fails, your visual aids will be useless.

Third, realize that the audience will be distracted if the transparencies are too complex, if the print is too small, if you use too many transparencies, or if you change them too rapidly. Above all, be sure to check in advance that the transparencies are in the order you plan to present them. You will break the audience's concentration if you stop either to rearrange the transparencies or to project some of them onto the screen to determine which is which.

transparencies
Celluloid sheets that are projected onto a screen with the use of an overhead projector.

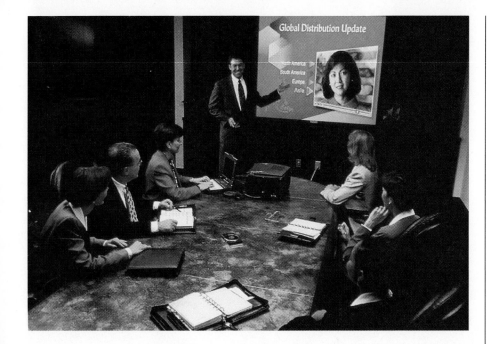

◄ *Visual aids and projection equipment need to be placed properly in the room, so that you can refer to the visual aid while also maintaining eye contact with the audience, and so that listeners can see you and the visual aid at the same time.*

For all their benefits, transparencies are effective only with an audience of about fifty or fewer people. With larger audiences, transparencies have to be enlarged so much to fit the screen that they lose their focus and impact.

Slides

Not all forms of visual aids lend themselves to projection by transparencies. Photographs and complex graphs may be easier to project with slides. In addition, if the audience is too large for you to use transparencies effectively, any visual aid on a transparency can be photographed and shown on a slide. But slides are harder to prepare than transparencies, and they are more expensive. You should shoot extra rolls of film so that you can select the slides that most clearly capture the images you want.

Most speakers who use slides arrange them in a **carousel**—a circular tray that fits onto a slide projector. The slides are placed in the desired order for presentation, and the carousel rotates to bring each slide into view. The rate of display can be set to a predetermined number of seconds, or you can change slides by pressing a button. It may not be necessary to stand at the projector while you speak. You can avoid being tied to that space if the projector has a remote control to advance the carousel or if you can find an assistant who will stand at the projector and advance it according to your directions.

As with transparencies, the positioning of the slide projector is critical to the success of the speech. It must be placed so that the slides will be enlarged to the proper size on the screen and so that the path of light from projector to screen is above the heads of the audience. For this reason you may want to place the screen in a corner at the front of the room rather than directly in the center. As in using an overhead projector, you should check the equipment carefully in advance; find out whether you need and can use an extension cord, and carry a spare lightbulb.

carousel
A circular tray that holds slides and fits onto a projector and is usually advanced by remote control.

Speakers who use slides often overuse them. They have more slides than their speech really requires, and they change them very quickly. This can be extremely distracting, both because audience members really do not have the time to absorb one slide before another is presented and because the constant clicking of the carousel as it advances calls attention to itself.[7]

Videotape

As was noted earlier, videotape makes it possible to present moving images as visual aids. As in using slides, you'll want to tape more material than you can use, to ensure that you get the most effective images. Because you can show only short segments of videotape, review and edit it carefully before the speech. Remove everything that is not directly relevant to the points you want to make. Today's technology makes it easy to tape with a portable camcorder and then to edit the tape for presentation. In fact, the results are so professional-looking that you'll need to exercise restraint. Your tape must do more than just entertain. Remember that it is a visual aid and that its purpose is to *support* the ideas you articulate.

APPLYING STRATEGIES

Choosing Appropriate Visual Aids

T. J. Brinkerhoff

I think the most appropriate visual aids for a speech are pre-prepared on posterboard and displayed as necessary in the speech, and videos. Too many of the other methods have problems. Using a chalkboard causes a speaker to have to turn his/her back to the audience too frequently, and it is dusty and messy. Transparencies have the tendency to be too problematic with focusing, with dead spots (white rabbit in a snow storm), and with readability. By having prepared posterboard you can ensure that the size will suit the audience and that the pictures and wording will be neat and legible. Videos are also useful visual aids because they combine visual and audio to present ideas to an audience. They usually keep the audience's attention better and

can reinforce or define an idea better or more clearly. I think visual aids are important to any speech to keep it from losing the audience's attention.

Latif Farag

Using a visual aid depends very much on the topic of the speech. When I talked about soccer in my informative speech, I used a videotape because this is the most effective way to show the audience how soccer is played. When I talked about decision making and problem solving, I used transparencies to show the audience the steps that need to be taken to solve a problem. The most important thing when you use visual aids is to check and try them out before you start the speech in order to avoid an embarrassing situation.

Carrie Biesel

I used one visual aid that I thought was very effective during my persuasive speech. My topic was automobile safety. . . . I put a big emphasis on seatbelts and then I used pictures from a serious car accident I had been in a few years ago as visual aids. I think seeing a "real life" accident that someone you know was in makes it sink in better than a bunch of statistics about people you don't know. A visual aid was not required with this speech, but I felt that it would help with my topic.

Laura Breland

When I was using my visual aids, I really thought about the appropriateness of them to the speech. I carefully went over my speeches and visualized in my head several possibilities for visual aids and thought about which ones I should eliminate and which ones I should use for my speech. On my speech about adoption, I used baby dolls— one had a sad expression, the other one had a big smile. I state in the speech when using the dolls, ". . . so help turn this sad, crying girl to this happy person over here . . ."

PREPARING VISUAL AIDS

Whatever materials you use in creating visual aids, the most important strategic consideration is that visual aids should be carefully matched to the contents of the speech.

Storyboarding

The process of matching visual aids to points in the speech is called storyboarding. A **storyboard** is a page containing the verbal outline for a single idea in the presentation, along with a sketch of the visual aid that will illustrate that idea. Taken together, the storyboards for a speech provide both a visual and a verbal outline. Storyboarding will force you to:

- Limit yourself to one visual aid per idea.
- Select the types of visual aids that will be most appropriate and most effective.

When you plan your storyboards, be conservative about the number of visuals to include. Not every idea needs to be illustrated, and you should give the audience enough time to absorb what you show and to listen carefully to your verbal information before you make them shift attention to another image.

Designing Visual Aids

The following design principles will help you to prepare effective visual aids that support your presentation.

1. *Visual aids should be seen easily by members of the audience.* If people must strain to see, if the visual aid is too small, or if it is too complex, the benefit of using the visual aid is lost. This principle dictates that visual aids be *simple*. Each visual aid should illustrate only one idea in the speech, and each should be as uncluttered as possible.

   This principle also requires that you pay attention to the size and proportion of visual aids. For example, the lettering in textual graphics should be at least two or three inches high. You should have a good sense of the distance from the visual aid to the back of the room; stand at that distance from the visual aid as you prepare it, and be certain that you can see and read it easily. Also, you should select the kind of visual aid that is appropriate to the situation. A flip chart or a chalkboard drawing might work perfectly for an audience of twenty-five, but for an audience of two hundred you probably need slides or videotape to ensure that everyone can see well.

2. *Visual aids should be easy for the speaker to handle.* Your aids should be portable, not heavy or cumbersome, and they should not restrict

storyboard
A page containing the verbal outline for a single idea, along with a sketch of the visual aid to illustrate that idea.

your movements or gestures during the speech. In addition, you should be able to set up and remove them quickly, since it is unlikely that the room will be available for any great length of time either before or after your speech. Finally, you should design the visual aids with an eye toward how they will be kept in place during your presentation. Imagine the "choreography" of your speech, and determine whether the aids need to be placed on an easel; if so, be sure that one is available. If you plan to mount your aids on the wall or to hand them out to the audience, consider carefully how best to do this and at what point during the speech you will need to use them. If you plan to hold the visual aids, be sure that their size and materials permit you to do so easily.

3. *Visual aids should be aesthetically pleasing without distracting from the speech.* This principle suggests that you determine what the central element of the visual aid is and what elements are in the background. You might use color to heighten the appeal and focus of your aids and to make points clearly. Color is more vivid than black and white and usually will grab the audience's attention. To make your meaning clearer, you might use variations of a single color (shades of green, for example), colors that are close to one another on a color wheel (to suggest similarities), or colors that are usually thought of as opposites (to emphasize distinctions). Aesthetic considerations might also lead you to choose, for example, whether to use a chart or a graph and whether a bar graph or a pie graph is a more compelling way to illustrate a central idea.

On the other hand, you do not want your speech to be like the movie that is remembered primarily for its special effects. Be careful that elaborate visual aids do not run away with your speech, causing listeners to remember your attractive charts and graphs rather than what you said. Follow two key principles: Restrict your visual aids to those that really are crucial, and keep the design of each visual aid as simple as possible. Although visual aids will help make your ideas clearer, remember that the speech is ultimately about those ideas, not about the visual aids.

Checklist

12.2 *Designing Visual Aids*

Keep in mind the following principles:

1. **Visual aids should be carefully matched to the contents of the speech.**

2. **Visual aids should be easily seen by members of the audience.**

3. **Visual aids should be easy for the speaker to handle.**

4. **Visual aids should be aesthetically pleasing without distracting from the speech.**

USING VISUAL AIDS IN THE SPEECH

To plan the effective use of visual aids, you must be sensitive to your audience, your purpose, and the physical circumstances. The composition and culture of the audience will affect your decisions about which visual aids are appropriate, and the size of the audience will affect how large or how complex the visual aids should be. You also need to think about how to use the aids during the speech—and to practice the speech including them.

One of the first decisions is where to place the visual aids. Will they be in the center of the room or to the side? Will they be mounted or free-standing? Will they be visible throughout the speech or concealed except when you refer to them? Make these decisions consciously, not by accident. Then gather whatever materials you need—thumbtacks, tape, extension cord, easel, light-bulb, and so on.

As you practice your speech incorporating the visual aids, keep two important considerations in mind:

1. *Do not obstruct the audience's view of the visual aid.* Position the aid so that, when you stand to speak, listeners will be able to see it as well as to see you. Otherwise, there is no point in preparing the visual aid. For example, if you plan to stand at the center of the room, place the visual aid to the side. If you are using a projection screen, try placing it in one of the front corners of the room rather than in the center.

   Remember, though, that you need to have access to the visual aid. If you plan to point to it, you must stand close enough that your pointer will identify the specific spot you want to highlight. If you plan to turn flip charts, you have to be able to reach them. If you need to be near the overhead projector, that should govern where the projector is placed.

   If possible, experiment with the placement of your visual aids in the room where you will speak. If you can arrive early, try out different locations for the visual aids, and find out what works best. If you can't do that because the room is occupied or because you must speak immediately after others, at least think ahead of time about what placement will make the most sense.

   If the visual aid is positioned some distance from you and you will need to point to it, select the type of pointer that will work best in the situation. You could consider using your hands, although some find that to be awkward or even impolite. You might use a ruler or a yardstick, or you could buy a retractable pointer that is made for the purpose. Laser pointers throw a beam of light onto the screen, but these must be used with care. They are hard to hold steady, and the audience may think you are nervous if the pointer moves back and forth. With a laser pointer it is usually best to circle the object you want to highlight rather than focusing directly on it; then turn the light off so it won't be distracting.

2. *Speak to the audience, not to the visual aid.* Many speakers forget this. They face the screen or the chalkboard, pointing to the visual aid, moving their arms around, but with their back to the audience. This is obviously

ineffective—first, because it prevents listeners from seeing the visual aid and, second, because the speaker cannot maintain eye contact with the audience. When you turn to the visual aid, do so briefly, to highlight or point out certain features, and then be sure to turn around to face the audience again.

These two considerations suggest the importance of practicing the use of visual aids. Plan where to put them, how and when to refer to them, how to use your hands, and how to put them away. If you practice these steps several times, the visual aids will become a natural part of the speech rather than a distraction.

If you can, simulate the actual conditions in the room where you will speak. Bring your visual aids, and make sure that all needed equipment is in place. Plan where to position yourself and your visual aids. Be prepared with extension cords, spare lightbulbs, and other things you may need. Go through the speech just as you would with the audience present. And if much time lapses between this pre-speech practice and your actual speech, check again that everything is still in working order. Even with the very best preparation, however, equipment sometimes fails during a speech, and you may not be able to use the visual aids as planned. If that happens, be confident that your practice has made you familiar with your visual aids and that you can either improvise some other ones or, if necessary, can even deliver the speech without visual aids.

COMPUTER-GENERATED VISUAL AIDS

Computers make it possible to produce high-quality, sophisticated visual aids and to present them imaginatively during the speech. Computer-generated visual aids have become the norm in many business and professional presentations. Even beginning speakers find many uses for computer technology.

Preparing Visual Aids on the Computer

The most common use of the computer is to generate visual aids that will be printed on slides or transparencies and then used in the speech. Almost any word-processing program can help you make attractive charts, tables, and textual graphics. Computers also can be used to produce images and representations. And, with the use of a scanner, you can retrieve photographs, maps, or documents electronically. Some programs also permit you to mix sound with graphics.

DESIGN PRINCIPLES   Beyond providing a wide range of visual aids, an obvious advantage to using the computer is that you can experiment with different sizes and shapes, and you can correct errors easily. You can vary the size and font (type style) of textual graphics and can modify the color, proportions, background, and other elements of an image. In fact, it is tempting to use too much of the computer's capability, leading to visual aids that ignore the principle of simplicity—too many colors, too many fonts, and too much information. The following suggestions should help you to resist this temptation.

1. *Choose a basic design and color scheme for the entire presentation.* You might repeat a word, symbol, style, or font throughout your visual aids, or maintain a consistent color scheme, or use consistent spacing. Any of these will help to create a sense of unity for your presentation.

2. *Select fonts carefully.* Designers usually divide typefaces into four basic classes of fonts: serif, sans serif, script, and ornamental (or decorative). *Serif* fonts, like the one you are reading, have little lines (serifs) at the tops and bottoms of letters, and the letters are usually made up of both thick and thin lines. *Sans serif* fonts do not have the extra lines at the tops and bottoms, and all lines in the letters are usually the same thickness. Of the two, serif fonts are easier to read for longer passages, because the serifs guide the eye from one letter to the next. *Script* fonts imitate handwriting but are far more precise and uniform. They can be very fancy and complicated, which can make them hard to read. Finally, *ornamental,* or *decorative,* fonts are designed not so much for ease in reading as to convey a particular feeling or tone. Figure 12.7 shows examples of each class of font.

Most designers agree that you should use no more than two typefaces on a single visual aid and that they should be from two different font categories. The most common combination is to use a sans serif font for displayed titles or headings and a serif font for text passages. Of course, designers sometimes violate these guidelines to achieve special effects.

FIGURE 12.7
Typefaces grouped by font type

Serif

Palatino
Times New Roman
Courier
Century Schoolbook

Sans Serif

Arial
Officina Sans
Century Gothic
Kabel

Script

Linoscript
Caflish Script
Brush Script

Decorative

Whimsy
LITHOS
Metropolis
Wonton

Title set 44 pt. or 36 pt.
Subtitle set 32 point or 24 point
Text (with a subtitle) 28 point or 18 point

SLIDES

24-point title
18-point subtitle
14-point text

FIGURE 12.8

Variations of a typeface

3. *Choose an appropriate type size.* Visual aids are of little use if the type is not large enough for everyone in the audience to see. Designers at Microsoft have specified general guidelines for visual aids. They recommend using 44-point type for titles, 32-point type for subtitles or text if there is no subtitle, and 28-point type for the text if there is also a subtitle. (To give a sense of what this means, there are 72 "points" in an inch.) The smallest sizes recommended for visuals other than slides are 36-point type for titles, 24-point for subtitles, and 18-point for text. Slides can be somewhat smaller, since projection enlarges the image. You might use 24-point for titles, 18-point for subtitles, and 14-point for text. Figure 12.8 shows how these sizes look in print. In any case, avoid using capital letters for emphasis except in short titles. Long stretches of all-capital text are hard to read, because our eyes rely on contrasting letter shapes to decode quickly.

4. *Use color to create a mood and sustain attention.* Graphic designers have long known that warm colors (oranges and reds) appear to come forward and have an exciting effect, whereas cool colors (greens and blues) seem to recede and have a more calming effect. When you choose colors, think about how you want your audience to react to your visual aid. Your topic, occasion, and purpose should influence this decision. For example, in a business setting you might use cool colors to convey disappointing news and warm colors to convey good news.

   It is also important to choose colors for backgrounds and for text or graphics that contrast with one another but do not conflict. Figure 12.9

Effective

Ineffective

FIGURE 12.9

Examples of effective and ineffective color combinations.

provides examples of an effective and an ineffective color combination. Using yellow against a blue background is effective; the colors contrast yet are harmonious. Using purple against a blue background, on the other hand, is not effective; both colors are dark, and so the purple letters do not stand out from the background. Be cautious about combining red and green. Some audience members may have a type of color blindness that makes these two colors indistinguishable. Even for those without color blindness, this combination is not effective because it is difficult to read.

MULTIMEDIA PRESENTATIONS It is now possible, with computer programs such as PowerPoint, to incorporate drawings, photographs, video segments, animation, and sound into your visual aids, along with charts, graphs, and text. Such a combination is called a *multimedia presentation*. PowerPoint, for example, contains a set of drawing tools that you can use to create professional-looking images. You can download photographs directly from the Internet, or you can import images that you have entered into your computer by using a scanner. Then you can produce a series of quick images that look like animation, integrating sound clips and even displaying short video clips.

USING VISUAL AIDS ON THE COMPUTER

With a multimedia presentation, you have to use the computer to present the visual aids during your speech, and you may wish to do this even if you have created "electronic slides" without multimedia. For a small audience, you can display the finished presentation on the computer monitor, but for most speeches you will need to project the visual aids onto a larger screen. You can set the computer to advance the visuals automatically at the pace you choose—to match where you expect to be in the speech—or you can advance the visuals manually. You can also use the "build" feature to control the information the audience sees. The presentation will begin with the first major bullet point on your slide and then display progressively more information as you speak about the various points. You can also vary the transitions between slides (how they move on and off the screen), such as making the slides fade in and out or move across, up, or down.

You always should rehearse the presentation on the equipment that you will actually use when you deliver the speech. Then you can deal in advance with any technical mishaps. Also be sure to bring backup diskettes with you to the speech, in case you run into problems with the files on your computer's hard drive. If you will not be using your own computer, be sure that the computers at the speaking site are compatible with your software.

As a precaution, you should have a backup plan in case the computer program fails to run. For instance, you might use your slides to make a set of transparencies that you could show on an overhead projector in an emergency. By anticipating technical difficulties, you can use the time right before the presentation to collect your thoughts, knowing that the technical aspects of your visual aids are under control.[8]

Summary

Although visual aids are not usually required, they can help make your message clear and hold the audience's attention. They permit an appeal to multiple senses, they add variety to the message, they focus the audience's attention, and they make it easier for listeners to remember the speech. If visual aids are not used carefully, however, they may call attention to themselves and distract from your message. The challenge is to reap the benefits of using visual aids while avoiding the pitfalls.

Virtually anything can serve as a visual aid, but it is useful to think in terms of primary categories. Charts can be used to present statistical material, to show the sequence of steps in a process, to reflect patterns of decision or action, and to introduce lists. Graphs show the relationships between variables and are usually depicted as line graphs, bar graphs, or pie graphs. Physical representations can include textual graphics, diagrams, maps, photographs, and film or videotape. Objects and models can be used as visual aids, and the body—whether the speaker's or someone else's—is often a powerful aid to demonstrate actions or processes.

Speakers must decide which materials to use in making visual aids. The main issue is what will be most effective in the given situation. Some possibilities include drawings on the chalkboard, flip charts, posters, handouts, transparencies, slides, and videotape. Each offers certain benefits and has possible drawbacks. Whatever materials are used, the most important consideration is that visual aids should be carefully matched to the contents of the speech. This can be accomplished through storyboarding.

In designing visual aids, key principles include visibility to the audience, ease of handling by the speaker, and aesthetic considerations. To take full advantage of well-prepared visual aids, it is important to practice the speech using the visual aids—if possible, simulating the conditions in the room where you will present the speech.

Computer technology makes it possible to design sophisticated visual aids and to present them from the computer during the speech. You can create text and graphics, making strategic choices about such matters as font, type size, and color. Some computer programs permit you to develop multimedia presentations combining text, clip art, drawings, photographs, video clips, and sound.

Not every speech needs visual aids, but some, such as a sales presentation, virtually require them. In most cases the decision to use visual aids is a strategic choice that is made to enhance the effectiveness of the speech.

1. During the 1992 presidential campaign, candidate Ross Perot was fond of using visual aids to support his messages. Recalling that campaign or watching a videotape of some of Perot's speeches, what do you make of those visual aids? Did they support or detract from the impact of his speeches? Was the use of visual aids appropriate for the situation? Which visual aid was the most effective? Which was the least effective?

2. Fifty years ago, people listened to the radio for news and entertainment. Today, most young people are raised on the visual medium of television. Do you think television's integral connection of image to oral message has changed people's expectations about visual support in speeches? Has the rise of the personal computer altered expectations about visual support in speeches? How do these modern considerations affect the strategic decisions you make about your speech?

3. What type of visual aid would be most appropriate for the following purposes? Could the speaker get away with not using a visual aid? What would visual aids add to these oral discussions?

   Describing your trip to Paris
   Informing your audience about the length of sentences for certain crimes and the length of time that criminals actually serve for those crimes
   Explaining the technique of crab picking
   Teaching an audience how to fill out a 1040EZ tax form
   Teaching the Heimlich maneuver
   Describing the change in expected life spans over the last 500 years
   Getting your audience excited about exploring the Internet

4. Sometimes visual aids not only increase interest, credibility, and memory, but also add to the persuasiveness of a message. Can you think of any examples of visual aids (in speeches, newspapers, advertisements, or the courtroom) that would have an especially powerful persuasive impact?

1. Take some statistics from one of your speeches, and try to display those statistics in the following forms:

   As a chart
   As a line graph
   As a bar graph
   As a pie graph

   Which form seems to best communicate the information that you want to get across in your speech? Why?

2. Evaluate each piece of support in your speech to determine whether or not a visual aid will contribute significantly to the message. In making this determination, be sure to consider the many types of visual aids that you might use.

3. Using the visual aids that you have chosen, practice your speech in the room where you are going to give it. Note the potential pitfalls (e.g., lack of an easel for the poster, unfocused overhead projector, low volume on a tape player), and be prepared to avoid them in the actual presentation.

Using the Internet

1. **Analyze a speech for potential use of visual aids.** Read Secretary of Health and Human Services Donna E. Shalala's speech entitled "Teenage Drug Use Report" that was delivered on December 19, 1996, as part of the Monitoring the Future conference. Point your browser to <http://www.hhs.gov/news/speeches/mtf.html>. After reading the speech, identify what kinds of visual aids would enhance the speech. What benefits of using visual aids could be achieved with the visuals that you recommend?

2. **Analyze the visual aids used at a Website.** To get to the Website **The Web as a Research Tool** by Janet Alexander and Marsha Tate from the Wolfgram Memorial Library at Widener University in Chester, Pennsylvania, point your browser to <http://www.science.widener.edu/~withers/advoc.htm>. Did their visual aids, created with PowerPoint, provide interest, enhance credibility, and improve the comprehension and retention of their points?

3. **Use online tools to create a computer-generated visual aid.** There are a host of software programs that you can use to develop effective visual aids. To explore some of these, go to the **Allyn & Bacon Public Speaking** Website page "Multimedia Tools." Point your browser to <http://www.abacon.com/pubspeak/deliver/webtools.html>.

 Notes

1. For more about these three benefits, see Virginia Johnson, "Picture-Perfect Presentations," *Training and Development Journal* 43 (May 1989): 45–47.
2. William J. Seiler, "The Effects of Visual Materials on Attitudes, Credibility, and Retention," *Speech Monographs* 38 (November 1971): 331–334.
3. Visual aids are often the norm in business speeches. For a good discussion of the minimal standards for visual aids in corporate presentations, see Michael Antonoff, "Presentations that Persuade," *Personal Computing* (July 1990): 60–68.
4. William J. Seiler, "The Conjunctive Influence of Source Credibility and the Use of Visual Materials on Communicative Effectiveness," *Southern Speech Communication Journal* 37 (Winter 1971): 174—185.

5. For more about the mechanics of constructing charts and graphs without the aid of a computer, see Robert Lefferts, *Elements of Graphics: How to Prepare Charts and Graphs for Effective Reports* (New York: Harper & Row, 1981).

6. Lawyers often use objects in their persuasive messages. For a description of one lawyer who was particularly skilled at the use of visual aids, see Edward Palzer, "Visual Materials with a Point," *Today's Speech* 10 (April 1962): 15–16.

7. More advice about the use of slides in a speech can be found in J. R. Van Pelt, "Lantern Slides and Such," *Quarterly Journal of Speech,* 36 (February 1950): 44–50.

8. For further practical advice about the design of computer-generated visual aids, see Dan Cavanaugh, *Preparing Visual Aids for Presentations* (Boston: Allyn & Bacon, 1997).

chapter 13
Informing

In This Chapter We Will:

- Refine our understanding of strategic planning as the process of determining how the speech can most effectively achieve its purpose.

- Distinguish between informing and persuading as purposes for a speech while recognizing that they often overlap.

- Consider how the goal of informing dictates clarifications or refinements in the specific purpose and the organizational pattern of the speech.

- Become familiar with various strategies that achieve the goal of educating the audience.

- Examine ways by which you can encourage listeners to remember the knowledge or insight your speech provides.

Now that we have explored audience analysis, research, reasoning, organization, language, and presentation, we are ready to bring these skills together into a complete speech. To do so, we should revisit two related concepts: *purpose* and *strategy*. A speech is designed to achieve a purpose, and strategic planning is the process of deciding how your speech can best do that.

In Chapter 4 we examined seven different kinds of purpose:

- Setting the agenda
- Providing new information or sharing a perspective
- Strengthening commitment to a position
- Weakening commitment to a position
- Converting the audience away from one belief and toward another
- Intensifying or weakening a feeling
- Inducing a specific action

Now the question is, which strategies are most appropriate for achieving these purposes?

MATCHING STRATEGY TO PURPOSE

Broadly speaking, speech goals are achieved through the strategies of *informing, persuading,* and *entertaining.* These are sometimes mistakenly seen as resulting in three fundamentally different kinds of speeches. In fact, though, because successful sharing of information also affects people's attitudes, informing and persuading occur together. Likewise, a successful persuasive speech is also entertaining and enjoyable to listen to, and an entertaining speech usually also conveys new information.

The broad strategies overlap, then, and they do not exclude each other. So if your assignment is to present "an informative speech," this does not mean that you should avoid saying anything entertaining or persuasive. Rather, you should achieve your purpose *primarily* through strategies of informing.

Defining Your Specific Purpose

But what if the assignment does not specify a purpose? Or what if you are speaking outside the classroom setting? Then you must decide what you want to achieve (for example, to teach people something new, to get them to contribute money to a cause, or to make them laugh). You will need to assess how the audience and the occasion create opportunities or constraints. Finally, based on this analysis, you will define your specific purpose.

For example, suppose that many of your listeners believe that the Internet should be regulated to protect children from indecent material. Your own opinion is exactly the opposite, and you would like to change their minds. But you know (or will learn in the next chapter) that people do not usually make major changes in their beliefs because of a single speech. You also realize that most of your listeners do not really understand exactly what the Internet is. Finally, you will be speaking at an educational conference that is exploring how the Internet can be used in the home. All these factors lead you not to try to convert your audience but to seek the more realistic goal of providing new in-

> ### 13.1 *Speech Purposes and Strategies*
>
> 1. **Purposes achieved primarily through informative strategies**
>   - *Agenda setting*
>   - *Providing new information or sharing a perspective*
> 2. **Purposes achieved through a balance of informative and persuasive strategies**
>   - *Intensifying or weakening a feeling*
> 3. **Purposes achieved primarily through persuasive strategies**
>   - *Strengthening commitment to a position*
>   - *Weakening commitment to a position*
>   - *Converting the audience away from one belief and toward another*
>   - *Inducing the audience to perform a specific action*

formation about the Internet, thus weakening commitment to the view that it should be regulated. To accomplish this, you will rely more on strategies to inform than on strategies to persuade.

On the other hand, sometimes an audience must be persuaded before it can be informed. Consider another example. During the Cold War years, most Americans approached foreign policy issues from the premise that the world was locked in a mortal struggle between freedom and communism. For a speaker even to discuss nationalism in Eastern Europe, it first was necessary to challenge the prevailing view that all of Eastern Europe was a monolith dominated by the Soviet Union. In order to share information effectively, it first was necessary to change listeners' attitudes.

Informing Your Audience

In this chapter we are concerned with informing. **Informative strategies** presume that the overall goal of the speech is to share ideas with the audience. They rely on the metaphor of the speaker as teacher and the speech as a lesson. Listeners are asked to be attentive, to understand what is being said, and to modify their knowledge and belief systems to take this new information into account.

In a speech about the microscopic world around us, Kimo Sanderson made his classmates think about something they had previously ignored:

> There are millions of living creatures in your house right now. They crawl through your carpet, reproduce under your bed, and snack in your closet. When examined under a microscope, they look like creatures from your worst nightmares. They are dust mites, and we live with them every day.

In her speech about the Beat Generation, Elizabeth Wright introduced her audience to an era that was unfamiliar to them:

> During the late 1940s and early 1950s, the Beat Generation began to explore the country in search of something to believe in. People like Jack Kerouac, Allen Ginsberg, and Gary Snyder listened to jazz, wrote "stream of consciousness" poetry, and celebrated freedom. Let's take a closer look at these people and their ideas.

informative strategies
Approaches to preparing a speech in which the overall goal is to share ideas with an audience.

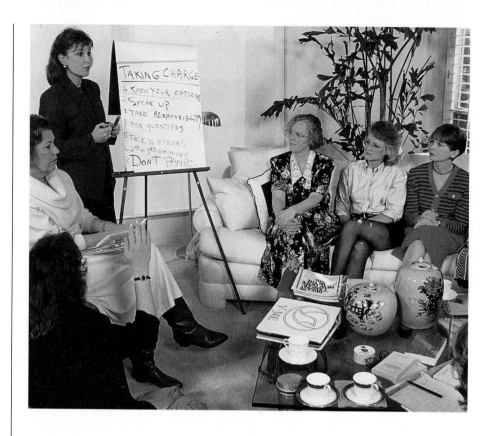

Providing information is one way to empower an audience by making listeners feel better about their abilities to control their own lives.

Informative strategies do not explicitly ask listeners to believe or do any particular thing. Of course, learning something new might stimulate them to take some action. For example, imagine that you heard a speech about the depletion of the ozone layer, knowing nothing previously about this scientific and ecological issue. The speaker's purpose was to share information about the extent of the thinning of the ozone layer so far, the role of the ozone layer in shielding us from the sun's ultraviolet rays, and projections for the future rate of ozone depletion. The speaker did not actually call on you to do anything; the goal was only to make you aware of a previously neglected issue. But it would not be surprising if, after hearing such a speech, you chose to stop using aerosol spray cans and to urge legislators to ban their use. In the next chapter we will contrast informative strategies with strategies of persuasion, which seek to influence listeners' beliefs, values, or actions.

Clarifying Your Informative Goal

Two of the speech purposes discussed in Chapter 4 rely primarily on informative strategies: agenda setting and providing new information or perspective. Information is essential if you are to induce listeners to think about something new, to view it from a unique perspective, or to take into account something they had previously ignored. In addition, the purpose of intensifying positive or negative feelings relies heavily on both informative and persuasive strategies, as well as on entertaining.

AGENDA SETTING   A speaker whose purpose is **agenda setting** wants to create awareness of a subject that listeners did not know about or think about before, thus putting it on the agenda of topics that warrant their concern. Until fairly recently, for example, most of us simply didn't think about the disposal of waste paper, glass, plastic, and aluminum. We tossed these materials in the trash can, counting on garbage collectors to get rid of them somehow. Because solid-waste landfills are being exhausted, the subject now warrants our attention, and most people are aware of recycling. Speakers and writers focused attention on a topic that had been ignored, and at some point it was put on the agenda.

PROVIDING NEW INFORMATION OR PERSPECTIVE   Common knowledge about a subject is often quite general. It is widely acknowledged, for example, that many eligible voters in the United States do not vote. But most people have little understanding of what lies behind this statement—whether the percentage of voters has been increasing or decreasing, how participation varies among different groups, factors that tend to increase or limit participation, the relationship between registration and voting, and so on. One informational goal for a speech would be to enrich the audience's common knowledge about voting rates, moving listeners from a broad understanding to a more detailed awareness of the issue.

Sometimes a speaker's objective is not merely to supply more details but to update and revise the audience's common knowledge. Part of what people generally believe may be mistaken, and social knowledge changes with the times. There is probably no clearer example than what people in the United States "know" about Russia. For most of the period from 1945 to 1990, people "knew" that the Soviet Union (which included Russia) was engaged in a deadly economic and political struggle with the United States. But in the years since 1990, people have come to "know" that this is no longer the case. You probably will not be able to alter your listeners' perspective so dramatically. But if your Internet speech gives listeners information that leads to a new way of thinking about "indecency," you will have accomplished the same purpose.

INTENSIFYING OR WEAKENING A FEELING   It borders on cliché to say that information gives people power. Knowledge and understanding enable people to perform competently and to make intelligent choices. Providing information empowers listeners to feel better about their ability to control their lives. Ellen Benson, for example, did not think that she was good at managing her time. She never seemed to have enough time to get everything done; tasks took much longer than she thought they should, and she often forgot what she needed to do. But then she attended a speech about time management skills, and the speaker's information helped Ellen to understand her problems and gave her some techniques to manage time better. After the speech she told a friend, "I feel like this speech has given me a new way to take power over my own life."

The ability to make intelligent choices is also a source of power. When you have to make a difficult choice—where to go to college, what to study, whether to return home or to stay on campus for the summer, whether to buy a stereo or to save the money—you will be frustrated if you do not know how to decide which alternative is better. Informative speeches do not tell the audience which option to choose. But if they lay out the costs and benefits of

agenda setting
Creating awareness about a subject that listeners did not know about or think about before.

alternatives, they may help listeners to form criteria for making a decision. By resolving a difficult question, people feel better both about the subject and about themselves.

Agenda setting, providing new knowledge, and creating a positive feeling are examples of speech goals that rely heavily on informative strategies. Now we will explore some of these strategies.

INFORMATIVE STRATEGIES

For ease of explanation, we shall examine informative strategies one at a time, as though speakers used only one strategy in a given speech. Although that is possible, informative strategies are seldom found in pure form. Most speeches combine a number of strategies to achieve the speaker's purpose and to make it more likely that listeners will remember the information.

Defining

Definition is a strategy to clarify a term or concept that is vague or troublesome. A speaker may use definition to pin down the meaning of a term so that everyone understands exactly what is being discussed. Or definition may be used to introduce a new or unexpected way of viewing the subject, so that the speech can develop the details and implications of this new approach. Definition is unnecessary when a term's meaning is clear-cut; it is used precisely because the term's usage cannot be settled just by consulting a dictionary.

Defintion is absolutely required, though, when a concept is not clear at all, as when new technical terminology makes its way into general usage. In the early 1980s, when personal computers came into use, most people suddenly needed to learn a whole new vocabulary: "floppy disk," "booting up," "bytes," "download," "modem," and so on. A speech entitled "Deciphering the Personal Computer"—defining such terms—would have been well received.

At other times definition is used to identify different or conflicting meanings of a common term and to establish the speaker's preferred meaning. Student Sonia Rubenstein, for example, believed that many of the unfortunate racial incidents and cases of "hate speech" on college campuses during the 1990s arose partly because the key concept "affirmative action" was misunderstood. She used the strategy of definition to clarify the concept and to establish a preferred meaning:

> Mention the term "affirmative action," and some people will tell you that it means special recruiting efforts to attract minorities and women. Others say it means identifying a specific goal for the number of minorities and women to be hired. Still others think it means reserving a specific number of places for minorities and women. And people speak so often of the mechanics of affirmative action that they lose sight of the goal: We all benefit from the perspectives offered by a culturally diverse student body. If we keep track of that goal, then the best way to think of affirmative action is as special efforts to seek out qualified students who will enable us to achieve the goal.

Intelligent discussion is unlikely when the participants have different ideas of what they are talking about. For that reason, Sonia Rubenstein's goals were to identify different possible meanings, to explain the implications of accept-

definition
A strategy to clarify a term or concept that is vague or troublesome.

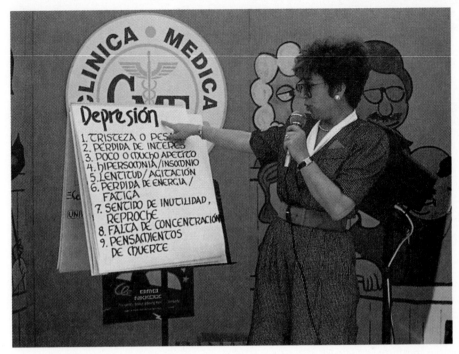

The goal of a speech of definition is to clarify a difficult concept. "Depression" is sometimes used as a very general term, but this speaker tries to explain precisely what it means.

ing one meaning or another, and to describe a preferred point of view. She organized the body of her speech like this:

I. Affirmative action has multiple meanings.

    A. It may mean aggressive recruiting.

    B. It may mean numerical goals.

    C. It may mean tie-breaking preferences.

    D. It may mean quotas.

II. Selecting a meaning makes a difference.

    A. It will influence how actively the government takes an interest in the question.

    B. It will clarify whom affirmative action seeks to help.

    C. It will determine whether it is fair to place at a disadvantage people who have not themselves caused previous discrimination.

    D. It will influence how actively committed we should be to the goal.

III. Affirmative action really means aggressive recruiting.

    A. This meaning is consistent with our belief that people should be evaluated as individuals, not as groups.

    B. It is consistent with our belief that decisions should ultimately be made on the basis of merit.

    C. It recognizes the historical underrepresentation of minorities and the fact that qualified minority candidates may not be identified through normal means.

In these examples the speaker uses definition to identify and explain a preferred meaning. As we saw in Chapter 10, however, such definitions are not neutral; they shape how we view or think about a subject. In educating listeners about a definition, the speaker is also influencing them to think

THE SITUATION

You work at a local retail clothing store and have been asked by your boss to prepare a ten-minute presentation on the information you gathered about a new store that opened around the corner from you. Primarily, your boss wants you to discuss the type and quality of merchandise, prices, and service. You will give your presentation before the upcoming executive board meeting.

MAKING CHOICES

1. What will be the major areas of your speech, and what organizational pattern will you choose?
2. Think about your introduction, transitions, and conclusion: What do you want to achieve with them and how will you accomplish those goals?
3. What types of evidence and supporting materials do you need/should you use?

WHAT IF . . .

How would your decisions about this speech change if . . .
1. the presentation is in front of all 200 employees?
2. you are in a casual meeting sitting among the audience members?
3. your presentation is only five minutes instead of ten?
4. you work at a fast-food chain or at a bank instead?

about the topic in a particular way. Although the strategy of definition is intended mainly to be informative, definitions also are persuasive.

Reporting

Reporting is journalism in the oral mode. It answers the question "What happened?" and usually does so in strict chronological order with little overt analysis or interpretation. Select this strategy if your analysis of audience, occasion, and purpose suggests that you need to explain a complex event by identifying each of its components.

If you were giving a speech about the recent visit to the campus of a world-famous artist and your goal was to share what happened, the body of the speech would report the major events of the visit:

   I. Arrival at the airport
     A. Time and place
     B. Reception party
     C. Welcoming remarks
  II. Visiting with classes
     A. Which classes were visited
     B. What topics were discussed in class
 III. Delivering a public lecture
     A. What the audience was like
     B. What the speaker's main topics were

reporting
A strategy to relate what happened with little analysis or interpretation.

C. How long the speech lasted

D. What the students thought of the speech

IV. Evaluating students' work

A. Which artworks were judged

B. The results

V. The departure ceremony

A. The gift given to the artist

B. The final words from the artist

Although the image of reporting is that it is purely factual, usually far more has occurred than can be conveyed in a relatively short speech. Selecting which items to include and which to leave out therefore involves the speaker in making subjective judgments; in turn, these can influence what listeners think about the topic. Even reporting, then, is not a purely informative strategy.

APPLYING STRATEGIES

The Informative Speech

Excerpts from Carrie's Informative Speech on Body Piercing

How many of you are curious about body piercing when you see a pierced ear, nose, or navel? (show navel ring) I contemplated getting my navel pierced a few years ago and decided to do research on this topic before I did it.

Perhaps you, too, are curious about this popular trend and would appreciate learning more about it. Today, I'll be discussing the history of body piercing, the most common piercing points, and the actual procedures involved.

People in every culture throughout history have enhanced their appearances by either injecting dye under their skin or piercing odd parts of their body. I wasn't sure whether some of them would be appropriate to talk about in class, so I won't. Archaeologists have found evidence of Egyptian and Macedonian jewelry for pierced earrings dated back to 2,000 B.C.

Dr. Marrow's Comments

I loved your attention getter of showing your navel. . . . It was definitely a good thing that you employed the "conceal, reveal, conceal" rule because if your navel ring was visible throughout the speech, no one would have listened to you!

I like the three main points of this speech—history, common piercing points, and actual procedures. You develop these points sufficiently for a 3- to 4-minute speech assignment.

Says whom? Don't forget to cite a source for this claim. Also, because this is such a visual topic, the speech could benefit from more visual aids. How about showing us some large photographs of body-pierced characters (close-ups) throughout history? Or a videotape from a recent movie where body-pierced-characters are shown? The visual influence would help tell your story and keep the audience's attention throughout your speech.

(continued)

Excerpts from Carrie's Informative Speech on Body Piercing

Dr. Marrow's Comments

Many contemporary cultures reserve piercing parts of the body for a rite of passage from child to adult. In the 1960s few women in the U.S. had their ears pierced and almost no men did.

And now in the '90s, it's become an everyday thing for the ladies and very many of the guys. Piercing was reintroduced to this generation by "bikers, punks, and skinheads," and then became a trend of contemporary fashion.

A common question is, does it hurt? It hurts. The body responds to acute pain by releasing endorphins, which is a natural pain killer. it only hurts for a moment or two, and it doesn't hurt after it heals. For me it took about a month to heal. I went to Lake Bower right after I had it done, and that didn't help things too much. it depends on how you get it pierced. The most common but the worst way of piercing is, a friend does it for a friend. We didn't do that. A bunch of my friends and I had gone and got it done by a technician, and she used the right pair of tools and a stainless steel ring, which is supposed to keep it from being infected.

Guns are only used on the earlobes, although some people have piercing guns available. Piercing guns on belly buttons can cause a lot of problems and disfigurement.

Needles are never to be reused, even on the same person. it took them twice to get through mine. And the patient is carefully instructed in aftercare, after the piercing. We were supposed to use Bactine on ours. A lot of people use different things. That worked for me.

A personal story could be useful and powerful during your speech, especially when discussing how friends should not perform body-piercing acts on other friends. You would not have to include gruesome details, but rather use a poignant example where the message is clear—go to a body-piercing professional for this procedure, not a friend.

Describing

Many passages in novels use words to try to paint a picture of the scene. When readers can "see" the characters, setting, and action in their minds, they become more actively involved in the novel.

This process of painting a mental picture is **description,** and it can benefit a speech as well as a novel.[1] In a speech about travel to the French Riviera, we are unlikely to hear a set of arguments about *why* we should go. Rather,

description

A strategy in which a cumulation of details characterizes, or evokes a mental image of, the subject.

the speaker will develop so appealing an image of the Riviera that we will *want* to go. Similarly, a speech about the San Francisco earthquake of 1906 might use description to convey a sense of what it was like rather than just reporting what happened.

A mental picture becomes vivid through its details. Instead of a general reference to a person, an effective speaker describes specific details—the color of the eyes or hair, whether the person was standing erect or leaning against a post, the expression on the person's face, and so on. But a steady stream of details quickly becomes tedious, so the speaker selects details that evoke a larger picture. The expression on the person's face, for example, might convey a certain attitude. In a speech about the professor who had the greatest influence on her life, student Janet Wickstrom described many such details to her audience:

> I walked into Professor Alvarez's office and immediately noticed her desk. Or, rather, I noticed that I couldn't *see* her desk. One corner was piled high with new books. The telephone was covered with reminder notes. Students' papers and memos were strewn across the desk. There was yesterday's newspaper opened to the crossword puzzle. A napkin with crumbs from a leftover bagel was on top. Somewhere nearby was a coffee cup. Class notes were piled on top of the computer. A grade book was buried underneath a stack of paper. "What a desk," I thought. Yet I soon would discover that behind that desk was the most organized woman I ever have met.

Description is an especially useful strategy when you believe that listeners will share your appraisal of the details and will regard them as signs or examples of some characteristic that you could not observe or report directly—such as, in this example, the generalization that first appearances can be deceptive. Stated directly, the claim would seem a cliché. But if it is developed indirectly through detailed description, listeners' interest in the details will help them to appreciate the generalization.

Explaining

Beyond simply defining a term or making an idea precise, speakers sometimes want to share with an audience a deeper understanding of events, people, policies, or processes. This is done through explanation, which goes beyond reporting to consider different views of what happened, to ask how or why it happened, or to speculate about what it means or implies.

For example, if you wanted to explain the 1962 Cuban missile crisis to listeners who were not yet born and who don't really understand that event, you would not simply report what took place from October 16 to October 28, 1962. You would discuss such topics as how and why Soviet missiles were placed in Cuba, why Americans regarded them as so threatening, what options for a response were weighed by President Kennedy and his advisers, how the crisis was resolved, and what it meant for U.S.–Soviet relations at the height of the Cold War. If your explanation is successful, listeners not only will know more of the facts but also will grasp the significance of the crisis and will appreciate why the issues it raised have fascinated people for nearly four decades.

Speeches that explain events or people often begin simply and then build toward greater richness or complexity. In contrast, speeches that explain policies or processes generally proceed in the opposite direction. For most of the years between 1945 and 1990, for example, the chief military policy of the United States toward the Soviet Union was deterrence. A speaker who wants to explain this abstract concept would have to break it down into its components: what weapons were developed and maintained, which diplomatic channels were important, how the United States tried to reassure the Soviet Union that it would not begin a war—while also inducing the belief that, if war started, the United States might use nuclear weapons—and so on. Only by understanding these components well could listeners really know what deterrence was and how it worked.

Similarly, speeches that explain a process proceed by breaking down complex operations into a simple sequence of steps. Such a speech enables listeners to understand how a complicated process works even if they cannot do it themselves. For example, because public opinion polls are reported so often in the news, you might want to speak about how such polls are conducted. You would explain all the steps in the process: the framing of the questions, identification of the population to be sampled, procedures for obtaining responses from the sample, recording and coding of responses, performing statistical analyses, and interpreting significant results. After hearing your speech, listeners will not be able to design and conduct polls themselves but they will recognize and understand the key steps in the polling process.

Demonstrating

Sometimes it is not enough to explain a process; it is necessary as well for the audience to *see* it. Or sometimes the goal is not just for listeners to understand something; the object is to enable them to do it themselves. In such a case a speaker may offer a demonstration, describing a seemingly mysterious or complicated procedure as a series of fairly simple steps performed in a particular order. Such a speech to demonstrate how to cook something, how to wallpaper a room, how to prepare a simple tax return, or how to organize a cluttered desk demystifies the topic for listeners, so that they learn to do something that they could not do before.

In preparing a speech of demonstration, the following considerations are particularly important:

1. *Do listeners really need to see the process to understand it?* If not, a demonstration may seem superfluous or boring; but if so, a demonstration will be strategically essential.

2. *Is the subject precise enough that it can be demonstrated in the time available?* Complicated operations, such as rebuilding an automobile engine, can't possibly be covered in a single speech. And even without a time limit, it's unlikely that an audience will attend to, much less remember, a long demonstration about how to rebuild an engine. On the other hand, such topics as how to make an apple pie, how to plan one's study time, and how to pack a suitcase efficiently lend themselves well to brief demonstrations.

Sometimes explanation is not enough; the speaker must show listeners how to do something. The speech of demonstration enables them to view a process so that they may be able to repeat it themselves.

3. *Are the steps of the process clear, distinct, and in proper sequence?* Listeners will not understand what they are supposed to do if your instructions are vague or incomprehensible or if you demonstrate the steps out of order. Start at the beginning, and go through all the steps leading to the finished product. Do not skip any necessary steps, and do not duplicate steps.

4. *Are your actions and your verbal instructions coordinated?* Avoid any long gaps in the speech while you are doing something or waiting for something to happen. You will lose both the continuity of the speech and the audience's attention if you must pause and wait for results. This problem often weakens a demonstration of how to cook something.

Checklist

13.2 *The Demonstration Speech*

In considering whether to give a demonstration speech, ask yourself these questions:

1. **Do listeners really need to see the process to understand it?**

2. **Is the subject precise enough that it can be demonstrated in the time available?**

3. **Are the steps of the process clear, distinct, and in proper sequence?**

4. **Are your actions and your verbal instructions coordinated?**

Demonstration speeches usually benefit from visual aids, which we examined in Chapter 12.

Comparing

The final informative strategy is comparing, which seeks to clarify for listeners the similarities and differences between the items compared. It can be used to make things seem more similar than an audience had imagined. For example, word-processing programs often are thought to be quite different from one another, but a speech comparing features of two leading programs could convince the audience that they are so similar that anyone who knows one can learn the other quickly. Alternatively, a comparison might heighten awareness of differences between things thought to be alike. If listeners think that all systems of Parliamentary procedure are basically the same, they might learn otherwise by hearing a speech that compares different systems. Or the strategy could accomplish both of these purposes. A speech comparing the curriculum in engineering with that in liberal arts could make listeners aware of both similarities and differences that they had not recognized.

Another use of the strategy of comparing is to decide in what category the topic of the speech should be placed. Deciding whether Social Security is basically an insurance program or basically a welfare program could be helped by a speech exploring its similarities to and differences from each of those concepts.

Finally, comparing can provide listeners with a basis for making a choice. The speaker does not tell them what to do or urge them to accept one perspective over another but instead identifies the options available and compares their benefits and costs.

The public debate about health care during the early 1990s provides a good example. The skyrocketing costs of health insurance, and the fact that more than thirty million Americans had none, prompted a variety of competing proposals for health-care reform. President George Bush favored modest changes in the system, combined with cost controls on two federal health programs, Medicare and Medicaid. President Bill Clinton offered a detailed program based on managed competition among health-care providers. Some Democratic members of Congress championed a "pay or play" system in which employers would either provide health insurance for all workers or else contribute to a national fund that would do so. Still other advocates supported a system of national health insurance. Few citizens, however, fully understood the details of these various proposals, none of which ultimately was adopted. When the health care issue resurfaced in the late 1990s, understanding these earlier proposals became important. A speech of comparison might have increased public understanding by identifying the problem, describing the proposed options, and determining the strengths and weaknesses of each. The purpose of the speech would not be to urge any particular choice but to make the alternatives clear so that listeners could apply their own criteria in deciding. In this case, the various reform proposals remained complex and were misunderstood. Along with political considerations, this helps to explain why none of the proposals was adopted, even given the widespread public support for some kind of change.

The body of a speech comparing the financing options for health care might be organized this way:

I. Modification of the current system is a possible solution.

  A. It offers certain benefits.

  B. It poses certain drawbacks.

II. Managed competition is a possible solution.

  A. It offers certain benefits.

  B. It poses certain drawbacks.

III. A "pay or play" plan is a possible solution.

  A. It offers certain benefits.

  B. It poses certain drawbacks.

IV. National health insurance is a possible solution.

  A. It offers certain benefits.

  B. It poses certain drawbacks.

V. Summary: The choices that we must consider are modification of the current system, managed competition, a "pay or play" plan, and national health insurance.

Although we have examined the informative strategies as though they were completely separate and distinct, remember that speakers often combine them. A speech may both report what happened and attempt to interpret what it means, or may both explain and compare, or may both define and describe, or may both demonstrate and explain. Always, however, the goal is to share understanding and insight in order to enhance listeners' awareness and their ability to make intelligent choices.

ENCOURAGING RETENTION

It might be said that the true test of learning is not how much knowledge or insight one takes in but how much one retains. There *are* cases in which the speaker seeks only an immediate response. If the purpose of the speech is to convince people to donate to a fund-raising effort, then the immediate response—Did people actually give money?—may be the sole test of success. But with informing it is different. Speakers want the audience not only to attend to and understand what they said but also to remember it.[2]

Over a century ago, psychologists explained what is called the **forgetting curve.** This concept is applied to public speaking in Figure 13.1 on page 350, where the horizontal axis represents the amount of time after the speech, and the vertical axis shows the percentage of content that is remembered. As you can see from the fast-falling curve, a large portion of the speech is forgotten

forgetting curve
A curve that displays the rate at which something learned is forgotten over time.

FIGURE 13.1
The forgetting curve.

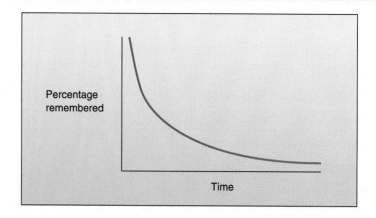

quickly; the line begins with a sharp negative slope and then levels out later. The forgetting curve applies both to the main points of the speech and to the sources of information. Over a short period of time listeners quickly forget who said what. We might say that the information conveyed in a speech typically has a short half-life. Indeed, this is the biggest constraint on the effectiveness of informative strategies.

Although the forgetting curve typically takes the shape shown in Figure 13.1, the sharp decline does not have to appear at the same place on the graph. It is possible to "shift the curve upward," to increase the likelihood that listeners will remember more content at any given time. In Chapter 3 we examined ways to gain and keep an audience's attention, such as making the speech personally relevant to listeners, making the message stand out, and making it easy to follow. Fortunately, the methods used to increase attention apply to retention as well.

Moreover, in Chapter 2 we learned the importance of active listening, which occurs when the speaker challenges listeners to think, to mentally role-play situations, and to ask and answer questions. Compared with passively receiving information, active listening requires a higher level of participation. And because participation enhances motivation, it should be no surprise that active involvement by listeners (rather than just passive hearing of the speech) increases the chances that they will remember the message.

Retention is also strengthened through **reinforcement,** a response by the speaker that rewards the listener and thereby strengthens the listener's positive attitudes toward the speech. In the public speaking classroom, listeners often reinforce speakers. If audience members nod their heads in agreement whenever a speaker expresses an opinion, the speaker is likely to increase the number of opinion statements.

As a speaker you also can use reinforcement strategically to ensure that the audience remembers the message. As you learned in Chapter 7, if your organizational pattern enables listeners to anticipate what will come next and the subsequent development of your speech confirms their guess, then by confirming their expectation you reward their shrewd judgment.

reinforcement
A response by a speaker that rewards the listener to strengthen the listener's positive attitude toward the speech.

You can also reinforce audience members by how you refer to them. Saying "we" instead of "you" conveys the message that you identify with listeners and regard them as your equals; you signal that they are in the know and that you respect their thoughtful judgment. Explicit references to them within the speech may have the same effect. A speaker whose transition says, "Since you've followed this complex topic so far, I'm sure you can see why the next point is valid," is speaking well of the audience and providing reinforcement. This, along with strategies that draw attention and encourage active listening, will shift the forgetting curve and improve the odds of ensuring retention.

Summary

In this chapter we have examined how informative strategies achieve several speech purposes: agenda setting, providing new information or perspective, and creating positive feeling by making listeners aware of how to do something or by involving them in making an important choice. Speeches that rely mainly on informative strategies do not seek directly to influence listeners' actions, and yet it would be unfair to say that they have no persuasive effects.

After completing your research, developing an outline, and testing your reasoning, you should review your speech plan in terms of your specific goals. Based on analysis of the audience, occasion, and purpose, you can select appropriate informative strategies. These include defining, reporting, describing, explaining, demonstrating, and comparing. Many speakers combine these strategies.

Because listeners quickly forget much of what was said in a speech, you will want to use strategies that encourage and reinforce retention. Providing information that draws attention, using an organizational structure that enables listeners to anticipate what is coming next, and making complimentary references to the audience are ways to improve retention.

Discussion Questions

1. In the public speeches that you've heard lately, were informative strategies or persuasive strategies dominant? Consider speeches from outside the public speaking classroom, such as:

   A presidential address

   A speech at a protest rally

   A lecture in your history class

   An oral research report presented by a student in another class

   The closing argument in a trial

   Was any of these speeches completely devoid of persuasive strategies? Was any completely devoid of informative strategies? Can a speaker inform listeners without influencing them in some way? Can a speaker persuade listeners without providing information?

2. Speakers encourage retention by reinforcing listeners, by drawing their attention, and by encouraging them to listen actively. Two strategies for doing these things are (a) to provide a clear organizational pattern and

(b) to refer to "we" instead of "you." What other strategies help a speaker to encourage retention in a speech with a primarily informative goal? Discuss the strategies that in your experience were most effective in making you remember the message long after the speech was over.

Activities

1. Watch a news report on television. In what ways is it like a speech to inform? In what ways is it different? Can you take anything from this model to help you create speeches with informative strategies?

2. Describe five strategies that you plan to use in your next speech to increase the audience's retention of information.

3. Create one of the following:
   a. A speech of explanation about the process of developing informative strategies in speeches
   b. A speech of comparison that discusses informative and persuasive strategies
   c. A speech of definition about the concept of "strategic planning" in speech preparation

Using the Internet

1. **Assess Webpages to determine their purpose.** Use the **IdeaList** to find Webpages of nonprofit organizations. Point your browser to <http://www.idealist.org>. Next, type in a search term if you know the name of an organization or for a topic. The IdeaList will provide a description of the organization and links to its Webpage. In your view, did the creators of the page emphasize informative strategies or persuasive strategies? Does the page inform or persuade—or do both? Insofar as the page is informative, how does it accomplish the goals of an informative message:
   • *Agenda setting*
   • *Providing new information or perspective*
   • *Intensifying or weakening a feeling*

2. **Search for informative strategies in an informative magazine.** Which informative strategies can you find examples of in the online version of *National Geographic?* Point your browser to <http://www.nationalgeographic.com/main.html> and select one or more of the "Features." Then consider which informative strategies you've found:
   • *Defining*
   • *Reporting*
   • *Describing*
   • *Demonstrating*
   • *Comparing*

1. For more about description in speeches, see Gerard A. Hauser, "Empiricism, Description, and New Rhetoric," *Philosophy and Rhetoric* 5 (Winter 1972): 24–44.
2. For more about retention, see Robert L. Greene, *Human Memory: Paradigms and Paradoxes* (Hillsdale, N.J.: Lawrence Erlbaum, 1992).

Notes

chapter 14
Persuading

In This Chapter We Will:

- Explore the differences between informative and persuasive strategies for speeches.

- Learn how audiences resist persuasion and what resources help a speaker overcome resistance.

- Determine how speakers can use those resources most effectively, focusing on the relationship between speaker and audience.

- Examine three basic types of persuasive messages: those that strengthen convictions and move listeners from belief to action, those that attempt to convert or actually change beliefs, and those that attack another position or rebuild one's own position after such an attack.

Being one of only two African American students in a public speaking class, Nicole Wesley was not surprised to discover that her classmates knew little about the history of African Americans. She decided to develop a speech that would inform them about soldiers of African descent who fought in the Revolutionary and Civil wars, former slaves who settled the West, the Tuskegee airmen, the Harlem Renaissance, and the civil rights movement.

On reflection, Nicole realized that her speech would not really address the underlying issue. The real need was for an educational system that taught such basic historical and cultural lessons to students before they reached college. What Nicole had begun as a speech with an informative strategy soon evolved into a persuasive message to change the local high school curriculum.

As Nicole discovered, informative goals are sometimes insufficient. A speaker may want not only to make listeners think about something but also to influence what they think about it; or may want to move listeners beyond having a belief to taking action; or may want listeners to change their minds, to abandon one belief and accept another. In all these cases the speaker's goal is to *persuade* the audience, to prompt listeners to feel, act, or believe in a particular way.

COMPARING INFORMATIVE AND PERSUASIVE STRATEGIES

Chapter 4 introduced seven specific speech purposes, and we saw in Chapter 13 that both agenda setting and providing new information or perspective are achieved mainly through informative strategies. The goals of strengthening commitment, weakening commitment, conversion, and inducing specific action all depend primarily on persuasive strategies.

As you know from Chapter 13, informing and persuading are not entirely separate goals, and both create positive or negative feelings in the audience. If you want listeners to remember new information, you need to persuade them that the information is important. And to persuade them to take action, you need to be sure that they understand what the action means. Nevertheless, there are differences between informative and persuasive strategies.

Asking for Commitment

One difference between informative and persuasive strategies is in the degree of commitment that the speaker requests from the audience. Informative strategies do not require listeners to commit themselves to any belief or action; the speaker mainly wants the audience to understand, think about, and remember the information in the speech. In contrast, persuasive strategies ask listeners to make a particular choice about believing or doing something—which to some degree eliminates another potential choice. In this sense, persuasive strategies ask listeners to put their beliefs or values on the line.

For this reason, speakers who seek to persuade must be sensitive to their ethical responsibility not to manipulate listeners. A speaker can so "load the deck" that the audience has an illusion of choice even though the speech predetermines what that choice will be. If a speaker moves listeners to action by persuasive but unsound appeals, or withholds crucial information or arguments because they might lead to an unwanted conclusion, or rushes listeners to judgment by pronouncing an issue more urgent than it actually is, then the audience has been manipulated.

Changing Degrees of Commitment

A speaker applies persuasive strategies because he or she assumes that listeners can be either more committed or less committed to a position. By reasoning with audience members, the speaker seeks to move them from one point to another along a scale reflecting degrees of commitment. As shown in Figure 14.1, the speaker might want to *strengthen commitment* to a belief, moving listeners farther along the scale in the direction toward which they are already headed. Or the speaker might want to *weaken commitment* to a belief, moving listeners closer to the other end of the scale. Or the speaker might even want to try to change listeners' minds, moving them from one end of the scale to the other—a process of *conversion* that seldom results from a single speech. Finally, the speaker might try to shift the entire scale, aiming to move listeners from a strong belief to approval of a *specific action*.

Both informative strategies and persuasive strategies seek to change the audience's perspective. But an informative speech seeks change by enlarging the audience's scope of concerns, whereas a persuasive speech seeks it by redirecting the audience's position.

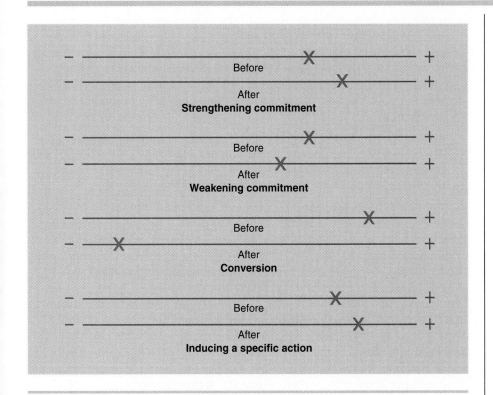

FIGURE 14.1
Belief intensity scales.

PLAN YOUR STRATEGY

Throughout our study we have emphasized speechmaking as strategic planning. Being able to analyze the audience, to size up the situation, and to determine its constraints and opportunities—the basic skills you learned in Chapters 3 and 4—will enable you to make the best use of persuasive strategies.[1]

In Chapter 13 we reviewed the steps in strategic planning. Because persuasive strategies seek an increased commitment from listeners, you need to perform a more detailed audience analysis aimed at identifying your target audience and at assessing that audience's motivation.

Determine Your Target Audience

If your audience is diverse and you are not seeking unanimity, the first step is to determine as precisely as possible which members are your **target audience.** For example, suppose you are speaking at a corporate meeting attended by upper management and by the heads of all departments that might be affected by your presentation—even though any decisions ultimately will be made by only the president and the chair of the board. It would be nice to influence the department heads by your speech, but your real target audience is the president and the board chair. They are the decision makers, and it is they whom you want to persuade.

Assess Your Audience's Motivation

Listeners will be *motivated* to let your speech influence them if they perceive that your appeal is linked to their own motives and needs.

Psychologists have offered many different accounts of the nature of human **motivation.** At the most general level, people seek to attain pleasure and to avoid pain. This motive is the basis for persuasive speeches about everything from the dangers of air pollution to the benefits of good nutrition—as student speaker Michael Masdea demonstrated in urging his audience to stop drinking so much caffeine:

> Caffeine can help us stay up during those frequent student all-nighters. But it can also cause severe headaches, stomachaches, and insomnia. The psychological and behavioral effects of caffeine are frightening. It is a highly addictive drug, and it may be the cause of many problems you are experiencing right now.

Another general account of human motivation was offered by psychologist Abraham Maslow, who theorized that human beings have a *hierarchy of needs;* we first seek to satisfy biological and safety needs, which include food, clothing, shelter, and protection from harm, and then proceed to higher-order needs, such as identity, meaningful relationships, and self-actualization.[1] Maslow argued that a person's higher-order motives become important only after lower-order needs are satisfied. It is useless, for instance, to discuss abstract ideals with someone who doesn't know where his or her next meal is coming from. On the other hand, people who have been able to satisfy their lower-order needs often find that they are not truly fulfilled; then higher-order needs and motives become important. According to this view of motivation, the persuasive speaker's task is to determine approximately where in Maslow's

target audience
Within a larger audience, those individuals whom a speaker especially wants to address, usually people whose response will determine if the speech succeeds.

motivation
The incentive to do something that requires effort, such as considering a persuasive message.

hierarchy listeners are, and then both to arouse the appropriate motive and to show how it can be satisfied by the recommended action or belief.

Student speaker Kevin Krebs appealed to motives on different levels of Maslow's hierarchy in a speech favoring the new NCAA policy of enforcing stricter rules about athletes' minimum grade-point averages and test scores. Kevin first appealed to the athletes' basic need to make a living:

> How many of you really think you're going to get a job playing professional sports? If you do, the odds are stacked against you. Only a small percentage will actually make a living playing the game. Chances are, when you get out of college, you're going to need the education being forced upon you by the new NCAA rules.

Then, for athletes and sports fans alike, Kevin appealed to the higher need to enjoy winning:

> The policy at this university is already stricter than the new NCAA rules. By accepting these new guidelines, some of our competitors with lower standards will be eliminated from the field. Our school will finally get a chance to win a game or two!

REQUIREMENTS FOR EFFECTIVE PERSUASIVE SPEAKING

Just as when you inform, to persuade you need a clear organizational structure and positive *ethos*. Likewise, successful persuasion requires that listeners remember what they heard. In addition, to persuade you must offer sound reasoning, and you must identify with your audience.

Follow Appropriate Organizational Patterns

Not only does being organized itself enhance persuasiveness, but the choice of one organizational pattern over another is significant. When seeking to influence others, the *problem-solution pattern* is often the structure of choice: Make the audience aware of a problem, and then provide a specific means to address that problem. Within this overall framework you can inject a number of other helpful patterns; narrative sequence lets you tell the story of how the problem developed, topical structure allows you to examine various dimensions of the problem, and biographical structure enables you to focus on key individuals in the evolution of the problem.

Also be astute in selecting supporting materials for a problem-solution speech.[2] A startling statistic, for example, might move listeners to take notice of an issue that is far more vast than they might think. Describing interest on the national debt as the largest single government expenditure—larger than national defense, larger than social welfare—might cause listeners to regard the debt as a more serious problem than they had realized. If you then divide the national debt into a $1,600 bill to be paid by every man, woman, and child in America, you might translate its vast size into meaningful terms and personalize the problem for listeners.

A personal narrative can be a potent form of supporting material, making an abstract problem concrete and showing its effects on the lives of real people. If you discuss how "taxpayer resistance has squeezed the public sector of the economy," the problem may seem distant, removed, and impersonal.

A speaker who wants to persuade an audience usually must establish positive ethos. James Brady, who was injured in the assassination attempt on President Ronald Reagan, speaks with experience and credibility to promote gun control.

Instead, you can make the issue more vivid and immediate by telling listeners, "the local elementary school has been forced to close its library, depriving children of books and the librarian of a job."

An effective speaker regards structure as an opportunity to sequence and highlight facts, leading his or her audience to a reasonable conclusion.

Establish Positive Ethos

Your ethos, or credibility, is a powerful resource in persuasive speeches. If listeners trust you, they will be more inclined to give your ideas a fair hearing. Particularly important among the many factors that engender trust are a speaker's previous record, association with trustworthy sources, and reluctant testimony.

PREVIOUS RECORD   A speaker who has established a record of being trustworthy is likely to be trusted in the specific situation at hand. If in earlier speeches you've convinced the audience that you are careful, faithful to the evidence, critical in reasoning, and don't make claims beyond what the evidence supports, you have created a strong presumption that what you say in this speech will be trustworthy as well.

ASSOCIATION WITH TRUSTWORTHY SOURCES   Particularly when your topic is something about which you are not yourself an expert, you need to draw on the statements of people who do have expertise in the subject. If your sources themselves have a reputation for trustworthiness, your association with them will suggest that you are trustworthy too.

RELUCTANT TESTIMONY Your statements will be weakened if listeners think that you have something to gain by stating them. If your audience believes that you have a vested interest—whether economic, political, or ideological—in a particular outcome of the speech, listeners will tend to discount what you say.

On the other hand, if you make a statement that is at odds with your own interest, that statement is considered to be **reluctant testimony.** Because you are working against your own interests by making this statement, listeners presume that you would not make it unless it were true.

Consider how reluctant testimony has worked in the political world. Only Ronald Reagan, for example—a Cold Warrior who had called the Soviet Union an "evil empire"—could really begin to dismantle the Cold War apparatus and seek arms reduction agreements with the Soviet Union. If someone else had attempted this, it might have seemed like a cave-in to Soviet demands. But President Reagan was trustworthy because people believed that he would not betray conservative interests. Similarly, Lyndon Johnson, although he came from the region that most resisted civil rights, convinced Congress to enact the most sweeping civil rights legislation in history.

Since reluctant testimony generally is more credible than is evidence reflecting the source's self-interest, you should look for it when conducting your research. Reluctant testimony is the opposite of **biased evidence,** which you should try particularly hard to avoid.

Reluctant testimony enhances the credibility of classroom speakers too. Western State University had a tradition of strong social fraternities, a system that had come under fire because several recent initiation rituals clearly had been excessive. A vocal group of faculty members charged that all fraternities were anti-intellectual, and the campus newspaper called frats "social clubs for the privileged rich." Two students of public speaking addressed this issue, arguing that major changes were needed if fraternities were to survive on campus. Ben Peters was an independent who was known to dislike fraternities. Although his speech was well prepared, it had little impact on his classmates; it said exactly what everyone expected Ben to say. But when Charles Thompson, a fraternity president, acknowledged that the system had serious problems, listeners noticed. If a prominent fraternity man criticized the system, his views had to be taken seriously.

Just as the insider was more persuasive in this example, so will a dorm resident who is a smoker be more credible than one who is a nonsmoker in urging a smoke-free dormitory environment. Similarly, a biology student who argues that animal experiments on campus need to be monitored and reduced will be more believable than an English major who makes the same argument. As a speaker, you can enhance your credibility by pointing out when you are offering reluctant testimony.

Encourage Retention through Reinforcement

We saw in Chapter 13 that the slope of the forgetting curve is steep, particularly when the message involves new, unfamiliar, or uncomfortable ideas (see Figure 13.1). Unless your persuasive goal is very specific and can be achieved through the speech itself, you should think creatively about how

reluctant testimony
Statements that are not in the speaker's self-interest.

biased evidence
Statements that are suspect because they are influenced by the self-interest of the source.

to reinforce what you want listeners to believe or to do. Your strategies might range from the simple act of thanking the audience for hearing you out to the extreme of asking listeners to participate actively in encouraging others to accept the view you propose.

Student Margaret Orsinger used an interesting metaphor to reinforce her message that bicyclists and motorcyclists should wear helmets:

> We do more to protect the melons in our grocery stores than we do to protect our own heads! Every time you see a cyclist without a helmet, take a good hard look at these "melon-heads." They are people in need of a good, solid crate around their ears.

There is no magic recipe for reinforcing a persuasive message. In general, though, you are more likely to succeed if you give listeners opportunities to rehearse and remind themselves of your conclusion and how you arrived at it, and if you can make acceptance of your position seem to enhance listeners' self-worth.

To create a speech based on persuasive strategies, you need to understand the ways by which people often resist efforts to persuade them. This will enable you to determine where your audience is positioned on the belief intensity scale (Figure 14.1). You also need to know what resources speakers have to overcome resistance.

Use Sound Reasoning

Because in a persuasive speech you are asking the audience to believe or to do something, it is particularly important that you use sound reasoning. If listeners think that your reasoning is shoddy, they will be far less likely to conclude that you have made a good case for what you want them to believe or do. And if your case is weak, it is easy for them to disregard your request for their response. You may wish to review the discussion of reasoning in Chapter 6. Remember that we have focused on reasoning with the audience in mind, not on reasoning as an abstract exercise in logic.

Achieve Identification

Establishing common bonds between speaker and audience is referred to as **identification.**[3] The more that listeners believe themselves to be basically like the speaker and to share the same values or experiences, the more willing they are to be influenced by what the speaker says. Speakers can develop common bonds explicitly, by stating the features they share with the audience. Or bonds can be developed implicitly, when the speaker relates a personal experience that many listeners also have had. Common bonds can even be developed with no mention at all. For example, the fact that a college student speaks to an audience of college students about concerns of college students is itself a source of common bonds. Not surprisingly, listeners are more likely to be persuaded by a peer than by a more distant figure with whom it is difficult to identify.

To keep identification from being perceived as pandering to the audience or telling listeners whatever they want to hear, apply the test you learned in Chapter 4: Use appeals that will satisfy not only the specific audience that is immediately present but also the broader audience of unseen critical listeners whom you might imagine as your court of appeal.

identification
Establishing common bonds between speaker and audience so that the speaker appears to be at one with listeners.

Even facing a potentially hostile audience, speakers enjoy *some* level of identification. The common bond that leads an audience at least to listen attentively to ideas with which they disagree might be a shared procedural value, such as a belief in fair play or a willingness to hear the speaker out. Or the bond might be a shared value, such as respect for a speaker who has the courage of his or her convictions.

Do not conclude, then, that you can't disagree with your audience. In fact, a speaker who always tailors the message to what listeners believe is suspect. But when you cannot achieve identification with the audience on the basis of your content, do so on the basis of some overarching value.

CONSTRAINTS ON EFFECTIVE PERSUASIVE SPEAKING

Even though the requirements for persuading are similar to those for informing, the constraints you face are far greater. Listeners often resist attempts to persuade them. They do so because their identities may be tied closely to their opinions; thus, an appeal to change their opinions might threaten their identities. The nature and strength of such resistance varies significantly among listeners and situations, and it often takes one of the following forms:[4]

- Selective listening
- Disposing of the message
- Compartmentalization
- The boomerang effect

Selective Listening

As we have seen, audiences typically attend to messages, interpret them, and remember them selectively. But a message that reinforces what the audience already believes does not arouse defensive reactions, perhaps because it is less threatening or because it offers reassurance. For example, if you already support national health insurance, you are more likely to attend to, understand, and remember messages that also support it. Moreover, if the focus of a speech is vague or unclear, listeners will "clarify" it by interpreting it in a way that supports what they already believe. Odd as it seems, a speech that decries the cost of health care and demands reform but does not propose a specific solution might be seen by supporters of national health insurance as "really" agreeing with their views.

Because these barriers to persuasion are potentially powerful, it is important to plan strategies that surmount them. One often-used approach is to begin with areas of agreement and gradually move to areas of difference. If your listeners were known to favor national health insurance but you opposed it, you could start by agreeing with them that costs are out of hand, that reform is needed, and that government must play a role. Only then would you make the case that national health insurance is an undesirable solution. The audience will react more favorably to this strategy than if you broadly attacked national health insurance without acknowledging the positive aspects of the issue or the intensity of their feelings.

However, when you acknowledge common ground in a persuasive speech, you have to be careful. Selective listening may lead the audience to hear the common ground but to ignore your message. For example, one student speaker thought that she was being considerate of opposing viewpoints when she began a pro-life speech by acknowledging, "A pregnancy at this point in my life would be a disaster." Somehow, half the audience failed to hear her later statements that abortion would make the disaster even worse and that adoption would make it bearable. The speaker did not move clearly enough from common ground to her own thesis; as a result, her confusing speech was made even more confusing by the selective listening of the audience.

Disposing of the Message

Even if your persuasive message urging listeners to change gets past the filters of selective listening, audiences have other ways to resist being persuaded. They can dispose of the message in several ways, thus not taking it seriously.

DENIAL   Listeners sometimes refuse to accept a message that challenges them to change, no matter how well that message is supported or defended. Wanting to believe otherwise, they simply will not accept the truth of the message; they are in **denial.**

For example, since the mid-1970s, various public figures have maintained that there are limits to what the United States can do in the world. Even when this message has been clearly explained, well supported, and articulately presented, it usually has not been well received. Many Americans—influenced by a two-century tradition that views the United States as a land of unlimited opportunity and promise—simply will not accept that there are limits to what they can achieve.

In a public speaking class, Christy Verneuil learned just how powerful a constraint denial can be. Her persuasive speech urged that gay couples be allowed to serve as adoptive parents. Christy presented study after study proving that children of homosexual parents are as happy and well adjusted as children of heterosexual parents. After the speech, the audience questioned her extensively about those studies. Yet, even though Christy answered every question, her classmates' strong beliefs about this issue kept them from accepting her proposal.

DISMISSAL   A second way that audiences can dispose of an unfavorable message is to dismiss it as not really applying to them. Unlike denial, in which they refuse to accept the *general* truth of the message, in **dismissal** they dispute that the truth applies *specifically* to them.

Dismissal is a common response to unsettling messages about health. A smoker, for example, may hear a speech that describes the harmful effects of nicotine and urges smokers to quit, may conclude that the speech was well reasoned and probably correct in its claims, and yet light a cigarette after the speech because, "It won't happen to me." If you can imagine reasons why your audience might dismiss the message, plan strategies that respond directly to those reasons. You may have to accept, however, that dismissal is sometimes purely self-delusion—and insurmountable.

denial
The refusal to accept the claim in a message no matter how strong its justification is.

dismissal
Disregarding a message (even if it is generally true) because one disputes that it applies to oneself.

BELITTLING THE SOURCE A third way to dispose of a threatening message is to attack the credibility of the source. If your persuasive appeal relies almost entirely on a single source, you run the risk that listeners might discredit the source and thereby avoid your message.

An example of disposing of the message by belittling the source occurred during the early months of 1998, when former White House intern Monica Lewinsky alleged that President Clinton had had an affair with her and then encouraged her to lie about it. Before the release of the Independent Counsel's report and before the President's admission of wrongdoing, some of Clinton's supporters responded to the allegations by suggesting that Lewinsky was an unstable person whose perceptions were warped by her infatuation with him. Because positive ethos is a requirement for persuasion and because there was no solid external evidence of the alleged events, belittling Lewinsky's credibility as a source was an effective way to belittle her accusations as well. Later, some of the President's supporters challenged the motives of the Independent Counsel…for the same reasons.

Compartmentalization

If a message challenges what listeners already believe, they may avoid its influence by keeping it separate from their conflicting belief, so that the two ideas do not seem at odds. This defense against persuasion is called **compartmentalization** because it is like putting the conflicting ideas into separate mental boxes.

People often have different compartments for their general beliefs and their specific beliefs. During the Cold War, for example, many people reported to interviewers that they believed in freedom of speech and yet also indicated that they did not think a Communist should be permitted to speak at a state university. The general belief about freedom of speech was kept separate from the specific belief about Communists having the freedom to speak. Similarly, many people who say they oppose racial discrimination at the same time support police departments that stop black motorists for driving through wealthy white neighborhoods.

Compartmentalization is especially effective as a defense against influence when listeners can distinguish between attitudes and behavior. If you were championing the virtues of a low-fat diet, you might succeed in convincing listeners that they ought to modify their eating habits (attitude) without actually altering what they choose to eat (behavior). Conversely, listeners might be induced to modify their behavior without changing their underlying attitudes. Thus a speech decrying racial slurs might persuade listeners to avoid them when speaking with members of other racial groups and yet not change in any way how they feel about race.

One approach to influencing people who are sustaining an inconsistent position is simply to make apparent to them that they are defending something in the abstract which they are unwilling to apply in practice. Student Robert Myers, for example, believed that everyone should have the right to speak; yet he was agitated when a campus group scheduled a speaker who claimed that white Americans were responsible for poverty in the Third World and who urged U.S. minority groups to revolt. Robert, like many white students on campus, resented the college giving this speaker a platform.

Classmate Susan Martinson decided to discuss this issue in her next speech. She began by identifying with her listeners, noting that they all shared the value of freedom of speech. She then argued that we diminish this value

compartmentalization
Keeping two conflicting beliefs separated so that one need not be conscious of the conflict between them.

by applying it only to easy cases and supporting free speech only for those whose messages we approve. The real test, she said, is whether we are secure enough in our own beliefs to extend freedom of speech to "disreputable" speakers whose ideas we hate. By focusing on this criterion for what makes freedom of speech really meaningful, Susan convinced Robert and her classmates to reexamine their opposition to allowing this controversial speaker to speak on campus.

In exposing listeners' inconsistencies to them, it is important to be gentle and sympathetic. If you are too direct, they naturally could become defensive and even deny that there is any inconsistency. Instead, you want to inspire them to recognize that they have not fully embraced their own ideals.

The Boomerang Effect

A final defense of listeners against being influenced is called the **boomerang effect,** because the message turns back on the speaker. This can happen if an appeal is so powerful that it overwhelms the audience. Concluding that nothing they can do will help matters, listeners may actually do the opposite of what the speaker has urged, thinking, "What I do won't matter anyway."

Julie Richardson knew that depletion of the ozone layer was a serious environmental and public health issue. In trying to convince listeners of its importance, she explained that much of this protective atmospheric layer has been lost already, resulting in great health risks both for us in the present and also for future generations. Specifically, Julie wanted her audience to stop using products in aerosol spray cans because many of them release fluorocarbons that deplete the ozone layer.

Several classmates reacted as Julie had hoped and were persuaded to stop using aerosol cans. But Jeff Martin had quite a different reaction. Julie's speech convinced him that the problem was so vast in scope that nothing he personally might do could affect it. His occasional use of aerosol cans couldn't possibly make much difference, Jeff reasoned, and if he changed his behavior and stopped using them, that would do hardly anything to improve such a serious situation. Moreover, he thought that the problem was already so far advanced that a change in his behavior wouldn't reverse the damage. Since his actions would be futile in the face of such a massive problem, why bother? Why not continue using the aerosol cans, which he likes and which are easy to use? Julie's speech boomeranged and had the opposite effect from what she desired. Hoping to persuade Jeff to stop using aerosol sprays, she actually convinced him to keep using them.

To avoid the boomerang effect, you must assess carefully just how much to arouse the audience about an issue. Obviously, you want to convey a sense of seriousness or urgency when discussing a significant problem. At the same time, however, your speech should leave listeners optimistic about their ability to contribute to the problem's solution and that concerted efforts along the lines recommended in the speech really can make a difference.

Fortunately, these methods by which audiences resist persuasion—selective listening, disposal of the message, compartmentalization, and the boomerang effect—are not absolute. Speakers can overcome them by meeting the requirements described earlier.[5]

boomerang effect
The opposite effect from that which a speaker intends.

THE PROBLEM-SOLUTION SPEECH

One of the most common types of speeches using persuasive strategies is the problem-solution speech, which establishes a serious problem and then identifies what should be done to solve it. The speaker uses persuasive strategies to create a positive feeling, to strengthen commitment, and to move the audience beyond concern to action.[6] Although problem-solution speeches can be organized in a variety of patterns, they typically follow the four-stage structure that you learned in Chapter 7:

- Describe the situation.
- Evaluate the situation as a problem.
- Propose a solution.
- Argue for the solution.

Describe the Situation

This part of the speech is primarily informative. Your goal is to make listeners aware of the magnitude or importance of the problem. For example, in discussing how people are threatened by crime, you might report how often crimes are committed, the number of people who have been victimized by crime, how people say that crime affects them psychologically, and what steps people have taken to try to deal with crime. The outline for this part of the body of your speech might be:

I. Crime is significant and growing.

   A. Rates of virtually all crimes are increasing.

   B. Loss of life and property because of crime are increasing.

   C. People in all segments of the community believe their neighborhoods to be unsafe.

   D. Crime is a growing problem even on this campus.

Evaluate the Situation as a Problem

The second stage is to convince listeners that the situation you described really does represent a problem—that it is cause for genuine concern. People will endure all sorts of inconveniences without taking action; they become concerned only about what they regard as serious problems.

To establish that a situation is a problem, you need to show that it violates a value that is important to your audience. In the case of crime, for instance, the rising crime rates might lead people to feel insecure, might undermine their sense of justice, and might threaten the stability of the community. Because people care about these values, they will be disturbed by rising crime rates.

Values are rooted in emotions, and so persuasive strategies must be concerned with emotional appeals. In Chapter 6 you learned that an inappropriate appeal to emotions is an error in reasoning. The key word here is "inappropriate." Although emotional appeals can be misused, there is nothing irrational about responding to an appropriate appeal. When you decide not to go out alone at night because of safety concerns, when you try to mend fences with

The problem-solution speech
requires you first to persuade
the audience that there is a
serious threat or problem,
and then to persuade them
that your solution is the best
approach to the problem.
This speaker is arguing that
handgun-related deaths
are excessive and that limitations must be placed on hand-
gun ownership.

parents or siblings because family harmony is important, or when you strive to do your best in response to competition, your choices are perfectly reasonable and sensible.

The second part of the speech's body might be outlined like this:

II. Rising crime is a serious problem.

  A. It causes people to feel insecure and unsafe.

  B. It undermines a sense of justice.

  C. It threatens the stability and peace of the community.

A speaker cannot create in listeners an emotion that they do not feel. However, the speaker can make audience members aware of their emotions and indicate the importance of those emotions. When you evoke fear, pride, anxiety, or any other emotion, you also create a need to satisfy that emotion. Some emotions, such as fear and anxiety, can become highly disturbing if they are left unrelieved. Your power as a speaker lies in the ability not only to arouse the emotion but also to satisfy it by providing a positive course of ac-tion. We have seen that arousing too much fear can cause a boomerang effect. But if you arouse an appropriate level of fear in the audience and you then of-fer the means to relieve the fear—by taking advantage of a campus escort ser-vice, by learning the art of self-defense, or by deciding not to go out alone at night—the speech is likely to be persuasive.

Propose a Solution

Having aroused an appropriate level of emotion, it is important to offer the audience a solution to the problem. Listeners will feel uncomfortable if you arouse fear, concern, or anxiety without also suggesting a solution that will restore their sense of harmony. Your solution might be simple (a single option) or complex (a range of options). You might identify it at once, or you might first rule out alternatives. But your solution should be detailed enough to address the problem as you have described it. If you have presented three separate dimensions of the problem, for instance, each should be addressed by your solution.

In the crime example few listeners would feel that a statement like "We have to have faith and hope that things will turn out for the best" is an appropriate solution. You are more likely to be persuasive if a section of the body of your speech details the solution, such as:

III. A successful solution to the problem has several components.

    A. It includes efforts to eliminate the root causes of crime.

    B. It includes more effective means to investigate crime.

    C. It includes making the justice system more efficient and more effective.

    D. It includes stiffer penalties for the most serious offenders.

Argue for the Solution

The final step in the problem-solution speech is to convince listeners that your solution really works—that it resolves the problem, is feasible, and produces benefits that outweigh its costs. Speakers too often neglect this final step, as though the value of the solution were self-evident. But if that were so, the solution would probably have been tried already!

Instead of taking the value of your solution for granted, give listeners reasons to believe that your solution is the best option. In the crime example this final section of the body of your speech might be organized in the following way:

IV. The comprehensive solution I have proposed is the best way to deal with crime.

    A. It will stop crime at the source when possible.

    B. It will deter crime when possible.

    C. It will keep criminals off the streets.

    D. It will cause the public to feel safer and more secure.

From this example you can see that the basic problem-solution organizational pattern adapts easily to persuasive speeches. Although each step of the structure includes informative elements, the principal purpose of the speech is to affect the audience's beliefs, attitudes, values, or actions.

OTHER GOALS FOR PERSUASIVE SPEECHES

Persuasive strategies sometimes are used to achieve more specific goals. Some speeches seek mainly to strengthen the audience's conviction. Others seek conversion (to weaken commitment to one belief and to lead listeners to another). Still others are speeches of refutation that dispute the ideas someone else has advanced or that respond to someone else's criticism of your ideas. These variations on the problem-solution speech are described next.

Strengthening Conviction

Speakers often address audiences that already agree with them. Why, then, do listeners need to be persuaded?

Suppose that you believe your school should hire more faculty to teach undergraduate courses, even if that means an increase in tuition. Since most students dislike tuition increases, objections from your classmates could outweigh support for more faculty. A speaker who favors hiring more faculty would know that the agreement of people like you is essential and would want to strengthen your conviction as well as insulate you from the possibility of conversion. The body of this speaker's outline might look like this:

I. A tuition increase would benefit undergraduate education.

   A. It would make it possible to hire more faculty.

   B. It would enable the university to offer more small classes and seminars.

   C. These, in turn, would enrich faculty-student interaction.

II. The risks of a tuition increase are slight.

   A. The size of the increase would be modest.

   B. Financial aid would be increased along with tuition.

   C. After a slight initial decline, applications for admission would increase in response to the improved faculty.

You may have been vaguely familiar with these arguments, but you had not considered them carefully. Therefore, the speaker succeeds in *strengthening your conviction* that the benefits of additional faculty are worth the cost of tuition increases.

Is this really a form of persuasion? Yes, because your attitude about the subject differs after the speech as a direct result of the speech. The speaker has influenced you to believe more strongly about the subject than you did before. Strengthening conviction is a very common approach to persuasion because it takes advantage of people's tendency to seek out and accept messages with which they already agree.

Following are several common ways by which speakers try to strengthen listeners' convictions.

CONSCIOUSNESS RAISING   You undoubtedly have beliefs or values that you are barely aware of because you take them for granted. Only when you deliberately focus attention on those values will you acknowledge and reaffirm support for them. For example, people often don't realize how important families and loved ones are until they are separated from them or someone becomes ill.

In the 1970s the emerging women's movement used the term **consciousness raising** to refer to the process of making people aware of values and commitments that they had taken for granted.[7] This process recently has become popular with the acknowledgment of sexual harassment in the workplace. Prior to this movement toward public awareness, many people believed that sexual harassment was wrong, but they were not aware of how this conviction applied to everyday occurrences at work. By bringing such values to the surface and applying them to a specific situation, a speaker

consciousness raising

Making people aware of values and commitments that they previously took for granted.

can cause listeners to identify with them consciously, thereby strengthening their convictions.

MOVING FROM EDUCATION TO COMMITMENT   Informative strategies might provide listeners the background that they need to understand an issue. For example, listeners need to be informed of the workings of the Electoral College to recognize the risk that it will not necessarily select as president of the United States the candidate favored by the voters. A persuasive speech would go further, building on listeners' new intellectual awareness of that risk and seeking to convince them that the issue is serious and should be addressed. The speaker's goal might be to convince listeners to support a Constitutional amendment that abolishes the Electoral College or maybe even to lobby for passage of such an amendment.

INCREASING THE SENSE OF URGENCY   Political campaign managers face the difficult problem of convincing a candidate's supporters that their ongoing support really matters. Tracy Baxter saw the need to fire up supporters when she was managing a political campaign for her neighbor, Martha Scott, who was running for the city council. Martha was well known in the neighborhood for such projects as increasing crime patrols, beautifying parks, and encouraging parents to volunteer at their child's school. She seemed certain to win the election—and that's what troubled Tracy. She was worried that Martha's supporters might think their efforts weren't needed and wouldn't bother to contribute to the campaign or even to vote. If enough people felt that way, Martha could lose the election. So Tracy addressed a rally of Martha's supporters, stressing that the race could go either way and that their efforts, money, and votes were essential to victory.

Tracy was worried that a **self-fulfilling prophecy** might derail Martha's campaign. If supporters believed that their efforts weren't needed and thus didn't contribute, the campaign wouldn't have the resources to advertise and mobilize voters; then, if Martha were defeated, supporters would conclude that they were right not to waste their money and time. To break this circular, self-fulfilling reasoning, Tracy needed to establish a sense of urgency among listeners. At the same time, she didn't want to overstate the situation because that might produce the boomerang effect. Instead, she convinced listeners that each person's action would make a real difference in averting defeat and ensuring victory. Her speech carefully balanced how serious the problem was and how easily listeners could be effective in solving it.

In such situations, speakers typically argue that (1) the issue is important, (2) it could be decided either way, (3) it will be decided soon, and (4) the listener's action could tip the scales. Properly crafted, such a message will jolt listeners out of complacency and intensify their commitment to the cause.

Conversion

Far more difficult than strengthening a conviction is *changing* it. Speakers who attempt **conversion** aim to alter listeners' beliefs, either by convincing them to accept something they had previously rejected or to reject something they had previously accepted.

Because people defend themselves against persuasion, no speaker is likely to achieve conversion through a single speech, unless listeners' opinions about

self-fulfilling prophecy
A prediction that comes true because of actions that people take upon hearing the prediction.

conversion
Abandoning one belief or value and replacing it with another.

Checklist

14.1 *Steps in Conversion*

1. **Chip away at the edges of beliefs.**

2. **Identify a pattern of anomalies.**

3. **Employ consciousness raising.**

4. **Seek incremental changes.**

the subject are not deeply held. Few if any speaking situations are like the old-time religious revivals in which the emotion of the situation and the magic of the preacher's words caused listeners to feel in a flash the seriousness of their situation and the need for reform.

How, then, can conversion ever take place? People do change their minds, do abandon positions that they have held and replace them with others. Typically, a speaker attempts conversion through the following steps:

1. CHIP AWAY AT THE EDGES OF BELIEFS Rather than attacking beliefs head-on, where they are most strongly defended, work first on the periphery. During the civil rights movement of the 1950s and early 1960s, for example, many resistant Southerners who did not abandon racial prejudice were nonetheless convinced by marches and demonstrations that inhumane treatment of blacks was wrong. That was often the first step toward conversion because it aroused sympathy for the demonstrators and led listeners to examine whether other aspects of the treatment of blacks were also wrong.

One effective way to chip away at the edges of beliefs is to defend a value that initially coexists with the value you want to challenge but that eventually will undermine it. Again the civil rights movement furnishes an example. Many who believed in racial segregation also revered the Constitution. These two values could coexist as long as the Constitution was not seen as prohibiting segregation; indeed, many opposed integration based on the belief that it violated the Constitution. When laws and court rulings indicated that it was segregation that was unconstitutional, President Lyndon Johnson appealed to many Southerners not so much by discrediting racial prejudice (although he attempted that as well) but by appealing instead to reverence for the Constitution. Suddenly, the two values were in opposition, and one was used to undermine the other.

2. IDENTIFY A PATTERN OF ANOMALIES People change beliefs when their old beliefs no longer explain things adequately. *Anomalies* are puzzling situations that an explanation does not fit. When we first discover them, we tend to dismiss them as freak coincidences or point to them as exceptions to the rule. But if anomalies continue, and especially if they intensify, they eventually call a position into question. Then the old view may collapse of its own weight, and the listener might convert to a new belief.

Such a pattern has been used to explain why many Democrats during the 1980s converted to support Republican Ronald Reagan. Believing in the effectiveness of government programs, they watched through the 1960s and 1970s as those programs grew; yet, in their view, social problems worsened rather than improving. At first this was just a puzzle for them. But as evidence (and their taxes) continued to mount, they eventually came to believe that government was not a solution to social ills but was itself part of the problem. This, of course, was the position advocated by President Reagan.

3. EMPLOY CONSCIOUSNESS RAISING   Besides being a means of strengthening convictions, consciousness raising can be used when a speaker wants the audience to change. Let's look again at the example of the women's movement. Early advocates of consciousness raising maintained that women had accepted their subordinate role because they had never regarded their role as subordinate. By raising women's consciousness about the dominant/submissive pattern in many of their existing relationships with men, advocates were able not only to sensitize them to their situation but also to evoke an alternative toward which they might strive.

In another example, student speaker Laura Davisson gave a speech to raise listeners' consciousness about their daily acts of discrimination against overweight people:

> You might just laugh at them behind their backs. Perhaps you call them names like "whale" or "pig." Maybe they are the butt of your jokes. Or maybe it's something much more subtle than that. Maybe you just assume that fat people have no self-control, that they eat too much and too often, or that they get no exercise.

By pointing out the existence of listeners' discriminatory feelings and actions, Laura was able to begin altering them. Consciousness raising made listeners sufficiently uncomfortable with their own actions that they could be induced to change.

4. SEEK INCREMENTAL CHANGES   Usually, conversion comes about slowly, in a series of small and gradual steps. Knowing that people typically change their views incrementally rather than radically, keep your goals modest. Don't ask for too much too soon.

Imagine, for example, that your goal is to defend public funding for the arts, even though you know that the audience is hostile to it, considers most contemporary art unnecessary or even perverse, and sees public funding as a waste of tax money. Successful persuasion will probably require several steps, beginning with asking the audience to acknowledge the importance of art both in fostering self-expression and advancing culture; then perhaps moving to the position that one need not like or support all examples of art to believe strongly in the value of the arts; then explaining why it is in the public interest to support art; then defending the overall administration of public funding programs and establishing that errors and mistaken judgments are few; and only then moving to the question of whether the government should reduce funding for the arts. Getting to this point might require several speeches, over a long period of time. But a frontal assault on the audience's values is likely to fail, whereas a gradual, incremental approach has at least a chance of success. People often accept in small doses a belief that they would reject outright if it were presented all at once.

Refutation

In addition to persuasive speeches that seek either to strengthen or to change convictions, **refutation** is a type of speech that tries to disprove or dispute the arguments or appeals made by others. This strategy is defensive

refutation
The attack and defense of a challenged statement or claim.

Checklist

in that it seeks to prevent listeners from being persuaded by someone else. Of course, if you convince them not to be persuaded by someone else, you have actually persuaded them yourself.[8]

GROUNDS FOR REFUTATION   Before you can refute an argument or appeal, you first need to be sure that you understand what it says. This is where the tests of reasoning that were offered in Chapter 6 are important. Once you have decided that the other person's argument is weak and should be refuted, you can use either or both of the following strategies.

1. *Object to the claim itself, and develop a contrary claim.* This form of refutation does not target the internal workings of the argument; instead, it suggests that the conclusion is mistaken and offers an alternative conclusion. For example, on hearing a speaker maintain that abortion should be restricted, you decide to refute the speaker by presenting your own arguments that restrictions should not be established. Your arguments are independent of the other speaker's. You develop them not by analyzing the internal workings of the speaker's argument but through your own careful and independent thought.

2. *Object to the speaker's inferences, and thereby refuse to accept the conclusion.* In this case you analyze the internal workings of the other person's argument, applying the same tests of reasoning (see Chapter 6) that you used in developing your own speech. If the speaker employs hasty generalization, confuses cause with sign, develops a faulty analogy, or commits any other error in reasoning, the conclusion may well be faulty even if supporting evidence is true. You will want to point out these deficiencies in reasoning if your goal is refutation.

DEVELOPING THE MESSAGE   Whether you want to refute a particular argument or an entire speech, the basic steps in developing your message are similar. You must specify what you are refuting, make your refutation convincing, and explain to listeners what the refutation has accomplished. To achieve these goals, the following steps are recommended.

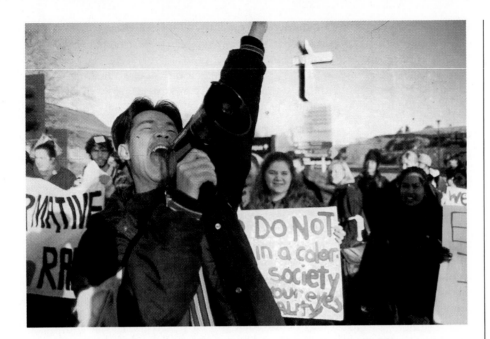

Refuting an opposing argument requires calling its claims into question and advancing your own.

1. Identify the position to be attacked. State the position as clearly and as fairly as you can. It is especially important to state the position in a way that its supporters would accept. Advocates who fail to do this usually end up speaking past each other rather than truly refuting each other's positions.

For example, if you opposed abortion and began to refute a pro-choice speech by stating, "Pro-choice speakers support the killing of innocent babies," you would not be stating the position fairly. You may regard the fetus as an innocent baby, but pro-choice supporters do not. In fact, that is probably the essential difference between those who support and those who oppose abortion. A fairer statement of the position might be, "Pro-choice supporters don't think the fetus is a human being, but I believe we must assume that it is."

Student speaker Bruno Campos very effectively identified the position he wanted to attack in a speech refuting President Bush's justification of the Persian Gulf War in 1990–1991. Taking the very words that Bush used to support his decision to send troops to Kuwait, Bruno created a visual aid: a chart listing the President's justifications for the war. Then, step by step, he responded to each item, crossing it off the list as he refuted it. When he finished the speech, nothing was left on the chart.

2. Explain the significance of the position you are attacking. This often-omitted step lets the audience know why your refutation is important. Most people dislike hearing disagreement for disagreement's sake. If your refutation can be granted and yet do no real damage to the opponent's position, then listeners will probably not take your speech seriously.

Consider the abortion example again, but this time imagine that the speaker is pro-choice and is refuting the statement that protesters stayed ten yards away from the entrance to an abortion clinic, instead insisting that they were within five yards of it. In this case, the refutation is probably not very important; it is hard to imagine why the difference between five and ten yards would matter. But suppose that the speaker were to say, "Pro-life supporters violated a local ordinance by entering the ten-yard radius and blocking the entrance to an abortion clinic," and then went on to explain, "This is important because the law was designed to balance the rights of protesters with the rights of women seeking abortions. If the ten-yard rule is too difficult to maintain, then it should be changed by the City Council, not by protesters." Now the speaker has both identified the argument to be refuted and explained why the refutation matters.

3. Present and develop the attack. State your position, and support it with appropriate materials. This step will probably take the most time. The process is basically the same as if you were developing a constructive position of your own. Pay special attention to the tests of evidence (Chapter 5) and reasoning (Chapter 6).

4. Explain the impact of the refutation. Having presented and supported your own claim, do not assume that the significance of your achievement is self-evident. Include a sentence or two to explain exactly what your refutation has accomplished. If you are refuting the argument that all students should have parking privileges on campus, and you show that there are not enough parking spaces to go around and that the cost of building additional space is prohibitive, you may believe that you have been very clear about what you've accomplished. But the audience often still needs help. It will not hurt to draw the argument together by saying, "So this proposal is infeasible with the current supply of parking spaces, and creating more spaces is out of the question. Even though the proposal appeals to your desire for parking privileges, therefore, you ought not to be swayed by it." Recognize that listeners will attend to the speech with different degrees of intensity, and provide a clear statement of what your refutation has accomplished.

REBUILDING ARGUMENTS   Refutation is not solely a process of criticizing arguments; it is also a means of rebuilding an argument that has been attacked. You can rebuild an argument by responding to criticism against it—either by showing that the attack was flawed or by developing independent reasons for the audience to believe the original claim.

If your thesis were "Many people have argued that space limitations make it infeasible to guarantee parking to all students, but I wish to defend the guaranteed-parking proposal against these attacks," your analytical process would be exactly the same as if you were developing the refutation. Both attack and defense therefore come under the heading of refutation, and both should be seen as basically alike in analysis and composition.

ORGANIZING FOR PERSUASION

Some writers describe persuasion as though it were a series of steps performed in a specific sequence. For example, social psychologist William J. McGuire holds that a person's attitudes are changed in a six-step process: receiving a communication, paying attention to it, comprehending it, yielding to it, retaining the new attitude, and performing the desired behavior.[9] Even if these steps are not always separate and do not always come in the same order, McGuire's scheme is useful for understanding what happens when someone is persuaded.

APPLYING STRATEGIES

Critique of a Persuasive Speech

Excerpts from T. J.'s Persuasive Speech on the Increase in Divorce Rates

"If you go to a panel discussion in Washington, D.C. on 'Reframing Family Values,' do not expect much attention to either family or values. Instead you will be flooded with charts and graphs about heads of household and income distribution. . . . behavior and values have nothing to do with the crisis of the American family. Everything is economic. If the awkward term 'family values' comes up, it will be discussed gingerly as some sort of mysterious optional product that some households have while others do not. Then back to the charts." This quotation was taken from the U.S. News and World Report in an article titled "Where Marriage Is A Scary Word," by John Leo.

Dropping out of school, poor reading, spelling and mathematical skills, emotional, behavioral problems, anxiety, aggressiveness, crime and even suicide are only some of the tendencies that are heightened in children who are affected by divorced families. All too often the adult quest for freedom, independence and choice in family relationships conflicts with the child's developmental need for stability, constancy, harmony and performance in family life. Family disruption creates a deep division between parents' interests and the interests of children, according to Barbara Defoe Whitehead in "Dan Quayle Was Right," in The Atlantic.

With the divorce rate steadily climbing and aided by new no-fault divorce laws in our country, many children are being raised without the advantage of an intact family.

Although intact families are not without their problems, evidence shows that two-parent families are preferable to the alternatives of single or step-parent families. Today, I'd like to heighten your awareness of the problem of divorce and its effects on children by showing you the immediate challenges that children face due to divorce, the solutions our country needs, and what we can do as individuals to help prevent this problem.

Dr. Marrow's Comments

Help me, T. J., I'm starting to yawn. Wake me up with a revised introduction. How about a rhetorical question like, "How are children affected by divorce?" Then answer it with information from your second quotation by Whitehead (Dropping out of school, poor reading, emotional problems, etc.). This is more attention-grabbing, as many of us in this classroom aren't likely to attend a D.C. conference, but we are likely to know about children of divorce. We'll be pulled into your topic right away. As you proceed with Monroe's Motivated Sequence, use your Leo quotation on "Reframing Family Values" in the Need Step. It will work better there instead of in the Attention Step in your introduction.

You state "although intact families are not without their problems, evidence shows that two-parent families are preferable to the alternatives of single-parent or stepfamilies." That's a provocative comment, T. J., that needs some support—where is the evidence? Your credibility is on the line. Also, don't you want to do more in a persuasive speech than "heighten our awareness"? Perhaps add "an action plan to consider." Now we're ready to be persuaded.

The Motivated Sequence

A sequential scheme for achieving persuasion in a speech was developed many years ago by Alan H. Monroe.[10] His **motivated sequence** is similar to the problem-solution speech, but instead of being organized with reference to the specific subject—health care or crime, for instance—it is organized in terms of the audience's motivation. The sequence has five steps and includes the introduction and conclusion of the speech as well as the body:

I. Attention step   Introduction

II. Need step

III. Satisfaction step   }   Body

IV. Visualization step

V. Action step   Conclusion

INTRODUCTION   The *attention step,* as its name suggests, is intended to engage listeners' attention. It serves as the introduction to the speech and includes such appropriate devices as visual narratives, engaging anecdotes, and startling statistics.

BODY   The *need step* is intended to convince the audience that something is amiss. The goal is to arouse listeners to believe that an important value is being lost, an opportunity is being wasted, or an objective is not being met. This belief will motivate them to take corrective action if they know what to do.

The *satisfaction step* provides listeners with the means to fulfill the motivation that the need step aroused. People seldom respond to broad and abstract generalizations, however, and so slogans like "Stimulate the economy" or "Get tough on illegal immigration" are unlikely to satisfy listeners. To avoid this problem, the speaker goes on to explain how the solution will work and how it will affect listeners personally.

The *visualization step* gives the audience a mental picture of the solution. Instead of saying, "Stimulate the economy," the speaker shows what the solution will mean: "Putting an extra $1,000 saved from taxes into the hands of the average family will make it easier for them to buy the things they need. Increased demand for those products will create millions of new jobs, so that even more people will be better off."

CONCLUSION   The final step in the motivated sequence is the *action step,* in which the speaker asks the audience to do specific things to bring about the solution that they have visualized: change your personal behavior, sign a petition, patronize some stores but not others, write to senators and representatives, make a donation, and so on. The action step resembles the final plea that is one of the traditional functions of the conclusion of a speech.

Using the Motivated Sequence

The earlier outline for the problem-solution speech about crime might be organized into the motivated sequence as follows:

I. Attention step

    A. Description of recent crime on campus.

    B. Statistics suggesting a dramatic increase in crime in recent years.

    C. Translation of these statistics into the odds that someone you know will be the victim of crime.

motivated sequence

A persuasive message that is organized in terms of steps in the audience's motivation rather than in terms of the specific subject.

II. Need step

    A. Crime undermines personal security and safety.

    B. Crime undermines your ability to control your life.

    C. Crime undermines your sense of justice.

    D. Crime weakens the fabric of society.

III. Satisfaction step

    A. Use technology to develop better databases about criminals.

    B. Increase the number of police officers on the street.

    C. Enact laws to compensate victims of crime.

    D. Increase penalties for the most serious offenders.

IV. Visualization step

    A. You will be able to walk safely at night on campus.

    B. You won't have to alter your schedule or routine because of fear of crime.

    C. You'll be able to trust other people more.

    D. You'll have support for your beliefs about what is right and wrong.

V. Action step

    A. Urge your public officials to support the crime legislation now before Congress.

    B. Urge five other people to write letters doing the same.

The criticisms that were raised against McGuire's theory of persuasion also apply to the motivated sequence. First, these steps are not always completely separate. It's possible, for example, that visualizing a solution is what alters the perception of a need. Second, not all listeners experience the steps in precisely the same order. Someone might be attracted to the satisfaction step, for example, without having grasped the full dimensions of the need. But even if the motivated sequence is not a universal account of human motivation, it still can provide a clear, coherent, and compelling way to organize speeches when the goal is persuasion.

Summary

Persuasive strategies aim not only to provide information but also to affect audience members' attitudes and behavior. They ask for a greater degree of commitment from listeners than informative strategies do, although no speaker can manipulate an unwilling audience. Listeners are often resistant to persuasion and may dispose of the message by denying it, by believing that it doesn't apply to them, or by belittling the source. They may compartmentalize the message in their minds so that it affects beliefs without affecting values or behavior. Or they may respond with a boomerang effect, becoming so upset by the persuasive message that they believe or do the opposite of what the speaker recommends.

Speakers, of course, have strategies to combat audience resistance. They need to understand that listeners must be motivated, must comprehend and agree with the message, and must incorporate the message into their overall system of beliefs and attitudes. To attain these results, speakers draw on their ability to analyze the audience and the situation, on their own credibility, and on the effective use of evidence, reasoning, and emotional appeals.

In using their resources, speakers first determine the target audience that they are trying to influence, which may not be identical to the sum of people who hear the message. They try to achieve identification by establishing common bonds with the audience. They may call upon listeners to be true to their own beliefs. They try to give listeners a sense of trust that they then can draw upon to support their message, which should reflect an appropriate organizational plan and include appropriate supporting materials. Finally, speakers should provide opportunities for listeners not only to say that they agree but also to perform some action.

The most common type of speech based on persuasive strategies is the problem-solution speech, which (1) describes a situation, (2) evaluates it as a problem, (3) proposes a solution, and (4) argues for the solution. The problem-solution speech may achieve one or more of the specific purposes that persuasive strategies advance.

Three general categories of messages are variations on the problem-solution speech and seek to achieve more specific goals. Some messages *strengthen convictions* by moving from education to commitment, from subconscious to conscious values, or from belief to action. When listeners' beliefs are strengthened, they move farther—in the same direction they currently are moving—on a scale of commitment. Speakers seeking *conversion* ask listeners to abandon one set of beliefs and to adopt another. Rarely can this be achieved in a single speech, but speakers attempt it by consciousness raising, by developing a pattern of anomalies, and by incremental appeals. Finally, messages of *refutation* try to prevent listeners from being persuaded by someone else. Refutation can be directed either at a position's conclusions or at its inferences. Although refutation is often described as an approach for attacking arguments, it is also used to rebuild them.

The motivated sequence offers another way to organize persuasive appeals. Similar to the problem-solution speech, it is organized for the purpose of arousing and then satisfying the audience's motivation. Including the introduction and conclusion, the message has five key parts: the attention step, need step, satisfaction step, visualization step, and action step.

Discussion Questions

1. What are the most urgent issues of controversy in the public forum of your classroom? List debate topics that most interest your community and your generation. Which of those topics would be good for a persuasive speech that:

   Strengthens commitment
   Weakens commitment
   Converts opponents
   Calls for a specific action

2. When a speaker has strong beliefs about a controversial issue, how can that speaker achieve identification with an opponent without compromising his or her own beliefs? What common bonds might

be established between the opposing sides on the following controversial topics?

Abortion
The death penalty
Affirmative action

How could a speaker use those common bonds as an aid to persuasion?

3. In what ways do persuasive strategies differ for the various speech purposes? As a class, create a chart that describes what you think would be likely differences in organization, choice of supporting material, and style for the following persuasive goals.

	Organization	Supporting Material	Style
Strengthening commitment			
Weakening commitment			
Conversion			
Inducing a specific action			

Activities

1. Identify a topic and develop a thesis statement for each of the persuasive goals in the chart above. In a sentence or two, explain why you think each of these would be a good topic and thesis statement for a speech aimed at your target audience.

2. Choose one of your thesis statements from Activity 1, and develop a persuasive speech. In a short essay, explain how you intend to motivate your audience. To which values do you plan to appeal?

3. From an opponent's perspective, examine the issue that you have chosen for your persuasive speech. Honestly try to step into the shoes of someone who disagrees with and might refute you.

   a. Which argument is most important for your opponent?
   b. What concerns would your opponent have if your position is argued successfully?
   c. How will your opponent view the supporting material that you plan to use in your speech?

4. Watch a debate. It can be a campaign debate, an academic debate, or a debate between two friends. In a short essay, answer the following questions about each speaker:

   a. Did the speaker fairly identify the opponent's position?
   b. Did the speaker refute the claims or the inferences being made by the other side?
   c. Did the speaker explain the significance of the position being attacked?
   d. Did the speaker explain the impact of the refutation?
   e. Who do you think won the debate, and why?

Using the Internet

1. **How persuasive were the Bradys?** At the 1996 Democratic Party Convention in Chicago, Sarah and Jim Brady spoke to the delegates in convention and to a national audience on television about gun control.

    Point your browser to <http://www.pbs.org/newshour/convention96/floor_speeches /brady.html>. After reading and/or listening to the speech, analyze how strategies of persuasion were used.

    -   *What seemed to be the specific persuasive goal of the speech?*

        To strengthen or weaken convictions?

        To convert opponents?

        To call for an action?

    -   *How well did Sarah and Jim Brady analyze their audience and the situation to adjust to these constraints?*

        Did they create identification with the audience?

        Did they call on the audience members to be true to their own beliefs?

        Did they create trust?

    -   *Were they effective in using evidence and reasoning?*

    -   *Did they effectively appeal to the audience members' emotions?*

2. **Take a side in the debate over whether tobacco companies bear responsibility for illnesses associated with smoking.** Point your browser to a debate on the BBC at <http://news.bbc.co.uk/hi/english/talking_point/newsid_50000/50727.asp/>. Which side presented a more persuasive case? Why?

3. **Resistance to persuasion.** How might audience members be unwilling to be persuaded by Jeff Jacobs, Director of Government Affairs for the AIDS Action Council, testifying before a subcommittee of the House Committee on Appropriations?

    Point your browser to <http://www.aidsaction.org/jefftest.html> to read Jacobs' statement. Then consider whether some audience members might be likely to dispose of the message by denying it, by believing that it does not apply to them, by belittling the source, by compartmentalizing their beliefs without affecting their values or behavior, or by responding with the boomerang effect.

Notes

1. A. H. Maslow, "A Dynamic Theory of Personality," *Psychological Review* 50 (July 1943): 370–396.
2. See John C. Reinard, "The Empirical Study of the Persuasive Effects of Evidence: The Status after Fifty Years of Research," *Human Communication Research* 15 (Fall 1988): 3–59.
3. See Kenneth Burke, *A Rhetoric of Motives,* New York: Prentice-Hall, 1950. For a discussion of Burke's theory of identification, see Dennis G. Day, "Persuasion and the Concept of Identification," *Quarterly Journal of Speech* 46 (October 1960): 270–273.

4. A review of the psychological literature about persuasion further explains the resistances discussed in this chapter. See Chester A. Insko, *Theories of Attitude Change,* New York: Appleton-Century-Crofts, 1967.

5. For more discussion of persuasive strategies, see Herbert W. Simons, *Persuasion: Understanding, Practice, and Analysis,* Reading, Mass.: Addison-Wesley, 1976.

6. A message that first arouses a need and then attempts to satisfy that need is more persuasive than a message organized in the reverse order. See Arthur R. Cohen, "Need for Cognition and Order of Communication as Determinants of Opinion Change," *The Order of Presentation in Persuasion,* New Haven, Conn.: Yale University Press, 1966, 79–97.

7. Consciousness raising often occurred in group discussions but could also be the result of a more formal speech. See Anita Shreve, *Women Together, Women Alone: The Legacy of the Consciousness-Raising Movement,* New York: Viking Press, 1989.

8. Research has shown that messages which provide both arguments for a position and refutation of the opposition are more persuasive than messages that simply present arguments for a position. Mike Allen, Jerold Hale, Paul Mongeau, et al., "Testing a Model of Message Sidedness: Three Replications," *Communication Monographs* 57 (December 1990): 275–291.

9. William J. McGuire, "Personality and Attitude Change: An Information-Processing Approach." In A. G. Greenwald, T. C. Brock, and T. M. Ostrom, ed., *Psychological Foundations of Attitudes,* Orlando: Atlantic Press, 1968, 171–196.

10. Alan H. Monroe, *Principles and Types of Speech,* Glenview, Ill.: Scott Foresman, 1935. The book has had multiple editions with various authors. In the most recent edition, the lead author is Bruce E. Gronbeck.

chapter 15
Occasions for Public Speaking

In This Chapter We Will:

- Explore how the nature of the speaking occasion influences the speech.

- Understand what expectations are raised for a speech by the concept of decorum, or "fittingness to the occasion."

- Identify the differences between deliberative and ceremonial speaking occasions.

- Examine various specific kinds of deliberative and ceremonial speaking.

I n preparing classroom speeches, you probably have been careful to follow specific instructions. If the assignment was to demonstrate a process, you made certain that your speech did that. If you were supposed to include three different types of supporting material, you probably paid extra attention to that aspect of preparation. And if the speech could not be longer than eight minutes, you most likely worked carefully with your outlines to be sure that you could cover the topic in that time.

FITTING YOUR SPEECH TO THE OCCASION

Although the requirements of an assignment may sometimes seem arbitrary, they help you to focus on your goals for a speech, and they make the point that all speeches—whether inside or outside the classroom—are given in specific situations. Strategies of informing and persuading are selected and combined so that you and your listeners will have the greatest chance of achieving your goals in a particular situation. (Although we have not focused specifically on them, the same is true of strategies of entertaining.) Now that you have mastered the general tools for constructing and presenting effective speeches, you are ready to explore some of these specific situations in which they take place.

What's needed in one situation is different from what's needed in another. Just as an hour-long lecture is out of place when an eight-minute speech is expected, so is self-congratulation inappropriate in a speech to accept an award. On the other hand, just as including variety of supporting material makes a persuasive speech effective, so does well-intentioned humor play an enhancing role in a "roast."

Influence of the Occasion

So far we have examined the *speech,* the *speaker,* and the *audience,* as well as the relationships among them. It is time to consider the final dimension of any rhetorical situation—the *occasion.* We begin with three premises:

1. SPEECHES ARE PRESENTED FOR SPECIFIC OCCASIONS   At its best, literature is meaningful regardless of the circumstances in which it is written or read. Speeches, however, achieve their power by responding effectively to a particular occasion.

Even an occasion that is as formal and well-defined as a president's State of the Union address can be influenced by specific circumstances. President Reagan's, for example, responded to special circumstances that the nation faced in 1986. His State of the Union address would have been his first televised speech since the astronauts died in the *Challenger* explosion, so he changed the address into a tribute that reflected the occasion. Had he ignored the circumstances and delivered his original State of the Union address, that response would have been far less appropriate. Similarly, in 1998 President Clinton believed that the occasion called for statesmanship, and he delivered his State of the Union address without commenting on allegations that he was involved in a personal scandal. Although the two presidents had the same "assignment," their responses were quite different. Yet both were appropriate to the occasion.

Some speeches—such as Lincoln's Gettysburg Address and Martin Luther King's "I Have a Dream"—resonate with great force and power long after delivery, largely because they both responded to the specific occasion and also made that response more universal.

2. OCCASIONS CREATE CONSTRAINTS   Certain expectations arise on any occasion. If you attend a commencement speech, for instance, you expect that it will do certain things and not others. Undoubtedly it will pose some challenge for the graduates; most likely it will not criticize their parents and families. At a funeral or memorial service, you expect speakers to talk about the noble character of the deceased and to recall significant events in the person's life; you do not expect anyone to urge the audience to see an important new movie.

Experienced speakers sometimes choose deliberately to violate the audience's expectations. For example, in a series of speeches thanking teachers and parents, one speaker might choose to be humorous to set the speech apart from the others and to entertain the audience. Deliberately violating the expectations of the occasion can sometimes be an effective strategy. But beginning speakers are wise to understand and fit a speech to the expectations of the occasion before seeking to subvert them.

3. CONSTRAINTS ARE NOT ABSOLUTE, HOWEVER   Satisfying the expectations of a particular occasion still leaves the speaker much room for making creative and strategic choices. Not only are there many different ways to meet expectations, but a speech might also go beyond them. In the process it could change listeners' understanding of a situation.

Consider the example of the commencement speech again. Once it has posed a challenge to the graduates, it might proceed to discuss an important issue of public policy. Secretary of State George Marshall used the 1947 Harvard commencement address to announce what became known as the Marshall Plan to rebuild Europe after World War II. President John F. Kennedy used the 1963 American University commencement address to urge Americans to change their attitudes about the Soviet Union. When First Lady Barbara Bush spoke at commencement at Wellesley College in 1990, she used the occasion to focus on life-style choices of women. And it is quite likely that speakers in 2000 and 2001, after proclaiming graduates to be the first of a new century, will proceed to predict its opportunities and challenges.

In each of these examples, the speech not only responded to but also altered the situation. It met the audience's expectations for what they should hear, and yet it transformed those expectations. Each speaker presented a commencement address but also announced or proposed policies, or placed significant public issues on the nation's agenda.

To a greater or lesser degree, we could make the same observation about any speech in any situation. Speakers both respond to and actively shape the rhetorical situation. That is why any occasion for public speaking requires not that you follow a prescribed formula but that you make strategic choices while also recognizing the constraints imposed by the occasion.[1]

The Concept of Decorum

Centuries ago, theorists of public speaking developed the concept of **decorum** to identify "fittingness to the occasion."[2] Decorum implies more than common courtesy. A *decorous* speech is one that conforms to the

decorum
Fittingness or appropriateness to the occasion.

expectations of a particular occasion. As we've just seen, these expectations differ from one occasion to another, but the following variables are important.

FORMALITY   Some occasions are highly formal, such as the inauguration of a president or the keynote address at a conference. These may call for a carefully worded speech delivered from manuscript. Other occasions are informal and call for a conversational delivery, use of familiar maxims, and plain language. Although neither approach is right or wrong in the abstract, either one can be successful or disastrous in the context of a specific situation.

LENGTH   Some occasions call for lengthy remarks; others demand brevity. If your campus organization spends thousands of dollars to present a distinguished guest speaker who talks for only two minutes about the topic and then asks, "Any questions?" the audience will feel cheated. On the other hand, a nomination speech should not go on for more than a few minutes because the speaker would eclipse the nominee.

For most occasions, brevity is preferred. Speeches that are too long challenge the audience's attention, undercut the import of the occasion, and may even expose the speaker to ridicule.

INTENSITY   If you are speaking at a dinner to honor a retiring faculty member, how lavish should your praise be? If you are extravagant, the honoree may be embarrassed, and the audience may not take you seriously. But if your remarks are perfunctory, listeners may think that you don't really know or care about the person.

Determining just how intense to make your remarks is a particularly difficult challenge. As you gain experience in speaking, however, you should develop an almost-intuitive sense of what an occasion calls for.

SUPPORTING MATERIAL   In a speech of introduction, you may decide to highlight an incident from the person's early life to characterize him or her for the audience. As supporting material, that anecdote should truly represent the person. Other occasions call for different types of supporting materials. Formal arguments might be appropriate in congressional testimony, narratives in a speech of tribute, and examples in a pep talk.

IDENTIFICATION   All speakers try to evoke a sense of common bonds among listeners and between the audience and themselves. Sometimes the bonding is explicit, as in a speech that commemorates an important occasion and seeks to draw attention to the community. At other times the bonding is implicit, as when the chair of a meeting summarizes a discussion. To be decorous, a speech also matches expectations about identification.

Considering the factors that we have just reviewed, the most general standard for decorum is the answer to the question: "Does the speech capture the thoughts and emotions appropriate to the occasion?" Every aspect of the speech—selection of materials, arrangement, language, and delivery—should help to express the sentiments which, if they thought about it, listeners would agree were the things that ought to be said on the occasion. This doesn't mean that audience members would necessarily agree with everything the speaker said, but rather that they would agree that the speaker, given his or her standpoint and purpose, selected the right topics and presented them in the right way.

Occasions for Public Speaking

The Value of Public Speaking Throughout Your Life

Laura: Public Speaking is very important and should be used when possible. Practice makes perfect. It can be used almost everywhere. Talking to friends is a form of public speaking. I may use public speaking skills to either teach or get my feelings about adoption out and to talk about why everyone should adopt at least one child, which was the subject of my persuasive speech.

Latif: My opinion is that public speaking is very important for students, and it should be a requirement for graduation for all students. The reason is that every student needs to speak in public regardless of his or her major. At work, you need to speak in meetings or to your boss or CEO. Also, students are considered the future leaders of society, and they need to speak to people in their communities.

Carrie: I feel that public speaking should be a course required in general education. The school that I spent my first two years of college at didn't even have a public speaking class. I feel that this class would benefit everyone. I know it's required for speech majors, recommended for journalism majors, and required for education majors. These professions obviously will use these skills on a day to day basis, but so will every other field. If you are a doctor, dentist, nurse . . . you will be required to communicate effectively with your patients and coworkers. If you are a lawyer, banker, receptionist . . . you will be required to communicate effectively with your clients and coworkers. If you are in sales, retail, food . . . anything, you will be required to work with others and be able to communicate effectively with them. Not just in careers but in everyday life, too. You will need to be able to communicate with your spouse, your children, your children's teachers . . . if you participate in any community functions/clubs, teach Sunday School, etc. Speaking skills always will be beneficial.

T. J.: I think public speaking is an important tool for any student and professional. No matter what field of study you pursue, there will come a time when you will have to interact with other people. Public speaking gives you the skills and confidence that you need to effectively communicate with others or in a group setting.

DELIBERATIVE SPEAKING

The Nature of Deliberative Speaking

In ancient Greece the earliest theorists of public speaking distinguished among three types of occasions: forensic, deliberative, and ceremonial (also called epideictic).[3] **Forensic speaking** occurs in a court of law and is concerned with establishing justice. Because this type of speaking is highly specialized and is largely the province of lawyers, judges, and legal panels, we will not examine forensic speaking here. But both deliberative and ceremonial speaking warrant our close attention. Also, many occasions, including pep talks, political campaigns, commencement speeches, and Inaugural addresses, call for combinations of deliberative and ceremonial speaking. We shall examine some of these situations as well.

Just as the law court is the model setting for forensic discourse, the legislature is the model for where deliberative speaking takes place. Actually, though, it occurs in any formal or informal decision-making group.

• • • • • • • • • • • • • • • • • • • •

forensic speaking
Speaking in a court of law; concerned with establishing justice.

Deliberative speaking deals with the question, "What shall we do?" and often is conducted before a group that has been commissioned to deal with a subject.

Deliberative speaking aims to answer the question "What shall we do?" Its focus is on action, and it occurs when two conditions arise:

1. The answer to "What shall we do?" is not self-evident. Matters are uncertain perhaps because they deal with the future, because they involve questions of value, or because the information needed for certainty is simply not available.

2. A decision is required. Action cannot be deferred until everything is known and the outcome is self-evident. Either that may never occur, or, if it does, it will happen too late.

Many of the examples discussed throughout this book involve deliberative speaking occasions. For instance, suppose you were addressing the topic "How to solve America's health care crisis." The topic itself is oriented to action and implies that you might choose among potential actions or at least review your solution options. Not everything about the topic can be known.

deliberative speaking
Speaking in a decision-making assembly; concerned with matters of expediency; addresses the question "What shall we do?"

Checklist

15.1 *Deliberative Speaking Occasions*

1. **Oral reports and presentations**

2. **Group presentations**
   - *Group reports*
   - *Speaking in small groups*
   - *Chairing a meeting*

3. **Public hearings and debates**
   - *Providing testimony*
   - *Debates*
   - *Responding to questions*

Even if you know how the current health care system works, you obviously will not know the results of untried alternatives. Yet a decision must be made because health costs represent a large and growing share of national expenditures and also increase the federal debt. Needing to make a decision under uncertain conditions, listeners turn to you for help in answering the question "What should we do?"

It should be apparent from this description that deliberative speaking uses the strategies of informing and persuading, which we examined in Chapters 13 and 14. By providing needed information or by giving good reasons to favor one choice over another, a deliberative speech helps the audience to determine what should be done. Following are some of the most common occasions that call for deliberative speaking.

Oral Reports and Presentations

Staff members in businesses and government agencies often have to brief their supervisors about important issues and situations. Such a briefing is simply an oral report in which the staff member identifies the topic or issue and gives background information to help the supervisor reach a decision. Similarly, when you describe a problem facing the company or explain to coworkers how to perform a task, you are presenting an oral report.

You probably have made oral reports in some of your classes in school. Although your purpose might not have been to help someone make a decision about what to do, such reports are much like the oral briefings expected in business and government settings. In preparing an oral report, the organizational pattern that you select is particularly important because you want to present the material in an order that is appropriate and easy to understand. If you are describing a process, for example, you want to be sure to list its specific steps in the right order. If you are proposing a solution, you want to be sure that the problem is explained first. Then, after establishing a clear organizational structure, you want to use effective transitions and signposting to help listeners to follow the speech. For example, you can hold their attention with vivid or unfamiliar details, and by including concise summaries you can tie together the main points.

Laura Winston was the project manager responsible for developing new information systems for her company. She and her staff were experts in handling the technical aspects of databases, networking, and data security, but these systems also were used by managers who did not understand them well. So when Laura was asked to describe a new system at a meeting of company executives, she wisely began with a clear forecast of her speech:

> The company will soon develop a new information system. Let me describe its key features, explain the major differences from the old system, and show you how it will benefit us all. I know that change is sometimes difficult, but once we get used to this new system, I think we'll find it to be a big improvement. So please follow along, and be sure to ask questions if there's something you don't understand.

Laura might have met the expectations for a briefing even without this careful preview. But by including it, she altered the occasion to make it also a time for reassuring her listeners in the face of uncertainty.

Laura's presentation was primarily informative, but sometimes a speech's goal is to be persuasive, not just to present information but to urge decision makers to select your proposal over others. Persuasive presentations are common in the sales environment in that they emphasize how the benefits of your proposal are most in line with the decision makers' values.

For example, if you know that a corporation's decision makers will select the advertising campaign that most appeals to the values of youthfulness and creativity, you will make primary reference to those values in presenting and defending your proposal. If you know that the city council will select the parking plan that makes parking easiest in the downtown area, you will point out that your proposal creates the greatest number of spaces at the lowest cost. And knowing that your professors represent diverse interests, you may want to defend a proposed research paper by pointing out that it will contribute to several different schools of thought. In cases like these, the principles of audience analysis and persuasion that we examined in earlier chapters will be of great help.

Jon Hobbs applied these principles when he was president of New Images, a student group that made films and videos. Appearing at a meeting of the Student Activities Funding Board, which was responsible for allocating all student activity fees, he made a convincing presentation. He emphasized the large number of students involved in New Images, the artistic merit of the group's previous work, the fact that the group had won production awards that brought prestige to the college, and the group's track record in attracting outside donors and staying under budget. These themes matched the values of the funding board, whose members were interested in benefiting large numbers of students, bringing favorable recognition and publicity to the college, and stretching its resources as much as possible. Although several other student organizations left the budget meeting unsatisfied, Jon's effective presentation resulted in full funding for New Images.

Group Presentations

GROUP REPORTS   It is quite common for people to join groups that investigate an issue, propose solutions, and then present the results of their work to others. Group reports are often presented orally, as the starting point for discussion by a larger public audience. For example, a citizens' panel might be asked to propose ways to improve public education in the community. When the group presents its findings for public discussion, one member might talk about curriculum, another might talk about extracurricular programs, another might discuss cultural diversity, another might stress the significance of parental involvement, and yet another might address matters of school finance.

An example of a group report on campus is one that focused on how fraternities and sororities were making the transition to alcohol-free rush as required by their national organizations. The report's purpose was to inform fraternity and sorority members of their responsibilities and options under the new plan. One panelist outlined the new regulations, a second talked about alcohol-free events being organized by her sorority, and a third discussed the values that would lead students to affiliate with fraternities and sororities in the absence of alcohol.

When a group report is presented in this fashion, the occasion is called a **symposium.** As in the example of the citizens' panel, the organizational structure of a symposium is usually topical. All participants in a symposium

symposium

A group presentation in which a subject is organized topically and each speaker addresses a limited portion of the subject.

should understand how the issue has been divided into topics and what will be discussed under each topic heading. That will make them less likely either to repeat each other's points or to omit some important dimension of the issue. Each participant should present only a limited number of main points, being careful that these relate to his or her portion of the larger discussion.

SPEAKING IN SMALL GROUPS   Although this discussion has emphasized formal occasions, people are far more likely to engage in deliberative speaking when they participate in small groups. The task of the group is to reach a decision or to propose a solution to a particular problem, and participants advocate specific suggestions in a collaborative effort to find the best solution.

In the previous example about an alcohol-free rush, the symposium was preceded by group meetings in the individual fraternities and sororities. Members discussed whether they should challenge, ignore, or observe the new regulations. They talked about the benefits and drawbacks of alcohol-free events. And they reflected on whether or not alcohol played any role in their own decisions to join a fraternity or sorority. Some argued that the houses would be at a real disadvantage without alcohol, while others said that they would be better off if their parties were "dry." As the groups worked through these issues, members made speeches advancing ideas and arguments for their point of view. Although their remarks were brief and quite informal, the students made use of the strategies of informing and persuading that we have considered in this book.

By participating in a group, members gain access to the thinking of many other people about the question at hand. They can draw on more information in reaching a decision, and those who participate in problem solving tend to have a better understanding of the issues and to be more committed to the group's solution. On the other hand, a member who has a particularly strong personality may dominate the discussion and influence others to go along unthinkingly. And people sometimes propose more extreme solutions within a group setting because they do not feel personally responsible for the outcome. Be especially alert in a group, and avoid these dangers, sometimes labeled **groupthink.** Make sure that in advocating a position you do not close the door to other possibilities, that you listen as carefully to other people's ideas as you want them to listen to yours, and that you do not urge the group to adopt any course of action that you would not adopt personally. The idea is to take advantage of the assets that a group offers while minimizing the risks.[4]

CHAIRING A MEETING   Deliberative decisions are often made during a meeting, whether small and informal or large and public. Unless the occasion is very informal or spontaneous, someone will act as the **chair,** or presiding officer, of the meeting. This person may be appointed or elected or may simply assume the role by performing its functions. Some of the chair's functions are themselves deliberative in nature, particularly stating the issues, summarizing what group members have said, and identifying the issues to be decided.

Chairing a meeting is an important skill in its own right. **Parliamentary procedure** is a set of rules for a public meeting to ensure that the majority

groupthink
The tendency for groups to approve more extreme solutions than would an individual because no one is personally responsible for the group's decision.

chair
The presiding officer of a meeting.

parliamentary procedure
Rules for the conduct of public meetings.

will reach the most effective decision while protecting the rights of the minority. It involves **motions,** or statements that propose what the group should do. But even in informal meetings the chair has such responsibilities as:[5]

1. Ensuring that the physical space is set up appropriately—that there are enough chairs, that they are arranged in the best pattern for the meeting (circle, theater style, and so on), that lighting is adequate, that noise is controlled, and that the temperature is comfortable.

2. Previewing what will be discussed or decided—the equivalent of preparing an agenda for formal meetings.

3. Stating the issues precisely.

4. Summarizing major points that emerge in discussion and indicating how they are related.

5. Stating clearly what has been decided.

People chair meetings far more often than you might think. You may emerge as the leader of an informal study group that is deciding on the best way to prepare for an examination. You may function as the leader of a current-events discussion group. Or you may be elected or appointed to a leadership position in student government. Experienced public speakers are often selected to chair meetings because their skills of analysis and argument are of great value in these situations as well as at a podium.

RESPONDING TO QUESTIONS   One situation that calls for deliberative speaking does not seem like a prepared speech at all. After you speak, listeners may ask questions. Or, in an informal situation like a campaign rally, they may interrupt your speech to ask questions. Sometimes, as in a press conference, the entire point of speaking is to respond to questions.

Answering questions can be a way to share information. After a speech, you may be asked to explain an idea in greater detail or to develop an interesting point further. Sometimes a questioner will confront you with an alternative or even an opposing view of your topic, and you will have the opportunity to defend your position.

Sometimes questions may not be so straightforward. Skeptics or critics may try to discredit your speech under the guise of asking a question. The classic example is the **loaded question,** one that presupposes an adverse value judgment. The comedian who asks, "Have you stopped beating your wife?" has loaded the question because it can't be answered satisfactorily if taken at face value. Instead, one must identify the shaky premise on which it is based—in this case, that the husband was ever beating his wife in the first place.

Another trick question is one that poses a **false dilemma** by identifying two unacceptable options and assuming that they are the only alternatives. Ellen Williams faced such a question after a speech urging her classmates to spend their vacations in the United States rather than abroad. She had pointed out the many natural wonders and historical sites that many Americans had never seen, and she had argued that domestic tourism could strengthen the U.S. economy and improve the balance of payments. After the speech she was

motion
A statement proposing what an assembly should do.

loaded question
A question that presupposes a value judgment adverse to the speaker's.

false dilemma
Identifying two unacceptable options and assuming that they are the only alternatives.

immediately confronted by another student who asked, "Well, Ellen, if you don't support foreign travel, are you saying that we should all be ignorant of the rest of the world?" Obviously, these are not the only alternatives available, and a speaker should identify the false dilemma rather than being trapped by attempting to answer such a question.

If a listener asks multiple questions or a complex question that requires multiple answers, it is usually wise to divide the question and respond to its parts separately. Doing so will keep your organizational structure clear and make it easy for listeners to follow you. Sometimes humor or even obvious evasion can deflect an inappropriate question without antagonizing the audience. One lecturer, after speaking about changes in political campaigns over the years, was asked, "Did you vote for Clinton or Dole in 1996?" Believing that his personal political choices were irrelevant to the discussion but not wanting to offend the questioner, he answered, "Yes." Chuckles from audience members signaled their recognition that the speaker had answered the literal question but chose not to provide the information the questioner sought. Since the speaker smiled and obviously was in good humor, listeners interpreted his response to mean that the question was inappropriate rather than that the lecturer was evasive.

Although no speaker can anticipate every possible question, it's a good idea in preparing a speech to think about what listeners may ask. Try particularly to imagine questions that will challenge your position, and be ready to answer those. People who hold press conferences often prepare in advance by asking others to act as hostile questioners; then they rehearse the answers they plan to give. Thinking about possible questions will allow you to plan your answers mentally and to select among different ways of responding.

During the question-and-answer session itself, remember that you are both answering questions and giving listeners more evidence of your ethos. If you become defensive, they may decide that you are not really confident about what you said in the speech. If you become aggressive or hostile, they may conclude that you are not being fair to your questioner. If you take advantage of a vague or unclear question, you may seem to be playing a game rather than being genuinely committed to your topic. As a general rule, use question-and-answer periods to enhance your image as being fair, genuinely interested in your subject, and committed to the goals of sharing information and making intelligent decisions.

CEREMONIAL SPEAKING

The third type of speaking occasion identified by ancient theorists was called **epideictic** (ep-uh-DIKE-tik), but **ceremonial** is probably a more meaningful synonym. Epideictic speeches are delivered at ceremonial occasions. Speeches of tribute at a retirement dinner, speeches introducing a distinguished guest, speeches upon receiving an award, and speeches commemorating a significant event are all examples of ceremonial speaking.

Although ceremonial speeches have informative and persuasive elements, their basic purpose is different from deliberative speeches. Instead of sharing in-

epideictic
Ceremonial.

ceremonial speaking
Speaking at ceremonial occasions that reaffirm a community's common bonds and values, strengthening ties between individuals and the group.

Checklist

15.2 *Ceremonial Speaking Occasions*

1. **Speeches of greeting**
   - *Introductions*
   - *Speeches of welcome*
2. **Speeches of tribute**
   - *Testimonials*
   - *Eulogies*

   - *Toasts*
   - *Roasts*
3. **Speeches marking awards**
   - *Presentation speeches*
   - *Acceptance speeches*

formation and guiding decisions, ceremonial speeches strengthen the bonds between speaker and listeners and among listeners themselves, building a sense of community. Epideictic speakers often use humor to entertain listeners and to make them more aware of their common bonds. To achieve that sense of community, they usually create a sense of **presence** for particular ideas and values. They bring to the forefront of consciousness some value or belief that a group holds but may not have thought much about, which makes people aware that they share important values and beliefs. Although deliberative speeches also may emphasize values, they do so to guide an audience in decision making. Ceremonial speeches tend to focus on values to draw people closer together.

Reexperiencing a Common Past

By recalling events or stories that are important to the group, the speaker enables the audience to relive its history vicariously. If the group faced or

presence
Conscious awareness, salience.

Weddings are a common occasion for public speaking. Toasts to the bride and groom often involve celebrating the joining of two individuals and wishing them a lifetime of happiness together. ▶

overcame a major obstacle, references to that obstacle strengthen a sense that the group has been tested and has met an important challenge. That common experience sustains the group's identity.

INVOKING COMMON VALUES   By explicitly reminding listeners of the principles or values they share, the speaker knits them together as a community. President Ronald Reagan frequently used this technique in speeches that identified positive values with Americans, reminding listeners that they shared these values.

REINTERPRETING EVENTS   It is often said that events do not speak; they must be spoken for. By giving meaning to events, the speaker may interpret them within a frame of reference that draws the group together. If, for example, the group's membership has declined over the past year, is that a life-threatening crisis or a challenge to be met creatively? If the group has a history of rallying in the face of challenges, the speaker will want to interpret the event as a challenge. That interpretation will bring the event within the group's shared values and frame of reference.

EMPHASIZING PEOPLE   In any community, some individuals play an especially important symbolic role. They may be the founders, or those who sustained the community in a time of trouble, or those who have been its leaders. Images of these heroic figures themselves become shared by the community. To suggest that the heroes would approve or disapprove of something or to imply that their memory is being carried forward or violated is to keep them alive, to draw upon their unifying power, and to add emotional force to the issue being discussed. For example, a civil rights group might invoke the memory of Martin Luther King, Jr.; a service organization might call forth a feeling of patriotism through reference to Revolutionary War heroes; and a football team might be asked to "win this one for the Gipper."

Guidelines for Ceremonial Speaking

The strength of a ceremonial speech does not depend primarily on its informative or persuasive dimensions, as a deliberative speech might, but on the speaker's ability to craft words and images that capture the occasion. The speaker's ability to articulate the audience's unexpressed feelings is called **resonance,** because the speaker's words echo listeners' feelings.

The speaker chooses a mix of stories, images, and arguments to use in responding to the occasion and enjoys great flexibility in the selection of specific purposes. But the tone must be appropriate for the occasion; the speech should build to an emotional climax; its length has to be controlled carefully; and humor must contribute to rather than weaken the presentation. Do not leave these elements and other key decisions to chance.

Because a ceremonial speech helps to define the occasion it marks, the audience usually has high expectations. Although successful ceremonial speeches seem natural, even effortless, they are actually difficult to prepare. The great variety of ceremonial occasions makes it impossible to explore them all, but the following sections describe some of the most common.

resonance
Articulating the unexpressed feelings of listeners, who then conclude that the speaker's message rings true with them.

CEREMONIAL SPEAKING OCCASIONS

Many of the most typical occasions for ceremonial speaking can be grouped under three broad headings: speeches of greeting, speeches of tribute, and speeches marking awards.

Speeches of Greeting

INTRODUCTIONS Early in this course you may have delivered a speech of introduction, either of yourself or of another student. This is a common type of ceremonial speech. When a group invites a speaker to address it, a member of the group usually introduces the speaker. The goals of such a speech of introduction are to make the speaker feel welcome, to give listeners relevant information about the speaker, and to contribute to the speaker's ethos.

These general purposes suggest guidelines for the speech of introduction. It should be selective, since a lengthy list of all the speaker's achievements may embarrass the speaker and bore the audience. Mention only significant accomplishments that are directly related to the occasion, carefully avoiding any incidents or information that might digress from the point. Also avoid lavish praise, which either might be embarrassing or might raise the audience's expectations to an unattainable level. Listeners who are told, "Our special guest is simply the most captivating speaker you will ever hear," are likely to be disappointed, which can only undercut the speaker's efforts.

A speech of introduction should not be read because a manuscript suggests that the introducer doesn't really know the speaker very well. In fact, if you are to introduce a speaker whom you don't know well, learn about him or her in advance. In particular, be absolutely certain that you use and correctly pronounce the speaker's preferred name. Finally, never anticipate or try to summarize what the speaker will say; besides stealing attention from the speaker, you might be mistaken. Few things weaken the introducer's ethos more than being corrected immediately by the speaker.

Here is how student Jonathan Cherry introduced a guest speaker on campus:

> Welcome, and thank you for coming tonight. Our guest has been called socially conscious, family-oriented, and a business wizard. She has served on planning commissions under the last three mayors of our city and has been responsible for innovations in housing, human relations, and education. Her many years of practical experience, combined with her undergraduate degree in sociology and her master's degree from Eastern State in urban planning, make her especially qualified to discuss "The Future of the City." Please join me in welcoming to our campus Laura Westerfield.

SPEECHES OF WELCOME A visiting individual or group is often greeted on arrival with a speech of welcome. This aims not only to introduce the guest to the host but also to make the guest feel comfortable and at ease. Your tone should be upbeat and optimistic. You should explicitly express greetings to the guest, identify some common bond or interest between you and the guest (such as "We look forward to learning more about each other"), and honor the guest by saying how pleased you are by the visit.

Speeches of Tribute

TESTIMONIALS One of the most common ceremonial speeches is the **testimonial,** a speech to honor someone. Testimonials are presented on many occasions, such as a significant wedding anniversary, a transition to new responsibilities, an outstanding achievement, retirement from a career or profession, and, of course, death.

The honoree's accomplishments are the organizing principle for a testimonial speech. You should discuss achievements that are significant in their own right as well as representative of the person's general character. To keep listeners interested, mention specific incidents and describe them vividly. If possible, select at least some incidents that might not be known to the audience. Be cautious about focusing on incidents or situations in which you played a part, since the point of the testimonial is to focus on the honoree rather than on you. And although your goal is to praise the person, you again should be careful not to exaggerate. Doing so could embarrass the honoree, cause listeners to doubt your sincerity, or suggest that you are so enthralled by the person that you cannot exercise independent judgment.

EULOGIES A **eulogy** is a special form of testimonial speech that is concerned with praising the dead. Eulogies are often delivered at funerals or memorial services or on special occasions such as the birthday of the deceased. Eulogies typically celebrate the essential character of the person, so the organizing principle is the person's virtues rather than accomplishments. Cite specific examples that illustrate the virtues. A caring individual, for example, might have donated much time and money to various charity organizations. Someone who was "ahead of her time" might have recognized a cultural trend before it became popular.

A eulogy is positive in tone, magnifying the person's strengths and minimizing weaknesses. Still, if it praises too lavishly, it may become maudlin or sound insincere. The goal is to help listeners recall the honoree's personality and character. As in a testimonial, in a eulogy you should limit personal references so that the focus remains on the honoree.

Earlier in this chapter we briefly mentioned President Ronald Reagan's eulogy for the astronauts killed in the 1986 explosion of the space shuttle *Challenger*. He spoke again five days later at a memorial service in Houston. His remarks on that occasion illustrate many of the characteristic features of a eulogy:

> We come together today to mourn the loss of seven brave Americans, to share the grief that we all feel and, perhaps in that sharing, to find the strength to bear our sorrow and the courage to look for the seeds of hope. . . .
>
> Their truest testimony will not be in the words we speak but in the way they lived their lives and in the way they lost their lives—with dedication, honor, and an unquenchable desire to explore this mysterious and beautiful universe.
>
> The best we can do to remember our seven astronauts—our *Challenger* Seven—remember them as they lived, bringing life and love and joy to those who knew them and pride to a nation.[6]

testimonial
A speech honoring a person.

eulogy
A special form of the testimonial speech, honoring someone who has died.

TOASTS   A **toast** is a miniature version of the testimonial speech. It is usually delivered in the presence of the honoree and often concludes by raising a glass to salute the person.

Many people who give toasts—at wedding receptions, at dinners honoring someone, or at the beginning of a new career or position—perform awkwardly. They are unsure of what to say, their remarks are often trite, and they don't do justice to the honoree. Such problems often result from failing to plan the toast in advance.

One useful way to think of the toast is as a variation of the one-point speech discussed in Chapter 1. It should celebrate one key characteristic of the honoree; supporting materials should include one or two incidents which illustrate that characteristic, talent, or virtue. A toast at a wedding reception, for example, might emphasize the devotion of the newlyweds by referring to an eight-year engagement that spanned three different states and two time zones. After stating the key characteristic and providing the examples, the person giving the toast should recognize the honoree, wish for continued strength and success, and conclude.

ROASTS   A slightly different variation on the speech of tribute is the **roast,** which both honors and pokes fun at a person. When you roast someone, your deft handling of the humor is essential to the success of the roast. Yet, the humor can backfire. Humor is used to put listeners at ease and also to demystify the honoree, suggesting that he or she is "just one of us." But it should never embarrass the person, nor should it distract from the fact that you and the audience are engaged in a tribute.

Like other forms of the speech of tribute, a roast should focus on only one or two key themes or incidents in the honoree's life. Select incidents that poke fun in a good-natured way and yet also have an underlying positive message. For example, the person you are roasting may have done something that seemed unusual or silly at the time, yet revealed a positive character trait. Avoid humor that could be misunderstood as prejudice. Although the roast may begin humorously, it should always end by pointing to the honoree's strengths. Like the toast, the roast should be relatively brief.

Speeches Marking Awards

PRESENTATION SPEECHES   Suppose that an organization to which you belong sponsors an award for a student who has done an outstanding job of community or volunteer service. The award is presented at a dinner at the end of the year, and your job is to present the award. Rather than just calling out the winner's name and handing over the certificate or trophy, which might suggest either that you don't care much about the award or that you think the wrong person won it, on most occasions the presentation of an award calls for a speech.

The **presentation speech** typically has two basic elements, and there are choices to make about each. First, it establishes the importance of the award itself. You might say something about the values it represents—in this case, community or volunteer service. If the award is named after someone, you might say a word or two about that person, to pay continuing tribute and to remind the audience of how he or she is connected to the award. Or you

toast
A brief testimonial speech, usually delivered in the presence of the person honored and accompanied by raising a glass in the person's honor.

roast
A speech of tribute that both honors and pokes fun at a person.

presentation speech
A speech marking the issuance of an award.

might emphasize the award's importance by stating how it relates to other awards that the organization presents—perhaps it is the oldest award, the most prestigious award, or the most competitive award.

Second, the presentation speech establishes the winner's fitness to receive the award by sharing with the audience the actions or achievements that render the person particularly qualified. Often this step can be linked directly to the preceding part of the speech. For example, if you have shown that scholastic achievement and participation in extracurricular activities are the qualities honored by the award, you then could describe the winner's accomplishments in these respects. This step of the speech symbolically links the winner with the award, establishing that the winner is a fitting recipient.

Besides these two basic elements, presentation speeches may include other components. It may be appropriate to explain the selection process for choosing the recipient. If the choice reflects the subjective judgment of a committee, for instance, you might want to discuss some of the criteria the committee used. If a large number of applicants or nominees were considered for the award, you might describe how they were screened down to the finalists. There is no need to describe the selection process if the criteria for the award are purely mechanical, such as an award to the student with the highest grade-point average.

If the finalists who did not win the award are known to the audience, it may be appropriate to praise them as well. You might indicate that anyone in this strong group could have received the award, that the choice of the selection committee was especially difficult, or that the judges wished they could have made multiple awards. Make such statements only if they are true, of course; insincerity can seldom be concealed. But if the competition for the award really was keen, it takes nothing away from the winner to suggest that other candidates were also highly qualified. If anything, winning may magnify the recipient's achievement.

If your speech concludes with the physical presentation of the award, manage your gestures carefully to avoid any awkwardness. Present the award with your left hand into the recipient's left hand so that you can use your right hands to shake.

ACCEPTANCE SPEECHES   The recipient of an award is usually expected to "say a few words." An honoree who just says, "Thanks," and sits down quickly may seem not to value the award or the audience very much. Such a brief acknowledgment is successful only when the recipient is genuinely overcome with emotion and cannot put his or her feelings into words.

Like the presentation speech, the **speech of acceptance** has certain basic elements. First, you should express gratitude for the honor that the award represents. Be modest; it is always more appealing to say that you are surprised by the award than to say that you know you deserve it. Thank those who presented the award for the honor they have shown you. If it is appropriate, praise the runners-up, or indicate that you are accepting the award on behalf of all the candidates. (This courtesy may be especially diplomatic if the selection process was close or if the runners-up are good friends or are highly regarded by the audience.)

Second, when appropriate, thank those who helped make it possible for you to receive the award. Few people are solely responsible for their own

speech of acceptance
A speech presented when one receives an award or a nomination for office.

Abraham Lincoln's second in-augural address, delivered in 1865, is one of the most eloquent. He used the cere-monial occasion to look be-yond the end of the Civil War and to call for a peace "with malice toward none."

achievements; most have been helped along the way by parents, teachers, friends, and colleagues. Worthy recipients usually seek to share the honor with those whose influence has led to their success. Yet this seemingly simple step has potential dangers. Mentioning a very long list of people not only might bore the audience but also might imply that no single person made a signifi-cant contribution to your success. And if you are too specific in identifying helpful people, you may omit someone unintentionally. Sometimes references to people in categories, such as "my parents, my teachers, and my coworkers," may be the safest approach, unless the influence of certain individuals truly was exceptional.

Third, you should indicate your understanding of the values that the award represents. This step not only makes clear that you understand why you are being honored but, more importantly, also makes the point that you appreciate and pay tribute to those same values in accepting the award. This statement gives the award symbolic significance that transcends you personally.

Probably the most prestigious award of all is the Nobel Prize, given annu-ally in several different fields for distinctive achievement. Accepting the 1986 Nobel Prize for Peace, Elie Wiesel began by speaking about the significance of the award:

> It is with a profound sense of humility that I accept the honor you have chosen to bestow upon me. I know: Your choice transcends me. This both frightens and pleases me.
>
> It frightens me because I wonder: Do I have the right to represent the multitudes who have perished? Do I have the right to accept this great honor on their behalf? I do not. That would be presumptuous. No one may speak for the dead, no one may interpret their mutilated dreams and visions.

It pleases me because I may say that this honor belongs to all the survivors and their children, and through us, to the Jewish people with whose destiny I have always identified.

Wiesel chose to put his selection for the Nobel Prize in the broader context of the survivors of the Holocaust. Taking a different approach, Toni Morrison, recipient of the 1993 Nobel Prize for Literature, spoke about the social significance of language and literature, for which she had been honored. Referring to a hypothetical woman writer, she said:

> She is convinced that when language dies, out of carelessness, disuse, and absence of esteem, indifference or killed by fiat, not only she herself, but all users and makers are accountable for its demise. In her country children have bitten their tongues off and use bullets instead to iterate the voice of speechlessness, of disabled and disabling language, of language adults have abandoned altogether as a device for grappling with meaning, providing guidance, or expressing love. But she knows tongue-suicide is not only the choice of children. It is common among the infantile heads of state and power merchants whose evacuated language leaves them with no access to what is left of their human instincts for they speak only to those who obey, or in order to force obedience.

Like most ceremonial speeches, a speech of acceptance should be brief. Audiences want to hear a few words of thanks, not a long speech. Indeed, an overly long acceptance speech may suggest that you are using the receipt of the award as a launching pad for a presentation of your own. Usually, a few minutes will be quite enough for an acceptance speech. Then quit while you are ahead, and return to your seat.

SPEECHES COMBINING DELIBERATIVE AND CEREMONIAL GOALS

We categorize speeches to help recognize differences among them. Some speeches clearly fit into the deliberative category (such as proposal presentations and oral reports); others clearly fit into the ceremonial category (such as introductions and roasts); and some speeches share the basic characteristics of both categories. This should not be surprising. A single speech may well attempt both to guide decision making and to celebrate values in a community. In fact, on certain occasions the two goals are expected to come together, and the speech should be designed to achieve both deliberative and ceremonial purposes.

Speeches Posing Challenges

PEP TALKS   A **pep talk** is virtually any speech that is intended to motivate and inspire, ranging from a seminar presentation for sales executives to a coach's locker-room address to professional athletes. This speech has two basic purposes: (1) to heighten a sense of community, so that listeners believe that they are "all in this together" and are working for one another, and (2) to increase motivation, so that listeners will put forth extra effort willingly.

To inspire enthusiasm, you need to be enthusiastic yourself. In a pep talk, your emotional tone, intensity, and body language will communicate

pep talk
A speech that is intended to motivate a group and inspire enthusiasm for a task.

at least as much as your words do. You should remind listeners of shared goals, both to strengthen commitment to the goals and to move listeners beyond belief to action. To help unify the audience, you may remind everyone of past successes. Recalling a shared experience in narrative form will bind the group together. Reference to past successes will suggest that future successes also are possible and are called for, to honor the successes of the past. Sometimes a pep talk will remind the audience of their shared sacrifices, suggesting that their efforts will be justified if success is forthcoming. Finally, the speech should end on a strong positive note. Indicate that success is possible in the task at hand, and directly exhort every listener to perform as well as possible, not only for personal gain but for the achievement of the group's goals.

AFTER-DINNER SPEECHES   A second example of a speaking occasion that challenges the audience is the **after-dinner speech,** so named because it typically follows a banquet or other meal, which could be anything from a continental breakfast to a state dinner. This type of speech is deceptively simple. On the surface it has no serious content but aims primarily to entertain. Like the roast, however, it is delivered with serious intent and ultimately does challenge listeners. It is a speech of celebration that also contains a serious message.

The theme of the after-dinner speech should be easy to state and easy for listeners to grasp. The speech's development should be lighthearted and humorous. Again, though, be careful in how you use humor. It cannot be forced; your stories or anecdotes must be genuinely funny. Your use of humor cannot involve religious, racial, gender, or ethnic jokes. Although all were commonplace in the past, today they are offensive to most audiences and will reflect negatively on you as a speaker. And humor should not become an end in itself, or the point of the speech will be lost. As a general rule, the safest humor is that which seemingly comes at one's own expense. Poking fun at yourself may cause listeners to see their own situations in a more lighthearted vein.[7]

Commencement Speeches

Few speaking occasions are more common—or more the object of satire and ridicule—than are graduation ceremonies. Although a formal speech is not essential, custom is strong enough that the absence of a commencement speaker is noted, usually negatively. Much energy goes into identifying just the right speaker, for the ethos of the speaker is somehow thought to transfer to the graduates. Yet most commencement speeches are eminently forgettable. Only a few—such as the speeches by George Marshall, John F. Kennedy, and Barbara Bush, all mentioned earlier in the chapter— outlive the occasion.

The obvious purpose of the commencement speech is to challenge the graduates, urging them to go out into "the real world" and dedicate themselves to a task that is larger than they. Yet the speech cannot be that simple. First, although it is directed primarily to the graduating students, it somehow must acknowledge the presence of others, particularly the parents and families of the graduates, who may be of different generations and who

after-dinner speech

A speech presented following a ceremonial meal, usually humorous in tone but with a serious message.

have had different experiences; for them, the same basic message may not be appropriate.

Second, although the speech is intended mainly for this specific occasion, it also needs to suggest a broader scope without sounding "canned." Presumably, the commencement speaker at Eastern State University would not give a dramatically different speech at Western State; and yet something must be said to the graduates of Eastern that distinguishes them from their counterparts at Western.

In 1990, as noted earlier, First Lady Barbara Bush spoke at Wellesley College's commencement about the challenges facing women and the variety of roles available to women in contemporary society. Her remarks are important not only because they offered advice and encouragement to the graduates and their families but also because they addressed a significant social issue:

> For several years you've had impressed upon you the importance to your career of dedication and hard work, and of course that's true. But as important as your obligations as a doctor, a lawyer, a business leader will be, you are a human being first, and those human connections with spouses, with children, with friends are the most important investment you will ever make. . . .
>
> For over fifty years, it was said that the winner of Wellesley's annual hoop race would be the first to get married. Now they say the winner will be the first to become a CEO. Both of those stereotypes show too little tolerance for those who want to know where the mermaids stand.

Some commencement exercises include a student speaker. If you perform this role, you will face additional challenges. You will appear presumptuous if you seem to have more experience or expertise than your classmates. You want to issue a challenge, and yet you do not want to talk down to an audience of your peers. Student speakers are most successful when they do not try to issue a challenge themselves but rather discover and articulate one that is already "out there"; it also helps to speak frequently in the first person rather than the second person, referring to challenges facing "us" rather than "you" and indicating what "we," not "you," must do to meet those challenges.

Summary

Just as the speaker, the speech, and the audience are important components of a rhetorical situation, so too is the occasion. Any occasion creates expectations that the speaker may want to observe or to modify, but in any case will need to understand. *Decorum,* or fittingness to the occasion, influences a speaker's decisions about the appropriate degree of formality, length, and intensity of a speech; about the representativeness and types of supporting materials to use; and how explicitly to identify with the audience. A decorous speech is one that gives voice to the heretofore unexpressed sentiments of the audience.

Speaking occasions can be classified in various ways. The ancients distinguished among forensic, deliberative, and epideictic (ceremonial) speaking. Forensic speaking, conducted in courts of law, today is the work of professionally trained advocates, but all public speakers engage in deliberative and ceremonial speaking.

Deliberative speaking aims to answer the question "What shall we do?" Its focus is on action, which involves sharing information to resolve matters that are uncertain but require decisions. It takes place in a wide range of settings and includes oral reports and presentations, group meetings and presentations of various kinds, public hearings, and debates.

Ceremonial speaking aims to emphasize common bonds among people and to give a greater sense of presence to particular ideas, beliefs, or values. These goals are achieved by recalling a common past, invoking shared values, interpreting past events within a frame of reference that ties them to the community, and paying tribute to a group's symbolic heroes. Ceremonial speaking is both argumentative and emotional in nature. It is seemingly simple yet requires difficult judgments and careful preparation. Many occasions for ceremonial speaking can be grouped into three broad categories—speeches of greeting, speeches of tribute, and speeches marking awards. Opportunities for ceremonial speaking arise often.

Some occasions call for speeches that serve both deliberative and ceremonial functions, often posing challenges to the audience. In particular we examined pep talks, after-dinner speeches, and commencement speeches.

Discussion Questions

1. What occasions have you experienced on which speeches were given? What were your expectations as an audience member? Did the speaker meet or neglect your expectations? Discuss your impressions with both deliberative and ceremonial speeches, including their appropriateness for the occasions at which they were presented.

2. In what ways might the strategic design of a speech differ for ceremonial and deliberative occasions? Identify the general goals of these two types of speaking, and discuss the various strategies that a speaker might use to achieve them. As part of your analysis, create a chart that identifies potential differences in the speaker's arrangement of ideas, choice of supporting materials, and stylistic decisions.

3. When you discussed questions 1 and 2, how did the group dynamic of your class work? Did one person dominate the discussion? Did groupthink become a problem? Did anyone provide testimony to guide decision making? Was an individual who offered a claim asked to respond to questions? Were there any debates? Discuss and evaluate the public speaking that occurs in the group discussions of your class.

Activities

1. Attend a ceremony at which at least one speech will be given. In a short essay, critique a speech that you heard at that ceremony. Was the speech decorous? In what ways was it designed to fit the constraints of the occasion?

2. Observe a group discussion, taking care not to engage in that discussion yourself. Write an essay describing what you learned from that experience. Considering the size of the group, the function of the meeting, and the particular dynamics of the group, comment on some of these speech goals:

   Drawing up a group report
   Speaking in small groups
   Chairing a meeting
   Providing testimony

Debating an issue
Responding to questions

3. Think about the expectations raised by the following real or imagined occasions, and prepare a decorous speech for one of them:

    a. A roast of your public speaking teacher
    b. An acceptance speech for an award that you hope to win someday
    c. A pep talk to your favorite sports team
    d. A eulogy for a friend, family member, or public figure

Using the Internet

1. Deliberative or Ceremonial? Choose one of the speeches presented in the **History Outloud Collection** by pointing your browser to <http://oyez.at.nwu.edu/history-out-loud>, where you will find texts and RealAudio links. Determine if it fulfills the expectations of a deliberative or a ceremonial occasion, or a combination of these forms.

    After selecting one of the speakers and reading or listening to the presentation, address some of the following points.

- *What was the occasion for the speech? How did the occasion influence what was said?*
- *Did the speaker fulfill the expectations of decorum?*
- *To what degree was the speech a deliberative speech?*
- *In what regard was the speech a ceremonial speech?*

2. Watch or Listen to Congress. While most speeches presented on the floor of the U.S. House of Representatives or the Senate deal with specific pieces of legislation, you may also observe speeches that have a ceremonial quality. Explore **FedNet** to find out the current issues being discussed on the Hill. You can watch or listen to floor debate or observe committee hearings.

    Point your browser to <http://www.fednet.net>. Scroll to your right to find links for debates, hearings, press conferences or special events to see or listen to RealVideo or RealAudio transmission. FedNet subscribers can also access the Archive of past Congressional activities.

Notes

1. Two articles together capture this balance between constraint and creativity. Lloyd F. Bitzer, "The Rhetorical Situation," *Philosophy and Rhetoric* 1 (Winter 1968): 1–14, focuses on the need to respond to a rhetorical situation. Richard E. Vatz, "The Myth of the Rhetorical Situation," *Philosophy and Rhetoric* 6 (Summer 1973): 154–161, emphasizes that choices made by speakers actually shape the rhetorical situation.

2. Cicero emphasized the concept of decorum and made much of it. See Marcus Tullius Cicero, *Orator,* trans. H. M. Hubbel, Cambridge, Mass: Harvard University Press, 1939, 70–74.

3. For example, see Aristotle, *The Rhetoric,* trans. W. Rhys Roberts, New York: The Modern Library, 1954, Book I, Chapter 3.

4. For more about speaking in small groups, see John K. Brilhart, *Effective Group Discussion,* Fifth Edition, Dubuque, Ia.: Wm. C. Brown, 1986.

5. For more about parliamentary procedure, see Henry Martyn Robert, *Robert's Rules of Order, Newly Revised,* Glenview, Ill.: Scott, Foresman, 1981.

6. The way in which Reagan's eulogy was designed to respond to the occasion is discussed in more detail in Steven M. Mister, "Reagan's *Challenger* Tribute: Combining Generic Constraints and Situational Demands," *Central States Speech Journal* 37 (Fall 1986): 158–165.

7. For more about the use of humor in speeches, see Charles R. Gruner, "Advice to the Beginning Speaker on Using Humor—What the Research Tells Us," *Communication Education* 34 (April 1985): 142–147.

Beyond the Classroom: Speaking in the Public Forum

In This Appendix We Will:

- Explore what the public forum is and how your study of public speaking prepares you to participate effectively in it.

- Describe a variety of speaking situations that are likely to arise as you move from the classroom to the public forum.

our public speaking skills are applicable beyond the classroom, of course. You will use them in addressing your neighborhood civic club, church group, or PTA. You'll use them when making presentations in your business or professional life. And you'll use them when a public issue matters to you and you decide to speak out about it.

A course in public speaking prepares you to express yourself and perhaps to influence others in each of these settings. Diverse as the settings are, they all embody a public forum; that is, they meet the conditions under which skilled speakers can conduct meaningful public discussion of important issues.

THE PUBLIC FORUM

The word **public** in "public speaking" is important in at least two respects. First, it designates speaking that is open and accessible by others. A person who speaks publicly is inviting others to listen carefully and to think about and appraise the message. The speaker's goal is that of informed choice, not forced compliance, on the part of the audience.

Second, speaking is public when it affects people beyond the immediate audience. If you urge classmates to lobby for higher student activity fees, your remarks will have consequences for people who are not even present to hear you. If you explain how to examine the terms of a lease before signing it, listeners can follow your directions in ways that will affect others.

From the speaker's point of view, giving a speech means entering into the **public forum.** Centuries ago, the forum was a physical place where citizens gathered to discuss issues affecting them. Today, the public forum is not an actual place to which we go; instead it is an imagined "space" that exists wherever people have the freedom to exchange ideas. The public forum is created whenever the following conditions are met:

1. *Some problem affects people collectively* as well as individually.

2. *Cooperative action is needed* to address the problem. Speakers and listeners participate in deciding what to do.

3. *The decision requires subjective judgment.* What should be done is not obvious; there is more than one possible solution, and there is no way for anyone to gather all the information that conceivably might bear on the decision.

4. Nevertheless, *a decision is required.* People stand at a fork in the road, and a choice cannot be avoided.

Just as the public forum exists in many places, so do many subjects call for communication in the public forum. The subject of health care is an example. Consider how it reflects each of the four conditions for a public forum:

1. For many years health care was seen as a private matter. People either did or did not obtain insurance, did or did not seek preventive care, did or did not receive treatment, and were healthy or ill—all as a series of individual choices and actions that were not seen as affecting others. Gradually, however, people realized that health care is *not just an individual*

public

Open to or accessible by others; affects others.

public forum

A space (imagined, rather than physical) in which citizens gather to discuss issues affecting them; discussion characterized by certain assumptions about the need for cooperative action and subjective judgment to resolve a problem.

matter. Many people are unable to obtain insurance on their own. If someone becomes seriously ill and goes without treatment, he or she may become a real burden to family members. And the cost of providing health care limits economic growth and hurts everyone.

2. When people came to see health care as more than a private matter, *speakers and listeners together began to discuss* how to provide and pay for it. Audiences heard descriptions of how various plans would work. They identified and evaluated speakers' claims, arguments, and evidence. They considered a variety of proposals, accepting some ideas and rejecting others. Speakers analyzed their audiences' beliefs and values and tried to adapt their ideas to what listeners regarded as most important.

3. *No one person can just impose a solution.* No one can be certain which proposal is best, and no one can ever get all the information that might help in making that decision. So there is a process of give-and-take as speakers and listeners consider alternative ideas and proposals, trying their best to decide which are the most sensible or compelling.

4. *And yet a decision has to be made,* because doing nothing will make the problems of health care worse—for individuals as well as for society as a whole.

Over time the participants in the public forum come to an understanding about which approach should be tried. The understanding that they reach is always tentative and always subject to revision if better ideas emerge into the forum. Indeed, because no final answer has been found, the subject of health care returns to the public forum every few years.

Public Speaking and Democracy

You may not have thought about it this way, but as you become skilled in public speaking, you become a more effective participant in the public forum. You are able to articulate your ideas and to relate them to others, to listen carefully and critically to other points of view, to weigh and evaluate arguments and evidence, and to bring your best judgment to issues that have no easy or automatic answer. As you exercise these skills, you strengthen the ties that unite participants in the public forum into a community or society.

Traditionally the public forum has been associated with large political questions. But the boundary between public and private is always shifting, and any subject might easily find its way into the public forum. Styles in popular music, for example, become more than just private or individual choices in response to claims that the noise level is harmful to health or that the content leads children to violence. Personal choices of deodorants or clothing are no longer just private matters when they are are alleged to cause destruction of the ozone layer or exploitation of Third World labor markets. And speculating in the stock market becomes a public matter when one's investment choices affect so many others. Whatever subject you discuss—whether or not it is usually regarded as political—you are entering into the public forum.

Discussion of public issues is best advanced when the public forum is active and vibrant. Unfortunately, there are many signs that today's public forum is not healthy. Increasing numbers of people claim to have little interest in public affairs. Many are put off by the complexity and difficulty of understanding important issues. Others are satisfied with sources of information that oversimplify issues and turn them into slogans. Large numbers of people see no point in participating in the public forum because they think they are powerless to affect any public change. Others generally perceive public figures to be deceptive or dishonest. Still others say that they are interested only in themselves.

These are warning signals for a free society. If the public forum is allowed to weaken, critical public decisions will be made unilaterally, whether by experts or by rulers, so those who are affected by the decisions really won't have any part in making them. Without a well-cultivated public forum, the two alternatives are autocratic rule and anarchy.

Fortunately, studying public speaking equips you to better participate in the public forum by enabling you to understand issues and evaluate claims. You'll be able to make decisions even about matters that do not directly affect you. And when an issue does affect you, your involvement and participation will count.

OCCASIONS FOR SPEAKING IN PUBLIC

In Chapter 15 we examined a number of occasions for public speaking outside of the classroom in which student speakers are likely to find themselves, such as making an oral report or presentation, chairing a meeting, or giving a speech of greeting or tribute. Here are additional speaking occasions you are likely to encounter as you move into the larger public forum. Even if you do not speak on all these occasions, you will listen to others who do. Your understanding of public speaking will enable you to listen critically, making you a more effective citizen when the time comes to express your preferences or to record your vote.

Public Hearings and Debates

PROVIDING TESTIMONY   A development firm is proposing to build a major shopping center in your neighborhood. The plan offers great potential economic benefits to the town, but it's likely to increase neighborhood traffic and will create a commercial presence in a residential area. The development firm seeks a zoning variance to build the center even though it will not comply fully with regulations. The zoning board holds a public hearing at which interested citizens can testify.

Individuals who testify in public hearings present deliberative speeches; their goal is to persuade those conducting the hearings to their point of view. Because many people testify at a hearing, each statement must be brief. An analysis of the decision makers helps a speaker to determine which points to emphasize and how best to be persuasive in the situation.

Janet Carpenter and Richard Brinkley were both well informed about the proposed shopping center. They both knew that the city would welcome the additional tax revenue from the center, especially since citizens had recently voted against higher taxes. But they were also aware that the shopping center might damage the residential character of the neighborhood. They both testified before the zoning board that would have to approve the project. Janet favored the development and began by saying:

> This shopping center will revive the sagging economy of our town. That's worth a lot. It will strengthen the value of our homes and make money available for schools and parks without our tax rates having to go up. Now, I know that the residential character of this area is important, but tough zoning regulations will still protect that, even after the shopping center is built.

Richard opposed the project. In his testimony he argued:

> We must be careful to avoid being lured too strongly by money. Sure, we all recognize the need to bring more money into the town, and let's find better ways to do that. But this shopping center will change the quality of our lives forever. That's a far more harmful effect, even though it can't be measured in dollars.

Both Janet and Richard focused on a small number of arguments and made each as clear and concise as possible. Those are excellent goals to strive for if you are called upon to provide testimony.

DEBATES Sometimes an organization will sponsor a debate about a controversial issue. You may be invited to advocate one side of the issue while someone else supports the other side. Debaters not only present speeches they have thought about in advance but also respond to the statements of their opponents. The purpose of a debate is to enable the audience, by hearing the opposing positions at the same time, to understand the issues better and to decide which side they wish to support.

Some debates are highly structured, with rules prescribing the number of speeches and the time limits. Other debates are loosely structured; one advocate presents a speech, the opponent responds, and then the speakers alternate their responses until everyone feels that the issue has been exhausted. Debates employ all the techniques of informative and persuasive speaking, with special emphasis on testing reasoning. Participants not only develop their own arguments but also refute opposing arguments.

In election campaigns, candidates appear in debates to enable voters to decide whom to support. In legislative bodies discussing a proposal, members engage in debates both to make a record for their constituents and to clarify issues to influence their undecided colleagues' votes. In local communities, civic organizations hold debates so that people will be informed about important issues and can decide what they believe. Although it may be some time before you participate in debates that will affect your community, school or campus organizations may give you practice in debating issues ranging from the nation's foreign policy to the allocation of student funds for campus activities.

Ceremonial Occasions

ANNIVERSARY CELEBRATIONS The most common example of an **anniversary celebration** is the Fourth of July oration, a patriotic speech delivered annually on the anniversary of American independence. Anniversaries of

anniversary celebration
A speech of remembrance delivered on the anniversary of an important event.

major historical events are often celebrated with speeches. For example, in 1994 President Clinton delivered an address to mark the fiftieth anniversary of the D-Day landing during World War II, just as President Reagan had done on the fortieth anniversary in 1984. Referring to D-Day, Clinton said:

> My fellow Americans, we have gathered to remember those who stormed this beach for freedom who never came home. We pay tribute to what a whole generation of heroes won here. But let us also recall what was lost here. We must never forget that thousands of people gave everything they were, or what they might have become, so that freedom might live.

Anniversary celebrations share common features. First, the speaker typically refers to the event being commemorated, perhaps recounting it as a narrative and perhaps emphasizing a few key points. This reminds listeners of their historical roots in the event. Second, the speaker may abstract certain virtues or special characteristics from the event. The Fourth of July orator may highlight the selflessness and farsightedness of the nation's founders, much as President Clinton noted the courage and dedication of those who landed at Normandy on D-Day. These virtues are discussed to remind listeners why the event is celebrated and to show that the event has significance beyond its historical details. Third, the speaker relates these features to listeners' lives, perhaps challenging the audience to adhere to the standards evidenced in the event, to behave as nobly today as their predecessors did in the event commemorated, or to keep the memory of the event alive as it recedes into history. Through these steps, the anniversary celebration combines tribute to the past with a challenge for the future.

Speeches Marking Candidacy and Election

NOMINATING SPEECHES   Every four years in the United States, each major political party holds a national convention to nominate its candidates for president and vice-president. Especially when there is a contest for these offices, the **nominating speech** becomes a centerpiece of the convention. Each candidate is nominated by a delegate who makes a speech on his or her behalf, concluding by formally placing the person's name in nomination. Candidates select their nominating speakers with care, and delegates who are chosen for this task consider it a great honor and prepare their speeches with equal care. A similar process occurs in any organization that proposes candidates for office and then deliberates and votes on them. Nominating speeches are made in student government, in housing units, and in civic and religious organizations of all kinds.

While a nominating speech has deliberative goals, it also has a ceremonial aspect that makes it somewhat different from other campaign speeches. Although the speech attempts to guide and persuade people in choosing a leader, it is usually presented at a formal celebration and is meant to draw an audience together in support of common values.

A nominating speech has three basic goals. The first is *to make the importance of the office clear.* A speaker usually does this by alluding to the responsibilities of the office, describing the issues that the victorious candidate will have to confront or explaining the traits and attitudes that a successful office holder must demonstrate. This part of the speech both magnifies the signifi-

nominating speech

A speech in which a person is named for an office or honor.

cance of the office and makes it clear that the nominating speaker understands what is involved.

The second goal should be apparent: *to show the fitness of the candidate for the office.* If certain traits and attitudes are important, then the candidate should be shown to have them. The goal is to link the candidate with the office so that listeners can imagine that outcome and will consider it natural. For example, if previous experience is important, you might emphasize the candidate's record in other positions. If the candidate shares your beliefs about important issues and how to handle them, it will be helpful to note that you have similar priorities.

To demonstrate your candidate's fitness for the office, you may find it desirable to say something about other candidates. Here you need to be careful. Several recent national elections have been marked by negative campaigns that emphasized the opponents' weaknesses rather than the candidate's strengths, and voters have begun to resist this approach. In any case, negative campaigning is almost always inappropriate in a nominating speech. Appeals that compare your candidate with others will be more effective if they are generic and emphasize the candidate's positive features without attacking opponents. Your own conviction and enthusiasm will convey a strong positive message about your candidate; attacks on others may suggest that you lack confidence about your choice and see your candidate simply as the least of evils.

The third goal of the nominating speech is *to formally place the candidate's name in nomination.* Speakers sometimes save this formality for the end of the speech, to build to a dramatic climax. At national political conventions, for instance, nominating speeches often avoid mentioning the candidate's name because it might set off a demonstration by the audience that would compete for attention with the speaker's intended message. Even when everyone already knows which candidate you will nominate, saving the formal step of the nomination for the very end focuses listeners on why you think your candidate is best suited for the job.

ACCEPTANCE OF CANDIDACY   Sometimes the nominating process selects the person who will actually occupy the office. In that case, election to office is similar to receiving an award, and the winner might make the sort of speech described in Chapter 15. But when the nominating process determines only who will run for office in an upcoming election, then the acceptance speech needs to be slightly different.

First, of course, the candidate should formally accept the nomination, pledging his or her best efforts in the subsequent campaign and, if elected, in office. It is appropriate to acknowledge the supporters who made it possible to gain the nomination. Particularly if the contest for the nomination was hard fought, the winning candidate should appeal to the losers for support in the race ahead and should express appreciation for their campaign and principles. If it is at all possible, incorporation of elements from the losers' positions into one's own campaign will help to draw the community together.

The acceptance speech should also acknowledge the magnitude of the tasks ahead: winning office and carrying out its duties. It takes a careful combination of modesty and self-confidence to emphasize how difficult and important the position is and yet to pledge to perform capably if elected. Finally, the acceptance speech often concludes with a direct appeal for help from the audience. In accepting the Democratic presidential nomination in 1960, for example, John F. Kennedy asked listeners, "Give me your help, and your hand, and your heart, and your vote."

A slight variation on the acceptance speech occurs when there is no election campaign but the person nominated must still be approved by others. In 1993, when President Clinton nominated Judge Ruth Bader Ginsburg for a seat on the U.S. Supreme Court, her remarks revealed the typical features of an acceptance speech, as these brief excerpts indicate:

> Mr. President, I am grateful beyond measure for the confidence you have placed in me, and I will strive with all that I have to live up to your expectations in making this appointment. . . .

> The announcement the President just made is significant, I believe, because it contributes to the end of the days when women, at least half the talent pool in our society, appear in high places only as one-at-a-time performers. . . .

> I am indebted to so many for this extraordinary chance and challenge: to a revived women's movement in the 1970s that opened doors for people like me, to the civil rights movement of the 1960s from which the women's movement drew inspiration, to my teaching colleagues at Rutgers and Columbia and for thirteen years my D.C. Circuit colleagues who shaped and heightened my appreciation of the value of collegiality.

INAUGURAL ADDRESSES If the acceptance speech marks only the acceptance of candidacy rather than the assumption of office, the latter event is also often celebrated with a speech. Every four years, at the beginning of a term, the president of the United States delivers an **inaugural address.** Presidents of other organizations—whether colleges or universities, business or civic clubs, or professional organizations—may also be called upon to deliver an inaugural address. The inaugural may actually define the assumption of office, but sometimes there is an interval of time between the president's taking over the office and delivering the inaugural address.

An inaugural address includes several basic elements. First, the leader formally accepts the responsibilities of the office, stating that he or she understands the duties and will make every effort to fulfill them. Second, the new leader explicitly seeks to unify the audience. This is especially important if the campaign for office has been divisive; in effect the new leader says that the campaign is over and reaches out for the help and support of everyone in the audience. After the bitter and close election of 1800, Thomas Jefferson introduced this aspect to the presidential inaugural address when he proclaimed:

> Let us then, fellow citizens, unite with one heart and one mind. Let us restore to social intercourse that harmony and affection without which liberty and even life itself are dreary things. . . .But every difference of opinion is not a difference of principle. We have called by different names brethren of the same principle. We are all Republicans, we are all Federalists.

President Jefferson's goal was to urge members of the two political parties of his day to overcome their differences and to unite for the common good.

inaugural address
A speech delivered when assuming an office to which one has been elected.

Most subsequent U.S. presidents have expressed similar sentiments in their inaugural address.

Third, the newly installed leader typically outlines the general goals to be pursued during his or her time in office. The inaugural address usually does not spell out specific proposals but rather identifies the general themes or goals to be pursued. For example, in 1997 President Bill Clinton spoke about "building a bridge to the twenty-first century" and emphasized the themes of opportunity, responsibility, and community.

Finally, the inaugural address often puts the new leader's service into a larger context. He or she may speak of perpetuating the ideals of the organization or of fulfilling a dream held since childhood. Presidents of the United States have often concluded their inaugurals with a plea for divine assistance, which not only suggests humility but also places the presidency in the larger context of carrying out God's will.

KEYNOTE SPEECHES   Meetings of business, academic, professional, or political organizations often feature a speaker near the beginning of the program to set the tone of the event. You may find yourself inviting a keynote speaker for a meeting that you organize, or you may be asked to deliver a keynote speech yourself.

Coming near the beginning of a meeting, the **keynote speech** has two special purposes. First, it *draws together and defines the diverse members of the audience as a community*. The individual delegates at a state convention of a civic organization, for example, have come from cities and towns that have diverse issues and concerns. The fact that the delegates all belong to the same organization may not seem important to them individually. But when they assemble at the convention, the keynote speech helps to focus their attention and energy on what they share.

Second, the keynote speech helps *to set the meeting's thematic agenda*. This refers not to the listing of specific items of business but to the larger matters of topics, themes, or issues that will dominate the meeting. Sometimes a meeting has a designated theme, for example, "achieving unity through diversity," and the keynote speaker is asked to address that theme. What the speaker says will help listeners to think about the meeting's theme and to refer to it in their deliberations. On other occasions the meeting itself may have no theme; the keynote speaker, if successful, will help to determine what listeners will be thinking and talking about for the rest of the meeting.

The keynote speech is a platform enabling you to identify what you deem important and to urge others to think about it as well. It also serves to rally or inspire listeners, presenting them with a challenge and the motivation to meet it. Although a keynote speaker has considerable latitude, some cautions are appropriate. Remember that the purpose of the keynote is to open, not close, discussion. A successful keynote address poses issues or questions for delegates to ponder; it does not offer dogmatic proclamations. Stating your own views too strongly, unless you know that the audience holds the same views, can hurt the keynote speech. Recognize that the audience is likely to be diverse, at least on some dimensions. Design the keynote so that it seems to speak to everyone without excluding significant segments of the audience. This means that the speech has to be somewhat **multivocal,** including terms and phrases that individual listeners can interpret in light of their own experi-

keynote speech
A speech presented near the beginning of a meeting to guide its thematic agenda and to help set its tone.

multivocal
Capable of being heard in different ways by different listeners, all of whom find the term or concept positive.

ences and concerns. A reference to "the American dream," for example, will mean different things to different listeners, and yet it can be a positive symbol for everyone.

Summary

Public speaking skills are applied not only in the classroom but also in a wide variety of situations that have the characteristics of the public forum. In these situations an issue confronts people collectively as well as individually, cooperative action is needed to address the issue, it is impossible to know with certainty the best course to take, and yet a decision is required. Examples of such situations include public hearings and debates, ceremonial speeches, and speeches marking candidacy and election. Your understanding of public speaking will help you both to speak effectively in situations like these and also to listen more carefully to others.

appendix B
Speeches for Analysis and Discussion

CHILDREN OF DIVORCED FAMILIES

T. J. Brinkerhoff, University of Northern Colorado

T. J. Brinkerhoff is one of the students from the University of Northern Colorado whom you have met throughout this book. In this speech, he aims to heighten awareness of a significant social problem, but he also advocates a solution and urges his audience to act. This example illustrates how informative and persuasive strategies are often combined in a single speech.

In the introduction, T. J. acknowledges that the topic is sensitive and that there are conflicting points of view. Notice that he carefully previews the major divisions of the speech and that these follow a problem–solution structure. T. J. uses a variety of supporting materials. Does it lend weight to his conclusions? Does he reason soundly from the evidence, or are there fallacies in his reasoning? Some of T. J.'s statements are controversial. How could he best come to grips with the possibility that listeners who disagree with him might not give him a fair hearing? How would he want to change the speech for a less neutral audience?

Finally, consider whether the conclusion is as strong as the introduction. After discussing solutions, T. J. returns to the problem, relating the effects of divorce on a hypothetical child. Does this add strength to the conclusion, or would it have been better placed elsewhere in the speech? Why?

If you go to a panel discussion in Washington, D.C. on the topic Reframing Family Values, do not expect much attention to either family or values. Instead you will be flooded with charts and graphs about heads of household and income distribution . . . behavior and values have nothing to do with the crisis of the American family. Everything is economic. If the awkward term *family values* comes up it will be discussed gingerly as some sort of mysterious optional product that some households have while others do not. Then back to the charts.

This quotation is from *U.S. News and World Report* in an article titled "Where Marriage Is A Scary Word" by John Leo. Increasing chances of dropping out of school; lack of reading, spelling, and mathematical skills; emotional and behavioral problems; anxiety, aggressiveness, crime, and even suicide are only some of the tendencies that are heightened in children who are affected by divorced families. "All too often the adult quest for freedom, independence and choice in family relationships conflicts with the child's developmental needs for stability, constancy, harmony and performance in family life . . . family disruption creates a deep division between parents' interests and the interests of children," according to Barbara Defoe Whitehead in "Dan Quayle Was Right" in *The Atlantic*.

With the divorce rate steadily climbing and aided by new "no-fault" divorce laws in our country, many children are being raised without the advantage of an intact family. Although intact families are not without their problems, evidence shows that two-parent families are preferable to the alternatives of single- or step-parent families. Today I'd like to heighten your awareness of the problem of divorce and its effects on children by showing you the immediate challenges that children face due to divorce, the solutions our country needs, and what we as individuals can do to help prevent this problem.

First let me explain the problems we're facing. "Half of all marriages end in divorce [today]," according to Barbara Defoe Whitehead. If current trends prevail, less than 50 percent of children born in the 1990s will be raised by a single parent; they won't have the advantages of a mother and a father. These figures have jumped from "8 percent of white children born in the 1950s and (spending) their childhood with one parent . . . and among black children from 22%," notes Joseph Adelson in an article titled "Splitting Up" in *Commentary*. The event of divorce, once considered to be strongly avoided, has now become an increasingly neutral subject, even when children are present.

This increase of neutrality on the subject of divorce presents some major problems for the children involved. In a comparative study by Joseph Adelson between intact families and single-parent families, he found, "Children in [single-parent] situations are twice as likely to drop out of high school . . . two to three times more likely to have emotional or behavioral problems [including aggressiveness and low self-control], and they show substantially higher crime rates . . . 60 percent of rapists, 72 percent of adolescent murders and 70 percent of long-term prison inmates come from [single-parent homes]." Also, "Their rates of teenage pregnancy and drug abuse are higher as well . . ." according to Brian Robertson. These problems and others are only a fraction of the total picture.

But now that I've shown you some of the problems that divorce can cause for children, let's look at what can be done about it. The first step in solving the problem of divorce is to re-emphasize the importance of the marriage contract. In our society today, there is an ever-increasing desire for freedom and self-expression. This, in turn, frees individuals from responsibility and commitment. To focus on self is a severe detriment to any situation involving a cooperative effort—as marriage is. John Leo tells us that to solve this problem today is "to restore gravity to both marriage and separation." By restoring the weight of responsibility to the marriage agreement, it is necessary for both people to fully recognize the step they're taking and to make the changes in their lives that are required for their new commitment. By joining your life with that of another, you must be willing to make the necessary sacrifices for family and forget about self.

The second step, to restore the gravity of separation, follows the first. The introduction of no-fault divorce has unexpectedly created its own accelerated culture of noncommitment. In order to remedy this problem, it is believed by Brian Robertson that "some measure of fault should be reintroduced to force couples to consider carefully before splitting up." According to Victoria Lytle's article, "Kids and Divorce" in *NEA Today,* ministers of religion should be trained for handling situations that may lead to possible divorce before they've gone too far. It is also the responsibility of parents to raise and teach children about the value of family and its importance and the need for commitment in our society.

Now let me show you in real terms what divorce can do to a child. Imagine a young child who begins to notice the way his or her parents interact with one another. Sometimes the child may hear loud voices, yells, and maybe even uncomfortable silences. The day finally comes when the mother or father comes to the child and says that the other parent has gone away. The child waits eagerly for the day of the return of the parent, but in vain. And as the months and years pass, the curious child begins to wonder if that parent will ever return. The child begins to imagine the parent and fantasize that the parent still exists and is still there with him or her, reading stories to the child, maybe even sleeping in bed with the child. The child's fantasies bring comfort to a soul that longs for the love of a lost parent. The emptiness lingers as the child grows older and emotions increase and lead to a desire to find satisfaction for the void that has come into the child's life. But whatever the path the child may choose, he or she will never be able to satisfy the need for the loss of a loved parent.

The things I've told you today about divorce and its effects on children are results obtained from general studies conducted by people who have looked at divorce and who have not singled out the individuals involved. Some of us today in this room may have come from families of single parents or divorced parents. And all of us, whether we have come from that situation or not, have experienced loss in our lives and maybe have even experienced a very painful loss. In any case, we all know that loss and loneliness hurts, and we don't like to be in situations that cause us pain. I would sincerely encourage each one of you to make the decision that, if you have the desire to have children and to be married, you prepare to make a lifelong commitment and be sure that you and your spouse are ready for that commitment as well.

Because I have talked today and emphasized the effects of divorce on children and the negative trends, I want to let you know that there is something you can do about the situation. We control our own destiny. The problem of divorce in our society is not only a problem for the children involved, but it makes us aware of the areas in which we're lacking as a nation. We must learn to be more forgiving and cooperative with one another in order for us to succeed collectively. And for us to raise future generations, we must be willing to make a commitment to ourselves and to those we love to do our part to strengthen our nation by starting at home.

Bibliography

1. Whitehead, Barbara. "Dan Quayle Was Right," *The Atlantic* (Apr. 1993): 47.
2. Robertson, Brian. "In Academia, New Praise for the Nuclear Family," *Insight on the News* (14 Mar. 1994): 18.
3. Lytle, Victoria. "Kids and Divorce," *NEA Today* (Oct. 1994): 11.
4. Adleson, Joseph. "Splitting Up," *Commentary* (Sept. 1996): 63.
5. Leo, John. "Where Marriage Is a Scary Word," *U.S. News and World Report* (5 Feb. 1996): 22.

TISSUE ENGINEERING

Patricia Ann Campos, University of Texas at Austin

One purpose for which informative strategies are well suited is that of conveying new information or perspective. Complex scientific discoveries, technological breakthroughs, or medical applications may be largely unknown to the average person. In this speech, Patricia Ann Campos seeks to explain tissue engineering to other students.

The speech describes the process and the history of tissue engineering and identifies potential benefits and applications ranging from medicine to cosmetics. A variety of supporting materials are used. After pointing out the benefits of tissue engineering, Patricia alludes to possible negative effects and to questions of ethics. How well is the speech adapted to the occasion? Are complex terms avoided or explained sufficiently for a classroom audience? What if the audience is composed entirely of premedical students? What if audience members are known to be skeptics on the issue? By asking about alternative possibilities, you can become more aware of the strategic choices that are embedded in any speech.

Scientists recently made national headlines after growing a human ear on the back of a mouse. Although it may resemble a bizarre carnival attraction, this rising star is allowing researchers to refine the technology that will forever change the medical landscape. A marriage of biology and chemistry has given birth to a new branch of medicine known as tissue engineering.

The *Annals of Biomedical Engineering* of April 1995 explain that the idea is to use our own living cells to grow new tissue. According to *Scientific American* of September, 1995, tissue engineering will not only regenerate body parts for the millions of Americans who have lost organs to injury or disease, but will also provide less costly therapy that can save lives.

The Congressional Task Force on Organ and Tissue Donation revealed on February 23, 1996, that each day eight people die waiting for an organ. In an age when the waiting list is becoming longer and transplants are plagued with problems of availability and staggering costs, a new treatment is desperately needed. Fortunately, this procedure will also help treat degenerative and neurological diseases and provide a safe haven for premature babies.

The impacts are far-reaching, so to better understand this "grow-your-own-organ" approach we will first examine the history of tissue engineering and how we must focus on its benefits and present applications. And finally, we must discuss the future implications of this young medical field.

Today, scientists correct tissue damage by transplanting synthetic parts or organs from humans or animals. However, the risk has left the medical community searching for new alternatives. Born only twelve years ago, tissue engineering is the most viable option. The November 6, 1995, issue of *Blood Weekly* describes how Dr. Robert Langer envisions ways to grow new cells for sick children. After collaborating with Dr. Joseph Vancati of MIT, the duo successfully developed a biodegradable scaffold to grow healthy cells into permanent tissue. The November 4, 1995, *British Medical Journal* professes that the duo has successfully grown skin, heart valves, and even liver tissue. The process involved is relatively simple.

Chemical and Engineering News of March 12, 1995,[1] points out that first, porous, biodegradable materials are sculpted into three-dimensional scaffolds. These scaffolds will resemble the organs and will help guide the growing tissues. Next, the 1995 American Chemical Society states, doctors remove the living cells from the patients and seed them into the porous materials. The cells will be fed oxygen and blood. As the cells multiply, they begin to take the shape of the scaffold and the organ. The scaffolds eventually dissolve. Finally, permanent healthy tissues will form bone, skin, muscles, and even full-fledged organs that may be transplanted back into the body.

Although tissue engineering may seem as easy as growing a chia pet, it is a highly sophisticated technology with practical benefits. It eliminates the risk of rejection and will not deteriorate in the body. But first, unlike current transplants, engineered organs will not be rejected by our immune systems. Our bodies recognize and reject foreign objects. As a result, patients must be administered immuno-suppressant drugs. The *Washington Post* of February 18, 1996,[2] contends that our bodies attack transplanted organs so viciously that they may be destroyed within minutes, and the drugs only leave our bodies vulnerable to disease. However, the May 15, 1995, *Journal of Transplantation* asserts that with this technology the tissue is not strange to the body. Maintenance drugs become unnecessary and rejection becomes irrelevant.

Next, fabricated tissue will not deteriorate in the body. Over time, man-made parts such as hips and knees must be replaced again. For example, artificial arteries will function as blood vessels for a while. But the blood soon realizes that it's been deceived and begins to clog the tube. Yet a length of artery grown from the patient's own tissue would be genetically the same. *Scientific American* of September, 1995, alleges that these living implants will merge easily with surrounding tissue, eliminating deterioration and repeated operations.

While it may not be readily apparent, engineered skin and cartilage have already improved our medical services. Scientists have grown skin that is treating burn victims and diabetic patients. The *Economist* of January 5, 1996,[3] estimates that 800,000 Americans suffer from chronic diabetic foot ulcers. Seventy-five thousand will have to undergo amputations. And the patients can expect to pay more than $60,000 a year for treatment. Because of this technology we'll be able to help these individuals. Additionally, this therapy will allow us to help the one million Americans who suffer from torn knee cartilage. According to the *Sunday*

Advocate of of October 22, 1995, more than one million Americans have torn knee cartilage. Until recently, patients' only alternative was to have the cartilage removed in order to decrease stress to the area. Now an actual cure has been found, restoring active lifestyles to patients everywhere.

There is no doubt that tissue engineering will provide lifesaving therapies now and in the future. But before we reach these future possibilities, we must overcome two obstacles. First, natural proteins often interfere with developing tissue. According to *Science* of October 13, 1995, the growing cells secrete protein, which prevents the tissue from taking the precise shape of the scaffold. The answer may be implants and chemicals that attract the growth cells and push away the proteins. However, more time is needed to perfect this procedure.

Second, new, advanced scaffolds will have to be designed before complex organs may be grown. Current scaffolds can shape only simple tissues such as skin. And they do not have the ability to attract nerve endings into tissue. However, the National Academy of Science, in August of 1995, revealed that new polymers may be the key to engineering full-fledged livers, pancreases, hearts, and even arms and legs by the turn of the century. After overcoming these obstacles, tissue engineering will move into the future quickly. It will help millions of people suffering from various diseases, such as cancer, arthritis, and osteoporosis. The Daily Mail[4] of November–December, 1995, states that two million diabetic patients could soon receive implants of encapsulated insulin-producing cells, reducing daily shots to once every three years. Additionally, the American Chemical Society announced in April of 1995 that engineered heart valves will soon restore rhythmic heartbeats to 60,000 Americans.

In less dire situations, tissue engineering will also revolutionize the cosmetic and obstetric industries. The *Daily Mail* of March 11, 1996, mentions that Americans pay billions of dollars each year for cosmetic surgery. This research makes it possible to customize noses, chins, and even breasts.

Finally, premature infants will be nurtured in an artificial womb until their birth. By 2020 babies may be grown from removed embryos, and women may opt for painless pregnancies. But a roomful of developing babies and engineered limbs raises chilling ethical and moral questions. The *National Times* of April, 1996, argues that, while scientists could engineer vital organs and limbs, they could possibly couple this with artificial intelligence to build the Frankenstein of the 21st century. While this technology promises to save lives, we must be aware of its future implications on our society.

After examining the history of tissue engineering and how it works, its benefits and important applications, and its future, we can now appreciate this method. Tissue engineering has the capacity to remove many Americans from a long, daunting waiting list and give them the gift of life. Additionally, it will help millions who struggle from genetic and degenerative diseases. The mouse with a human ear on its back may have made national headlines, but tissue engineering, the heartbeat of the medical industry, is a constant reminder that we are living in a remarkable age.

These citations should have been spoken as follows:

[1]March 13, 1995
[2]January 6, 1996
[3]January 16, 1996
[4]*Healthcare Forum*

COLLEGE CREDIT CARD CRISIS

Jeni Pruitt, Kansas State University

Sometimes problem–solution speeches deal with national or international issues about which it is hard to imagine what an individual could do. This speech, however, deals with a matter that affects college students directly and on which they can take action. Jeni Pruitt is concerned about the growing problem of debt brought about by students' irresponsible use of credit cards.

Jeni confronts interesting strategic problems in crafting this speech. First, most listeners will not like being told that they are irresponsible. Notice how Jeni uses humor to deal with this situation and how she discusses extreme cases. Humor allows an audience to laugh at itself and extreme cases can make listeners aware of the problem without necessarily feeling that it affects them personally. Second, Jeni discusses a problem whose magnitude is unknown. She explains why precise information is unavailable and then appeals to the personal experience of her listeners. Are these good strategic choices?

Finally, in assigning responsibility for a solution, Jeni refers to both credit card companies and to students. To make her point, she uses the metaphor of drug abuse: companies are pushers and students are addicts. What does this metaphor illustrate about the ability of language to shape the way we think about issues? Is it a good choice?

Ask any seasoned college student how to study and they'll tell you, just scan it. Pay attention to the bold print. You'll be fine. Unfortunately, for a rising number of college students this strategy is catching up with them—not necessarily in their classes, but with their credit card applications. And when students flunk this econ. class, the least of their concerns is a grade.

According to a report by the Education Resources Institute recorded in the December 24, 1995, *Rocky Mountain News,* in the past five years alone college students have borrowed more money than the total borrowed by the general population in the 1960s, '70s, and '80s combined. In an age in which being debt-free means paying off your MasterCard with your VISA, Jocelyn Evans, an assistant professor of finance at Georgia State University, told the August 21, 1995, *Atlanta Journal and Constitution* that this generation is going to run into a crisis. Depending on credit is like building a house of cards. The higher it gets, the more likely it is to come crashing down. And we'll all feel the ripples—except for the credit card companies, who will simply pass their debts on to all of us. No wonder they continue to lure college students into a life of debt.

Credit card companies do indeed help many college students master their possibilities—their possibility of financial ruin. It's time to start playing our cards right. In order to do so, I would first like to examine the depth of the college credit card crisis; next, the causes; and finally, how we can take charge of our cards once again.

Of course, a casual glance at credit card misuse tells us that the problem is, this problem extends well beyond the college campus. Credit spending habits are formed on our campuses, and the habits we develop here will become the spending habits of an entire nation.

So, how big is the college credit card crisis? The exact numbers aren't clear, but reasonable estimates are disturbing. According to the April 30, 1995, *New York Times,* MasterCard International estimates that 80 percent of college students have credit cards by their senior year. And students with seventeen cards aren't unheard of. The problem is, this gives too much purchasing power to some people who simply aren't ready for it. Just ask Jesse Cantu. He told the September 11, 1995, *Pittsburgh Post Gazette* that things got so bad he started using his MasterCard to make cash advances to pay off his MasterCard. This sophomore at University of Houston filed for bankruptcy. His major . . . Finance. How many Jesse Cantu's are on our campuses? The *San Francisco Examiner* of February 25, 1995,[1] explains that there are no statistics because the people who could possibly put those statistics together—credit card companies—have no interest in doing so, and justly so. Their interest lies elsewhere . . . like in the 18.9 percent they collect from students monthly. But if the exact numbers aren't clear, the suspicions are. Ruth Suswein, executive director of the Bankcard Holders of America, told the *Pittsburgh Post Gazette,* "I defy you to go on any college campus and find any student who doesn't know some other student who's messed up using credit cards."

Now, credit cards can be a good thing. But misuse is a double-edged sword. First, students face huge debts. The August 23, 1995, *Wall Street Journal* explained that if a student owes only the national average debt per card, $1700, and pays only the minimum each month, in the time that it takes to pay it off they can earn three bachelor degrees and two master's. On top of that, students can easily end up with poor credit ratings. The August 20, 1995, *Palm Beach Post* appropriately explained no one will ever know if you skip that early morning biology lecture, but huge credit bureaus are waiting to tell the world about the time you skipped a payment. Landlords, banks, and employers all check credit ratings, which is why the February 25, 1996, *Dallas Morning Newsletter* says that for a student, a credit report is just as important as your grades. But this isn't a college student's only lesson in the school of hard knocks. In a personal interview on March 2, 1996,[2] Cindy Peterson of Consumer Credit Counseling Service said that she actually found some students who, when they can't pay their debts, don't pay the debts. They simply pass it on to all of us with higher interest rates and higher late fee payments. Not a pretty picture unless you work for VISA.

Well, what's next? Let's examine the two major causes of this crunch. Let's begin with an easy target . . . credit card companies. In the last decade these companies launched an aggressive marketing plan. According to the December 6, 1995, *Kansas City Star,* students received 2.4 billion applications in 1995. These companies are banking on students' future earning power. And, as the September 12, 1995, *American Banker* explained, students are very brand-loyal: once hooked to a particular brand, we tend to be hooked for life. That's why the *New York Times* explains that parents often bail students out, making them as good a risk as the general population.

No wonder the September, 1995, *Management Review* called college campuses "corporate circuses." Students can't help if they find applications everywhere they turn. You'll find them stuffed into your bags at campus bookstores, on tables in the union, offering free T-shirts if you'll simply fill out an application. And this campus is bombarded with credit card applications. I found six on one bulletin board outside. They don't care if you have a job or even an ID, which is why one student told the March 6, 1996,[3] *New York Times,* "I signed up as Lee Harvey Oswald, got a nice mug." Huge profit and, hey . . . thanks to mom and dad, risk free.

But if credit card companies are the pushers, college students are the willing addicts. First, there is ignorance. Judy McCoid of the Consumer Credit Counseling Service told the January 10, 1995, *Christian Science Monitor* that she actually found some students who believed they didn't have to pay the credit back. Now, while you might have figured that one out pretty quickly, most students at best are concerned about their classes and at worst, about beer and parties. No wonder *The Journal of Consumer Education* pointed out that students simply aren't aware that we're already forming our credit history. But on top of that, there's a lack of discipline. The August 20, 1995, *Arizona Republic* explained that students tend to think of their credit cards as sexy and intriguing, reassuring symbols of their adulthood. We simply start using our credit cards instead of deferring the purchase. This lack of discipline can be a disaster, which is why the *Wall Street Journal* called credit cards in the hands of college students the quickest route to financial ruin. I'm not going to say students should avoid credit cards all together. The August 20, 1995, *Phoenix Gazette*[4] said, "Credit is a game. Those who know the rules can play and win."

So finally, how can we help college students start winning at the credit game? We can do so by three means. First, legislatively. We should support Massachusetts representative Joseph Kennedy in his efforts to place limitations on issuers' ability to provide cards to students. Rus Maxham, a sophomore at the University of Texas, told the *New York Times* that giving a student seventeen cards "is like saying 'Here's a rope, kid. Go hang yourself.'" But are we going to have to dwell on the irony of our federal government helping us control our deficit spending? That's next. Look to what our schools can do.

While not the entire answer, most schools provide a freshman orientation program. Credit card abuse should be one of the topics. Encouraging preemptive strikes by our school officials could save everyone future trouble. And, finally, did you hear the one about the college student whose credit card was stolen? When asked why his father hadn't canceled his card yet, he replied, "Well, the thief's spending less than I was." There's probably more truth than humor to that joke. You see, we spend more time protecting our cards from thieves than from the number one offender . . . ourselves.

As college students, we have to change our attitudes and habits. First, we need only one card. If we're using our cards correctly, we shouldn't need $10,000 cumulative in credit limits. Second, track your spending. Most of us who've been in credit trouble were using our cards for impulsive buys. For those of us who are less disciplined, this may mean simply not bringing your card everywhere you want to be. Leave home without it. Finally, if you're already in credit trouble, consider consolidating your bills under your student loans, where you'll pay 7 to 9 percent interest instead of the 18 percent you may already be paying. For further help call the Consumer Credit Counseling Service listed in your Yellow Pages. But most importantly, parents of someone in debt should heed the advice of Michael Waldron in the *Wall Street Journal:* "Let them suffer." Parents can and should provide emotional support, but bailing them out will only ensure that generations to come will continue to follow the buy now–pay later road to destruction.

For too long, we as college students have bought the sky-is-the-limit credit card lie. Thorough study of the debt, causes, and solutions to the college credit card crisis can help us avoid the quickest route to financial ruin. Now we can sit and gripe about the federal deficit or we can begin by balancing our own. If Kenny Rogers can figure it out, so can we. We've just got to know when to hold them, when to fold them, and when to walk away.

These citations should have been spoken as follows:
[1]February 27, 1995
[2]March 4, 1996
[3]March 10, 1996
[4]*Arizona Republic*

ADDRESS TO THE NATIONAL WOMEN'S RIGHTS CONVENTION, 1855

Lucy Stone

The movement for women's rights had its beginnings in the United States in the early nineteenth century. For many women, even being able to speak in public required overcoming obstacles, especially a particular interpretation of the Bible that held that women should remain quiet. Women who became involved in the antislavery movement came to believe that their position in society was, in some respects, not too different from that of the slaves. With their sensitivities thus heightened, leaders of the women's rights movement held conventions during the 1850s all across the nation.

Lucy Stone spoke at one of these meetings. She was educated at Oberlin College, where she studied rhetoric and became the first woman from Massachusetts to earn a college degree. She was a popular lecturer on both abolitionism and women's rights. In this speech she is responding to another speaker at the 1855 Cincinnati women's rights convention who had claimed that the movement was nothing more than a few disappointed women. Rather than denying the charge, she turns the image of the "disappointed woman" to her advantage. How does she do it? How well?

Although not ignoring ideology or principles, Stone tries to emphasize the practical aspect of the women's rights issue by talking about the economic and legal harms suffered by women. In doing so, how is Stone able to avoid trivializing the larger issues? How do her appeals compare with those of the contemporary women's movement?

The last speaker alluded to this movement as being that of a few disappointed women. From the first years to which my memory stretches, I have been a disappointed woman. When, with my brothers, I reached forth after the sources of knowledge, I was reproved with "It isn't fit for you; it doesn't belong to women." Then there was but one college in the world where women were admitted, and that was in Brazil. I would have found my way there, but by the time I was prepared to go, one was opened in the young State of Ohio—the first in the United States where women and negroes could enjoy opportunities with white men. I was disappointed when I came to seek a profession worthy an immortal being—every employment was closed to me, except those of the teacher, the seamstress, and the housekeeper. In education, in marriage, in religion, in everything, disappointment is the lot of woman. It shall be the business of my life to deepen this disappointment in every woman's heart until she bows down to it no longer. I wish that women, instead of being walking show-cases, instead of begging of their fathers and brothers the latest and gayest new bonnet, would ask of them their rights.

The question of Woman's Rights is a practical one. The notion has prevailed that it was only an ephemeral idea: that it was but women claiming the right to smoke cigars in the streets, and to frequent barrooms. Others have supposed it a question of comparative intellect; others still, of sphere. Too much has already been said and written about woman's sphere. Trace all the doctrines to their source and they will be found to have no basis except in the usages and prejudices of the age. This is seen in the fact that what is tolerated in woman in one country is not tolerated in another. In this country women may hold prayer-meetings, etc., but in Mohammedan countries it is written upon their mosques, "Women and dogs, and other impure animals, are not permitted to enter." Wendell Phillips says, "The best and greatest thing one is capable of doing, that is his sphere." I have confidence in the Father to believe that when He gives us the capacity to do anything He does not make a blunder. Leave women, then, to find their sphere. And do not tell us before we are born even, that our province is to cook dinners, darn stockings, and sew on buttons. We are told woman has all the rights she wants; and even women, I am ashamed to say, tell us so. They mistake the politeness of men for rights—seats while men stand in this hall to-night, and their adulations; but these are mere courtesies. We want rights. The flour-merchant, the house-builder, and the postman charge us no less on account of our sex; but when we endeavor to earn money to pay all these, then, indeed, we find the difference. Man, if he have energy, may hew out for himself a path where no mortal has ever trod, held back by nothing but what is in himself; the world is all before him, there to choose; and we are glad for you, brothers, men, that it is so. But the same society that drives forth the young man keeps woman at home—a dependent—working little cats on worsted, and little dogs on punctured paper; but if she goes heartily and bravely to give herself to some worthy purpose, she is out of her sphere and she loses caste. Women working in tailor-shops are paid one-third as much as men. Some one in Philadelphia has stated that women make fine shirts for twelve and a half cents apiece; that no woman can make more than nine a week, and the sum thus earned, after deducting rent, fuel, etc., leaves her just three and a half cents a day for bread. Is it a wonder that women are driven to prostitution? Female teachers in New York are paid fifty dollars a year, and for every such situation there are five hundred applicants. I know not what you believe of God, but I believe He gave yearnings and longings to be filled, and that He did not mean all our time should be devoted to feeding and clothing the body. The present condition of woman causes a horrible perversion of the marriage relation. It is asked of a lady, "Has she married well?" "Oh, yes, her husband is rich." Woman must marry for a home, and you men are the sufferers by this; for a woman who loathes you may marry you because you have the means to get money which she can not have. But when woman can enter the lists with you and make money for herself, she will marry you only for deep and earnest affection.

I am detaining you too long, many of you standing, that I ought to apologize, but women have been wronged so long that I may wrong you a little. [*Applause*]. A woman undertook in Lowell to sell shoes to ladies. Men laughed at her, but in six years she has run them out, and has a monopoly of the trade. Sarah Tyndale, whose husband was an importer of china, and died bankrupt, continued his business, paid off his debts, and has made a fortune and built the largest china warehouse in the world. [*Mrs. Mott here corrected Lucy. Mrs. Tyndale has not the largest china warehouse, but the largest assortment of china in the world.*] Mrs. Tyndale, herself, drew the plan of her warehouse, and it is the best plan ever drawn. A laborer to whom the architect showed it, said: "Don't she know e'en as much as some men?" I have seen a woman at manual labor turning out chair-legs in a cabinet-shop with a dress short enough not to drag in the shavings. I wish other women would imitate her in this. It made her hands harder and broader, it is true, but I think a hand with a dollar and a quarter a day in it, better than one with a crossed ninepence. The men in the shop didn't use tobacco, nor swear—they can't do those things where there are women, and we owe it to our brothers to go wherever they work to keep them decent. The widening of woman's sphere is to improve her lot. Let us do it, and if the world scoff, let it scoff—if it sneer, let it sneer—but we will go on emulating the example of the sisters Grimke and Abby Kelly. When they first lectured against slavery they were not listened to as respectfully as you listen to us. So the first female physician meets many difficulties, but to the next the path will be made easy.

Lucretia Mott has been a preacher for years; her right to do so is not questioned among Friends. But when Antionette Brown felt that she was commanded to preach, and to arrest the progress of thousands that were on the road to hell; why, when she applied for ordination they acted as though they had rather the whole world should go to hell, than that Antionette Brown should be allowed to tell them how to keep out of it. She is now ordained over a parish in the state of New York, but when she meets on the Temperance platform the Rev. John Chambers, or your own Gen. Carey [APPLAUSE] they greet her with hisses. Theodore Parker said: "The acorn that the school-boy carries in his pocket and the squirrel stows in his cheek, has in it the possibility of an oak, able to withstand, for ages, the cold winter and the driving blast." I have seen the acorn men and women, but never the perfect oak; all are but abortions. The young mother, when first the newborn babe nestles in her bosom, and a heretofore unknown love springs up in her heart, finds herself unprepared for this new relation in life, and she sends forth the child scarred and dwarfed by her own weakness and imbecility, as no stream can rise higher than its fountain.

SECOND INAUGURAL ADDRESS, 1865

Abraham Lincoln

By the time Lincoln took the Presidential oath of office a second time, the outcome of the Civil War was certain. The disagreement was not about who would win the war but about the nature of the postwar Union. Lincoln needed to articulate how he planned to bring the nation back together, knowing that his approach would be highly controversial. To provide context for his reconstruction plan, he needed to explain or to account for the war. His Second Inaugural Address is devoted to this task. He both reaffirms that the war was about preservation of the Union and acknowledges that slavery was the underlying cause.

Lincoln's explanation fuses secular and sacred. He sees the war as divine punishment for human sins. By implication, changing attitudes about slavery was necessary to atone for sin, and only when that was done would "the scourge of war" pass away. It recalls values drawn from the past, puts forward the broad political principles of reconstruction, and acknowledges Executive limitations by placing the ultimate outcome in the hands of God.

Six weeks after delivering this speech, Abraham Lincoln lay dead, the first President to fall victim to assassination. In retrospect, the Second Inaugural Address takes on added significance as a kind of valedictory or farewell address, although it surely was not constructed with these purposes in mind.

Fellow Countrymen: At this second appearing to take the oath of the Presidential office there is less occasion for an extended address than there was at the first. Then a statement somewhat in detail of a course to be pursued seemed fitting and proper. Now, at the expiration of four years, during which public declarations have been constantly called forth on every point and phase of the great contest which still absorbs the attention and engrosses the energies of the nation, little that is new could be presented. The progress of our arms, upon which all else chiefly depends, is as well known to the public as to myself, and it is, I trust, reasonably satisfactory and encouraging to all. With high hope for the future, no prediction in regard to it is ventured.

On the occasion corresponding to this four years ago all thoughts were anxiously directed to an impending civil war. All dreaded it, all sought to avert it. While the inaugural address was being delivered from this place, devoted altogether to *saving* the Union without war, insurgent agents were in the city seeking to *destroy* it without war—seeking to dissolve the Union and divide effects by negotiation. Both parties deprecated war, but one of them would make war rather than let the nation survive, and the other would *accept* war rather than let it perish, and the war came.

One-eighth of the whole population were colored slaves, not distributed generally over the Union, but localized in the southern part of it. These slaves constituted a peculiar and powerful interest. All knew that this interest was somehow the cause of the war. To strengthen, perpetuate, and extend this interest was the object for which the insurgents would rend the Union even by war, while the Government claimed no right to do more than to restrict the territorial enlargement of it. Neither party expected for the war the magnitude or the duration which it has already attained. Neither anticipated that the *cause* of the conflict might cease with or even before

the conflict itself should cease. Each looked for an easier triumph, and a result less fundamental and astounding. Both read the same Bible and pray to the same God, and each invokes His aid against the other. It may seem strange that any men should dare to ask a just God's assistance in wringing their bread from the sweat of other men's faces, but let us judge not, that we be not judged. The prayers of both could not be answered. That of neither has been answered fully. The Almighty has His own purposes. "Woe unto the world because of offenses; for it must needs be that offenses come, but woe to that man by whom the offense cometh." If we shall suppose that American slavery is one of those offenses which, in the providence of God, must needs come, but which having continued through His appointed time, He now wills to remove, and that He gives to both North and South this terrible war as the woe due to those by whom the offense came, shall we discern therein any departure from those divine attributes which the believers in a living God always ascribe to Him? Fondly do we hope, fervently do we pray, that this mighty scourge of war may speedily pass away. Yet, if God wills that it continue until all the wealth piled by the bondsman's two hundred and fifty years of unrequited toil shall be sunk, and until every drop of blood drawn with the lash shall be paid by another drawn with the sword, as was three thousand years ago, so still it must be said "the judgments of the Lord are true and righteous altogether."

With malice toward none, with charity for all, with firmness in the right as God gives us to see the right, let us strive on to finish the work we are in, to bind up the nation's wounds, to care for him who shall have borne the battle and for his widow and his orphan, to do all which may achieve and cherish a just and lasting peace among ourselves and with all nations.

FIRST INAUGURAL ADDRESS, 1933

Franklin D. Roosevelt

Like Lincoln's Second Inaugural, this speech was delivered in a time of national crisis. By 1932, after the stock market crash and the ensuing Depression, industrial production had been cut by half and more than 13 million people were unemployed. Many were without homes; more were without hope. The situation actually worsened during 1932 after a brief recovery during the summer. Five thousand banks failed; nine million savings accounts were lost; unemployment rose to fifteen million.

Where Roosevelt stood on most issues was not clear, and he had the reputation of being a vacillating politician who would temper his principles to the requirements of the situation. During the campaign he sounded inconsistent themes, and his advisers were divided about what he should do. Many people said the country had reached the end of an era, and some even predicted revolution.

Nearly 100,000 people gathered for the inaugural ceremonies at the Capitol, and millions listened on their radio sets. The new President's first task was to restore confidence, and he spoke to that need early in the speech. He promised action, called for sacrifice, promised to seek whatever powers he would need, and asked for the help of God. The President had promised to take charge, and from that moment the restoration of national confidence began.

I am certain that my fellow Americans expect that on my induction into the Presidency I will address them with a candor and a decision which the present situation of our Nation impels. This is preeminently the time to speak the truth, the whole truth, frankly and boldly. Nor need we shrink from honestly facing conditions in our country today. This great Nation will endure as it has endured, will revive and will prosper. So, first of all, let me assert my firm belief that the only thing we have to fear is fear itself—nameless, unreasoning, unjustified terror which paralyzes needed efforts to convert retreat into advance. In every dark hour of our national life a leadership of frankness and vigor has met with that understanding and support of the people themselves which is essential to victory. I am convinced that you will again give that support to leadership in these critical days.

In such a spirit on my part and on yours we face our common difficulties. They concern, thank God, only material things. Values have shrunken to fantastic levels; taxes have risen; our ability to pay has fallen; government of all kinds is faced by serious curtailment of income; the means of exchange are frozen in the currents of trade; the withered leaves of industrial enterprise lie on every side; farmers find no markets for their produce; the savings of many years in thousands of families are gone.

More important, a host of unemployed citizens face the grim problem of existence, and an equally great number toil with little return. Only a foolish optimist can deny the dark realities of the moment.

Yet our distress comes from no failure of substance. We are stricken by no plague of locusts. Compared with the perils which our forefathers conquered because they believed and were not afraid, we have still much to be thankful for. Nature still offers her bounty and human efforts have multiplied it. Plenty is at our doorstep, but a generous use of it languishes in the very sight of the supply. Primarily this is because the rulers of the exchange of mankind's goods have failed, through their own stubbornness and their own incompetence, have admitted their failure, and abdicated. Practices of the unscrupulous money changers stand indicted in the court of public opinion, rejected by the hearts and minds of men.

True they have tried, but their efforts have been cast in the pattern of all outworn tradition. Faced by failure of credit they have proposed only the lending of more money. Stripped of the lure of profit by which to induce our people to follow their false leadership, they have resorted to exhortations, pleading tearfully for restored confidence. They know only the rules of a generation of self-seekers. They have no vision, and when there is no vision the people perish.

The money changers have fled from their high seats in the temple of our civilization. We may now restore that temple to the ancient truths. The measure of the restoration lies in the extent to which we apply social values more noble than mere monetary profit.

Happiness lies not in the mere possession of money; it lies in the joy of achievement, in the thrill of creative effort. The joy and moral stimulation of work no longer must be forgotten in the head chase of evanescent profits. These dark days will be worth all they cost us if they teach us that our true destiny is not to be ministered unto but to minister to ourselves and to our fellow men.

Recognition of the falsity of material wealth as the standard of success goes hand in hand with the abandonment of the false belief that public office and high political position are to be valued only by the standards of pride of place and personal profit; and there must be an end to a conduct in banking and in business which too often has given to a sacred trust the likeness of callous and selfish wrongdoing. Small wonder that confidence languishes, for it thrives only on honesty, on honor, on the sacredness of obligations, on faithful protection, on unselfish performance; without them it can not live.

Restoration calls, however, not for changes in ethics alone. This Nation asks for action, and action now.

Our greatest primary task is to put people to work. This is no unsolvable problem if we face it wisely and courageously. It can be accomplished in part by direct recruiting by the Government itself, treating the task as we would treat the emergency of a war, but at the same time, through this employment, accomplishing greatly needed projects to stimulate and reorganize the use of our natural resources.

Hand in hand with this we must frankly recognize the overbalance of population in our industrial centers and, by engaging on a national scale in a redistribution, endeavor to provide a better use of the land for those best fitted for the land. The task can be helped by definite efforts to raise the values of agricultural products and with this the power to purchase the output of our cities. It can be helped by preventing realistically the tragedy of the growing loss through foreclosure of our small homes and our farms. It can be helped by insistence that the Federal, State, and local governments act forthwith on the demand that their cost be drastically reduced. It can be helped by the unifying of relief activities which to-day are often scattered, uneconomical, and unequal. It can be helped by national planning for and supervision of all forms of transportation and of communications and other utilities which have a definitely public character. There are many ways in which it can be helped, but it can never be helped merely by talking about it. We must act and act quickly.

Finally, in our progress toward a resumption of work we require two safeguards against a return of the evils of the old order; there must be a strict supervision of all banking and credits and investments; there must be an end to speculation with other people's money, and there must be provision for an adequate but sound currency.

There are the lines of attack. I shall presently urge upon a new Congress in special session detailed measures for their fulfillment, and I shall seek the immediate assistance of the several States.

Through this program of action we address ourselves to putting our own national house in order and making income balance outgo. Our international trade relations, though vastly important, are in point of time and necessity secondary to the establishment of a sound national economy. I favor as a practical policy the putting of first things first. I shall spare no effort to restore world trade by international economic readjustment, but the emergency at home can not wait on that accomplishment.

The basic thought that guides these specific means of national recovery is not narrowly nationalistic. It is the insistence, as a first consideration, upon the interdependence of the various elements in all parts of the United States—a recognition of the old and permanently important manifestation of the American spirit of the pioneer. It is the way to recovery. It is the immediate way. It is the strongest assurance that the recovery will endure.

In the field of world policy I would dedicate this Nation to the policy of the good neighbor—the neighbor who resolutely respects himself and, because he does so, respects the rights of others—the neighbor who respects his obligations and respects the sanctity of his agreements in and with a world of neighbors.

If I read the temper of our people correctly, we now realize as we have never realized before our interdependence on each other; that we can not merely take but we must give as well; that if we are to go forward, we must move as a trained and loyal army willing to sacrifice for the good of a common discipline, because without such discipline no progress is made, no leadership becomes effective. We are, I know, ready and willing to submit our lives and property to such discipline, because it makes possible a leadership which aims at a larger good. This I propose to offer, pledging that the larger purposes will bind upon us all as a sacred obligation with a unity of duty hitherto evoked only in time of armed strife.

With this pledge taken, I assume unhesitatingly the leadership of this great army of our people dedicated to a disciplined attack upon our common problems.

Action in this image and to this end is feasible under the form of government which we have inherited from our ancestors. Our Constitution is so simple and practical that it is possible always to meet extraordinary needs by changes in emphasis and arrangement without loss of essential form. That is why our constitutional system has proved itself the most superbly enduring political mechanism the modern world has produced. It has met every stress of vast expansion of territory, of foreign wars, of bitter internal strife, of world relations.

It is to be hoped that the normal balance of executive and legislative authority may be wholly adequate to meet the unprecedented task before us. But it may be that an unprecedented demand and need for undelayed action may call for temporary departure from that normal balance of public procedure.

I am prepared under my constitutional duty to recommend the measures that a stricken nation in the midst of a stricken world may require. These measures, or such other measures as the Congress may build out of its experience and wisdom, I shall seek, within my constitutional authority, to bring to speedy adoption.

But in the event that the Congress shall fail to take one of these two courses, and in the event that the national emergency is still critical, I shall not evade the clear course of duty that will then confront me. I shall ask the Congress for the one remaining instrument to meet the crisis—broad Executive power to wage a war against the emergency, as great as the power that would be given to me if we were in fact invaded by a foreign foe.

For the trust reposed in me I will return the courage and the devotion that befit the time. I can do no less.

We face the arduous days that lie before us in the warm courage of the national unity; with the clear consciousness of seeking old and precious moral values; with the clean satisfaction that comes from the stern performance of duty by old and young alike. We aim at the assurance of a rounded and permanent national life.

We do not distrust the future of essential democracy. The people of the United States have not failed. In their need they have registered a mandate that they want direct, vigorous action. They have asked for discipline and direction under leadership. They have made me the present instrument of their wishes. In the spirit of the gift I take it.

In this dedication of a Nation we humbly ask the blessing of God. May He protect each and every one of us. May He guide me in the days to come.

I HAVE A DREAM, 1963

Martin Luther King, Jr.

After months of organization and planning, civil rights leaders held a "March on Washington for Jobs and Freedom" on August 28, 1963. A civil rights bill seemed stalled in Congress, and leaders hoped the march would spur legislative action. Two hundred thousand people, black and white, massed in peaceful protest in front of the Lincoln Memorial, where they heard a series of speakers. Each speaker had to decide whether to appeal to the conscience of white Americans, regarding them as potential allies, or to regard them as the adversary who should be blamed for the problems in race relations.

The last speaker of the day, the Reverend Dr. Martin Luther King, Jr., delivered a speech that has become one of the most famous of the twentieth century. King walked a tightrope between militancy and moderation, stres-sing the urgency of the moment but avoiding attacks on whites and repudiating violence. He stressed the ideals to be achieved but rooted them in "the American dream" so that they would not seem new or radical. And he merged political oratory with the preaching style of the Southern black church.

How did King accomplish these objectives? What role was played by the metaphor of "cashing a check" or of "the American dream"? How did King's use of his voice contribute to his effect? What did King accomplish through parallel structure and repetition? It is clear that the speech was effective, at least for a time, in unifying the various elements of the civil rights movement. What factors in the speech help us to understand why it is also considered a masterpiece of public speaking?

I am happy to join with you today in what will go down in history as the greatest demonstration for freedom in the history of our nation.

Five score years ago, a great American, in whose symbolic shadow we stand today, signed the Emancipation Proclamation. This momentous decree came as a great beacon light of hope to millions of Negro slaves, who had been seared in the flames of withering injustice. It came as a joyous daybreak to end the long night of their captivity.

But one hundred years later, the Negro still is not free. One hundred years later, the life of the Negro is still sadly crippled by the manacles of segregation and the chains of discrimination. One hundred years later, the Negro lives on a lonely island of poverty in the midst of a vast ocean of material prosperity. One hundred years later, the Negro is still languished in the corners of American society and finds himself an exile in his own land.

And so we've come here today to dramatize a shameful condition. In a sense we've come to our nation's Capitol to cash a check. When the architects of our republic wrote the magnificent words of the Constitution and the Declaration of Independence, they were signing a promissory note to which every American was to fall heir. This note was a promise that all men—yes, black men as well as white men— would be guaranteed the unalienable rights of life, liberty, and the pursuit of happiness.

It is obvious today that America has defaulted on this promissory note insofar as her citizens of color are concerned. Instead of honoring this sacred obligation, America has given the Negro people a bad check—a check which has come back marked "insufficient funds."

But we refuse to believe that the bank of justice is bankrupt. We refuse to believe that there are insufficient funds in the great vaults of opportunity of this nation. And so we've come to cash this check—a check that will give us upon demand the riches of freedom and the security of justice.

We have also come to this hallowed spot to remind America of the fierce urgency of now. This is no time to engage in the luxury of cooling off or to take the tranquilizing drug of gradualism. Now is the time to make real the promises of democracy. Now is the time to rise from the dark and desolate valley of segregation to the sunlit path of racial justice. Now is the time to lift our nation from the quicksands of racial injustice to the solid rock of brotherhood. Now is the time to make justice a reality for all of God's children.

It would be fatal for the nation to overlook the urgency of the moment. This sweltering summer of the Negro's legitimate discontent will not pass until there is an invigorating autumn of freedom and equality. Nineteen sixty-three is not an end, but a beginning. Those who hope that the Negro needed to blow off steam and will now be content will have a rude awakening if the nation returns to business as usual. There will be neither rest nor tranquility in America until the Negro is granted his citizenship rights. The whirlwinds of revolt will continue to shake the foundations of our nation until the bright day of justice emerges.

But there is something that I must say to my people, who stand on the warm threshold which leads into the palace of justice. In the process of gaining our rightful place, we must not be guilty of wrongful deeds. Let us not seek to justify our thirst for freedom by drinking from the cup of bitterness and hatred.

We must forever conduct our struggle on the high plane of dignity and discipline. We must not allow our creative protest to degenerate into physical violence. Again and again we must rise to the majestic heights of meeting physical force with soul force.

The marvelous new militancy which has engulfed the Negro community must not lead us to a distrust of all white people. For many of our white brothers, as evidenced by their presence here today, have come to realize that their destiny is tied up with our destiny. They have come to realize that their freedom is inextricably bound to our freedom. We cannot walk alone.

As we walk, we must make the pledge that we shall always march ahead. We cannot turn back. There are those who are asking the devotees of civil rights, "When will you be satisfied?" We can never be satisfied as long as a Negro is the victim of the unspeakable horrors of police brutality. We can never be satisfied as long as our bodies, heavy with the fatigue of travel, cannot gain lodging in the motels of the highways and the hotels of the cities. We cannot be satisfied as long as a Negro in Mississippi cannot vote and a Negro in New York believes he has nothing for which to vote. No, no, we are not satisfied, and we will not be satisfied until justice rolls down like waters, and righteousness like a mighty stream.

I am not unmindful that some of you have come here out of great trials and tribulations. Some of you have come fresh from narrow jail cells. Some of you have come from areas where your quest for freedom left you battered by the storms of persecution and staggered by the winds of police brutality. You have been the veterans of creative suffering. Continue to work with the faith that unearned suffering is redemptive.

Go back to Mississippi, go back to Alabama, go back to South Carolina, go back to Georgia, go back to Louisiana, go back to the slums and ghettos of our Northern cities, knowing that somehow this situation can and will be changed. Let us not wallow in the valley of despair.

I say to you today, my friends, so even though we face the difficulties of today and tomorrow, I still have a dream. It is a dream deeply rooted in the American dream.

I have a dream that one day this nation will rise up and live out the true meaning of its creed, "We hold these truths to be self-evident, that all men are created equal."

I have a dream that one day on the red hills of Georgia the sons of former slaves and the sons of former slaveowners will be able to sit down together at the table of brotherhood.

I have a dream that one day even the state of Mississippi, a state sweltering with the heat of injustice, sweltering with the heat of oppression, will be transformed into an oasis of freedom and justice.

I have a dream that my four little children will one day live in a nation where they will not be judged by the color of their skin but by the content of their character. I have a dream today.

I have a dream that one day, down in Alabama, with its vicious racists, with its governor having his lips dripping with the words of interposition and nullification, one day right there in Alabama little black boys and black girls will be able to join hands with the little white boys and white girls as sisters and brothers. I have a dream today.

I have a dream that one day every valley shall be exalted, every hill and mountain shall be made low, the rough places will be made plain and the crooked places will be made straight, and the glory of the Lord shall be revealed, and all flesh shall see it together.

This is our hope. This is the faith that I go back to the South with. With this faith we will be able to hew out of the mountain of despair a stone of hope. With this faith we will be able to transform the jangling discords of our nation into a beautiful symphony of brotherhood. With this faith we will be able to work together, to pray together, to struggle together, to go to jail together, to stand up for freedom together, knowing that we will be free one day.

This will be the day—this will be the day when all of God's children will be able to sing with new meaning, "My country 'tis of thee, sweet land of liberty, of thee I sing. Land where my fathers died, land of the pilgrim's pride, from every mountainside, let freedom ring." And if America is to be a great nation, this must become true.

So let freedom ring from the prodigious hilltops of New Hampshire. Let freedom ring from the mighty mountains of New York. Let freedom ring from the heightening Alleghenies of Pennsylvania!

Let freedom ring from the snowcapped Rockies of Colorado! Let freedom ring from the curvaceous slopes of California!

But not only that. Let freedom ring from Stone Mountain of Georgia!

Let freedom ring from Lookout Mountain of Tennessee!

Let freedom ring from every hill and molehill of Mississippi. From every mountainside, let freedom ring.

And when this happens, when we allow freedom to ring—when we let it ring from every village and every hamlet, from every state and every city—we will be able to speed up that day when all of God's children, black men and white men, Jews and Gentiles, Protestants and Catholics, will be able to join hands and sing in the words of the old Negro spiritual, "Free at last! Free at last! Thank God Almighty, we are free at last!"

EULOGY FOR THE CHALLENGER ASTRONAUTS, 1986
Ronald Reagan

Giving meaning to tragic events is one key function of the eulogy. It honors the memory of the dead by finding a message for the living. Eulogies typically stress the virtues of the deceased to guide the beliefs and actions of listeners. Most eulogies are of interest to only a small number of people. When the tragedy is public, the eulogy takes on added significance.

Such a highly public tragedy occurred on the morning of January 28, 1986, when the space shuttle *Challenger* exploded barely a minute after liftoff, killing all seven astronauts aboard. Schoolchildren and families across the country especially watched the launch because one of the astronauts was a teacher, Christa McAuliffe, the first civilian to travel in space. The explosion of the spacecraft was seen by millions of people on live television.

President Ronald Reagan had been scheduled to give a State of the Union address, but he postponed it and eulogized the *Challenger* astronauts instead. Concerned that the tragedy might cause listeners to doubt the value of the space program, he chose instead to emphasize the pioneer virtues of the astronauts and to regard their death as an unfortunate but necessary price for progress. Did Reagan select an appropriate meaning to give to this tragedy? How did his choices in the speech work to accomplish his effect? Were better choices available? Was Reagan the most appropriate spokesperson on this occasion? Why or why not?

Ladies and gentlemen, I'd planned to speak to you tonight to report on the state of the Union, but the events of earlier today have led me to change those plans. Today is a day of mourning and remembering. Nancy and I are pained to the core by the tragedy of the shuttle *Challenger*. We know we share this pain with all of the people of our country. This is truly a national loss.

Nineteen years ago, almost to the day, we lost three astronauts in a terrible accident on the ground. But we've never lost an astronaut in flight; we've never had a tragedy like this. And perhaps we've forgotten the courage it took for the crew of the shuttle. But they, the *Challenger* Seven, were aware of the dangers, but overcame them and did their jobs brilliantly. We mourn seven heroes: Michael Smith, Dick Scobee, Judith Resnik, Ronald McNair, Ellison Onizuka, Gregory Jarvis, and Christa McAuliffe. We mourn their loss as a nation together.

For the families of the seven, we cannot bear, as you do, the full impact of this tragedy. But we feel the loss, and we're thinking about you so very much. Your loved ones were daring and brave, and they had that special grace, that special spirit that says, "Give me a challenge, and I'll meet it with joy." They had a hunger to explore the universe and discover its truths. They wished to serve, and they did. They served all of us. We've grown used to wonders in this century. It's hard to dazzle us. But for twenty-five years the United States space program has been doing just that. We've grown used to the idea of space, and perhaps we forget that we've only just begun. We're still pioneers. They, the members of the *Challenger* crew, were pioneers.

And I want to say something to the schoolchildren of America who were watching the live coverage of the shuttle's take-off. I know it is hard to understand, but sometimes painful things like this happen. It's all part of the process of exploration and discovery. It's all part of taking a chance and expanding man's horizons. The future doesn't belong to the fainthearted; it belongs to the brave. The *Challenger* crew was pulling us into the future, and we'll continue to follow them.

I've always had great faith in and respect for our space program, and what happened today does nothing to diminish it. We don't hide our space program. We don't keep secrets and cover things up. We do it all up front and in public. That's the way freedom is, and we wouldn't change it for a minute. We'll continue our quest in space. There will be more shuttle flights and more shuttle crews and, yes, more volunteers, more civilians, more teachers in space. Nothing ends here; our hopes and our journeys continue. I want to add that I wish I could talk to every man and woman who works for NASA or who worked on this mission and tell them: "Your dedication and professionalism have moved and impressed us for decades. And we know of your anguish. We share it."

There's a coincidence today. On this day 390 years ago, the great explorer Sir Francis Drake died aboard ship off the coast of Panama. In his lifetime the great frontiers were the oceans, and an historian later said, "He lived by the sea, died on it, and was buried in it." Well, today we can say of the *Challenger* crew: Their dedication was, like Drake's, complete.

The crew of the space shuttle *Challenger* honored us by the manner in which they lived their lives. We will never forget them, nor the last time we saw them, this morning, as they prepared for their journey and waved goodbye and "slipped the surly bonds of earth" to "touch the face of God."

ADDRESS ON AIDS:
REPUBLICAN NATIONAL CONVENTION, 1992

Mary Fisher

Acquired immunodeficiency syndrome (AIDS) was discovered in the early 1980s. By 1992 it had reached epidemic proportions; thousands had been infected and died from complications of the disease. Although medical researchers dedicated themselves to the task, they had been unable to find a cure. AIDS is spread primarily through blood and semen. Originally, intravenous drug users and homosexual men were the groups most often infected.

Like any disease about which little is known, AIDS inspired fear and prejudice. Some moralized that the illness was divine punishment for sexual deviance or drug use. Others shunned anyone who had AIDS, believing that even casual contact might transmit the disease. AIDS victims were seen as a group separate from society, sometimes pitied and sometimes scorned.

One way to increase attention to the disease and pressure for a cure was to break down this separation between AIDS sufferers and the general population. In her speech to the 1992 Republican national convention, AIDS activist Mary Fisher sought to do that by stressing that the disease was a great leveler; it could happen to anybody. What was needed, therefore, was sympathy and understanding rather than prejudice and stereotype.

Did Fisher make a wise choice in urging her listeners to identify with those suffering from AIDS? What were the devices she used to suggest that she and her listeners were basically alike? How effective were her personal references? Does portraying the threat of AIDS as universal help or hurt Fisher's position? Were there more persuasive appeals that she could have used?

Less than three months ago, at Platform Hearings in Salt Lake City, I asked the Republican party to lift the shroud of silence which has been draped over the issue of HIV and AIDS. I have come tonight to bring our silence to an end.

I bear a message of challenge, not self-congratulation. I want your attention, not your applause. I would never have asked to be HIV-positive. But I believe that in all things there is a purpose, and I stand before you, and before the nation, gladly.

The reality of AIDS is brutally clear. Two hundred thousand Americans are dead or dying; a million more are infected. Worldwide, forty million, sixty million, or a hundred million infections will be counted in the coming few years. But despite science and research, White House meetings and congressional hearings; despite good intentions and bold initiatives, campaign slogans and hopeful promises—it is, despite it all, the epidemic which is winning tonight.

In the context of an election year, I ask you, here, in this great hall, or listening in the quiet of your home, to recognize that the AIDS virus is not a political creature. It does not care whether you are Democrat or Republican. It does not ask whether you are black or a white, male or female, gay or straight, young or old.

Tonight, I represent an AIDS community whose members have been reluctantly drafted from every segment of American society. Though I am white, and a mother, I am one with a black infant struggling with tubes in a Philadelphia hospital. Though I am female, and contracted this disease in marriage, and enjoy the warm support of my family, I am one with the lonely gay man sheltering a flickering candle from the cold wind of his family's rejection.

This is not a distant threat; it is a present danger. The rate of infection is increasing fastest among women and children. Largely unknown a decade ago, AIDS is the third leading killer of young adult Americans today. But it won't be third for long, because, unlike other diseases, this one travels. Adolescents don't give each other cancer or heart disease because they believe they are in love. But HIV is different.

And we have helped it along. We have killed each other—with our ignorance, our prejudice, and our silence. We may take refuge in our stereotypes, but we cannot hide there long. Because HIV asks only one thing of those it attacks: Are you human? And this is the right question: Are you human?

Because people with HIV have not entered some alien state of being. They are human. They have not earned cruelty and they do not deserve meanness. They don't benefit from being isolated or treated as outcasts. Each of them is exactly what God made: a person. Not evil, deserving of our judgment; not victims, longing for our pity. People. Ready for support and worthy of compassion.

My call to you, my party, is to take a public stand no less compassionate than that of the President and Mrs. Bush. They have embraced me and my family in memorable ways. In the place of judgment, they have shown affection. In difficult moments, they have raised our spirits. In the darkest hours, I have seen them reaching not only to me, but also to my parents, armed with that stunning grief and special grace that comes only to parents who have themselves leaned too long over the bedside of a dying child.

With the President's leadership, much good has been done. Much of the good has gone unheralded. As the President has insisted, "Much remains to be done." But we do the President's cause no good if we praise the American family but ignore a virus that destroys it. We must be consistent if we are to be believed. We cannot love justice and ignore prejudice, love our children and fear to teach them. What-ever our role, as parent or policy maker, we must act as eloquently as we speak, else we have no integrity.

My call to the nation is a plea for awareness. If you believe you are safe, you are in danger. Because I was not hemophiliac, I was not at risk. Because I was not gay, I was not at risk. Because I did not inject drugs, I was not at risk. My father has devoted much of his lifetime to guarding against another holocaust. He is part of the generation who heard Pastor Niemoeller come out of the Nazi death camps to say, "They came after the Jews and I was not a Jew, so I did not protest. Then they came after the Trade Unionists, so I did not protest. Then they came after the Roman Catholics, and I was not a Roman Catholic, so I did not protest. Then they came after me, and there was no one left to protest."

The lesson history teaches is this: If you believe you are safe, you are at risk. If you do not see this killer stalking your children, look again. There is no family or community, no race or religion, no place left in America that is safe. Until we genuinely embrace this message, we are a nation at risk.

Tonight, HIV marches resolutely toward AIDS in more than a million American homes, littering its pathway with the bodies of the young. Young men. Young women. Young parents. And young children. One of the families is mine. If it is true that HIV inevitably turns to AIDS, then my children will inevitably turn to orphans.

My family have been a rock of support. My 84-year-old father, who has pursued the healing of the nations, will not accept the premise that he cannot heal his daughter. My mother refuses to be broken. She still calls at midnight to tell wonderful jokes that make me laugh. Sisters and friends, and my brother Phillip (whose birthday is today), all have helped carry me over the hardest places. I am blessed, richly and deeply blessed, to have such a family.

But not all of you have been so blessed. You are HIV-positive but dare not say it. You have lost loved ones, but you dared not whisper the word AIDS. You weep silently. You grieve alone.

I have a message for you. It is not you who should feel shame, it is we. We who tolerate ignorance and practice prejudice, we who have taught you to fear. We must lift our shroud of silence, making it safe for you to reach out for compassion. It is our task to seek safety for our children, not in quiet denial but in effective action. Some day our children will be grown. My son Max, now four, will take the measure of his mother. My son Zachary, now two, will sort through his memories. I may not be here to hear their judgments, but I know already what I hope they are.

I want my children to know that their mother was not a victim. She was a messenger. I do not want them to think, as I once did, that courage is the absence of fear. I want them to know that courage is the strength to act wisely when most we are afraid. I want them to have the courage to step forward when called by their nation, or their party, and give leadership, no matter what the personal cost. I ask no more of you than I ask of myself, or of my children.

To the millions of you who are grieving, who are frightened, who have suffered the ravages of AIDS firsthand: Have courage and you will find support. To the millions who are strong, I issue the plea: Set aside prejudice and politics to make room for compassion and sound policy.

To my children, I make this pledge: I will not give in, Zachary, because I draw my courage from you. Your silly giggle gives me hope. Your gentle prayers give me strength. And you, my child, give me the reason to say to America, "You are at risk." And I will not rest, Max, until I have done all I can to make your world safe. I will seek a place where intimacy is not the prelude to suffering.

I will not hurry to leave you, my children. But when I go, I pray that you will not suffer shame on my account. To all within the sound of my voice, I appeal: Learn with me the lessons of history and of grace, so my children will not be afraid to say the word AIDS when I am gone. Then their children, and yours, may not need to whisper it at all.

God bless the children, God bless us all. Good night.

NOBEL PRIZE LECTURE, 1993

Toni Morrison

This speech was delivered by Toni Morrison after she won the Nobel Prize for Literature. She made much briefer remarks to accept the award, and then delivered a formal lecture. Morrison both describes and illustrates the power of storytelling. An extended example serves to develop her thesis that narrative is a means of knowledge as well as entertainment.

After introducing the story on a literal level, Morrison then treats it metaphorically. A bird stands for language; an old woman, for writers. At this level, Morrison is able to explain the writer's responsibility to keep language alive in the face of threats to its "nuanced, complex" character. As she points out, attending to language does not serve to displace experience but rather to imbue it with meaning. How well do you think she establishes her claim?

Successful speeches often blend forms—in this case narrative and exposition. Morrison does not simply talk about storytelling; she tells stories. The variety in her approach and her supporting materials add interest and power to the speech. Also, although the speech is not about any specific policy or proposal, it does address an issue of significant concern that is appropriately discussed in the public forum.

Members of the Swedish Academy, Ladies and Gentlemen:

Narrative has never been merely entertainment for me. It is, I believe, one of the principal ways in which we absorb knowledge. I hope you will understand, then, why I begin these remarks with the opening phrase of what must be the oldest sentence in the world, and the earliest one we remember from childhood: "Once upon a time . . . '

"Once upon a time there was an old woman. Blind but wise." Or was it all old man? A guru, perhaps. Or a *griot* soothing restless children. I have heard this story, or one exactly like it, in the lore of several cultures.

"Once upon a time there was an old woman. Blind. Wise."

In the version I know the woman is the daughter of slaves, black, American, and lives alone in a small house outside of town. Her reputation for wisdom is without peer and without question. Among her people she is both the law and its transgression. The honor she is paid and the awe in which she is held reach beyond her neighborhood to places far away; to the city where the intelligence of rural prophets is the source of much amusement.

One day the woman is visited by some young people who seem to be bent on disproving her clairvoyance and showing her up for the fraud they believe she is. Their plan is simple: they enter her house and ask the one question the answer to which rides solely on her difference from them, a difference they regard as a profound disability: her blindness. They stand before her, and one of them says,

"Old woman, I hold in my hand a bird. Tell me whether it is living or dead."

She does not answer, and the question is repeated. "Is the bird I am holding living or dead?"

Still she does not answer. She is blind and cannot see her visitors, let alone what is in their hands. She does not know their color, gender, or homeland. She only knows their motive.

The old woman's silence is so long, the young people have trouble holding their laughter.

Finally she speaks, and her voice is soft but stern. "I don't know," she says. "I don't know whether the bird you are holding is dead or alive, but what I do know is that it is in your hands. It is in your hands."

Her answer can be taken to mean: if it is dead, you have either found it that way or you have killed it. If it is alive, you can still kill it. Whether it is to stay alive is your decision. Whatever the case, it is your responsibility.

For parading their power and her helplessness, the young visitors are reprimanded, told they are responsible not only for the act of mockery but also for the small bundle of life sacrificed to achieve its aims. The blind women shifts attention away from assertions of power to the instrument through which that power is exercised.

Speculation on what (other than its own frail body) that bird in the hand might signify has always been attractive to me, but especially so now, thinking as I have been about the work I do that has brought me to this company. So I choose to read the bird as language and the woman as a practiced writer.

She is worried about how the language she dreams in, given to her at birth, is handled, put into service, even withheld from her for certain nefarious purposes. Being a writer, she thinks of language partly as a system, partly as a living thing over which one has control, but mostly as agency—as an act with consequences. So the question the children put to her, "Is it living or dead?," is not unreal, because she thinks of language as susceptible to death, erasure, certainly imperiled and salvageable only by an effort of the will. She believes that if the bird in the hands of her visitors is dead, the custodians are responsible for the corpse. For her a dead language is not only one no longer spoken or written, it is unyielding language content to admire its own paralysis. Like statist language, censored and censoring. Ruthless in its policing duties, it has no desire or purpose other than to maintain the free range of its own narcotic narcissism, its own exclusivity and dominance. However moribund, it is not without effect, for it actively thwarts the intellect, stalls conscience, suppresses human potential. Unreceptive to interrogation, it cannot form or tolerate new ideas, shape other thoughts, tell another story, fill baffling silences. Official language smitheried to sanction ignorance and preserve privilege is a suit of armor, polished to shocking glitter, a husk from which the knight departed long ago. Yet there it is; dumb, predatory, sentimental. Exciting reverence in schoolchildren, providing shelter for despots, summoning false memories of stability, harmony among the public.

She is convinced that when language dies, out of carelessness, disuse, indifference, and absence of esteem, or killed by fiat, not only she herself but all users and makers are accountable for its demise. In her country children have bitten their tongues off and use bullets instead to iterate the void of speechlessness, of disabled and disabling language, of language adults have abandoned altogether as a device for grappling with meaning, providing guidance, or expressing love. But she knows tongue-suicide is not only the choice of children. It is common among the infantile heads of state and power merchants whose evacuated language leaves them with no access to what is left of their human instincts, for they speak only to those who obey, or in order to force obedience.

The systematic looting of language can be recognized by the tendency of its users to forgo its nuanced, complex, midwifery properties, replacing them with menace and subjugation. Oppressive language does more than represent violence; it is violence; does more than represent the limits of knowledge; it limits knowledge. Whether it is obscuring state language or the faux language of mindless media; whether it is the proud but calcified language of the academy or the commodity-driven language of science; whether it is the malign language of law-without-ethics, or language designed for the estrangement of minorities, hiding its racist plunder in its literary cheek—it must be rejected, altered, and exposed. It is the language that drinks blood, laps vulnerabilities, tucks its fascist boots under crinolines of respectability and patriotism as it moves relentlessly toward the bottom line and the bottomed-out mind. Sexist language, racist language, theistic language—all are typical of the policing languages of mastery, and cannot, do not, permit new knowledge or encourage the mutual exchange of ideas.

The old woman is keenly aware that no intellectual mercenary or insatiable dictator, no paid-for politician or demagogue, no counterfeit journalist would be persuaded by her thoughts. There is and will be rousing language to keep citizens armed and arming; slaughtered and slaughtering in the malls, courthouses, post offices, playgrounds, bedrooms, and boulevards; stirring, memorializing language to mask the pity and waste of needless death. There will be more diplomatic language to countenance rape, torture, assassination. There is and will be more seductive, mutant language designed to throttle women, to pack their throats like pâté-producing geese with their own unsayable, transgressive words; there will be more of the language of surveillance disguised as research; of politics and history calculated to render the suffering of millions mute; language glamorized to thrill the dissatisfied and bereft into assaulting their neighbors; arrogant pseudo-empirical language crafted to lock creative people into cages of inferiority and hopelessness.

Underneath the eloquence, the glamour, the scholarly associations, however stirring or seductive, the heart of such language is languishing, or perhaps not beating at all—if the bird is already dead.

She has thought about what could have been the intellectual history of any discipline if it had not insisted upon, or been forced into, the waste of time and life that rationalizations for and representations of dominance required—lethal discourses of exclusion blocking access to cognition for both the excluder and the excluded.

The conventional wisdom of the Tower of Babel story is that the collapse was a misfortune. That it was the distraction or the weight of many languages that precipitated the tower's failed architecture. That one monolithic language would have expedited the building, and heaven would have been reached. Whose heaven, she wonders? And what kind? Perhaps the achievement of Paradise was premature, a little hasty if no one could take the time to understand other languages, other views, other narratives. Had they, the heaven they imagined might have been found at their feet. Complicated, demanding, yes, but a view of heaven as life; not heaven as post-life.

She would not want to leave her young visitors with the impression that language should be forced to stay alive merely to be. The vitality of language lies in its ability to limn the actual, imagined, and possible lives of its speakers, readers, writers. Although its poise is sometimes in displacing experience, it is not a substitute for it. It arcs toward the place where meaning may lie. When a president of the United States thought about the graveyard his country had become, and said, "The world will little note nor long remember what we say here. But it will never forget what they did here," his simple words were exhilarating in their life-sustaining properties because they refused to encapsulate the reality of 600,000 dead men in a cataclysmic race war. Refusing to monumentalize, disdaining the "final word," the precise "summing up," acknowledging their "poor power to add or detract," his words signal deference to the uncapturability of the life it mourns. It is the deference that moves her, that recognition that language can never live up to life once and for all. Nor should it. Language can never "pin down" slavery, genocide, war. Nor should it yearn for the arrogance to be able to do so. Its force, its felicity, is in its reach toward the ineffable.

Be it grand or slender, burrowing, blasting or refusing to sanctify; whether it laughs out loud or is a cry without an alphabet, the choice word or the chosen silence, unmolested language surges toward knowledge, not its destruction. But who does not know of literature banned because it is interrogative; discredited because it is critical; erased because it is alternate? And how many are outraged by the thought of a self-ravaged tongue?

Word-work is sublime, she thinks, because it is generative; it makes meaning that secures our difference, our human difference—the way in which we are like no other life.

We die. That may be the meaning of life. But we *do* language. That may be the measure of our lives.

"Once upon a time . . . " Visitors ask an old woman a question. Who are they, these children? What did they make of that encounter? What did they hear in those final words: "The bird is in your hands"? A sentence that gestures toward possibility, or one that drops a latch? Perhaps what the children heard was, "It is not my problem. I am old, female, black, blind. What wisdom I have now is in knowing I cannot help you. The future of language is yours."

They stand there. Suppose nothing was in their hands. Suppose the visit was only a ruse, a trick to get to be spoken to, taken seriously as they have not been before. A chance to interrupt, to violate the adult world, its miasma of discourse about them. Urgent questions are at stake, including the one they have asked: "Is the bird we hold living or dead?" Perhaps the question meant: "Could someone tell us what is life? What is death?" No trick at all; no silliness. A straightforward question worthy of the attention of a wise one. An old one. And if the old and wise who have lived life and faced death cannot describe either, who can?

But she does not; she keeps her secret, her good opinion of herself, her gnomic pronouncements, her art without commitment. She keeps her distance, enforces it and retreats into the singularity of isolation, in sophisticated, privileged space.

Nothing, no word follows her declaration of transfer. That silence is deep, deeper than the meaning available in the words she has spoken. It shivers, this silence, and the children, annoyed, fill it with language invented on the spot.

"Is there no speech," they ask her, "no words you can give us that help us break through your dossier of failures? through the education you have just given us that is no education at all because we are paying close attention to what you have done as well as to what you have said? to the barrier you have erected between generosity and wisdom?

"We have no bird in our hands, living or dead. We have only you and our important question. Is the nothing in our hands something you could not bear to contemplate, to even guess? Don't you remember being young, when language was magic without meaning? When what you could say, could not mean? When the invisible was what imagination strove to see? When questions and demands for answers burned so brightly you trembled with fury at not knowing?

"Do we have to begin consciousness with a battle heroes and heroines like you have already fought and lost, leaving us with nothing, in our hands except what you have imagined is there? Your answer is artful, but its artfulness embarrasses us and ought to embarrass you. Your answer is indecent in its self-congratulation. A made-for-television script that makes no sense if there is nothing in our hands.

"Why didn't you reach out, touch us with your soft fingers, delay the sound bite, the lesson, until you knew who we were? Did you so despise our trick, our modus operandi, that you could not see that we were baffled about how to get your attention? We are young. Unripe. We have heard all our short lives that we have to be responsible. What could that possibly mean in the catastrophe this world has become; where, as a poet said, "nothing needs to be exposed since it is already barefaced"? Our inheritance is an affront. You want us to have your old, blank eyes and see only cruelty and mediocrity. Do you think we are stupid enough to perjure ourselves again and again with the fiction of nationhood? How dare you talk to us of duty when we stand waist deep in the toxin of your past?

"You trivialize us and trivialize the bird that is not in our hands. Is there no context for our lives? No song, no literature, no poem full of vitamins, no history connected to experience that you can pass along to help us start strong? You are an adult. The old one, the wise one. Stop thinking about saving your face. Think of our lives and tell us your particularized world. Make up a story. Narrative is radical, creating us at the very moment it is being created. We will not blame you if your reach exceeds your grasp; if love so ignites your words that they go down in flames and nothing is left but their scald. Or if, with the reticence of a surgeon's hands, your words suture only the places where blood might flow. We know you can never do it properly—once and for all. Passion is never enough; neither is skill. But try. For our sake and yours forget your name in the street; tell us what the world has been to you in the dark places and in the light. Don't tell us what to believe, what to fear. Show us belief's wide skirt and the stitch that unravels fear's caul. You, old woman, blessed with blindness, can speak the language that tells us what only language can: how to see without pictures. Language alone protects us from the scariness of things with no names. Language alone is meditation.

"Tell us what it is to be a woman so that we may know what it is to be a man. What moves at the margin. What it is to have no home in this place. To be set adrift from the one you knew. What it is to live at the edge of towns that cannot bear your company.

"Tell us about ships turned away from shorelines at Easter, placenta in a field. Tell us about a wagonload of slaves, how they sang so softly their breath was indistinguishable from the falling snow. How they knew from the hunch of the nearest shoulder that the next stop would be their last. How, with hands prayered in their sex, they thought of heat, then sun. Lifting their faces as though it was there for the taking. Turning as though there for the taking. They stop at an inn. The driver and his mate go in with the lamp, leaving them humming in the dark. The horse's void steams into the snow beneath its hooves and the hiss and melt are the envy of the freezing slaves.

"The inn door opens: a girl and a boy step away from its light. They climb into the wagon bed. The boy will have a gun in three years, but now he carries a lamp and a jug of warm cider. They pass it from mouth to mouth. The girl offers bread, pieces of meat, and something more: a glance into the eyes of the one she serves. One helping for each man, two for each woman. And a look. They look back. The next stop will be their last. But not this one. This one is warmed."

It's quiet again when the children finish speaking, until the woman breaks into the silence.

"Finally," she says. "I trust you now. I trust you with the bird that is not in your hands because you have truly caught it. Look. How lovely it is, this thing we have done—together."

Name Index

Subject Index

Constraints
  defined, 92
  identifying, 105–106
  of occasions, 387
  on persuasive speaking,
    363–366
Conversion, 103–104, 371–372
Conviction, strengthening, 370
Coordination, in outline, 239
Credibility, 13, 306
Critical appraisal, of audience,
    82
Critical thinking, 6
  applying to the speech
    situation, 50–52
  and characteristics of critical
    thinkers, 49–50
  and critical listening, 49–50
  skills of, 49
Cultural diversity, 29–30, 73, 289
Cultural facts, 71
Culture
  audience, 67–74
    beliefs and values, 69
    common knowledge and
      experience, 71
    and cultural diversity, 73–74
    prior understanding, 70–71
    roles and reference groups,
      72
    self-interest, 67–74
  and organizational pattern,
    195
Culture style type, 254

D

Data, as supporting material,
    16
Debates, in a public forum, 413
Decimal outline, 235
Decision tree, 309–310
Decorum, 387–388
Definition
  as an informative strategy,
    340–342
  defined, 260
  denotation and connotation,
    261–262
  neutral, 261
  persuasive, 262–263
Deliberative, defined, 11

Deliberative speaking
  and group presentations,
    392–395
  the nature of, 389–391
  and oral reports and
    presentations, 391–392
Deliberative speech occasion,
    93–94
Delivery, 90. *See* Presentation
Demographics
  audience, 65–67
    composition of, 67
    heterogeneity, 66
    size, 65
    voluntary *versus* captive, 66
Demonstration, 346–348
Denial, 364
Denotation and connotation,
    261–262
Description, 268, 344–345
Diagram, 313
Dialect, 289
Dialogue, 270
Dictionaries, 129
Direct observation
  and audience analysis, 80
  as supporting material,
    120–122
Discreteness, of main ideas, 185
Discussion, informal, 56–57
Dismissal, 364
Distractions
  listener, 40
  situational, 42–43
Distributed practice, 300
Documents, as supporting
    material, 122
Domain name, 137
Douglass Archive of American
    Public Address, 251
Dress. *See* Physical appearance

E

Editor & Publisher MediaInfo
    Links, 145
Effectiveness standard, 55
Ellipsis, 143
Empathy, 283
Empowerment, 339–330
Encyclopedias, 129–130
Entertaining, 26

Enunciation, 288
Epideictic, 395
Equivocal, 172
Ethics, and public speaking,
    27–31
Ethnocentrism, 30
Ethos, 4, 11
  absence of visual aids and,
    307
  and belittling the source, 365
  defined, 13
  establishing, 13–14
  and identifying constraints,
    105–106
  and persuasive speaking, 359,
    360–361
  and your audience, 82–84, 94
Eulogies, 399
Evaluation
  of classroom speeches, 56–57
  of messages, 39
  and rhetorical criticism, 57–58
  and the rhetorical situation,
    54–55
  and the speaker's purpose,
    55–56
  of speeches in the field, 57
  standards of, 53–54
Events, reinterpreting, 397
Examples
  defined, 153
  guidelines for reasoning
    through, 156–157
  inference from, 154–155
  tests for inference from, 156
  types of, 121
Excite, 136
Experience
  and choosing a topic, 98
  as supporting material, 16
  topic based on, 90
Experiments, 124
Expert testimony, 166
Explaining, as an informative
    strategy, 345–346
Explanation, as an inference
    from cause, 163
Extemporaneous
  defined, 21
  presentation, 90, 298
Eye contact, 295

Narrative *(continued)*
  structure of, 169
  tests for inference from, 170
Narratives, as supporting material, 16
National Geographic website, 352
Need step, in the motivated sequence, 378
Netscape Navigator, 134
Neutral definition, 261
Newspapers, as supporting material, 131–132
Nominating speeches, 414–415
Non sequitur, 171
Note taking, 47–48, 127–128, 141–143

O

Objects and models, 316
Occasion
  ceremonial speaking
    defined, 395–396
    guidelines for, 397
    and reexperiencing a common past, 396–397
    speeches marking awards, 400–403
    speeches of greeting, 398
    speeches of tribute, 399–400
    speeches of welcome, 398–399
  and choice of topic, 91
  deliberative speaking and, 389–394
    group presentations, 392–395
    the nature of, 389–391
    oral reports and presentations, 391–392
  as determinant of rhetorical situation, 10–11, 93–94
  ethics and, 27–31
  fitting your speech to the
    and the concept of decorum, 387–388
    influence of the occasion, 386–388
  and the introduction, 210

speeches combining deliberative and ceremonial goals
  commencement speeches, 404–405
  speeches posing challenges, 403–404
One-point speech, 18–19
Onomatopoeia, 269
Open-ended question, 127
Operational definition, 261
Opinion
  defined, 6, 49
  as supporting material, 16–17
  as testimony, 124
Oral practice, 300
Oral *versus* written style, 256–257
Organization. *See also* Body; Conclusion; Introduction; Transitions
  defined, 180
  importance of, 180–181
  of main ideas, 181–199
  and persuasive speaking, 359
  strategies for, 14–18
Ornamental fonts, 327
Outline
  defined, 234
  note taking and, 47, 243
  preparation, 234–240
  presentation, 234, 241–249, 299–300
  and rhetorical proof, 151–152
  samples of, 236–237, 244–249

P

Parallel structure
  of main ideas, 185–186
  and transitions, 228
Parallel wording, 267
Paraphrasing, 143, 166
Parliamentary procedure, 393–394
Partition, 208
Passive voice, 265
Pauses, 286–288
People
  in ceremonial speaking, 397
  hypothetical, 270

supporting materials and, 125–128
  use in visual aids, 316–318
Pep talks, 403
Perception, 77–78
Periodicals
  general-interest, 130–131
  indexes to, 131
  special-interest, 131
  as supporting material, 130–131
  technical, 131
Personal commitment, 90
Personal experience, as supporting material, 119–120, 125–126
Personal interests, and audience analysis, 68–69
Personal inventory, 98–99
Personal reference, in the conclusion, 220
Personification, 269–270
Perspective, 102, 339
Persuasive definition, 262–263
Persuasive strategies
  compared with informative strategies, 356–357
  constraints on persuasive speaking, 363–366
  and deliberative speaking, 391
  organization of the persuasive speech, 376–379
  persuading, defined, 26
  planning, 358–359
  the problem-solution speech, 359, 367–368
  requirements for effective persuasive speaking, 359–363
  variations on the problem-solution speech, 369–376
Photographs, 314–315
Phrases, stylistic, 273
Physical appearance, 292–293
Physical observation, as a sign, 160
Pie graphs, 313
Pitch, 284–285
Plagiarism, 30, 140
Plain style, 272

Platitudes, 66
Polls, 123
Pontificating, 168
Posterboard, 319
Post hoc fallacy, 164–165
Practicing
  the conclusion, 223
  delivery, 22–23
  distributed, 300
  outlining, 20–21, 244
Prediction, as an inference from
    cause, 163
Preparation outline, 21,
    234–240
Presence, 396
Presentation
  body in
    facial expression,
      295–296
    gesture, 294–295
    movement, 293–294
    physical appearance,
      291–293
  characteristics of effective,
    282–283
  defined, 282
  modes of
    extemporaneous, 298
    impromptu, 297
    manuscript, 297–298
    memorized, 297
  outline, 21, 234, 241–249
  practice, 20–23
    and the mental rehearsal,
      300
    oral, 300
    simulation, 301
    using the presentation
      outline, 299–300
  voice in
    articulation and enunciation,
      288
    pauses, 286–288
    pitch, 284–285
    pronunciation, 288–289,
      288–290
    rate, 285–286
    volume, 283–284
Presentation speeches, 400
Presumption, 120
Primacy effect, 189

Problem-solution
  as an organizational pattern,
    17
  pattern, of main ideas,
    191–192
  and persuasive speaking, 359
Project Vote Smart, 114
Pronunciation, 288–289
Proof. *See* Rhetorical proof
Psychological order, of main
    ideas, 192
Psychology, audience, 74–78
  perception, 77–78
  selective exposure and
    selective attention, 74–76
Public forum, 410–411
  and occasions for speaking in
    public
    candidacy and election,
      414–418
    ceremonial, 413–414
    public hearings and debates,
      412–413
  public, defined, 410
  public speaking and
    democracy, 411–412
Public issues, and selecting a
    topic, 98
Public speaking
  and beginning assignments,
    18–20
  benefits of, 4–6
  and communication, 6–8
  and ethics, 27–31
  and goals and strategies for a
    first speech, 12–14
  and overcoming speech
    anxiety, 23–25
  and practicing the speech,
    20–23
  and quality, 25–27
  and the rhetorical situation,
    8–12
  strategies for organizing a
    speech, 14–18
Purpose
  and clarifying informative
    goal, 338–340
  and critical evaluation, 55–56
  defined, 12, 101
  defining a specific, 336–337

  and evaluation, 56
  identifying, 101–107
  and the introduction, 207–208,
    210
  and the occasion, 11
  and organizational pattern,
    194
  in preparation outline, 235,
    238
Purpose statement, 108

Q

Q • Notes, 141
Quality
  feedback and, 27
  of Internet information, 137
  and purpose, 26
Questions
  in interviews, 127
  loaded, 394
  responding to, 394
Quotations, 130, 143
  in the conclusion, 220
  in the introduction, 214
  and testimony, 166–167

R

Rate, of speaking, 285–286
Rate of change, 123–124
Rating forms, 57
Reasonableness, 150
Reasoning
  avoiding errors in, 170–173
  examples and, 153–157
  and persuasive speaking, 362
  proof, support, and, 148–152
  in public speaking, 173–174
  through analogy, 157–160
  through cause, 162–165
  through narrative, 169–170
  through signs, 160–162
  through testimony, 165–169
Recency effect, 189
Red herring, 172
Reference groups, 72
Reference works, as supporting
    material, 129–130
Reflective, 50
Reflective judgment, 50
Reflexivity, 257–258
Refutation, 373–376

defined, 254
and definition
    denotation and connotation,
        261–262
    neutral, 261
    persuasive, 262–263
finding the right pace and
    proportion, 273
and language, 255–256
and memorable phrases,
    273–274
oral *versus* written,
    256–258
rhythm, 267–268
in a speech, 254–255
types of, 254
vividness, 268–271
Subject, and organizational
    pattern, 194
Subordination, in outline, 238
Summaries
    in the conclusion, 220
    internal, 226–227, 258
Supporting materials
    arranging of, 198–199
    for body of speech, 15–17
    common knowledge, 120
    defined, 15
    direct observation, 120–122
    documents, 122
    electronic, 133–137
    interviews, 126–128
    for the occasion, 388
    and the outline, 243
    personal experience, 119–120,
        125–126
    and persuasive speaking,
        359
    in preparation outline, 240
    in print, 128–132
    selection of, 195–198
    speech material file,
        140–141
    statistics, 123–124
    as support of conclusions,
        148–149
    testimony, 124
Surveys, 123
Symbols, in note taking,
    47
Symposium, 392–393

T
Tape recording, in interviews,
    127–128
Target audience, 358
Technical term, 265
Testimonials, 399
Testimony
    guidelines for using inference
        from, 169
    in a public forum, 412–413
    as supporting material, 124
    tests for inference from,
        167–168
    types of inference from
        testimony, 166–167
Textual graphic, 313
Thesis, 12–14
    analyzing the thesis statement,
        110–112
    identifying the main ideas in,
        44–45, 47
    in preparation outline, 235,
        238
    selection of, 44
    thesis statement defined
The Web as a Research Tool
    (website), 332
Thomas website, 114
Time order
    as an organizational pattern,
        17
    chronological, 190
Toasts, 400
Topic
    choosing a, 97–100
    criteria for a good, 95–97
    defined, 90
    ethics and, 27–31
    in preparation outline, 235,
        238
    and the rhetorical situation,
        91–94
Topical structure, as an
    organizational pattern, 17
Transitions
    defined, 223
    elements of effective, 225–227
    in presentation outline,
        242–243
    purposes of, 223–225
    strategies for preparing, 228

Transparencies, 320–321
Tribute, speeches of,
    398–400
Trustworthiness, and persuasive
    speaking, 359–360
Types, of styles, 254

U
Uniform Resource Locator
    (URL), 134
Unit of proof, 150
Universal audience, 82
Urgency, increasing sense of,
    371
Utopian vision, as a conclusion,
    221–222

V
Value judgments, and common
    knowledge, 120
Values, 69, 83, 397
Variety
    and rate of speaking,
        285–286
    stylistic, 273
    of supporting materials,
        197
Videotape, 315, 322
Visual aids
    benefits of using, 306–308
    computer-generated
        preparing, 326–329
        using, 329–330
    materials for
        chalkboard, 318
        flip charts, 318–319
        handouts, 319–320
        posterboard, 319
        slides, 321–322
        transparencies, 320–321
        videotape, 315, 322
    preparing
        designing, 323–324
        storyboarding, 323
    types of
        charts, 308–311
        graphs, 311–313
        objects and models, 316
        people, 316–318
        representations, 313–315
    using in a speech, 325–326